AN INTRODUCTION
TO FINANCIAL
MANAGEMENT

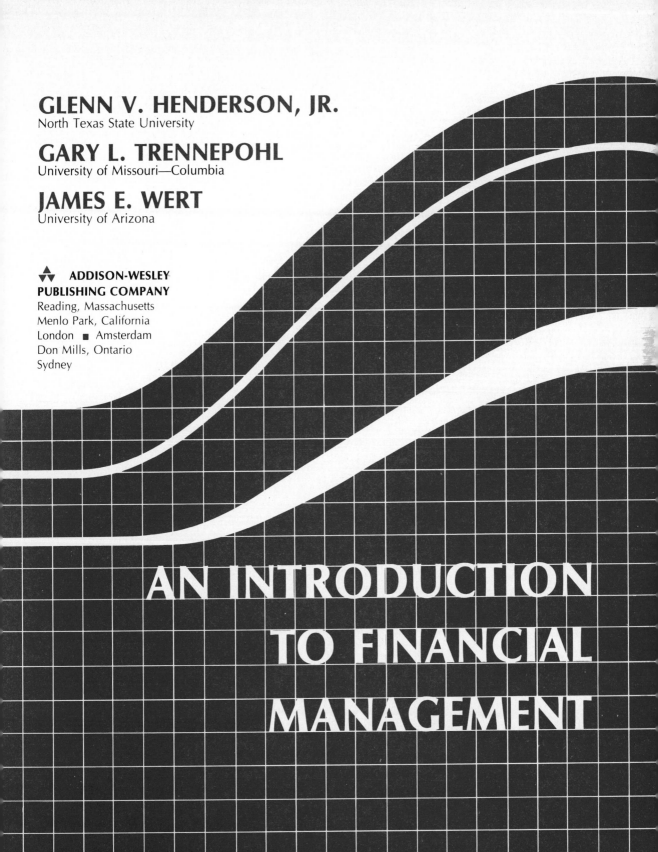

GLENN V. HENDERSON, JR.
North Texas State University

GARY L. TRENNEPOHL
University of Missouri—Columbia

JAMES E. WERT
University of Arizona

**ADDISON-WESLEY
PUBLISHING COMPANY**
Reading, Massachusetts
Menlo Park, California
London ■ Amsterdam
Don Mills, Ontario
Sydney

AN INTRODUCTION TO FINANCIAL MANAGEMENT

Sponsoring Editor ■ *William H. Hamilton*
Developmental Editor ■ *Patricia Peat*
Production Manager ■ *Martha K. Morong*
Production Editor ■ *Marilee Sorotskin*
Cover and Text Designer ■ *Vanessa Piñeiro*
Illustrator ■ *Textbook Art Associates*
Art Coordinator ■ *Kristin Belanger*
Copy Editor ■ *Helen Greenberg*
Manufacturing Supervisor ■ *Hugh J. Crawford*

Library of Congress Cataloging in Publication Data

Henderson, Glenn V.
  Introduction to financial management.

  1. Corporations—Finance.   I. Trennepohl, Gary L.
II. Wert, James Edward.   III. Title.
HG4026.H46   1984   658.1′5   83-7239
ISBN 0-201-10576-4

ABCDEFGHIJ-DO-8987654

PREFACE

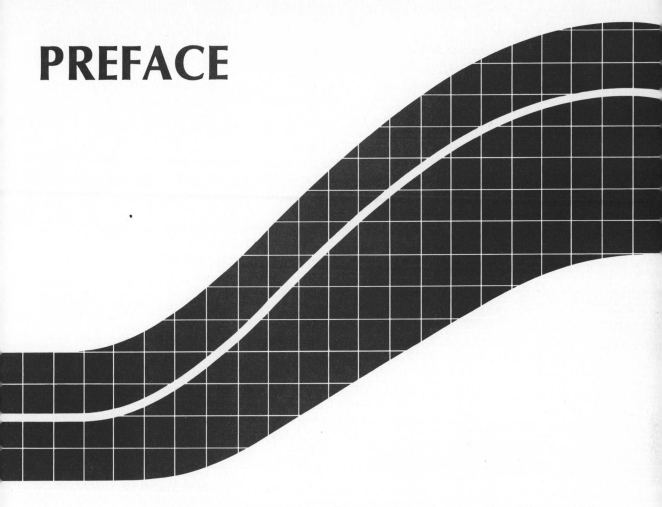

It is customary for a textbook's preface to indicate that the order of the material can be rearranged to suit users' preferences. All experienced instructors already know that. This book is especially amenable to such rearrangements in that each chapter is a tightly organized discussion of one set of closely related topics.

However, the book's order was chosen for reasons both practical and pedagogical. Surveys of business employers suggest that they expect finance courses to prepare students in two specific areas: financial analysis (Part I) and capital budgeting (Part II). Those are our first two topics. Most, if not all, finance courses require accounting as a prerequisite. Experience has convinced us that a quick review of financial statements is justified. Chapter 2, therefore, discusses accounting statements before explaining financial analysis in detail.

We consider the Appendix, Federal Income Taxes, as part of the introductory material. Taxes can be covered immediately following Chapter 2 if the instructor wants to include the topic. The tax appendix was put at the back where we can incorporate the very latest tax information and forms without reordering the rest of the book.

After the introduction, accounting reviews, and taxes, Part II discusses the time value of money, valuation, cost of capital, and capital budgeting. Financial literature indicates that U.S. capital markets are largely efficient. This implies that businesses make their money on their capital investment decisions not on their financial decisions. Further, theory is better developed in capital budgeting than it is in financing (e.g., capital structure, dividend policy). We see a first course in financial management as a place to teach usable techniques that have evolved from the application of financial theory. We have left discussion of current theoretical explorations for the more advanced courses that finance majors take.

The sequence in capital budgeting is self defining. Understanding the time value of money is necessary for valuation. Understanding valuation is necessary to comprehend the cost of capital—its derivation and its meaning. A discount rate is necessary to perform discounted cash flow analyses—that is, capital budgeting. Capital budgeting under risk is covered last.

The first six chapters (Parts I and II, plus the Appendix if wanted) make a natural block of test material. Admittedly, this "front loads" the course. By covering financial analysis, cost of capital and capital budgeting early, students are allowed to quickly assess their readiness, aptitude, and willingness to do the work necessary to learn finance. The size of this material block is also convenient for exam scheduling. Such an exam would typically be scheduled a week or so before midterm, allowing time for grading before any required midterm progress (or grade) reports are due.

If a firm produces goods and/or services, it needs more than just capital assets. Firms must have and manage working capital. Part III covers working capital management, again starting with a review of the necessary accounting tools—budgets and *pro forma* statements. The four-chapter working capital section can be used for a second exam. Such a schedule can be especially convenient in the spring when working around spring break can create problems for both instructors and students.

Part IV covers financing. This coverage has a decidedly practical perspective. That does not mean it is watered down. All of the necessary analytical material on lease-or-borrow, leverage, financial break-even, refunding, and analysis of long-term financing decisions is covered in depth, with example calculations. What *is* missing are the theoretical considerations concerning optimal capital structure and dividend policy decisions. It is not that we consider this material unimportant. Quite the opposite. However, theory in these areas is still being refined. Our experience has been that rather than being enlightened by exposure to such theory, beginning students are merely confused. We minimized coverage of these "frontier" areas. Instead we describe, in detail, the attributes of the available financing choices, the factors to be considered in a practical, point-in-time decision, and explain the mechanics of the investment banking and underwriting process.

The placement of descriptive material at the end of the course has a number of benefits. After being heavily involved in analysis for two-thirds of the course, the descriptive material is a change of pace. It can also be covered quickly to make up for any ground lost earlier. Further, invariably such material can be enlivened with real-world examples.

Having a heavy dose of description at the end of the course also has some advantages for testing. If circumstances (small classes) afford the luxury, the material is suitable for an essay final. On the other hand, if the more typical circumstances prevail (oversize classes and short grade deadlines), the material lends itself to testing by objective, machine-graded exams. Instructors will find the availability of the Addison-Wesley TESTGEN services to be a real time-saver.

Section V covers topics that should be included in a beginning textbook although most classes never cover them. However, each chapter in the section is current and technically correct. None of these topics can be adequately covered in a chapter. Each could legitimately be a course in itself. However, the student can derive a basic understanding of the material from our chapters. One or more of these can be included as a logical extension of the existing chapter sequence. International finance as discussed in Chapter 16 should prove especially convenient for programs striving to include some topical international coverage in each of their core courses.

Our textbook organization was largely dictated by the logic of the discipline and what we assess as its trends. The organization and presentation of the material within each chapter was dictated by pedagogical objectives. We wanted a book to study from—not a book to read and reread. The secret to an easy-to-study book is organization. We used every trick we could find. Some examples include

1. Every chapter was completely outlined before we started to write. To help the student grasp that structure each chapter starts with a topical outline.

2. Every chapter begins with the statement of well-defined learning objectives.

3. Illustrations and examples are numerous and detailed. Where students are expected to learn to do a particular type of problem, the solution technique is explained with a detailed numerical example.

4. All new terms are italicized when first mentioned and bold faced when defined. In addition, an extensive glossary is provided.

5. All important formulas are summarized and highlighted.

6. All chapter questions and problems were written *by the authors* at the time the chapter was written to assure they were internally consistent. Answers to selected problems are provided at the end of the book. Again, these were worked out by the authors not by graduate assistants.

One other thing is critical to an effective text—readability. We decided early to use active voice to reduce unnecessary words that accompany passive voice.

After that we had lots of help. The entire text was copyedited and revised before going out for professional review. We had five thorough, dedicated reviewers. Each made numerous suggestions about content and presentation that undoubtedly improved the book. After revisions were incorporated, the entire manuscript was reedited. Again the overriding considerations were style and pace. We wanted the material to be understandable and to get to the points quickly.

Ancillary materials include a useful student study guide and comprehensive instructor's resource guide.

The *Student Study Guide,* coauthored by Glenn Henderson and Sharon Garrison, reviews the textbook chapters, answers the questions posed at the beginning of each chapter, defines terms, lists important formulas, provides sample problems and solutions like those in the text, and gives the student self-test questions that assist in preparing for exams. We are confident the student will benefit from its use.

The *Instructor's Resource Guide* that we prepared offers the instructor chapter outlines, solutions to all chapter questions, transparency masters of key text exhibits and illustrations, and an extensive test bank made up of true/false, multiple-choice, and short problem solving questions. Instructors will find the supplement an invaluable aid.

No one pretends finance is easy. We simply want to make it understandable and palatable. Further, we want to highlight what is important, not bury it in details and alternative methods or theories. If our approach is successful we'll soon know. Markets are efficient—generally.

Acknowledgements

We were blessed with unbelievably good support. Regina DeRose (Tempe), Phillis Leiby (Columbia), Mary Wilson (Tucson), and Barbara Burmeister (Tucson) typed drafts and rewrites of the various chapters. They tolerated our poor handwriting, corrected our spelling, and generally turned out better work than we turned in. In addition to helping on the manuscript, Rita Nenaber typed the entire *Instructor's Resource Guide* to be camera ready, coordinating corrections and rewrites, while two of the authors were moving around the country. In addition to being a dependable tireless worker, she is a dear friend.

The help of several graduate students and associates is appreciated. Although we did the *Instructor's Resource Guide* ourselves, we are not foolish enough to believe ourselves infallible. Different parts of the manual were proofed (and reproofed) by anyone we could enlist. Of particular note are Dave Campbell, an MBA student at Arizona State University, and Nora Welsh, a teaching associate in economics at University of Arizona. Each took to the task with a dedication we still find hard to comprehend. (They found some mistakes.)

Special thanks are due to some of our colleagues. Stephen E. Skomp of Louisiana Tech University was coauthor of the paper (and recently accepted article) that is the basis for Appendix 6A. James Rauschkolb, Senior Vice President of Valley

National Bank in Phoenix, and Maurice Sandfort, President of Centerre Bank in Cape Girardeau, Missouri, provided valuable input on the working-capital-management chapters. John T. Emery, University of Arizona, and Allen A. Abrahamson, University of Denver, reviewed early versions of Chapters 7, 15, 17, and 18 and offered numerous suggestions that were incorporated in the final manuscript. Fred Zamon, Vice President of Centerre Bank of St. Louis (International Division), reviewed and made several constructive suggestions for Chapter 16. Alan P. Stein, librarian and lawyer at California State University at Los Angeles, reviewed Chapter 18 to assure its technical accuracy. Rich Panich, an Arizona State University doctoral student in tax, wrote the first draft of the tax appendix.

Patricia B. Peat did a super job of homogenizing our writing styles. To the extent that it appears that the three authors write in a similar style she deserves much credit. She cannot be held responsible for any remnants of our own poor grammar or syntax.

Our professional reviewers were just that—professional. They did not pull any punches and the book is better because of it. Our thanks to Russel P. Boisjoly of Simmons College, Severin C. Carlson of University of Rhode Island, Randolph A. Pohlman of Kansas State University, Joseph D. Vinso of University of Southern California, and (especially) Joseph E. Finnerty of University of Massachusetts.

It is supposedly poor form to thank the publisher's staff. That's too bad. We want to single out some people. We appreciate the efforts of Vanessa Piñeiro for coming up with what we think is an unusually attractive design. Bill Hamilton, our sponsoring editor, never cut a corner on us; in every instance the criterion was the same—do it the right way. Last, because she was always there to the bitter end— Marilee Sorotskin, our production editor: She is the most thoroughly dedicated professional we have ever worked with.

Finance is a demanding but exciting field. We hope that this text will convey some of this excitement to the student. More important, we hope it contributes to a better understanding of financial management. As we say in the first chapter, in the U.S. everyone must be a financial manager regardless of training. Good financial management is critical to our system's continued existence and growth.

Denton, Texas   G. V. H., Jr.
Columbia, Missouri   G. L. T.
Tucson, Arizona   J. E. W.
                                                                      February 1984

CONTENTS

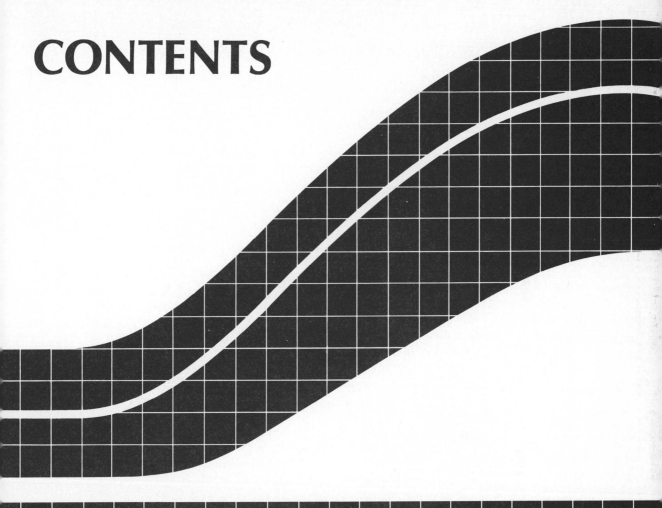

xi

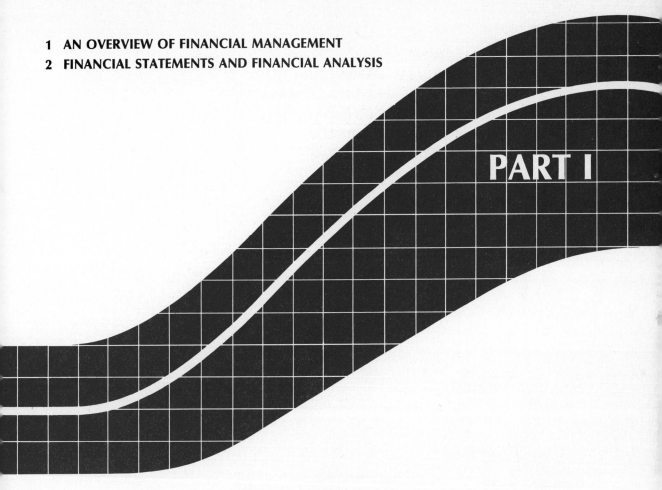

PART I

INTRODUCTION

DEFINITIONS
FINANCIAL MANAGEMENT FUNCTIONS
THE OBJECTIVE OF FINANCIAL MANAGEMENT
THE IMPORTANCE OF FINANCIAL MANAGEMENT
ORGANIZATION OF THE TEXT
TYPES OF TOPICAL MATERIAL

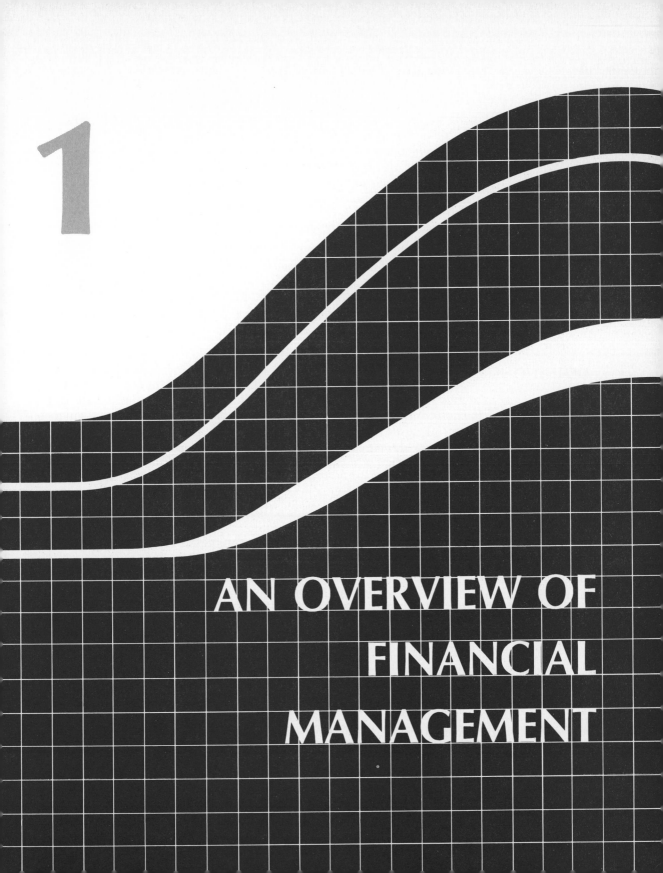

1

AN OVERVIEW OF FINANCIAL MANAGEMENT

This chapter will introduce you to some elementary definitions and concepts in finance. We have also provided a brief description of how the text is organized and the rationale for this organization.

After careful study of the chapter, you should understand

1. What finance is.
2. The three main areas of finance in the typical college finance curriculum.
3. The functions of financial management.
4. The objective of financial management decisions.
5. The reasons sound financial management is important.
6. The three types of material that might be presented in discussing a financial management topic.

DEFINITIONS

Like most introductory courses, this course requires you to learn quite a few definitions. We have included a glossary at the back of the book for convenience. Some terms, however, must be defined at the beginning to allow you to put this course in the proper context and to indicate our own perspective about the nature of financial management.

Finance

Finance is the study and practice of making dollar-denominated decisions. The distinguishing concepts here are *decision making* and *dollar denomination*. Finance professionals are always trying to figure out how or whether to do something; finance is a prescriptive, not a descriptive, discipline. This difference in emphasis distinguishes it from economics.

Finance is similar to accounting in that it attempts to quantify everything in dollars. But again, its difference from accounting lies in its emphasis. Finance is not a method of measuring for accounting or reporting purposes; the goal of finance is to reach a decision concerning some future course of action based on its dollar consequences.

In the classroom, we study dollar-denominated decision making—finance. Outside the classroom, we must make those decisions, whether or not we are trained in finance. Our economic system requires, in effect, that every producer and consumer be a practicing financial manager.

Our definition of finance is very broad, including the total discipline. Academic programs normally divide finance into three main areas: investments, markets and institutions, and financial management.

Investments

Investments courses consider the choices facing a securities investor. **Securities** are the stocks (equities) and bonds (debts) of companies and governments. The sequence may consist of one or two courses, depending on the nature of a particular program. In a two-course sequence, the first course is normally **security analysis,** which deals with how to evaluate the expected profitability of a company and assess the investment worthiness of its stock. Bonds are evaluated to determine the probability that the issuer will be able to honor its contractual commitments.

The second investments course is normally **portfolio management.** Whereas security analysis considers stocks (and, less frequently, bonds and other securities, such as options) one at a time, portfolio analysis considers how to form efficient *combinations* of securities. If only one course is offered at an institution, it is usually called "Investments," and covers both topics, with emphasis usually on security analysis.

Markets and Institutions

U.S. **financial markets** are necessary to ensure that companies and governments have access to the (long-term) *capital* and (short-term) *liquidity* they need to do business. The function of the markets is to make possible an orderly and relatively low-cost flow of funds from savers to investors—real capital investors, those who buy productive equipment. Some **financial institutions** that ensure that these needs are met are banks, stockbrokerage firms, insurance companies, savings and loan associations, pension funds, and investment bankers. Often colleges may offer one course on the operation of the markets and another on the nature of the institutions.

Because of the importance of banks as financial institutions, a separate course on money and banking may be taught in the finance department or, more frequently, the economics department. The emphasis will differ depending upon which department offers the course.

Financial Management

Financial management is the study and practice of dollar-denominated decision making *within a business firm*. Financial managers are the members of the management team responsible for assessing the financial implications of any decision made by the firm. As any action by the company can, and probably will, affect the firm's profitability, its liquidity (bill-paying ability), and its financial position (indebtedness), the financial manager is responsible for anticipating the impact of corporate actions upon these attributes of the firm.

Financial management is the topic of this text. We will study the types of decisions a financial manager must make while operating in our economy.

Although many of the same principles apply, we will not study how financial firms (such as banks) or not-for-profit entities (government and charities) operate.

FINANCIAL MANAGEMENT FUNCTIONS

The functions of financial managers are the *allocation* (investment) and *acquisition of funds* (financing) using techniques of their own design based on forecasts. Financial managers are ultimately responsible for the accuracy of their techniques and forecasts. Financial managers cannot pass the buck: they derive or select the forecasts; they design or choose an analytical technique; they must accept responsibility for the financial consequences of a right or wrong decision. Financial management is a challenging, rewarding, high-pressure career.

Allocation

By allocation of funds, we mean that financial managers decide where corporate money is invested. Generally, money should be invested where it will do the most good. In a corporate setting, this means being profitable.

There are two main types of expenditures: capital investments and investments in working capital. *Capital investments* are big-ticket, long-lived investments in plant and equipment. While capital investment decisions may not be made every day, their effect on the firm is critical. Capital investment determines the nature of a business: Utilities own power plants, railroads own locomotives, and steel manufacturers own steel mills.

Working capital refers to the current assets (and liabilities) of a firm. These are to a large degree dependent on the industry in which the firm operates; working capital requirements accompany capital investments. To be a manufacturer, one must have inventory. Selling on credit generates accounts receivable. Because payments from accounts receivable do not exactly match required payments for inventories, the firm must carry cash. Financial managers must manage working capital investments effectively, or the cost of carrying such assets will erode the profits from operations.

Acquisition

Before the company can spend money, it must have some. Financial managers are responsible for estimating the firm's financing requirements and then raising those funds on as attractive and timely a basis as possible. This is an extremely difficult task. Forecasting a firm's financial needs alone is difficult. Capital projects can involve very long lead times, and inflation and new technology constantly affect the costs of capital goods.

Even if the amount of capital needed and the timing of needs can be determined precisely, the problem is formidable. Corporations have two primary sources of capital—stock and borrowed money (debt: bonds). Acquiring funds on favorable terms means trying to sell stock when prices are high and/ or borrowing money when interest rates are low. This requires forecasting of stock prices and interest rates; neither is an easy task.

THE OBJECTIVE OF FINANCIAL MANAGEMENT

The unifying principle of financial management is that all financial decisions should *maximize the value of the firm*. When buying assets, we endeavor to choose those that will add the most to the value of the firm. When we finance, we try to do so in a manner that will result in the lowest overall cost to the firm.

This text does not present a great deal of theory. However, all the techniques we describe were derived the same way. When possible, someone modeled the value of the firm and figured out what would maximize it. Depending on how well we can specify the problem, we use one of the hierarchy of internally consistent, value-maximizing models. The hierarchy is as follows:

- Minimize costs.
- Maximize profits.
- Maintain firm value.
- Maximize firm value.

Whenever possible, financial models are applied as far down the list as possible. If a problem is so complex that its impact on the firm cannot be modeled, we follow a simpler rule, for example, maximize profits or minimize costs.

THE IMPORTANCE OF FINANCIAL MANAGEMENT

One way to appreciate the importance of financial management is to sample business news reported in the *Wall Street Journal*. Business news provides examples of the topics we will cover in this text, highlights interrelationships between investment and financing decisions, and illustrates how corporate business decisions can affect the nature and quality of our lives. We have collected here a few examples from the news of only one month, August 1982.

There are reports of huge capital outlays: Armco, Inc., has invested about $30 million to upgrade its Baltimore stainless steel works; the Columbia Broadcasting System (CBS) has bought the Ideal Toy Company for $58 million; Arizona Power Service (APS) is building a nuclear power plant; and ARCO's 1983 capital expenditures will total about $4.4 billion.

Frequently, reports of capital investment are closely linked to reports of new financing: APS sold 4 million shares of new common stock at $22.75, and ARCO registered an offering of about $400 million worth of debt with the Securities and Exchange Commission (SEC). APS's new investments and financing, along with construction, safety, pollution control, and energy costs, prompted it to request a $101 million rate hike.

The automobile industry continues to have problems. U.S. automobile manufacturers fear that their three-year slump has permanently damaged the industry. The industry's weakened position translates into trouble for auto workers: Fringe benefits are cut, General Motors (GM) extends new-model changeover closings due to lack of demand, and GM closes plants and cuts capacity, laying off 9,100 workers. The U.S. automobile industry's problems have international implications: GM also closed two British plants, and there are rumors of a small-car joint venture by GM and Toyota.

Automobile manufacturers are not the only ones with problems. Farm machinery manufacturers are in deep trouble. International Harvester (IH) is trying to restructure its $4.2 billion credit arrangement because of inability to service its debt. Massey Ferguson (MF) submitted a second proposal to lenders seeking debt service relief; MF lost $186 million in the first nine months of 1982. Again, the employees feel the impact of the company's financial problems: IH cut its white-collar staff by nearly 10%, and MF announced extended plant closings and layoffs.

The suppliers of those heavy industries are also feeling the pinch. The steel industry has been hurt by resulting low demand for steel. U.S. Steel's bond ratings have been lowered. As a result, the firm is financing with less traditional forms of securities; it sold 4 million shares of *adjustable-rate* preferred stock at $50. Again, the industry's problems are felt by its workers: Labor relations in the steel industry are becoming hostile as the firms take a tougher stand on labor issues.

In some industries there have been major shakeups caused by changes in government regulations. Airlines deregulation is an example. United Airlines' (UA) revenue passenger miles were up 11% for July 1982; Braniff has gone bankrupt. Such shifts have serious implications for aircraft manufacturers, such as Boeing, whose second-quarter profits fell 49%. USAir agreed to remarket seven Boeing 727-200s that Braniff had used. Fortunately for Boeing, government preservation of the sale-leaseback tax break persuaded UA to accept 19 Boeing 767s.

August's reports reveal that not all industries are suffering equally in the recession. Video game sales prospects continue to look good. Technology-based amusement is generally doing well, with the expected result of intensified competition in fields such as cable TV.

Computer and communications technology (and investment) is increasing at an astounding rate. More than 150 new computer programs hit the market monthly. International Business Machines (IBM) has lent 300 talking computers to schools in order to test the educational market. Firms are assessing the profitability of private-venture space shots for setting up satellite communications. Atari won a $13.4 million Army contract for microcomputers to be used in Department of Defense educational programs.

The recession, however, is generally widespread, and it is traceable directly to reduction of industrial inventories. Increases in such working capital investments are necessary to pull the country out of the recession. Further, our recession is felt throughout the world; because of it, U.S. firms have reduced overseas investments, which has caused some countries to put up retaliatory trade barriers.

All these events, their causes and their consequences, were reported in just one month. The implication should be clear: Businesses make decisions about capital investments and financing. If they guess right, the firms are profitable, consumers are offered products and services they want, and the firms' employees have work. If firms guess wrong or business conditions change unexpectedly, profits can drop. If things get too bad, firms, even very large ones, can go bankrupt. When profits drop or the firm goes bankrupt, its employees and perhaps those in related industries are hurt: They lose fringe benefits, take pay cuts, are laid off, or lose their jobs.

The general welfare of the population depends on sound financial management. The United States has a free-market economy (at least to a large degree). Financial managers make decisions based on perceptions of what they think consumers want. Anything that improves the quality of these decisions benefits everyone—consumers, employees, investors, the government (through taxes), and even citizens of other countries through resulting foreign investment. It is profitable firms that contribute the most to the economy.

Corporate decisions affect more than paychecks. In the long run, financial management decisions influence the type of work available, the location of jobs, the way we communicate, the size of our utility bills, the way we entertain ourselves, and the way in which education is provided. In short, such decisions play a big part in determining the quality of our lives.

ORGANIZATION OF THE TEXT

Section I of this textbook is introductory, including this chapter, which outlines where we are going. Chapter 2 reviews accounting and how to dissect financial statements. Familiarity with accounting is necessary to be comfortable with the later chapter on forecasting (Chapter 7) and the material on financing (Chapters 12 through 15).

The textbook's appendix on federal income taxes should actually be considered part of the introductory material. You must be familiar with taxes in order to understand certain elements of capital investment analysis (Chapters

5 and 6). Prior experience, though, has led us to put the discussion of taxes in an appendix to avoid any disruption that would be caused by a major change in the tax code.

Section II deals with capital investment. A firm's capital investment decisions are the most important choices it makes. These decisions determine the nature, profitability, and survival of the firm. It is widely believed that U.S. financial markets are relatively *efficient*, that is, that a firm pays prevailing market rates for the money it uses. Real capital markets cannot be efficient, in an economic sense; businesses buy capital assets in order to make money by using them. Since capital investment determines the winners and the losers to a great degree, we study it first.

With capital investment come working capital requirements, which are studied in Section III. Since planning for working capital uses budgets and *pro forma* statements, we present them there.

Asset acquisitions require financing, which is covered in Section IV from a practical perspective. Substantial descriptive material is included to ensure that you become familiar with practical terminology and understand what happens in the capital markets.

In today's world economy, all businesses, even relatively small ones, must be concerned about international finance. If businesses do well, they grow; if they do poorly, they die. Section V covers the three topics of international finance, growth and firm size, and reorganization and liquidation of the firm.

TYPES OF TOPICAL MATERIAL

For any topic to be studied, we have the choice of presenting three types of material: techniques, theory, and description of business practice. When you study a topic or chapter, you will often find it helpful to consider consciously which type of material is emphasized.

Techniques

Techniques are tools used for analysis. Generally, we present techniques when theory on a topic is most completely developed. In these areas, such as the cost of capital, although there may be academic disagreement on some relatively minor issues, there is consensus on the main ideas.

Everywhere techniques are presented, it is necessary to do the problems. Throughout the chapters, we give problems and solutions dealing with the techniques to be learned. The end-of-chapter problems follow the text examples very closely.

Techniques are emphasized in Chapters 2 (financial statements and financial analysis), 3 (time value of money), 4 (cost of capital), 5 and 6 (capital budgeting), 7 (budgets and *pro forma* statements), and 11 (lease-or-borrow analysis). There is also some material on techniques in Chapters 9 (credit standards analysis and economic order quantity), 10 (trade credit, factoring, and loan cost analysis), 12 (leverage analysis and measurement, refunding), and 15 (which uses techniques from earlier chapters to analyze long-term financing decisions).

Theory

A **theory** is a plausible or acceptable explanation of a phenomenon or set of relationships. In many cases, we do not know exactly what is going on in a financial situation, but we generally have a theory, an explanation that seems to fit the observed circumstances reasonably well. Such an explanation, even if imperfect, can be a productive way of thinking about and dealing with problems in that area.

A number of theories in finance fit this description, including valuation theory, the cost of capital, the capital asset pricing model, and the option pricing model. Whenever a theory appears useful in explaining how to deal with a problem, we have included it. Some theories are included simply because they are expected to be covered in a finance text. Although theoretical derivations may be abstract and symbolic, we have kept the mathematics as straightforward as possible while at the same time preserving the integrity of the theory.

Descriptions of Business Practice

It is impossible to fully understand financial management unless you learn how businesses handle their investments and financing. In the chapters that present techniques, we have used fictional and simplified examples to make problem solving easier. This allows us to avoid the many complicating details that one encounters in real world investments and financing.

However, when it is not necessary to work extensively with financial figures, real examples and descriptions are used. This text includes more descriptive material than most current texts because we believe that it will help you to understand business practice. Examples include Chapters 9 (management of cash and other current assets), 10 (short-term financing), 12, 13, and 14 (corporate securities), 15 (investment banking), 16 (international operations), 17 (mergers and other forms of corporate growth), and 18 (corporate distress, including bankruptcy).

SUMMARY

Finance is the discipline of dollar-denominated decision making. Investment analysis allows one to analyze firms in order to see if they are worth owning or lending to. Markets and institutions courses show how capital and credit are channeled from savers to businesses and government. Financial management is the study of how businesses are run.

The financial manager raises and invests funds in order to maximize the value of the firm. If the manager is successful, the owners and creditors of the firm benefit, and so does everyone else. Successful firms produce useful goods and services, employ people, pay taxes, and provide the essential ingredient that makes the U.S. economy thrive.

QUESTIONS AND REVIEW ACTIVITIES

1. Define or discuss
   a) Finance.
   b) Investments.
   c) Security analysis.
   d) Portfolio management.
   e) Financial markets.
   f) Financial institutions.
   g) Financial management.
2. Distinguish between
   a) Finance and economics.
   b) Finance and accounting.
3. Discuss the functions of financial management.
4. What is the objective of financial management decisions?
5. What three types of material should you anticipate with regard to any topic in this textbook?
6. Why is financial management important, and why is capital investment (capital budgeting) presented first in this textbook?

ADDITIONAL READINGS

Donaldson, G. "Financial Goals: Management versus Shareholders," *Harvard Business Review* (May–June 1963), pp. 116–129.

Findlay, C. M., and G. A. Whitmore. "Beyond Shareholder Wealth Maximization," *Financial Management* (Winter 1974), pp. 25–35.

Grossman, S. J., and J. E. Stiglitz. "On Value Maximization and Alternative Objectives of the Firm," *Journal of Finance* (May 1977), pp. 389–415.

Haley, C. W. "A Theoretical Foundation for the Basic Finance Course," *Journal of Financial and Quantitative Analysis* (November 1975), pp. 691–94.

Hill, L. W. "The Growth of the Corporate Finance Function," *Financial Executive* (July 1976), pp. 38–43.

Levy, H., and M. Sarnat. "A Pedagogic Note on Alternative Formulations of the Goal of the Firm," *Journal of Business* (October 1977), pp. 526–28.

Petty, W. J., and O. D. Bowlin. "The Financial Manager and Quantitative Decision Models," *Financial Management* (Winter 1976), pp. 32–41.

Wert, J. E. "Content Orientation in the Introductory Finance Course," *Journal of Financial and Quantitative Analysis* (November 1975), pp. 695–98.

Weston, J. F. "A Managerial Orientation in the First Finance Course," *Journal of Financial and Quantitative Analysis* (November 1975), pp. 699–704.

Weston, J. F. *The Scope and Methodology of Finance*. Englewood Cliffs, N. J.: Prentice-Hall, Inc., 1966.

- **FINANCIAL STATEMENTS**
  - **BALANCE SHEETS**
  - **INCOME STATEMENTS**
  - **AUDITOR OPINION**

- **FINANCIAL ANALYSIS**
  - **LIQUIDITY RATIOS**
  - **ACTIVITY RATIOS**
  - **LEVERAGE RATIOS**
  - **PROFITABILITY RATIOS**
  - **INTERPRETATION**
  - **SOURCES OF COMPARATIVE DATA**
  - **COMMON-SIZE STATEMENTS**
  - **TREND ANALYSIS AND ANALYST PERSPECTIVE**
  - **LIMITATIONS AND BIASES**

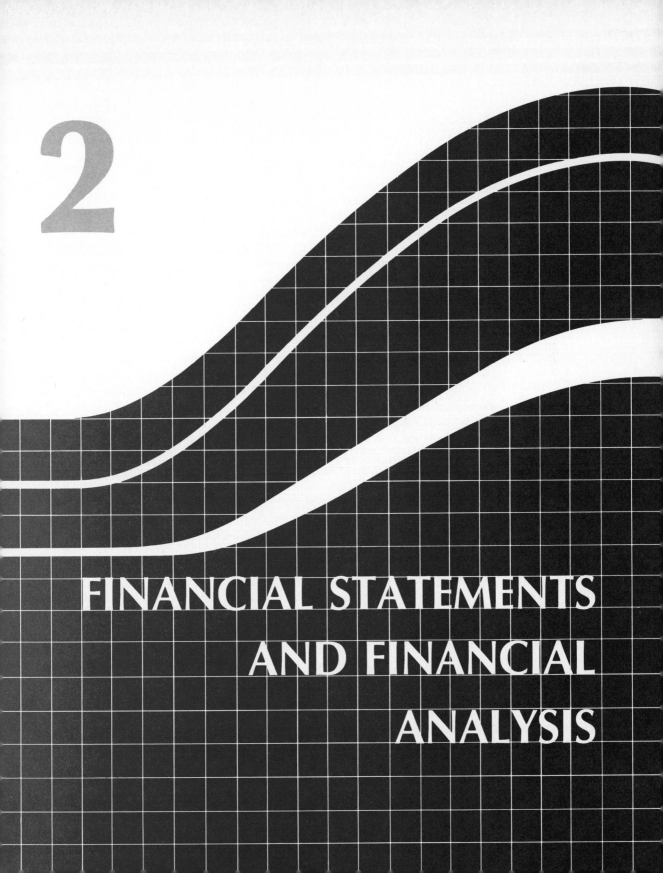

2

FINANCIAL STATEMENTS AND FINANCIAL ANALYSIS

The complexity of modern business requires the use of well-developed information systems for reporting and analysis. Such systems are based on accounting techniques that can provide a condensed and internally consistent picture of the firm. The *balance sheet* is a capsule summary of the financial status of the firm on a specified statement date. The *income statement* summarizes the results of the firm's operations during the period between two balance sheets.

Ratio analysis is a means of interpreting these accounting statements that examines the relationships between various accounting totals. A ratio may be constructed by dividing one balance sheet amount by another. Other ratios deal with relationships between asset (or liability) amounts from the balance sheet and revenue (or expense) flows from the income statement.

This chapter defines, discusses, and illustrates a number of ratio calculations. In reading about ratios, keep in mind that (1) a ratio is affected by any change in either the numerator or the denominator and that (2) a ratio is only a number; interpretation depends on judgment based on additional information about the company, the industry, and the economic environment.

Throughout this chapter, we utilize a hypothetical company, Electrodynamic Corp., as an example. Electrodynamic is patterned on several medium-sized electronics manufacturers. However, the example balance sheet and income statement are simplified; round numbers are used, atypical company-specific accounts and expense classifications are eliminated, and immaterial (small) accounts are omitted. The result is a sanitized set of accounting statements that are easier to use in examples. The relationships in this firm are, however, typical of what might be expected in an electronics manufacturer of this size. All ratios are calculated in decimal form; the results are sometimes restated or interpreted as percentages where this form is more intuitively appealing.

This chapter starts by reviewing Electrodynamic's financial statements. Financial analysis is then explained by analyzing Electrodynamic's statements. Some interpretation is provided with the calculation of each ratio. However, ratios should not be interpreted one at a time. Ratio analysis should be considered as a whole and in the context of industry comparison. An interpretation section uses Electrodynamic to illustrate the process.

After careful study of this chapter, you should

1. Understand the data presented in a balance sheet and income statement.
2. Be able to calculate and interpret ratios in order to answer the following questions about a company:
   a) How liquid is the firm?
   b) How well does the firm use its resources?
   c) How heavily debt financed is the firm?
   d) Are profits reasonable for the sales level and resources employed?
3. Be able to construct and analyze *common-size financial statements*.

FINANCIAL STATEMENTS

BALANCE SHEETS

Assets

The **balance sheet** reports the assets, liabilities, and stockholder equity (net worth) of a business firm as of a given reporting date. Assets must equal the sum of creditor and owner claims on those assets: assets = liabilities + stockholder equity. (This equation can also be written as: assets − liabilities = stockholder equity. If liabilities exceed assets, the equity amount is negative and the firm is technically bankrupt.) Table 2.1 presents a balance sheet for Electrodynamic Corp.

Definition

An **asset** is any item a firm owns that is expected to generate future benefits and is measurable in dollar terms. Tangibles such as cash, receivables, and plants are easy to understand: They have value, are expected to generate future benefits, and are dollar denominated. Intangibles are slightly more difficult to envision but can be illustrated by examples. Consider that Electrodynamic has developed a patentable electronic device. Development of such a device would entail research and development costs, and getting the patent would involve legal fees. The sum of these costs would be carried on the balance sheet as an asset, because having the patent is expected to produce future benefits.

The same rationale explains carrying prepaid expenses as assets. Sound accounting practice requires that costs be matched with the revenues they

---

TABLE 2.1
Electrodynamic Corp. Balance Sheet December 31, 1983 (in 000s).

Cash	$ 600	Accounts payable	$ 8,250
Marketable securities	1,050	Notes payable	4,225
Accounts receivable	14,500	Current portion of long-term debt	1,375
Inventories	21,250	Accruals	3,300
Other current assets	330	Total current liabilities	17,150
Total current assets	37,730	Long-term debt	15,345
Plant and equipment	19,500		
Accumulated depreciation	2,890	Common stock	10,630
New plant and equipment	16,610	Retained earnings	11,875
Intangibles	660	Net worth	22,505
Total assets	$55,000	Total liabilities and net worth	$55,000

help to produce. If a cost has been incurred but the revenues have not yet been realized, such costs are carried as an asset until a later date, when they are then charged off against the revenue they helped to create. This procedure produces a more representative measure of income in both the current and future accounting periods.

Assets are of two types—current and fixed. **Current assets** are those that would normally be converted into cash within the next 12 months, including cash, marketable securities, accounts receivable, and inventories.

Cash. Cash includes checking account balances, cash receipts not yet deposited, and currency on hand. Firms must spend money to sustain operations; they will incur cash outflows to pay for goods, services, rent, utilities, and labor. When the firm is paid for its own goods and services, cash inflows will result. Rarely, however, will outflows and inflows exactly match; sometimes there will be excess cash inflows, while at other times there will be excess cash outflows. In the latter case, the firm must use its cash reserves or borrow to meet the short-run imbalance. When the firm has temporary excess cash, it may invest such funds in marketable securities.

Marketable securities. Keeping idle cash is expensive. Pure cash generates no income. For temporary investment, safety is the first consideration; return is secondary, so the appropriate securities for temporary investments are as safe as possible. Temporary investments are usually in short-term, low-risk, highly marketable securities of the strongest firms and the U.S. government, which are near-money forms of investment.

Receivables. Most sales between businesses are on credit—short-term credit. The amount of money that the firm is owed for its credit sales of goods and services is the accounts receivable balance.

Inventories. Inventories include the *finished goods* a firm holds for sale to its customers. If the firm is a manufacturer, part of its inventories will not be ready for sale, being uncompleted; these inventories are called *work-in-progress*. The *raw materials* the manufacturer uses to make its product are also a component of inventories. Inventories usually represent the highest dollar value current asset of a business.

Inventories are valued according to the accounting convention of "lower of cost or market," which means that they are generally recorded at cost. If, however, the market value of the product has dropped below cost, the inventory should be written down to what could actually be received for it.

The method of accounting for inventory affects not only book value but also the company's profits. Two common inventory accounting procedures are LIFO (last in, first out) and FIFO (first in, first out). LIFO assumes that the most recently received or produced units are the first sold; FIFO assumes that old units are sold first. These two procedures can produce markedly different balance sheets and income statements.

Under LIFO, inventories sold during the period are valued at the near replacement cost rather than at the purchase cost. If prices are rising, this results in on-hand inventories that are carried at conservative (low) values, while those sold are valued at more current (high) prices. This increases the cost of goods sold and reduces profits (and income taxes). On the other hand, when FIFO is used during periods of rising prices, the higher-priced inventories stay on the balance sheet while the less expensive ones go through cost of goods sold, increasing reported income (and taxes).

Unless a company is speculating in inventories (holding excess inventory in anticipation of price increases), the objective of inventory management is to minimize costs while maintaining adequate inventory to sustain production and supply customer needs. The actual amount kept on hand will depend on the nature of the business; longer and more complicated production processes require larger investments in inventory. The quantity of finished goods kept on hand should also reflect any cyclical or seasonal variation in the demand for the product. Seasonal or cyclical patterns must be anticipated in production scheduling, which also affects work-in-process and raw materials inventories.

Efficient inventory management is a determining factor in the success of a business. In our current economy, product life cycles are shorter than they have ever been. Some products are salable for years; others have an economic life measured in days. Obsolescence is an endemic problem in high-technology markets such as electronics; a mistake can kill a company. Chapter 9 discusses inventory management in greater depth.

Plant and equipment. Plant and equipment are the fixed assets that the firm uses to produce the goods and services it sells to generate revenues. These assets are reported at original cost less depreciation. Accumulated depreciation is the sum of all past and current-period depreciation charges on plant and equipment currently owned by the company. Subtracting accumulated depreciation from the cost of these assets yields net plant and equipment.

Other noncurrent assets. Intangible assets increase the profit potential of a business, but they are not of a physical nature. They include such items as goodwill, patents, trademarks, licenses, franchises, and other items that may be presumed to endow the firm that owns them with extra rights, privileges, or advantages. Intangibles are recorded only when they have been acquired at cost, and they may be written off (**amortized**) in much the same way as plant and equipment. For example, the $660,000 on Electrodynamic's balance sheet represents development and legal fees associated with patenting some electronics devices. These costs would be amortized against future revenues the patents help generate.

Other assets. Some assets are classified as neither current assets nor fixed assets. To illustrate: An investment in common stock of a subsidiary company would not be classified as either a current asset or a fixed asset. Although common stock could be sold within a year, it does not follow that it would be sold in the normal course of business. Among the other forms of long-term investments owned by a business firm that are classified as noncurrent assets are preferred stock, bonds, mortgage notes, and real estate not used in business operations. Investments appear on the balance sheet at cost. Other noncurrent assets owned may include the cash surrender value of life insurance policies, advances to subsidiaries, and other items not classified as current or fixed assets.

Deferred charges, which are classified as noncurrent assets, are similar to prepaid expenses, but their nature justifies their amortization over a period of years. Deferred charges include costs that are expected to affect income for a number of years, such as advertising expenditures that will benefit the firm for a period of time, costs of factory layouts or removal to new locations, and discounts and expenses associated with long-term capital financing. (The present trend is to minimize or eliminate the deferred charges classification.)

Liabilities

Liabilities are debts of the firm. They may either be short-term (**current liabilities**) or stretch out for as long as 30 years. Current liabilities include accounts and notes payable, the current obligations on long-term debt, and accruals of expenses not yet paid.

Accounts and notes payable. Accounts payable are for the purchase of goods and services. Businesses customarily extend credit to one another as a matter of convenience. Periodically, usually once a month, a firm pays its suppliers. Until these bills are paid, they appear on the balance sheet as accounts payable.

If a loan (or note) has a maturity of less than one year, it is a current liability. The total of such obligations is the notes payable balance.

Current portion of long-term debt. Installment payments of term loans, serial bonds, mortgage notes, and other long-term obligations that are due within a year are current liabilities. Reclassification of such amounts is necessary if the *net working capital* position of the business is to be determined or if a *current ratio* is to be calculated correctly.

Accruals. Not all expenses are paid as charges are incurred. A good example is payroll. Workers are not paid every day; payrolls are usually disbursed every week or two, and sometimes monthly. Those expenses already incurred but not yet paid are recorded as a liability, an accrual.

Accrued income taxes are another common example. Federal income tax prepayments are made quarterly. At the end of the fiscal year, three quarterly payments normally have been made. The remaining balance, based on the period's income, is shown as an outstanding accrual.

Long-term debt. Long-term debt includes term bank notes, mortgage loans, bonds, notes, purchase obligations, and other debts having a maturity of more than one year from the statement date. Such debts, or portions of them, become current in the fiscal period when they mature; they are then recorded as current liabilities. The long-term balance is shown separately to indicate the difference in the immediacy of the payment obligation.

Stockholder Equity

Customarily, stockholder equity has three elements: the **par value** or stated value of outstanding shares of capital stock; contributed capital in excess of par or stated value (called *paid-in capital* in legal terminology); and **retained earnings**. Common and preferred issues are reported separately, as are any other classes of stock outstanding. The number of authorized shares of each class is disclosed parenthetically.

Capital in excess of the par or stated value may result from (1) issuance of shares at an amount in excess of par, (2) gifts or donations of assets or shares of the company's own stock to the corporation, (3) reduction of par, and (4) reacquisition of fully paid shares from stockholders. When transactions involving this account are numerous or especially significant, a separate supplementary statement may be prepared, such as the one shown in Table 2.2.

Retained earnings. Retained earnings is the sum of all of the corporation's income (including that of the current year) that has not been paid out to the shareholders as dividends. Payment of dividends to stockholders is presumed

TABLE 2.2
Electrodynamic Corp. Stockholder Equity (in 000s).

Capital Stock	1982	1983
Common stock, $.50 Par value: Authorized, 5,000,000 shares; Outstanding 1982, 1,750,000 shares; 1983, 2,000,000 shares	$ 875	$ 1,000
Paid-in capital	6,880	9,630
Retained earnings	9,385	11,875
	$17,140	$22,505

TABLE 2.3
Electrodynamic Corp. Accumulated Retained Earnings for Fiscal Year 1983 (in 000s).

Balance January 1	$ 9,385
Net profit for year	3,320
Total	12,705
Less: Dividends paid on	
Common stock	(830)
Balance December 31	$11,875

to be a distribution of retained earnings, not a return of capital. Some states allow dividends to be charged (partially) to contributed capital; if this is the case, sound accounting requires that the dividend be described, in part, as a liquidating dividend.

If a company's accounting policy is to report extraordinary and nonrecurring items of gain or loss on the income statement, direct charges or credits to retained earnings are restricted to the transfer of net income for the period and distributions of appropriations. An alternative treatment (generally accepted) permits extraordinary gains or losses to be entered in the Retained Earnings account without passing through the income statement. For this reason, a separate statement of changes in retained earnings is necessary to complete financial reporting. A statement of retained earnings for Electrodynamic, which had no extraordinary gains in 1983, is shown in Table 2.3.

INCOME STATEMENTS

Income statements summarize the operations of a company during a fiscal period, showing revenue and the expenses incurred in earning that revenue. Expenses are deducted from revenue in order to arrive at net income or net loss for the accounting period. The income statement explains the change in retained earnings caused by operations from one balance sheet to the next. It usually encompasses 12-month operations, although interim statements may be issued for shorter periods, such as a quarter.

The primary source of revenue is sales. Gross sales figures are reported, with any adjustment for returns, allowances, and discounts deducted to give net sales. In a merchandising or manufacturing concern, gross profit on sales is found by deducting the cost of the product sold from the net revenue. Several ratios are calculated using gross profit and are used to compare firms' profitability. High gross profits relative to sales indicate that the firm is selling merchandise at high prices, is effectively controlling costs, or some combination of the two.

TABLE 2.4
Electrodynamic Corp. Income Statement for Fiscal Year 1983 (in 000s).

Sales	$ 78,300
Less: Returns and allowances	800
Net sales	77,500
Cost of goods sold	(47,275)
Gross margin	$ 30,225
Selling and administrative expense	16,800
Depreciation	1,625
Amortization	130
Research and development	2,170
Total operating expense	$(20,725)
Earnings before interest and taxes	9,500
Interest expense	(3,350)
Earnings before taxes	6,150
Taxes	(2,830)
Net income	$ 3,320

Typical treatment of expenses is by function, with selling expenses grouped, general administrative expenses next, and finally income tax expense stated separately. Table 2.4 depicts an income statement for Electrodynamic for fiscal year 1983.

Most corporations' annual financial statements include comparative statements from prior years. The ability to compare this year's balance sheet, or income statement, to last year's adds perspective. By comparing the two statements, an investor can better assess the firm's position and progress.

AUDITOR OPINION

Evaluating a company by examining its financial statements presumes that these statements fairly present the financial position of the firm and the results of its operations. The financial community's reliance on accounting statements is largely due to its faith in the integrity of the accounting process.

The financial statements of publicly owned firms are generally prepared by independent accountants, outsiders, who are responsible to the public for ensuring that these statements are prepared in accordance with generally accepted accounting principles and represent the firm fairly. Such statements always include an auditor opinion or certification of their validity. When examining accounting statements, one should always read the auditor opinion. Auditors are required by their professional ethics to disclose any unusual accounting that might mislead the reader. If the auditor opinion contains any disclaimer, caution and further investigation are in order. If the statements are prepared "without audit," let the user beware.

Footnotes to a financial statement are also important in interpreting the meaning of the statement. Such footnotes must fully disclose the nature of any unusual facet of a firm's assets, liabilities, revenues, and/or expenses. The footnotes, as part of the statements, are also audited. A careful analyst of financial statements cannot overlook the footnotes; often they contain significant information about the company and its operations.

FINANCIAL ANALYSIS

Financial analysis is a natural extension of and an adjunct to accounting. Accounting procedures aggregate data and eliminate detail in order to present a clear picture of the firm. Ratio analysis omits even more detail. Ratios are relationships between different account balances, or between account balances and various income statement amounts. Each ratio calculation is intended to highlight some aspect of the firm's performance. Some of the main concerns of a business analyst are (1) a firm's ability to pay its short-term obligations, (2) the extent to which a business effectively uses its assets, (3) the way in which the business is financed, and (4) the profitability of the firm's operations. The four main types of ratios measure *liquidity, activity, leverage,* and *profitability.*

After study of this material, you should understand how to use ratios to answer some important questions about a company. If you understand ratio analysis, you should be able to use a firm's financial statements to answer the following questions:

1. How liquid is the firm; that is, can it pay its short-term bills?
2. Does the firm use its assets effectively; that is, is it generating enough sales compared to the assets it employs?
3. How leveraged is the company; that is, how much borrowed money is used in financing the business?
4. Are profits high enough compared to the assets and equity investment in this firm?

LIQUIDITY RATIOS

Liquidity ratios measure a firm's short-term bill-paying ability. They compare the assets available for meeting current obligations with the level of those obligations.

Current Ratio

Current obligations must be paid when they come due. Liquidity ratios evaluate the firm's ability to satisfy its creditors in the near term, and the **current ratio** is one of the most widely used liquidity ratios. It is calculated by dividing total current assets by total current liabilities. Electrodynamic's current ratio (see Table 2.1) is

$$\frac{\text{Current assets}}{\text{Current liabilities}} = \frac{\$37,730}{\$17,150} = 2.20.$$

A convenient intuitive interpretation of the current ratio is that Electrodynamic has $2.20 in assets that could be liquidated (converted to cash) this year for each dollar of current obligations.

There is no single correct benchmark for the current ratio. Traditionally, a current ratio of 2 to 1 has been considered appropriate. Recently, though, long production cycles coupled with shorter product life cycles have undermined the validity of this rigid standard. Now greater reliance is placed on comparison to industry norms. You will see how industry comparisons aid in ratio interpretation as you learn more about ratio analysis.

A low current ratio may be improved, or raised, in several ways: by repaying current debts, borrowing on longer terms, collecting tax refunds, converting noncurrent assets into current assets, and increasing investments in current assets by retaining earnings. On the other hand, the current ratio may be reduced by short-term borrowing, buying goods and materials on account, accruing federal income taxes and other expenses, converting current assets into noncurrent assets, and paying cash dividends.

The chief advantage of having a high current ratio is that it cushions a firm against difficulties that arise when accounts receivable become noncollectible or inventories unsalable. When there is insufficient cash to meet maturing liabilities, a business firm is at the mercy of its creditors. As bankers are interested in making loans that will be repaid, a business firm with a low current ratio will find it difficult to borrow when its need may be greatest. The current ratio is not an infallible measure of short-term liquidity, but it is an easy-to-calculate index of the ability of a business firm to pay its short-term debts.

Since we have noted that the current ratio is fallible, it seems appropriate to provide some warning about the danger of having too high a current ratio. A firm's current ratio may be high because of too large an investment in accounts receivables or excess inventory. An inflated accounts receivable balance can indicate that there are collection problems or that some accounts should be written off as uncollectible.

Excess inventories can be especially dangerous. The cause of such excess might be temporary lack of demand or, worse, the company may be stuck with technologically obsolete or outdated products. One purpose of activity ratio analysis is to detect such problems.

Acid-Test (Quick) Ratio

The current ratio measures a firm's liquidity, but there is a problem with it—inventories. The current ratio implicitly considers inventories as liquid and, on occasion, they may not be. The mistaken consideration of inventories as a highly liquid asset could lead to a serious misestimate of a firm's near-term liquidity. Rapid liquidation of inventories is generally costly to a firm, forcing it to reduce the prices for its products.

The **acid-test**, or **quick, ratio** applies a more severe measure of liquidity by subtracting the value of inventories from the current ratio numerator. This ratio is calculated by dividing "quick assets" by current liabilities. For Electrodynamic the ratio would be

$$\frac{\text{Current assets} - \text{inventories}}{\text{Current liabilities}} = \frac{\text{quick assets}}{\text{current liabilities}} = \frac{\$37,730 - 21,250}{\$17,150} = .96.$$

The interpretation of the measure is straightforward. Electrodynamic has $0.96 in truly liquid assets for each dollar of near-term liabilities. An acceptable quick ratio has been a minimum of $1 of liquid assets for each dollar of liabilities. Industries may differ, though, and in an industry with highly predictable cash receipts, firms can generally afford to maintain lower liquidity, that is, lower quick ratios.

ACTIVITY RATIOS

Activity ratios evaluate how well the company is using its assets. Comparisons are between level of activity (sales) and investment in some type of asset. Many of the activity ratios are referred to as turnover ratios, meaning that the analyst has divided some measure of sales by some asset. The two most common turnover ratios are **total asset turnover** and **inventory turnover**.

Total Asset Turnover

This ratio evaluates how well the firm is utilizing its total resources. For Electrodynamic, the ratio is

$$\frac{\text{Net sales}}{\text{Total assets}} = \frac{\$77,500}{\$55,000} = 1.41 \text{ to } 1.$$

This figure by itself is meaningless. To determine if the company is performing well, the ratio must be compared to those for other firms, or averages, in the same industry during the same time period. The ratio is also very sensitive to prevailing economic conditions. Even after taking into account industry and economy influences, there are problems in comparing one firm with another. For example, a low-turnover company may be suffering a loss of sales or have an inflated asset base. Further, the loss in sales may be due to low volume, depressed product prices, or a combination thereof.

There are many reasons why the ratio denominator can cause problems. Accounting decisions can create difficulties with comparability. The speed with which bad debts are written off affects the value of receivables. Use of LIFO versus FIFO affects inventory value. Old plants, because of the effects of inflation, are carried at a lower cost than new ones. Accelerated depreciation methods reduce book values for plants and equipment. Each of these accounting decisions affects total assets and as a result influences a firm's total asset turnover.

Examination of total asset turnover trends for a firm compared to some appropriate norm can provide valuable insights. This insight, in turn, can be heightened by examination of the use of particular assets.

Inventory Turnover Ratio

Avoiding excessive investment in materials, merchandise, and supplies is an elementary rule of financial management, but probably no rule is violated more frequently. Usually, inventory is not only the largest but also the least liquid of a firm's current assets. One widely used measure of investment in inventory is net sales divided by inventory value, which for Electrodynamic is as follows:

$$\frac{\text{Net sales}}{\text{Inventories}} = \frac{\$77,500}{\$21,250} = 3.65 \text{ times.}$$

This inventory turnover ratio is overstated by the amount of the gross profit on sales. The inventory turnover ratio based on the cost of goods sold is as follows:

$$\frac{\text{Cost of goods sold}}{\text{Inventories}} = \frac{\$47,275}{\$21,250} = 2.22 \text{ times.}$$

Ideally, inventory turnover should be based on the cost of goods sold. However, many sources of comparative figures use the net sales calculation. Obviously, for valid comparisons, your ratio should be calculated as it is in the published report.

Comparing a firm's turnover ratio to that of other companies in the same industry gives some indication of whether the business has too much money tied up in inventory. An analyst cannot ignore how the company values its inventories; if the firm uses LIFO while the rest of the industry uses FIFO, the comparison will be distorted. The same thing can happen if the firm uses an atypical fiscal year. When this occurs, the balance sheet inventories are atypical (e.g., in retail businesses, end-of-year inventories are usually low, while mid-year inventories may be high in anticipation of back-to-school demand).

The conclusion usually reached about inventory turnover ratios is that the more rapid the turnover, the smaller the amount of working capital needed in terms of net sales and the larger the total profits (unless the apparent rapidity of sales is due to an excessive markdown in prices, understocking, and other factors). Holding more inventories than needed is a form of speculation that is usually criticized. Sometimes, however, speculation in inventories is profitable (as during the OPEC oil embargo). The inventory turnover ratio is intended to indicate the liquidity of the inventory, the degree to which management tends to overstock, and the efficiency with which inventory is handled. Any decrease in the inventory turnover ratio will raise doubts about the efficiency of inventory management.

Average Collection Period (Days' Sales)

Average collection period, sometimes called *days' sales*, is a measure used to evaluate the level of investment in receivables compared to the volume of sales. For Electrodynamic, the ratio is

$$\frac{\text{Receivables}}{\text{One day's sales}} = \frac{\text{receivables}}{\text{annual sales}/360} = \frac{\$14,500}{\$77,500/360} = 67 \text{ days.}$$

Electrodynamic's 1983 sales were $77,500,000. Using 360 days as a year, sales were approximately $215,000 per day. As of December 31 the firm had $14,500,000 tied up in accounts receivable—slightly more than 67 days' sales.

We have suggested that calculating inventory turnover using cost of goods sold is more correct. Similarly, average collection period would be more informative if calculated using only credit sales. Total sales, though, is the more generally used measure. The reason is the same as for the inventory turnover ratio: Agencies that report industry averages use total sales in their calculations. An individual firm's ratio should be calculated the same way. However, in any company with an unusually high (or low) proportion of credit sales, the comparison can be materially distorted.

There is another problem with the average collection period calculation. Year-end receivables may be atypical because of seasonal patterns in sales or collections. A more accurate method would be to use a monthly (or weekly or even daily) average for receivables. This, however, would be difficult for a single firm and even more so for an industry. To the extent that firm-to-industry relationships remain relatively constant, it is possible to assess a firm's receivables policy by examining its average collection period relative to the industry and relative to its own performance over time. When the average collection period is longer than that of the industry, and when it is increasing over that of previous years, it is time for management to review its credit and collection policies.

Aging of Accounts Receivable

The days' sales calculation is a quick way of evaluating a firm's accounts receivable investment and its collection procedures. Greater understanding of receivables can be gained by aging them. To prepare an **aging schedule** of accounts receivable, the total amount is broken down into age groups, for example, less than 30 days, 30–60 days, 60–90 days, and over 90 days. These amounts can also be expressed as percentages. The aging pattern adds perspective to the less detailed days' sales calculation.

For Electrodynamic the breakdown is as follows:

Under 30	30–60	60–90	Over 90
$8,845	$2,900	$725	$2,030
61%	20%	5%	14%

The added detail reveals a problem that would have otherwise gone undetected. As we will see later, Electrodynamic's days' sales pattern is in line with the industry. However, the aging schedule indicates that the company has some problem accounts; 14% of its accounts are over 90 days old, and some are probably uncollectible. The aging schedule indicates that some immediate attention to this problem is in order.

LEVERAGE RATIOS

Leverage ratios measure the extent to which a company is financed with debt. There are two types of leverage ratios: (1) those based on balance sheet accounts and (2) those derived from income statements.

Balance Sheet Leverage Ratios

Balance sheet leverage measures compare the amount of debt outstanding to how much the firm has in assets or in equity capital. There are a number of such ratios. The calculation is easy to understand because the name usually makes it clear how the calculation is to be done. These ratios normally have debt in the numerator and some measure of assets (or equity) in the denominator. Examples of this type of ratio include long-term debt to net worth, total debt to net worth, long-term debt to fixed assets, and total debt to total assets.

The ratios an analyst uses depends on his or her personal tastes and the availability of comparison figures. Total debt to total assets is a commonly used measure; comparison figures are generally available, and the interpretation is straightforward. This ratio indicates what proportion of the firm's total financing is borrowed money. For Electrodynamic the proportion is

$$\frac{\text{Total debt}}{\text{Total assets}} = \frac{\$32,495}{\$55,000} = .59 \quad \text{or} \quad 59\%.$$

Total debt includes current liabilities and long-term debt. In Electrodynamic 59% of all financing is debt. A firm with a low debt ratio is less risky than one that finances heavily with debt. When the economy slumps, making debt payments can be difficult. In good times, though, creditors do not get part of the profits. Whether heavy debt financing can be used depends on the nature of the business. Electric utilities are examples of firms that can and have used extensive debt financing. Their assets are long-lived plant and equipment. Their cash flows are highly predictable; customers need electricity, and if they do not pay their bills, electric service will be discontinued. Long-term financing needs and predictable cash flows both encourage heavy debt financing. Many firms' financing needs are based on their asset needs and the dependability of their cash flows. These characteristics vary from industry to industry. For this reason, leverage ratios are industry sensitive; a firm's leverage ratios should be compared to industry averages.

Income Statement Leverage Ratios

Income statement leverage ratios compare a firm's ability to pay some form of leverage expense to the amount of that expense. This is done by dividing earnings (before the expense) by the amount of the expense. Since these ratios show how well the expense is covered, they are also called *coverage ratios*.

One leverage expense that firms must cover is interest. The **times-interest-earned ratio** is calculated by dividing **EBIT (earnings before interest and taxes)** by interest charges. Electrodynamic's times-interest-earned ratio is

$$\frac{\text{EBIT}}{\text{Interest charges}} = \frac{\$9,500}{\$3,350} = 2.84 \text{ times.}$$

This ratio shows how far earnings can fall before the firm will run into difficulty in meeting its annual interest costs. Electrodynamic's operating earnings could fall to approximately one-third (1/2.84 = .35) of its current level and still cover the interest expense. Since payments must be made from earnings over a period of time, this ratio measures the company's ability to service its debt. Trends in this ratio are usually watched carefully by long-term creditors. In addition, when the company has bonds outstanding, the times-interest-earned ratio is a partial determinant of its bond rating.

PROFITABILITY RATIOS

To stay in business, a company must generate reasonable profits. Whether profits are high enough is obviously important. Creditors are concerned about profits because profitability partially determines whether they will be repaid. Shareholders invest in the hope of participating in profits in the form of dividends. Managers are concerned that if profits are too low, they may be fired.

Each ratio discussed in this section has the same numerator—income. Each ratio is concerned with the same issue: Are profits high enough compared to sales, compared to assets employed, and compared to the level of equity investment?

Return on Sales

The **return on sales** ratio measures the percentage profit on each dollar of sales. For Electrodynamic this is

$$\frac{\text{Net income}}{\text{Sales}} = \frac{\$3,320}{\$77,500} = .043 \quad \text{or} \quad 4.3\%.$$

Because net income is affected by interest expense and tax rates, the percentage may be affected by factors other than operations. To eliminate these effects the **operating margin ratio** is sometimes used instead; it is:

$$\frac{\text{EBIT}}{\text{Sales}} = \frac{\$9,500}{\$77,500} = .123 \quad \text{or} \quad 12.3\%.$$

Return on Total Assets

The **return on total assets** ratio measures the return on the firm's total asset base. Again, the ratio may be calculated using net income or EBIT. For Electrodynamic the figures would be

$$\frac{\text{Net income}}{\text{Total assets}} = \frac{\$3,320}{\$55,000} = .060 \quad \text{or} \quad 6.0\%$$

$$\frac{\text{EBIT}}{\text{Total assets}} = \frac{\$9,500}{\$55,000} = .173 \quad \text{or} \quad 17.3\%.$$

These profitability ratios are performance measures widely used by stockholders and creditors, as well as by management.

Return on Net Worth

Shareholders are generally concerned about the return they make on invested capital. This may be determined by comparing net income to net worth. For Electrodynamic the **return on net worth** ratio is

$$\frac{\text{Net income}}{\text{Net worth}} = \frac{\$3,320}{\$22,505} = .148 \quad \text{or} \quad 14.8\%.$$

A company that has preferred stock outstanding will require adjustment to the figures to reflect the effect of this form of financing. Net income would be reduced for preferred stock dividends, and net worth would be reduced for the preferred outstanding.

INTERPRETATION

We have frequently mentioned comparison to industry norms while discussing individual ratios. We have postponed actual comparisons until now for good reason. Ratios should not be analyzed one at a time. It is when all the ratios are considered together, in comparison to industry norms, that the picture emerges.

In this section, we will put the pieces together for Electrodynamic. Table 2.5 summarizes the ratios we have calculated, with the comparable industry figures and capsule summary interpretations.

Considered together, Electrodynamic's ratios reveal things about the company that would not be apparent if the ratios were considered one at a time. Electrodynamic's current ratio looks acceptable, maybe even good. The quick ratio, however, suggests that meeting short-term bills could cause problems. The two ratios together indicate a possible inventory problem; that is the only way a firm could have both a high current ratio and a low quick ratio. The low inventory turnover figure reinforces this interpretation.

Total asset turnover is almost exactly average. With low inventory turnover, Electrodynamic must be compensating in some way. Actually, it is compensating in several ways. It is carrying less cash and marketable securities than the average electronics firm of this size. At first glance, Electrodynamic appears to be squeezing its accounts receivable. However, our previous aging of these accounts suggests a different interpretation. Most of Electrodynamic's customers pay quickly; however, a troublesome minority result in only an average collection period. The firm appears to be using fewer fixed assets than average to generate sales.

Electrodynamic is financing with a fair amount of debt—more than average. Further, it is paying a lot of interest, as indicated by the low times-interest-earned ratio. This characteristic explains some rather unusual profitability ratios. The firm's EBIT-to-sales and EBIT-to-total-assets ratios are above

TABLE 2.5
Summary of Ratio Analysis

Ratios	Electrodynamic	Industry	Interpretation
Liquidity			
Current			
$\dfrac{\text{Current assets}}{\text{Current liabilities}}$	2.20	2.10	Slightly higher than the average company in this industry.
Quick			
$\dfrac{\text{Current assets} - \text{inventories}}{\text{Current liabilities}}$	.96	1.0	A little low.
Activity			
Total asset turnover			
$\dfrac{\text{Sales}}{\text{Total assets}}$	1.41	1.40	Almost exactly the same as the industry average.
Inventory turnover			
$\dfrac{\text{Cost of goods sold}}{\text{Inventories}}$	2.22	3.20	Very low.
Days' sales			
$\dfrac{\text{Receivables}}{\text{Sales}/360}$	67	68	Almost average.
Leverage			
Debt to assets			
$\dfrac{\text{Total debt}}{\text{Total assets}}$	59%	55%	A little high.
Times interest earned			
$\dfrac{\text{EBIT}}{\text{Interest charges}}$	2.84	7.20	Extremely low.
Profitability			
Operating margin			
$\dfrac{\text{EBIT}}{\text{Sales}}$	12.3%	11.4%	Above average.
Operating return on assets			
$\dfrac{\text{EBIT}}{\text{Total assets}}$	17.3%	15.9	Above average.
Return on net worth			
$\dfrac{\text{Net income}}{\text{Net worth}}$	14.8%	16.2%	Below average.

TABLE 2.6
Electrodynamic Corp. ROI Analysis.

	Total asset turnover	×	Return on sales	=	Return on assets	÷	1 − Debt ratio	=	Return on net worth
	$\dfrac{\text{Sales}}{\text{Total assets}}$	×	$\dfrac{\text{Net income}}{\text{Sales}}$	=	$\dfrac{\text{Net income}}{\text{Total asset}}$	÷	$\left(1 - \dfrac{\text{Debt}}{\text{Assets}}\right)$	=	$\dfrac{\text{Net income}}{\text{Net worth}}$
Electrodynamic	$\left(\dfrac{77,500}{55,000}\right.$	×	$\dfrac{3,320}{77,500}$	=	$\dfrac{3,320}{55,000}$	÷	$\left(1 - \dfrac{32,495}{55,000}\right)$	=	.148
	$\left. 1.41 \right.$	×	.043	=	.060	÷	$(1 - .59)$	=	.148
Electronics industry	1.40	×	.052	=	.073	÷	$(1 - .55)$	=	.162

average, but return on net worth is low. Because of the level of debt financing and the high interest rates, returns to the stockholders are reduced.

Knowing ratio interrelationships is helpful in understanding patterns like those in Electrodynamic's return figures. One of the most useful sets of relationships is specified in the **DuPont Return-on-Investment (ROI)** system. The system can be stated concisely as follows:

$$\frac{\text{Sales}}{\text{Total assets}} \times \frac{\text{net income}}{\text{sales}} = \frac{\text{net income}}{\text{total assets}}$$

$$\frac{\text{Net income}}{\text{Total assets}} \div \left(1 - \frac{\text{debt}}{\text{total assets}}\right) = \frac{\text{net income}}{\text{net worth}}.$$

The ROI system was originally developed to encourage managers to think through all the implications of a particular decision. Here, we use it merely as an organizing concept for ratio analysis, and our brief discussion of the process does not do it justice. Its use as a planning tool is more important. Table 2.6 shows how the ROI system might be used to highlight ratio inter-relationships and to compare a company to its industry.

Together, the information in Tables 2.5 and 2.6 tells us quite a bit about Electrodynamic. Table 2.5 shows that it has some liquidity problems and large inventories. We also see that the firm uses a lot of debt financing, with consequent high interest costs. While the firm seems to generate good operating returns (on sales and assets), net returns are low because of interest expense. Turnover is about normal and will not offset these low returns. The result is the low *net* return on assets and net worth shown in Table 2.6.

SOURCES OF COMPARATIVE DATA

The previous example shows a way to use industry averages to help interpret ratios. Sources for such data include Dun & Bradstreet (D&B), Robert Morris Associates, the Federal Trade Commission (FTC), and the Securities and Exchange Commission (SEC). Probably the most widely known and used are the industry averages published by D&B, which provides 14 key ratios, by quartiles, for 125 selected industries. Table 2.7 contains excerpts from a recent D&B ratio summary. The FTC and SEC jointly publish quarterly data on manufacturing companies. The ratios are relatively current, as they are usually published within six months after the corporations publish financial statements.

COMMON-SIZE STATEMENTS

Ratio analysis is one way to analyze financial statements. Common-size statements are another. These statements use percentages instead of dollar figures to facilitate comparison to industry norms, such as those provided in the Robert Morris *Annual Statement Studies*.

TABLE 2.7
Dun and Bradstreet Key Business Ratios for Selected Manufacturers, 1982–83
(upper quartile, median, and lower quartile

Two-digit SIC Code Type of Manufacturer (Number of Respondents)	Quick Ratio	Current Ratio	Current Liabilities to Inventory	Assets to Sales	Sales to Inventory	Collection Period
	Times	Times	Percent	Percent	Times	Days
SIC 20	1.7	3.2	84.7	20.6	34.1	13.8
Food and kindred products	0.9	1.8	147.6	32.3	18.0	20.9
(1,861)	0.5	1.2	276.4	52.0	9.6	30.2
SIC 28	1.9	3.6	70.3	33.5	14.9	29.9
Chemicals and allied	1.1	2.2	122.1	45.4	8.8	41.5
products (1,467)	0.7	1.4	196.7	66.6	5.8	56.5
SIC 29	1.4	2.5	116.4	28.8	27.0	22.9
Petroleum refining and	0.9	1.6	195.3	43.1	14.5	37.5
related industries (227)	0.6	1.2	334.4	64.9	9.2	54.7
SIC 36	1.9	3.7	67.6	34.7	13.6	33.9
Electrical and electronic	1.1	2.3	116.1	49.5	7.2	49.2
machinery, equipment, and supplies (2,493)	0.7	1.5	203.3	71.9	4.5	66.9
SIC 37	1.5	3.3	60.8	33.3	13.0	16.7
Transportation equipment	0.9	2.0	106.7	47.5	7.0	32.1
(1,185)	0.4	1.3	183.2	68.9	4.5	49.6

Source: By permission of Dun and Bradstreet Credit Services, a company of the Dun and Bradstreet Corporation.

Common-Size Balance Sheet

In a **common-size balance sheet,** all account balances are stated as a percentage of total assets. When a common-size balance sheet includes comparable percentages from industry averages, comparison will disclose any odd features of a company's financial position. In Table 2.8, a common-size balance sheet for Electrodynamic is compared to a similar statement for the electronic components industry.

Table 2.8 reveals problems about Electrodynamic that ratio analysis should have led us to expect. The percentage of current assets is about right, but its components are not: The firm has too little cash and too much inventory. On the liabilities side, the firm has more than normal debt outstanding, and the majority of it is interest-bearing.

Operating Income Statement

The **common-size income statement** is often referred to as an operating income statement. **Operating income statements** show each revenue and expense

Sales to Net Working Capital	Accounts Payable To Sales	Total Liabilities to Net Worth	Current Liabilities to Net Worth	Fixed Assets to Net Worth	Return on Sales	Return on Assets	Return on Net Worth
Times	Percent	Percent	Percent	Percent	Percent	Percent	Percent
25.2	1.7	37.5	24.6	37.4	5.8	13.1	24.7
12.0	3.7	88.2	55.8	68.9	2.5	7.0	14.7
6.6	6.2	184.0	117.7	117.7	0.8	2.5	5.9
11.5	3.5	33.4	25.7	21.4	9.2	14.6	27.6
6.3	5.8	80.5	52.7	47.1	4.9	7.8	15.2
4.0	9.6	172.9	112.7	85.0	1.9	3.6	7.7
22.1	4.6	59.7	39.9	24.4	5.0	9.0	21.6
10.1	7.5	124.6	70.9	60.1	2.3	4.6	11.8
5.2	11.0	242.1	147.6	132.9	0.5	0.6	1.7
9.9	3.2	38.1	27.0	18.2	10.7	15.4	34.5
5.2	5.7	88.7	58.8	37.4	5.9	8.9	18.0
3.2	9.2	188.1	131.3	72.0	2.3	3.2	8.0
12.7	2.8	40.1	28.0	26.9	8.2	13.9	29.1
6.7	5.1	101.5	63.5	51.6	4.3	6.8	14.5
4.0	8.0	213.4	142.5	96.8	1.5	2.2	5.7

entry as a percentage of net sales. Comparison to industry averages allows the analyst to spot ways in which the firm might improve its operations. Table 2.9 provides common-size income statements for the industry and Electrodynamic.

Table 2.9 shows that Electrodynamic's cost of goods sold is lower than average. This is generally good; it indicates that the firm is effectively controlling costs or is able to sell its products at a slightly higher than average markup. Selling and administration costs for the firm are a little high, and depreciation and amortization are a little low. Such slight deviations from industry averages would not normally cause concern, although they would suggest areas for further investigation of company practices. (Differences in depreciation and amortization are to be expected; depreciation depends on the age and cost of the plant and equipment and on the choice of depreciation method. Similar differences in amortization accounting can explain variations there.)

The relatively low research and development (R&D) percentage should be investigated. In high-technology industries, low R&D costs are not necessarily good; firms must keep up if they are to stay competitive.

TABLE 2.8
Common-Size Balance Sheet, Electrodynamic and Industry, Fiscal Year 1983

	Electrodynamic	Industry
Cash and marketable securities	3.0%	6.3%
Receivables	26.4	28.1
Inventories	38.6	31.7
Other current	.6	1.2
Total current assets	68.6	67.3
Fixed assets	30.2	28.1
Intangibles	1.2	.7
Other noncurrent	0	3.9
Total assets	100.0%	100.0%
Notes payable	7.7%	6.3%
Current portion long-term debt	2.5	2.8
Accounts payable	15.0	12.4
Accruals	6.0	7.1
Other current	0	4.6
Total current liabilities	31.2	33.2
Long-term debt	27.9	17.9
Other noncurrent	0	2.7
Net worth	40.9	46.2
Total liabilities and net worth	100.0%	100.0%

TABLE 2.9
Operating Income Statement, Electrodynamic and Industry, Fiscal Year 1983

	Electrodynamic	Industry
Sales	101.0%	
Returns and allowances	1.0	
Net sales	100.0	100.0%
Cost of goods sold	61.0	62.1
Gross margin	39.0	37.9
Selling and administrative expense	21.7	20.7
Depreciation	2.1	2.6
Amortization	.2	
Research and development	2.8	3.6
Total operating expenses	26.8	26.9
Earnings before interest and taxes	12.3	11.0
Interest expenses	4.3	1.5
Earnings before taxes	7.9	9.5
Taxes	3.7	4.3
Net income	4.2%	5.2%

The most alarming figure in Electrodynamic's operations is the interest expense. It is unusually high. Although we cannot, from financial analysis alone, consider it a problem, we can say that it deserves further investigation. Any analyst would want to know why this expense is so high. Has there been a conscious decision to finance so heavily with debt, or has the company been forced into this position? Some explanation must be found for this unusual variation from industry practice.

TREND ANALYSIS AND ANALYST PERSPECTIVE

Our example, Electrodynamic, illustrates how financial analysis might be interpreted. However, the discussion was simplified to make it easier to follow. This simplification caused two important omissions. In the analysis, we have failed to consider trends in the company's performance or the perspective of the person doing the analysis.

Trend Analysis

Ratio analysis should not consider merely where the company is at the moment. The analysis and its interpretation should be done in the context of how the company has done over time compared to the industry—**trend analysis.**

As an example, consider Electrodynamic's current ratio. At the time of the analysis, it was slightly higher than that of the average company in the industry. However, this evaluation should be tempered by a consideration of how the firm has fared over time. In Fig. 2.1, panels A and B present two different scenarios that could drastically alter the interpretation of this ratio.

In panel A, Electrodynamic has shown a steady increase in its current ratio over the last five years. In panel B, Electrodynamic's current ratio has declined from 3.0 in 1979 to the current 2.20. The same industry trend is used in both panels; the industry's current ratio has stayed close to 2.0, currently being slightly higher at 2.10.

You can readily understand how these two trends would put the present current ratio in a different light. However, do not be too quick to decide which panel paints the better picture of the firm. Trend analysis, like all ratio analysis, must be tempered with judgment based on a total picture.

The overly hasty might conclude that panel B indicates trouble and that panel A pictures a firm of growing strength. Our analysis of accounts receivable and inventory shows that the opposite might be true. Panel A could depict a firm whose accounts receivable (remember the aging schedule) and inventory investments are becoming too large. On the other hand, Panel B could indicate that these problems were previously much worse and are now being brought under control.

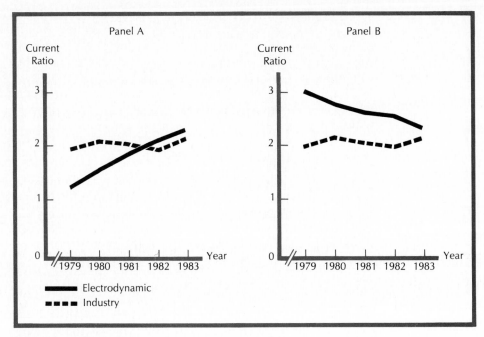

Figure 2.1 Trend analysis.

The point here is that you should not jump to conclusions. Ratios are diagnostic devices that must be used in combination. Using trend analysis adds perspective, as do industry averages, but the interpretation cannot be mechanical. Each company is different and must be analyzed in the context of its differences. The definition of a good ratio varies from one firm to the next. For internal management, a company should establish its own criteria for what is good and bad rather than trying to match industry averages.

Analyst Perspective

Throughout our discussion, we have implicitly assumed a financial management perspective. For this reason, we have looked at several types of ratios in attempting to assess where the company stands and how it is doing.

Management is not the only group that keeps an eye on a company. Every firm has several groups watching its performance. A firm's creditors, stockholders, and competitors are all keenly interested in how well it is doing. The emphasis of financial analysis changes depending upon the group to which an analyst belongs.

Creditors can be of two types, short-term and long-term. Short-term creditors tend to be more concerned about liquidity. Because they are the firms to which short-term liabilities are owed, they are concerned with the company's ability to service such near-term obligations.

Long-term creditors look at liquidity, but because of the nature of their loans to the company, they must also worry about the long term. For this reason, long-term creditors look at leverage and profitability ratios in addition to the liquidity measures. The likelihood that such creditors will be repaid depends on more than current liquidity. The ability to satisfy long-term indebtedness depends on how much of such debt is outstanding (leverage) and how effectively the firm is competing in its markets (profitability).

Shareholders put greater emphasis on profitability. As the last group to have a claim on company profits, shareholders are necessarily concerned about the relative size of those profits. Leverage is also a concern because creditors have a prior claim on the company's income (and assets in the case of a troubled firm).

Shareholders also use another type of ratio that we have not previously discussed—stock market ratios. These ratios are based on the market price of the company's stock. Investments classes spend considerable time examining such measures. For now, we will mention only two of them. **Dividend yield** and **price earnings (PE) ratio** are defined as follows:

$$\text{Dividend yield} = \frac{\text{per share dividend}}{\text{market price of stock}} \times 100$$

$$\text{PE ratio} = \frac{\text{market price of stock}}{\text{earnings per share}}.$$

The dividend yield expresses the annual cash dividend as a percentage of the stock price; this provides investors with one measure of the rate of return on an investment in a company's stock. Dividend yield is more important for some types of stock than others. Utility stocks have typically been considered income stocks, that is, stocks that are bought for their annual cash dividends. Dividend yield is important for income stocks.

Investors buy stock for more than the dividends. Price appreciation is one of the major attractions of investing in stocks. PE ratios indicate the multiple of earnings for which a company's stock is selling. This ratio is considered to be an important gauge of market sentiment with regard to a stock. Stocks that are expected to do well have high PEs. Growth stocks, those that are expected to experience above-average growth in earnings and price appreciation, normally have relatively high PE multiples. For this reason, a company's PE tells management what the market thinks of its performance and the company's future prospects.

Competitors are another group that is always keenly interested in how a company is doing. Further, every firm is continually monitoring the competition. If competitors are more profitable and are growing faster, it is possible that they can use their size and the related economies of scale and market position to further exploit their advantage. Extremely successful firms have even been known to buy less successful ones to further accelerate their growth. Invariably, some managers of acquired firms are relocated (or fired) in the process. This provides added incentive to watch the competition. Any change in the nature of their operations could signal an opportunity or a challenge.

LIMITATIONS AND BIASES

Financial analysis using ratios and common-size statements can be a very efficient way to dissect a firm's accounting statements. The techniques we have discussed help the analyst to better understand a company and to identify potential trouble spots. There are limitations to such techniques, and as a potential analyst, you must recognize some of the pitfalls.

Limitations

Financial analysts typically compare company ratios (or common-size statements) to industry norms. The usefulness to such comparison depends on (1) the correct identification of a firm's industry; (2) the quality of the firm's accounting data; (3) the similarity of the firm's accounting procedures to those of most other firms in the industry; and (4) the similarity of the firm's operations to the norm in the industry. Variability or error in any of these areas can limit the value of comparison.

Many companies are involved in more than one line of business and can be in more than one industry. Therefore, the choice of appropriate industry ratios can represent something of a compromise. The analyst can only hope to select the industry that can provide the most appropriate comparison. This problem exists to some degree even with single-line businesses; some of the firms that contribute to the industry averages may well be multi-industry businesses.

The results of analyzing a firm from its accounting data depend on the quality of those data. If the firm's statements are audited and attested to by a certified public accountant, you are assured that the statements have been prepared in compliance with generally accepted accounting principles (GAAP). However, accountants have quite a bit of latitude under GAAP; there is often more than one accepted method of accounting for a transaction.

There are various ways in which one firm's accounting practices could differ from an industry's. A few examples should be sufficient. The speed with which a firm writes off bad debts affects accounts receivable and therefore days' sales. Inventory valuation (LIFO as against FIFO) affects inventory turnover. Depreciation methods affect net plant and equipment and, therefore, total asset turnover.

Operating differences can produce similar comparability problems. If a firm has more (or less) than a normal percentage of credit sales, it would expect to have a nonnormal collection period. An unusual seasonal pattern of sales for an individual company would undermine comparison to an industry unless the fiscal year were in some way adjusted to reflect that seasonality.

These limitations are related to either accounting conventions or the nature of firm operations. One other source of distortion can be company age. Inflation has increased the price of most things, and capital assets are no exception. An older firm may often have plant and equipment on the books at acquisition prices far below their replacement costs. This will distort current versus fixed asset percentages, debt ratios, and profitability ratios. The firm will appear to have a smaller investment in fixed assets than it actually does, based on current value. Debt will seem to be high relative to old (low) asset values. Profitability will look relatively good because asset (and, consequently, net worth) values are understated.

Biases

In addition to limitations or distortions that can affect comparisons of a company to an industry, you should be aware of *status quo* and *one-way* biases.

The status quo bias results from using industry averages as a benchmark. The analyst assumes implicitly that what the industry is doing is acceptable and to be emulated. However, if an industry itself is in the doldrums, matching that performance is of questionable worth to a firm. If a whole industry is experiencing rapid growth and high profits, a firm that appears to be only average may actually be an outstanding performer when viewed in the context of the entire economy.

The one-way bias results from interpreting ratios too absolutely. A high current ratio is good; too high a ratio, though, might be as much (or more) of a problem than too low a ratio. A very high ratio could result from excess liquidity, long collection periods, excess inventories, or any combination of the three. In ratio analysis you are looking for abnormality; it is not a case of the greater the liquidity or the lower the leverage the better. Aberrations in either direction can indicate problems in a firm's financial condition.

SUMMARY

Financial statements are the primary sources of financial information about a firm. General-purpose financial statements include the balance sheet, income statement, and statement of retained earnings. Such accounting statements provide condensed summary information about a company so that an analyst can assess its current status and the nature of its operations.

Financial analysis involves extracting more information from such statements by explicitly considering certain interrelationships between account balances or between accounts and revenue (or expense) items. This is done by constructing ratios or restating the statements in percentage form (common-size statements).

Ratio analysis normally reveals the firm's liquidity, activity, leverage, and profitability. Comparisons of company figures to industry averages are invaluable to the analyst. Common-size (percentage) statements also help to uncover relationships in the accounting data; again, comparison to industry norms is helpful.

Financial analysis is not without its traps, however. You as an analyst must recognize its limitations and biases.

QUESTIONS AND REVIEW ACTIVITIES

1. What are the three general-purpose financial statements that a firm normally includes in its annual statement?

2. What is the purpose of each of these financial statements?

3. The main purpose of financial accounting is the determination of net income; therefore, the procedure for matching revenue and expenses is the main problem of accounting. Discuss.

4. Why are industry averages important in financial analysis?

5. Discuss briefly the purpose of (a) liquidity ratios, (b) activity ratios, (c) leverage ratios, and (d) profitability ratios.

6. In the U.S. economy a firm must have some characteristic, or combination of characteristics, that allows it to generate a competitive return. Discuss this in the context of the DuPont ROI system.

7. Utilities such as electricity companies often have low liquidity ratios, low activity ratios, and high leverage ratios. What characteristics of utilities allow them to carry on what would seem to be very high-risk operations?

8. Discuss some of the biases and problems in ratio analysis.

PROBLEMS

1. Given the following financial statement:

	Baker Mfg. Co. (in 000s)	Able Mfg. Co. (in 000s)
Cash	$ 1,670	$ 10,500
Accounts receivable	4,100	24,660
Inventory	14,250	37,600
Net fixed assets	53,730	43,550
Other assets	26,250	16,090
Total assets	$100,000	$132,400
Current liabilities	7,540	20,300
Long-term debt	53,940	40,000
Net worth	38,520	72,100
Total claims	$100,000	$132,400

(Cont.)

	Baker Mfg. Co. (in 000s)	Able Mfg. Co. (in 000s)
Sales	47,100	166,600
Cost of goods sold	27,000	115,900
Operating expenses	10,600	34,500
Operating profit	9,500	16,200
Interest expenses	2,500	2,000
Taxes	3,000	5,900
Net profit	$ 4,000	$ 8,300

Compute the following ratios for both companies:

a) Current ratio.

b) Average collection period.

c) Inventory turnover.

d) Debt to total assets.

e) Net profit to sales.

f) Times interest earned.

g) Return on net worth.

h) Operating ratio.
Compare the performance of the two firms from the information provided from the ratios.

2. Construct the balance sheet and income statement from the following information:

a) Total assets = $1,000,000.

b) Current assets as a percentage of total assets (CA/TA) = 60%.

c) Current ratio = 1.50.

d) Debt to total assets = 50%.

e) Total asset turnover = 2.

f) Gross profit rate (GP/total sales) = 50%.

g) Return on total assets = 20%.
Set up a balance sheet and income statement as shown below:

Current assets	_____
Fixed assets	_____
Total assets	$1,000,000
Current liabilities	_____
Term debt	_____
Net worth	_____
Total liabilities and net worth	_____

Total sales	_____
Cost of goods sold	_____
Gross profit	_____
Other expenses	_____
Net profit after taxes	========

3. Construct a balance sheet from the following data:

Net profit/net worth	25%
Long-term debt/net worth	1:2
Inventory turnover (using cost of goods)	4×
Average collection period	72 days
Current ratio	2.5
Total asset turnover	1.25
Return on total assets	12.5%
Sales (all credit)	$10,000,000
Cost of goods sold	6,000,000
Gross margin	4,000,000
Expenses	2,000,000
Earnings before taxes	2,000,000
Taxes	1,000,000
Net profit	$ 1,000,000
Cash	_____
Accounts receivable	_____
Inventory	_____
Total current assets	_____
Fixed assets	_____
Total	========
Current liabilities	_____
Bonds	_____
Net worth	_____
Total	========

4. Given the following information, analyze Wynot, Inc.:

Balance Sheet

Cash	$ 9,500
Accounts receivable	62,500
Inventory	120,000
Current assets	192,000
Net fixed assets	8,000
Total assets	$200,000

(Cont.)

Current liabilities		$ 80,000
Long-term debt		20,000
Common stock	$ 60,000	
Retained earnings	40,000	
Net worth		100,000
Total claims		$200,000

Income Statement

Net sales		$500,000
Cost of goods sold		400,000
Gross profit on sales		100,000
Selling expenses	$ 21,000	
General and administrative expense	25,000	46,000
Earnings before interest and taxes		54,000
Less: interest		4,000
Income before taxes		50,000
Less: taxes		20,000
Net income		$ 30,000

Industry Averages

Current ratio	2.5	Debt/total assets	.30
Quick ratio	1.3	Times interest earned	15
Total asset turnover	3	Return on sales	3.5%
Inventory turnover	6	Return on total assets	10.5%
Days' sales	30	Return on net worth	15.0%

5. Below are two income statements for Whitneys, Inc. Construct common-size statements for the firm and interpret your statements.

	1982		1983	
Gross sales		$530,000		$471,000
Less: returns and allowances		30,000		31,000
Net sales		500,000		440,000
Cost of goods sold		350,000		317,000
Gross profit		150,000		123,000
Selling expense	$25,000		$22,000	
General administrative expense	35,000	60,000	33,000	55,000
Income before taxes		90,000		68,000
Income taxes		22,750		14,650
Net income		$ 67,250		$ 53,350

ADDITIONAL READINGS

Altman, E. I. "Financial Ratios, Discriminant Analysis and the Prediction of Corporate Bankruptcy," *Journal of Finance* (September 1968), pp. 589–609.

Beaver, W. H. "Financial Ratios as Predictors of Failure," *Empirical Research in Accounting: Selected Studies in Journal of Accounting Research* (1966), pp. 71–111.

Benishay, H. "Economic Information on Financial Ratio Analysis," *Accounting and Business Research* (Spring 1971), pp. 174–79.

Bierman, H., Jr. "Measuring Financial Liquidity," *Accounting Review* (October 1960), pp. 628–32.

Donaldson, G. "New Framework for Corporate Debt Capacity," *Harvard Business Review* (March–April 1962), pp. 117–31.

Foster, G. *Financial Statement Analysis.* Englewood Cliffs, N. J.: Prentice-Hall, Inc., 1978.

Helfert, E. A. *Techniques of Financial Analysis*, 5th ed. Homewood, Ill.: Richard D. Irwin, Inc., 1982.

Horrigan, J. O. "A Short History of Financial Ratio Analysis," *Accounting Review* (April 1968), pp. 284–94.

————. "The Determination of Long-Term Credit Standing and Financial Ratios," *Empirical Research in Accounting: Selected Studies in Journal of Accounting Research* (1966), pp. 44–62.

Jaedicke, R. K., and R. T. Sprouse. *Accounting Flows: Income, Funds, and Cash.* Englewood Cliffs, N. J.: Prentice-Hall, Inc., 1965.

Lev, B. *Financial Statement Analysis: A New Approach.* Englewood Cliffs, N. J.: Prentice-Hall, Inc., 1974.

Murray, R. F. "The Penn Central Debacle: Lessons for Financial Analysis," *Journal of Finance* (May 1971), pp. 327–32.

Pinches, G. E., A. A. Eubank, K. A. Mingo, and J. K. Caruthers, "The Hierarchial Classification of Financial Ratios," *Journal of Business Research* (October 1975), pp. 295–310.

Pohlman, R. A., and R. D. Hallinger, "Information Redundancy in Sets of Financial Ratios," *Journal of Business Finance and Accounting* (Winter 1981), pp. 511–28.

Sorter, G. H., and G. Benston, "Appraising the Defensive Position of a Firm: The Internal Measure," *Accounting Review* (October 1960), pp. 633–40.

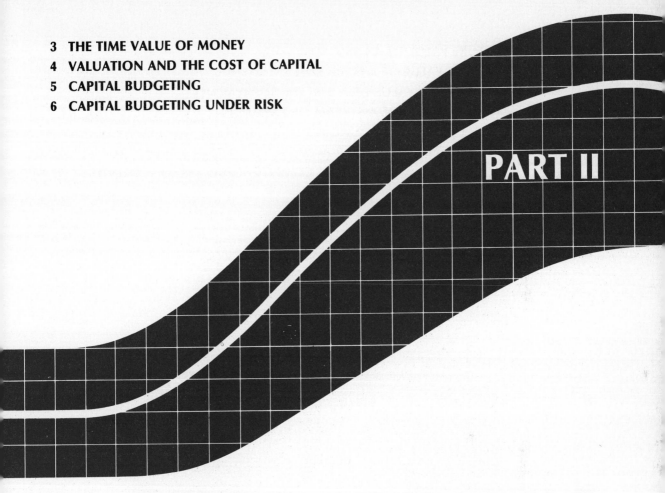

PART II

CAPITAL INVESTMENT ANALYSIS

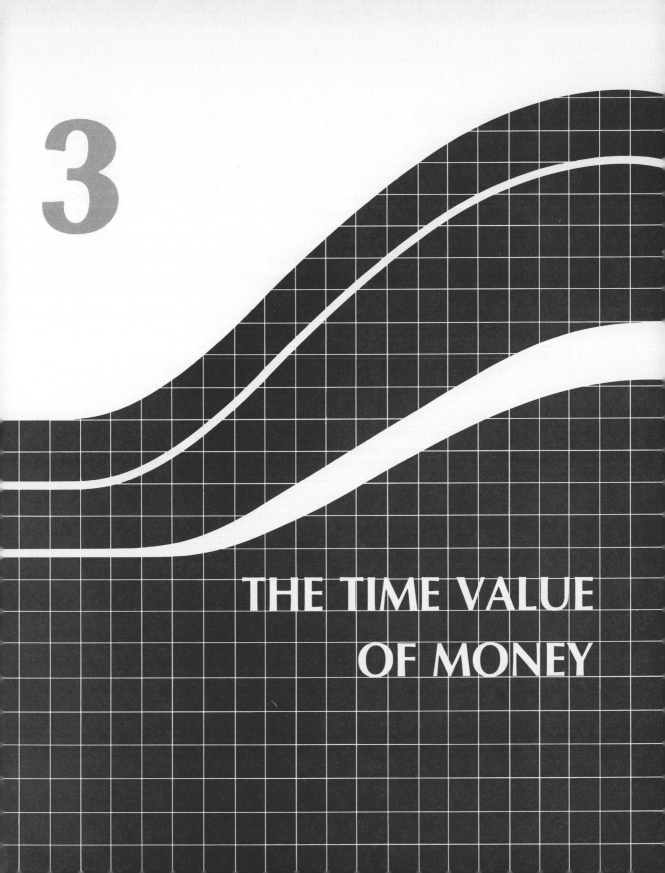

3

THE TIME VALUE
OF MONEY

One of the most important financial concepts you will need to understand is the *time value of money*. The techniques described in this chapter incorporate the dimension of time in financial analysis and enable you to compare alternative decisions using time-adjusted dollars. Evaluation of long-term investments under consideration by the firm (capital budgeting) uses the techniques to be discussed. Consideration of the timing of cash flow is also basic to the valuation procedure for stocks, bonds, and other financial assets.

Time value adjustments to cash flows consist of calculating either **future value**, which is the worth at some point in the *future* of a series of cash flows, or **present value**, which is the worth *today* of all future cash flows to be received. For both situations, you will learn to apply techniques for single payments and multiple payments spread over a period of time. A thorough familiarity with the procedures presented in this chapter is necessary to understand the principles of financial management.

To illustrate the application of time-adjusted cash flows, consider finding the value of a corporate bond. The most straightforward bond valuation problem involves what are called **zero coupon bonds**. With a zero coupon bond the bondholder receives no annual interest payments; rather, the difference between the purchase price and the value at maturity, $1,000, represents the interest paid by the corporation (hence, the name *zero coupon bond*). In July 1981 IBM issued $150 million in zero coupon bonds that mature in 1988. Each bond could be redeemed for $1,000 at maturity, and market interest rates were 14%. Using techniques presented later in the chapter, you will be able to determine that IBM should have received $400 for each bond issued in July 1981.

After careful study of the chapter, you should know:

1. Definitions of the following terms:
   a) Compounding.
   b) Discounting.
   c) Discount rate.
   d) Annuity.
   e) Perpetuity.
   f) Present value interest factor, (PVIF).
   g) Future value interest factor (FVIF).
   h) Present value interest factor of an annuity (PVIFA).
   i) Future value interest factor of an annuity (FVIFA).
2. How to calculate the future value or present value of a lump sum.
3. How to calculate the future value or present value of a series of cash flows.
4. Under what situations to use Tables A, B, C, and D in the back of this book.

5. How to perform compounding and discounting operations under the assumption of nonannual compounding periods.

6. How to rearrange the time value of money relationships to solve for time, interest rate, or yearly payment amounts.

FUTURE VALUE OF A LUMP SUM

Assume that I offer you a choice of $1,000 today or $1,125 three years from today. Any funds received today can be deposited in a savings account earning 5% interest. Which alternative is most attractive? (Ignore the fact that you harbor some doubts about my ability to pay you in three years, and concentrate on the timing of the cash flows). The technique of finding the future value of a lump sum, or **compounding,** can be used to answer this question.

If you receive $1,000 today, call this amount the principal, P. If it is deposited in your savings account and earns 5% interest, i, the future value, FV, at the end of year one is $1,050:

$$FV = \$1,000\,(1 + .05)$$
$$= \$1,050.$$

The compounding process can be expressed mathematically as P deposited, plus the interest, i, received on P at year's end:

$$FV = P + iP \qquad\qquad (3.1)$$
$$= P(1 + i).$$

If the $1,050 remains on deposit for a second year, the compound value after two years would be $1,102.50:

$$FV = \$1,050(1 + .05)$$
$$= \$1,102.50$$

Notice that the end-of-the-year-one value of $1,050 could be expressed as $1,000(1.05), so that the compound value after two years could be written as

$$FV = \$1,000(1.05)(1.05)$$
$$= \$1,000(1.05)^2.$$

Interest earned on interest (the $50 of interest earned the first year becomes part of the principal at the start of the second year) is called **compound interest.** If the second year's balance of $1,102.50 remained on deposit for a third year, the compound value would equal

$$FV = \$1,102.50(1.05)$$
$$= \$1,157.60,$$

which could be written alternatively as

$$FV = \$1,000(1.05)^3$$
$$= \$1,157.60.$$

We can now answer the question posed earlier. By taking the $1,000 today and investing it at 5%, you will accumulate $1,157.60, which is greater than the $1,125 I offered you in three years.

The mathematical calculation used to find the compound value of a lump sum, P, earning an interest rate, i, over n years can be expressed as

$$FV = P(1 + i)^n. \tag{3.2}$$

The value of $(1 + i)^n$ may be determined by using an electronic calculator and multiplying $(1 + i)$ to the nth power. However, Table C in the Tables section shows values of $(1 + i)^n$ calculated for many combinations of i and n. (A portion of Table C is reproduced here as Table 3.1).

The quantity $(1 + i)^n$ that appears in Table C is often called a **future value interest factor** (**FVIF**). To find the future value of a lump sum, multiply the principal by the FVIF from the table for the appropriate interest rate and period. The principal, P, usually is termed a present value, PV, because it is immediately available.

$$FV = PV \times FVIF_{\%,n}. \tag{3.3}$$

To solve the previous problem of the future value of $1,000 on deposit for three years at 5% interest, find the 5% column and read down to the third period row, where you will find the interest factor of 1.158. Multiply the principal by this figure; the result, $1,158, is the future value after three years.

TABLE 3.1
Selected Future Value Factors (FVIF).

Years	Rates						
	2%	4%	5%	6%	8%	10%	12%
1	1.020	1.040	1.050	1.060	1.080	1.100	1.120
2	1.040	1.082	1.103	1.124	1.166	1.210	1.254
3	1.061	1.125	1.158	1.191	1.260	1.331	1.405
4	1.082	1.170	1.216	1.263	1.261	1.464	1.574
5	1.104	1.217	1.276	1.338	1.469	1.611	1.762
6	1.126	1.265	1.340	1.419	1.587	1.772	1.974
10	1.219	1.480	1.629	1.791	2.159	1.594	3.106
15	1.346	1.801	2.079	1.397	3.172	4.177	5.474

(The $.40 difference from the previous results is due to rounding.)

$$FV = \$1,000(1.158)$$
$$= \$1,158.$$

To evaluate another situation, calculate the amount you will accumulate by investing $1,500 at 12% for six years. Using Table 3.1 the answer is calculated as

$$FV = \$1,500 \times 1.974$$
$$= \$2,961.00.$$

This particular problem illustrates the **Rule of 72,** a rule of thumb that can be used to approximate the time period or interest rate required for a sum to double in value. Note that the FVIF in the previous equation is very close to 2.0 (i.e., 1.974) and that the product of the time on deposit, six years, and the interest rate, 12%, is 72 (6 × 12 = 72). It is a mathematical curiosity that any product of interest rate and time that equals 72 produces an interest factor of approximately 2.0, representing a doubling of the original investment. For example, if you deposit $2,000 at 7%, how long will it take to accumulate $4,000? Slightly over 10 years (72/7 = 10.28 years).

PRESENT VALUE OF A LUMP SUM

Lump sum present value techniques are the reverse of compound value calculations. They are used to determine the equivalent value today of an amount to be received at a future date. Consider once again the example of $1,000 received today versus $1,000 received one year from now. An additional comparison of these alternatives can be made by finding the present value of the $1,000 to be received at the end of the year.

Mathematically, the calculation of present value is the inverse of compound value, as can be seen by rearranging Eq. (3.2) and solving for PV. We find that the present value, PV, of a future cash flow, FV, is the future dollar amount multiplied by $1/(1 + i)^n$:

$$FV = PV(1 + i)^n .$$

$$PV = \frac{FV}{(1 + i)^n} = FV \frac{1}{(1 + i)^n} . \tag{3.4}$$

The present value of $1,000 received one year from today if interest rates are 5% is calculated as $952.

$$PV = \$1,000 \frac{1}{(1 + .05)^1}$$
$$= \$1,000 \times .952$$
$$= \$952.$$

TABLE 3.2
Selected Present Value Interest Factors (PVIF).

Years	Rates						
	2%	4%	5%	6%	8%	10%	12%
1	.980	.962	.952	.943	.926	.909	.893
2	.961	.925	.907	.890	.857	.826	.797
3	.942	.889	.864	.840	.794	.751	.712
4	.924	.855	.823	.792	.735	.683	.636
5	.906	.822	.784	.747	.681	.621	.567
10	.802	.676	.614	.558	.463	.386	.322
15	.743	.555	.481	.417	.315	.239	.183

This means that there is no difference between the alternatives of receiving $952 today or $1,000 in one year, because you can deposit the $952 at 5% and it will grow to $1,000 by year's end. However, there is a difference between $1,000 today and $952 today. The technique of calculating present value, commonly called *discounting*, enables comparison of investment alternatives that have different timing of cash flows.

Tables of **present value interest factors** (**PVIF**), $[1/(1 + i)^n]$, have been constructed to facilitate our calculations. Table A, "Present Value Interest Factors," in the Tables section contains the values of $(1/1 + i)^n$ for a wide range of interest rates and time periods. When interest factors from Table A are used, the present value relationship can be expressed as follows:

$$PV = FV \times PVIF_{\%,n}. \tag{3.5}$$

The value in the table $[1/(1 + i)^n]$, the PVIF, is multiplied by the future dollar amount to determine present value.

For example, we can use Table 3.2, which contains selected Present Value Interest Factors, from Table A to determine the present value of $1,000 to be received in three years. If the interest rate is 5%, the PVIF of .864 is found at the intersection of the 5% column and the three-year row. The present value of $1,000 received in three years is $864:

$$PV = FV \times PVIF_{5\%,3}$$
$$= \$1,000(.864)$$
$$= \$864.$$

The issue price for the IBM bonds described earlier can be determined using present value of a lump sum technique. The selling price in July 1981 represents the present value of $1,000 discounted at 14% for seven years.

Using Table A, the present value factor is .400 and the present value of the bond is $1,000 × .400 = $400.

Comparing the values in Tables 3.1 and 3.2 will illustrate the difference between compounding and discounting. The compound value interest factor, $(1 + i)^n$, increases in value as i and n increase. Thus, the values in Table 3.1 are all bigger than 1.0 and grow larger at higher interest rates or after long periods. Conversely, the PVIF, $1/(1 + i)^n$, declines as i or n increases. All values in Table A are smaller than 1.0 and grow smaller as the period or interest rate is increased.

COMPOUND VALUE OF A STREAM OF PAYMENTS

Frequently in financial analysis, it is necessary to evaluate investments consisting of a series of payments rather than a single lump sum. If the payments are of equal amounts and the time between each payment is identical, the series of payments is called an **annuity.** A stream of payments that does not meet both criteria is an *uneven stream* of cash flows. Techniques for calculating the compound value of annuities and uneven streams are described in the following sections.

Future Value of an Annuity

There are two types of annuities. Our primary concern is the **immediate annuity,** which assumes that the cash flows occur at the end of each period. A second type of annuity, an **annuity due,** assumes payment at the beginning of each period. All annuity examples in this chapter are immediate annuities because this is the most prevalent type in financial analysis.

Consider investing $1,000 a year in a savings account at the end of each of the next four years. The account pays 5% interest. How much money will you have immediately after making the fourth deposit of $1,000? Table 3.3 presents the situation and the answer.

**TABLE 3.3
Future Value of an Annuity at 5%.**

	0	1	2	3	4
Payments		$1,000	$1,000	$1,000	$1,000.00
				$(1.05)^1 \rightarrow$	1,050.00
			$(1.05)^2$ ———————		$\rightarrow$ 1,103.00
		$(1.05)^3$ ———————————————			$\rightarrow$ 1,158.00
Compound amount					$4,311.00

The first deposit of $1,000 at the end of the first year earns interest for three years, the second deposit earns interest for two years, the third year deposit earns interest for one year, and the last deposit earns no interest. The dollars are moved right to represent their values at the end of the fourth year. To understand how tables containing annuity factors are developed, consider finding the future value of this annuity by compounding each payment by the appropriate lump sum factor shown in Table 3.3, a tedious process for long annuities.

The future value of the four-year annuity FV_A, described in Table 3.3, can be expressed mathematically as

$$FV_A = 1,000(1.05)^3 + 1,000(1.05)^2 + 1,000(1.05)^1 + 1,000$$
$$= 1,000(1.158) + 1,000(1.103) + 1,000(1.050) + 1,000$$
$$= \$4,311.$$

To derive a simpler form, first attach an interest factor $(1.05)^0$ to the last $1,000 (any value raised to the zero power equals 1).

$$FV_A = 1,000(1.05)^3 + 1,000(1.05)^2 + 1,000(1.05)^1 + 1,000(1.05)^0.$$

Factor the yearly $1,000 payment and write the expression in compact notation:

$$FV_A = \$1,000 \sum_{t=1}^{4} (1.05)^{4-t}.$$

Defining n as the term of the annuity, R as the period payment or receipt (rent), and i as the interest rate, the general equation for future value of an annuity can be written as

$$FV_A = R \sum_{t=1}^{n} (1 + i)^{n-t}. \tag{3.6}$$

Table D contains values for $\sum_{t=1}^{n}(1 + i)^{n-t}$, **future value interest factors for an annuity (FVIFA)**, so that the future value of an annuity can be calculated more easily using the relationship shown in Eq. (3.7):

$$FV_A = R \times FVIFA_{\%,n}. \tag{3.7}$$

A portion of Table D is reproduced in Table 3.4. It is used in the same fashion as the two tables already discussed. The compound value of a four-year annuity of $1,000 is found by multiplying the $FVIFA_{5\%,4}$ of 4.310 by $1,000, obtaining $4,310, which differs by $1 from the results above due to rounding.

TABLE 3.4
Selected Future Value Interest Factors for an Annuity (FVIFA).

Year	Rates						
	2%	4%	5%	6%	8%	10%	12%
1	1.000	1.000	1.000	1.000	1.000	1.000	1.000
2	2.020	2.040	2.050	2.060	2.080	2.100	2.120
3	3.060	3.122	3.153	3.184	3.246	3.310	3.374
4	4.122	4.247	4.310	4.375	4.506	4.641	4.779
5	5.204	5.416	5.526	5.637	5.867	6.105	6.353
10	10.950	12.006	12.578	13.181	14.487	15.937	17.549
15	17.293	20.023	21.578	23.276	27.152	31.772	37.280

To try another example, how much would you accumulate in a savings account if you deposit $2,500 per year for 10 years at 12%? Using Table 3.4 the answer is

$$FV_A = \$2,500 \times 17.549$$
$$= \$43,872.50$$

Future Value of an Uneven Stream

Consider depositing the cash flows presented in Table 3.5, in a savings account earning 10%. In many financial decisions, cash flows are unequal, and the solution procedure becomes more complicated.

To find the compound value of an uneven stream, each cash flow must be adjusted for the period during which it is earning interest. If every cash flow is different, appropriate interest factors from Table C must be used to determine the compound value for each. In other situations, an annuity may occur in conjunction with uneven cash flows, so both Tables C and D can be used. As shown in Table 3.6, the $300 at the end of year one is on deposit for five years and is multiplied by the FVIF of 1.611. Year two and year three cash flows are also multiplied by FVIF factors for four years and three years,

TABLE 3.5
Uneven Payment Stream

Year	0	1	2	3	4	5	6
Cash flow	0	$300	$200	$100	$400	$400	$400

TABLE 3.6
Compound Value of an Uneven Stream.

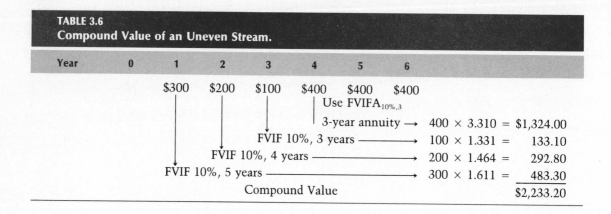

Year	0	1	2	3	4	5	6

respectively. The $400 deposited at the end of years four, five, and six represent an immediate annuity starting at the beginning of year four, and the compound value of the last three payments is calculated most easily by multiplying $400 by the FVIFA of 3.310. Summing the compound values provides a future value for the uneven stream of $2,233.20.

When presented with a problem involving future value of a stream of payments, you can solve it more easily by diagramming the cash flows on a time line similar to Table 3.5. Appropriate interest factors from Tables C and D can then be easily identified.

PRESENT VALUE OF A STREAM OF PAYMENTS

Instead of determining the future value of a payment series, we may need the worth today of a future cash flow stream. Most problems in finance, such as valuing stocks and bonds and determining the worth of long-term investments, involve finding the present value of a stream of payments.

Present Value of an Annuity

To understand why you might want to find the present value of an annuity, consider the following problem. An insurance company will sell you an annuity paying $1,000 a year for each of the next four years. The purchase price is $3,300. If equally secure investments are earning 10%, should you purchase the annuity or look for another investment?

To answer this question, you must compare the present value of the annuity to its cost of $3,300. The present value of the annuity can be thought of as the investment required today, earning the assumed rate of return, to provide payments of $1,000 at the end of each of the next four years.

Calculating the present value of an annuity is the inverse of finding the annuity's future value. The cash flows are discounted (instead of compounded) to arrive at the present value.

The present value of the annuity in the preceding problem could be determined by discounting each cash flow by the appropriate PVIF to arrive at the present value of $3,169 as shown in Table 3.7. (The dollars are moved to the left to represent their values at time 0, their present value.)

$$PV_A = 1,000 \left[\frac{1}{(1.10)^1} + \frac{1}{(1.10)^2} + \frac{1}{(1.10)^3} + \frac{1}{(1.10)^4} \right]$$

$$= 1,000(.909) + 1,000(.826) + 1,000(.751) + 1,000(.683)$$

$$= \$3,169.$$

However, the calculations can be simplified by factoring the $1,000 and writing the series as

$$PV_A = 1,000 \sum_{t=1}^{4} (1/1.10)^t$$

$$= 1,000(3.170)$$

$$= \$3,170.$$

In general, the relationship for present value of an annuity is described by Eq. (3.8):

$$PV_A = R \times \sum_{t=1}^{n} \frac{1}{(1 + i)^t}. \tag{3.8}$$

To facilitate computation, the **present value interest factor for the annuity, (PVIFA)**, representing the term

$$\sum_{t=1}^{n} \frac{1}{(1 + i)^t}$$

TABLE 3.7
Present Value of a Four-Year Annuity: $R = \$1,000$; Interest = 10%.

	0	1	2	3	4
		$1,000	$1,000	$1,000	$1,000
$ 909		(.909) ←			
826		(.826) ←			
751		(.751) ←			
683		(.683) ←			
$3,169					

TABLE 3.8
Selected Present Value Interest Factors for an Annuity (PVIFA).

Year	Rates						
	2%	4%	5%	6%	8%	10%	12%
1	.980	.952	.943	.943	.926	.909	.893
2	1.942	1.886	1.859	1.833	1.783	1.736	1.690
3	2.884	2.775	2.723	2.673	2.577	2.487	2.402
4	3.808	3.630	3.546	3.465	3.312	3.170	3.037
5	4.714	4.452	4.330	4.212	3.993	3.791	3.605
6	5.601	5.424	5.076	4.917	4.623	4.355	4.111
10	8.983	8.111	7.722	7.360	6.710	6.145	5.650
15	12.849	11.118	10.380	9.712	8.560	7.606	6.811

is given in Table B, a portion of which is reproduced in Table 3.8. The present value of an annuity is found by multiplying the PVIFA from the table by the yearly cash flow, R.

$$PV_A = R \times PVIFA_{\%,n}. \tag{3.9}$$

A special annuity: The perpetuity. A distinguishing feature of the preceding annuities is their finite life. Cash flows occur over a defined time period and then the annuity ceases. If the annuity provides cash flows over an infinite time period it is termed a *perpetuity*. The technique for finding the present value of a perpetuity is simpler than finding the present value of an immediate annuity.

The present value of a perpetuity paying R dollars per year and earning a rate of return of $i\%$ is given by Eq. (3.10):

$$PV_A = \frac{R}{i}. \tag{3.10}$$

For example, assume that you could buy a bond which promises to pay $50 per year forever. If interest rates are 10% the present value of that bond is $500:

$$PV_A = \frac{\$50}{.10}$$
$$= \$500$$

The concept of perpetuities is useful for valuing many types of financial assets. For example, the British "consul" bonds issued in the 1800s are a true perpetuity, paying a fixed amount of interest each year but having no maturity date. These bonds are still traded and price quotes appear frequently in the *Wall Street Journal*. Preferred and common stock often are treated as perpetuities because they have no stipulated maturity. A preferred stock that pays $9 per year in dividends at a time when investors require a 12% return is worth $75 (i.e. $9/.12 = $75). Frequently a firm can be valued by treating its projected earnings stream as a perpetuity and dividing expected yearly earnings by the discount rate appropriate for the risk level of the firm. Consider finding the value of a small, privately held business that is projected to generate $100,000 per year forever. If the appropriate discount rate is 20%, its value is $500,000 (i.e. $100,000/.20 = $500,000).

Present Value of an Uneven Stream

Most investments by firms do not produce a series of equal payments each period, but rather generate a stream of uneven cash flows. The HTW Corp. is evaluating the purchase of a machine to resole jogging shoes. Expected yearly cash flows from the investment are depicted in Table 3.9. The machine costs $2,000, and alternative investments of equal risk are yielding 10%. Should HTW purchase the machine? The answer can be determined by comparing the present value of the future cash flows to the cost of the investment. If the present value is greater than the cost, the investment is acceptable.

The present value of an uneven stream is the sum of the discounted values of each payment. If each cash flow is different, it is necessary to use present value interest factors from Table A. In cases including both annuities and uneven cash flows, you will need to use Tables A and B.

Table 3.9 illustrates the solution procedure. Note that the cash flows for years one through three, 100, −200, and 300, are uneven, and one is negative.

TABLE. 3.9
Present Value of an Uneven Stream: Interest Rate = 10%.

	0	1	2	3	4	5	6	7	8	9	10
		$100	−$200	$300	$500	$500	$500	$500	$500	$500	$1,000

$ 90.90   .909⟵⎦

−165.20   .826⟵

225.30   .751⟵

1,635.30   .751 × $2,177.50⟵⎯ 4.355⎦

386.00   .386⟵

$ 2,172.30

PVIFs from Table 3.2 are used to determine the present value of each cash flow. Be certain to attach the negative sign to the $165.20 to represent the negative impact of the -200 cash flow in the present value of the stream of payments. Next, observe the six-year, $500 per year immediate annuity starting at the beginning of year four. Calculating the present value of this six-year annuity that begins in three years can be accomplished by combining factors from Tables 3.8 and 3.2 as follows.

First, multiply $500 by the PVIFA for six years at 10%: $500 $\times$ 4.355 = $2,177.50. Interpret the $2,177.50 as the value of the annuity three years from today. Next, discount the $2,177.50 by $PVIF_{10\%,3}$, .751, to find its present value: $2,177.5 $\times$ .751 = $1635.30. The result indicates that there is no difference between receiving a lump sum payment today of $1,635.30 and receiving $500 a year for six years, with the first payment made four years from today.

Other procedures can be used to find the present value of the six-year, $500 annuity. For example, the PVIFA of a three-year annuity at 10%, 2.487, could be subtracted from a nine-year, 10% annuity factor, 5.759 − 1.487 = 3.272, and the result multiplied by $500: $500 $\times$ 3.272 = $1,636. Except for a 70-cent rounding error, this is the same result obtained above. After working several problems of this type, you will be able to develop procedures for solving any type of uneven cash flow problem you encounter.

The last cash flow in our example is $1,000 in year 10. Use the PVIF from Table 3.2 to discount the $1,000 received in year 10 back to the present. Summing the present values of the individual calculations (and remembering the negative sign) gives a present value of $2,172.30 for the uneven stream.

Comparing the $2,172.30 to the investment required, $2,000, reveals that the machine should be purchased. Given a 10% discount rate, a current receipt of $2,172.30 is equivalent to the future cash flows shown in Table 3.9. Since the same cash flows can be obtained with only a $2,000 investment, the machine should be purchased.

NONANNUAL COMPOUNDING

So far, we have assumed that compounding occurs only once, at year's end. However, in many situations compounding occurs more frequently. For example, many banks compound interest on savings accounts quarterly or even daily. Interest payments on bonds are received semiannually, so bond values are calculated assuming semiannual compounding.

Assume that you deposit $1,000 on December 31 in a savings account paying 8% annual interest compounded (and paid) quarterly. How much will you accumulate by the end of one year? The 8% annual interest rate must be restated as a quarterly rate. This is accomplished by dividing 8% by the four quarters in a year, resulting in a 2% interest rate per quarter. At the end of each quarter, interest payments will be credited to the principal, so that interest is compounded four times during the year. Table 3.10 illustrates the timing of the interest payments and the terminal wealth achieved.

For nonannual compounding, Eq. (3.2) can be modified to conform to the observed cash flow in Table 3.10 by making two adjustments. First, define the interest rate as a per-period rate calculated by dividing the annual rate by the number of compounding periods in a year, i/m. Second, multiply the exponent n, which is dimensioned in years, by the number of compounding periods occurring each year, m. Equation (3.11) results:

$$FV = PV\left(1 + \frac{i}{m}\right)^{nm}. \tag{3.11}$$

The problem presented in Table 3.10 can be solved with Eq. (3.11) as follows:

$$FV = \$1,000(1 + .08/4)^{1 \times 4}$$
$$= \$1,000(1.02)^4$$
$$= \$1,082.42.$$

More easily, Table C could be used if you interpret the interest rate as the per-period rate $(i/m = 2\%)$ and the exponent, $(n \cdot m = 4)$, as the number of compounding periods. Using the $FVIF_{2\%,4}$ of 1.082 from Table C (or Table 3.1) yields the future value calculation

$$FV = \$1,000 \times 1.082$$
$$= \$1,082.00,$$

which differs due to rounding by 42 cents from the previous calculations.

As many banks and savings and loan institutions now pay interest on a daily basis, you can calculate future value assuming daily compounding of

---

TABLE 3.10
Compound Value of $1,000 at 8%, Assuming Interest Is Paid Quarterly.

Jan.	Mar.	June	Sept.	Dec.
$1,000 ⟶	$20 interest			
	$1,020 ⟶	$20.40 interest		
		$1,040.40 ⟶	$20.80 interest	
			$1,061.20 ⟶	$ 21.22
			Terminal Wealth =	$1,082.42

TABLE 3.11
Examples of the Effect of Compound Period on the Terminal Value of $1,000 at 8% Annual Interest Rate.

Compounding Period	Interest Factor	Terminal Value
Yearly	$(1.08000)^1$	$1,080.00
Six months	$(1.04000)^2$	1,081.60
Three months	$(1.02000)^4$	1,082.43
One month	$(1.00667)^{12}$	1,083.04
Daily	$(1.00022)^{365}$	1,083.60

interest. Define m as 365 and use Eq. (3.11).

$$FV = \$1,000\left(1 + \frac{.08}{365}\right)^{365}$$

$$= \$1,000(1.00022)^{365}$$

$$= \$1,083.60.$$

As expected, the increased compounding results in a higher terminal wealth. Table 3.11 allows comparison of future values under different compounding period assumptions. Appendix 3A at the end of this chapter considers an even shorter compounding interval in a concept called **continuous compounding**, a procedure frequently used in theoretical financial analysis.)

The nonannual compounding period adjustments are identical for all the tables. To find present or future value of any payment stream, convert the annual interest rate to a compounding period rate and interpret time as the total number of compounding periods. You can then find the correct interest factor from the appropriate Tables A, B, C, or D.

SOLVING FOR OTHER VARIABLES

To this point, our problems have involved finding the present or future value of a lump sum or stream of dollars. It is also possible to use the interest tables to solve for other variables in financial problems. For example, suppose your banker will lend you $5,000 today and requires you to repay $10,000 in eight years. What rate of interest is being charged? [Actually, the Truth-in-Lending Act requires lenders to divulge the effective interest rate of a loan. Most institutions refer to this rate as the **annual percentage rate (APR)**.]

Or consider a mortgage on a house. What yearly payment would be required to repay a $90,000, 20-year loan at 12% interest? If the loan value, interest rate, and term of the loan are known, you can calculate the yearly payment necessary to repay the loan. A loan that is repaid in equal installments over time is termed an *amortized loan*. Individual loans (such as home mortgages or car loans) usually are amortized loans, and so are many corporate borrowing arrangements. The following examples illustrate how the interest tables can be used to solve for (1) interest rate, (2) investment period, (3) yearly payment, and (4) investment required to fund a stream of payments.

Before proceeding with these examples, it is useful to outline a solution methodology with which to approach these problems. Realize that four variables are present in each time value equation that we have discussed:

$$FV = PV \times FVIF_{\%,n} \qquad (3.3)$$

$$PV = FV \times PVIF_{\%,n} \qquad (3.5)$$

$$FV_A = R \times FVIFA_{\%,n} \qquad (3.7)$$

$$PV_A = R \times PVIFA_{\%,n}. \qquad (3.9)$$

The four variables are two dollar amounts: (1) FV and PV or (2) FV_A or PV_A with R, (3) time, and (4) the rate of interest, which is impounded in the interest factor. If any three of the variables are known, the fourth can be determined by solving the appropriate time value equation. In problems involving lump sums, you can use either Eq. (3.3) or (3.5). For annuities, either the future value of an annuity (Eq. 3.7) or the present value of an annuity (Eq. 3.9) will be correct depending upon the type of cash flows given. Problems such as those described in the following sections can be solved most easily by following these steps:

1. Determine what the problem is (which variable is unknown).
2. Identify the types of cash flows given (present or future dollars) and the known variables.
3. Identify which of the four time value equations contains the three known variables.
4. Solve the equation for the unknown quantity.

The following examples show how to solve for different variables in the time value of money equations.

Determining interest rates—An example. Belchfire Motors will finance your new car under the following terms: You pay 20% down on the purchase price of $10,000, with the balance, $8,000, to be repaid in four annual installments of $2,802.10. What rate of interest are you being charged?

Solution

1. Unknown variable: Interest rate
2. Given
   PV_A of an annuity: $8,000
   Time: four periods
   Yearly payment (R): $2802.10

3. Applicable equation

$$PV_A = R \times PVIFA$$

4. Solution

$$\$8,000 = \$2,802.10 \times PVIFA$$

$$\frac{8,000}{2,802.10} = 2.855.$$

Look up 2.855 in Table B in the four-period row.
Answer: The interest rate is 15%.

When the problem involves an annuity, be sure to identify whether the present or future value of the annuity is given. The interest factor will be found in Table D if the future value is given and in Table B for present value of an annuity.

Calculating the investment period—An example.   In January 1981, you purchased IBM stock at $50 a share, believing that it would grow at a 15% compound annual rate. How many years will pass before the stock is worth $100?

Solution

1. Unknown variable: Time
2. Given

   Present value: $ 50
   Future value: $100
   Interest rate: 15%

3. Applicable equations

   a) $FV = PV \times FVIF$

   b) $PV = FV \times PVIF.$

   (Either equation can be used as long as you obtain the interest factor from the applicable table)

4. Solution.

   a) $\$100 = \$50 \times FVIF$

   $$\frac{100}{50} = 2.000 = FVIF.$$

   Look up 2.000 under the 15% column in Table C. You will find 2.011, the value closest to 2.000, in the five-year row. *Answer:* Approximately five years.

   b) $\$50 = \$100 \times PVIF$

   $$\frac{50}{100} = .5000 = PVIF.$$

   Look up .5000 under the 15% column in Table A. *Answer:* Approximately five years.

Determining Period Payments (R)—An Example.   Youben Took Mortgage Company will finance your $125,000 house under the following arrangement. A down payment of $25,000 is required, with a loan balance of $100,000. An interest rate of 12% is charged against the declining balance over a 30-year term. What *even* yearly payment is required to repay the loan?

Solution

1. Unknown variable: Yearly cash flow (R)

2. Given

    PV of an annuity: $100,000
    Interest rate: 12%

    (Do not be misled by the phrase "charged against the outstanding balance." The PVIFA table incorporates exactly this assumption.)

3. Applicable equation

    $PV_A = R \times PVIFA$.

4. Solution

$$\$100,000 = R \times 8.055$$

$$\frac{100,000}{8.055} = R$$

$$\$12,414.65 = R.$$

Answer: A yearly payment of $12,414.65 will repay the loan over a 30-year period.

Calculating the investment required to fund a stream of payments—An example. Rich Uncle Ebenezer Scrooge has offered to finance your college education. You have determined that a yearly sum of $5,000 is needed to pay for room, board, and tuition at a school in sunny Arizona. How much should Uncle Scrooge deposit in your account today so that you can withdraw $5,000 at the end of each of the next four years? The money will earn 10%.

Solution

1. Unknown variable: Present value of an annuity

2. Given

    Yearly payment (R): $5000
    Time: 4 years
    Interest rate: 10%

3. Applicable equation

    $PV_A = R \times PVIFA$.

4. Solution

$$PV_A = \$5,000 \times 3.170$$
$$= \$15,850$$

Answer: A deposit today of $15,850 will enable you to withdraw $5,000 at the end of each of the next four years, assuming your money earns 10%.

The preceding examples illustrate how different variables contained in the time value of money equations can be determined using the interest tables. The end-of-chapter problems provide practice in applying the techniques described to a wide range of situations.

SUMMARY

This chapter has presented techniques that enable cash flows to be adjusted for the time at which they occur. Future value calculations involve compounding cash flows to a point of time in the future. Finding present value, or discounting, is the process of determining the value today of cash flows to be received in the future. An annuity is a stream of equal cash flows with the same time between each flow. Examples were given of finding future values and present values for situations involving a lump sum payment and a stream of cash flows.

Tables A, B, C, and D in the Tables section at the back of the book facilitate present value and future value calculations. If compounding is assumed to occur other than annually, these tables can be used by interpreting the headings as the per-period interest rate and the number of compounding periods that occur.

Each time value of money equation is composed of four variables: (1) FV or PV, (2) FV_A or PV_A with R, (3) interest rate, and (4) time. Once any three variables are known, the fourth can be determined.

Several of the chapters that follow will draw on your knowledge of the time value of money calculations. For example, valuation of stocks and bonds, presented in Chapter 4 is based on present value, as is the valuation process for the firm itself. Chapters 5 and 6 discuss the evaluation of long-term investments (called *capital budgeting*), which is also based on the present value of future cash flows. A good comprehension of the concepts presented in this chapter will greatly enhance your understanding of the principles of financial management.

PROBLEMS

1. If you deposit $1,000 in a savings account today, how much will you have at the end of four years if:
   a) The account earns 5% compounded annually?
   b) The account earns 8% compounded annually?
   c) The account earns 10% compounded annually?

2. You plan to deposit $500 per year in a savings account for each of the next four years. What will be the value of your account after the fourth-year deposit if

   a) You earn 6% compounded annually?
   b) You earn 10% compounded annually?
   c) You earn 12% compounded annually?

3. IBM stock currently sells for $70 a share. If the price appreciates by 12% a year, how many years will it take for the stock to double in value?

4. Penney's is issuing a bondlike security that will pay you a lump sum of $5,000 in seven years. If current market interest rates are at 12%, what is the present value of this bond? How much should you pay for the bond?

5. An insurance company offers you an annuity paying $5,000 per year at the end of each of the next 10 years. What is the present value of this annuity if market interest rates are 10% for an investment of equivalent risk? How much should you pay for this annuity?

6. Joe Sharkey, your neighborhood banker, will lend you $10,000 to purchase a new car. Your payments are $3,502 per year for the next four years. What rate of interest is Joe charging?

7. Your fraternity has found a house that costs $150,000. It can be purchased by paying $25,000 down and financing the balance over a 25-year period at 12%. What yearly payments are required to repay the loan?

8. Using annual and semiannual compounding, calculate the future value of $5,000 two years from today, assuming that the rate of return that could be earned is

   a) 12%.

   b) 8%.

   c) (Optional) Assume a 12% rate compounded daily. (Use your calculator for this one.)

   d) (Optional) Assume a 12% rate compounded continuously.

9. Hank's Bank pays interest quarterly at a rate of 8%. Last National Bank pays interest annually at a rate of 9%.

   a) What will be the value one year from today of $10,000 deposited in Hank's Bank? In the Last National Bank?

   b) What annual rate must Last National pay to be competitive with Hank's Bank?

10. You have found the house of your dreams, which costs $135,000. It can be yours for $20,000 down and $13,655 a year for the next 25 years. What rate of interest are you paying on your loan?

11. The Fuzzyworm Tractor Company is establishing a fund to repay $10,000,000 in debt five years from today. Fuzzyworm can earn 9% on its money. What are the equal annual payments required, beginning one year from today, that will enable the firm to accrue $10,000,000 by the end of the fifth year?

12. AT&T is offering a security that pays $120 a year at the end of each of the next 20 years, plus a lump sum payment of $1,000 at the end of the 20th year.

    a) What is the present value of this stream of payments if market interest rates are 10%? What should you pay for the security?

    b) If interest rates change to 12%, what is the present value of the cash flow?

13. This year IBM will pay a dividend of $4.50 a share on its common stock. Five years ago, the dividend was $2.14. What is the average annual rate of growth in the dividend payment?

14. Your company is evaluating the following investments:

Year	Cash Flows X	Cash Flows Y
1	$500	$100
2	400	200
3	300	300
4	200	400
5	100	500

a) Without discounting the cash flows, which investment do you believe will have the higher present value?

b) Now calculate the present value of the cash flows for each investment at a discount rate of 10%.

15. To increase the sale of new houses in the early 1980s, some building contractors advertised 0% financing. Under a typical contract for a $90,000 house, the buyer pays $30,000 down and $10,000 a year for the next six years. Mortgage interest rates at the time were 15%.

a) Is there really such a thing as a 0% loan?

b) Assuming mortgage interest rates are 15%, what should the house sell for to someone who pays cash for it?

16. To provide for your retirement, you decide to invest in an Individual Retirement Account (IRA) offered by your local bank. The account earns 9% per year, and you will deposit the maximum of $2,000 per year. What will be the future value of your fund, assuming that you have 40 years to retirement?

17. Tab Collar is sixty-five years old and has received a lump sum retirement payment from his company of $200,000. An insurance company has offered him an annuity paying $27,174 a year for the next 10 years in exchange for the $200,000. What rate of interest is he earning on his investment of $200,000?

18. Assume that you can invest in only one of the following four investments, all of which have equal risk. The interest rate is 12%.

	Cost	Cash Inflows
W	$ 7,000	$1,941/year for 5 years
X	$ 9,000	$1,675/year for 10 years
Y	$ 5,500	$34,375 lump sum in the 15th year
Z	$11,320	$2,325/year for 7 years

a) Calculate the rate of return from each investment.

b) Calculate the net present value (present value of cash inflow less cost) of each investment.

c) Which investment is preferable?

19. Three years from today, Jerry Donalds plans to take a European vacation that will cost $3,000. He consults you, his banker, about methods of providing for the trip. In one of your many plans, you explain that he can deposit a single amount today and allow it to collect interest so that the account equals $3,000 in three years. Assuming that your bank pays an 8% interest rate compounded semiannually, how much must he deposit now? (Use Table C to interpolate the amount.)

20. Find the compound value of a $125, 10-year immediate annuity at 12% annual interest if the payment at the end of year 6 is omitted.

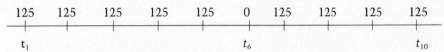

21. A father is planning to provide a 20-year trust fund for his son. The amount deposited today will remain untouched until the end of the 20th year but will gain interest at a rate of 10% compounded annually. The money will then be transferred to another account, which pays 5%. The son plans to withdraw the money in six equal annual payments of $4,000 each starting at the end of the year 20. The fund will be completely depleted after six payments. What amount should the father deposit today?

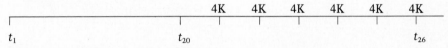

22. You have been offered an investment which will pay $75 per year forever. Calculate the present value of this income stream at the following rates:

a) 8%

b) 12%

c) 16%

23. An investment promises to pay $115 per year forever. What rate of return are you making if you pay the following amount for the investment?

a) $1,000

b) $985

c) $750

d) $1,250

APPENDIX 3A

CONTINUOUS COMPOUNDING AND DISCOUNTING

The time value of money calculations presented in Chapter 3 assume that interest is credited to the earning stream at discrete time intervals. At first, annual compounding was assumed. The section entitled "Nonannual Compounding" presented the equation†

$$FV = PV\left(1 + \frac{i}{m}\right)^{tm}, \tag{3.11}$$

which allows calculation of future values for any discrete interval of time. Most financial institutions pay interest daily, and some compound interest continuously. It is appropriate and interesting to ask, what will happen if the compounding period is increased to every hour, every second, and so on? The answer is that a mathematical limit to this process can be determined that defines the meaning of continuous compounding and discounting. Many theoretical problems in finance are best solved by assuming that continuous compounding occurs. The following four sections describe how to calculate future value and present value of a lump sum and annuities under the assumption of continuous rates.

FUTURE VALUE OF A LUMP SUM: CONTINUOUS COMPOUNDING

The formula for continuous rates is developed from the following mathematical expression, which may remind you of Eq. (3.11):

$$Y = \left(1 + \frac{1}{X}\right)^{x}. \tag{3A.1}$$

It will soon be shown that Eq. (3.11) contains the expression $(1 + 1/X)^x$. Table 3A.1 describes what happens to Y as X increases in value. As X increases beyond 1,000, the increase in Y becomes less and less. Mathematically, it is said that $(1 + 1/X)^x$ approaches a limiting value as X approaches infinity.

---

† In this section the number of time periods is denoted by t, a continuous variable, rather than n as was used in the chapter where n denoted the number of *discrete* time periods.

TABLE 3A.1
Values of $Y = (1 + 1/X)^x$.

$Y = (1 + 1/X)^x$	when X is
$= 2.00000$	1
$= 2.25000$	2
$= 2.37035$	3
$= 2.44141$	4
$= 2.48832$	5
$= 2.59374$	10
$= 2.70481$	100
$= 2.71692$	1000

Because Eq. (3A.1) occurs frequently in mathematical problems, the limiting value of this equation has been given the label e.

$$e = \lim_{X \to \infty} \left(1 + \frac{1}{X}\right)^x = 2.71828.$$

Note: e is an irrational number whose value to five decimal places is 2.71828.

The importance of e to continuous compounding and discounting is shown by some algebraic manipulation of Eq. (3.11). The objective is to isolate the factor $(1 + 1/X)^x$ in the equation.

1. Begin with Eq. (3.11):

$$FV = PV\left(1 + \frac{i}{m}\right)^{tm}.$$

2. First multiply the exponent (tm) by i/i [equivalent to (1)] and write $(t \cdot i)(m/i)$.

3. Realize that i/m is equivalent to $1/(m/i)$, so we can write

$$FV = PV\left[\left(1 + \frac{1}{m/i}\right)^{m/i}\right]^{ti}.$$

4. Define a new variable, $X = m/i$, and substitute X for m/i. Observe that as the number of compounding periods, m, increases, X increases.

$$FV = PV\left[\left(1 + \frac{1}{X}\right)^{x}\right]^{ti}.$$

5. If it is assumed that the compounding period increases toward infinity, the term in brackets becomes the value e. The formula for future value under an assumption of continuous compounding becomes

$$FV = PV\, e^{ti}. \tag{3A.2}$$

6. To find the future value of a lump sum, multiply the lump sum by e to the power of the period times the interest rate. For example, if t = two years, i = 8%, and PV is $1,000, the calculation is

$$FV = 1,000 \times e^{2 \times .08}$$
$$= \$1,173.51.$$

Note that values of t and i must be based on the same time dimension. If 8% is an annual rate, t must be stated in years. Conversely, a daily rate of interest would require t to be dimensioned in days. Problems of future value are solved easily with hand-held calculators containing an e^x function. On standard-notation calculators (such as those of Texas Instruments), first multiply the interest rate by the time to get the value of X. Punch the e^x button to obtain the value of e^{ti} in order to determine the future value.

PRESENT VALUE OF A LUMP SUM: CONTINUOUS DISCOUNTING

Solving for present value under continuous discounting involves determining an amount that, if invested today, would grow to the known future sum when interest is continuously credited to the account. Present value under continuous discounting is determined by rearranging Eq. (3A.2) to solve for PV.

$$FV = PV\, e^{ti}$$
$$PV = \frac{FV}{e^{ti}} \qquad (3A.2)$$

Recall that a value in the denominator can be transferred to the numerator by changing the sign of its exponent. Present value of a lump sum usually is written in the form of Eq. (3A.3), with the discount factor as e^{-ti}:

$$PV = FV\, e^{-ti}. \qquad (3A.3)$$

The present value of $1,000 to be received two years hence, with an interest rate of 8% assuming continuous discounting, is solved as

$$PV = 1,000\, e^{(-2 \times .08)}$$
$$= 1,000\, e^{-(.16)}$$
$$= 1,000\,(.85214)$$
$$= \$852.14.$$

FUTURE VALUE OF AN ANNUITY: CONTINUOUS COMPOUNDING

Calculating the future value of an annuity is more complex, as it is necessary to perform integration in conjunction with the e^{ti} operation. In equation form, future value of an annuity is defined as Eq. (3A.4) with the variable of integration being time and the limits of integration going from time 0 to n.

$$FV_A = \int_0^n Re^{ti}\, dt. \tag{3A.4}$$

Solution of Eq. (3A.4) by substitution yields the following general expression for future value of an annuity, assuming continuous compounding. Solution of $FV_A = R \int_0^n e^{it}\, dt$ proceeds as follows:

1. Define

$$u = it$$
$$du = i\, dt$$
$$\frac{1}{i} du = dt.$$

2. Substitute u and $(1/i)\, du$ into the original expression:

$$FV_A = \frac{R}{i} \int_x^y e^u\, du.$$

3. Recall that $e^u\, du = e^u$; the solution becomes

$$\frac{R}{i} e^u \bigg|_x^y.$$

4. Redefining u as $i \cdot t$ and inserting limits for t,

$$FV_A = \frac{R}{i} e^{i \cdot t} \bigg|_0^n = \left(\frac{R}{i} e^{i \cdot n} - \frac{R}{i} e^0 \right).$$

5. Equation (3A.5) is obtained by factoring R/i:

$$FV_A = \frac{R}{i} (e^{in} - 1)$$

or $\hspace{8cm}$ (3A.5)

$$= \frac{R}{i} (e^{it} - 1).$$

For example, consider finding the future value of the four-year $1,000 annuity at 5% described previously in Table 3.3. Using Equation (3A.5), we obtain

$$FV_A = \frac{1,000}{.05} (e^{(.05)(4)} - 1)$$
$$= 20,000\,(1.22140 - 1)$$
$$= \$4,428.$$

As should be expected under the assumption of more frequent (continuous) compounding, the future value of \$4,428 is greater than the \$4,310 achieved with yearly compounding.

PRESENT VALUE OF AN ANNUITY: CONTINUOUS DISCOUNTING

Finding the present value of an annuity under continuous discounting is the inverse of determining the future value. Consequently, all that is required is to use e^{-it} in place of e^{it} in Eq. (3A.4) to derive Eq. (3A.6):

$$\begin{aligned} PV_A &= R \int_0^n e^{-ti}\, dt \\ &= R\left(\frac{1 - e^{-it}}{i}\right). \end{aligned} \tag{3A.6}$$

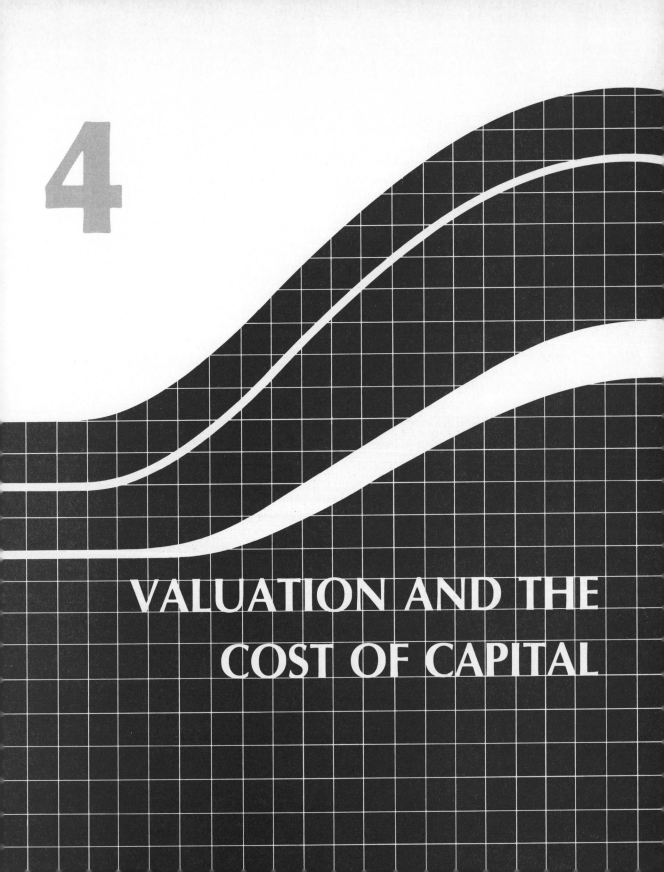

4

VALUATION AND THE COST OF CAPITAL

The *cost of capital* is the minimum rate of return that a firm must earn on new investments so that the value of the firm is not reduced. In order to derive the cost of capital, we must start with a specification of firm value. The value of a firm is the sum of the values of its outstanding securities.

All economic assets are valued according to the same rule: The value of an economic asset is the present value of its cash flows. Using this rule, we can find the value of a firm's stocks and bonds and, in turn, the value of the firm itself. From this **valuation** model we can derive the cost of capital, the cutoff rate for all new corporate investments.

After careful study of this chapter, you should understand:

1. What determines the value of economic assets such as stocks and bonds.
2. What is meant by the valuation of a firm.
3. How a cost of capital is derived from the value of the firm.
4. How to calculate a number, the cost of capital, that can be used to evaluate potential firm investments.

VALUATION

The value of an economic asset is the present value of the benefits it generates over time. Anything that increases the present value of an asset increases the worth of that asset. Corporate securities are economic assets. By applying present value analysis techniques learned in the last chapter to the cash flows generated by bonds and stocks, we can define their economic worth, that is, their price.

BONDS

A **bond** is a long-term corporate debt in which the borrower, the firm, agrees to pay the lender, or investor, periodic interest plus an amount equal to the original loan. Bonds generate two types of cash flows for investors. Periodically, every 3, 6, or 12 months, they pay interest. At maturity, usually 20 to 30 years after issue, the originally borrowed amount, the principal, is repaid to the current owner of the bond. By taking the present value of these two components, we can determine the price of a bond. The equation for the calculation is

$$\text{Price of the bond} = \text{present value of interest payment} + \text{present value of principal} \qquad (4.1)$$

$$P_\text{B} = \sum_{i=1}^{n} \frac{I_i}{(1 + K_d)^i} + \frac{P_n}{(1 + K_d)^n},$$

where P_B is the price of the bond, I is the dollar amount of interest per period, i is the period, n is the total number of periods, P_n is the principal, and K_d is the market rate of interest for a bond of this quality (riskiness).

When bonds are sold, their **coupon rate,** or stated rate of interest, is usually at (or close to) the prevailing market rate; $I = K_d P_n$. If such is the case, the bond will sell at a price equal to its **par value,** or stated value. For example, consider a 12% (annual interest), 30-year, $1,000 bond selling in a 12% market. It would be worth

$$P_B = \sum_{i=1}^{30} \frac{\$120}{(1.12)^i} + \frac{\$1,000}{(1.12)^{30}}$$

$$= \$966.62 + \$33.38 = \$1,000.$$

Market interest rates, however, change frequently. Consequently, bond prices also change frequently. If interest rates drop, bond values rise. For example, if market rates dropped to 10%, this same bond would be worth

$$P_B = \sum_{i=1}^{30} \frac{\$120}{(1.10)^i} + \frac{\$1,000}{(1.10)^{30}}$$

$$= \$1,131.23 + \$57.31 = \$1,188.54.$$

On the other hand, if the market rate rose, say, to 14%, bond values would drop. For example, this bond would be worth

$$P_B = \sum_{i=1}^{30} \frac{\$120}{(1.14)^i} + \frac{\$1,000}{(1.14)^{30}}$$

$$= \$840.32 + \$19.63 = \$859.95.$$

As this example shows, the value of a bond is determined not only by what it promises to pay (interest and principal) but also by what the market currently demands as a level of return—the market rate of interest. By examining the price of a bond relative to its coupon rate and maturity, we can determine the market rate of interest (for a bond of that quality).

STOCKS

Stock is the ownership interest of a corporation. Each share of stock is a fraction of the rights and privileges that belong to the owners of a business. A stock certificate is evidence of that fractional ownership; it is tangible evidence, a certificate of title, to part of the company.

There are two types of stocks—*common* and *preferred*. Both are economic assets, and their worth is determined by the present value of the cash flows they receive, dividends. The valuation model for common stocks and preferreds is the same. The preferred stock model is simply a specific application of the more general common stock valuation model.

A person buying a stock invests on faith, in the hope of receiving dividends. The common stock certificate makes no mention of ever repaying the "principal," or purchase price. The purpose of investing in equities, or stocks, is to participate in the earnings of the firm through dividends when (and if) the firm should decide to distribute them. The value of a share of stock is the present value of the expected dividends. Algebraically,

$$P_s = \sum_{i=1}^{n} \frac{D_i}{(1 + K_e)^i},$$ (4.2)

where P_s is the price of the stock, D is the expected per-period divided, i is the period, n is the total number of periods, and K_e is the market rate of return required on equity investments of this riskiness.

Equations (4.1) and (4.2) are very similar. The main differences are that Eq. (4.2) has no provision for principal repayment and that the market discount rates are different because debt and equity investments carry different risks.

Another difference in the equations is less apparent. Interest payments, I_i, are usually the same in every period. Dividends, D_i, grow (the investor hopes) over time. If dividends were to grow at a *constant* per-period rate, Eq. (4.2) could be expanded to

$$P_s = \frac{D_1}{(1 + K_e)} + \frac{D_1(1 + g)}{(1 + K_e)^2} + \frac{D_1(1 + g)^2}{(1 + K_e)^3} + \cdots \frac{D_1(1 + g)^{n-1}}{(1 + K_e)^n}.$$ (4.3)

Equation (4.3) is what is called a *geometric series;* each term in the series differs from the prior term by a common ratio. The common ratio in this case is $(1 + g)/(1 + K_e)$. The equation for the sum of n terms of a geometric series is

$$S = \frac{t_1 - t_1 r^n}{1 - r},$$ (4.4)

where S is the sum, t_1 is the first term, r is the common ratio, and n is the number of terms.

When we substitute the first term, $D_1/(1 + K_e)$, and the common ratio, $(1 + g)/(1 + K_e)$, in the equation we get

$$P_s = \frac{D_1\{1 - [(1 + g)/(1 + K_e)]^n\}}{K_e - g},$$ (4.5)

which would be the price of the stock *if it matured,* that is, if n were finite. Stocks, however, do not mature; n is infinite. If the rate of growth of the dividend, g, is less than the required return on equity investment, K_e, the value of the common ratio will be less than 1, $(1 + g)/(1 + K_e) < 1$. If we take a number less than 1 to a very high power it becomes insignificant, that is, zero. If n is equal to infinity, the stock valuation model is simplified to

$$P_s = \frac{D_1}{K_e - g}.$$ (4.6)

Equation (4.6) is called the **Gordon model.** It was derived and popularized by Professor Myron J. Gordon, and it is one of the best-known formulas in finance.

The same equation applies to preferred stock. The difference is that preferred stock dividends do not grow; that is, g equals zero. This further simplifies the equation as follows:

$$P_p = \frac{D_p}{K_p}.$$ (4.7)

All the variables are subscripted with a p to indicate that they apply to preferred stock.

COMPANY VALUATION

The value of a company is the sum of the values of its outstanding securities. So far, we have looked at the valuation of individual securities; now we shall consider the total value of a firm.

To make things easier, we will make some simplifying assumptions. We will assume that the firm has no preferred stock outstanding. Bonds will be assumed to be perpetual; they are issued once at a stated rate of interest and then never mature. Finally, it will be assumed that the firm distributes all earnings (dividends equal after-tax earnings) and that the level of earnings is constant (no growth).

Although these assumptions are restrictive, they allow us to build a simple model of a firm, to derive a cost of capital, and to better understand the logical link between valuation and the cost of capital.

Bonds

A company issuing bonds agrees to pay an interest rate, r, on the face value, D, of those debts. For any individual bond, the coupon I will be equal to the rate times the par value (usually \$1,000) of the bond. That is,

$$I = rD.$$ (4.8)

The market value of the bonds (B) will be the present value of the interest payments. If a bond is perpetual (no repayment of principal), the valuation formula is the same as that used for preferred stock (Eq. 4.7). Therefore the market value of the firm's outstanding debts would be

$$B = \frac{I}{K_d} = \frac{rD}{K_d},$$ (4.9)

where I now refers to the *total* interest payments the company must make on its outstanding bonds.

Stocks

Stockholders own all earnings that exceed the interest payments and that the government does not claim in taxes. If the company had operating earnings (EBIT) of X dollars, earnings before taxes would be $(X - rD)$; that is, EBIT minus total interest payments. After-tax earnings would be $(1 - t)$ times that amount where t is the company's tax rate. The market value of the stock, S, is the present value of these earnings:

$$S = \frac{(X - rD)(1 - t)}{K_e}. \tag{4.10}$$

Firm Value

The value of the company, V, is the sum of the *market values* of its outstanding securities—its stocks and bonds.

$$\begin{aligned} V &= S + B \\ &= \frac{(X - rD)(1 - t)}{K_e} + \text{B}. \end{aligned} \tag{4.11}$$

Further, as shown in Eq. (4.11), the market value of the stock is the present value of the after-tax earnings, capitalized at the required return or equity rate, K_e.

COST OF CAPITAL

THEORY

This section develops the concept of a firm's cost of capital. As will become clear, the idea derives directly from the definition of firm value, and its application uses many of the security valuation equations.

Definition

Numerous authors have defined the **cost of capital.** Among the most explicit of these definitions is the following one supplied by Myron J. Gordon:

> The cost of capital for a firm is the discount rate with the property that an investment with a rate of profit above (below) this rate will raise (lower) the value of the firm.[†]

[†] Myron J. Gordon, *The Investment Financing and Valuation of the Corporation* (Homewood, Ill.: Richard D. Irwin, Inc., 1962), p. 218.

To paraphase, the cost of capital is the *minimum rate of return* that the firm must receive on new investments so that the *value of the firm* will not be reduced. Note that the key to the concept is maintaining the value of the firm.

Derivation

One of the advantages of this definition of the cost of capital is that it implies a procedure for mathematically deriving the cost of capital. The derivation has four steps:

1. Define the value of the firm.
2. Derive the relationship between changes in investment and changes in the value of the firm.
3. Impose the minimum return requirement; that is, require that the value of the firm cannot be reduced.
4. Isolate the return variable; the cost of capital is a measure of required return on investment.

The valuation formula expressed as Eq. (4.11) is correct, but it contains one component that is awkward for present purposes. Interest expense is stated in *book value* terms; that is, total interest expense is rD. It would be more convenient if this expense, like the equity cost (K_e), were defined as a market capitalization rate. Fortunately, we can make an easy substitution. From Eq. (4.9) we can see

$$rD = K_d B.$$

Making the appropriate substitution in Eq. (4.11) yields a firm valuation equation expressed in terms of only market values and market capitalization rates:

$$V = \frac{(X - K_d B)(1 - t)}{K_e} + B. \qquad (4.12)$$

Mathematically, we can find the change in firm value with respect to changes in investment. The procedure is called partial differentiation. Assuming that the new investment is of average riskiness (i.e., that it does not change K_e or K_d), the change in the value of the firm with respect to new investment would be

$$\frac{\partial V}{\partial I} = \frac{\partial X (1 - t)}{\partial I \, K_e} - \frac{K_d (1 - t)}{K_e} \frac{\partial B}{\partial I} + \frac{\partial B}{\partial I}. \qquad (4.13)$$

If an investment is not to penalize existing security holders, the value of the firm must increase by an amount equal to the cost of the investment. Otherwise, existing owners would, in effect, subsidize the investment. Mathematically, this means that $\partial V/\partial I$ must be at least 1. To accomplish the third step in the derivation, imposing the return constraint, set $\partial V/\partial I$ equal to 1, as follows:

$$1 = \frac{\partial X(1 - t)}{\partial I \, K_e} - \frac{K_d(1 - t)}{K_e} \frac{\partial B}{\partial I} + \frac{\partial B}{\partial I}. \tag{4.14}$$

The fourth step in the cost of capital derivation, isolating the return variable, requires rearrangement of the equation. At a minimum, the required after-tax rate of return $[\partial X(1 - t)/\partial I]$ on new investments must be

$$\frac{\partial X(1 - t)}{\partial I} = K_e\left(1 - \frac{\partial B}{\partial I}\right) + K_d(1 - t)\frac{\partial B}{\partial I}. \tag{4.15}$$

One more change will make the formula more logical. The variable $\partial B/\partial I$ is the proportion of the new investment that is financed with bonds. Therefore $(1 - \partial B/\partial I)$ is the proportion of the investment that would be equity financed; this quantity could also be indicated as $\partial S/\partial I$. Now the formula makes sense: a new investment must earn enough to satisfy the return requirements of the firm's investors weighted in proportion to the amount of each of the types of capital that is employed. The formula is simply a weighted average cost of capital (WACC):

$$\text{WACC} = K_e\frac{\partial S}{\partial I} + K_d(1 - t)\frac{\partial B}{\partial I}. \tag{4.16}$$

Interpretation

Considering the cost of capital as a weighted average makes interpretation easier. You might very well have reached a similar conclusion without the mathematical derivation. For example, suppose you were told that a company was financed with equal amounts of debt and equity. The cost of the firm's debt is 12% (after taxes), and the cost of the equity is 24%. What is the company's cost of capital? Your instinctive response would be 18% (the average of 12 and 24%)—and that is correct.

The calculation using Eq. (4.16) simply formalizes the process. To be consistent, using more complete information, assume that the firm's cost of debt (K_d) is 20% before taxes of 40% $(t = .4)$; the cost of equity (K_e) is 24%; and the proportions of debt and equity are equal (both $\partial S/\partial I$ and $\partial B/\partial I$ are .5).

Note that although we speak of percentages, all calculations are done in decimals, both for costs and for weights. Consistently working in decimals avoids confusion and reduces the likelihood of making a decimal point error. The calculation using Eq. (4.16) is

$$\text{WACC} = .24(.5) + .20(1 - .4)(.5) = .18 \quad \text{or} \quad 18\%.$$

An 18% *after-tax* rate of return is the *minimum* that can be accepted. Eighteen percent will barely satisfy the demands of security holders; it produces nothing extra that will raise the price of the firm's stock.

This point can be made clear by using a numerical example. Assume that the firm is considering a marginal investment, one that earns exactly 18%. The investment costs $1,000, and it will earn 18% after taxes each year in perpetuity (forever); an 18% after-tax return is the same as 30% before taxes of 40%; that is, $.30 = .18/(1 - .40)$. Examining an income statement *for this investment alone* demonstrates that such an investment just repays the suppliers of the necessary capital:

EBIT (30% on $1,000)	$300.00
Interest ($500 @ 20%)	100.00
Earnings before taxes	200.00
Taxes (40%)	80.00
Net income (24% on $500)	$120.00

A 30% return on a $1,000 investment is $300. Half of the investment ($500) is debt financed at a cost of 20%. Interest expense would be $100; earnings before taxes would be $200; earnings after taxes of 40% would be $120, or exactly a 24% rate of return on the $500 equity investment.

The cost of capital defines the minimum after-tax rate of return such that each security holder receives his or her necessary percentage return. Anything less than this minimum will not satisfy the security buyers. Their dissatisfaction will result in lower demand for the company's stock, and stock prices will decline. The cost of capital is, therefore, the minimum rate of return that can be accepted on new investments.

APPLICATION

Application of the cost of capital concept follows the theory *exactly*. To derive a company's cost of capital, we must define each of the components in Eq. (4.16) and then calculate the weighted average. The process has three steps:

1. Determine the costs (K_e and K_d).

2. Determine the weights for each component ($\partial S/\partial I$ and $\partial B/\partial I$).
3. Calculate the weighted average.

Actually, the calculation is a little more complicated than indicated in Eq. (4.16). A company may have more than bonds and stocks; it may have preferred stock outstanding. Further, the common equity may be retained earnings in addition to common stock. As a result, we may have more than two costs (and weights), but the process is essentially unchanged: Fill in the blanks in Eq. (4.16) and calculate the weighted average. The sections that follow discuss how to complete each step: finding the costs, finding the weights, and calculating the average.

Illustrating the calculations requires an example. For simplicity, a hypothetical company will be used. We can then use round numbers and avoid a variety of complications than are unnecessarily confusing at this point.

Component Costs

We have already seen the equations necessary for calculating the component costs; they are the valuation formulas presented at the beginning of this chapter. At that point they were stated in terms of price, that is, with price on the left-hand side of the equation. Now we will rearrange the equation to solve for K, the security buyers' required rates of return.

Logically, what we are doing is implicitly defining the security holders' return requirements. We cannot ask all the bondholders and stockholders what rates of return they expect, but we can observe bond and stock prices. We know the levels of interest and dividend payments. What we will do is work backward to determine what discount rates must have been used in the valuation process.

Cost of bonds. Equation (4.1) specifies the valuation formula for a bond. If we know the price of a bond, P_B, its annual coupon, I, its principal amount, P_n (normally $1,000), and the time to maturity, n, we can solve for the discount rate, K_d. This is a rate-of-return calculation of the type illustrated in the previous chapter. However, because the calculation involves both an annuity (of amount I) and a lump sum (P_n), it can be tedious. Fortunately, there is a shortcut approximation. The rate, K_d, is approximately†

$$K_d = \frac{I + [(1,000 - P_B)/n]}{(P_B + 1,000)/2} . \tag{4.17}$$

To illustrate the use of the formula, assume that a firm has bonds

---

† The formula assumes that P_n = $1,000. If this is not the case, substitute the principal amount of the bond for the $1,000.

outstanding that are selling currently for $800. The original coupon was 11%; that is, I is $110. The bond will mature in 25 years. The approximate yield on this bond (the bondholders' implied discount rate) is 13.11%:

$$K_d = \frac{110 + [(1,000 - 800)/25]}{(1,000 + 800)/2} = .1311 \quad \text{or} \quad 13.11\%.$$

This is the K_d that would be used in the cost of capital calculation. Note, however, that the cost of debt must be tax adjusted (it is the only component requiring this adjustment). If the firm is in a 40% tax bracket, the after-tax cost of its debt would be less; $K_d(1 - t) = .1311(1 - .4) = .0787$ or 7.87%.

Cost of preferred stock. The cost of preferred stock is found by again rearranging the valuation formula, Eq. (4.7). The result is

$$K_p = \frac{D_p}{P_p}. \tag{4.18}$$

Assume that our company has preferred stock outstanding earning an annual dividend of $8 and selling currently for $50 (its par value is $100). The implied cost of the preferred stock (the implicit valuation discount rate) is 16%:

$$K_p = \frac{8}{50} = .16 \quad \text{or} \quad 16\%.$$

Cost of common equity. There are two types of common equity—internal and external. Internal common equity is generated as profits and accounted for as retained earnings. External common equity comes from the sale of common stock. Determining the cost of both of these components uses the same measure, Eq. (4.6). Solving for the cost of equity as retained earnings,

$$K_{er} = \frac{D_1}{P_s} + g. \tag{4.19}$$

The same formula is used to determine the cost of external equity, that is, new stock. There is only one slight difference. When a company sells new stock, it gets less than the full market price. Sales of new stock generally involve a middleman called an *investment banker*. Investment bankers do not donate their services; they must be paid. Payment to the investment banker and other administrative costs, such as the cost of printing the stock certificates and the registration fees, are called **flotation costs.** Flotation costs, F, are a percentage of the sales price of the new stock that serves to reduce the net sales price of new stock, P_{sn}, below the market price. Symbolically, the relationship is

$$P_{sn} = (1 - F)P_s. \tag{4.20}$$

To determine the cost of new common stock, K_{en}, we use the net sales price in Eq. (4.19). Either definition of net sales price (in Eq. 4.20) will work. The cost of new equity is then

$$K_{en} = \frac{D_1}{P_{sn}} + g$$

or

(4.21)

$$K_{en} = \frac{D_1}{P_s(1 - F)} + g.$$

To illustrate, assume that our firm's expected next-period dividend is $4. The dividend has historically grown at a rate of 10% per year. The current market price of the stock is $50. Using Eq. (4.19), we get a cost of retained earnings of

$$K_{er} = \frac{\$4}{\$50} + .10 = .18 \quad \text{or} \quad 18\%.$$

If the company sold new stock, flotation costs would be 10%; that is, it would net only $45 a share on the sale of new stock. This is consistent with the relationship in Eq. (4.20):

$$P_{sn} = (1 - F)P_s$$
$$\$45 = (1 - .1)\$50.$$

Using either of the calculations in Eq. (4.21), the cost of new stock is

$$K_{en} = \frac{\$4}{\$45} + .10 = .189 \quad \text{or} \quad 18.9\%$$

$$= \frac{\$4}{\$50(1 - .1)} + .10 = .189 \quad \text{or} \quad 18.9\%.$$

Component Weights

The second step in the cost of capital calculation is to determine the weights for each of the components, based on the proportions of debt and equity used in financing the new investment—the marginal weights. There is a problem in applying such a procedure; although work is in progress, we have not yet determined how to measure the amount of debt capacity associated with each individual investment.

For this reason, we sidestep the problem by assuming that each investment is traditionally financed, that is, using the same proportions of debt and equity as the firm as a whole. Even this assumption does not solve all the problems. The question remains of whether to use **market value** weights (proportions based on the relative market values of the firm's outstanding securities) or

ILLUSTRATION **93**

historical weights (**book values**). It can be shown that either set of weights is correct if the costs are defined in an internally consistent manner. If we use costs derived from market prices, internal consistency demands that we use market value (MV) weights. The formulas for the weights are as follows:

$$\text{Weight for debt} = \frac{\text{MV of outstanding bonds}}{\text{MV of all outstanding securities}}$$

$$\text{Weight of preferred stock} = \frac{\text{MV of outstanding preferred stock}}{\text{MV of all outstanding securities}}$$

$$\text{Weight for common equity} = \frac{\text{MV of outstanding common stock}}{\text{MV of all outstanding securities}}.$$

There is only one more problem to deal with before calculating the weighted average cost of capital. We know that common equity has two components: retained earnings and new stock. How much of the equity weight should be attributed to stock and how much to retained earnings? Although various approaches have been suggested, none of them is beyond question. A common expedient is to apportion the weight for common equity based on book values (BV) as follows:

$$\text{Weight for new stock} = \text{Weight for common equity} \times \frac{\text{BV of common stock}}{\text{BV of common equity}}$$

$$\text{Weight for retained earnings} = \text{Weight for common equity} \times \frac{\text{BV of retained earnings}}{\text{BV of common equity}}.$$

ILLUSTRATION

Given procedures for calculating each of the costs and weights, the third step in the cost of capital calculation, finding the weighted average, is a matter of mechanics. Market value for each of the components is determined, and weights are calculated. Equity weight is apportioned to new stock and retained earnings. Each component cost is calculated. An illustration will show how the average is calculated. (The equations are summarized in Table 4.1.)

Assume that each of the capital-cost calculations already done applies to our example firm. We already know that

$$K_d(1 - t) = 7.87\% \quad \text{or} \quad .0787$$

$$K_p = 16\% \quad \text{or} \quad .1600$$

$$K_{en} = 18.9\% \quad \text{or} \quad .1890$$

$$K_{er} = 18\% \quad \text{or} \quad .1800.$$

Further, we have specified the market prices of our outstanding securities. To get the *total market value* of each type of security, we restate the capital

TABLE 4.1
Summary of Cost and Weight Formulas.

Component	Cost	Weight
Debt	$(1 - t)K_d = (1 - \text{tax rate})\left[\dfrac{I + (1{,}000 - P_B)/n}{(P_B + 1{,}000)/2}\right]$	$\dfrac{\text{MV of outstanding bonds}}{\text{MV of all outstanding securities}}$
Preferred stock	$K_p = \dfrac{D_p}{P_p} = \dfrac{\text{preferred stock dividend}}{\text{preferred stock price}}$	$\dfrac{\text{MV of outstanding preferred stock}}{\text{MV of all outstanding securities}}$
Common equity weight (CEW)		$\dfrac{\text{MV of outstanding common stock}}{\text{MV of all outstanding securities}}$
Common stock	$K_{en} = \dfrac{D_1}{P_{sn}} + g$ $= \dfrac{\text{common stock dividend}}{\text{net per share proceeds on sale of new stock}} + \text{growth rate}$	$\dfrac{\text{BV of common stock}}{\text{BV of common equity}} \times \text{CEW}$
Retained earnings	$K_{er} = \dfrac{D_1}{P_s} + g = \dfrac{\text{common stock dividend}}{\text{common stock price}} + \text{growth rate}$	$\dfrac{\text{BV of retained earnings}}{\text{BV of common equity}} \times \text{CEW}$

ILLUSTRATION   **95**

structure of the firm (the right-hand side of the balance sheet, excluding current liabilities) in market value terms, as in Table 4.2.

The book value of the company's bonds is $4 million. Recall, however, that these same bonds are now selling for only $800 even though their original par (and principal amount) is $1,000 *per bond*. The market value of the firm's bonds is found by multiplying the $4 million by .8(.8 = 800/1,000). The market value of the outstanding bonds is $3.2 million.

A similar calculation is used for preferred stock. Par is $100; current market value is $50. The market value of the original $1 million worth of preferred stock is $500,000.

Figuring out the market value of the common stock is a little more complicated for a hypothetical company. For a real company, it would be easier. Annual reports indicate how many shares a firm has outstanding; to determine the market value of outstanding common stock, simply multiply that number by the current market price. Our example requires an extra step. We determine the number of shares outstanding using the common stock account and par value. The common stock account indicates a book value of $3 million. Dividing by $20 par determines the number of common shares outstanding: 150,000 = $3 million/$20. To derive the market value, multiply by the current market price, $50. The market value of our firm's common equity is $7.5 million. Note that this is the market value of both the common stock and retained earnings. Retained earnings contributes to the market value of the stock; it has no market value of its own.

The total market value of the firm's outstanding securities is $11.2 million. Using the formulas in Table 4.1, we calculate the market weights for each of the components by dividing each component market value by $11.2 million. The results are shown in column 3 of Table 4.2.

Next, the common equity weight is apportioned for common stock and retained earnings. The market value of our company is 67% equity. *Based on*

TABLE 4.2
Cost of Capital Sample Calculation (Value Figures in 000s).

Type of Funds	(1) Book Value	(2) Market Value	(3) Market Weights	(4) Component Weights	(5) Component Costs	(6) Weighted Costs
Bonds	$4,000	$ 3,200	.286	.286	.0787	.0225
Preferred stock	1,000	500	.045	.045	.1600	.0072
Common stock ($20 par)	3,000 ⎱	7,500	.670	.402	.1890	.0760
Retained earnings	2,000 ⎰			.268	.1800	.0482
		$11,200	1	1		.1539 or 15.39%

book values, 60% of that equity is common stock and 40% is retained earnings. Apportion the common equity weight (CEW = .67) 60/40 based on the book value proportions. The weight for common stock is .402 = (.67)(.60). The weight for retained earnings is .268 = (.67)(.40). These results are shown in column 4 of Table 4.2.

Each of the component costs was calculated earlier. These are simply inserted in column 5 of Table 4.2 (again, use the decimal form). Next, column 4 is multiplied by column 5, and the weighted costs are summed to get the weighted average. The example firm's weighted average cost of capital is approximately 15.39%. It should make no new investments that earn less than that figure. To do so would reduce the value of the company and disappoint the firm's security owners.

SUMMARY

The concepts of valuation and the cost of capital are very closely related. A model of firm value is the starting point for deriving the cost of capital. Deriving the cost of capital involves several steps: valuing the firm, determining the relationship between investment and firm value, and deriving an investment rule based on the investment–firm-value relationship.

Implementing the cost of capital concepts also uses valuation; to derive the cost of each capital component (debt, preferred, and common equity), we work the valuation models backward to determine the implicit discount rate of the security buyers. This chapter has examined valuation formulas for each form of corporate security from which we put together a simplified model of firm value and then derived one widely recognized cost of capital model—the weighted average cost of capital.

An illustration has shown that calculating the weighted average cost of capital involves three steps: finding the component costs, determining component weights, and taking the average. Formulas for each of the costs and weights are summarized in Table 4.1. An example of how to find the average is illustrated in Table 4.2.

The previous chapter presented discounted cash flow analysis. This chapter shows how to find the discount rate—the cost of capital. The next chapter shows how discounted cash-flow analytical techniques and discount rates, used together, can analyze long-term, real asset (capital) investments. That is called *capital budgeting*.

QUESTIONS AND REVIEW ACTIVITIES

1. What determines the value of an economic asset? How does this concept apply to bonds and stocks?
2. Discuss the relationship between valuation and the cost of capital.
3. What is the definition of cost of capital?
4. What are the steps in a cost-of-capital derivation? How do these steps relate to the definition of cost of capital?
5. If a firm says that it has an 18% cost of capital, what does this statement mean?
6. What are the steps in calculating the cost of capital?

7. Why do retained earnings and new stock have different costs?
8. Explain the rationale for using the formula

$$K_{er} = \frac{D_1}{P_s} + g$$

to calculate the cost of common equity (retained earnings).
9. Discuss the relationship between the cost of capital and capital budgeting.

PROBLEMS

1. Market Products, Inc., wants to know the cost of each of its capital components. The company intends to use current yields and prices as a basis for the calculation. The information is summarized as follows:

Market price of outstanding bonds	$980
Coupon rate of bonds	9%
Maturity value of bonds	$1,000
Years to maturity	7
Corporate tax rate	40%
Market price of outstanding preferred stock	$70
Par value	$100
Dividend	$8
Market price of outstanding common stock	$25
Common stock dividend	$1
Growth rate	8%
Percentage flotation cost on sale of new shares	7%

a) Calculate the after-tax cost of debt.
b) Calculate the cost of preferred stock.
c) Calculate the cost of new common stock.
d) Calculate the cost of retained earnings.

2. Using the component costs calculated for Problem 1, calculate a weighted average cost of capital using the following weights:

	Weight
Bonds	30
Preferred stock	10
Common stock	40
Retained earnings	20

3. Middleman Supply & Co. intends to calculate its cost of capital. To do so, it has asked an investment banker to supply estimates of what prices and yields the

firm might expect to offer on new securities in order to sell them. The estimates, along with certain other data, can be summarized as follows:

Expected offering price of bonds net of underwriting concessions	$960
Anticipated coupon rate	8.25%
Maturity value	$1,000
Term (in years)	30
Corporate tax rate	40%
Net proceeds on sale of new preferred stock	$96
Par value	$100
Dividend rate (percentage of par)	9%
Current market price of outstanding common stock	$40
Common stock dividend	$0.60
Growth rate	11%
Net proceeds per share on sale of new stock	$34

Calculate the cost of (a) debt; (b) preferred stock; (c) common stock; and (d) retained earnings.

4. Using the component costs from Problem 3 and the following weights, calculate a weighted average cost of capital.

	Weight
Bonds	40
Preferred stock	5
Common stock	35
Retained earnings	20

5. Marketimer, Ltd., needs to determine its cost of capital for capital budgeting purposes. The company has assembled the following information:

Market price of outstanding bonds	$940
Coupon rate of bonds	8.25%
Maturity value of bonds	$1,000
Years to maturity	12
Corporate tax rate	40%
Market price of outstanding preferred stock	$57.25
Par value	$100
Dividend (percentage of par)	6%
Market price of outstanding common stock	$72
Common stock dividend	$5
Growth rate	6%
Net proceeds per share on sale on new stock	$65.50

The current capital structure, based on book value, is as follows:

Bonds	$2,500,000
Preferred stock	1,500,000
Common stock (par $50)	3,700,000
Retained earnings	2,300,000

Calculate the weighted average cost of capital based on market value weights (allocate common equity by book value, as was done in the chapter).

Note: *Problems 6 and 7 relate to the material on CAPM in Appendix 4A.*

6. Calculate a beta for a stock given the following information:

Security Return(%)	Market Return(%)
4	3
6	4
−1	0
2	1
3	1
4	3

7. Using the values given, calculate
   a) The beta of the firm's stock (β_s).
   b) Its cost of equity.
   c) The cost of capital using Eq. (4A.14).
   d) The cost of capital using the weighted average technique.
   The values are as follows:

   Return on the market, R_M = 18%   or   .18

   Risk-free rate, R_F = 10%   or   .10

   Beta of operating earnings, β_x = 1.2

   Corporate tax rate, t = 40% (or .4)

   Percentage debt financing $\partial D/\partial I$ or $D/(D + S)$ = 40%.

ADDITIONAL READINGS

Arditti, F. D., and M. S. Tysseland. "Three Ways to Present the Marginal Cost of Capital," *Financial Management* (Summer 1973), pp. 63–67.

Beranek, W. "Some New Capital Budgeting Theorems," *Journal of Financial and Quantitative Analysis* (December 1978), pp. 809–23.

————. "The Weighted Average Cost of Capital and Shareholder Wealth Maximization," *Journal of Financial and Quantitative Analysis* (March 1977), pp. 17–31.

Bower, R. S., and J. M. Jenks. "Divisional Screening Rates," *Financial Management* (Autumn 1975), pp. 42–49.

Gordon, M. J. *The Investment Financing and Valuation of the Corporation.* Homewood, Ill.: Richard D. Irwin, Inc., 1962.

Hamada, R. S. "Portfolio Analysis, Market Equilibrium, and Corporation Finance," *Journal of Finance* (March 1969), pp. 13–31.

Henderson, G. V., Jr. "In Defense of the Weighted Average Cost of Capital," *Financial Management* (Autumn 1979), pp. 57–61.

————. "Shareholder Taxes and the Required Rate of Return on Internally Generated Funds," *Financial Management* (Summer 1976), pp. 25–31.

Lewellen, W. G. *The Cost of Capital.* Belmont, Calif.: Wadsworth Publishing Co., Inc., 1969.

Lintner, J. "The Valuation of Risk Assets and the Selection of Risky Investments in Stock Portfolios and Capital Budgets," *Review of Economics and Statistics* (February 1965), pp. 13–37.

McConnell, J. J., and C. M. Sandberg. "The Weighted Average Cost of Capital: Some Questions on Its Definition, Interpretation, and Use: Comment," *Journal of Finance* (June 1975), pp. 883–86.

Markowitz, H. M. "The Optimization of a Quadratic Function Subject to Linear Constraints," *Naval Research Logistics Quarterly* (March and June 1956), pp. 111–33.

————. "Portfolio Selection," *Journal of Finance* (March 1952), pp. 77–91.

Mossin, J. "Equilibrium in a Capital Asset Market," *Econometrica* (October 1966), pp. 768–83.

Nantell, T. J., and C. R. Carlson. "The Cost of Capital as a Weighted Average," *Journal of Finance* (December 1975), pp. 1343–55.

Rubinstein, M. E. "A Mean-Variance Synthesis of Corporate Financial Theory," *Journal of Finance* (March 1973), pp. 167–81.

Sharpe, W. F. "A Simplified Model for Portfolio Analysis," *Management Science* (January 1963), pp. 277–93.

————. "Capital Asset Prices: A Theory of Market Equilibrium under Conditions of Risk," *Journal of Finance* (September 1964), pp. 425–42.

Solomon, E. *The Theory of Financial Management.* New York: Columbia University Press, 1963.

Weston, J. F. "Investment Decisions Using the Capital Asset Pricing Model," *Financial Management* (Spring 1973), pp. 25–33.

APPENDIX 4A

THE CAPITAL ASSET PRICING MODEL
AND THE COST OF CAPITAL

Over the last 20 years, work has proceeded on an important theory that promises to add new precision to the concept of cost of capital. The **capital asset pricing model (CAPM)** is a rigorously developed, comprehensive statement of the relationship between security risk and the level of return that investors should receive. You have learned that the value of any economic asset is the present worth of its expected cash flows; the CAPM defines the *discount rates* and, therefore, the appropriate prices for such securities, or capital assets.

In the sections that follow, we will review the development of the CAPM and show how it became part of cost of capital theory. We will then describe and illustrate how CAPM-based measures can be used to define a cost of capital.

With careful study of this material you should know

1. What the CAPM is and how it is relevant to the theory of financial management.
2. What beta is and how it is calculated.
3. The manner in which *cost of capital* is derived using the CAPM.
4. The way to calculate a CAPM-based cost of capital.
5. How the calculated cost of capital is interpreted—that is, what it means.

HISTORY OF THE CAPM

The origins of the CAPM are in the investments literature. In 1952, Professor Harry Markowitz changed portfolio management theory by suggesting that traditional statistical measures could be used to define concepts that had previously been discussed only in generalities. It has long been suggested that investments be evaluated with regard to their risk and return. Markowitz pointed out that return was simply "expected value," the mean of a probability distribution of anticipated returns. Risk could be thought of as the variance (or standard deviation) of this same distribution.

Although Markowitz was not the first to suggest using statistical measures for risk and return, he was able to formulate a model for calculating expected values and variances for combinations of securities—in other words, for portfolios. This was the birth of what has since been called *modern portfolio theory, (MPT)*.

Markowitz noted that since the returns on individual securities did not move exactly in unison, investors could reduce the riskiness of their portfolios by diversifying. Further, through mathematical examination of how portfolio returns and risks behave, Markowitz provided a conceptual description of the choices open to security investors, illustrated in Fig. 4A.1 as the "feasible set." Investors could choose any combination of risk and return within the shaded area. The risk and return of any particular portfolio would depend upon the securities it contained. The expected return would be simply a weighted average of the returns of the individual stocks:

$$R_p = \sum_{i=1}^{n} X_i R_i , \qquad (4A.1)$$

where

R_p = the return of the portfolio,

X_i = the proportion of the portfolio invested in stock i (e.g., if 10% of the portfolio is in stock 1 then $X_1 = .10$),

R_i = the return on stock i.

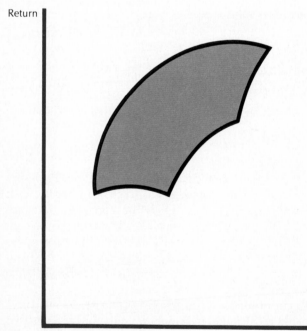

Figure 4A.1 The feasible set.

Calculation of portfolio variances is more difficult. If many securities are involved, normally a computer is used to perform the actual calculations. The equation for portfolio variance is

$$\sigma_p^2 = \sum_{i=1}^{n} \sum_{j=1}^{n} X_i X_j \rho_{ij} \sigma_i \sigma_j \tag{4A.2}$$

where

σ_p^2 = the portfolio variance,
X_i = the proportion invested in security i,
X_j = the proportion invested in security j,
ρ_{ij} = the correlation between the returns of securities i and j (correlation is a statistical measure of association that tells the degree to which two random variables move together),
σ_i = the standard deviation of security i returns,
σ_j = the standard deviation of security j returns.

Markowitz supplied these equations for calculating portfolio returns and risk (variance). However, investors need not look at all possible portfolios. Only those on the upper left edge of the feasible set are worthwhile; they offer the highest return for a given risk or, alternatively, the lowest risk for a given return. Markowitz called this surface the **efficient frontier** (**EF**) and supplied a mathematical technique for finding all portfolios on it.

The technique, called constrained quadratic programming, essentially involved finding a tangent to the curve for each possible portfolio on the frontier. In going from one tangency point to the next, the computer had to examine different portfolios (which could differ from the previous tangency point by only one security). For each new tangency point, numerous expected values and variances had to be calculated. By the time all possible efficient portfolios were found, a great deal of computer time (and money) could be spent.

A way of doing the job more quickly was needed. Calculating expected values was not the problem; they were a simple weighted average. It was calculation of variances that used computer time. The statistical requirements were enormous. To do the calculations, one had to know the correlation between the returns on every security and *every other security*.

Professor William Sharpe (acting upon a suggestion from Markowitz) found a way to avoid both difficulties. If it is assumed that every security is associated with every other security *only* to the extent that these securities are related to the general market (as might be measured by an index), the whole procedure is simplified.

Define a measure, **beta**, as the sensitivity of an individual security to changes in the market. If a stock has a beta of 1.0, its return goes up 1% when the market return goes up 1%; if the market goes down 1%, so does the security. If a security's beta is 2.0, it goes up 2% when the market goes up 1%, and vice versa. A stock with a beta of .5 would be only half as volatile as the market; if the market returns are up 1%, the security returns go up .5%; likewise, returns would go down by only half as much when the market dropped.

Beta measures only the market-related component of a security's returns. Each security will have a market-related component and a random component—an element in its return that is not related to the market. However, recall that, by assumption, individual securities are interrelated only through their relation to the market. The random components are not interrelated and, in a portfolio, they would tend to cancel each other out. As a result the variance, or standard deviation (which is easier to work with), becomes much easier to calculate. The risk of a well-diversified portfolio can now be calculated as

$$\sigma_p = \sigma_m \cdot \sum_{i=1}^{n} X_i \beta_i , \qquad (4A.3)$$

where

σ_p = the standard deviation of the portfolio,
σ_m = the standard deviation of market returns (as measured by an index),
X_i = the proportion of the portfolio invested in security i, and
β_i = the beta of security i, a measure of the security's sensitivity, or covariation, with the market.

Sharpe's shortcut accomplishes two things. First, it saves a lot of computer time by simplifying the calculation of portfolio risk; the portfolio's beta is simply a weighted average of the betas of the individual securities. This weighted average multiplied by the standard deviation of the return on the market gives the standard deviation of the portfolio *assuming that sufficient stocks are in the portfolio to eliminate the random (nonmarket-related) components.* Second, it reduces the data requirements. It is no longer necessary to know the correlation between the returns of each and every security. All that is needed is the measure of market sensitivity, beta, and a measure of the volatility of the market, σ_m.

Even though the use of betas drastically reduced the computations, Sharpe used another device to eliminate consideration of some portfolios; he limited the EF. Sharpe showed that if investors can borrow at rate R_B, any portfolio past B is not worth considering (see Fig. 4A.2). Combining portfolio B with borrowing produces returns superior to those that would be achieved by "following the EF around." If investors want to follow a high-risk strategy, their returns are greater if they use a combination of borrowing and portfolio B than they are picking the higher-risk portfolios.

The less adventurous investors are in a similar situation. If they can lend at (or buy debt securities that yield) rate R_L, then no portfolio below L is

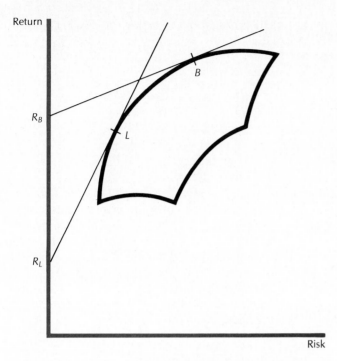

Figure 4A.2 Reducing the efficient frontier.

worth considering. Combining L with lending produces lower risks for any level of return below that of portfolio L.

By delimiting the EF in this way, Sharpe produced an even more efficient computer algorithm. These savings, combined with those of using beta, greatly aided the application and adoption of MPT.

Soon after publication of Sharpe's article on the shortcut to the application of MPT, another implication of Markowitz's theory was recognized. Implicit in his prescriptive model was a descriptive model of market equilibrium. Developing the model required explicit detailing of the assumptions:

1. All investors are rational Markowitz-type investors; they like return and avoid risk.

2. Further, if any agreement is to be reached, all investors must hold the same beliefs about the future prospects for every stock. Called *homogeneous expectations*, this condition implicitly requires that all investors have free and equal access to all available information.

3. Markets are perfectly competitive; there are no transaction costs (e.g., brokerage fees, taxes), total available assets are given and perfectly divisible, and no one buyer or seller alone is large enough to affect the overall equilibrium.

4. *There is one borrowing and lending rate that applies to all market participants;* all such borrowing is, by assumption, riskless and takes place at the risk-free rate, R_F.

The last element is the one that creates the pricing model. If everyone borrows at the same risk-free rate, then Sharpe's borrowing and lending rates (Fig. 4A.2) are equal, $R_B = R_L = R_F$, and there is only one tangent portfolio, M (see Fig. 4A.3). This portfolio is denoted M because it must be the market portfolio. Any security that is not in M is mispriced; if its price is too high it will drop, and if it is too low it would be bid up. In equilibrium, the price of every security must be such that supply and demand are equal.

Figure 4A.3 describes an explicit pricing equation for the market portfolio (and all other portfolios). At point M the coordinates are known. The return of the market portfolio must, by definition, be the expected return on the market, R_M. The riskiness of the portfolio is σ_M, the standard deviation of market returns. This line, called the **capital market line (CML)**, is a pricing equation for all efficiently diversified portfolios. We can derive the equation for the line by inspection. The intercept is the risk-free rate, R_F. The slope, with respect to risk, portfolio standard deviation (σ_p), can be calculated by using the familiar rise-over-the-run formula. Consider point M, the market

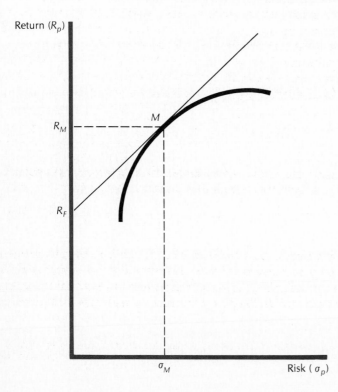

Figure 4A.3 The capital market line.

portfolio; its coordinates are R_M, σ_M. The market portfolio, by definition, yields the market return, R_M, and has the market level of risk, σ_M. To that point, the rise is $R_M - R_F$. The run is σ_p. The slope of the CML is

$$\frac{R_M - R_F}{\sigma_p}. \tag{4A.4}$$

Given the intercept and the slope, we can algebraically specify the capital market line. It is

$$R_p = R_F + \left(\frac{R_M - R_F}{\sigma_M}\right)\sigma_p. \tag{4A.5}$$

This is a rigorously developed, internally consistent pricing equation for efficiently diversified portfolios. As a start, a portfolio must generate a return equal to the risk-free rate: Every investment should earn interest. As the risk of a portfolio (σ_p) increases, investors should receive additional compensation proportionate to the riskiness. The reward for risk bearing should be the same as that received in the market generally. All investors should get the same incremental return for assuming risk; this reward is the same as that in the market portfolio $(R_M - R_F)/\sigma_M$. The slope of the CML is called the *market price of risk* and is sometimes denoted λ:

$$\lambda = \frac{R_M - R_F}{\sigma_M}. \tag{4A.6}$$

The CML is a pricing model for well-diversified portfolios. We also need a pricing model for inefficient capital assets, that is, individual securities. For portfolios, risk can be measured by the standard deviation of returns. For individual securities, this is not appropriate. Recall from the earlier discussion that the risk of a single security has two components, market-related riskiness and a random component. These two components are referred to as the **systematic** and **nonsystematic risk** of a security. The total risk of a security equals the sum of these components:

Total risk = systematic risk + nonsystematic risk.

The same relationship can be expressed algebraically as follows:

$$\sigma_i^2 = \beta_i^2 \sigma_M^2 + \sigma_{\epsilon i}^2, \tag{4A.7}$$

where

σ_i^2 = the standard deviation of the ith security's returns,

β_i = the beta of security i,

σ_M = the standard deviation of market returns, and

$\sigma_{\epsilon i}^2$ = the random component of security i returns, or the part of the security's returns that does not follow the market.

Although investing in a *single* security subjects the buyer to risk equal to σ_i^2, the buyer will not be compensated for that level of risk. Part of the risk is avoidable; the random component $(\sigma_{\epsilon i}^2)$ can be avoided by diversification. There will be no compensation for bearing the risk $\sigma_{\epsilon i}^2$. A rational market will not reward foolishness.

We now have all the necessary components for building a pricing model for single securities. The relevant risk for a single security is the nondiversifiable component $\beta_i^2 \sigma_M$ or $\beta_i \sigma_M$ if we use standard deviations as before. The reward for risk bearing in a single security would be the difference between that security's return R_i, and the risk-free rate, R_F. The reward for risk taking in a single security would be the ratio of these two:

$$\text{Reward for risk taking} = \frac{R_i - R_F}{\beta_i \sigma_M}.$$

For the market to be in equilibrium, every security must offer the same reward for risk taking. Fortunately, we already know what that reward must be; every security must reward risk taking at the market price of risk, λ. Using the definition of λ, we can find the pricing model as follows:

$$\frac{R_i - R_F}{\beta_i \sigma_M} = \frac{R_M - R_F}{\sigma_M} = \lambda$$

$$R_i - R_F = \left(\frac{R_M - R_F}{\sigma_M} \right) \beta_i \sigma_M \qquad (4A.8)$$

$$R_i = R_F + \beta_i (R_M - R_F).$$

Equation (4A.8) is the pricing equation for all securities or combinations of securities. Called the **security market line (SML)**, it shows that every security should earn an expected return equal to the risk-free rate plus (or minus) a risk premium proportionate to its beta. The relationship can be depicted graphically, as in Fig. 4A.4, which looks much like the CML in Fig. 4A.3. There are, however, important differences. The SML applies to individual securities (as well as to portfolios), and the measure of risk has changed. Risk is now defined as beta—market sensitivity. The relevant risk for an individual investment is its contribution to a well-diversified portfolio—its beta.

Beta was a revolutionary concept. It virtually changed the definition of risk. It was not long before it was recognized as relevant to the theory of financial management, and many scholars have contributed to its refinement. Professor Robert Hamada added precision to a number of financial management theories through use of CAPM concepts and derived a capital budgeting criterion based on the SML. Hamada's model was not exactly a cost of capital model, but it was conceptually similar. Professor Mark Rubinstein provided an overall synthesis of finance theory based on the CAPM and showed how

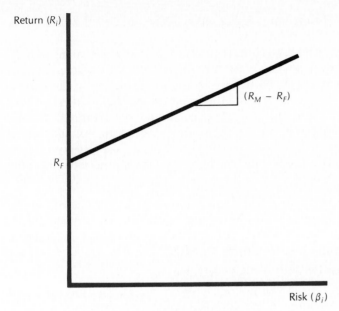

Figure 4A.4 The security market line.

the SML might be used to define a cost of capital. Professor Fred Weston went even further, suggesting such an application. Beta has become part of cost of capital theory.

BETA
Definition

Beta is a measure of the sensitivity of an individual security to changes in the market; it is an elasticity coefficient. *Beta is the percentage change in an individual security's return for a 1% change in the return of the market.*

Measurement

There are several ways to find betas. For large companies, they can be looked up. Investment services such as *Value Line Investment Surveys* publish betas for the stocks of companies traded on the national exchanges and for the more active over-the-counter stocks. Stockbrokerage houses such as Merrill Lynch also calculate betas for securities.

Knowing that betas are published still does not explain how *Value Line* and Merrill Lynch derive them. Although judgment is involved in the application of the technique, betas are simply regression coefficients. Plot the returns of the security against the returns of the market, and estimate a line of best fit to the scatter diagram (see Fig. 4A.5). The slope of the line is the beta.

Generally, the regression equation is fitted mathematically using a computer program. The most frequently used method is the ordinary-least-squares technique. Although the mathematics of the technique can be intimidating, the concept is simple. The computer fits the line through the points such that the sum of the squared errors (the differences between each point and the line squared) is as small as possible. This line minimizes the errors of estimation (squared).

Betas can also be calculated by hand. The procedure is illustrated in Table 4A.1. The steps are as follows:

1. Record the returns on the security and the market for a certain number of periods. (The example uses six hypothetical quarters; this is too few to produce meaningful results, but the reduced number of observations simplifies the example.) See columns 1 and 2.

2. Calculate the mean for each of these returns.

3. Calculate and record the deviations (each observation minus its respective mean) for each observation. See columns 3 and 4.

4. Calculate a variance for the market (σ_M^2). This is the average squared deviation of the market returns. See column 5.

5. Calculate the *covariance* (σ_{iM}) of the security's returns with the market. Covariance is a statistical measure of association that indicates the degree to which two variables covary (move together). It is calculated as the

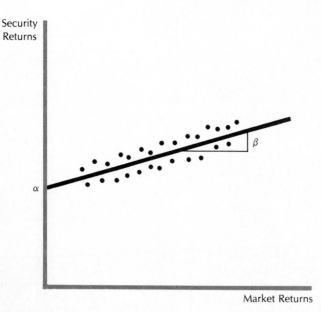

Figure 4A.5 Deriving beta.

TABLE 4A.1
Calculating a Beta.

(1) Security Return (%)	(2) Market Return (%)	(3) Security Deviation (1) − Mean	(4) Market Deviation (2) − Mean	(5) (4)^2	(6) (3) × (4)
3	2	.5	.5	.25	.25
2	1	− .5	− .5	.25	.25
0	− 1	− 2.5	− 2.5	6.25	6.25
6	4	3.5	2.5	6.25	8.75
1	2	− 1.5	.5	.25	− .75
3	1	.5	− .5	.25	− .25
15	9			13.50	14.50
2.5	1.5	Mean		$\sigma_M^2 = 2.25$	$\sigma_{iM} = 2.42$

$$\beta \equiv \frac{\sigma_{iM}}{\sigma_M^2} = \frac{2.42}{2.25} = 1.07$$

average cross product of the deviations. Multiply each deviation in column 3 by each deviation in column 4 (this is, the figure in column 6). Add them and divide by the number of observations (six in this case).

6. Calculate the beta; it can be calculated as the ratio of the covariance to the variance of the market:

$$\beta_i \equiv \frac{\sigma_{iM}}{\sigma_M^2}.$$

Obviously, calculating betas by hand is tedious, especially if you have a realistic number of data points and numerous securities. Fortunately, modern computers can handle the problem quickly. The availability of published betas on most companies eliminates even the need to do that.

VALUATION AND THE COST OF CAPITAL

As demonstrated in this chapter, the cost of capital is derived from a valuation model for the firm. The CAPM provides a specific pricing model (the SML) that can be used to define discount rates for the securities' cash flows and, consequently, their values.

Valuation

A valuation model for the firm, similar to Eq. (4.12), is

$$V = \frac{(X - K_d B)(1 - t)}{R_F + \beta_s (R_M - R_F)} + \frac{K_d B}{K_d}, \tag{4A.9}$$

where all the terms are defined exactly as they were in the chapter, except that the cost of equity is determined by plugging the beta of the stock, β_s, into the SML:

$$K_e = R_F + \beta_s(R_M - R_F). \tag{4A.10}$$

With the CAPM, each cash flow can be valued on the basis of its own riskiness. This allows Eq. (4A.9) to be rewritten as

$$V = \frac{X(1 - t)}{R_F + \beta_x(R_M - R_F)} + \frac{K_dB(1 - t)}{R_F + \beta_{K_d}(R_M - R_F)} + \frac{K_dB}{K_d}. \tag{4A.11}$$

In this valuation model, the discount rate for operating earnings, $X(1 - t)$, would be determined by the riskiness of those earnings as measured by their beta, β.

The discount rate for the interest flows, K_d, is determined similarly. That is, K_d is determined by the SML and the beta of the interest rate, β_{K_d}:

$$K_d = R_F + \beta_{K_d}(R_M - R_F). \tag{4A.12}$$

Recall assumption 4 of the CAPM. Everyone borrows at the same interest rate; all debt flows are riskless—that is $\beta_{K_d} = 0$. Therefore

$$K_d = R_F. \tag{4A.13}$$

Substituting this into Eq. (4A.11) simplifies the valuation model considerably:

$$V = \frac{X(1 - t)}{R_F + \beta_x(R_M - R_F)} - \frac{R_FB(1 - t) + R_FB}{R_F}$$

$$= \frac{X(1 - t)}{R_F + \beta_x(R_M - R_F)} + tB. \tag{4A.14}$$

COST OF CAPITAL

Derivation

Now that we have a CAPM-based valuation model, deriving the cost of capital is just a matter of following the given steps: Differentiate with respect to investment (I), set $\partial V/\partial I$ equal to 1, and solve for $\partial X(1 - t)/\partial I$. Assume, as was done before, that new investments are of average riskiness; therefore $\partial \beta_x/\partial I = 0$. Further, the effect of one firm's investments has a negligible impact on market equilibrium $(\partial R_M/\partial I = 0$ and $\partial R_F/\partial I = 0)$.

These conditions simplify the cost of capital derivation to the following:

$$V = \frac{X(1-t)}{R_F + \beta_x(R_M - R_F)} + tB$$

$$\frac{\partial V}{\partial I} = 1 = \frac{\partial X(1-t)}{\partial I}\left[\frac{1}{R_F + \beta_x(R_M - R_F)}\right] + \frac{t\partial B}{\partial I}$$

$$\frac{\partial X(1-t)}{\partial I} = \left[R_F + \beta_x(R_M - R_F)\right]\left(1 - \frac{t\partial B}{\partial I}\right). \qquad (4A.15)$$

The minimum rate of return that the firm can accept is specified by the right-hand side of Eq. (4A.15). To use this equation, you must know (or estimate) the market return values (R_F, R_M), the beta of the firm's operating earnings (β_x), its tax rate (t), and the proportion of debt employed in financing new investments $(\partial B/\partial I)$.

Application

The easiest way to show how this cost of capital calculation works is to use a numerical example. Assumed values for the necessary components are provided in Table 4A.2.

The expected return on the market is 13% and the interest (risk-free) rate is 8%. The firm is in the 40% tax bracket and finances with equal amounts of debt and equity, that is, it uses 50% debt financing $(\partial B/\partial I = .5)$. The beta of the firm's operating earnings is 1.4. Plugging these figures into the CAPM cost of capital model yields a figure of 12%. Undertaking any investment with a return of less than 12% would lower the value of the firm.

CAPM AND THE WACC

Equation (4A.15) looks different from the cost of capital calculation derived and illustrated in this chapter. It is not. The weighted average cost of capital

---

TABLE 4A.2
CAPM Cost of Capital: Illustration.

$$R_M = .13 \qquad t = .4$$
$$R_F = .08 \qquad \partial B/\partial I = .5$$
$$\beta_x = 1.4$$

$$\text{Cost of capital} = [R_F + \beta_x(R_M - R_F)]\left(1 - t\frac{\partial B}{\partial I}\right)$$
$$= [.08 + 1.4\,(.13 - .08)][1 - .4(.5)]$$
$$= (.08 + .07)\,(.8)$$
$$= (.15)(.8) = .12$$

still works. The beta in Eq. (4A.15) is not the beta of the firm's stock (β_s). The beta in Eq. (4A.15), β_x, is the beta of the firm's operating earnings. These two betas are related as follows:

$$\beta_s = \beta_x \left[1 + (1 - t)\frac{B}{S} \right] \qquad (4A.16)$$

The beta of the firm's stock (β_s) is larger than the beta of the operating earnings (β_x). The stock beta is magnified by the use of debt, as shown by the bond value (B) to stock value (S) ratio. This magnification is mitigated somewhat by the effects of taxation where t is the company's tax rate.

Recall that in our example company 50% debt financing was assumed; therefore $B = S$ and $B/S = 1$. For the company examined in Table 4A.2 the stock beta would be

$$\beta_s = \beta_x \left[1 + (1 - t)\frac{B}{S} \right]$$

$$= 1.4 \left[1 + (1 - .4)\frac{50\%}{50\%} \right]$$

$$= (1.4)(1.6) = 2.24.$$

If we plug this result into the SML, we get a cost of equity (see Eq. 4A.10) of 19.2%, as shown in Table 4A.3. As that table also shows, the weighted average cost of capital calculation will yield the same result as that of Table 4A.2. Either way, we find that the firm must earn a 12% rate of return to satisfy its investors. The chapter illustration (Table 4.1) for the traditional calculation provides the numerical proof.

TABLE 4A.3.
BETA-Based WACC Calculation.

$$K_e = R_F + \beta_s(R_M - R_F)$$
$$= .08 + 2.24(.13 - .08)$$
$$= .08 + .112$$
$$= .192 \quad \text{or} \quad 19.2\%$$
$$K_d = R_F = .08 \quad \text{or} \quad 8\%$$
$$\text{WACC} = K_e \frac{\partial S}{\partial I} + K_d(1 - t)\frac{\partial D}{\partial I}$$
$$= .192\,(.5) + .08\,(1 - .4)\,(.5)$$
$$= .192\,(.5) + .048\,(.5)$$
$$= .096 + .024 = .12$$

WARNINGS

The theoretical rigor of the CAPM is enticing. Everything seems to fit together so nicely. Investors like return and dislike risk. Some risk is avoidable, and beta measures that which is unavoidable. Therefore expected return should be a function of beta. This provides a theory for what investors' expectations of return, and therefore the cost of capital, should be.

But there are traps in this logic. CAPM is a theory of what investors should be looking for if their preferences can be measured with expected values and risk can be measured as variance (or standard deviation). If investors actually react differently, our cost of capital calculations are not adequate to measure these differences.

Even if the theory is entirely correct, there are problems. Betas must be estimated. Estimates will depend upon our measures of return (security and market), how frequently we take the observations, over how long a period, and a host of other considerations (some of which we probably do not yet recognize). Further, many betas are not stable over time.

These warnings are not given to denigrate the CAPM, which represents a major step forward in finance theory. However, you should be aware that all the problems have not yet been worked out.

SUMMARY

The CAPM is a major new development in finance theory that started in investments but is now being integrated into financial management and, most notably, cost of capital theory. Using the CAPM, the cost of capital can be calculated in two ways. If you have the beta for operating earnings (β_x), you can use Eq. (4A.15). If you have the stock beta (β_s) you can use it to calculate the cost of equity (Eq. 4A.10) and calculate the firm's weighted average cost of capital, just as before. The results should be the same. If you are not given betas, you can calculate them as illustrated in Table 4A.1.

The CAPM cost of capital measures have the same purpose as those covered in the chapter: to define the minimum acceptable return on new investments. The additional element that the CAPM provides is an explicit definition of what constitutes risk, which helps us better to define the level of returns necessary to keep the firm's owners, the shareholders, happy. Our cost of capital measure gives the minimum return that the company must earn on its new investments so as to meet these shareholder expectations.

CAPITAL BUDGETING: CONCEPTS AND DEFINITIONS
TECHNIQUES OF ANALYSIS
SPECIAL PROBLEMS IN CAPITAL BUDGETING

5

CAPITAL BUDGETING

Capital budgeting is the analysis of proposed long-term (capital) investments; it is the decision-making process that determines the type of plant and equipment a firm will own, how much will be invested in such assets, and when the expenditures will be made. Capital investment decisions are among the most, if not the most, important decisions that financial managers must make.

The very nature of capital investments makes them important. Capital investments involve relatively large dollar amounts. They represent commitments that extend over long periods of times (sometimes as long as 50 years or more); and once a capital investment has been made, it is largely irreversible—or at least it is hard to undo without making a major sacrifice.

It does not take much research to see how capital investments affect a firm's success or failure. Braniff International airline, decided to undertake a major capital expansion shortly after deregulation of the airline industry. The timing of this capital investment (and its financing) resulted in the company's bankruptcy.

On the other hand, several recent fortunes have been amassed by pioneers in small computers and electronic games. The success of these originators has enticed others (large and small) to copy their decisions. Some of these investments will pay off handsomely; others will not.

Capital investment (or the lack of it) has profound effects on industry suppliers and on the economy in general. A sluggish economy, record high interest rates, and the effects of trucking deregulation and high fuel costs have severely reduced heavy truck sales; several manufacturers of such equipment have failed or have been acquired by competitors.

Similar factors have reduced the sales of construction and farm equipment. The combined reduction of capital spending in different sectors has crippled the industrial giant International Harvester Company. If International goes under, numerous small manufacturers selling primarily to the company will be hurt. Some of them will survive; several will not.

Many of the current problems of American automobile manufacturers are traceable to capital budgeting decisions made earlier. Delayed industry reaction to high fuel prices and to the resulting demand for a different type of automobile allowed foreign competitors to increase their market share. High interest rates then depressed sales of all new models. During the worst slump in recent history, unemployment in the automobile industry (and related suppliers) has been at record levels.

The point of this discussion is obvious. Good capital budgeting decisions are critical to the growth (or survival) of a business. Capital expenditures are the basis of our economic system. In our capitalist economy, it is imperative that firms make good capital budgeting decisions. Their success and the overall health of the economy depend upon it.

This chapter discusses what is involved in capital budgeting, beginning with a review of some definitions and central concepts. The techniques used in analyzing capital investments are then demonstrated. A subsequent section covers some special problems in capital budgeting, for example, how to rank competing projects, how to compare investments with different maturities, and how to handle the problem of *capital rationing* (limited capital investment funds).

After careful study of this chapter, you should:

1. Understand what capital budgeting is and, more specifically, how to use discounted cash flow analysis to analyze investment projects.
2. Know what payback, average rate of return, net present value, profitability index, and internal rate of return mean, and how these measures are used.
3. Be able to calculate and interpret the various capital budgeting measures.
4. Be able to handle some special problems that may be encountered in capital budgeting analysis.

CAPITAL BUDGETING: CONCEPTS AND DEFINITIONS

In capital budgeting you will encounter a number of terms that, at first, sound the same. Further, several concepts are referred to by multiple names. The purpose of this section is to clarify the use of these terms.

The Capital Budget

The **capital budget** is an internal corporate document that lists the accepted investment projects for a given fiscal period, for example, a year. The term *capital budget* is also used to refer to the total dollar amount of a firm's capital investments.

Firms sometimes use the term to define the total amount of *allowable* capital investments for a period. If a manager says that the capital budget is $3 million for 1984, he or she is indicating that this amount is available for capital investment in 1984. This use of the term is commonplace in government.

Capital Budgeting

Capital budgeting is the process of determining which capital investments will be undertaken. There are three stages of capital budgeting: proposal generation, analysis, and implementation. Of these the first is the most important, even though generally we do not spend much class time on it. The firms that come up with innovative, profitable new projects are the ones that make the front page of the *Wall Street Journal*. The reason we do not discuss proposal generation is that the process is essentially creative and is difficult, if not impossible, to approximate in a classroom. If we could teach you how to develop a successful new electronic calculator, microcomputer, electronic game, or patent medicine, it is unlikely that we would be in the classroom. This sort of creative talent results in new products and produces millionaires.

Implementation of capital investments is obviously important too. Good ideas and well-analyzed decisions are worthless if not put into practice. After all the forecasting, number crunching, soul searching, and analysis are done, someone must decide to commit funds to the accepted projects. After a decision is reached, management must act on it promptly.

Although these two stages of capital budgeting are (possibly more) important, our discussion will concentrate on analysis—because that is the job of financial managers. Capital budgeting analysis itself involves three steps: estimating the cost of the project, forecasting its benefits, and combining these two sets of estimates in a reasoned analysis. The different types of analysis are called *techniques*—payback, net present value, and so on. Each of these is discussed later in the chapter. For now, it is important that we understand what is meant by cost and benefits.

Cost

For purposes of analysis, the cost of a capital asset is the price that would be paid for the asset if it were bought for cash. This would be reduced (or, in some odd cases, increased) by trade-ins. Cost would also be adjusted for any tax consequences of the trade-in.

Although this definition of cost seems straightforward, it contains some subtle, and sometimes difficult, analytical assumptions. Regardless of *how* the asset in question is acquired, the analysis *assumes* that the firm would buy it outright. The purpose of the current analysis is to determine whether an asset should be acquired. If analysis shows that investment in the asset (or project) is justified, then the manager can address financing.

The assumption of cash purchase is more than an expedient; there is theoretical justification for it. As will be explained, benefit estimates are developed in a way that assumes that an asset is bought outright. There is another reason for excluding financing considerations. The previous chapter showed how to calculate the cost of capital based on the assumption of a particular financing mix. To include financing considerations again in analyzing costs or benefits would be double counting.

Trade-ins can cause problems that generally can be dealt with by remembering that equipment would be considered a trade-in only if it were released from service by the proposed acquisition. It is the logical relationship between acquisition and trade-in that counts, not the actual transaction. Consider the following example. A company is analyzing the installation of a new materials handling system. Six months later, after implementing the system, the firm could sell its current forklift trucks on the resale market. Although the seller of the new system is not taking the forklifts in trade, they constitute a logical trade-in and should be considered as such in the analysis.

The opposite situation can also be envisioned. A trucking company has 10 old trailers on the back lot. The trailers were not licensed this year because they are no longer compatible with the firm's other equipment. Their current market value is $800 each. The firm is considering acquiring some new tools. The tool manufacturer can use the trailers and agrees to allow an $8,000 trade-in for them.

Although the trailers actually would be traded in, they are not a logical trade-in because they are not being replaced by the new tools. Presumably, the trailers could be sold for $8,000 without acquisition of the tools. Analysis of the tool acquisition should not entail a lower cost because of a trade-in.

Trading-in or selling old equipment normally has tax consequences. The effect of any transaction on the current year's tax bill should be considered as part of the cost of investment.

To clarify the proposed definition of cost, again consider the example of the firm evaluating a new materials handling system. The system would cost $45,000 if purchased outright. The market value of the forklift trucks that would be released from service, and that could be sold, is estimated to be $10,000. This makes the net outlay, excluding immediate tax effects, $35,000.

To illustrate the tax calculations, assume that the book value of forklifts is $15,000. The tax loss on their sale would be $5,000 (market value of $15,000 minus book value of $10,000).† Writing off the loss this year would reduce the firm's taxable income and therefore its taxes. If the firm is in the 40% tax bracket (a rate that will be used throughout the chapter), the loss write-off will save the firm $2,000 in taxes this year (.40 tax rate × $5,000 tax loss = $2,000).

The new project is not saddled with the loss, which is referred to in accounting and finance as a *sunk cost*. This means that the cost has already occurred; it cannot be recaptured, so it should not affect future decisions. The only consideration is its tax effect, which is part of the new project analysis. For this project the cost would be $33,000, as shown:

Cash price	$ 45,000
Less: Trade-in	(10,000)
Less: Tax loss	(2,000)
Net cost	$ 33,000

Estimating Benefits

Generally, capital acquisitions are undertaken because they increase profits, either by increasing revenues or by decreasing expenses, or both. In analyzing

---

† An appendix on Federal Income Taxes is provided at the end of the textbook.

capital proposals, though, financial analysts speak in terms of cash flows—not profits.

The difference between the two is relatively simple. Cash flow includes profit on investments *and* return of capital. An example will help clarify the distinction. Assume party B (for banker) lends party C (for client) $1,000 for one year at 10% interest. At the end of the year, C repays $1,100. B's end-of-year profit is $100. B's end-of-year cash flow is $1,100, which represents profit ($100) plus the return of capital ($1,000). B's time-zero cash flow was a negative $1,000—the investment.

In banking, return of the original capital by the borrower is referred to as *repaying the principal*. The return of invested capital by a fixed capital investment is accounted for as depreciation. The previous example could have shown party B (a business executive) investing in project C (a capital acquisition, a machine). The machine costs $1,000, has only a one-year economic life, and is depreciated accordingly. During the year, B spends $400 on materials and $500 for labor, and produces and sells $2,000 worth of goods for cash. The profit, ignoring taxes, would be as follows:

Revenues		$2,000
Less:		
Direct labor	500	
Direct materials	400	
Depreciation	1,000	
Cost of goods sold		1,900
Net income		$ 100

At the end of the year, party B would have more than $100 in cash on hand. Recall that the machine was purchased outright. The depreciation expense would involve no cash outflow. The sale of the goods would bring in $2,000. Paying for materials and labor would require only $900, leaving $1,100, the cash flow. The cash flow is the profit of $100 plus the $1,000 return of capital, which is accounted for as depreciation.

This example illustrates the purpose of depreciation accounting. *Depreciation* is the systematic allocation of the cost of capital equipment to the revenues it helps to generate. More simply, *depreciation accounting* is the process of writing off the cost of the means of production. This keeps the company from confusing return of capital with income.

The distinction is important from a tax standpoint. Income is taxable. Return of capital is not; with the return of capital, the investors are simply getting their own money back. The fact that capital return is nontaxable (depreciation is deductible) preserves the definition of cash flow. With a 40% tax rate, party B's income would be

Revenues	$2,000
Less: Cost of goods sold	
(including $1,000 depreciation)	1,900
Earnings before taxes	100
Less: Taxes	40
Net income	$ 60

The end-of-year cash flow would be $1,060, net income plus depreciation.

In addition to net income and depreciation, there are off-income-statement cash flows. These are flows that involve the investment or the return of capital in ways other than through depreciation. The original investment usually involves a cash outflow. Two other cash flows are frequently encountered. Working capital investment and the salvage value of capital equipment do not affect income, but they are cash flows.

The investment cash flow is determined by the cost calculation. If a project requires added inventory or receivables, these costs should be considered part of the investment. If equipment has value at the end of the related project's life, the estimated proceeds from its sale should be considered an added benefit and figured into the analysis. This is also true of any residual values associated with working capital investment. These flows should be considered net of any related taxes.

To recapitulate, when speaking of the benefits from a capital investment, a financial analyst will normally refer to cash flows. This is the total flow generated by the acquisition—both parts, income and return of capital. Cash flow, net income plus depreciation, is the amount of cash the firm would have on hand if the asset were purchased for cash and no other accounts were changed, that is, if there were no changes in working capital and no changes in any other asset or liability accounts.

Stated in this way, the cash flow concept seems highly artificial, which it is. Cash flow is an analytical construct. Its purpose is to isolate the change due to one investment devoid of financing considerations. Financing determines the firm's cost of capital, which, in turn, determines which projects are acceptable.

The analyst is not naive enough to believe that this will be the actual cash flow. The problem at this point is to determine the benefits of the one project alone. The cash flow concept is very helpful in doing this. It allows the analyst to concentrate on only those changes that will affect revenues, expenses, or depreciation. If working capital flows or salvage are involved, they can be added separately.

To appreciate how project benefits might be quantified, recall the earlier example of materials handling equipment. The equipment would not affect sales revenue, but it is estimated to reduce physical handling costs by $14,000

TABLE 5.1
Illustrative Cash Flow Calculation.

Increase in revenues	$ 0
Decrease in expenses	14,000
Net contribution	14,000
Less: Increased depreciation	6,000
Change in income	8,000
Less: Taxes	3,200
Change in net income	4,800
Plus: Increased depreciation	6,000
Incremental cash flow	$10,800

a year. Assume that either the new system or the old forklifts could perform the task for five years, and that both would be depreciated over a five-year life, straight-line, to a zero salvage value. The new system would generate depreciation of $9,000 a year ($45,000 divided by a five-year life). The forklifts would have $3,000 a year in depreciation (their book value is $15,000 divided by five years). The change in depreciation would be $6,000 a year.

Changes in revenues, expenses, and depreciation, along with the firm's tax rate provide the basis for the calculation of the incremental *per-year* cash flow, as illustrated in Table 5.1.

Even with the cost and benefit estimates, the problem is not solved. The figures must be combined in some way to provide useful guidance for the decision.

Before we proceed to the methods of analysis, a warning is in order. An introductory text cannot simulate information-gathering and estimation processes. Some of these processes are highly sophisticated and relatively precise; others are almost entirely subjective. A revered tenet in all decision making is that analysis can be no better than the information that goes into it (GIGO—garbage in, garbage out). While we have only referred to the estimation process, remember that the quality of the analysis is no better than the quality of the estimates.

Discounting

Discounting in capital budgeting means finding the present value. To discount a cash flow, we multiply it by a **present value** factor to find its present worth. The present worth can then be compared to the cost, which is already expressed in current dollars, to see if an investment is worthwhile.

Required Rate of Return

In capital budgeting there is frequent reference to the **required rate of return** or the **discount rate.** These two terms are synonymous and interchangeable. Both mean the minimum acceptable return on a new investment; as was shown in the prior chapter, this is the **cost of capital.** These three concepts are the same.

TECHNIQUES OF ANALYSIS

There are basically two types of capital budgeting techniques—discounted cash flow (DCF) methods and non-DCF methods. The DCF methods are theoretically superior: They include *net present value (NPV)*, *profitability index (PI)*, and *internal rate of return (IRR)*.

The non-DCF methods are *payback period* and *average rate of return (ARR)*. Although we would like to omit them, we cannot. Since they continue to be widely used by managers, we will discuss them first and demonstrate their weaknesses.

Payback Period

Payback remains a widely used method of analysis. The **payback period** is the estimated time it will take to recover invested capital. To determine payback, calculate a cumulative cash flow total. When the total reaches zero; that is, when the cost is recovered, payback is achieved. Table 5.2 illustrates the calculations for a hypothetical example. (Although it costs $33,000, this is not the materials handling project. The figures were made up merely to illustrate the calculation, but if you compare this example with the materials handling system, you will see one of payback's weaknesses.) This project achieves payback between the third and fourth years.

TABLE 5.2
Payback Calculation for a Project with a Net Cost of $33,000.

Year	Cash Flow	Cumulative
0	$(33,000)	$(33,000)
1	7,000	(26,000)
2	10,000	(16,000)
3	15,000	(1,000)
4	12,000	11,000

It is common practice to interpolate in order to give the appearance of greater precision. Given a cash flow of $12,000 in year four, the project would pay out $1/12$th of the way into the fourth year. Its payback period is 3.08 years.

If a project has the same cash inflow each year, the payback period can be calculated directly using the formula

$$\text{Payback period} = \frac{\text{net cost}}{\text{annual cash inflow}}.$$

In the case of the earlier materials handling example, this would be

$$\text{Payback period} = \frac{33,000}{10,800} = 3.06.$$

The obvious question is whether three years is an acceptable payback period. There is no standard of acceptance for the payback method; management must define arbitrarily what is acceptable.

This lack of a logical cutoff value is one of the weaknesses of the payback method. In addition, payback does not consider the timing of cash flows during the payback period, and it ignores cash flows after this period. The two examples so far discussed illustrate this weakness. The materials handling project had greater total cash flows and greater early cash flows, yet its payback period is approximately the same as that of the example investment used in Table 5.2. This point is dramatized in Table 5.3. These three projects all have a three-year payback.

Table 5.3 is enlightening. If management accepted all projects with a three-year payback (or less), Project A would be acceptable even though it merely returns invested capital. It looks so good, from a payback perspective, as Project B, which does more than return the capital and has better early cash flows.

Project C is an example of the type of investment that is most severely penalized by the payback method. Where a long period of product development is involved, and where early R & D costs are high, payback can be slow. Yet,

TABLE 5.3
Cash Flows for Three Projects, Each with a Net Cost of $6,000.

Year	Project A	Project B	Project C
1	$2,000	$3,000	$(4,000)
2	2,000	2,000	(5,000)
3	2,000	1,000	15,000
4	0	1,000	20,000
5–20	0	0	25,000

the long-run benefits of investment in such projects can be quite high (e.g., in synthetic fibers, ethical drugs, and electronics product development).

Payback survives because it is quick, easy to apply, and easy to understand, and because many businesses investments are of a nature that minimizes the problems of the technique. If the projects under analysis have relatively level cash flows and similar economic lives, rankings achieved by the payback method may be similar to those achieved by DCF methods. Results can be misleading, though, and therefore costly.

Average Rate of Return (ARR)

Logically this method is more defensible than payback in that it attempts to calculate a rate of return rather than determine the time necessary to recapture the original investment. It considers both the amount invested and the *profits* generated. **Average rate of return (ARR)** is defined as average annual net income after taxes divided by average investment. The technique utilizes income rather than cash flow in its evaluation of investment worthiness. For the materials handling project, the calculation would be

$$\frac{\text{Average annual net income}}{\text{Average investment}} = \text{ARR}$$

$$\frac{4,800}{(33,000/2)} = .291 \quad \text{or} \quad 29.1\%.$$

The denominator, the average investment, is derived by averaging the initial investment of $33,000 and the end-of-life value (zero). It is sometimes suggested that using average end-of-year book values is better. However, because of other problems with the technique, this is a waste of time.

The numerator is an average of the after-tax income figures for each year of the project's life. As with payback, the time value of money and the greater importance of early flows are ignored. For this reason, the ARR calculated by this method will generally mistate the true return on invested capital, the IRR.

In some cases, ARR may approximate the true rate. If a project is long lived (greater than twice the payback), if salvage values are negligible, and if annual income is fairly uniform, this technique occasionally may approximate the results from IRR analysis. Still, its usefulness is limited. ARR's importance is historical; it represents an early method of making decisions based on rate-of-return projections.

Long-lived, low-salvage investments may be correctly ranked by ARR. Many business investments have had these attributes, so use of the technique persists. However, an analyst cannot count on ARR. Few projects have truly uniform inflows or insignificant salvage values. Accelerated depreciation and shortened product lives make the need to deal accurately with the time value of money all the more important. Averages are insufficient; DCF techniques are far superior.

Net Present Value (NPV)

The **net present value (NPV)** of a project is the present value of the future benefits minus the cost. It is the difference between what is to be received, in current worth, and what will be paid for it. NPV quantifies the benefit from a particular investment by comparing the current dollar value of the future benefits with the cost. To make the comparison, the firm must specify what rate of return it wants on its money—that is, what discount rate to use in translating future benefits into current dollar equivalents. The correct rate for average-risk investments is the cost of capital.

The materials handling project can again be used as an illustration. Assume that the company has a 15% cost of capital; use a 15% discount rate.

Recall that the project generates cash flows of $10,800 a year for five years. The present value of the benefits can be calculated as the present value of an annuity of $10,800 per year discounted at 15%. Using the calculation from Chapter 3, we find that:

$$PV_A = 10,800 \times PVIFA_{15\%,5}$$
$$= 10,800 \times 3.352$$
$$= 36,202.$$

If the company spends $33,000 to receive benefits with a current worth of $36,202, it has a good deal. NPV simply quantifies how much of a bargain the firm is getting for its money.

$$NPV = \text{present value of benefits} - \text{cost}$$
$$= 36,202 - 33,000 = 3,202.$$

As the example illustrates, the actual calculation of NPV is easy once the cost and benefits have been specified. Problems arise in making certain to count everything once and count nothing twice. A worksheet can serve as a checklist of the potential costs and benefits.

The cost section of the worksheet is identical to the earlier calculation. The benefits section derives the cash flows slightly differently; the reasons for this will be explained. The bottom-line result is the same, but the derivation differs. The easiest way to explain the calculations is to use the materials handling data. The two approaches are illustrated in Table 5.4.

Both approaches arrive at the same bottom-line figure, $10,800. With the tax-shield method, the after-tax value of the contribution and the depreciation are each calculated separately. If the firm saved $14,000 in expenses *and there*

TABLE 5.4
Quantifying Benefits—Two Alternatives.

Cash Flow		Tax Shield	
Net contribution	$14,000	Net contribution	$14,000
Less: Depreciation	6,000	Less: Taxes	5,600
Change in income	8,000	After-tax contribution	8,400
Less: Taxes	3,200	Depreciation	6,000
Change in net income	4,800	Times: Tax rate	.40
Plus: Depreciation	6,000	Tax shield	2,400
			8,400
			2,400
Total benefit	$10,800	Total benefit	$10,800

were no changes in depreciation, the entire amount would be taxed, resulting in an after-tax benefit of $8,400 per year. However, additional depreciation of $6,000 reduces the taxes from $5,600 (which would have been paid on $14,000) to $3,200, under "Cash Flow." Having a $6,000 depreciation deduction reduces taxable income by that same amount, $6,000. The taxes on $6,000 in income at a 40% rate would be $2,400, so having an added $6,000 in deductible depreciation will save the firm $2,400 in taxes per year. This amount can be calculated directly as the added depreciation times the tax rate.

The main benefit of the tax shield method is its convenience. The approach allows the effect of each change in revenues, expenses, and depreciation to be handled separately, eliminating the need for setting up a *pro forma* statement for each year of the project's life, as in Table 5.1. The tax shield method is especially helpful if projects are long lived, if accelerated depreciation is used, if maintenance and rehabilitation costs vary over the life of the project, and if the analysis is replicated using various cost and benefit estimates. Such complications require an analytical format that is capable of expanding with the complexity of the analysis. Table 5.5 illustrates such a worksheet. This method of analyzing capital investment is very general. It is capable of handling a wide variety of problems. (It is used again in Chapters 11 and 12.)

The worksheet has two sections. In the first, the cost of the investment is defined; in the second, the expected benefits are detailed. Within each section the entries can vary. The materials handling project provides a fairly typical replacement problem. The price of the investment is, as explained before, the cash purchase price of the asset regardless of how it is actually financed. Price is the same before and after taxes. Capital acquisitions are not immediately deductible. They must be depreciated. The depreciation allowances are accounted for in the benefits section.

TABLE 5.5
Analysis of Materials Handling System Using the Tax Shield Worksheet.

	Before Tax	After Tax	Time	Discount Factor	Present Value
Cost					
Price	$ 45,000	$ 45,000	0	1	$ 45,000
Trade-in	(10,000)	(10,000)	0	1	(10,000)
Tax loss	(5,000)	(2,000)	0	1	(2,000)
					$ 33,000
Benefits					
Revenues	0	0	1–5	3.352	0
Expenses	$ 14,000	$ 8,400	1–5	3.352	$ 28,157
Depreciation	6,000	2,400	1–5	3.352	8,045
Salvage	0	0	5	.497	0
					$ 36,202

$$NPV = \text{present value of benefits} - \text{cost}$$
$$= \$36,202 - 33,000 = \$3,202.$$

The trade-ins are logical trade-ins, as we explained earlier. Trade-ins are also the same before and after taxes. The tax consequences of trade-ins are entered separately on the next line. Losses would arise when the market or trade-in value was lower than the book value. Gains would occur if the asset sold for more than book value. Unless otherwise specified, the firm's normal tax rate will be applied to such gains and losses. (Generally, gains would be depreciation recapture, and losses are Section 1231 losses that are deducted from ordinary income. See the Appendix, "Federal Income Taxes.")

Increases in revenues and reductions of expenses constitute net contributions to fixed expenses and profits and are fully taxable. For this reason, the after-tax value is derived by multiplying the before-tax amount by *one minus the applicable tax rate* $(1 - .4 = .6)$. Depreciation is beneficial because it reduces taxes. For depreciation, the after-tax value is the depreciation amount *times the tax rate.*

In every case, the time column indicates when the flow occurs. For convenience, it is assumed that all flows occur at year's end. The discount (present value) factor is determined by the time and the discount rate. If the flow is annual, the factor is an annuity factor. If the flow occurs only once, such as in the case of salvage, the factor would be the present value of a dollar. (Note that the entry for salvage is the *increase* in salvage between the acquisition and the trade-in equipment.) The present value amounts are the product of the discount factor and the after-tax amount.

To calculate the project's NPV, add up the benefits, determine the cost, and take the difference. If the NPV is positive, the project generates more than the required rate of return and should be undertaken.

Profitability Index (PI)

The **profitability index** (**PI**) is simply a different way of presenting the results of the same analysis. Every calculation *except the last one* is the same. In calculating NPV, the analyst must find the difference between the present value of the benefits and cost. When the PI is derived, the results are presented as a ratio of present value of benefits to cost. For the materials handling project the profitability index would be

$$\frac{\text{Present value of benefits}}{\text{Cost}} = \text{PI}$$

$$\frac{\$36,202}{\$33,000} = 1.10.$$

The purpose of the PI is to allow a different interpretation of the results. The NPV indicates that the expected benefits are worth more than the amount invested. The PI shows that for every dollar invested, the firm expects future benefits with a current worth of $1.10 if it discounts future returns at 15%.

Like NPV, the PI has a built-in acceptance value. If a project had a PI of 1.0, the firm would be getting exactly its required return on capital. If a project's PI is greater than 1.0, it is expected to return more than a dollar for each dollar invested, over and above the required rate of return—the cost of capital. For this reason, the firm should undertake all projects with PIs of 1.0 or greater.

Note that the PI calculated is valid only for the rate used in the discounting process. Thus, the discount rate should be specified when speaking of a project's PI. This will avoid confusing the PI with a project's rate of return. A PI of 1.10 is *not* a rate of return of 10%. The PI depends on the discount rate used, and a project's rate of return is independent of the assumption of an external rate. That is why it is referred to as an *internal* rate of return.

Internal Rate of Return (IRR)

Recall that the NPV indicates how much a project is expected to generate in present dollar terms *over and above* the required rate, the discount rate. Therefore, if a project has an NPV of zero, it will generate a return exactly equal to the discount rate. This provides both a definition of and a way to solve for the **internal rate of return** (**IRR**). The IRR of a project is that discount rate that makes the project's NPV zero.

Finding the IRR is, therefore, a trial-and-error process. Different discount rates must be tried until one gives an NPV of zero. Actually, the process can be somewhat more systematic. If the NPV for a given discount rate is positive, this indicates that the return is greater than the discount rate used and that a higher rate must be tried. The size of the NPV can indicate how much to increase the discount rate on the next trial.

TABLE 5.6
Analysis of Materials Handling System: Internal-Rate-of-Return Method.

	Before Tax	After Tax	Time	15% Discount Factor	15% Present Value	18% Discount Factor	18% Present Value	20% Discount Factor	20% Present Value
COST									
Price	$ 45,000	$ 45,000	0	1	$ 45,000	1	$ 45,000		
Trade-in	(10,000)	(10,000)	0	1	(10,000)	1	(10,000)		
Tax loss	(5,000)	(2,000)	0	1	(2,000)	1	(2,000)		
					$ 33,000		$ 33,000		$ 33,000
BENEFITS									
Revenues	14,000	0							
Expenses	6,000	8,400	1–5	3.352	28,157	3.127	26,267	2.991	25,124
Depreciation		2,400	1–5	3.352	8,045	3.127	7,505	2.991	7,178
		10,800							
Salvage	0								
NPV					$ 36,202		$ 33,772		$ 32,302
					$ 3,202		$ 772		$ (698)

The worksheet can also help to organize this analysis. Each trial can be calculated by simply repeating the last two columns, the discount factor and the present value. Using the materials handling project again, recall that the project had an NPV of $3,202 at a discount rate of 15%, which indicates that the project's rate of return *exceeds* 15%. Table 5.6 illustrates trial solutions increasing the discount rate to 18 and 20%.

The analysis indicates that the project's return is between 18% (a positive NPV) and 20% (a negative NPV). For greater accuracy, the exact rate can be approximated† through interpolation as follows:

Discount Rate	NPV	Difference
18%	$ 772	
20%	$(698)	
		$1,470

$$\frac{772}{1,470} \times 2\% = 1.05\% + 18.00\% = 19.05\%.$$

The logic of interpolation is sometimes easier to understand if it is presented in a diagram:

Difference		2%	
Discount rate	18%	X%?	20%
NPV	$772	$0	($698)
Difference		$1,470	

At some discount rate between 18 and 20%, this project will have a NPV of zero. Zero is 772/1,470s of the "distance" between the 18 and 20% discount rates. Multiplying 772/1,470 by 2% (the difference between 18 and 20%) indicates that the same proportion of the percentage distance is 1.05%. Adding that to the starting point, 18%, indicates that at a discount rate of approximately 19.05% this investment will have an NPV of zero.

The materials handling project will generate a return of 19.05% per year on invested capital *if all the estimates are correct*. Table 5.7 illustrates this return to help interpret the IRR measure.

In the beginning, $33,000 is invested in the project. A 19.03% return on $33,000 is $6,280;‡ the other $4,520 of the first-year cash flow of $10,800

---

† The interpolation is approximate because the present value of a dollar decreases at an increasing rate as the discount rate is increased. Thus, the discount factors are not linear between the 18 and 20% rates used. In this case the true rate is 19.03% instead of the interpolated value of 19.05%.

‡ The true rate is used to avoid rounding errors.

TABLE 5.7
IRR Illustration for the Materials Handling Project.

Year	Invested Capital	Return on Investment	Capital Return	Cash Flow
0	$33,000	—	—	$(33,000)
1	28,480	$6,280	$4,520	10,800
2	23,100	5,420	5,380	10,800
3	16,695	4,396	6,404	10,800
4	9,073	3,177	7,623	10,800
5		1,727	9,073	10,800

constitutes a repayment of invested capital. This reduces the invested capital to $28,480; a 19.03% return on this amount would be $5,420, so almost half of the second-year cash flow is capital recapture—reducing the investment to $23,100. This division of each year's cash flow can be continued for the life of the project. At the end of the project's life it will have generated each year a 19.03% return, and over the life of the project it will repay all the original invested capital.

As indicated, the IRR solution generally involves trial and error. However, when annual inflows are equal, the solution can be derived directly.† In this situation, you can utilize the determining interest rates calculation from Chapter 3.

If a project is expected to generate a level benefit stream, such as the $10,800 a year in our materials handling project, some present value of annuity factor exists that will make the present value of those benefits equal to the project's cost of $33,000. The factor can be found by substituting into the present value of an annuity equation.

$$PV_A = R \times PVIFA_{x\%,5}$$

$$\$33,000 = 10,800 \times PVIFA_{x\%,5}$$

$$\frac{\$33,000}{\$10,800} = PVIFA_{x\%,5} = 3.06.$$

The implied discount rate can be ascertained by looking up this factor in the present value of annuity table. Using the table, go across the five-year row until you find a factor of approximately 3.06. As it turns out, this is almost exactly halfway between the 18 and 20% factors (3.127 and 2.991), implying a 19% rate of return as found earlier. (Again, interpolation can be used for rates between those in the tables.)

---

† The IRR can also be solved directly when there is only one inflow by using an analogous solution utilizing the present-value-of-a-dollar table.

Although the technique is truly accurate only for level-flow projects, it can also provide a starting point for those with nonlevel flows. Consider a project with the following flows:

t_0	t_1	t_2	t_3
$(1,800)	$1,000	$800	$600

Recognizing that the flow averages $800 a year allows one to approximate the IRR by direct solution.

$$PV_A = R \times PVIFA_{x\%,3}$$

$$\$1,800 = \$800 \times PVIFA_{x\%,3}$$

$$\frac{\$1,800}{\$800} = PVIFA_{x\%,3} = 2.25.$$

The table shows that the project returns approximately 16%. Using the 16% factors demonstrates that the approximation identified a relatively efficient first-trial discount rate:

	t_0	t_1	t_2	t_3
	$(1,800)	$1,000	$800	$600
	862 ←	.862	.743	.641
	594 ←			
	385 ←			
NPV	$ 41			

One more iteration would provide the basis for the IRR interpolation. Many computer installations have, as part of their standard software, IRR programs eliminating the need for this time-saving approximation. However, when hand calculations are necessary for complex problems, such a technique can help reduce the drudgery.

As with the other discounted cash flow techniques, a logical acceptance rule for projects follows naturally from the analysis. If a project's IRR exceeds the company's cost of capital, it is acceptable and should be undertaken.

SPECIAL PROBLEMS IN CAPITAL BUDGETING

If capital investments were analyzed one at a time, we would not encounter special problems. All the DCF techniques (NPV, PI, and IRR) will give the same accept-reject decisions for investments considered one at a time; if an investment has a positive NPV, it will have a PI greater than 1.0 and an IRR greater than the cost of capital.

It is when we are forced to choose between investments that problems arise. Different techniques may *rank* investments differently. This is especially true when the investments have *different lives*, when one lasts longer than the other. The problem is accentuated in a *rationing* situation in which the firm is limited to some maximum dollar level of investment that might rule out otherwise worthwhile investments. Each of these problems is discussed separately in an attempt to provide some guidance on how to solve the problems.

Ranking

A ranking criterion is implied in each DCF technique. The higher the NPV, PI, or IRR, the better. Therefore if two or more projects are to be ranked, they can be placed in descending order by these measures. This ranking procedure would cause the firm to undertake the "best" projects first. Generally, the techniques produce the same rankings. However, because they have slightly different underlying assumptions, they can produce conflicting ranks. The techniques differ in their assumptions regarding (1) the assumed **reinvestment rate** for interim cash flows and (2) recognition of the existence of external constraints.

Cash flows are discounted in DCF analysis to recognize the earning power that one has foregone by not having the money now. If money did not have this earning power (if it could not be invested), there would be no need for discounting. Future dollars would be just as valuable as current dollars.

The DCF techniques make different assumptions on the rate of return that can be earned on the interim investments. To illustrate the difference, a simple numerical example is helpful. Assume that a firm that requires a 15% return is reviewing an investment with the following cash flows:

t_0	t_1	t_2	t_3
$(2,100)	$1,000	$1,000	$1,000

The NPV can be calculated quickly because of the level flow. The NPV is $183 because the present value of the inflows is $2,283, calculated as the present value of a $1,000, three-year annuity at 15%. But why is the present value of $1,000 a year for three years $2,283?

The answer is found in Table 5.8; if $2,283 were invested at 15% for three years, the balance, principal and interest at the end of three years, would be $3,473. If, on the other hand, the individual $1,000 flows are invested as they are received, the ending balance is the same. The amount $2,283 is called the *present value of the annuity* because it will generate the same terminal amount as the annuity if invested at 15%. NPV and its alter ego, PI, both

---

TABLE 5.8
Present and Compound Values of a Three-Year, $1,000 Annuity at 15%.

Year	Cash Flow	Present Value	Future Value
1	$1,000	$ 870	$1,323
2	1,000	756	1,150
3	1,000	658	1,000
		$2,284	$3,473

$$\$2,284 \times (1.15)^3 = \$3,473$$

---

implicitly assume that interim flows are reinvested at the discount rate, that is, the cost of capital.

Because of the way IRR is calculated, it uses a different discount rate and therefore assumes a different reinvestment rate. This example problem is capable of direct IRR solution:

$$PV_A = R \times PVIFA_{x\%,3}$$

$$\$2,100 = \$1,000 \times PVIFA_{x\%,3}$$

$$2.100 = PVIFA_{x\%,3}$$

$$X \simeq 20\% = IRR$$

The return on the project is approximately 20% (actually 20.2%) because $2,100 invested at 20% will generate the same terminal amount as the interim flows if they too are invested at 20% (see Table 5.9). The IRR method assumes that interim flows are reinvested at the IRR rate, not at the cost of capital.

NPV and PI also differ with regard to recognition of outside constraints. NPV, as it stands, ignores outside constraints, especially possible capital constraints; it implicitly suggests that all positive NPV projects be undertaken

---

TABLE 5.9
Present and Compound Values of a Three Year, $1,000 Annuity at 20%.

Year	Cash Flow	Present Value	Future Value
1	$1,000	$ 833	$1,440
2	$1,000	694	1,200
3	$1,000	579	1,000
		$2,106	$3,640

$$\$2,106 \times (1.20)^3 = \$3,640$$

TABLE 5.10
Comparison of Projects A, B, and C Using a Discount Rate of 15%.

Project A	t_0	t_1
	$ (1,000)	1,400
	1,218 ←	.870
NPV	$ 218	
IRR	40%	PI = 1.22

Project B	t_0	t_1
	$(100,000)	120,000
	104,400 ←	.870
NPV	$ 4,400	
IRR	20%	PI = 1.04

Project C	t_0	t_{10}
	$ (1,000)	6,192
	1,536 ←	.248
NPV	$ 536	
IRR	20%	PI = 1.54

assuming the money will be available at the cost of capital used in the discounting.

These differences create certain biases. NPV favors large projects. Table 5.10 provides an exaggerated illustration.

The NPV method shows that Project B is more attractive than Project A, even though it has a lower rate of return. For a firm with unlimited capital, this conclusion is defensible. With unlimited funds, a firm would be better off investing $100,000 at 20% than investing $1,000 at 40%. However, it is important to be aware of this bias in the NPV method. This is one of the main reasons PI was developed; it retains the NPV reinvestment rate assumption but at the same time takes account of the amount of money invested.

The reinvestment rate assumption creates another bias. Because the IRR on all acceptable projects (IRR greater than the required rate) would be higher than the reinvestment rate used in calculating the NPV (and PI), the IRR tends to favor projects with earlier returns. In Table 5.10, Projects A and C are of the same size, but they have a different time pattern of returns. Project A is expected to generate a 40% return at the end of the year. Project C does not generate any returns until the tenth year, but the cash flow in that year constitutes a 20% compound rate of return per year for the life of the project. This level of return makes Project C more attractive than Project A from both an NPV and a PI perspective. However, because the IRR method implicitly assumes that Project A's cash flow can be reinvested at a rate of 40%, it strongly favors Project A.

Generally, theorists suggest that NPV is superior to IRR and PI. *If the cost of capital has been correctly calculated*, the firm should invest *as much as possible* at beneficial rates of return. It should maximize NPV, which in turn maximizes the value of the firm.

However, NPV alone does not always supply the best answer with regard to the time bias. The IRR solution is sometimes correct, although for the wrong reasons. When two investments with unequal lives are to be compared, the appropriate analysis is a modified NPV analysis, which follows.

Unequal Lives

Although it is not at first apparent, the unequal lives problem is a variant of the size problem; a $10,000, 10-year investment is larger than a $10,000, 5-year investment. The longer investment has the same amount of money tied up for more years. The conflicting results of the techniques are predictable: NPV tends to favor longer (larger) investments. The reinvestment rate assumption of the IRR accentuates its bias in favor of shorter projects.

In discussing the ranking of investments, we suggested that theory favored NPV. In different-lived investment comparisons, NPV needs to be modified. Without this alteration, IRR is sometimes correct when NPV is wrong, as the following example illustrates.

Table 5.11 describes two $10,000 investments. Assume that the $10,000 could be spent to buy either of two machines that do exactly the same job. The short-lived (SL) machine lasts only 5 years but generates cash flows of $3,345 per year. The long-lived (LL) machine costs the same but will last 10 years, generating benefits of $2,225 per year.

TABLE 5.11
Comparison of 5-Year and 10-Year Investments Using a Discount Rate of 12%.

		t_0	$t = 1, 5$
Short-lived (SL)			
		$(10,000)	3,345
		12,059 ←	3.605
	NPV	$ 2,059	
	IRR	20%	
		t_0	$t = 1, 10$
Long-lived (LL)			
		$(10,000)	2,225
		12,571 ←	5.650
	NPV	$ 2,571	
	IRR	18%	

Which of the two investments is better? The results are contradictory but predictable. SL has the better IRR, but LL has the higher NPV.

At this point, it might be well to ask two fundamental questions:

1. Is it better to produce a net benefit (NPV) of $2,571 over 10 years or to make $2,059 over 5 years?
2. Is the additional profit (NPV) worth having the capital tied up 5 years longer?

One way of handling the problem is to recognize that the company could buy two short-lived machines, one now and another 5 years from now. The results would be as shown in Table 5.12. Using two 5-year machines produces a higher NPV than one 10-year machine.

This method of analysis is one approach to handling the unequal lives problem: Stretch the two alternatives out to the same number of years, and analyze them over the same time period. That was easy in this case because there was a convenient common multiple. Such is not always the case. If two machines have lives of 9 and 11 years, the lowest common multiple is 99 years.

What we need is a per-year NPV. In our example, the average NPV per year for the two machines was

$$SL = \frac{NPV}{5} = \frac{2,059}{5} = 412$$

$$LL = \frac{NPV}{10} = \frac{2,571}{10} = 257.$$

Now we see why SL is the better of the two investments; it produces more NPV per year. Regrettably, the calculation of the per-year NPV is not quite this easy. Simply dividing by the number of years of investment overlooks the time value of money. Net benefits in the tenth year are not as valuable as benefits in the first year. Rather than using the number of years as the divisor, we use the PVIFA for that number of years at the cost of capital.

TABLE 5.12
Analysis of Two 5-Year, Back-to-Back Investments Using a Discount Rate of 12%.

	t_0	$t = 1$–5	t_5	$t = 6, 10$
	$(10,000)	$3,345	$(10,000)	$3,345
	12,059 ←	3.605	↓	(5.650 − 3.605)
	(5,674) ←		.567	↓
	6,840 ←			2.045
NPV	$ 3,225			

TABLE 5.13
Calculation of Equivalent Annual Economic Profits.

Short Lived:
$$\frac{\text{NPV}}{\text{PVIFA}_{12\%,5}} = \frac{\$2,059}{3.605} = \$571$$

	1	2	3	4	5
	$571	$571	$571	$571	$571

$2,059 ← ———————————————— 3.605

Long Lived:
$$\frac{\text{NPV}}{\text{PVIFA}_{12\%,10}} = \frac{\$2,571}{5.650} = \$455$$

1	2	3	4	5	6	7	8	9	10
$455	$455	$455	$455	$455	$455	$455	$455	$455	$455

$2,571 ← ———————————————— 5.650

This calculation converts the NPV of a project into an **equivalent annual economic profit** (**EAEP**). Table 5.13 shows both the mechanics and the logic of the calculations. Making an NPV of $2,059 in 5 years is the equivalent of making a net economic profit of $571 a year for each of the 5 years. An NPV of $2,059 for 10 years is the equivalent of clearing $455 a year. Obviously, making $571 a year is better, and the short-lived machine is the better investment.

The mechanics of comparing unequal-lived investments can be summarized very briefly:

1. Calculate the NPV in the usual manner.
2. Divide each investment's NPV by the PVIFA for the number of years involved.
3. The result is a per-year NPV, referred to as the equivalent annual economic profit (EAEP). Select the alternative with the highest EAEP.

Capital Rationing

If a firm can raise sufficient capital, it should undertake all acceptable projects, that is, all projects where NPV $\geq$ 0, all those where PI $\geq$ 1.0, or all those whose IRR exceeds the cost of capital. Conflicting rankings of mutually exclusive investments (either-or investments in which acceptance of one means rejection of the other) normally should be based on NPV or on EAEP for unequal-lived alternatives.

If a firm cannot raise sufficient capital, the problem is different. A firm that is limited in its ability to finance new projects is operating under conditions of **capital rationing.** Under such circumstances, analysis must consider the capital constraint, or limit.

Capital rationing may be externally or internally imposed. If requirements are externally imposed, the size of the firm's capital budget is dictated by an outside authority or conditions. Examples include limited outside capital availability (because of economic conditions) or limitations written into previously negotiated contracts that are still in force.

In addition to operating under such outside constraints, firms may limit capital investment voluntarily. Such internally imposed rationing may be attributable to managers' or owners' fears of debt financing. Reluctance to incur excessive debt is observable today in a number of firms that survived the Depression. Reluctance to issue new equity can also constrain capital investment; this sometimes occurs when owners wish to protect their voting control.

Regardless of the origin of the constraint, any limit on the size of the capital budget should be explicitly considered in the analysis. Three approaches can be used. Two of them, the IRR and the PI, are approximations. The third, which uses the NPV, is theoretically correct but more difficult.

The IRR approach ranks all projects by their IRRs and finances as many projects as possible. This approach selects projects that generate the highest return *per dollar.* It will arrive at approximately the same result as the theoretically correct approach unless there are marked differences in either (1) the dollar size of individual projects or (2) the time patterns of their returns. Because of the reinvestment rate assumption, the IRR approach favors projects with high rates of return. Yet its application could result in fewer dollars being invested now or, more importantly, in the future when the early-return projects pay out.

The PI approach ranks all projects by their PIs and finances as many as possible. If all projects were divisible, that is, if the firm could take on part of a project, this approach would identify the same one-year solution as the correct method. However, because projects are not divisible, application of the PI approach can result in less than optimal capital allocation. Its results are reasonably efficient approximations when individual projects are relatively small.

The best method of handling capital rationing is a constrained maximization of the NPV of the capital budget. Although that sounds imposing, the idea is not complex. Find the capital budget that gives the highest NPV without exceeding the number of dollars available. This provides the firm with the highest possible net benefit, in current dollars, that it can purchase with its constrained budget.

Development and discussion of this approach generally make use of linear programming, but a reasonably efficient solution for a one-year problem can be obtained by systematic trial-and-error examination of the potential capital budgets. The procedure follows these steps:

1. Identify the dollar size of the capital budget, that is, the constraint.
2. Calculate the NPV of all projects, eliminating those with negative NPVs.
3. List all projects in increasing order by cost and, using the constraint, determine the maximum number of projects that can be financed. This is the upper bound.
4. List all projects in descending order by NPV, with the highest NPV project first, the next highest second, and so on. Use the constraint to determine how many of the projects, so ordered, could be financed. This is the lower bound. No budget with fewer than this number of projects need be considered. Further, the budget defining the lower bound is the best budget for this number.
5. List all feasible combinations between the upper and lower bounds. Any combination that would cost more than the constraint is nonfeasible.
6. Calculate the NPV of each feasible solution.
7. Select the combination with the highest NPV, which is the optimal solution given the constraint.

Although the process sounds involved, it really is nothing more than a way of eliminating many useless possible solutions. To better envision the process, examine the hypothetical capital budget in Table 5.14.

This example illustrates the logic behind the programming solution to capital rationing. Application can be more complex, of course, for comprehensive capital planning requires consideration of more than one year's investments. When multiple-year planning horizons are considered, the problem grows. The investments made in the first year (partially) determine how much is available for the following years. Further, investments can be undertaken now, a year from now, or later. Additionally, some projects are interdependent: Different ways of handling production scheduling at a new plant are irrelevant if the plant is not built. It is when a great number of interactions must be considered that the strength of the programming models can be fully exploited. The increased availability of computer software for such problems should make future use of the programming models more commonplace.

Considering the number of dollars involved, programming's application to capital budgeting is long overdue. The possible increases in company worth could be thousands (or millions), which would more than compensate for any additional analysis expense.

TABLE 5.14
Determination of a Constrained Capital Budget.

1. Maximum capital budget: $250,000
2. NPV of individual projects:

Project	Cost	NPV	
A	$ 50,000	$ 22,000	
B	100,000	47,000	
C	80,000	32,000	
D	40,000	14,000	
E	120,000	(30,000)	Eliminated
F	60,000	17,000	
G	25,000	10,000	

3. Establish upper bound:

Project	Cost	
G	$ 25,000	
D	40,000	
A	50,000	Four maximum
F	60,000	
C	80,000	
B	100,000	

4. Establish lower bound:

Project	NPV	Cost	
B	$ 47,000	$100,000	
C	32,000	80,000	Three minimum
A	22,000	50,000	
F	17,000	60,000	
D	14,000	40,000	
G	10,000	25,000	

5. List all feasible solutions.
6. Calculate their NPVs:

Sets of Three	Cost	NPV
ABC	$ 230,000	$101,000

All other sets of three will have lower NPVs.

Sets of Four	Cost	NPV
ABCD	$ 270,000*	$ —
ABCF	290,000*	—
ABCG	255,000*	—
ABDF	250,000	100,000
ABDG	215,000	93,000

(Continued)

TABLE 5.14 **(Cont.)**		
ABFG	235.000	96,000
ACDF	230,000	85,000
ACDG	195,000	78,000
ACFG	215,000	81,000
ADFG	175,000	63,000
BCDF	280,000*	—
BCDG	245,000	103,000†
BCFG	265,000*	—
BDFG	225,000	88,000
CDFG	205,000	74,000

7. Select the constrained maximum.

* Not feasible.
† Note that combination BCDG has the highest NPV.

SUMMARY

Capital budgeting is the process of determining which capital (long-term) investments will be undertaken. A firm will often refer to the total dollar amount of planned capital investment as *the* capital budget.

Good capital budgeting is critical to the value, and even the survival, of the firm. Capital investments are big-ticket items; they are long-lived and difficult to reverse once financial commitments have been made. The current financial press is filled with examples of firms whose futures have changed because of a single capital budgeting decision.

Capital budgeting involves three stages: proposal generation, analysis, and implementation. Although analysis is not necessarily the most important, we have concentrated on it because it is generally the responsibility of financial managers.

Analysis involves three steps: (1) estimation of cost, (2) estimation of benefits, and (3) consideration of both through some form of reasoned analysis. We have covered two main forms of analysis, or techniques. Non-DCF techniques are payback and ARR. While they have faults, we have included them because they are still used.

The better techniques are the DCF methods—NPV, PI, and IRR. These techniques use the time value of money analysis covered in Chapter 3 and the cost of capital calculated in Chapter 4. They are among the most valuable tools to be described in this course.

NPV, PI, and IRR always give the same accept-reject decisions for single investments. As long as the same cost, benefit, and cost of capital estimates are used, they will give consistent answers. However, because of their implicit assumptions, the techniques may not agree on the *relative* merit of two competing investments. NPV favors big projects, whereas IRR prefers less lengthy ones. Use of the PI serves to reduce NPV's bias toward bigness.

Examination of the reasons for these biases suggests that NPV produces results that are generally best. If two projects have unequal lives, the NPV technique must be applied in modified forms to preserve its superiority. This is also true if the firm has limited capital investment funds, a condition called capital rationing.

In this chapter we have ignored differences in investment riskiness, which the next chapter will explore.

QUESTIONS AND REVIEW ACTIVITIES

1. Define or discuss
   a) Capital budgeting.
   b) Capital budget.
   c) Cash flow.
   d) Discounting.
   e) Required rate of return.
   f) Payback.
   g) Average rate of return.
   h) Net present value.
   i) Profitability index.
   j) Internal rate of return.
   k) Reinvestment rate assumption.
   l) Equivalent annual economic profit.
   m) Capital rationing.

2. What are the three stages of capital budgeting? Which is the most important? Which did the text emphasize and why?

3. Why is cost defined in terms of the cash purchase price of an asset?

4. What is the purpose of depreciation accounting, and why must depreciation flows be considered in capital budgeting analysis?

5. Explain the advantages and disadvantages of payback as a capital budgeting technique.

6. Distinguish between the ARR and the IRR.

7. In your own words, tell what the results found by the three discounted cash flow techniques—NPV, PI, and IRR—mean to a financial analyst.

8. Under what conditions might the DCF technique give inconsistent rankings to two projects and why?

9. What does equivalent annual economic profit (EAEP) mean, and is it a logical decision criterion for unequal-lived investment alternatives?

10. Explain briefly what is accomplished by applying the programming approach to capital budgeting under rationing.

11. Why is assembling data so important in capital budgeting?

PROBLEMS

1. Find the present value of the following cash flows (assuming the required rate of return equals 10%):

Year	X	Y	Z
1	$1,000	$1,000	$1,000
2	1,000	1,000	1,000
3	1,000	1,000	1,000
4	1,000	1,000	2,000
5	5,000	5,000	3,000
6		5,000	5,000
7		5,000	5,000
8		5,000	0
9			5,000
10			5,000

2. If the cash flows in Problem 1 represent the benefits from three different investments, and if the cost of each investment (cash outflow occurring in year 1) is $4,000 for X, $9,000 for Y, and $13,000 for Z, find the

a) Payback.

b) NPV.

c) PI.

3. Find the internal rate of return of the following investment proposals:

	X	Y	Z
Outflow	$4,100	$ 250	$5,250
Benefits in year			
1	1,000	0	1,000
2	1,000	0	1,000
3	1,000	0	2,000
4	1,000	0	2,000
5	1,000	1,000	4,000

4. Elco Manufacturing, Inc., is contemplating the purchase of a new computer-controlled processing machine. The machine, including installation, would cost the company $60,000 if purchased out-right. If the company bought the machine, it could trade in its two old processors for $8,000. This would involve a small loss, as the book value of the old machines is currently $10,000.

Either the old or the new machines would be usable for 10 years. Depreciation on either would be straight-line to a zero salvage. (The company figures that either would be worthless after 10 years.) The principal reason for the changeover would be cost. Although no increases in revenue would be attributable to the new machine, its use would cut labor costs by $13,000 a year before taxes, which are 40%. The firm's required rate of return is 10%.

a) Calculate payback and ARR.

b) Calculate the NPV.

c) Calculate the PI.

d) Calculate the IRR. Use the direct solution and report to the nearest whole percent (do not interpolate).

5. Elco Manufacturing, Inc., could buy an updated version of a piece of equipment currently in use. It would cost $25,000. The purchase would allow the firm to dispose of one of its old processors and some related machinery. The old equipment could be sold for $5,000 (its current book value is $6,000). The new machinery would reduce labor costs by $5,500 a year before taxes.

Either the new equipment or the old processor would last for 10 years. Depreciation is straight-line to a zero salvage, which is a realistic estimate of the future worth of either setup. The company is in a 40% tax bracket and requires a 10% rate of return.

a) Calculate the NPV.

b) Calculate the PI.

c) Calculate the IRR.

6. A new processing system has been developed that is compatible with Elco Manufacturing's operations. The manufacturer would sell the system to the firm for $27,800, installed, if Elco purchases it outright. The manufacturer agrees to take the company's old equipment in trade upon completion of the installation, which would facilitate the changeover. However, the manufacturer will allow the firm only $7,000 for the equipment, even though its book value is $10,000.

The benefits of the equipment are twofold. It produces more, and it is cheaper to operate. Elco is certain that it can sell the increased number of products. The equipment is expected to have a useful life of five years. The expected revenues and cost savings it would generate per year are as follows:

Year	Added Revenues	Reduced Expenses
1	$5,000	$5,500
2	5,000	4,300
3	5,000	3,100
4	4,000	1,900
5	4,000	1,800

For purposes of analysis, it is assumed that both the old and the new equipment would be worthless after five years.

Depreciation on either would be straight-line over a five-year life toward a zero salvage. The firm is in a 40% tax bracket and expects a 10% return on invested capital.

a) Calculate the NPV.

b) Calculate the PI.

c) Calculate the IRR. (Do not forget the shortcut.)

7. The projects in Problems 4 and 5 could be mutually exclusive alternatives. Discuss the inconsistent rankings achieved with the NPV and IRR measures. Why did the inconsistency occur, and how would you resolve it?

8. The projects in Problems 5 and 6 could be mutually exclusive alternatives. Discuss the inconsistent rankings achieved by the different methods. Why did this inconsistency occur, and how would you resolve it?

9. The Tucson Company is considering the replacement of a piece of molding equipment in its household appliance division. Company accountants have provided the following information. If you were the president, what action would be appropriate?

	Present Machine	Proposed Machine
Book value	$20,000	
List price		$65,000
Expected remaining life	5	
Expected life		5
Salvage value	0	5,000
Trade-in value	15,000	
Cash operating expense	30,000	30,000
Revenues	75,000	90,000

Assume that both machines are depreciated on a straight-line basis. The firm is in a 40% tax bracket and has a required rate of return of 10%.

a) Calculate the NPV.

b) Calculate the PI.

10. Double-Whammy, Inc., is considering the use of industrial robots as part of its manufacturing process. Using three robots to work in the acid-bath section of the production line would solve a number of problems: It would reduce wages, eliminate the need for a high-volume ventilation system (as required by the U.S. Occupational Safety and Health Administration), and eliminate a continuing personnel problem (no one likes the acid-bath job, and some workers have quit after a short period).

The annual savings would be as follows:

Labor savings (including fringes)	$ 75,000
Reduced job-safety costs	22,000
Reduced insurance costs	8,000
Total	$105,000

There would be other savings, but these are almost exactly offset by the cost of the robots' service contract; $105,000 is a good estimate of the annual before-tax benefits.

However, the robots are not cheap. They cost $100,000 each. Further, they will require some revamping of the production line, which will cost another $18,000. To ensure orderly progress of work to the robots, slightly higher work-in-process and raw materials inventories will be needed; the estimated added investment would be $20,000.

The robots and the production line changes will be depreciated straight-line over 10 years. The robots' estimated tenth-year salvage value is $10,000 each. By installing robots, the company could eliminate and sell some safety equipment that is now necessary. This equipment has a zero book value but should sell for about $15,000 on the open market.

The robots and equipment costs qualify for a 10% investment tax credit. The company is in the 40% tax bracket and requires a 16% rate of return on new investments. Calculate the NPV on this investment.

11. Wishy Washee, Inc., a laundromat, is considering two different types of washing machines. Both would generate the same cash flows, about $3,000 a year. (This is revenue less expenses and taxes plus depreciation. It is your cash flow figure; do not use the worksheet.)

    The difference in the machines is their cost and useful life. The less expensive machine costs $3,000 and will last three years in a laundromat. The Heavy Duty Wonder Washer costs $5,500 but will last five years. Which should Wishy Washee buy, assuming its required rate of return is 15%?

12. Given a required rate of return of 14% and a $25,000 maximum capital budget, which projects (X, Y, or Z) would you select using the following?

    a) Payback.

    b) IRR.

    c) Constrained NPV (the book method).

	X	Y	Z
Outlay	$9,000	$12,000	$16,000
Benefits in year			
1	3,000	5,875	5,250
2	3,000	5,875	5,250
3	3,000	5,875	5,250
4	3,000	0	5,250
5	3,000	0	5,250

ADDITIONAL READINGS

Bernhard, R. H. "Mathematical Programming Models for Capital Budgeting—A Survey, Generalization, and Critique," *Journal of Financial and Quantitative Analysis* (June 1969), pp. 111–58.

Bierman, H., Jr., and S. Smidt. *The Capital Budgeting Decision*, 5th ed. New York: The Macmillan Company, 1980.

Dudley, C. L., Jr. "A Note on Reinvestment Assumptions in Choosing between Net Present Value and Internal Rate of Return," *Journal of Finance* (September 1972), pp. 907–15.

Fogler, H. R. "Ranking Techniques and Capital Rationing," *Accounting Review* (January 1972), pp. 134–43.

Fremgen, T. M. "Capital Budgeting Practices: A Survey," *Management Accounting* (May 1973), pp. 19–25.

Haynes, W. W., and M. B. Solomon, Jr. "A Misplaced Emphasis in Capital Budgeting," *Quarterly Review of Economics and Business* (February 1962), pp. 39–46.

Herbst, A. F. *Capital Budgeting: Theory, Quantitative Methods, and Applications*. New York: Harper & Row, Publishers, Inc., 1982.

Kim, S. H., and E. J. Farragher. "Current Capital Budgeting Practices," *Management Accounting* (June 1981), pp. 26–30.

Klammer, T. "Empirical Evidence of the Adoption of Sophisticated Capital Budgeting Techniques," *Journal of Business* (July 1972), pp. 387–97.

Levy, H., and M. Sarnat. *Capital Investments and Financial Decisions*. Englewood Cliffs, N. J.: Prentice-Hall International, 1978.

Lorie, J. H., and L. J. Savage. "Three Problems in Rationing Capital," *Journal of Business* (October 1955), pp. 229–39.

Osteryoung, J. *Capital Budgeting: Long-Term Asset Selection*, 2nd ed. Columbus, Ohio: Grid, Inc., 1979.

Petty, J. W., D. F. Scott, and M. M. Bird. "The Capital Expenditure Decision-Making Process of Large Corporations," *Engineering Economist* (Spring 1975), pp. 159–72.

Schall, L. D., G. L. Sundem, and W. R. Geijsbeek. "Survey and Analysis of Capital Budgeting Methods," *Journal of Finance* (March 1978), pp. 281–87.

Schwab, B., and P. Lusztig. "A Comparative Analysis of the Net Present Value and the Benefit-Cost Ratios as Measures of the Economic Desirability of Investments," *Journal of Finance* (June 1969), pp. 507–16.

Tilles, S. "Strategies for Allocating Funds," *Harvard Business Review* (January–February 1966), pp. 72–80.

Vandell, R. F., and P. J. Stonich. "Capital Budgeting: Theory or Results?" *Financial Executive* (August 1973), pp. 46–56.

Weingartner, H. M. "Capital Rationing: Authors in Search of a Plot," *Journal of Finance* (December 1977), pp. 1403–31.

STATISTICAL PROBABILITY
CERTAINTY, RISK, AND UNCERTAINTY
RISK-ADJUSTED CAPITAL BUDGETING
**APPENDIX 6A. THE CAPITAL ASSET PRICING MODEL AND
RISK-ADJUSTED DISCOUNT RATES**

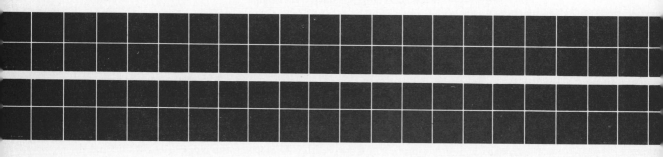

6

CAPITAL BUDGETING
UNDER RISK

Chapter 5 described how to analyze capital investments—capital budgeting. Throughout that chapter, we used the cost of capital as the discount rate in NPV analysis and as the hurdle rate for IRR analysis.

We derived the cost of capital in Chapter 4 under the assumption that new investments would not alter firm riskiness, that is, that all new investments were of the same and average risk. What does the financial manager do if investments are of differing and nonaverage risk? That is the topic of this chapter.

After careful study of the chapter, you should understand

1. What risk is, and the way that probability and statistics help to analyze risky capital investments.
2. How to calculate expected values, standard deviations, and coefficients of variation.
3. The differences in decision making under certainty, decision making under risk, and decision making under uncertainty.
4. The difference between capital budgeting under risk and capital budgeting analysis that formally incorporates risk considerations.
5. How to analyze capital investments using risk-adjusted discount rates.
6. How certainty equivalents are used to analyze risky capital investments.
7. How to use decision trees to calculate capital investment NPV statistics for more complicated cash flow patterns.

STATISTICAL PROBABILITY

Risk analysis uses probability concepts. Probability is a branch of mathematics that helps any decision maker to make choices when the exact outcome of an event cannot be specified but the expected frequency of each outcome can be defined. Traditionally, probability has been applied to repetitive process in which there is a limited number of known outcomes. In such circumstances, while it is not possible to predict the outcome of any individual trial, over a large number of trials the expected frequency of occurrence of each outcome can be predicted fairly accurately.

For example, if you were to draw one capsule at random from a bottle holding four red and six white ones, you could not guess consistently which color you would draw. However, over a large number of draws, you could be assured that you would draw white capsules nearly 60% of the time.

Sixty percent, the expected frequency of drawing a white capsule, is said to be the *probability* of that outcome, or *event*. The mathematics of probability specifies rules for describing such situations:

1. The probability of each event is between 0 and 1.
2. All events must be included.
3. Events must be mutually exclusive with no overlap.
4. The probabilities, consequently, must add up to 1.

Originally, probability was applied only to situations in which theory allowed specification of relative frequencies (e.g., the fair coin has a 50% probability of coming up heads) or those in which empirical (statistical) evidence about the relative frequency of the outcomes was obtainable. This is referred to as *traditional, empirical,* or *objective* probability.

However, probability concepts are so useful that they have come to be applied when hard evidence of frequencies is not available. In such instances, probability is merely a numerical expression of someone's belief about what will happen. Such probabilities are referred to as *subjective*.

A business person who says that the probability of success in a venture is 60% actually has no idea of the number of successes or failures that are "in the bottle." However, probability expressions are a very convenient way of indicating one's degree of belief in a project.

Probability Distributions

The **probability** of an event is the expected frequency of occurrence of that event. A **probability distribution** (**PD**) is a rule relating all possible events and their expected frequency of occurrence. Such a rule can take the form of a graph, a chart, a complete listing, or a mathematical expression.

An expression of the probability of an event as a function of its numerical value is a **probability density function** (**PDF**). Essentially, PDs and PDFs are shorthand expressions stating the expected frequency of all possible events for the particular process under consideration.

Statistics

PDs have the virtue of being complete, as they list the probability for each possible outcome. Such completeness, however, actually can be a disadvantage. The mathematics can be cumbersome if there are a large number of possible outcomes. Further, the resulting mass of numbers can be confusing rather than enlightening; one can lose sight of the forest for the trees.

Rather than consider the entire PD, it is sometimes more convenient to isolate summary descriptions of the distribution, that is, statistics. Frequently used statistics include **expected value** ($\hat{E}$), **variance** (σ^2), **standard deviation** (σ), and **coefficient of variation** (**CV**).

TABLE 6.1
Expected Profits from Selling Ice Cream under Varying Conditions.

Weather Conditions	(1) Probability $P(S_j)$	(2) Conditional Profit E_j	(3) Expected Value (1) × (2)
Hot and clear	.70	40	28.00
Hot and rainy	.10	(10)	(1.00)
Cool and clear	.15	0	.00
Cool and rainy	.05	(15)	(.75)
			$\hat{E}$ = 26.25

The formulas for deriving these statistics are as follows:

$$\hat{E} = \sum_{j=1}^{n} [P(S_j) \times E_j] \qquad (6.1)$$

$$\sigma^2 = \sum_{j=1}^{n} [P(S_j) \times (E_j - \hat{E})^2] \qquad (6.2)$$

$$\sigma = \sqrt{\sigma^2} \qquad (6.2a)$$

and

$$CV = \frac{\sigma}{\hat{E}} \qquad (6.3)$$

where there are n possible outcomes, each with a probability $P(S_j)$ and a payoff (or efficiency measure) E_j for each possible outcome j.

To illustrate these calculations, consider the case of an ice cream vendor trying to estimate the expected daily profit. The vendor knows the events that can occur (in this case, limited to the weather), the probability of each, and the profit that will be made under each set of weather conditions. These are summarized in Table 6.1.

The profit per day, over a large number of days, would be expected to be $26.25. The variability of profits can be quantified through calculation of the standard deviation or CV, as illustrated in Table 6.2.

The results indicate that the vendor's profits have their ups and downs. The expected profit is $26.25, but the variability is high; the standard deviation is $21.26, or 81% of the expected value.

CERTAINTY, RISK, AND UNCERTAINTY

Precise definitions of these terms are derived from the model of a decision. The decision model describes all situations involving a reasoned choice among

TABLE 6.2
Standard Deviation and Coefficient of Variation for Ice Cream Profits.

Weather Conditions	(1) Probability $P(S_i)$	(2) Deviation $(E - \hat{E})$	(3) Deviation Squared $(E - \hat{E})^2$	(4) Variance (1) × (3)
Hot and clear	.70	13.75	189.05	132.34
Hot and rainy	.10	(36.25)	1,314.06	131.41
Cool and clear	.15	(26.25)	689.06	103.36
Cool and rainy	.05	(41.25)	1,701.56	85.08
				$\sigma^2 = 452.19$

$$\sigma = \sqrt{\sigma^2} = \sqrt{452.19} = 21.26$$

$$CV = \sigma/\hat{E} = 21.26/26.25 = .81$$

competing courses of action, that is, when one must choose the best course of action, based on a prediction about the future and on a specified criterion. The different courses of action are **alternatives.** Each possible future set of circumstances that might occur is called a **state of nature.** Each state of nature has a certain likelihood of occurrence—the *probability* of that state of nature. The basis of choice is called the **efficiency measure** or *decision variable.* Making a decision involves choosing the best alternative based on the value of the efficiency measure.

Decisions are made under conditions of certainty, risk, and uncertainty, depending on the amount of information the decision maker has, or assumes, about the probabilities of the states of nature. If the decision maker knows which state of nature will occur (i.e., the probability of that state equals 1), the situation is **certain.** If more than one state is likely *and the probabilities can be specified,* the situation is **risky.** If the states can be specified *but their probabilities cannot,* the situation is **uncertain.**

An example helps make these concepts clearer. A street vendor near an amusement center needs to decide which product line to carry on a given day. The vendor's insulated cart can carry either cold goods such as ice cream or hot products such as coffee and hot dogs. The sale of ice cream is potentially more profitable because of the higher margin and greater sales on hot days, but sales are poor on cool or rainy days. The vendor knows the probable profits for each product line under each set of circumstances. The predictions for the alternatives are presented in Table 6.3, where the payoffs for ice cream are identical to those in the earlier example.

The table makes the nature of the vendor's problem clearer. If the vendor knew which state of nature was going to occur, the problem would be solved—

TABLE 6.3
Expected Profits under Varying Conditions for Two Different Product Lines.

Alternatives	States of Nature			
	Hot and Clear	Hot and Rainy	Cool and Clear	Cool and Rainy
Cold goods	40	(10)	0	(15)
Hot goods	15	(5)	20	15

the correct choice would be the alternative with the greater profits. This is decision making under certainty. Certainty prevails when the analyst knows, or assumes, that the probability of some state of nature is 1.

If the vendor did not know which state was going to occur, yet could assign probabilities to the various states, the decision could be based on the *expected value* of the efficiency measure as illustrated in Table 6.4. Decisions based on expected values are decision making under risk.

In this instance, the expected profit is higher with ice cream. Note that decision making under risk is not synonymous with decision making that considers the *degree* of risk. Carrying ice cream is riskier in the sense that the potential error of the prediction is larger, as indicated by the standard deviation (or σ^2 or CV). Decision making under risk means only that probability estimates are used. If the *degree of riskiness* is to be incorporated into the analysis, measures such as the standard deviation can be helpful.

If probabilities cannot be specified, the vendor is making a decision under uncertainty. There is no clear-cut decision rule for such a problem. Some attempts have been made to provide guidance, but each proposed rule can be shown to have logical weaknesses.

The **maximax** rule proposes that a decision maker take the alternative with the highest potential reward. In this case, carrying ice cream offers a potential $40 profit if the weather cooperates, while no more than $20 can be made by selling coffee and sandwiches. The maximax approach is appropriate only for an optimist; it overlooks the greater potential losses that might occur with ice cream.

The pessimist's decision rule, **maximin,** says, take the alternative that has the highest low payoff. Coffee and hot dogs never lose more than $5 under any state, whereas ice cream can produce a $15 loss. The pessimist minimizes potential losses by carrying coffee and hot dogs.

There are other proposals for dealing with uncertainty; however, each has logical weaknesses. As a result, uncertainty must be met by the decision maker's personal evaluation of such problems. The lack of probabilities does

	States of Nature				
Alternatives	**Hot and Clear**	**Hot and Rainy**	**Cold and Clear**	**Cold and Rainy**	**Expected Value Standard Deviation**
Cold goods	40	(10)	0	(15)	26.25 21.26
Hot goods	15	(5)	20	15	13.75 6.50
Probability of state	.70	.10	.15	.05	

TABLE 6.4
Decision Making under Risk.

not stop one from considering the *degree of uncertainty*. Table 6.3 shows that the range of outcomes is wider when selling ice cream and that the potential losses are greater. It can be said, therefore, that the degree of uncertainty is greater with that alternative. Because *degree of risk* and *degree of uncertainty* both refer to the magnitude of potential estimation error, it is common practice to use the terms *risk* and *uncertainty* as synonyms in this context.

The distinction between decision making under uncertainty and decision making that considers the degree of uncertainty is important, because uncertainty is the decision situation that financial managers encounter most frequently. Most cash flows depend on overall economic conditions that are uncertain.

Lacking the necessary probability information to develop precise statistical decision rules for capital budgeting, managers have developed techniques that can be applied using only subjective estimates of the *degree of uncertainty* in future cash flows. These techniques also work when better probability information is available.

RISK-ADJUSTED CAPITAL BUDGETING

There are two types of capital budgeting techniques that consider project riskiness, or uncertainty: formal and informal. The *formal* techniques incorporate specific and explicit adjustments for riskiness in the analysis. The *informal* approach is the adjustment or tempering of the results of the analysis, *after it has been completed*, by a consideration of project riskiness.

The two formal techniques use **risk-adjusted discount rates (RADRs)** and **certainty equivalents (CEs)**. We can demonstrate their application in an NPV example. The NPV of a project is the present value of *expected future* cash flows minus the cost:

$$NPV = \sum_{t=1}^{n} \left[\frac{\hat{C}_t}{(1 + K)^t} \right] - C_0,$$ (6.4)

where

$\hat{C}_t$ = expected cash flow in period t (C_0 = cost)

K = discount rate (cost of capital)

t = time period from zero to n, the life of the investment.

To take account of riskiness in the analysis, we can change either the discount rate or the expected cash flows. Changing the discount rate (K) is accomplished by using RADRs (pronounced rad-R); the more uncertain the cash flows, the higher the discount rate used. CEs are the means for altering cash flows ($\hat{C}_t$). For each uncertain cash flow, we substitute the guaranteed minimum amount we would take willingly in exchange for the uncertain cash flow; the more uncertain $\hat{C}_t$, the smaller the necessary guaranteed amount— the CE. Once cash flows are converted to CEs, or riskless flows, they are discounted at a riskless rate.

Generally, RADRs and CEs are determined subjectively. The financial manager assesses the degree of uncertainty involved and sets the figures considered appropriate to reflect the potential error in the forecasts. Subjectivity or individual judgment, however, is not inevitable. If risk information can be developed, and a valuation model formulated based on that type of risk, the techniques can be made precise. Appendix 6A demonstrates that this can be done when beta measures risk and the capital asset pricing model holds. What we will describe here covers only the more subjective application of the techniques.

Risk-Adjusted Discount Rate (RADR)

In the last chapter, we assumed implicitly that all investments were of the same riskiness (uncertainty). For this reason, it was possible to use the same hurdle rate for all IRRs and the same discount rate (cost of capital) for all NPVs. In actuality, the outcomes of some investment proposals are relatively certain, while others entail a high degree of uncertainty regarding future cash flows. In evaluating either sort of investment, it would be inappropriate to apply a discount factor that implies an average degree of risk. Instead, a lower rate would be logical when an investment proposal is low risk. Likewise, when future cash flows are highly uncertain, the discount rate should be higher. How much higher would be determined by management's judgment. In any case, the general formula for finding acceptable investment projects must be altered. When the adjustment is made to the discount rate, the result is

$$\text{NPV} = \sum_{t=1}^{n} \left[\frac{\hat{C}_t}{(1 + K^\star)^t} \right] - C_0 \tag{6.5}$$

$$K^\star = \text{RADR}.$$

Use of RADR—An example. The ABC Corporation is trying to determine whether to introduce a new product. The initial production cost will be $100,000, with net operating cash inflows estimated to be $10,000 for each of the first two years and $30,000 annually for the remaining eight years the product is expected to sell. While the firm's cost of capital is 14%, the financial manager believes that this figure actually understates the risk of the project because the company has little information on the demand and possibility of obsolescence of the product. Therefore, the manager assigns the project a discount rate of 18%.

Using Eq. (6.5), one arrives at an NPV of $3,500.

$$\text{NPV} = \sum_{t=1}^{2} \frac{\$10,000}{(1 + .18)^t} + \sum_{t=3}^{10} \frac{\$30,000}{(1 + .18)^t} - \$100,000$$

$$= \$15,660 + \$87,840 - \$100,000 = \$3,500.$$

There are some problems in using RADRs. Increasing the discount rate penalizes projects whose cash flows are larger in the later years of the project.† For this reason, this method should be applied only when there is an increase in uncertainty in future years. In the ABC Corporation example, obsolescence and uncertainty about demand were the significant factors that made application of this technique appropriate; more distant projections were more error prone.

Although we have illustrated RADR approach using NPV, RADRs also can be used with the IRR. The IRR application is even easier. The only change is in the last step of the analysis; the hurdle rate (the acceptance criterion) changes. To use RADRs with the IRR, calculate the IRR as usual, and then use the RADR as the acceptance rule. If IRR ≥ RADR, accept the project; if not, reject it.

Certainty Equivalent (CE)

The RADR approach adjusts for uncertainty in the discount rate in the denominator of the NPV formula. The CE method allows for uncertainty by

---

† A particular problem arises when using RADRs with cost data; risky costs should be discounted at lower, not higher, discount rates. This somewhat technical issue is beyond the scope of this textbook. For elaboration, see Thomas E. Copeland and J. Fred Weston, *Financial Theory and Corporate Policy* (Reading, Mass.: Addison-Wesley Publishing Company, 1983), Chapter 11.

adjusting the cash flow itself, which means that a different discount rate is then appropriate. The NPV formula using the CE adjustment is

$$NPV = \sum_{t=1}^{n} \left[\frac{A_t \cdot \hat{C}_t}{(1 + R_F)^t} \right] - C_0, \tag{6.6}$$

where

A_t = CE coefficient for period t

R_F = riskless discount rate.

The logic of the CE approach is similar to the logic that underlies RADRs. That is, both approaches penalize risky flows by making them worth less than the same certain cash flows. However, in the case of CE analysis, greater uncertainty reduces the size of the adjustment factor, A_t. The CE coefficient, A_t, takes on values from 0 to 1. If a future cash flow were certain, $A_t \equiv 1$. Lower values would be assigned as future cash flows became more uncertain, that is, riskier.

Note that the CE-adjusted cash flows are discounted at a riskless rate. This rate can be used because all elements of uncertainty are incorporated in the CE coefficient. If a higher discount rate such as the cost of capital were used, the investment would be doubly penalized. Recognize that a different CE may be used for each period's cash flows. It would appear logical, for example, for CEs to diminish over time in the case of most investments.

When the IRR is used to make capital budgeting decisions, the problem involves finding the discount rate that equates the present value of the cash inflows and outflows adjusted for uncertainty with the CE coefficient. This rate is then compared with the riskless rate. An acceptable project would be one in which the CE-IRR is higher than this riskless rate.

Use of CEs—An example. Big D Corp. has $9,000 to invest for two years. The investment under consideration has expected cash inflows of $7,000 in each of these years. However, because of the riskiness of these cash flows, the financial manager would be willing to take smaller, guaranteed cash flows in exchange for each of the cash flows. The CE coefficients assigned for the two years are $A_1 = .90$ and $A_2 = .80$, respectively. At the present time, U.S. Treasury bills are yielding 12%, which we use as the riskless rate.

The CE NPV would be

$$NPV = \sum_{t=1}^{n} \left[\frac{A_t \cdot C_t}{(1 + R_F)^t} \right] - C_0$$

$$= \frac{.9(\$7,000)}{1.12} + \frac{.8(\$7,000)}{(1.12)^2} - \$9,000$$

$$= \$5,625 + \$4,464 - \$9,000 = \$1,089.$$

The NPV of the discounted, uncertainty-adjusted cash flows exceeds the cost of the investment by $1,089. The project has a positive CE NPV and, therefore, should be undertaken.

Informal Risk Adjustment

Financial managers following the informal approach to risk adjustment would carry out all preliminary analysis just as we described in Chapter 5. They would calculate the NPV (or IRR or PI) of all projects without explicitly adjusting any input for riskiness.

After completing the preliminary analysis, managers would decide on individual projects, or between competing projects, on the basis of their investment attractiveness versus their perceived riskiness. Some companies go so far as to categorize and rank different types of investments in terms of their riskiness. One company's ranking might be as follows:

- Replacing existing equipment.
- Modernizing production facilities.
- Expanding existing product lines.
- Expanding within existing markets.
- Entering new but existing markets.
- Introducing a new product for a currently undefined market.
- Introducing a new product based on a new technology for a currently undefined market.

The further down the list you go, the less precise (or more risky) will be the estimates of future cash flows. The effect of these riskier cash flows is allowed for by requiring different categories of investments to offer greater and greater returns (IRRs or PIs).

Experienced managers do not need such a specific list to be made aware of what is risky. They know that offering a new product to an untapped or unknown market is hazardous. Although they may not be able to quantify risk, or express precisely the way in which they incorporate its effects into their decisions, managers must decide continually whether the potential payoff from a capital outlay is profitable enough to warrant taking on the risk of loss.

Statistical measures of dispersion can be helpful in an informal assessment of risk, even though they are not explicitly worked into the analysis. And where a capital investment involves a series of decisions, as is often the case, a decision tree is a useful device for organizing the analysis.

Use of statistics in informally risk-adjusted capital budgeting—An example. Whiz Corporation is trying to determine whether a particular investment project should be undertaken. The initial investment will be $1,000. As Table 6.5 shows, only three states of nature are possible. Each has an expected probability and a conditional cash inflow. The firm's required rate of return is 18%, and the life of the project is six years.

The analysis is done as follows:

1. The expected annual cash flow is calculated as shown in Table 6.5.
2. The standard deviation is calculated as shown in Table 6.6.
3. The NPV of the project is calculated using Eq. (6.4).

$$\text{NPV} = \sum_{t=1}^{n} \frac{\hat{C}_t}{(1 + K)^t} - C_0$$

$$= \sum_{t=1}^{6} \frac{\$500}{(1.18)^t} - \$1,000$$

$$= 3.498(500) - \$1,000$$

$$= \$749.$$

This particular project is relatively risky; the standard deviation ($\sigma = \$190$) is high compared to the expected cash flow ($\hat{C} = \$500$). Such results suggest that caution is in order and that the analyst should carefully evaluate the accuracy of the cash flow estimates.

TABLE 6.5
Expected Value of Annual Cash Inflows.

State of Nature	(1) Probability	(2) Conditional Cash Flows	(3) Expected Value (1) × (2)
Boom	.20	$800	$160
Normal	.60	500	300
Recession	.20	200	40
			$\hat{C} = \$500$

TABLE 6.6
Standard Deviation of Annual Cash Flows.

State of Nature	(1) Probability	(2) Deviation $(E - \hat{E})$	(3) Squared Deviation $(E - \hat{E})^2$	(4) Variance (1) × (3)
Boom	.20	300	90,000	18,000
Normal	.60	0	0	0
Recession	.20	−300	90,000	18,000
				$\sigma^2 = 36,000$

$$\sigma = \sqrt{\sigma^2} = 190$$

Expected values and dispersion measures can also be used to choose between competing investments. In simple situations, some of the choices are obvious. For example,

1. If two or more investment proposals have the same expected values, select those with the lowest standard deviations.
2. If two or more investment proposals have the same standard deviations, choose those with the highest expected values.

This procedure is proper to follow for decisions with comparable expected returns or standard deviations. Historically, however, returns vary proportionally with the degree of uncertainty regarding future cash flows; and typically, all investment proposals under consideration will not have the same expected return or standard deviation. Therefore, the analyst must develop some method for relating each proposal's measure of risk to the expected value of its cash flows; that is the purpose of the CV. The CV can be used for assigning investments to risk classes and for choosing among competing investments offering different returns. The lower the CV, the less risky the investment.

This interpretation can be understood more easily if the CV is thought of as the percentage error. That is, a project with cash flows of $1,000 and a CV of .5 can be thought of as a project with a cash flow of $1,000, give or take 50%. This interpretation is not exact; with normally distributed flows, the actual probability that the flows would be between $500 and $1,500 is 68%.† However, this interpretation of the CV may demonstrate why a lower CV is preferable. The lower the margin of error relative to the estimate, the better off the analyst is, that is, the less uncertainty exists.

Application of the standard deviation, expected value, and CV to capital budgeting decisions—An example. The KBA Corporation is trying to choose between two investment proposals. Project A has a standard deviation of $650, while project B has a standard deviation of $800. The firm's financial manager wants to know which investment to choose, given each of the following combinations of expected values.

1. Project A and project B both have expected cash flows of $12,500; or
2. Project A has expected cash flows of $9,000, while project B has expected cash flows of $12,500.

In the first situation, it is clear that project A would be preferable, for the expected value of the projects is the same, while the standard deviation, and therefore the uncertainty, of project A is smaller. The second situation requires a comparison of their CVs. The result is that project B would be selected because it has a lower CV, as you can see from the following calculations.

---

† For a normal distribution, 68% of the outcomes will fall within ±1 standard deviation from the mean.

Project A	Project B
$CV = \dfrac{\$650}{\$9,000} = .072$	$CV = \dfrac{\$800}{\$12,500} = .064$

Actually, calculating dispersion measures for capital investments is harder than our examples indicate. To analyze an investment's riskiness, the standard deviation (or CV) of the *per-period* cash flow is not enough. What the analyst needs is a standard deviation for the NPV, and this depends on the degree of interdependence between the annual flows. If one good year tends to be followed by more good years throughout the project (or if a bad first year tends to mean that the whole project will be a flop), then the standard deviation for the project will be greater than it would be if bad and good years tend to offset each other.

The statistical term for the situation in which good years are followed by more good years is *correlation*, or *interdependence*. The dispersion of the NPV distribution will depend on the interdependence among a project's annual cash flows. High correlation increases dispersion, and low or negative (high followed by low) correlation reduces dispersion. Unfortunately, the mathematics for most realistic levels of interdependence is complicated. Where the relationship is not perfect (one good year is not *always* followed by another) and is not 0 (there is no association between years), it is easier to work with decision trees.

Decision Trees

Decision trees depicit cash flows over sequential events or states of nature. The events can be managerial decisions or specific time periods. Decision trees graphically illustrate the pattern of the cash flows and can be used to depict a wide variety of cash flow patterns. They can be used to derive the necessary information to calculate wanted statistics for such decisions.

Use of decision trees—An example. An investment costing $3,000 lasts two years. First-year cash flows have a 50-50 chance of being either $4,000 or $1,000. If the first year is good, the second-year probabilities change to 70-30 for the same cash flows. If the first year is bad, the probabilities are 70% for a zero second-year payoff and 30% for $2,000. This information is summarized in Table 6.7.

Each path has a probability and an NPV, assuming a cost of capital. From this information, an expected NPV and dispersion statistics can be calculated. Using a 15% cost of capital, the calculations would appear as illustrated in Table 6.8. The expected NPV is 572.

TABLE 6.7
Cash Flow Decision Tree.

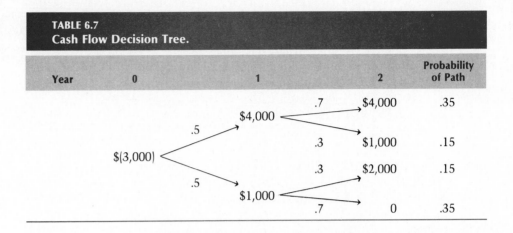

Year	0	1	2	Probability of Path
	$(3,000)	$4,000 (.5)	.7 → $4,000	.35
			.3 → $1,000	.15
		$1,000 (.5)	.3 → $2,000	.15
			.7 → 0	.35

TABLE 6.8
Expected Net Present Value.

State of Nature (Path)	(1) Probability	Calculation	(2) NPV	(3) Expected Value (1) × (2)
1	.35	− 3,000 + .870 (4,000) + .756 (4,000)	3,504	1,226
2	.15	− 3,000 + .870 (4,000) + .756 (1,000)	1,236	185
3	.15	− 3,000 + .870 (1,000) + .756 (2,000)	(618)	(93)
4	.35	− 3,000 + .870 (1,000) + .756 (0)	(2,130)	(746)
			$N\hat{P}V =$	572

Table 6.9 shows the dispersion statistic calculations. The figures indicate that although the NPV of the project is positive, this is a very risky proposition. The example also indicates how the interdependence of annual cash flows increases riskiness. Such interdependence is not at all unusual in investments. Its presence should indicate how important it is for managers to learn how to assess project riskiness very carefully.

TABLE 6.9
Calculation of the Standard Deviation and Coefficient of Variation of Net Present Value.

Path	(1) Probability $P(S_j)$	(2) Deviation $(NPV - \hat{NPV})$	(3) Deviation Squared $(NPV - \hat{NPV})^2$	(4) Variance (1) × (3)
1	.35	2,932	8,596,624	3,008,818
2	.15	664	440,896	66,134
3	.15	(1,190)	1,416,100	212,415
4	.35	(2,702)	7,300,804	2,555,281
			$\sigma^2 =$	5,842,649

$$\sigma = \sqrt{\sigma^2} = \sqrt{5,842,649} = 2,417$$
$$CV = \sigma/\hat{NPV} = 2,417/572 = 4.23$$

SUMMARY

Risk analysis uses probability mathematics. Probability theory was developed to describe and analyze situations in which the outcome of a single event is not predictable but the frequency of different outcomes over repeated trials is. The convenience of probability mathematics has led to its use when the numbers indicate only degrees of belief unrelated to hard statistical evidence.

Probability distributions specify the probability of all possible outcomes for a particular process. For convenience, analysts often use summary measures of such distributions—statistics. Three useful statistics are expected value, standard deviation, and coefficient of variation.

Risk is only one condition a decision maker may face. If only one outcome is possible, the situation can be described as certainty. If more than one outcome is possible but the probabilities of these states of nature are unknown, decisions are made under conditions of uncertainty. Different decision rules are followed in each decision situation. Decision making under risk is different from decision making that considers the degree of risk or uncertainty.

Capital budgeting analysis that incorporates consideration of risk may do so either formally or informally. The formal risk-adjusted capital budgeting techniques use RADRs and CEs. Either technique can be used in conjunction with the NPV or IRR method.

Informal risk adjustments can be based on investment characteristics or on statistical measures of dispersion. Interperiod associations between or among cash flows complicate the calculation of statistical measures. Decision trees help organize the necessary calculations.

In short, uncertainty and risk describe the conditions most financial managers face. Probability and statistics provide useful methods for describing such situations. Financial theory often equates dispersion statistics and risk. A project with a large standard deviation (or CV) is relatively risky. Having a way of quantifying an attribute as vague as riskiness can be of immeasurable value in dealing with risk in all decisions. Capital budgeting has progressed further than most areas of financial management in coming to grips with risk. The techniques most frequently used are those described—RADRs, CEs, and the informal adjustment for riskiness after applying standard capital budgeting techniques to non-risk-adjusted data.

QUESTIONS AND REVIEW ACTIVITIES

1. Define or discuss
   a) Probability.
   b) Probability distribution.
   c) Probability density function.
   d) Statistic.
   e) Expected value.
   f) Variance.
   g) Standard deviation.
   h) Coefficient of variation.
   i) Decision making under certainty.
   j) Decision making under risk.
   k) Decision making under uncertainty.
   l) Alternatives.
   m) State of nature.
   n) Efficiency measure.
   o) Risk-adjusted discount rates.
   p) Certainty equivalents.
   q) Informal risk adjustment.
   r) Decision trees.
2. Explain the difference between decision making under conditions of certainty, risk, and uncertainty.
3. Distinguish between decision making *under* risk and decision making that *considers* the degree of risk.
4. Explain why the terms *degree of risk* and *degree of uncertainty* can often be used interchangeably.
5. We suggested use of RADRs and CEs to analyze investment proposals under uncertainty. Would you use the techniques under conditions of risk, and if so, how?
6. How is the CV used for choosing between alternative investment proposals?
7. Under what conditions is decision tree analysis useful?

PROBLEMS

1. Phlashin Pan, Inc., is considering an investment with annual cash flows as described here. What is (a) the expected annual cash flow, (b) the standard deviation, and (c) the CV of the annual cash flow?

State of Nature	Probability	Conditional Cash Flow
Boom	.20	$3,500
Normal	.50	2,000
Recession	.30	1,000

2. Begs, Inc., is faced with investing in one of the following proposals (all three have the same cost and same expected life).

Proposal A		Proposal B		Proposal C	
Probability	Net Cash Flow	Probability	Net Cash Flow	Probability	Net Cash Flow
.1	$1,000	.2	$1,000	.4	$1,000
.2	2,000	.2	2,000	.4	2,000
.3	3,000	.3	3,000	.1	3,000
.4	4,000	.3	4,000	.1	4,000

If the company is averse to risk, which proposal should it undertake?

3. a) If Begs were not averse to uncertainty, which proposal would it select? Why?

   b) If the probability distribution for Proposal C were as follows, would your answer change? Assume that Begs is averse to uncertainty.

Proposal C Revised	
Probability	Net Cash Flow
.1	$1,000
.2	2,000
.5	3,000
.2	4,000

4. A merchant is contemplating starting a business located next to a new apartment complex. He is deciding whether to open a laundromat or a video game arcade. The laundromat will do reasonably well in all circumstances; if the renters are working single people and young married couples, however, it will do better than average. If there were a reasonable number of video game aficionados in the complex, though, the arcade could be extremely profitable. Table 6.10 shows the expected payoffs.

TABLE 6.10
Expected Monthly Profits for Two Different Operations with Different Markets.

	State of Nature	
Alternatives	Single People and Young Married Couples	Numerous Video Game Players
Laundromat	$4,000	$2,000
Video game arcade	300	7,000

a) If you were a maximax (or maximin) decision maker, what would you do?

b) Which alternative is more uncertain?

c) Assume that the two states of nature are equally likely (the probability of both is .5). What is the expected monthly profit, standard deviation, and CV for each alternative? Which is the more risky?

5. The financial manager of a corporation has determined that the company's cost of capital is 20%. In the past, the company has used 80 or 120% of the required rate as the discount rate for investments that are *not* of average uncertainty. The manager is evaluating the following two proposals.

	Project A	Project B
Expected life	Ten years	Ten years
Uncertainty factor	Below average	Above average
Cost	$35,000	$40,000
Expected net cash flow	6,500	12,000

Which project(s) would be selected applying the RADR approach?

6. Assuming that the financial manager in problem 5 would be equally satisfied with the risky cash flows of Project B or the following certain cash flows, determine whether Project B should be accepted. Assume a risk-free rate of 16%.

Year	Certain Cash Flows
1–2	$10,000
3–7	9,000
8–10	8,000

7. The Carpet Manufacturing Co. uses a CE approach in its capital budgeting decisions. The company is currently evaluating three proposals. The expected values of the net cash flows are as follows:

Year	A	B	C
0	− $30,000	− $25,000	− $20,000
1	10,000	12,000	8,000
2	10,000	12,000	9,000
3	10,000	12,000	10,000
4	8,000	12,000	10,000

In analyzing the three proposals, the financial manager provided the following CE coefficients.

Year	A	B	C
0	1.00	1.00	1.00
1	.95	.95	.95
2	.90	.80	.90
3	.80	.70	.90
4	.70	.50	.90

If U.S. Treasury bills are currently yielding 12%, which proposal(s) should be selected?

8. A two-year project has expected cash flows as depicted in the following decision tree. Calculate the expected NPV and the standard deviation and CV. Use a 16% discount rate.

Year	0	1	2	Probability of Path
		.7	$9,000	.42
		$8,000		
	.6	.3		
			$7,000	.18
$(5,000)		.3	$4,000	.12
	.4			
		$3,000		
		.7	$3,000	.28

Note: Problem 9 involves calculating a RADR based on the CAPM. This material is covered in Appendix 6A.

9. The Chicago Mfg. Co. is evaluating a new capital investment. This project would be economically independent of all existing investments by the firm. To calculate a CAPM-based RADR, the company has assembled the following data:

Corporate tax rate	40%
Firm's debt ratio	50%
Project beta	1.0
Return on the market	18%
Risk-free rate	10%

a) Calculate the risk-adjusted hurdle rate.

b) Set up an income statement for a marginal $2,000 investment of this type (assume a perpetual investment—no depreciation, no capital recapture).

c) Calculate the beta of the new stock $(\beta_{\Delta S})$ that would be issued.

d) Calculate a cost of equity using the security market line (SML) and $\beta_{\Delta S}$.

e) Show that the calculated RADR preserves the value of the firm (replicate Table 6A.1).

f) Calculate a weighted average cost of capital for *this project alone.*

ADDITIONAL READINGS

Bierman, H., Jr., and J. E. Hass. "Capital Budgeting under Uncertainty: A Reformulation," *Journal of Finance* (March 1973), pp. 119–29.

Bower, R. S., and J. M. Jenks. "Divisional Screening Rates," *Financial Management* (Autumn 1975), pp. 42–49.

Byrne, R., A. Charnes, A. Cooper, and K. Kortanek. "Some New Approaches to Risk," *Accounting Review* (January 1968), pp. 18–37.

Copeland, T. E., and J. F. Weston. *Financial Theory and Corporate Policy.* Reading, Mass.: Addison-Wesley Publishing Company, 1983.

Farrar, D. E. *The Investment Decision under Uncertainty.* Englewood Cliffs, N.J.: Prentice-Hall, Inc., 1962.

Greer, W. R., Jr. "Theory versus Practice in Risk Analysis: An Empirical Study," *Accounting Review* (July 1974), pp. 496–505.

Henderson, G. V., Jr., and S. E. Skomp. "A Pedagogical Note on CAPM-Based Capital Budgeting," *The Financial Review* (Spring 1981), pp. 51–58.

———. "The Security Market Line, Constrained Leverage, Value Additivity, and Determination of Capital Budgets: Geometric Exposition," A paper presented at the 1981 Financial Management Association conference.

Hertz, D. B. "Risk Analysis in Capital Investment," *Harvard Business Review* (January–February 1964), pp. 95–106.

Hillier, F. S. "The Derivation of Probabilistic Information for the Evaluation of Risky Investments," *Management Science* (April 1963), pp. 443–57.

Hillier, F. S., and D. V. Heebink. "Evaluation of Risky Capital Investments," *California Management Review* (Winter 1965), pp. 71–80.

Lerner, E. M., and A. Rappaport. "Limit DCF in Capital Budgeting," *Harvard Business Review* (September–October 1968), pp. 133–39.

Magee, J. F. "Decision Trees for Decision Making," *Harvard Business Review* (July–August 1964), pp. 126–38.

Myers S. C. "Procedures for Capital Budgeting under Uncertainty," *Industrial Management Review* (Spring 1968), pp. 1–19.

Myers, S. C., and S. M. Turnbull. "Capital Budgeting and the Capital Asset Pricing Model: Good News and Bad News," *Journal of Finance* (May 1977), pp. 321–33.

Robichek, A. A. "Interpreting the Results of Risk Analysis," *Journal of Finance* (December 1975), pp. 1384–86.

Robichek, A. A., and S. C. Myers. "Risk-Adjusted Discount Rates," *Journal of Finance* (December 1966), pp. 727–30.

Schall, L. D. "Asset Valuation, Firm Investment and Firm Diversification," *Journal of Business* (January 1972), pp. 11–28.

Van Horne, J. C. "Capital Budgeting Decisions Involving Combinations of Risky Investments," *Management Science* (October 1966), pp. 84–92.

APPENDIX 6A

THE CAPITAL ASSET PRICING MODEL
AND RISK-ADJUSTED DISCOUNT RATES

Appendix 4A discussed how a current theoretical model, the CAPM, could be used to measure a firm's cost of capital. It reviewed the history of the CAPM and showed how the security market line (SML) could be used to measure a firm's cost of capital.

This appendix assumes that you have read Appendix 4A, which showed how a firm's beta could be used to calculate the firm's cost of capital, which we use as the cutoff rate for average-risk investments. This appendix shows how a single *project's* beta can be used to calculate a RADR applicable to that project alone.

After studying this appendix, you should understand

1. What value additivity means and its importance to derivation of project-specific RADRs.
2. How leverage enters into the calculation of RADRs.
3. How capital budgets are determined using RADRs.
4. Differences between the CAPM and traditional approaches to capital budgeting.

RADRs FOR INDIVIDUAL INVESTMENTS

The Chapter 4 review of CAPM history ended with a proposal that the SML be used as a model for project RADRs. Early work in this area was sometimes less than precise. The CAPM was often borrowed, in total, as analysts assumed that what was appropriate for evaluating security investments was also appropriate for evaluating capital investments within firms. The importance of the riskiness of the firm's operations and its financing were often overlooked by those proposing to use the SML as a RADR model.

Security returns are additive. If you receive a return of $100 from investing $1,000 in stock A and $200 from investing $1,000 in stock B, the return from investing $2,000 in stocks A and B will be $300. If NPVs based on RADRs are to be theoretically legitimate, the risk of projects must be additive. If the risks are additive, so are the NPVs.

Fortunately, the *value additivity principle* (*VAP*) was developed at about the same time the CAPM was being integrated into capital budgeting theory. Myers makes a number of points that are particularly important to the current theory of capital budgeting: "[T]he cost of capital is defined as the minimum expected rate of return on a project . . ."; "a hurdle rate with the height of the barrier depending on the risk characteristics of the project . . ."; and "the NPV approach presumes projects to be risk-independent." Myers demonstrates that risk independence is a necessary condition for capital market equilibrium as implied by the CAPM, and "that capital budgeting projects are risk independent, and thus that procedures using a variable hurdle rate are entirely appropriate from a theoretical standpoint."[†]

Schall uses investor arbitrage arguments to make similar points: "*The marginal project is therefore evaluated solely in terms of its returns. . . . The increment to the investing firm's value is V_n and firm-investment diversification considerations are irrelevant.*"[‡] Schall asserts that this result holds in the existence of corporate taxation and for firms that issue risky debt if tax losses are sold in an efficient market. Schall labeled this relationship the **value additivity principle** (**VAP**). Succinctly stated, VAP says that the *value* of the returns from any new investment is independent of any *statistical* interrelationship of such returns with existing firm investments.

DERIVATION OF SML-VAP HURDLE RATES

As noted, using specific hurdle rates for individual investments implicitly assumes value additivity; this is appropriate if investments are not *economically* interrelated to each other or to existing investments of the firm. If the projects have no effect on each other's returns, they may be evaluated separately. The justification for this is essentially the same as that underlying Sharpe's portfolio management model. If the projects are interrelated only through their common relationship to the market, their contribution to portfolio (the postinvestment company real-asset portfolio) risk will be measured by each asset's beta.

VAP does not change the firm valuation model; Eq. (4A.14) still holds. Derivation of VAP hurdle rates is simplified because a similar model applies to new investments without regard to any *statistical* interrelationship with the firm's existing earnings. The value of the incremental investment would be

$$\Delta V = \frac{\Delta X(1 - t)}{R_F + \beta_i(R_M - R_F)} + t \, \Delta B, \tag{6A.1}$$

[†] S. C. Myers, "Procedures for Capital Budgeting Under Uncertainty," *Industrial Management Review* (Spring 1968), pp. 1–2.

[‡] L. D. Schall, "Asset Valuation, Firm Investment and Firm Diversification," *Journal of Business* (January 1972), p. 20.

where

ΔV = the value of the incremental investment i,

DX = the change in the firm's operating earnings (X) due to this investment,

β_i = the beta of the *incremental* earnings,

ΔB = the change in outstanding debt (market value),

t = the firm's tax rate,

R_M = the return on the market, and

R_F = the risk-free rate.

To be acceptable, ΔV must exceed the cost of the new investment, ΔI, that is, $\Delta V > \Delta I$ or, equivalently, at a minimum, $\Delta V/\Delta I = 1$. To find the hurdle rate, divide through Eq. (A6.1) by ΔI, set $\Delta V/\Delta I = 1$, and isolate the required after-tax, rate-of-return variable, $\Delta X(1 - t)/\Delta I \equiv RADR_i$.

$$1 = \frac{\Delta V}{\Delta I} = \frac{\Delta X(1 - t)}{\Delta I[R_F + \beta_i(R_M - R_F)]} + t\frac{\Delta B}{\Delta I}$$

$$RADR_i = \frac{\Delta X(1 - t)}{\Delta I} = [R_F + \beta_i(R_M - R_F)]\left(1 - t\frac{\Delta B}{\Delta I}\right). \qquad (6A.2)$$

This hurdle rate specifies the minimum after-tax rate of return on a single new investment such that firm value will be maintained. The formulation takes into account the riskiness of the project (β_i) and the beneficial effects of debt financing (due to deductibility of interest payments). If the project (investment i) earns at least this rate of return, the wealth of existing shareholders will be undiminished.

NUMERICAL EXAMPLE

A numerical example helps illustrate the logic of the SML-VAP hurdle rate. Table 6A.1 lists hypothetical parameter values for the market and a marginal $1,000 investment. The hurdle rate is calculated using Eq. (6A.2); it is 16.8% after taxes or 28% before taxes of 40%. Table 6A.1 also includes an incremental income statement. Since the investment is marginal, it generates a return of exactly 28%, that is, $280 before interest and taxes. The interest expense is $56—14% (the same for all issuers under CAPM) on the incremental debt of $400.

The values of issued securities are obtained by capitalizing their returns at the appropriate SML-determined rates. The value of the riskless debt, ΔB, is its book value of $400 = $56/.14.

The stock's value is found the same way. However, finding the capitalization rate is not quite as straightforward. The problem is the beta of the new stock, $\beta_{\Delta S}$, which is issued to finance the new investment. The relationship between this beta, $\beta_{\Delta S}$, and the beta of the new investment's returns, β_i, is the same as that given in Eq. (4A.16):

$$\beta_{\Delta S} = \beta_i \left[1 + (1 - t) \frac{\Delta B}{\Delta S} \right],$$

or in terms of the individual investment:

$$\beta_{\Delta S} = \beta_i \left(\frac{\Delta I - t\Delta B}{\Delta I - \Delta B} \right). \tag{6A.3}$$

Under the conditions given, the new common stock would have a beta of 1.68 even though the investment had a beta of 1.2. Substituting this value into the SML yields a capitalization rate of 22.4% and a stock value of $600.

TABLE 6A.1
A Numerical Example.

1. Parameter values:

$R_M = .19$	$\Delta B = \$\ 400$
$R_F = .14$	$\Delta I = 1,000$
$\beta_i = 1.2$	$t = .4$

2. Hurdle rate calculation:

$$RADR_i = [R_F + \beta_i(R_M - R_F)] \left(1 - t\frac{\Delta B}{\Delta I} \right) \tag{6A.2}$$

$$= [.14 + 1.2(.19 - .14)] \left(1 - .4\frac{400}{1,000} \right) = .168.$$

3. Calculation of valuation determinants:

   a) Pretax return $= .168/(1 - .4) = .280$

   b)
EBIT ($1,000 @ .28)	$280.00
Interest ($400 @ .14)	56.00
Earnings before taxes	224.00
Taxes (40% rate)	89.60
Net income	$134.40

   c) $\Delta B = \$56/.14 = \$400$

   d) $\Delta S = \$134.40/[R_F + \beta_{\Delta S}(R_M - R_F)]$,
   where $\Delta S =$ the change in outstanding equity (market value).

   e) $\beta_{\Delta S} = \beta_i \left(\dfrac{\Delta I - t\Delta B}{\Delta I - \Delta B} \right) = 1.2 \left[\dfrac{1,000 - .4(400)}{1,000 - 400} \right] = 1.68$

   f) $\Delta S = \$134.40/[.14 + 1.68(.19 - .14)] = \$600$

4. Determination of change in firm value:

   $$\Delta V = \Delta B + \Delta S = \$400 + \$600 = \$1,000.$$

5. Conclusion:

   $$\Delta V = \Delta I = \$1,000.$$

The value of the issued securities would total $1,000, equaling the cost of the investment; this demonstrates the internal consistency of the hurdle rate formulation. If individual investments are valued separately, that is, if the VAP holds, Eq. (6A.2) defines the required returns on investments under CAPM conditions. Only by accepting investments that generate an after-tax return of RADR or greater will the firm maintain its value.

DETERMINING THE CAPITAL BUDGET

Using project-specific RADRs simplifies determination of the capital budget. Project NPVs, based on their appropriate RADRs, determine the relative attractiveness of the firm's investments. The sum of the positive NPV investments is the capital budget. As straightforward as it sounds, this result is a complete reformulation of the capital budgeting process. In the sections that follow, we will examine the steps in the capital budgeting process through the use of geometric figures. Then we will discuss how this process differs from the traditional cost of capital model.

The Hurdle Rate Surface

Equation (6A.2) can be rearranged to simplify explanation of the figures as follows:

$$\text{RADR}_i = R_F\left(1 - t\frac{\Delta B}{\Delta I}\right) + \beta_i(R_M - R_F)\left(1 - t\frac{\Delta B}{\Delta I}\right). \qquad (6A.2a)$$

From this equation, a three-dimensional picture of the hurdle-rate surface is developed in which a project's RADR increases as a function of its risk (β_i) and decreases as a function of leverage $(\Delta B/\Delta I)$. These relations are illustrated in Fig. 6A.1. Leverage can be no greater than 1; no more than 100% of any asset can be debt financed. The required return on riskless investments in projects would be $R_F(1 - t\Delta B/\Delta I)$. Riskless investments must generate a return of R_F if unleveraged (as suggested by the SML) and need to generate a return of $R_F(1 - t)$ if totally debt financed. Thus, the "riskless rate" consists of the line R_F, $R_F(1 - t)$ shown in the figure. The zero-leverage trace is found by setting $\Delta B/\Delta I = 0$, regenerating the SML (Fig. 6A.1). This shows the shortcoming of the SML alone as an RADR—it does not consider leverage.

The forward edge of the hurdle rate surface is found by setting $\Delta B/\Delta I = 1$;

$$\text{RADR}_i = [R_F + \beta_i(R_M - R_F)](1 - t). \qquad (6A.4)$$

With total debt financing, the intercept is $R_F(1 - t)$ and the slope with regard to β_i is $(R_M - R_F)(1 - t)$. The hurdle rate is less than the SML. Leverage reduces both the minimum acceptable return and the risk premium.

The three traces indicating the riskless rate R_F, $R_F(1 - t)$, the zero leverage edge (SML), and the maximum leverage edge SML$(1 - t)$ inscribe the hurdle rate surface depicted in Fig. 6A.1. The surface is theoretically unbounded in the β direction, although it can be delimited by assuming some maximum reasonable beta. At this point, the hurdle rate development is complete. However, this does not show the logical difference between the CAPM approach and the traditional cost of capital model.

The Cost of Capital Plane

To make the transition from a hurdle rate model to a capital budgeting model, something must be done to translate the hurdle rate model (which is in return-risk-leverage space) into a cost of capital model (in return-risk-budget space where $C is used to denote the total capital budget in dollars). Assuming a target debt ratio for the firm allows such a translation.

Note that the hurdle rate surface slopes downward at all points with respect to leverage ($\Delta B/\Delta I$). This slope suggests that with tax-deductible debt and perfect markets, optimum financing is all debt. This result has been

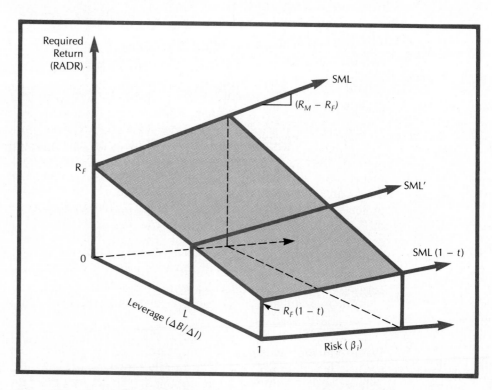

Figure 6A.1 The hurdle-rate surface.

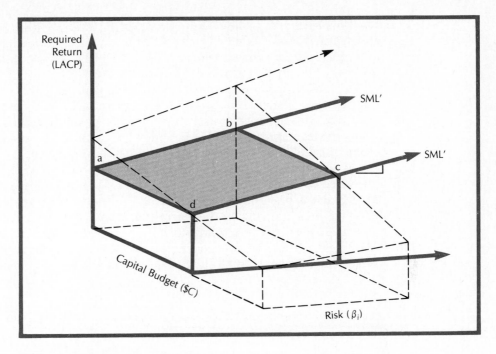

Figure 6A.2 The cost of capital plane.

reported by many theorists.† Realistically, firms cannot finance completely with debt. Lenders simply will not lend to the firm after a certain point. It is assumed that the firm will not borrow more than some maximum reasonable, or "target," amount denoted L. It is assumed that the firm finances a constant proportion (L) of its capital investments with debt; *this proportion is maintained for every investment.*

Point L is indicated on Fig. 6A.1. The hurdle rate surface is now redefined using the target leverage ratio, L. The leverage-adjusted, cost of capital plane (LACP) is defined by the equation

$$\text{RADR}_i = R_F(1 - tL) + \beta_i(R_M - R_F)(1 - tL). \qquad (6A.5)$$

The LACP is depicted in Fig. 6A.2. The leverage effect has now been incorporated into the cost of capital. The RADR for riskless investments

† The best-known of the all-debt models is found in Franco Modigliani and Merton H. Miller, "The Cost of Capital, Corporation Finance and the Theory of Investment," *American Economic Review* (June 1958), pp. 261–97, and Franco Modigliani and Merton H. Miller, "Corporate Income Taxes and the Cost of Capital: A Correction," *American Economic Review* (June 1963), pp. 433–43. The authors recognized the implausibility of a firm's financing entirely with debt and suggest the external constraint, L, used here.

$(\beta_i = 0)$ is $R_F(1 - tL)$. The premium for risk (β_i) is $(R_M - R_F)(1 - tL)$. Market capitalization rates can now be converted into project hurdle rates, including the leverage effect, by multiplying by $(1 - tL)$. The LACP is the SML multiplied by $(1 - tL)$, denoted SML'.

This cost of capital plane can now be depicted in the R_i, β_i, \$C space because, if a constant leverage ratio (L) is assumed, the $\Delta B/\Delta I$ argument is eliminated. Hurdle rates for individual projects are now functions of only risk (β_i) and the leveraged-adjusted SML', allowing geometric representation of the cost of the individual projects, $\$C_i$, and determination of the total capital budget, \$C. The LACP is perpendicular to the zero budget wall (along the line a, b) where \$C = 0, with an intercept and slope as indicated. The cost of capital plane (a, b, c, d) is also shown in Fig. 6A.2 and is replicated in subsequent figures with capital (\$C) on the diagonal axis. As long as financing continues to be available (with a constant leverage ratio), the maximum size of the capital budget, \$C, is dependent solely on the availability of acceptable investments. There is no capital rationing under CAPM assumptions.

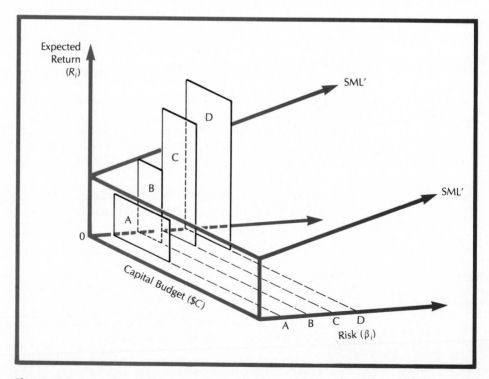

Figure 6A.3 Capital investments ranked by expected risk (β_i).

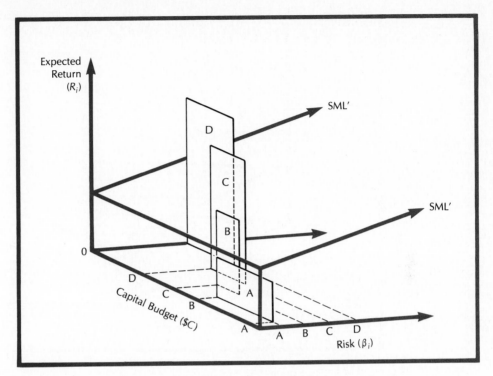

Figure 6A.4 Capital investments ranked by expected NPV.

Risk/Return Ranking of Investments

To determine the acceptability of investments graphically, we must rank them by their risk/return characteristics. Figure 6A.3 illustrates the ranking of four investments (A, B, C, and D) according to their respective betas, β_i. Note that each alternative has two dimensions—expected return (R_i) and risk (β_i)—in addition to its cost $(\$C_i)$. Alternative D promises greater returns than C, but it also requires a larger investment. Risk (β_i) is a third dimension; alternative D is aligned with a beta farther from the origin than that of C; D is riskier than C.

To illustrate the capital budgeting process using SML-VAP hurdle rates, assume that the firm is considering only projects A, B, C, and D as investments. First, the projects are ranked according to their risk-adjusted NPVs from the highest to the lowest. The project with the highest NPV is most preferred and is accepted first.

NPV refers to the difference between project return, R_i, and the RADR$_i$ for the project, multiplied by the project's cost, $\$C_i$. Project risk would be measured by beta, β_i. Figure 6A.4 shows that project D has the highest NPV,

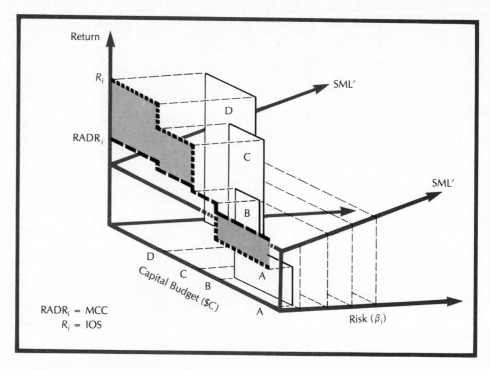

Figure 6A.5 Capital budget determination.

while project A has the lowest. The maximum possible budget (for all four investments) would be at point A measured on the $C axis. The ranking procedure, where individual investments are accepted in the order of their contribution to firm value, is consistent with the theory of capital investment generally and with recently developed CAPM-based models.

The Capital Budget

Once investment projects have been ranked by their risk-adjusted NPVs, the optimal capital budget is determined. Figure 6A.5 indicates that projects D and C have positive NPVs, project B has a zero NPV (marginally acceptable), and project A has a negative NPV. Because only project A is unacceptable, the capital budget size would be at B measured on the $C axis.

Figure 6A.5 includes several concepts similar to those in traditional capital budgeting models. The bold dashed line (RADR$_i$) represents the marginal cost of capital (MCC) for a firm considering this package of investments *under VAP assumptions*. Each investment must earn a return commensurate with its particular riskiness. The required return is lower than the SML due to leverage and the tax deductibility of interest. However, the leverage effect is constrained by the firm's maintenance of a target debt ratio.

The dotted line (R_i) represents the ranked returns on these investments. Under the assumption of investment in perpetuities, this line would also represent the IRR of these investments. Under these conditions, R_i is an investment opportunities schedule (IOS) when projects are ordered by their IRRs as traditionally depicted.

CAPM VERSUS TRADITIONAL CAPITAL BUDGETING

CAPM-based capital budgeting contains the same elements as more traditional models, but the pieces fit together differently. To understand the differences, we must review the traditional model as depicted in Fig. 6A.6.

In the traditional model, there are two components—an investment opportunity schedule (IOS) and a marginal cost of capital (MCC) schedule. The traditional IOS is a downward-sloping stairstep in which investments are ranked in descending order by their IRRs.

The traditional MCC is an upward-sloping stairstep. The explanation for the rising MCC is that the firm has to pay more and more for capital as it uses increasingly expensive sources of funds.

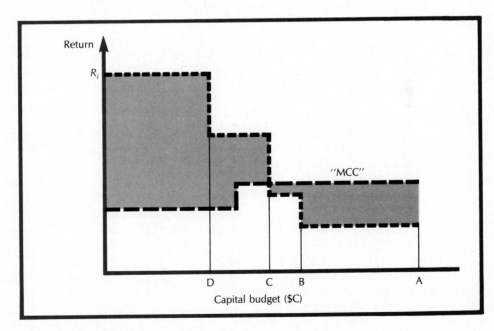

Figure 6A.6 Traditional IOS/MCC analysis.

The capital budget is determined by the intersection of the IOS and the MCC. The firm keeps investing until the marginal IRR equals the marginal cost of capital. This is an application of standard economics; expand until marginal return equals marginal cost. The same end result obtains under CAPM, but everything else is different.

The CAPM IOS ranking is not based on the IRR. It is an NPV schedule. The project with the highest IRR may not have the highest NPV because of differences in investment size. After risk adjustment, a high-IRR investment may have a negative NPV, which is easy to demonstrate mathematically. For perpetual-return investments, $IRR = R_i$, and the risk-adjusted NPV is proportional to $(R_i - RADR_i)\$C$ where the $RADR_i$ depends on β_i, as explained earlier. This definition of NPV makes it clear how the NPV could be negative even when R_i is highly positive. If a high-return project were extremely risky (high β_i), it is quite possible for $RADR_i$ to exceed R_i and the NPV to be negative.

A related yet separate difference between the two approaches is illustrated by the cost of capital lines. The hypothetical, upward-sloping MCC in Fig. 6A.6 assumes that the firm is a monopsonistic acquirer of capital, meaning that it faces a rising cost of capital schedule; the firm's capital costs increase as more funds are required from the market. Such a relationship is contrary to CAPM and VAP assumptions. Under these assumptions, the firm is a price taker with respect to new funds, and its needs are negligible compared with the total market supply of funds. In this model, the firm's marginal cost of capital is *totally unrelated to the size of the capital budget.* The cost of capital for each project is determined solely by its riskiness.

Under CAPM, both the IOS and the MCC can have almost any shape. The shape of these lines would depend entirely upon the nature of the firm's investment opportunities. Figure 6A.7 depicts the IOS-MCC picture from our earlier (Fig. 6A.5) example. Note that it has a downsloping MCC. With the CAPM hurdle rate model, the cost of capital curve can have almost any shape: unsloping, downsloping, high in the middle, or whatever. These possibilities exist because the size of the capital budget ($\$C$) does not affect the hurdle rate for individual projects.

Recognizing that capital budget size has no effect on individual hurdle rates serves to eliminate some problems that arise with the approach used in the 1960s and 1970s. The traditional approach may suggest project rejection for the wrong reasons, as in the case of project B. Also, note that in Fig. 6A.6 project C is assigned not one but two discount rates. The step in the MCC schedule near the middle of project C suggests that part of the project must earn one rate and the rest of the project must earn another. This is illogical; such an unrealistic problem does not arise with the CAPM approach as illustrated in Fig. 6A.7.

The traditional capital budgeting model has three components: (1) a declining IOS because of lower and lower (internal rates of) return as more

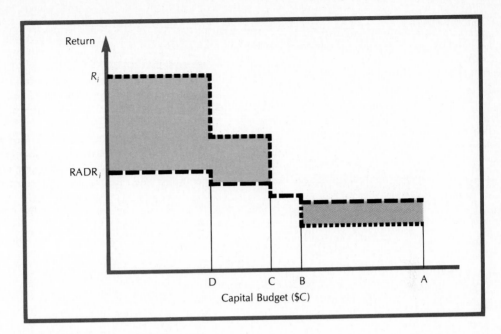

Figure 6A.7 CAPM IOS/MCC analysis.

dollars are invested, (2) an increasing MCC curve, which is a function of capital budget size, and (3) project selection based on a comparison of these two factors. The capital budget is established where the IOS intersects the MCC.

CAPM-based capital budgeting is different on all counts. The CAPM IOS is defined by the NPV, not the IRR. The CAPM cost of capital is different for each project; it is based on project risk (beta) and is unrelated to the size of the capital budget. Project selection is based on the NPV (not the IRR), which in turn is determined by market rates. The capital budget is simply the sum of the costs of the acceptable projects.

Traditional figures are inappropriate for describing CAPM-based capital budgeting. CAPM-based techniques ignore the IRR, use a different cost of capital concept, and imply a different method for determining the capital budget. The logic of the two approaches is totally different. Both expand investment until the last investment generates a return equal to the hurdle rate. In the traditional model, the cost of capital depends on the size of the capital budget. In the VAP-SML model, the MCC for the last investment will depend solely on the riskiness of that investment; the size of the capital budget is not an issue.

SUMMARY

Using the CAPM to define project-specific hurdle rates has several theoretical advantages: (1) it is not limited to average-risk investments, as is the cost of capital; (2) an investment's riskiness determines its required rate of return; (3) projects need not be evaluated with multiple hurdle rates due to steps in the MCC schedule; and (4) inappropriate and internally inconsistent hurdle rates will not be applied because of a rising MCC schedule.

There is also a practical advantage to using project-specific hurdle rates. Projects become available one at a time at different times. The firm does not evaluate all of its potential investments at the same time once a year. Under such conditions, the financial manager needs project-specific hurdle rates based on current market conditions.

All the concerns about beta that we mentioned in Appendix 4A, such as the assumption that investors think of risk as standard deviations, hard to estimate, and possibly unstable betas, are still valid. The CAPM approach is not without problems, but it has a lot to recommend it.

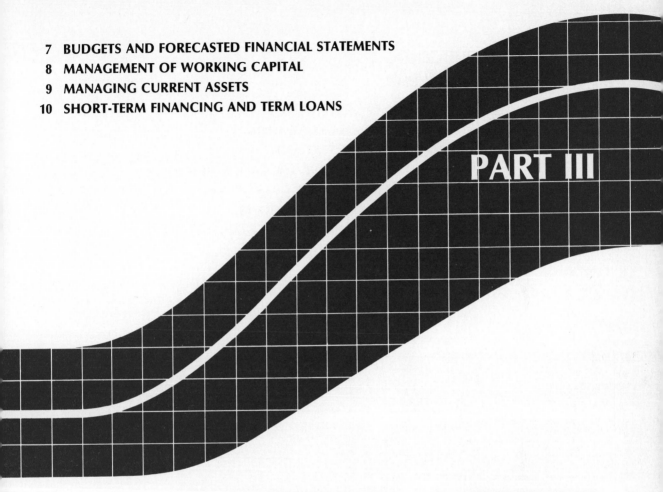

PART III

WORKING CAPITAL MANAGEMENT

- **BUDGETING**
  CASH BUDGET

- **FORECASTING STATEMENTS**
  ROLES OF *PRO FORMA* STATEMENTS
  ***PRO FORMA* INCOME STATEMENT**
  INCOME STATEMENT USING THE CASH BUDGET
  ***PRO FORMA* BALANCE SHEET**
  GAUGING UNCERTAINTY IN BUDGETS
  QUALITY OF THE ASSUMPTIONS

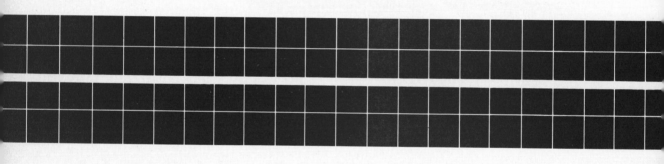

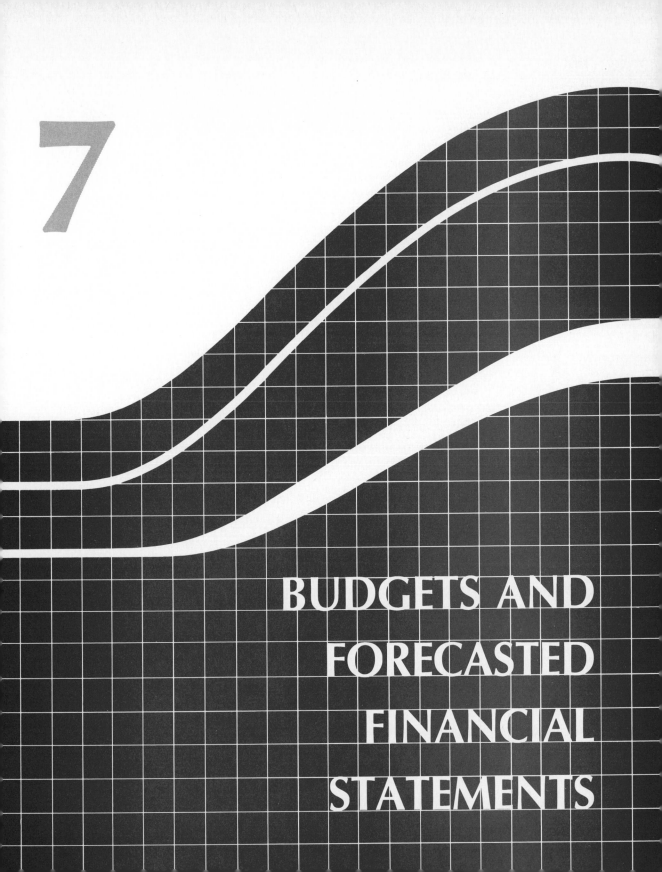

7

BUDGETS AND
FORECASTED
FINANCIAL
STATEMENTS

Financial planning is one of the most important responsibilities of financial managers in achieving the firm's objectives. Financial planning requires detailed budgets and projections of financial statements as the mechanism for looking ahead to coordinate the firm's activities and financing requirements. Budgets and financial projections provide the information needed to maintain control, and they serve as a standard of comparison for evaluating the performance of the firm. This chapter provides insight into the key elements involved in financial planning.

The most important tools in financial planning, as we have said, are the budgeting of cash flows and the projection of financial statements. A cash budget details the timing and amount of cash inflows and cash outflows, as well as the scheduling of all financing requirements. From the cash budget, managers project future financial statements showing the balances in the asset, liability, and equity accounts, as well as estimated profitability.

An understanding of the material in this chapter will provide you with

1. An overview of the financial planning and budgeting process and how it applies to the management of the firm's activities.
2. An introduction to the most widely used forecasting methods and their application to financial planning.
3. The ability to construct a cash budget and to establish a firm's financing requirements from a forecast of anticipated sales with some knowledge of the firm's production process.
4. The ability to project financial statements from the cash budget.
5. An understanding of how to interpret and use these statements and budgets for financial planning and control.

BUDGETING

Budgets are plans for allocating resources to future events. The allocation of time to the various activities a person wishes to complete and the distribution of financial resources among competing uses are examples of everyday budgeting problems. Budgets serve several functions. First, a budget is a planning device that indicates when management needs to take action on future events. A cash budget identifies the amount and timing of future financial needs. Second, a budget provides a vehicle for monitoring activities. Should actual results not conform to budget expectations, management can take corrective measures. Third, a budget provides a standard for measuring the performance of a department, a division, or individual managers. In these ways a budget is a planning, control, and evaluation aid for management.

Several types of budgets are used throughout a business organization. Physical budgets are employed for marketing products and services, allocating labor, managing the production process, controlling inventories, and maintaining physical facilities. The capital budget for new investment is an important example. Cost budgets are used for each major expense category. Cost budgets commonly found in manufacturing firms include production cost, administrative overhead, research and development costs, and financing costs. Ultimately, of course, what management is planning and budgeting for is the profitability of the firm: a profitability budget. Taken together, these budgets provide the input for preparing the cash budget.

CASH BUDGET

The **cash budget** presents a detailed plan of the cash flows that management anticipates during a particular period. Included in the cash budget are all transactions creating cash inflows or cash outflows, plus a determination of any net change in the cash position and the amount of any new financing required. The construction of the cash budget can be illustrated by the example of the Tempe Manufacturing Co., a firm with a distinct seasonal sales pattern. We will refer to this example throughout the chapter.

To prepare the cash budget, management must make a number of assumptions about future sales and operations. The resulting budget is good for this particular set of assumptions only, so one must take care in interpreting the budget if the assumptions are changed. For instance, a 10% decrease in sales may not imply a 10% decrease in all components of the firm's cash flows, because there may be differences between fixed and variable costs, as well as aspects of operations that influence cash flows.

A key assumption to be made in budget preparation is the level of sales. A six-month cash budget requires sales forecasts not only for those six months but also for the following two months. Management must provide for purchasing two months in advance of sales to be made. Table 7.1 shows Tempe's July–December cash budget with projected sales for January–February.

From experience, managers assume that sales are collected as 20% cash in the month the sale is made, 60% the first month after the sale, and the final 20% the second month after the sale. Accordingly, it is necessary to know sales from the two months preceding the budget period. Table 7.1 shows that July collections are composed of $14,000 from July sales (20% of $70,000), $36,000 from June sales (60% of $60,000), and $10,000 from May sales (20% of $50,000).

TABLE 7.1
Tempe Manufacturing Co. Cash Budget for the Six Months Ending December 31, 1984.

	May	June	July	August	September	October	November	December	January	February
Cash inflow										
Sales	$50,000	$60,000	$70,000	$90,000	$110,000	$150,000	$100,000	$70,000	$50,000	$40,000
Collections										
Cash sales (20%)			14,000	18,000	22,000	30,000	20,000	14,000		
Accounts receivable first month (60%)			36,000	42,000	54,000	66,000	90,000	60,000		
Accounts receivable second month (20%)			10,000	12,000	14,000	18,000	22,000	30,000	20,000	$14,000
Total cash inflow			$ 60,000	$ 72,000	$ 90,000	$ 114,000	$ 132,000	$ 104,000		
Cash outflow										
Purchases (60% of sales)		$54,000	$ 66,000	$ 90,000	$ 60,000	$ 42,000	$ 30,000	$ 24,000		
Payment for purchases (30 days)			54,000	66,000	90,000	60,000	42,000	30,000		
Direct labor										
First month (5% of sales)			5,500	7,500	5,000	3,500	2,500	2,000		
Second month (5% of sales)			4,500	5,500	7,500	5,000	3,500	2,500		
Salaries			3,000	3,000	3,000	3,000	3,000	3,000		
Sales expenses (5% of sales)			3,500	4,500	5,500	7,500	5,000	3,500		
Other operating expenses			2,000	2,000	2,000	2,000	2,000	2,000		
Income taxes			3,000			10,803			$23,865	
Interest expense on long-term debt			200	200	200	200	200	200		
Loan repayment										
New equipment purchase					10,000	30,000		10,000		
Total cash outflow			$ 75,700	$ 88,700	$ 123,200	$ 122,003	$ 58,200	$ 53,200		
Beginning cash balance			$ 10,000	$ 10,000	$ 10,000	$ 10,000	$ 10,000	$ 10,000		
Net monthly change (inflows − outflows)			(15,700)	(16,700)	(33,200)	(8,003)	73,800	50,800		
Less: Interest on short-term borrowing			300	460	632	970	1,060	332		
Ending cash balance (no new borrowing)			(6,000)	(7,160)	(23,832)	1,027	82,740	60,468		
Ending cash balance (after borrowing)			10,000	10,000	10,000	10,000	10,000	27,243		
Net new funds required			16,000	17,160	33,832	8,973	(72,740)	(33,225)		
Cumulative borrowing		$30,000	$ 46,000	$ 63,160	$ 96,992	$ 105,965	$ 33,225	$ 0		

Under cash outflow, purchases are matched to the forecast of future sales. Current pricing practices have been designed to create a level of purchases equal to 60% of sales. Purchases are made two months in advance of anticipated sales, but they are paid for in the month following the purchase. For instance, July purchases of $66,000 are based on 60% of the $110,000 sales forecast for September; November purchases of $30,000 represent 60% of January's $50,000 sales forecast; December purchases of $24,000 represent 60% of February's $40,000 planned sales. At any time, Tempe's inventory should represent the last 60 days' purchases. Notice that the $96,000 in inventory shown on the June 30, 1984, balance sheet (Table 7.5) is 60% of combined sales for July and August of $160,000.

As purchases are paid for in 30 days, accounts payable can be determined from purchases made in that month. The $54,000 for materials purchased in June will be paid during July. The balance sheet for June 30 will show accounts payable of $54,000. Likewise, the $24,000 of purchases during December will be shown as accounts payable on the *pro forma* balance sheet (Table 7.6) for December 31, and the amount will be paid in January.

During the 60 days from the time of purchase until sale, the production process uses direct labor to convert raw materials to finished goods. In the month that the material is purchased, direct labor costs totaling 5% of the planned sales price are incurred. The same amount is budgeted for in the second month. Consider September sales of $110,000. Purchases of $66,000 (60% of $110,000) are made in July, and $5,500 (5% of $110,000) in direct labor expenses is incurred in both July and August. The finished products are sold in September.

Certain expenses such as salaries, rent, and a multitude of other operating expenses are more closely related to the passage of time than to sales volume. Salary expense of $3,000 per month and other operating expenses of $2,000 per month are anticipated. Further, sales expenses equaling 5% of that month's sales are paid in the month the sale is made.

In order to present an example for six months, we have had to adjust the treatment of income tax payments. Federal regulations actually require corporations to estimate income tax liability for the entire year and to pay the tax in quarterly installments. For convenience, we have assumed in this example that the tax liability is calculated quarterly and paid in the month following the end of the quarter. An average income tax rate of 40% is assumed for this example. The tax of $10,803 for July, August, and September is paid in October. The opening balance sheet, dated June 30, 1984, shows an accrual of $3,000 that is paid in July. On the *pro forma* balance sheet (Table 7.6) for December 31, 1984, accrued income taxes of $23,865 will be reported. Other cash out-flows include $200 in interest on long-term debt that must be paid every month, plus loan payments of $10,000 in September and December. Also, the company plans a new equipment purchase of $30,000 in October.

The cash budget allows financial managers to establish the amount and timing of financing required. In our example, management wishes to maintain a minimum cash balance of $10,000. The beginning cash balance for each month is adjusted for the net monthly change (cash inflows minus cash outflows) less any interest due on short-term borrowing. The ending cash balance (with no new borrowing) is used to determine the amount of new borrowing that is required to bring the ending cash balance up to at least $10,000. Any excess cash is used to repay short-term borrowing. Interest of 1% per month is applied to cumulative short-term borrowings.

The influence of the seasonal sales pattern is evident in the pattern of net cash flow. Sales peak in October, cash inflows peak in November, and cash outflow is highest in September. Beginning with cumulative short-term borrowing of $30,000 on June 30, the amount of borrowing required increases to $105,965 in October to pay for purchases incurred earlier in anticipation of the peak sales season. As Tempe's purchases decline following the peak, and as accounts receivable from the peak period sales are collected, cash inflows increase, allowing the repayment of short-term borrowing and an ending cash balance of $27,243 on December 31.

FORECASTING STATEMENTS

After the cash budget has been completed, the final planning process should include two *pro forma*, or projected, financial statements, the *pro forma* income statement and the *pro forma* balance sheet. The financial manager constructs these statements at the end of the entire process because both depend upon cash budget data. Essentially, both statements summarize all the forecasts and assumptions made by management for the forecast period. These statements are the result of a point estimate. A financial manager may wish to construct a range of estimates using at least a best case, worst case, and most likely set of assumptions. This is a simple form of sensitivity analysis and it is discussed later. These forecasts follow the format of the usual financial position and income statements.

ROLES OF *PRO FORMA* STATEMENTS

Forecasting statements are used most often for planning and control. In its planning, management initially uses *pro forma* statements to evaluate plans it may adopt for the upcoming period. By incorporating effects of planned decisions into standard financial statements, management can see how these decisions will affect firm value. In the event that results differ from expectations or goals, the company can change its plans to achieve better results.

Another role of *pro forma* statements is in financial control. When they are used in conjunction with other forecasting budgets, *pro forma* financial statements can be compared after the fact to the actual outcome. Divergences of *pro formas* from the actual situation are evaluated to identify unforeseen events or to modify existing forecasting techniques.

PRO FORMA INCOME STATEMENT

The **pro forma income statement** estimates future net income based upon forecasts and assumptions about sales and costs. To do this, it incorporates much of the data contained in the cash budget, but it is based on an accrual rather than on a cash accounting basis.

The cash budget accounts for income and expenses in the period in which revenues and expenses are actually received or disbursed. The income statement, on the other hand, accounts for revenues and expenses in the period in which sales occurred. Because collections normally lag behind sales, as we have seen, the cash budget is not a good predictor of net income for any period.

Other adjustments to cash budget data must be made for noncash expenditures, such as depreciation or as an allowance for uncollectible accounts. Likewise, prepaid items, such as prepaid interest or insurance, must be apportioned to account for the part applicable to the forecast period. Once made, these adjustments on the income statement are carried over to the balance sheet to reflect these allocations on the *pro forma* income statement.

Expenditure Control

A *pro forma* income statement will permit the firm's management to develop plans for controlling expenses that might deviate from the projections in the cash budget. The projected expenses, in addition, can serve as a basis for rating manager or department performance. This is done by comparing the *pro forma* income statement with actual results at the close of the estimating period. By taking appropriate corrective measures, management can attempt to control expenditures.

Management may find it necessary to revise the various statements as time passes, taking into consideration any significant deviations from expense or revenue projections. In fact, it may anticipate different outcomes by using sensitivity analysis based upon a range of possible sales levels (lowest, most likely, and highest expected sales).

TABLE 7.2
ABC Merchandise Co.
***Pro Forma* Income Statement for the Period Ending December 31, 1984.**

Estimated sales		$1,000,000
Less: Estimated cost of goods sold		
(60% × $1,000,000)		600,000
Estimated gross margin (100% − 60%)		400,000
Less: Estimated expenses		
Selling and administrative	$100,000	
Interest	25,000	
Other expenses	15,000	140,000
Estimated net income before taxes		260,000
Less: Income taxes (40%)		104,000
Total estimated net income		$ 156,000

Use of Historical Ratios

Given the sales estimate for the period, management can now complete the income statement by use of historical ratios and trends in expenses based upon past income statements. For example, if the cost of goods sold has been stable in relation to sales, management readily can estimate the cost of goods sold or the gross profit margin. This method is used in the statement shown in Table 7.2 where the gross profit margin is 40% of sales, calculated by subtracting the cost ratio of 60%.

Unfortunately, such a simple approach frequently does not produce accurate results. Fluctuating prices caused by uncertain economic and business conditions are only one factor that can affect the relationship between sales and the cost of sales. Also, some costs, such as labor or energy costs, may be growing at rates significantly different from historical trends.

Estimating Components

A widely used method of constructing a *pro forma* income statement calls for estimating its components directly from the cash budget. Keeping in mind the distinction between cash and accrual methods of accounting, the analyst restates all data from the cash budget to reflect the costs incurred in producing and selling the product or service.

In contrast to Table 7.2, which presented the ratio approach, Table 7.3 depicts a *pro forma* income statement in which each expense is estimated directly. We have simplified it for our illustration by assuming a single-product firm. A company producing many different product lines would construct separate schedules to accumulate costs for each one.

All the expenditures requiring a cash outlay appear in the cash budget. Adjustments to the cash budget data in Table 7.1 are required in some of the categories to reflect the actual cost of goods produced and sold. For instance, depreciation is a noncash expense. It is estimated from the beginning balance sheet (June 30, 1984, shown in Table 7.5), with adjustments made for new assets acquired during the period. Likewise, income taxes are based upon forecasted earnings even though payment of the taxes will lag behind the recognition of the tax liability. Management forecasts a net income of $52,003 based upon its $590,000 sales estimate.

INCOME STATEMENT USING THE CASH BUDGET

A *pro forma* income statement is developed from the information contained in the cash budget plus information about certain noncash expenditures such as the depreciation of physical assets and the amortization of intangibles such as goodwill. The *pro forma* income statement for Tempe Manufacturing is presented in Table 7.3.

TABLE 7.3
Tempe Manufacturing Co.
***Pro Forma* Income Statement for the Six Months Ending December 31, 1984.**

Sales		$ 590,000
Cost of goods sold (60% of sales)		(354,000)
Gross operating profit		$ 236,000
Operating expenses		
Depreciation	$30,375	
Direct labor	54,500	
Salaries	18,000	
Sales expenses	29,500	
Other operating expenses	12,000	(144,375)
Net operating income		$ 91,625
Interest expense		
Long-term debt	$ 1,200	
Short-term debt	3,754	(4,954)
Earnings before taxes		$ 86,671
Income taxes (40%)		(34,668)
Net income		$ 52,003

Sales of $590,000 are the sum of the monthly sales from July through December. The cost of goods sold is calculated as 60% of sales and amounts to $354,000. The cost of goods can also be calculated as follows:

Beginning inventory (6/30)	$ 96,000
Plus: Purchases	312,000
	408,000
Less: Ending inventory (12/31)	54,000
Cost of goods sold	$354,000

Sales less the cost of goods sold yields a gross operating profit of $236,000.

Operating expenses include depreciation (a noncash expense) in the amount of $30,375. Assuming that depreciation is calculated over 20 years on a straight-line basis on an asset base of $1,200,000, the six-month income statement shows annual depreciation of $60,000, or $5,000 per month ($1,200,000/12 = $60,000 yearly; $60,000/12 = $5,000 per month). Also, depreciation on the $30,000 in new equipment to be acquired in October must be recognized. Depreciation for this equipment is calculated on the same 20-year straight-line basis, as follows: $30,000/20 years = $1,500 per year; $1,500/12 = $125 per month. The $30,375 in depreciation for the forecast period is made up of $5,000 × 6 months = $30,000, plus $125 × 3 months = $375, equals $30,375. If the financial manager had used the Accelerated Cost Recovery System (ACRS) rather than the straight line method to calculate depreciation, the result would be different than the one presented here. Straight line depreciation is used for computational simplicity. Other expenses for which cash was disbursed include direct labor, $54,500; salaries, $18,000; sales expenses, $29,500; and other operating expenses, $12,000. Operating expenses total $144,375. Subtracting total operating expenses of $144,375 from a gross operating profit of $236,000 gives a net operating income of $91,625.

Interest expense is separated from operating expenses to emphasize the influence of financing requirements. Long-term debt expense of $1,200 represents six months at $200 per month. Interest expense for short-term borrowing of $3,754 is the sum of the monthly charges from June through December. Net operating income less interest expense of $4,954 gives earnings before taxes of $86,671. Income taxes at 40% amount to $34,668, yielding an after-tax net income of $52,003 that is available for distribution to stockholders. As no provision has been made for the payment of dividends, this amount will be transferred to the retained earnings account. From the cash budget and *pro forma* income statement, the financial manager can construct the *pro forma* balance statement for the end of the forecast period.

PRO FORMA BALANCE SHEET

A *pro forma* **balance sheet** covers the same period as the *pro forma* income statement, be it a month, a quarter, or a year. The length of the period depends on management's use of the statement. For example, if the balance sheet is drawn up to provide information for obtaining a 90-day bank loan, a quarterly projection is appropriate. Normally, management makes a six-month or yearly projection as a control measure.

Use of Historical Ratios

As was true in the *pro forma* income statement, net sales is the most important input required to project the balance sheet using historical ratios. Over a period of time, many firms develop a relatively consistent relationship between sales volume and certain items of current assets and liabilities, so that they can develop a *pro forma* balance sheet based on their sales forecasts. Fixed assets can be estimated from the most recent balance sheet and the cash budget so as to account for any new acquisitions or disposals of existing fixed assets.

Assume that the X Corp. prepares a *pro forma* balance sheet based on net sales. A three-year historical review (1981–1983) reveals that current assets and liabilities vary consistently with net sales. The firm can prepare a balance sheet based on these relationships, as shown in Table 7.4. The percentages

---

TABLE 7.4
X Corp. *Pro Forma* Balance Sheet, December 31, 1984.

Current Assets		Current Liabilities	
Cash (5%)	$ 100,000	Acounts payable (12%)	$ 240,000
Receivables (15%)	300,000		
Inventory (8%)	160,000	Provision for income	
		tax (6%)	120,000
Total current assets	$ 560,000	Total current liabilities	$ 360,000
Fixed Assets		**Net Worth**	
Gross	$1,500,000	Capital stock	$ 980,000
Accrued depreciation	440,000	Retained earnings	280,000
Net fixed assets	1,060,000	Total net worth	1,260,000
Total assets	$1,620,000	Total claims	$1,620,000

are shown in parentheses. However, since all firms operate in a dynamic and changing environment, they must adapt the data to conform to current conditions.

Estimating Components

We can now construct the balance sheet for the Tempe Manufacturing Co. by using cash budget forecasts and the balance sheet dated June 30, 1984, which represents the beginning of the forecast period (Table 7.5).

The cash budget and the *pro forma* income statement give the manager all the information needed to complete the *pro forma* balance sheet. The *pro forma* balance sheet as of December 31, 1984, is presented in Table 7.6.

TABLE 7.5
Tempe Manufacturing Co.: Balance Sheet as of June 30, 1984.

Assets

Current assets		
Cash	$ 10,000	
Accounts receivable	58,000	
Inventory	96,000	
Total current assets		$ 164,000
Fixed assets		
Gross plant and equipment	$1,200,000	
Less: Accumulated depreciation	300,000	
Net plant and equipment		900,000
Land		150,000
Total assets		$1,214,000

Liabilities and Stockholders' Equity

Current liabilities		
Accounts payable	$ 54,000	
Short-term notes	70,000	
Accrued income tax	3,000	
Total current liabilities		$ 127,000
Long-term liabilities		
Long-term debt		20,000
Stockholders' equity		
Common stock ($5 per share)	$ 200,000	
Paid-in capital	600,000	
Retained earnings	267,000	
Total stockholders' equity		1,067,000
Total liabilities and stockholders' equity		$1,214,000

TABLE 7.6
Tempe Manufacturing Co.: *Pro Forma* Balance Sheet as of December 31, 1984.

Assets

Current assets		
Cash	$ 27,243	
Accounts receivable	76,000	
Inventory	54,000	
Total current assets		$ 157,243
Fixed assets		
Gross plant and equipment	$1,230,000	
Less: Accumulated depreciation	330,375	
Net plant and equipment		899,625
Land		150,000
Total assets		$1,206,868

Liabilities and Stockholders' Equity

Current liabilities		
Accounts payable	$ 24,000	
Short-term notes	20,000	
Accrued income tax	23,865	
Total current liabilities		$ 67,865
Long-term liabilities		
Long-term debt		20,000
Stockholders' equity		
Common stock ($5 per share)	$ 200,000	
Paid-in capital	600,000	
Retained earnings	319,003	
Total stockholders' equity		1,119,003
Total liabilities and stockholders' equity		$1,206,868

The first entry is the cash account. The entry is merely the $27,243 ending cash balance from the cash budget in Table 7.1. Accounts receivable of $76,000 consists of the uncollected $42,000 of December's $70,000 sales (60%), plus the uncollected $20,000 of November's $100,000 sales (20%), which is expected to be received in January, and the remaining 20% of December sales ($14,000), which is to be collected in February. An alternative method for calculating accounts receivable is as follows:

Accounts receivable (6/30/84)	$ 58,000
Plus: Credit sales (80% of $590,000)	472,000
Less: Collection of accounts	454,000
Accounts receivable (12/31/84)	$ 76,000

At any time, the value of the inventory should represent the last 60 days' purchases. Purchases of $30,000 and $24,000 for a total of $54,000 were made in November and December. Another method for determining the ending inventory is as follows:

Inventory (6/30/84)	$ 96,000
Plus: Purchases	312,000
Less: Cost of goods sold	354,000
Inventory (12/31/84)	$ 54,000

Purchases were obtained by totaling monthly purchases from the cash budget in Table 7.1. The cost of goods sold comes from the *pro forma* income statement in Table 7.3.

Acquisition or sale of fixed assets is taken from the cash budget. Depreciation expense can be found in the *pro forma* income statement. During the period being forecast, $30,000 in new equipment was acquired and added to $1,200,000, and $30,375 in depreciation expense was recognized and added to $300,000 (Table 7.5). No changes in landholdings occurred. The figure for net plant and equipment is the difference between gross plant and equipment ($1,230,000) and accumulated depreciation ($330,375), or $899,625. Another method would be as follows:

Net plant and equipment (6/30/84)	$900,000
Plus: Purchase of equipment	30,000
Less: Depreciation expense	30,375
Net plant and equipment (12/31/84)	$899,625

Total assets on December 31, 1984, are expected to be $1,206,868.

As payment for purchases is due in the following month, accounts payable should equal that month's purchases. December purchases of $24,000 are shown on the *pro forma* balance sheet as accounts payable. An alternative procedure is as follows:

Accounts payable (6/30/84)	$ 54,000
Plus: Purchases	312,000
Less: Payments	342,000
Accounts payable (12/31/84)	$ 24,000

The entry for short-term notes payable represents the net change in short-term borrowings. The $70,000 in short-term notes on the June 30 balance sheet represents $30,000 in cumulative borrowings to maintain the $10,000 minimum cash balance and an additional $40,000 in short-term borrowing being repaid with a $10,000 payment at the end of each quarter. The $20,000 in short-term debt still outstanding at the end of 1984 can be calculated as the remaining balance due on the loan. The separate line of credit for maintaining the cash balance has been repaid. Also, the balance due can be calculated as follows:

Short-term notes (6/30/84)	$ 70,000
Plus: Additional borrowing	75,965
Less: Loan repayments	125,965
Short-term notes (12/31/84)	$ 20,000

No changes were made in the $20,000 of long-term debt outstanding at the beginning and end of the forecast period.

Accrued taxes are obtained directly. The income tax liability for the last three months of the forecast period remains unpaid and should be shown as an accrual in the amount of $23,865. A different method of accounting for the tax liability is as follows:

Accrued income taxes (6/30/84)	$ 3,000
Plus: Tax liability incurred	34,668
Less: Tax payments	13,803
Accrued income taxes (12/31/84)	$23,865

Except for retained earnings, none of the stockholders' equity accounts changed during the period being forecast. Retained earnings increased by the amount of net income after taxes, $52,003. The change in retained earnings can be accounted for as follows:

Retained earnings (6/30/84)	$267,000
Plus: Net income	52,003
Less: Cash dividends	0
Retained earnings (12/31/84)	$319,003

Stockholders' equity totals $1,119,003. The sum of liabilities and stockholders' equity amounts to $1,206,868, the same as total assets.

Once the cash budget and *pro forma* financial statements are complete, management can see how the anticipated results meet the objectives of profitability and maintaining the financial integrity of the firm. We must emphasize again that *pro forma* results are based on a particular set of assumptions. If actual experience proves to be different from the forecast, or if management or economic conditions cause any of the operating variables to change, the analysis must be altered to reflect these changes. Budgeting is a dynamic rather than static process. Management should update budgets to reflect the differences between anticipated and actual experience plus make efforts to incorporate the implications of new developments on the budgets. Due to continuing revision of budgets, some financial analysts describe the process as one of creating rolling budgets.

GAUGING UNCERTAINTY IN BUDGETS

Forecasts, both short- and long-run, are requisite to operating any firm efficiently. Production and other operating budgets are necessary to ensure that plant, equipment, and personnel are available to handle the projected level of operations. Financial budgets attempt to translate these operational budgets into forecasts of cash flows in order to anticipate the financial requirements. One of the goals of the process is to determine whether cash requirements are seasonal or longer-run. Seasonal financing requirements may be met with commercial bank loans. Longer-run needs may require the firm to bridge the financial gap with long-term bonds or an equity issue.

QUALITY OF THE ASSUMPTIONS

The most important forecast item, and the one that affects all the other budget estimates, is sales. Typically, this estimate comes from a number of separate forecasts using different approaches based upon differing assumptions. Inputs used to estimate sales include internal data generated by the sales department and external data compiled from government or industry sources.

After the various estimates are generated, they are analyzed and reconciled into a reasonable sales forecast for the upcoming budget period. It is then possible to formulate the other financial statements and to determine where the firm will be *if* the sales forecast is fulfilled. The quality of the result depends to a great degree on the care and understanding exercised by the people entrusted with making the forecasting assumptions.

Use of Sensitivity Analysis

Regardless of how much painstaking care is taken in making the forecasting statements, the final product is nothing more than the most likely outcome. As anyone who has ever forecasted an athletic contest or an investment well knows, the results can be a far cry from the forecast. Two factors may be responsible for the divergence of actual results from those forecast for the business. The first is external; there may be shifts in interest rates, for example, or in the competitive structure of the industry over which the firm has no control. The second is internal and therefore susceptible to control; wages and hours, which tend to vary with changes in output, would be an example. Internal influences are quite amenable to the use of **sensitivity analysis.** This involves running computer **simulations** that vary the values of casual variables in an attempt to determine the extent to which operating results are affected by such individual changes. In this manner, the firm is able to forecast alternative levels of outlays for differing assumptions. The practice gives managers some insight into the effects of changing costs with shifts in demand for the firm's goods or services.

As an illustration, assume that three levels of sales are projected. Historical data reveal that beyond a certain level of production both wages and hours increase at a nonlinear rate as output increases at a declining rate due to lower productivity and additional payments for overtime. As output climbs, computer simulations based upon past relationships make it possible to estimate labor costs at varying levels of production. The objective is to analyze the impact of a range of labor inputs on the profitability of the firm. Thus, the firm's managers can elect to operate the business at the level that best maximizes profits, that is, assuming the demand is present for the service or product at the desired level.

Low-cost interactive computers and programs designed specifically to allow decision makers to vary forecast assumptions easily have greatly simplified the tasks of sensitivity analysis and simulation. In the past, sensitivity analysis often required management to work directly with a mathematical model of the forecast. Today modern computer programs allow the manager to make one change, say, in labor costs, and instantly receive a whole set of new forecasts and budgets that will show the impact of that change. Of course, this technology merely provides flexibility; it does not improve the quality of the forecasts.

Evaluation of Multiple-Outcomes Planning

Another method of coping with inaccurate assumptions in forecasting budgets involves assuming various sequences of events and then tracing their effects on the firm. In this approach to planning, several "what if" sequences can be developed to determine their impact on the firm's operations. For example, if interest rates are an important factor affecting the consumer's ability to buy a firm's primary product—say, motors used in filtering systems for swimming pools—it might be feasible for the company to project various interest rates and to determine their impact on pool construction. After the firm estimates the number of new swimming pools that can be built at various interest rates, it determines its share of the market in order to estimate sales. Carrying the analysis one step further, it may then be feasible to calculate the inputs required to produce at these estimated levels, allowing the manager to determine the availability and costs of both labor and materials. By working through a series of output possibilities, the manager can estimate the effects on costs of various output levels. Plans can be made to ensure adequate sources of supply or to avoid long-term commitments if there is no urgent need to make them.

Effective Forecasting

Effective budgeting and forecasting is totally dependent on the quality of the forecasts that enter the budgeting process as assumptions. Typically, forecasting is not included in the discipline of financial management. In practice, responsibility for forecasts usually falls to other departments of the firm. For example, the sales forecast comes from the marketing department, and the operating expense forecast usually comes from the cost accounting function. Errors in the forecasts used for budgeting, however, can cause a serious loss of efficiency, profitability, or control of the firm, and as the financial manager is directly responsible for maximizing the wealth of the firm's owners, he or she should be familiar at the very least with the techniques needed to develop the forecasts.

Forecasting Techniques

The ultimate test of a forecast is how close the estimate made before the fact, or *ex ante*, is to the actual result, *ex post*. This measure of quality or efficiency is, in turn, determined by three things: the model developed, the methodology employed to develop the forecast from the model, and the quality of the inputs into the model.

A **model** is a *formal relationship* between activities or economic events. For example, the statement, "Our level of sales growth is related to the growth in Gross National Product (GNP)" is not a model. The statement does not *specify* the relationship between sales and the GNP. That is, it does not answer the vital question, "What is the nature of the relationship?" Effective forecasting should be based only on models that define, as completely as possible, the formal relationship between observable events and the event being forecast.

A common error in forecasting is to neglect the development of a model altogether and to seek simply *correlation* between events without giving much thought to the economic relationships that would induce that correlation. For example, the cost of goods sold will usually exhibit excellent correlation with sales. Yet there is a tendency for the *ex post* cost of goods to break out and rise upward from *ex ante* forecasts based on this simple relation if a marked expansion in sales occurs. This could result from bottlenecks in production, from inefficiency in production caused by new employees, or from inventory or raw material shortages. If these were the only factors causing a change in the relationship between the cost of goods sold and sales, then a marked *contraction* of sales would not be expected to influence the correlation originally observed. This simple example, however, clearly indicates how important it is to model not only *why* an observed correlation between two events exists, but also *how* the conditions under which that observed relationship occurs might change.

Ideally, models of the firm's activities should not only define the relationships between activities, thereby resulting in efficient forecasts, but also be capable of sensitivity analysis and simulation. For example, a model of sales should permit simulation of sales losses due to customer cancellations resulting from poor operating efficiency or lack of product due to a strike.

The **methodology** of a forecast refers to the mathematical techniques that are used to develop the forecasts from the model. The most common methodology is **linear regression.** Regression is related to correlation in principle; in practice, regression methodology results in an equation that relates one activity—for example, sales—to other events or activities—for example, GNP, industry sales levels, imports, or personal income. Sales, in this case, is termed the *dependent variable*. That is, the methodology is based on a model that asserts that sales depend upon the other events. These other events are termed the *independent variables*. Each independent variable has a **regression coefficient** that is generated by the regression methodology. A forecast is made from a regression model by taking the values for each independent variable and multiplying each value by the variable's correlation coefficient. When this is done for each variable in the equation, the sum is the forecast level of sales.

Regression presupposes that the relationship between two events is *linear* as they are mathematically defined in the model.† The efficiency of the forecast is dependent upon the accuracy of this assumption. The single most serious potential problem in using regression is forecasting beyond the range of data used to develop the coefficients. For example, usually the model's

---

†Even if a relationship is not linear, a mathematical transformation can make it so. For example, suppose a model predicts that the outcome of event y is dependent on a power of the outcome of event x, or $y = x^b$. Then $\log y = b \log x$. Regression methodolgy would yield an *estimate* of the power b as the coefficient of the logarithm of x.

inputs are historical data. If a forecast is made outside the range of these data, there may be an error, for reasons similar to those we mentioned in discussing the relationship between the cost of goods sold and sales. Further, the relationships specified in the model must be the same in the period for the forecast as they were in the periods of the historical data. This is true not only for all the relationships specified in the model but also for all the dependent relationships that are *not* explicit in the model.

Many alternative methodologies to regression are known in management science and operations research, including linear programming, smoothing, and moving average prediction. In using any of them, the forecaster must make sure that the methodology is appropriate for the model developed.

The final determinant of the efficiency or quality of a forecast is the quality of the inputs to the forecasting model itself. A familiar term in computer science is *GIGO*: "garbage in, garbage out." No matter how elegant a model of sales is, the forecast will be in error if the forecasts of the values of the events that sales are dependent upon are wrong. As *ex ante* sales forecasts normally rely on *ex ante* forecasts, this is a major problem.

Forecasting in practice is best viewed as a combined effort of the firm's management and specialists and experts in forecasting. Management's expectations, outlooks, and targets are converted by the specialists' models into forecasts of the firm's activities. The specialists' models must be flexible and general enough to give management valid indications of the effects of changes or errors in their expectations, so that the firm can be prepared to respond effectively to changing conditions of supply and demand.

SUMMARY

Financial planning is necessary if a firm is to survive. Planning for the future requires *guessing* what the future has in store—that is it requires forecasting. In a business forecasts are made, in general, by using the familiar reporting format, the financial statement. This chapter reviewed how and why such statements are prepared.

The need for cash is common to all business firms, and management must know the firm's cash position. Because a shortage of cash may cause a firm to cease operations, management must plan for adequate cash flows as well as for total income. The cash budget is an indispensable aid because it requires a forecast of income, expenditures, and a cash balance for a future period.

Cash budgeting permits the timing of disbursements to coincide with receipts, thereby possibly avoiding some short-term borrowing that might otherwise be necessary. The cash budget is a forecast of anticipated cash receipts, expenditures, and the resulting cash balance that can be constructed for one month and then extended month by month. In addition to drawing up a monthly cash budget, firms frequently make yearly cash budgets. Although it is prudent for management to follow a cash budget for control purposes, policies must be flexible enough to permit necessary adjustments in response to changing conditions.

Pro forma statements aid the financial manager in forecasting the effects of current decisions upon future operations. Basically, *pro forma* statements summarize future plans within the familiar framework of financial position and income statements. Thus, *pro forma* statements can be used as mechanisms for financial control. Like budgets, *pro forma* statements can be compared with actual results. Differences between the expected and the actual can be identified, and corrective action may be taken if required.

When a company is contemplating external financing, *pro formas* such as cash budgets, balance sheets, and income statements are useful to test the possible effects on the firm of prospective borrowing or issuing of equity. A projected balance sheet can disclose possible weaknesses of proposed plans, such as a low current ratio. The key item in *pro forma* statements is the estimate of sales, as the level of sales most often has a direct bearing on many of the expenditures likely to be incurred by the firm during the forecast period.

QUESTIONS AND REVIEW ACTIVITIES

1. What is the most likely effect on a firm's cash balance of each of the following?
   a) An increase in sales.
   b) Stretching the payment of accounts payable.
   c) Applying relaxed credit standards to the firm's customers.
   d) The sale of excess land.
   e) A decision to carry a larger raw materials inventory.
   f) A requirement by the firm's bank that it maintain a larger cash balance.
   g) A decrease in the corporate income tax rate.
2. Why would management be interested in sensitivity analysis?
3. Why is the sales forecast basic to the entire budgeting system?
4. Explain how a downturn in a firm's sales could have the effect of generating excess cash.
5. Explain this statement: "Depreciation of fixed assets, amortization of patents, estimated uncollectibles, and other valuation accounts do not affect cash but do reduce profits."
6. Is it necessary to make cash budgets if the firm typically carries sufficient cash to handle all but extraordinary needs?
7. How would you correct an unsatisfactory cash position that is due to a volume of business that is too large relative to the firm's assets?
8. Why are bankers interested in cash budgets and *pro forma* balance sheets?
9. "Since accurate forecasts of cash are difficult, cash budgets of over a month's duration are not meaningful." Why is this attitude questionable?
10. How can *pro forma* statements be used as a means of financial control?

PROBLEMS

1. The controller of the J Corp. wants to construct a cash budget for the month ending July 31, 1984. The following information is given to him by the various departments:

   a) Cash balance on July 1, 1984, is $3,250.

   b) July sales are forecast at 800 units.

   c) Sales price per unit is $10.

   d) Fifty percent of the sales are in cash and receive a 3% discount.

   e) Credit sales are 3/15, net 30 days.

   f) Collections from previous sales should be $3,750 during July.

   g) Operating expenses will be $6,750.

   h) A $1,000 loan payment is due on July 23, 1984.

   i) Twenty percent of net sales goes toward payment of purchases.

   What is the end-of-the-month cash balance?

2. X Manufacturing Co. intends to replace an operating machine on April 1, 1984. Given the following figures, will the firm have sufficient cash on that date to cover the cost of $10,000? (Prepare monthly cash budgets for the first quarter of 1984.)

   a) Actual and forecasted sales are as follows:

November	$28,000
December	35,000
January	15,000
February	$20,000
March	25,000
April	22,000

   b) All sales are made on credit, and accounts receivable are collected entirely in the month after the sale. Purchases each month are made to satisfy next month's forecasted sales and are paid the month after incurred.

   c) The gross margin historically has been 30%, and it is expected to remain so over the next year. Other cash expenses amount to $5,000 per month.

   d) Accrued taxes must be paid January 1 and July 1 of each year.

   e) Annual mortgage interest is due on March 1.

   f) X's balance sheet as of December 31, 1983, is as follows:

Assets		Liabilities and Owner's Equity	
Cash	$ 3,000	Accounts payable	$10,500
Accounts receivable	35,000	Accrued taxes	5,400
Inventory	10,500	Mortgage note at 8%	10,000
Fixed assets	40,000	Common stock	15,000
		Retained earnings	47,600
Total	$88,500	Total	$88,500

3. A company has approached the M Bank about a $250,000 loan. The loan would be repaid in five annual installments of $50,000 each. Proceeds from the loan would be used as follows:

a) $50,000 to reduce trade payments.

b) $25,000 to increase the cash balance.

c) $50,000 to purchase inventory.

d) $25,000 to repay a bank note to the Q Bank.

e) $100,000 to purchase fixed assets

Given the current balance sheet (Table 7.7) and the uses of the loan, prepare a *pro forma* balance sheet.

TABLE 7.7
Balance Sheet as of December 31, 1983 (in 000s).

Assets		Liabilities and Net Worth	
Cash	$ 100	Notes payable—A Bank	$ 300
Receivables	500	Notes payable—B Bank	100
Inventory	600	Trade payables	200
Current assets	1,200	Accruals	200
		Current liabilities	800
Building and fixed assets	800	Term debt	500
Other assets	200	Common stock	200
		Retained earnings	700
Total assets	$2,200	Total claims	$2,200

4. Prepare a cash budget for the MJW Co. for the first quarter of 1984 from the following data.

a) Actual and forecasted sales are

December	$35,000
January	20,000
February	22,000
March	24,000
April	30,000

b) All sales are made on credit, and accounts receivable are collected in the month after sale.

c) Purchases each month are made to satisfy the next month's forecasted sales, and are paid in the month after purchase.

d) The gross profit margin is 40%.

e) Wages and salaries are paid in the month incurred:

January	$4,000
February	5,000
March	7,000

f) Rent is $1,500 a month.

g) Administrative and general expenses are $2,000 a month and paid immediately.

h) The MJW Balance Sheet as of December 31, 1983 is as follows:

Assets		Liabilities and Equity	
Cash	$ 10,000	Accounts payable	$ 12,000
Accounts receivable	35,000	Bank note 10%, due 3/31/84	25,000
Inventory	12,000	Common stock	25,000
Fixed assets	50,000	Retained earnings	45,000
Total assets	$107,000	Total claims	$107,000

i) The bank loan is due March 31, 1984, including interest for three months. Assuming the MJW Co. needs a $5,000 cash balance, will it be able to pay off the $25,000 bank loan as scheduled?

5. Using the data from problem 4 for the MJW Co. and the following information, prepare a *pro forma* income statement for the period ending March 31, 1984.

a) Depreciation is $800 per month.

b) The corporate tax rate is 20%.

6. Using the data from problems 4 and 5, prepare a *pro forma* balance sheet for March 31, 1984 including the following assumptions:

a) The firm maintains a $5,000 cash account.

b) The firm borrows enough to maintain the cash balance.

ADDITIONAL READINGS

Chambers, J. C., S. K. Mullick, and D. D. Smith. "How to Choose the Right Forecasting Technique," *Harvard Business Review* (March–April 1971), pp. 45–74.

Grinyer, P. H., and J. Wooller. *Corporate Models Today—A New Tool for Financial Management*. London: Institute of Chartered Accountants, 1978.

Pan, J., D. R. Nichols, and O. M. Joy. "Sales Forecasting Practices of Large U.S. Industrial Firms," *Financial Management* (Autumn 1977), pp. 72–77.

Pappas, J. L., and G. P. Huber. "Probabilistic Short-Term Financial Planning," *Financial Management* (Autumn 1973), pp. 36–44.

Parker, G. C., and E. L. Segura. "How to Get a Better Forecast," *Harvard Business Review* (March–April 1971), pp. 99–109.

Traenkle, J. W., E. B. Cox, and J. A. Bullard. *The Use of Financial Models in Business.* New York: Financial Executives' Research Foundation, 1975.

THE WORKING CAPITAL CYCLE
THE NET WORKING CAPITAL POSITION
THE APPROPRIATE LEVEL OF NET WORKING CAPITAL

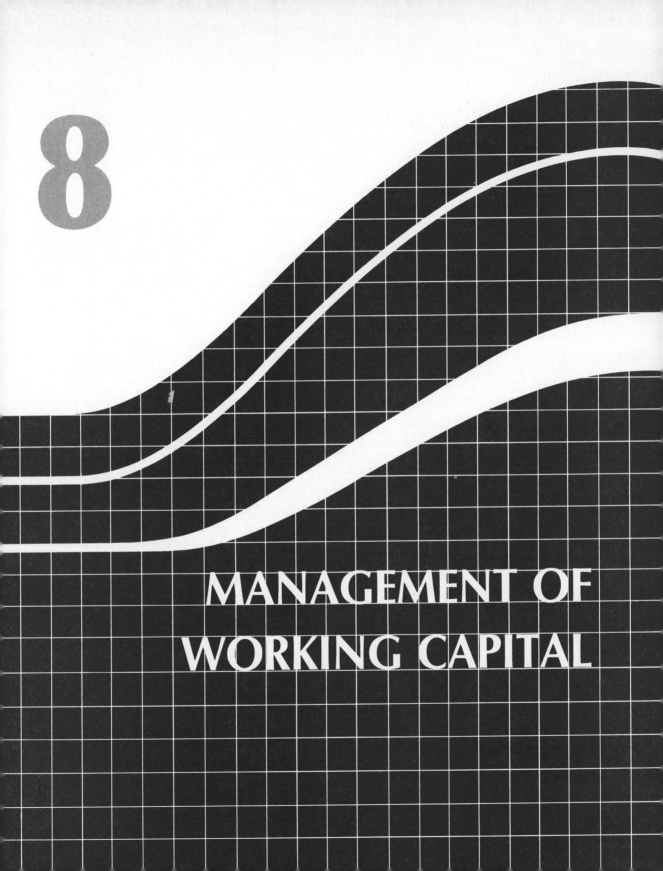

8

MANAGEMENT OF WORKING CAPITAL

Current assets of any firm consist of cash and marketable securities, accounts receivable, and inventory. These are assets that are related directly to the production cycle of the firm, and they are called **working capital. Current liability** accounts, which are used to finance current assets, consist of accounts payable, notes payable, and taxes payable. Current liability accounts are also related directly to production and sales. The difference between current assets and current liabilities is called **net working capital.**

In this chapter, we will focus on the interrelationship between the amount of investment in current assets and the level of financing provided by current liabilities. One important function of the financial manager is to determine what the net working capital position should be. Decisions regarding net working capital are important because they affect the expected return and risk incurred by the firm.

This chapter explains the risk-return principles underlying net working capital management. Careful study of it should enable you to

1. Define the following terms:
   - Working capital.
   - Current liability.
   - Current assets.
   - Net working capital.
   - Working capital cycle.
   - Term structure of interest rates.
   - Yield curve.
   - Matching principle.
   - Permanent current assets.
   - Temporary current assets.
2. Explain why current liabilities have a lower average cost than long-term funds.
3. Explain why current assets provide less return than fixed assets.
4. Know why the level of working capital affects risk in the firm.
5. Know why a low net working capital position can increase profits.
6. Distinguish between permanent and temporary current assets.
7. Understand the principle of matching the sources and uses of funds.
8. List factors that influence the level of working capital in the firm.

THE WORKING CAPITAL CYCLE

To start an enterprise, owners and lenders provide cash. Part of this cash is invested in machinery, furniture, buildings, and other fixed assets that are not sold during the normal course of business. The remainder of the cash is kept available as working capital to meet day-to-day expenses such as payment of wages, purchases of raw materials or merchandise, and other daily requirements. As production ensues, inventories of finished goods become available for sale. Cash sales provide an immediate source of cash to the firm. Credit sales result in accounts receivable, which are collected normally within 30 days after billing. When payment is received, the circular flow of working capital is complete: from cash to inventory, to accounts receivable, and back to cash. This is the **working capital cycle**, a process depicted in Fig. 8.1.

If the business is profitable, the firm's assets at the end of each cycle will be greater than the original investment. In this manner, each cycle will produce a gross profit, and the amount of net earnings for the year will depend, in part, on the number of times the cycle occurs or how often working capital is turned over. Turnover of working capital is measured by the ratio of sales to current assets. The higher the ratio, the more efficient the operations; fewer current assets are needed to support each dollar of sales.

Unfortunately, the flow of working capital through different stages of the cash cycle does not always proceed as planned. For example, if sales decline because the economy slows or consumer tastes change, or if receivables become more difficult to collect, the working capital cycle is interrupted. Profitability will decline, and the firm ultimately could suffer bankruptcy if adverse conditions prevail for some time.

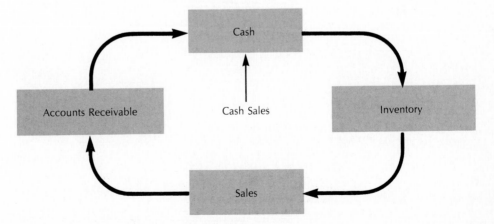

Figure 8.1 Working capital cycle.

THE NET WORKING CAPITAL POSITION

So far, we have defined net working capital as the difference between current assets and current liabilities. It is more descriptive to state that net working capital is the amount of short-term assets (current assets) that are financed by long-term funds (long-term debt or equity). In other words, the level of net working capital in the firm is a measure of liquidity. Table 8.1 shows this graphically in the conservative balance sheet of the Fuzzyworm Tractor Co. The shaded area represents the amount of long-term funds financing short-term assets.

Almost all firms prefer to maintain a positive net working capital level because of the liquidity it provides the firm. Recall the financial ratios of

TABLE 8.1
Conservative Balance Sheet—Fuzzyworm Tractor Co.

Assets	Liabilities and Equity
Current assets $ 400,000	Current liabilities $ 200,000
Net fixed assets $ 600,000	Long-term debt and equity $ 800,000
Total $1,000,000	$1,000,000

Assets			*Liabilities*	
Cash	$ 50,000		Accounts payable	$ 80,000
Marketable securities	70,000		Notes payable	60,000
Accounts receivable	100,000		Accruals	60,000
Inventory	180,000		Total current liabilities	200,000
Total current assets	400,000			
Net fixed assets	600,000		Long-term debt	200,000
Total assets	$1,000,000		Equity	600,000
			Total claims	$1,000,000

Net working capital = $200,000
Current ratio = 2.0

TABLE 8.2
Aggressive Balance Sheet—Fuzzyworm Tractor Co.

Assets	Liabilities and Equity
Current assets $ 400,000	Current liabilities $ 300,000
Net fixed assets $ 600,000	Long-term debt and equity $ 700,000
Total $1,000,000	$1,000,000

Assets		Liabilities	
Cash	$ 50,000	Accounts payable	$ 80,000
Marketable securities	70,000	Notes payable	160,000
Accounts receivable	100,000	Accruals	60,000
Inventory	180,000	Total current liabilities	300,000
Total current assets	400,000		
		Long-term debt	100,000
Net fixed assets	600,000	Equity	600,000
Total assets	$1,000,000	Total claims	$1,000,000

Net working capital = $100,000
Current ratio = 1.33

liquidity discussed in Chapter 2. There we suggested that a current ratio (current assets/current liabilities) of 2.0 was a good rule of thumb to indicate financial liquidity. There is a direct relationship between net working capital and the current ratio. As net working capital declines, so does the current ratio. To illustrate the decline in liquidity that accompanies a lower net working capital balance, consider the aggressive balance sheet for Fuzzyworm Tractor presented in Table 8.2. When the net working capital has been reduced to $100,000, the current ratio becomes 1.33, or less than the desirable current ratio of 2.0.

The balance sheet in Table 8.2 describes a more risky financial position, because even slight changes in the working capital cycle can affect liquidity significantly. For example, assume that the economy slows. The collection period of the accounts receivable begins to lengthen because firms owing money to Fuzzyworm Tractor are generating less cash and paying more slowly. Inventory increases because of fewer sales and cash flows into the firm are reduced. The creditors of Fuzzyworm Tractor still must be paid, however. Accounts payable must be kept current: taxes on prior sales remitted, payrolls met, and bank loans repaid. With the reduced level of net working capital shown in the balance sheet in Table 8.2, the generation of cash from the collection of receivables and new sales must keep pace with the cash outflows required by the current liabilities; otherwise the firm may default on its obligations. In contrast, the $200,000 of net working capital financed by long-term liabilities shown in the conservative balance sheet in Table 8.1 represents a cushion for the firm in the event of reduced cash inflows. This is so because payments on long-term debt do not have to be made every month; a greater proportion of the firm's cash can be used for payment of current liabilities.

Risk of Using Current Debt versus Long-Term Debt or Equity

The use of short-term liabilities rather than long-term debt or equity to finance assets increases the firm's risk for two reasons:

1. The cost of short-term funds is more variable than that of long-term funds.
2. There is always uncertainty about the firm's ability to replace or increase maturing short-term debt with new funds (called *rolling over* the debt).

Long-term funds, such as those raised by selling long-term bonds, carry a fixed rate of interest until the bond issue matures. Their cost is known to the firm. By contrast, the cost of short-term funds can fluctuate even over short periods. For example, in September 1981, short-term funds cost 20.5%, as measured by the prime rate, while only one year later, in September 1982, the prime rate had declined to 13.5%. Even though short-term funds are sometimes less expensive and other times more expensive than long-term funds, the *variability* of short-term rates is much greater than that of long-term rates. Figure 8.2 illustrates the relationship between the prime rate and long-term corporate bond yields over a recent five-year period, in which the prime rate is taken to represent the base cost of a firm's short-term borrowing. Because of compensating balance requirements (see Chapter 10), the actual short-term rate would probably be slightly higher.

The second risk, uncertainty regarding the firm's ability to obtain new or additional financing when current loans come due, exists because it is impossible to predict future conditions. Consumer demand may change, labor may strike, or the economy may slow. The ability to roll over or increase

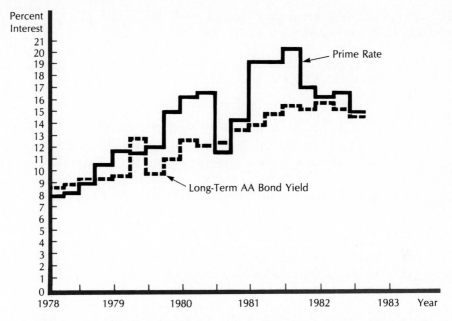

Figure 8.2 Prime rate and long-term AA bond yield (quarterly average, 1978–1982)

short-term debt becomes especially difficult during general economic declines. As cash inflows are reduced, firms tend to borrow from banks to maintain liquidity. Increased demand for cash reduces loanable balances, making funds more expensive to all firms and all but unobtainable by marginal borrowers. On the other hand, when a firm uses long-term debt, it obtains funds for a known period of time, usually several years. Even when firms must amortize long-term debt with periodic payments, as may be required under a sinking fund agreement, the payments can be planned well in advance. The firm has more flexibility in repaying or refunding long-term sources of funds than short-term ones.

The risks incurred when firms operate at a low level of net working capital can be illustrated by the many bankruptcies that occurred during the 1981–1982 recession. The number of bankruptcies in October 1982 reached 900, a level not seen since the Great Depression. One reason was the low working capital position of many firms. As the economy slowed, these firms were unable to generate enough cash to repay current liabilities; when they could not obtain additional bank loans, they went bankrupt.

The firm's risk increases as the level of net working capital is reduced. However, most firms choose to finance a majority of current assets with current liabilities because the average cost of short-term liabilities is less than that of long-term funds.

Cost of Current Liabilities versus That of Long-Term Debt or Equity

Using current liabilities to finance assets is less expensive than using long-term funds for two reasons:

1. Many current liabilities are "free."
2. Short-term borrowing is usually less costly than long-term debt or equity.

Consider the current liabilities of Fuzzyworm Tractor shown in Table 8.1. Accounts such as accrued wages, taxes, and accounts payable (which represent 70% of Fuzzyworm's current liabilities) are carried at no direct cost to the firm and therefore can be classified as free funds. Short-term bank borrowing does subject the firm to an interest cost, but the average cost of short-term funds over several years is usually lower than the cost of long-term funds. Since 1978, short-term borrowing costs have often exceeded long-term interest rates because of severe inflationary pressures in our economy. However, before 1978, the average cost of short-term funds was usually below that of long-term funds. The relationship between the cost of short-term and long-term debt is explained by the phrase *term structure of interest rates.*

Term structure of interest rates refers to the relationship between yield and time to maturity of debt instruments. It is represented by a graph called a **yield curve,** which plots the yield against the time to maturity of debt instruments having identical risk characteristics. Most yield curves are derived from yields on U.S. government securities, because they are homogeneous in all respects except time to maturity. Figure 8.3(a) depicts the usual shape of the yield curve, sloping upward to the right. Long-term securities carry a higher yield than short-term securities because (1) the lender is exposed to more uncertainty as maturity on a bond is increased, and (2) the lender anticipates some degree of inflation and expects additional compensation for expected price increases.

While the yield curve generally slopes upward, changes in economic conditions can alter the relationship between short- and long-term interest rates. Figure 8.3(b) illustrates downward-sloping yield curves, which have been common since 1978. Greater uncertainty about future economic conditions motivated most borrowers to borrow for the short term, which had the effect of increasing the cost of short-term funds.

Even when the cost of short-term debt exceeds that of long-term debt, however, the *average* cost of all current liabilities will be below that of long-term funds because, as you have seen, a large proportion of current liabilities incurs no direct interest costs. For this reason, it may be expected that using current liabilities to finance current assets will increase a firm's profitability.

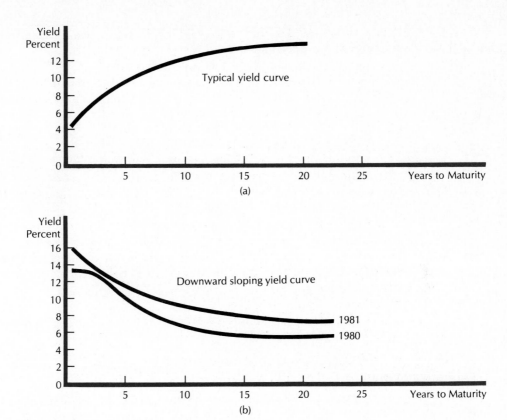

Figure 8.3 Yield curves.

Earning Power of Short-Term and Long-Term Assets

Compared to fixed assets, current assets generally provide a lower return; however, the relative importance of fixed assets varies among industries. For a manufacturing firm such as Fuzzyworm Tractor, long-term or fixed assets represent the basis of its production capability. Investment in plant and machinery is necessary in order to be able to manufacture a product. Long-term assets as the foundation of production provide the highest return to an industrial or manufacturing firm, but they are less important to service and professional industries, which base their sales on the competency and skill of their workforce. All firms require current assets to support daily operations. Cash earns nothing, yet it is required for day-to-day transactions. While the firm can invest in short-term marketable securities when it has excess cash balances, the yield is usually below that on long-term funds, as illustrated by the yield curve. Accounts receivable and inventories exist only to facilitate sales. Without fixed assets or a professional workforce to produce the products, inventory and accounts receivable are unnecessary.

The relative earning power of current assets versus fixed assets suggests why a reduction in net working capital should increase the firm's profitability. The $200,000 of net working capital in Table 8.1 represents long-term funds financing short-term assets. The cost of the funds probably exceeds the return earned by the current assets; hence profitability suffers. Shifting $100,000 of financing to short-term borrowing, as shown in Table 8.2, lowers the overall financing costs. As long as the firm can meet the principal and interest payments, its profitability will be higher under the financing arrangement depicted in Table 8.2.

As an extreme example, suppose a firm sells 10-year bonds with an interest rate of 12% and invests the cash proceeds in six-month marketable securities. Liquidity will increase but profitability will decline because the average return on marketable securities is likely to be less than the 12% cost of the bonds over the 10-year period.

Impact of the Net Working Capital Level on Firm Profitability

By combining specific data on the cost and earning power of various assets and liabilities, the financial manager can analyze how different net working capital strategies will affect firm profitability and risk. Table 8.3 presents comparative balance sheets and income statements for Fuzzyworm Tractor to illustrate very conservative to extremely aggressive net working capital positions. In all cases, total assets and EBIT are assumed to be independent of the working capital level.

The extremely aggressive position uses no long-term debt financing; all borrowing is with current liabilities. As long-term debt is substituted for current liabilities, the firm becomes more conservative in its working capital position. The increasing current ratio and net working capital indicate greater liquidity and lower risk.

It is in the income statements, however, that we can see the greater net profit and higher return on common stock that the aggressive net working capital position makes possible. Lower interest costs of current liabilities are responsible for the increase in net profit. The aggressive and extremely aggressive net working capital positions produce higher returns, assuming that sales and collections are generated as expected, but they expose the firm to a greater possibility of financial difficulty if the working capital cycle is interrupted.

TABLE 8.3
Effect of Working Capital Levels on Risk and Profitability.

	Very Conservative	Conservative	Aggressive	Extremely Aggressive
	Balance Sheet			
Assets				
Current assets	$ 400,000	$ 400,000	$ 400,000	$ 400,000
Fixed assets	600,000	600,000	600,000	600,000
Total assets	$1,000,000	$1,000,000	$1,000,000	$1,000,000
Liabilities and net worth				
Current liabilities*	$ 100,000	$ 200,000	$ 300,000	$ 400,000
Long-term debt†	300,000	200,000	100,000	0
Common stock	600,000	600,000	600,000	600,000
Total debt and equity	$1,000,000	$1,000,000	$1,000,000	$1,000,000
	Income Statement			
Sales	$ 610,000	$ 610,000	$ 610,000	$ 610,000
EBIT	120,000	120,000	120,000	120,000
Interest expense				
Current liabilities	6,000	12,000	18,000	24,000
Long-term debt	30,000	20,000	10,000	0
EBT	84,000	88,000	92,000	96,000
Taxes (50%)	42,000	44,000	46,000	48,000
Net profit	$ 42,000	$ 44,000	$ 46,000	$ 48,000
Return on common stock	7.0%	7.3%	7.7%	8.0%
Net working capital	300,000	200,000	100,000	0
Current ratio	4.0	2.0	1.33	1.00
Net working capital turnover	2.03	3.05	6.1	Undefined

* Average cost = 6%.
† Average cost = 10%.

THE APPROPRIATE LEVEL OF NET WORKING CAPITAL

So far, we have discussed only general concepts of risk and return associated with working capital management. We have not identified any specific level of working capital, because the unique characteristics of individual firms make this impossible. To illustrate the divergent approaches toward working capital in different firms, Table 8.4 presents abbreviated balance sheets for three large corporations.

Emerson Electric is a St. Louis-based manufacturer of electrical and electronic equipment for industrial, military, and consumer markets. IBM is the world's largest computer and office equipment manufacturer. APS is a publicly owned gas and electric utility company serving Arizona. All three

TABLE 8.4
Selected 1981 Balance Sheets Illustrating Various Net Working Capital Levels (millions of dollars).

	Emerson Electric	IBM	APS
Assets			
Cash	$ 21.0	$ 454.0	$ 6.8
Marketable securities	104.2	1,575.0	0
Accounts receivable	530.4	4,792.0	95.8
Inventory	872.0	2,805.0	70.6
Other	59.0	677.0	8.8
Current assets	1,586.6	10,303.0	182.0
Net fixed assets	615.1	19,283.0	3,214.8
Total assets	$2,201.7	$29,586.0	$3,396.8
Liabilities and equity			
Current liabilities	$ 651.1	$ 7,320.0	$ 295.7
Long-term liabilities	164.2	4,105.0	1,420.4
Equity	1,386.4	18,161.0	1,680.7
Total claims	$2,201.7	$29,586.0	$3,396.8
Sales	$3,429.2	$29,070.0	$ 882.2
Net working capital	935.5	2,983.0	(113.7)
Current ratio	2.437	1.408	.615
Sales/net working capital	3.666	9.745	(7.759)

firms have a long history of sound management and growth in sales and earnings; however, each has a different philosophy regarding net working capital. Emerson Electric maintains the most conservative net working capital level and current ratio of all three firms. Management is willing to forgo potentially larger profits for the safety provided by a larger amount of net working capital. IBM has chosen an aggressive net working capital position and current ratio compared to Emerson. APS can operate with a negative net working capital position, due to the predictability of its sales.

While the level of net working capital may vary widely, as Table 8.4 illustrates, all firms should consider one financial principle when determining the appropriate level of working capital for their circumstances. This is the **matching principle:** matching the maturity of sources and the uses of funds.

Matching Sources and Uses of Funds

Current assets have a lower rate of return than fixed assets, as we have seen, and current liabilities cost less than long-term funds. Current assets, by definition, are more liquid than fixed assets, and the generation of funds from current assets more nearly matches the payment cycle of current liabilities than does the generation of funds from fixed assets. These facts motivate financial managers to match the maturity structure of the source of funds to the timing of cash flows expected from the investment of those funds. That means financing current assets with current liabilities and fixed assets with long-term sources of funds.

Complete adherence to this principle, though, would result in a current ratio of 1.0 and a net working capital of zero, a level of liquidity much lower than most firms would find prudent. However, it is possible to match permanent uses of funds with long-term sources of funds and temporary requirements of funds with short-term sources of funds to achieve an acceptable degree of liquidity. To understand the application of this matching principle, it is necessary to distinguish between permanent and temporary current assets.

Permanent and temporary current assets. **Permanent current assets** represent the required investment in current assets that supports the minimum sales level of the firm for a given period. **Temporary current assets** are needed to meet seasonal or cyclical expansion of sales. Figure 8.4 illustrates the distinction between permanent and temporary current assets over a firm's operating cycle. It can be used to represent a toy manufacturer who sells 80% of his yearly production between September and November. At the beginning of the cycle in August, current assets increase as inventories expand to support anticipated sales. Inventories continue to increase during September and October, sales rise, and accounts receivable grow. The need for temporary working capital increases to a peak in November. Collection of receivables extends from October through January, and current assets decline to minimum operating levels until a subsequent cycle starts the process again.

The matching principle. Following the matching principle, the toy manufacturer would finance permanent assets (fixed assets plus permanent current assets) with long-term sources of funds, as shown in Fig. 8.4(a). Some long-term funds are used to finance current assets, producing a positive net working capital position and a current ratio above 1.0. *Aggressive* management in search of higher profits might use some short-term funds to finance permanent current assets, as shown in Fig. 8.4(b), thereby increasing the firm's risk. *Conservative* management might finance some temporary current assets with long-term sources, as shown in Fig. 8.4(c), thus reducing both the risk and the profitability of the firm.

Whether or not the firm should adopt a conservative or an aggressive net working capital policy depends on three factors:

1. *Expected volatility of sales*—The greater the uncertainty regarding cash flows from sales, the higher the level of working capital required. A utility, for instance, can maintain a lower net working capital level than an electronics firm can.

2. *Working capital cycle of the firm*—The longer the time required to convert raw materials into collected accounts receivable, the more the firm is

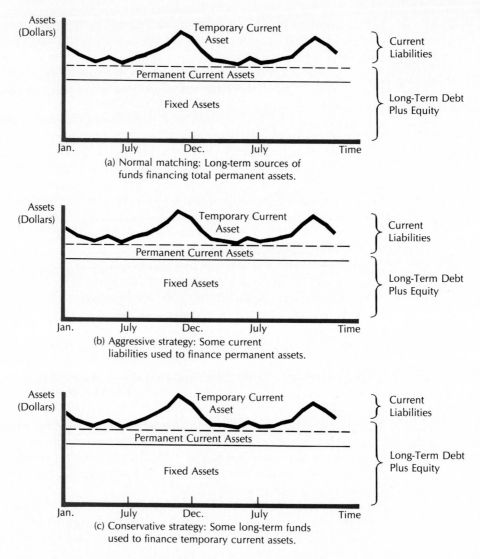

Figure 8.4 Normal, aggressive, and conservative financing of temporary and permanent assets.

exposed to disruption of the working capital cycle. A lower level of net working capital can be maintained by firms with short working capital cycles.

3. *Risk preferences of management*—Greater amounts of net working capital increase the firm's ability to meet unforeseen disruptions in the working capital cycle. The more risk averse the management, the higher the working capital balance required.

Working capital management involves many simultaneous decisions about the level and financing of current assets. While it is impossible to maintain a specific amount of net working capital over each operating cycle, most firms find it useful to follow general guidelines and principles when establishing net working capital levels. Financial managers will consider the three factors just discussed and the principle of matching sources and uses of funds when they make working capital policy decisions.

SUMMARY

Net working capital can be defined as the amount of long-term capital financing short-term assets. It is a measure of the liquidity of the firm. Determining the appropriate net working capital level requires a risk-return analysis by the financial manager. Reducing net working capital causes risk to rise because slight interruptions in the working capital cycle may prevent the firm from repaying short-term obligations. However, because short-term funds generally are cheaper than long-term debt, a lower net working capital level can increase profitability. To achieve an appropriate level of working capital, firms should consider the principle of matching sources and uses of funds. That means financing permanent current assets and fixed assets with long-term sources of funds and temporary current assets with short-term sources of funds. How closely the matching principle is followed will depend on the firm's sales volatility, working capital cycle, and risk preferences of management.

QUESTIONS AND REVIEW ACTIVITIES

1. What is the working capital cycle of the firm?
2. Explain why management of the net working capital level is more important than management of the working capital level.
3. Why is short-term debt generally less costly than long-term debt?
4. Explain why profitability will be maximized when working capital is held to a minimum value.
5. What is meant by the matching principle in working capital management?
6. Why does an increase in net working capital reduce risk?
7. Why does an increase in net working capital increase the expected return?
8. What risks are incurred by the firm when short-term debt is used to finance assets?
9. What is the relative earning power of current assets and fixed assets?
10. What factors should be considered when determining the appropriate net working capital level of a firm?

PROBLEMS

1. The current balance sheet of Teeney Weeney Airplanes (TWA), a toy manufacturer, is Table 8.5.

   Evaluate the liquidity and working capital investment of TWA's position.

TABLE 8.5
Teeney Weeney Airplanes Balance Sheet December 31, 1984.

Cash	$ 20,000	Accounts payable	$ 20,000
Accounts receivable	180,000	Taxes payable	40,000
Inventory	10,000	Short-term bank loans (8%)	70,000
Total current assets	210,000	Total current liabilities	130,000
Net fixed assets	90,000	Long-term debt (10%)	20,000
		Common stock	150,000
Total assets	$300,000	Total claims	$300,000

Sales in 1984: $750,000
EBIT in 1984: $74,000
Earnings available to common stock: $30,000.

a) Determine:
    i) Net working capital.
    ii) Working capital.
    iii) Current ratio.
    iv) Sales/net working capital.
    v) Sales/working capital.
    vi) Return on common stock.
b) Industry norms for these values are

$$\frac{\text{Sales}}{\text{Net working capital}} = 13.4$$

$$\text{Current ratio} = 2.4$$

$$\frac{\text{Sales}}{\text{Working capital}} = 6.0.$$

2. TWA, whose financial data are shown in problem 1, believes that it should increase its liquidity and is evaluating two plans. Plan G involves the sale of $50,000 of bonds at 12% interest. Plan T is a $50,000, one-year bank loan at 8%. The proceeds would be used to increase current assets in support of projected 1984 sales of $800,000 and an EBIT of $78,933. Short-term bank loans and long-term debt already on the books would remain at their current costs. Assume that current assets expand to offset the increase in the common stock account caused by retained earnings.

a) Prepare a *pro forma* income statement and balance sheet for each plan. (Assume a 50% tax rate.)

b) Calculate the net working capital, working capital, and current ratio of each alternative. Which plan has the greater effect on liquidity?

c) Which plan should produce the greatest net profit after taxes in 1984?

d) What is the difference in risk in Plan G and Plan T?

3. Booth's Tool and Die Company is just beginning business. Current plans call for a $500,000 investment in fixed assets and a $300,000 allocation for working capital. The owners are considering three financing alternatives as follows.

	X	Y	Z
Current liabilities	$300,000 at 9%	$200,000 at 6%	$100,000 at 8%
Long-term debt	100,000 at 12%	0	300,000 at 12%
Common stock	400,000	600,000	400,000

Sales are projected at $1,200,000, and EBIT should be $120,000. Taxes will be 50% of earnings.

a) For each alternative use beginning of year figures to calculate the
   i) Net working capital.
   ii) Projected sales/net working capital.
   iii) Current ratio.
   iv) Expected return on common stock.
   v) Debt/assets ratio.

b) Compare the financial risks involved in all plans.

c) Justify one plan to management.

ADDITIONAL READINGS

Aigner, D. J., and C. M. Sprenkel. "On Optimal Financing of Cyclical Cash Needs," *Journal of Finance* (December 1973), pp. 1249–53.

Bean, V. L., and R. Griffith. "Risk and Return in Working Capital Management," *Mississippi Valley Journal of Business and Economics* (Fall 1966), pp. 28–48.

Beranek, W. *Working Capital Management.* Belmont, Calif.: Wadsworth Publishers, 1966.

Budin, M., and R. J. Van Handel. "A Rule-of-Thumb Theory of Cash Holdings by Firm," *Journal of Financial and Quantitative Analysis* (March 1975), pp. 85–108.

Emery, G. W. "Optimal Liquidity Policy: A Stochastic Process Approach," *Journal of Financial Research* (Fall 1982), pp. 273–83.

Knight, W. D. "Working Capital Management—Satisfying versus Optimization," *Financial Management* (Spring 1972), pp. 33–40.

Mehta, D. R. *Working Capital Management.* Englewood Cliffs, N.J.: Prentice-Hall, 1974.

Nunn, K. "The Strategic Determinants of Working Capital: A Product Line Perspective," *Journal of Financial Research* (Fall 1981), pp. 207–19.

Petty, J. W., and D. F. Scott. "The Analysis of Corporate Liquidity," *Journal of Economics and Business* (Spring–Summer 1980), pp. 206–18.

Silvers, J. B. "Liquidity, Risk, and Duration Patterns of Corporate Financing," *Financial Management* (Autumn 1976), pp. 54–64.

Smith, K. V. *Guide to Working Capital Management.* New York: McGraw-Hill Book Company, 1979.

- **CASH MANAGEMENT**
  SHORT-TERM AND DAILY CASH MANAGEMENT DECISIONS
  THE CASH MANAGEMENT SYSTEM
  CASH COLLECTION PROCEDURES
  CASH DISBURSEMENT

- **MARKETABLE SECURITIES**
  CRITERIA FOR INVESTMENT OF EXCESS CASH BALANCES
  INSTRUMENTS CLASSIFIED AS MARKETABLE SECURITIES

- **ACCOUNTS RECEIVABLE MANAGEMENT**
  CREDIT STANDARDS
  CREDIT TERMS
  COLLECTION POLICIES
  EVALUATION OF ACCOUNTS RECEIVABLE BALANCES

- **INVENTORY MANAGEMENT**
  CLASSIFICATION OF INVENTORY
  INVENTORY COSTS
  OPTIMAL ORDER SIZE
  OPTIMAL REORDER POINT

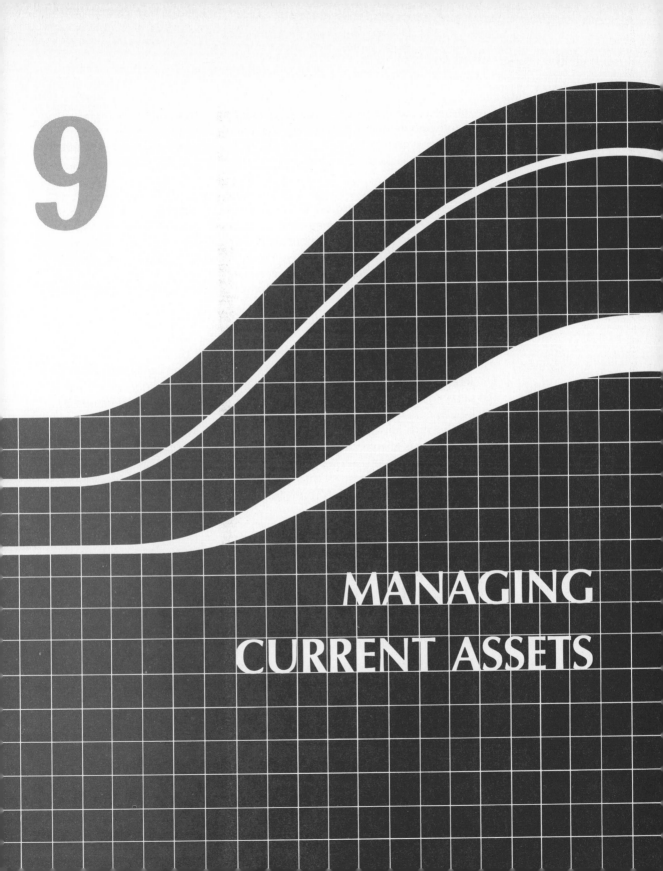

9

MANAGING
CURRENT ASSETS

The previous chapter introduced the principles of net working capital management and outlined the factors influencing a firm's net working capital investment.
This chapter presents specific techniques for managing the elements of working
capital assets: (1) cash, (2) marketable securities, (3) accounts receivable, and (4)
inventory.

Cash refers to all of a business's coin and currency plus bank demand
deposits. **Marketable securities,** also called **money market securities,** are short-
term investments made with temporary excess cash. Smaller firms may invest in
money market mutual funds or money market savings accounts instead of purchasing marketable securities directly. The interest rate earned on marketable securities or money market funds is higher than that paid by an interest-
bearing savings account; therefore most firms hold such account balances to an
absolute minimum.

Accounts receivable result from credit sales by the company. Determining
accounts receivable policy requires an analysis of the benefits from increased
credit sales and the costs of carrying higher receivables.

Inventory represents the largest investment in working capital for many firms.
Efficient inventory management is aimed at minimizing inventory costs while at
the same time avoiding production delays and potential sales losses caused by
stock-outs.

The relative importance of each working capital asset varies in different lines
of business. This chapter does not prescribe current asset levels for any particular
industry, but it does present several techniques for efficient management that can
be applied to any business. As with every financial issue, decisions about cash,
marketable securities, accounts receivable, and inventory should be analyzed in a
risk-return framework.

Careful study of this chapter should enable you to

1. Define the following terms:
   - Good funds balance.
   - Ledger balance.
   - Float.
   - Disbursement float.
   - Disbursement float balance.
   - Invoicing float.
   - Mail float.
   - Processing float.
   - Collection float.
   - Lockbox.
   - Preauthorized check.

- Wire transfer.
- Depository transfer check.
- Concentration bank account.
- Disbursement float analysis.
- Payable-through-drafts.
- Zero balance accounts.
- Controlled disbursing.
- Marketable securities.
- Credit policy.
- Credit standards.
- Credit terms.
- Credit period.
- Inventory costs.
- Economic order quantity (EOQ) model.
- Transit stock.
- Safety stock.

2. Explain several cash collection procedures that will increase cash flow.
3. Describe how a firm can control cash disbursements.
4. Be familiar with the criteria used for selecting money market securities.
5. List the common instruments of the money market.
6. Analyze the impact on profitability of a change in credit standards or credit terms.
7. Be familiar with collection efforts commonly used for overdue accounts.
8. Be familiar with the costs associated with inventory.
9. Know how to determine the optimal order quantity.
10. Know how to calculate the optimal reorder point.

CASH MANAGEMENT

Cash is essential for all businesses because it is used to acquire assets for production and to pay wages, taxes, interest, and dividends. Cash sales, the collection of accounts receivable, borrowing from banks, and the sale of stocks and bonds generate cash for the firm. A cash balance held by a firm is an investment representing funds that could be allocated to other assets. Consequently, firms seek to hold the minimum level of cash necessary to conduct daily operations. Managing cash flows and cash balances involves careful planning and the routine use of cash-expediting techniques. Here we will discuss the objectives of a cash management system, explain the importance of float, and discuss various cash-gathering and cash-disbursing techniques.

SHORT-TERM AND DAILY CASH MANAGEMENT DECISIONS

Figure 9.1 shows elements of a typical firm's cash flow. Cash balances will rise and fall daily throughout the firm's operating cycle. The cash manager must anticipate cash requirements over, say, the coming three to six months, as well as make daily decisions about the size of bank account balances and the need for short-term lending or borrowing.

Short-Term Cash Management

Short-term cash management is based on the cash budget, as described in Chapter 7. Recall that the cash budget is a forecast, usually over the next three to six months, of cash balances on a weekly or monthly basis. For

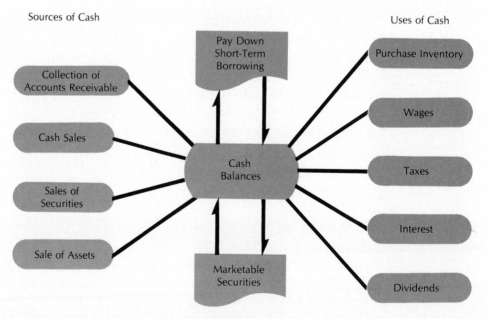

Figure 9.1 Sources and uses of cash in the firm.

months in which the cash manager projects cash deficits, arrangements must be made for a line of credit from the bank to cover the shortage. In months when excess cash is expected, the cash manager will pay down any short-term borrowing and plan short-term investments with excess cash balances. Many items in the cash budget can be forecast with relative accuracy: interest, tax, and debt payments. Other elements, such as forecasted sales and purchases, are highly uncertain in amount and timing. Unforeseen demands for cash may arise, such as major equipment repair or increased purchases of raw materials for which the cash budget makes no provision. Consequently, the cash budget can be viewed only as a general estimate of future borrowing requirements or lending opportunities. Firms should revise and update their cash budgets weekly or every other week to reflect the most current information available to them.

Daily Cash Management

Daily cash management enables the firm to pay its bills, retain a minimal level of excess cash, and obtain the highest returns with minimum risk from short-term investments. The cash manager must make sure that the firm's bank accounts have sufficient "good funds" to cover all checks expected to clear the bank on any particular day. Banks maintain two balances for every checking account. One balance, called the **good funds** or **available funds balance,** reflects cash that can be withdrawn from the account. The **ledger balance** shows deposited checks that have not yet cleared the payee's bank. Ledger balances, therefore, are not available for use by the business.

Any excess good funds over compensating balances should be withdrawn from the checking account daily and invested. (Banks frequently require firms to maintain a minimum cash amount called *compensating balances* in their checking accounts as a cost for bank services or loans. Such compensating balances are unavailable to the firm for investment and therefore are not considered part of excess balances. In some cases, firms may avoid the requirement for compensating balances by paying a cash fee to the bank.)

Each morning the firm's cash manager will analyze the firm's bank account to determine (1) the available good funds in the checking account, (2) the dollar value of deposited checks expected to clear during the day, thereby providing good funds to the firm, and (3) the dollar amount of checks already *written* by the firm that are expected to clear the account during the day, thus reducing the firm's cash balance.

After considering any compensating balance requirement, and a small extra amount to cover unforeseen demands, the cash manager then determines whether the firm will have an excess or a deficit cash position in the account. Excess cash will be invested, while deficits must be covered through the sale of investments or bank borrowing.

THE CASH MANAGEMENT SYSTEM

Cash managers should follow certain principles of good cash management:

1. Forecast cash requirements for each day and over the short term (three to six months).
2. Make sure that sufficient funds are available daily to pay all cash demands placed on the firm.
3. Develop short-term sources of funds (such as a bank line of credit) that can be used to meet unexpected cash requirements. Borrowing funds for only 24 hours is not uncommon in firms that use sophisticated cash management systems.
4. Make sure that customers' payments and other receipts are converted into cash that can be used by the firm as good funds as efficiently as possible.
5. Minimize the level of idle cash balances.

Cash is a nonearning asset. Good cash management improves a firm's profitability because it allows greater investment in productive assets. To design a cash management system, it is necessary to understand the concept of float.

The Concept of Float

In banking, the term **float** is defined as cash items in the process of collection. For example, you can write a $200 check on Thursday with $10 in your account; knowing that the check will not clear your account until Monday. As long as your payroll check will be deposited on Friday, the lack of money in your account today, *when you write the check*, does not matter. You have just taken advantage of what is called **disbursement float**—the use of funds paid someone else but not removed from your possession until your check clears your bank. The **disbursement float balance** is the difference between your checkbook balance and the bank's good funds balance for your account.

Five different kinds of float can be identified:

1. **Invoicing float**—the time it takes for a firm to bill receivables. This is a function of a company's internal accounting and the efficiency of its billing procedures.
2. **Mail float**—the time the firm's bill spends in the mail to the customer, and the time the customer's check spends in the mail back to the firm.
3. **Processing float**—the time between receipt of payment by the billing firm and deposit of the check for collection.
4. **Collection float**—the time between deposit of a check and the availability of good funds in the firm's checking account.

5. **Disbursing float**—the time that funds are available in a bank account until a check that has been written clears the account.

The first four floats are negative floats; that is, they hinder the firm's ability to turn collection items into cash. Disbursing float, on the other hand, is positive float because it reduces cash needs.

When interest rates are high, the benefits of reducing float by even one day are impressive. For example, a firm with annual credit sales of $500 million can make $1,369,863 available by reducing float by one day ($500,000,000/365 days). If the firm is borrowing at 18% (a common rate in 1981), then $246,575 before taxes in interest costs per year could be saved by the float reduction.

Good cash management attempts to reduce negative float and lengthen disbursement float. Invoicing and processing floats are directly controllable by the company, and the firm must ensure that internal procedures reduce these to a minimum. Control of mail float is out of the hands of most firms, although some firms are using delivery systems other than the U.S. Postal Service. For example, a few companies collect large payments ($500,000 and above) by courier, while some utilities are using their own personnel to deliver bills. Collection or disbursement float can be modified using cash collection and disbursement services provided primarily by the banking system.

CASH COLLECTION PROCEDURES

The following four banking mechanisms are used widely to turn collection items into cash.

Lockbox Systems

Under a **lockbox** arrangement, a firm's customers mail payments directly to a post office box instead of to the company's mailing address. A bank collects checks from the box one or more times a day, immediately depositing them for collection. Figure 9.2, which portrays the collection process with and without a lockbox, shows the advantages of using a lockbox.

Beginning with the transaction (step 1 in Fig. 9.2), the company sells a product and invoices the buyer. In the absence of a lockbox, the buyer mails the payment to the seller, who processes the payment and deposits the check in the bank. One to three days later, on average, the deposited check will become good funds to the firm.

When the seller uses a lockbox, the buyer sends the payment directly to the lockbox. Processing float is reduced, usually by at least one day, and the payment enters into the clearing system more quickly. More sophisticated banks will capture invoice data daily on magnetic tape and forward it to

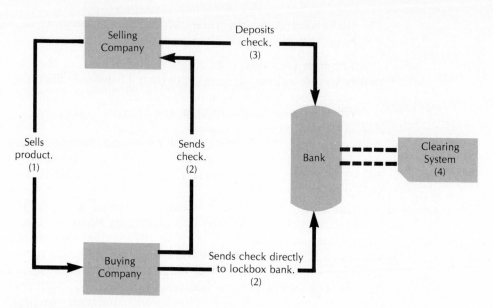

Figure 9.2 Lockbox System.

company headquarters, reducing the accounts receivable staff that the firm needs. For example, a regional lockbox bank in Phoenix, Arizona, may collect invoice information from paying customers, transmitting it daily to company headquarters in Lubbock, Texas, where posting of accounts receivable occurs.

Preauthorized Checks

While a lockbox system is important to many businesses, other firms, such as insurance, finance, leasing, and mortgage companies, may find that a **preauthorized check** (**PAC**) is a more useful method of collecting receivables. A PAC is a commercial instrument used to transfer funds between demand deposit accounts. The collecting firm is authorized to draw a check at specified intervals and in specified amounts on the customer's demand deposit account. An indemnification agreement between the bank and the individual authorizes payment of the PAC. The PAC reduces mail float and collection float and ensures that the company receives payments on a specified date.

Decentralized Collection Points

Firms with national sales can reduce mail and collection float by using decentralized collection points for receivables. The decentralized collection locations are usually lockboxes tied to demand deposit accounts with local banks. They are for collection specifically; only deposits from the lockbox are made to these accounts, and no checks are written against them. Each day, the collection bank services the lockbox and deposits checks into the collection account. At the end of each day, all good funds are withdrawn from the account and transferred to the company's concentration bank account. Transfer of the funds is accomplished by a wire transfer or depository transfer check.

Wire transfer.   **Wire transfer** is an electronic bank-to-bank transfer of funds. It is the fastest method available to move funds. Large cash balances can be transferred within an hour and made available immediately to the firm. The Federal Reserve wire system transfers funds between Federal Reserve Banks, while a commercial bank wire system transfers funds and other security data between various financial institutions.

Depository transfer check.   A **depository transfer check** (**DTC**) is another instrument for transferring funds between financial institutions. For example, the collection bank just described would complete a DTC for the daily deposits into the checking account and submit the DTC to the collection system. While the DTC is cheaper than a wire transfer, it is also slower. To reduce the time involved in using a DTC, banks generally use an automated DTC (ADTC) system. The collection bank telephones the information to the concentration bank, which prepares the DTC and credits it to the firm's account.

Decentralized collection procedures and transfer of funds to a concentration account reduce two types of float. First, mail float is reduced because the customer mails the payment to a local bank, not the seller's bank across the country. Second, and perhaps more important, the customer's check received for payment usually will be drawn on a bank in the same Federal Reserve District as the collection bank. Thus, collection float is reduced by at least one day because the check does not have to be transferred between Federal Reserve Districts. It is no surprise that many firms locate decentralized collection points near cities with Federal Reserve Banks.

Concentration Banks

The final element in the cash collection system is a **concentration bank** account. In an ideal situation only one concentration account is needed; all deposits and fund transfers flow from decentralized collection locations into the account, and all disbursements of funds by the company are made from that account. A concentration account is essential in the cash management system because it reduces excess cash balances held for precautionary reasons, thereby making forecasts of daily cash balances easier.

Cash-Gathering Techniques—Summary

Only the largest firms find it cost effective to use all possible cash-gathering techniques. Usually a lockbox is profitable only for firms with monthly receivables of over $300,000. PACs work best for utilities and for mortgage and insurance companies with fixed monthly billings. Cash concentration procedures are important to firms with dispersed operating locations, but are of no value to single-location businesses.

CASH DISBURSEMENT

Four techniques used to manage the firm's disbursement of cash include (1) disbursement float analysis, (2) payable-through drafts, (3) zero balance accounts, and (4) controlled disbursing.

Disbursement Float Analysis

Disbursement float analysis examines the time required for checks written by the firm to actually clear through the firm's account. Its objective is to provide only enough funds each day to cover checks that will clear that day. Excess funds made available in this manner can be invested in marketable securities or used in other ways by the firm.

Disbursement float analysis uses checking account data that show the time between the writing of a check and its clearing of the account. Data for the HTW Corp. in Table 9.1 can be used as an example. Notice that $4,140,000 worth of checks, representing 26% of the value of all checks written, took five days to clear the account. By waiting until the morning of the fifth day after writing the checks before depositing the $4,140,000 in the account, the firm has use of the money for four extra days. Study of a firm's disbursement float data for a few months can reveal ways to reduce daily excess cash balances to a minimum, thereby freeing funds for profitable opportunities.

Payable-Through-Drafts

A **payable-through-draft** looks like a check and works like a check. However, a draft is drawn on the issuing *company* rather than on the company's bank. The bank's main function is to act as the collection agent. The difference between a draft and a check is seen in the clearing process. When a check is received by the bank upon which it is drawn, available funds are removed automatically from the firm's checking account to pay the check. When a draft is received by the paying firm's bank, it is not paid. Rather, the bank must receive authorization from the company to remit payment. In practice, each day the bank presents drafts that it has received to the company for

TABLE 9.1
Disbursement Float Analysis (Period Ending October 1984).

Account #123456-20   Date 11/10/84

Number of Days Outstanding	Amount of Checks Paid	Number of Checks Paid	Checks Paid by Total Amount
2	$ 28,684.78	2	.18
3	762,060.48	11	4.78
4	1,653,456.92	84	10.38
5	4,141,107.10	141	26.01
6	1,409,658.36	122	8.85
7	562,237.97	39	3.53
8	1,205,903.36	42	7.57
9	1,357,390.44	63	8.52
10	320,237.00	31	2.01
11	1,352,603.23	34	8.49
12	2,272,597.68	39	14.27
13	37,477.05	10	.23
14	78,742.16	8	.49
15	2,025.00	1	.01
16	7,018.72	1	.04
17	233,509.28	3	1.46
19	20,381.11	4	1.23
21–30	275,601.05	9	1.73
31–40	561.00	1	.00
Totals	$15,917,586.49	652	100.00%

payment. The firm must return that same day all items it does not wish to pay; all drafts not returned are paid by the payable-through bank.

The draft is an excellent instrument for providing central control over several disbursing entities, because corporate headquarters can review the disbursement before it is paid. Payable-through-drafts are widely used by field representatives of large firms to pay expense account charges and by insurance companies to pay claims. As drafts are more costly to use than checks, firms must compare the costs and benefits of using a payable-through-draft system.

Zero Balance Accounts

Concentration banks and disbursement analysis can reduce excess cash balances. However, to facilitate accounting and to control disbursement, operating divisions of large firms often prefer to have their own checking accounts. The banking system provides a service that achieves both objectives; a firm can have a single master corporate checking account, but separate disbursement accounts for each division. Such an arrangement is called a **zero**

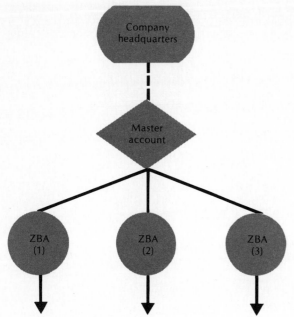

Figure 9.3 Zero balance account (ZBA) disbursing system.

balance account (**ZBA**) system. As Fig. 9.3 illustrates, the corporate head-quarters maintains a master account that is tied to the divisional ZBAs. *Zero balance* means that the account is zeroed out, or justified, at the end of each day. As checks clear during the day, a negative balance builds up in the account. At day's end, money is deducted from the master account and credited to the ZBA to restore a zero balance. The benefits of a ZBA system are that each division has accounting and control for its disbursements, while cash balances are concentrated into a single account until the firm's checks are presented for payment.

Controlled Disbursing

For several years, businesses have used **controlled disbursing** to increase their disbursement float. To institute controlled disbursing, a Phoenix business would open a checking account at a bank in a distant city, say the Boone County Bank in Columbia, Missouri. All checks used to pay the Phoenix firm's liabilities are drawn on the Boone County Bank. As Columbia, Missouri, is some distance from Phoenix, and as it is served by a different Federal Reserve District, the Phoenix company's checks will take at least two days longer to clear than they would if it had paid its bills with checks drawn on a Phoenix bank. Business publications such as the *Wall Street Journal* carry many advertisements to West Coast businesses by East Coast banks (and vice versa) offering to set up a controlled disbursement system for corporate clients.

Cash Disbursement Techniques—Summary

Managing disbursement float is essential to a cash management system. Any firm, regardless of size, can use disbursement float analysis to free excess cash balances for investment. ZBAs are advantageous only to larger firms whose operating divisions desire autonomous control over disbursements. The greatest benefit of the payable-through-draft is the cash control they provide. Controlled disbursing is cost effective only for firms with a large volume of payables. Regardless of the cash management procedures used, any system must have timely information about current bank balances and checking account activity. One popular system, Bank Link, allows corporate cash managers to accurately estimate investable cash balances early each morning and make appropriate investment decisions.

MARKETABLE SECURITIES

Maintenance of cash reserves involves a cost in the form of interest foregone on an investment. Any temporary cash balance should be used first to pay down short-term borrowing balances because the cost of borrowing will exceed the return on short-term investments. Excess cash can then be placed in short-term investments, even for only one day, to maximize the company's profitability.

CRITERIA FOR INVESTMENT OF EXCESS CASH BALANCES

The term *temporary* excess cash balances implies that in the near future the firm will again need the cash for operations. Consequently, four criteria become very important to the cash manager considering investment of these funds: (1) certainty of principal, (2) maturity, (3) liquidity, and (4) yield.

Certainty of Principal

When a firm invests in a marketable security, it is buying a debt instrument issued by either a bank, the U.S. government, or another firm. The two factors that directly influence the value of that debt instrument through time are default risk and interest rate risk.

Default risk refers to the ability of the issuer to repay the debt. Treasury bills issued by the U.S. government have very low default risk, while short-term debt securities (commercial paper) sold by large corporations entail some default risk (consider the case of W. T. Grant).

Interest rate risk refers to fluctuation in the security's price caused by changes in market interest rates. Consider the equation for the value of a bond presented in Chapter 3, where i is the market interest rate and n is the time to maturity.

$$\text{Bond value} = \sum_{t=1}^{n} \frac{\text{interest}}{(1 + i)^t} + \frac{\text{principal}}{(1 + i)^n}.$$

As the market interest rate, i, changes, the value of a debt security will change in the opposite direction. Thus, uncertainty exists about the market value of a debt security unless it is held to maturity and redeemed for par. Because price changes in short-term securities are smaller than they are for long-term issues, interest rate risk can be minimized by keeping the maturity short and holding the instrument to maturity.

Maturity

Because of the interest rate risk, longer maturities generally carry higher interest rates. Maturity dates of marketable securities purchased should coincide with the length of time funds are available. The value of the security at maturity is known with certainty (assuming no default), and the longest possible investment period will maximize returns.

Liquidity

Liquidity refers to the ease with which a company can sell a financial instrument on short notice at a price close to its market value. Treasury bills are highly liquid—their market is broad, with many participants, commission costs are low, and price is primarily a function of market interest rates. Real estate, on the other hand, is an illiquid investment characterized by a thin market, high transaction costs, and prices that are determined to a great extent by the relative bargaining position of the buyer and seller. No responsible cash manager would invest temporary cash balances in real estate.

Yield

Because marketable securities are low in risk, they generally yield less than many other securities. Safety of principal is the main criterion for excess cash investments, so yield is considered only after safety, maturity, and liquidity have been evaluated and deemed acceptable.

INSTRUMENTS CLASSIFIED AS MARKETABLE SECURITIES

Marketable securities meeting the above criteria or appropriate for investment of temporary excess cash often are called *money market securities*. The term *money market* refers not to a physical location but rather to financial assets with *less than one year to maturity*. (The term *capital market* is used to describe securities with more than one year to maturity, including common stock, bonds and mortgages.)

U.S. Treasury Bills

Treasury bills (T-bills) are the most important money market instrument. The Federal Reserve sells T-bills by auction every Monday; they have maturities of 91 days and 182 days. Once a month, 365-day T-bills also are offered. Denominations range from $10,000 to $100,000 per bill, and responsibility for repayment rests with the U.S. government.

T-bills are sold at a discount; the difference between the price paid and the value at maturity is the investor's interest. If a $10,000 T-bill with 182 days to maturity is selling for $9,428, its rate of return can be calculated using Eq. (9.1).

T-bills usually are the lowest-yielding of all marketable securities. However, they are quite liquid and virtually default free, and they can be purchased with a maturity very close to what the investor wants. To minimize transaction costs, large quantities of T-bills are best purchased directly from a Federal Reserve Bank or branch or through a government securities dealer. Smaller transactions can be handled by banks and brokers.

$$\text{Annual yield} = \frac{\$10,000 - \text{price}}{\text{price}} \times \frac{360 \text{ days}}{\text{days to maturity}} \qquad (9.1)$$

$$= \frac{\$10,000 - 9,428}{9,428} \times \frac{360 \text{ days}}{182 \text{ days}} = .1200.$$

Negotiable Certificates of Deposit

Negotiable certificates of deposit (NCDs) originate by investors depositing funds in a bank for a fixed period of time that earn a fixed and prespecified rate of interest. Banks developed NCDs to obtain needed funds when market interest rates were higher than the maximum rate that banks were allowed to pay for deposits. NCDs are issued in denominations of $100,000 or over, which exempts them from government regulations pertaining to interest rate ceilings.

NCDs bought for marketable security portfolios generally are sold by major money center banks (e.g., Citicorp, Bank of America). Smaller regional banks and savings and loan associations offer certificates of deposit (CDs), but no market exists in which these securities can be sold before they mature.

Maturities for NCDs range from 1 to 18 months, with 4 months being most common. Their yields are higher than those of T-bills for two reasons—the market is less liquid, and their risk is greater, for NCDs represent unsecured debt obligations of the issuing bank. (One only need recall the Franklin National Bank failure of 1974 to realize that the possibility of default risk exists.) The difference in yield between NCDs and T-bills will be largest when the economy is strong and banks need funds for lending. A narrower spread will exist when the demand for loans is low. In contrast to T-bills, NCDs are sold at face value; the principal plus interest is paid to the holder at maturity.

Commercial Paper

Commercial paper refers to unsecured promissory notes sold by large, financially sound companies. Because the notes are unsecured, firms with the highest credit ratings dominate the borrowing side of the commercial paper market.

Commercial paper issues are more heterogeneous than T-bills or NCDs. Borrowing corporations usually sell several million dollars worth of paper per issue to major dealers such as Salomon Brothers or Merrill Lynch. The dealers, in turn, sell the paper to investors in denominations ranging from $5,000 to $5 million.

Maturities for commercial paper range from 30 to 270 days. Paper usually is sold as bearer securities at a discount, just like T-bills; however, many corporations now are selling paper that repays the principal plus interest at maturity. The secondary market for commercial paper is not as liquid as that for T-bills or NCDs, primarily because of the heterogeneous nature of the issuing firms. Yields on commercial paper are usually similar to those on NCDs.

Banker's Acceptance

A **banker's acceptance** is a time draft (essentially a postdated check) drawn on and accepted by a bank. It is created by the seller in a foreign trade or agricultural commodity transaction to cover the cost of goods sold to the buyer. Once the time draft is accepted by a bank, the piece of paper becomes a banker's acceptance, which the bank then sells at a discount to an investor. On the due date, the investor tenders the acceptance to the bank and receives the face value of the instrument. At the same time, funds are removed from the buyer's account on which the draft is drawn. (Banker's acceptances are described in more detail in Chapters 10 and 16.)

Maturities on banker's acceptances range from 30 to 180 days, with 90 days being the norm. Because they are used to finance specific transactions, denominations are variable, ranging from $25,000 to over $1 million. They are guaranteed by the issuing bank as well as by the firm on which they are drawn. Generally, their yields are higher than those of NCDs, probably because of the wide range of denominations and the number of issuing banks. In addition, it is more difficult to sell a banker's acceptance before maturity compared to a T-bill or NCD.

Repurchase Agreements

Repurchase agreements (repos) are contracts to buy and sell back specific securities rather than being a true security. They can be described best by an example. Assume that the HTW Corp. has $1.5 million in excess cash available for three days. The company could buy T-bills and sell them three days later, or it could create a repurchase agreement with its bank as follows. HTW would agree to "purchase" $1.5 million worth of marketable securities (usually T-bills or other U.S. government securities) and "sell" the same securities back to the bank three days later for $1.5 million plus three days' interest. "Buy" and "sell" are in quotation marks because physical transfer of the securities does not take place. The entire transaction process consists of bookkeeping entries on the firm's and the bank's accounts.

Two advantages accrue from using a repo instead of buying and selling T-bills. First, the maturity can be tailored to the exact period of fund availability, from overnight to 30 days or more. Second, interest rate risk is avoided because the selling price of the securities is predetermined by agreement between the buyer and seller. Since repos are very similar to a T-bill investment, their yield is very close to but usually slightly less than T-bills.

Money Market Mutual Funds

Money market mutual funds are a product of security market ingenuity and the high interest rates of the 1970s. They did not exist in 1973, but by the spring of 1982 investment in these funds had surpassed $200 billion. Money market mutual funds pool investor dollars to buy money market securities. Their popularity may be attributed to the high interest rates on money market instruments and the access to these securities that they provide the small investor.

Characteristics of money market funds vary greatly, but they may be summarized as follows. Minimum deposits to open an account range from $200 to $1,000, and deposits into existing accounts may be as small as $100.

Interest, which is calculated daily, is a function of the returns being earned on the fund's portfolio of money market securities. Some funds invest only in one type of security, (e.g., T-bills or U.S. government issues), while others purchase a broader spectrum of money market instruments.

Liquidity is a primary reason for investing in money market funds, since withdrawals can be made daily on demand, with one-day delivery of funds. Many funds provide checks that can be used to withdraw funds, as in ordinary checking accounts. Money market mutual funds offer professional investment management, high liquidity, and low minimum transaction amounts.

Bank Cash Investment Services

Many businesses with $100,000 to $500,000 of investable balances may find that direct purchase of money market securities is not cost effective. As an alternative, many banks now offer a variety of **cash investment services** for such small businesses. Because interest rate ceilings on savings accounts were removed by the Depository Institution and Monetary Control Act of 1980, banks are allowed to offer money market savings accounts. These accounts pay a competitive rate of interest that is compounded daily, and funds may be removed at any time with no interest penalty. Transactions, however, are limited to three per month. (At this time, businesses are not allowed to establish interest-bearing checking accounts.)

Another alternative is a cash management investment plan offered by many banks that works as follows. At the beginning of each day, the company treasurer decides how much money to invest for the day and notifies the company's bank of the amount. The bank pools this amount from its clients and invests in money market securities. Funds are invested for one day only, so each morning a new investment amount must be determined. Yields on these investment plans are below T-bill rates and are usually quoted in relation to the bank's prime rate (i.e., a certain number of points below prime). Smaller companies find this procedure a low-cost way to increase the yield from excess cash balances that they cannot invest otherwise.

Marketable Securities—Summary

Marketable securities are instruments for short-term investment of excess cash balances. To maximize firm value, the cash manager should minimize cash balances and invest in relatively risk-free marketable securities whenever temporary excess cash exists. Money market instruments must meet certain criteria of safety, maturity, liquidity, and yield.

ACCOUNTS RECEIVABLE MANAGEMENT

Another working capital asset is accounts receivable, which might be seen as a less liquid, short-term investment by the firm. Proper management of accounts receivable is necessary for firms with a large proportion of credit sales to achieve maximum profitability. Accounts receivable result from credit sales made to the firm's customers. Many retail businesses have eliminated accounts receivable while still making credit sales by the exclusive use of bank credit cards. Accounts receivable are eliminated because the bank card sales tickets are deposited to the firm's bank just like a check, and funds are credited to the firm within one day. Collection risk is assumed by the bank, which charges the business 1 to 4% of each credit sale for its services.

Except for retail sales firms using bank cards, most firms carry accounts receivable balances. Investment in extending credit or in accounts receivable represents dollars that could be allocated to other earning assets. Consequently, investment in accounts receivable must meet the same criterion as any other investment decision: What is its expected contribution to shareholder wealth? The firm should be willing to increase its investment in accounts receivable as long as marginal returns exceed marginal costs. Marginal returns usually are derived from increased sales. Marginal costs include bad debts and investigation and collection expenses, as well as the cost of funds required to make the investment.

The basis of accounts receivable management is determined by the firm's **credit policy.** The three components of credit policy are (1) credit standards, (2) credit terms, and (3) collection policies. Keep in mind that the level of accounts receivable is *influenced* by the firm's credit policy, but *credit policy does not determine* that level. Current economic conditions beyond the firm's control can affect accounts receivable balances to a significant degree. Once the firm establishes its credit policy, it can make changes as conditions warrant.

CREDIT STANDARDS

Credit standards are the criteria used to determine which customers are extended credit. Whether or not a firm is granted credit will be influenced by (1) its credit rating, (2) its credit references, (3) its outstanding debt, and (4) the strength of its financial statements. In response to economic conditions or a desire to increase its market share, a firm may elect to tighten or loosen credit standards.

Loosening credit requirements should lead to increased sales because marginal accounts would be accepted. Costs associated with less stringent credit standards include (1) greater bad debt expense, (2) increased investigation and collection expenses, and (3) a greater investment in accounts receivable. A higher accounts receivable balance would result because of more credit sales and because marginal accounts take longer to pay. Tightening credit standards would have the opposite effect: decreased sales and less investment in accounts receivable.

To illustrate the marginal cost/benefit analysis of changing credit standards, we will consider the case of the Fuzzyworm Tractor Co. The firm, which maintains rather stringent credit standards, currently sells $2 million per year of tractors and components (all sales are made on credit). Investigation and

---

TABLE 9.2
Analysis of Fuzzyworm Tractor Company's Proposal to Relax Credit Standards.

I. Marginal costs of additional receivables.
   A. Determine the capital costs of additional investment in accounts receivable.
   1. Additional accounts receivable balance.

$$\frac{\text{Annual credit sales}}{360 \text{ days}} \times \text{collection period}$$

$$\frac{\$1,500,000}{360 \text{ days}} \times 50 \text{ days} = \qquad \$\ 208,333$$

   2. Actual investment in additional receivables. This step is important and sometimes overlooked. It does not cost $100 to create $100 of accounts receivable because the profit margin is included in the sales price. The additional investment required is only 80% (variable cost proportion) of sales.

Additional receivables	208,333
Times variable cost percent (80%)	.80
	166,667

   3. Capital costs of additional investment in receivables.

Actual receivables investment	166,667
Times before-tax cost of capital (%)	.20
	33,333

   B. Calculate other costs.

Increased collection and investigation costs	15,000
Bad debt costs (5% of additional sales)	75,000
Total cost of proposed credit standards change	$\ 123,333$

II. Calculate the marginal revenue of additional sales.

Marginal sales	$1,500,000
Times gross margin (20%)	.20
	300,000

III. Compare marginal revenue and marginal costs.

	300,000
	− 123,333
Net increase in profit	$\ 176,667$

collection expenses for the year total $3,000, and bad debt expenses are 1% of sales ($2,000). The average collection period is 30 days.

John Fuzzyworm, son of the company's founder, is the new head of marketing. John, a recent business administration school graduate from a large state university, believes that relaxing credit standards will increase sales by $1.5 million.

To help decide whether or not to relax credit standards, John collects the following data:

1. In performing a *marginal* analysis, we assume that fixed costs are covered, and we ignore them. *Variable* production, administration, and marketing costs are estimated to be 80% of additional sales. Thus, incremental profit is $1 - .80 = .20$ (20%) of incremental sales. Each dollar of incremental sales will contribute 20 cents to profit. (John has already determined that production capacity exists to meet the increased sales. If this were not true, the analysis would have to be modified to include all additional costs.)

2. Bad debt expenses on the additional sales are estimated to be 5%.

3. Collection and investigation costs would increase by $15,000.

4. The **opportunity cost of funds** is 20% before tax. Opportunity costs represent the return that could be earned on the next most profitable investment.

5. The average collection period of the increased sales will be 50 days.

The analysis presented in Table 9.2 indicates that the new credit policy should be adopted, assuming the estimates of underlying additional costs and benefits are correct. Explicit analysis of these changes in accounts receivable policy is necessary, as the costs of extending credit are very visible, while the benefits often are not. Similar techniques can be tailored to evaluate most accounts receivable policy decisions.

CREDIT TERMS

Credit terms refer to payment procedures to be followed by firms granted credit. Credit terms include (1) the **credit period** (length of time until payment is due), (2) any cash discount offered for early payment, and (3) interest costs for not paying within the credit period.

Credit terms are expressed in a shorthand notation such as "2/10 net 30, 18% over 30." This means that a 2% discount from the invoice amount can be taken if payment is made within 10 days (not including transportation charges and taxes). The full amount is due within 30 days. If payment is not made within 30 days, interest on the invoice amount is assessed at an 18% annual rate.

In many cases, credit terms are dictated by industry standards. If terms such as 2/10 net 30 are customary, any firm that shifts to a less liberal credit policy probably would suffer a loss of goodwill and a decline in business. Analysis of changes in credit period or cash discounts shown in Tables 9.3 and 9.4 is similar to that for relaxing credit standards.

Credit Period

Lengthening the credit period should increase sales. Whether the change is cost effective can be determined by modifying somewhat the marginal cost/ marginal revenue analysis shown in Table 9.2. The primary cost of an extended credit period would be additional investment in accounts receivable. The percentage of bad debt expenses and collection costs would increase only slightly (if at all).

For example, the Hotrock Tire Co. is considering lengthening its credit period from 30 to 45 days. Credit sales are expected to increase from $3 million to $3.5 million. The profit contribution margin is 25%; the variable cost ratio is 75%, and the before-tax cost of capital is 18%. The bad debt expense will remain at 5% of sales (an additional $25,000 on the new sales), and no additional collection costs are anticipated.

Analysis of the change in credit period from 30 to 45 days is presented in Table 9.3. The calculation of the marginal cost of additional receivables is slightly more complicated than the example in Table 9.2 because the receivables balance increases for two reasons. First, current customers will now take 45 days instead of 30 days to remit payment; thus, Hotrocks will lose the use of funds from 15 days of current credit sales. The opportunity cost of delaying collection for 15 days is the full value of 15 days of receivables less any bad debt losses times the opportunity cost of funds. The firm's cost of capital is the appropriate opportunity cost of these funds. Second, new customers who are attracted to the firm will increase yearly credit sales by $500,000, causing the accounts receivable balance after adjustment for bad debts to increase by $59,375, as shown in Part I of Table 9.3. The marginal cost of carrying these additional receivables, however, is based only on the variable cost proportion of the sale. The $59,375 of new receivables requires an investment equal to the variable cost of these sales, or $44,531, which is multiplied by the firm's cost of capital. Adding the cost of investment in additional credit sales to the opportunity cost of delayed payment by current customers, plus the bad debts, produces a marginal cost of $54,390.62 for extending the credit period.

If estimated sales, profits, and capital costs are accurate, the profit contribution from the additional sales will exceed the marginal cost by $70,609.38. But what cannot be included in this analysis is the reaction to the credit period change by other firms in the tire industry. If major competitors also lengthen their credit period, increased sales may not materialize.

TABLE 9.3
Analysis of Hotrock Tire Company's Proposal to Extend the Credit Period from 30 to 45 Days.

I. Marginal cost of additional receivables. Determine the capital costs of additional investment in accounts receivable.

$$\frac{\text{Annual credit sales} - \text{bad debts}}{360 \text{ days}} \times \text{collection period} = \text{average receivables}$$

A. Calculate the opportunity cost of extension of payment by current customers from 30 to 45 days.

$\dfrac{\$3,000,000 - 150,000}{360 \text{ days}} \times 45 \text{ days} =$	$ 356,250.00
$\dfrac{\$3,000,000 - 150,000}{360 \text{ days}} \times 30 \text{ days} =$	$-237,500.00
Total funds delayed	118,750.00
Times opportunity cost of funds	.18
Cost of delayed collections	21,375.00

B. Calculate the cost of additional receivables resulting from increased sales.

$\dfrac{\$500,000 - 25,000}{360 \text{ days}} \times 45 \text{ days} =$	59,375.00
Times variable cost percent (75%)	.75
Additional investment in receivables	44,531.00
Times cost of capital	.18
Cost of increased credit sales	8,015.62
Cost of extension of payment by current customers	21,375.00
Cost of additional bad debts	25,000.00
Total costs of policy change	$ 54,390.62

II. Compute the marginal profit from additional sales.
Additional sales × profit contribution (25%)

	$ 500,000.00
	.25
	125,000.00

III. Compare marginal benefits to marginal costs:

Profit	125,000.00
Costs	54,390.62
Increased profit	$ 70,609.38

Cash Discounts

Most firms provide cash discounts as an incentive for early payment. Whether a cash discount is cost effective can be determined by comparing the savings resulting from a decrease in accounts receivable to the revenues lost from the discount. Table 9.4 shows how International Monkey Business Machines can

TABLE 9.4
Analysis of International Monkey Business Machines Proposal to Offer a 2% Cash Discount.

I. Marginal return from reducing accounts receivable.
  A. Determine the reduction in receivables.

$$\frac{\text{Annual sales}}{360 \text{ days}} \times \text{average collection period}$$

  1. Current receivables

$$\frac{\$2,000,000}{360 \text{ days}} \times 30 \text{ days} = \qquad \$166,666.67$$

  2. Projected receivables

$$\frac{\$2,000,000}{360 \text{ days}} \times 20 \text{ days} = \qquad 111,111.11$$

  Reduction in receivables $\qquad$ 55,555.56
  B. Calculate the earning power of funds released from accounts receivable balances.
  Funds released $\qquad$ 55,555.56
  Times cost of capital (25%) $\qquad$ .25

$\qquad$ 13,888.89

II. Determine the marginal cost of allowing the discount.

  Annual credit sales times percent of customer's taking a discount times discount percent.

$$\$2,000,000 \times .50 \times .02 = \qquad 20,000.00$$

III. Compare the marginal return to the marginal cost of the discount.
  Marginal return $\qquad$ 13,888.89
  Marginal cost $\qquad$ 20,000.00
  Change in profit $\qquad$ $\$-6,111.11$

evaluate the effect of instituting a 2% cash discount for accounts paid within 10 days, as compared to its current policy of no cash discount for early payment.

Part I of Table 9.4 shows the marginal profit resulting from the decreased investment in accounts receivable. It is expected that 50% of current customers will pay within the discount period, so the average collection period will decline to 20 days (.50 × 10 days + .50 × 30 days = 20 days). The reduction in average accounts receivable means that $55,555.56 can be invested elsewhere in the firm at a yield equal to the company's cost of capital. If the company can earn 25% on invested funds, the firm would realize an additional return of $13,888.89 by reinvesting these dollars in assets other than accounts receivable.

The costs of implementing the discount are shown in Part II. If 50% of all customers take the 2% discount, revenues will decline by $20,000. As the lost revenue will be $6,111 more than the $13,888.89 increased earnings, the company should not establish a cash discount.

COLLECTION POLICIES

The task of collecting accounts receivable is usually a routine one, because most businesses pay their obligations promptly. Collection begins with the first billing sent to the customer, and in the majority of cases no further collection efforts are required. When timely payment is not received, however, the company may consider the following steps:

1. Mail a second bill indicating that the account is overdue. (Second bills frequently are on red or pink paper or have "overdue" stamped in red letters on them.)

2. Telephone the customer to say that payment is expected immediately or legal action may be taken. If time permits, a personal visit may produce the desired results.

3. Turn the account over to a collection agency or initiate legal action against the customer.

Care must be exercised when enforcing a company's collection policies. Overdue accounts can result from unintentional customer oversight or billing errors by the seller, as well as from deliberate nonpayment. Bills must be collected from good customers in a manner that retains their goodwill yet does not compromise the firm's credit procedures. Changing economic conditions also affect a company's enforcement procedures. During an economic downturn, for instance, it may be better to carry some customers for a longer than normal period in order to prevent a total loss of the account balance because of customer bankruptcy.

In the final analysis, the total cost of collection efforts should be weighed against the estimated collection receipts. Second billings or telephone reminders are relatively inexpensive, but the use of a collection agency or legal action is not; such procedures should not be considered until all others have been exhausted. If the expenses exceed the recoverable cash, the account should be written off immediately as being uncollectible.

EVALUATION OF ACCOUNTS RECEIVABLE BALANCES

Two ratios typically are used to measure the quality of accounts receivable—the *average collection period* and the *relative age* of accounts receivable balances. The average collection period, which indicates the time required to collect receivables, can be compared to the firm's stated credit period. The monthly or quarterly financial statements of most firms contain sufficient information to permit the calculation of the average collection period. More detailed data are required to construct a schedule of the age of accounts receivable. Aging of accounts receivable is accomplished by calculating the proportion of receivables that is 0 to 30 days old, 31 to 60 days old, and so on. Table 9.5 presents two months of receivables aging data for the HTW Corporation.

Comparison of the data reveals an improved collection picture for April. Although the accounts receivable balance is higher that month, no accounts are over 90 days old and the 61–90 days category has been reduced, both in dollars and as a percentage of the total. The April figures reflect a more current accounts receivable balance.

Most firms find it helpful to determine the ratio of the dollar value of bad debt expenses to credit sales, as well as to use an aging analysis. Trends in the bad debt ratio indicate whether established credit standards are being followed. Comparison of actual to predicted bad debt expenses reveals whether the credit standards are too generous or too severe. In summary, careful monitoring of accounts receivable on a monthly or more frequent basis is a necessary part of accounts receivable management.

Accounts Receivable—Summary

Accounts receivable, like marketable securities or inventory, are a short-term investment by the firm. This investment must earn a return at least equal to the before-tax cost of capital to justify credit sales. A firm's investment in

TABLE 9.5
Aging of Accounts Receivable for the HTW Corporation.

	March		April	
	Accounts Receivable	% of Total	Accounts Receivable	% of Total Sales
0–30 days	$ 75,000	26.20	$116,300	33.75
31–60 days	165,000	57.63	204,000	59.20
61–90 days	36,500	12.75	24,300	7.05
Over 90 days	9,800	3.42	0	0.00
Total accounts receivable	$286,300	100.00	$344,600	100.00

accounts receivable is influenced by its credit policy, which is defined by its (1) credit standards, (2) credit terms, and (3) collection policies.

Credit standards are the criteria used to determine which customers receive credit. Credit terms refer to the payment procedures to be followed by firms that buy on credit. Collection policies are the procedures to be followed in collecting overdue receivables. Close monitoring of accounts receivable balances is a necessary part of accounts receivable management. The average collection period, aging of accounts receivable, and bad debt expense ratio are useful measures of accounts receivable quality.

INVENTORY MANAGEMENT

The objective of inventory management is to improve profitability by minimizing the costs associated with investment in inventory. Like most financial decisions, the inventory management problem involves a trade-off between risk and return. Carrying larger inventories reduces the risk of lost sales, customer ill will, and production delays. At the same time, though, income declines, because total costs associated with holding inventory rise. Although most financial managers are not involved directly in setting inventory levels, they do have responsibility for efficient overall investment of the firm's scarce resources.

CLASSIFICATION OF INVENTORY

The classes of items held in inventory vary across industries, but for most firms inventory can be categorized as follows:

Raw Materials

Raw materials represent items used to produce a finished product. Raw material inventory must be large enough to support the production process over a production cycle, because production delays are expensive, but too large a raw material inventory ties up capital that could be invested more profitably elsewhere.

Work in Process

Work in process refers to items in various stages of the production cycle but not yet ready for sale. The size of the work-in-process inventory is primarily a function of the time required to manufacture the finished item. Large generators used by electric utility plants require more than a year of production time. In contrast, several production runs of plastic toys can be made in one day.

Finished Goods

Finished goods are completed items awaiting sale. The size of the finished goods inventory depends mainly on forecasted demand. Too little an inventory will lead to missed sales or customer ill will because of long delivery times for ordered goods. Too much inventory represents inefficient investment and increased inventory carrying costs.

Manufacturing firms will show inventory in all three classes on their balance sheets, and inventory generally will comprise 20 to 30% of their total assets. Nonmanufacturing firms (both retail and wholesale) will carry only finished goods as inventory, and their inventory may represent 35 to 50% of the firm's total assets. Regardless of the class or size of inventory, all companies incur several costs when holding it.

INVENTORY COSTS

Costs of holding inventory fall into one of three categories.

Carrying Costs

Carrying costs include all expenses incurred in holding inventory over a given time period. These include insurance, storage obsolescence, pilferage, and the cost of funds invested in the inventory. Total carrying costs *rise* when the average inventory level increases, as shown in Fig. 9.4.

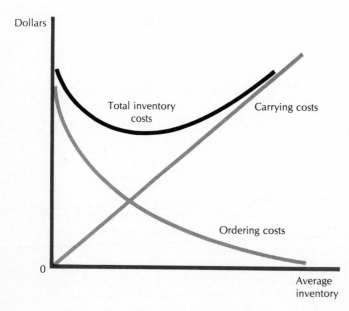

Figure 9.4 Inventory Costs.

Ordering Costs

Ordering costs are the costs related to placing and receiving an order. Included are order form preparation, receiving and handling of the shipment, and the costs of preparing the payment. In manufacturing firms, order costs include the production setup costs required to arrange equipment for a production run. Total ordering costs per time period *fall* as average inventory *rises*, as shown in Fig. 9.4.

Stock-Out Costs

Stock-out costs refer to lost sales or production down time caused by insufficient inventory. Stock-out costs can be the most difficult to determine, for few firms know when sales are lost because of insufficient inventory.

Total inventory costs are found by combining carrying costs and ordering costs, as shown in Fig. 9.4. (In basic inventory analysis, stock-out costs are assumed to be zero and are not included in the graphs.) The optimal average inventory is the one that minimizes total inventory costs. The optimal level of inventory is achieved by ordering the appropriate amount of inventory, termed the *optimal order size*, at the proper time, called the *optimal reorder point*.

OPTIMAL ORDER SIZE

A mathematical formula, the **economic order quantity (EOQ) model,** can be used to calculate the order size that minimizes total inventory costs. Simplicity of the EOQ model depends on four rather unrealistic assumptions:

1. Constant and uniform demand over the planning period.
2. Instantaneous delivery of orders.
3. Constant cost per unit regardless of the number of units ordered.
4. Constant carrying and ordering costs.

Under these assumptions, inventory size follows the sawtooth graph shown in Fig. 9.5. The model is valid for any time period as long as all variables are defined for the time period considered. For simplicity, assume the time horizon to be one year.

To determine the optimal order quantity, Q, we need to know the per unit carrying costs for one year, I, the cost of placing one order, O, and the yearly demand for the product, R. The economic order quantity is calculated with Eq. (9.2):

$$Q = \sqrt{\frac{2RO}{I}}. \qquad (9.2)$$

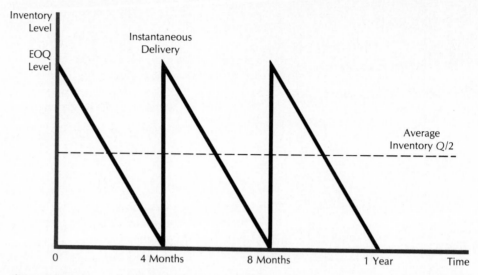

Figure 9.5 Inventory level under EOQ assumptions.

If the company orders Q units each time, it will minimize total inventory costs. The following example shows how the calculation can be used.

The large car manufacturer, Major Motors, uses 100,000 tires (R) a year for production of their Z238 sports car. The ordering cost, O, is \$135, and the per unit carrying cost, I, is \$0.75. The optimal order quantity turns out to be 6,000 units.

$$Q = \sqrt{\frac{2(100,000)(\$135)}{\$0.75}}$$

$$= 6,000 \text{ units.}$$

Because Major Motors requires 100,000 tires, it will be necessary to place 17 orders per year to satisfy the demand (100,000/6000 = 16.7).

OPTIMAL REORDER POINT

Because instantaneous delivery and constant demand are assumed in the basic EOQ model, the inventory reorder point is not considered. When we relax these assumptions to more closely approximate real world conditions, the optimal reorder point must be established using the following procedure.

As long as delivery is not instantaneous, an order must be placed so that inventory is not depleted before the new shipment arrives. This required inventory level is termed **transit stock** and represents the amount of inventory that would be used (or sold) between the time an order is placed and the time it is delivered:

Transit stock = stock used per time period × transit time.

Assume that Major Motors uses 400 tires per day (based on 250 work days in a year, 100,000/250) and that five days are required for delivery of new orders. The reorder point is reached when inventory is reduced to the transit stock level of 2,000 tires.

$$\text{Transit stock} = 400 \times 5 \text{ days}$$
$$= 2,000 \text{ tires.}$$

Uncertainty in demand can be accommodated by adding safety stock to the transit stock level. **Safety stock** refers to extra inventory held as a hedge or protection against the possibility of a stock-out. Safety stock reduces or eliminates the costs incurred by a stock-out, but it adds to carrying costs. Models for the appropriate size of safety stock can become very complex because they rely heavily on probability concepts, but while the mathematics may be complicated the idea is simple. The appropriate level of safety stock is determined by comparing the costs of carrying various levels of safety stock to the *expected* loss that would be incurred because of a stock-out.

The reorder point, then, is determined by adding transit stock to the safety stock level that the company determines to be cost effective.

$$\text{Reorder point} = \text{transit stock} + \text{safety stock.}$$

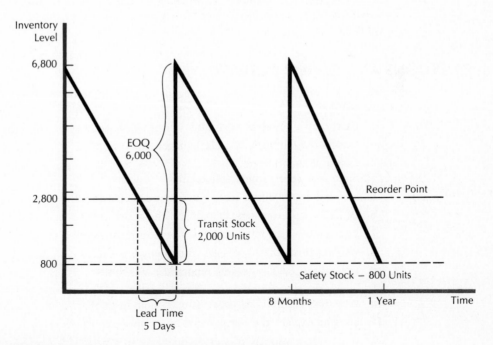

Figure 9.6 Inventory level with transit stock and safety stock.

If Major Motors decides that a safety stock of 800 tires is optimal, it will place a new order for the EOQ of 6,000 tires when inventory falls to 2,800 units.

$$\text{Reorder point} = 2,000 + 800 = 2,800.$$

Figure 9.6 depicts inventory levels over time when transit and safety stock are taken into account.

Inventory—Summary

Optimal investment in inventory should be analyzed in a risk-return framework. The risks of incurring production delays, customer ill will, or lost sales are compared to the costs incurred with carrying higher levels of inventory. These costs include carrying, ordering, and stock-out costs. Optimal average inventory is determined by calculating the optimal order size and the optimal reorder point.

SUMMARY

Cash, marketable securities, accounts receivable, and inventory are the working capital assets of a firm. Proper management of these assets enables the firm to operate on a day-to-day basis, paying its employees, owners, and creditors, collecting credit sales, and meeting customer demands for its products. We have described various techniques for efficient management of the working capital assets. The next chapter examines current liabilities, which represent a significant portion of the financing for working capital assets.

QUESTIONS AND REVIEW ACTIVITIES

1. How does efficient cash management contribute to maximizing shareholder wealth?
2. Distinguish between good funds and ledger balances in a checking account.
3. List five objectives of a cash management system.
4. Define float, indicate where float occurs, and illustrate the importance of float reduction with a numerical example.
5. List and describe four techniques that can speed up the cash collection process.
6. Describe wire transfers and explain their usefulness to a cash manager.
7. List and describe four procedures for controlling cash disbursements.
8. What criteria should be used when investing excess cash balances?
9. Evaluate U.S. T-bills and repurchase agreements as investments by the cash manager.
10. Why does commercial paper usually yield more than T-bills?
11. List and explain the components of a firm's credit policy.
12. What might you say to a credit manager in a firm with over $5 million in sales who had no bad debt losses last year?

13. What calculations enable the firm's management to monitor accounts receivable balances?

14. What procedures would you suggest for collecting overdue accounts receivable?

15. Describe and graph the behavior of costs associated with carrying inventory.

16. What assumptions must be made when using the EOQ formula?

17. Describe how the EOQ model can be modified to relax the assumptions of instantaneous delivery and uncertainty in demand.

18. Why do you believe that some people refer to overinvestment in inventory as the "graveyard of business firms?"

PROBLEMS

1. Terell Construction Co. has credit sales of $100 million per year. It is currently running an excess cash balance and believes that any additional cash should be invested in marketable securities earning 10%. If the collection float can be reduced by two days, what pretax change in annual earnings will result? (Use a 365-day year.)

2. The Foundation for Irrelevant Information has a weekly payroll of $100,000. Because of a drastic cut in its budget, it is seeking ways to save money. A proposal has been made to pay its employees biweekly instead of weekly. If the foundation can earn 10% on its invested funds, how much can it save over the next year if the change is implemented? Recalculate the savings if employees are paid monthly.

3. The Ajo Ice Co. is considering using a lockbox for its East Coast sales of $9 million. Sales occur evenly throughout the year, and it is estimated that float could be reduced by four days using a lockbox. The cost to the firm would be $6,240 per year. Released funds would be invested at 10%. (Use a 365-day year.)

   a) Should the firm use the lockbox?

   b) Assuming all estimates are correct, what is the maximum Ajo should pay for a lockbox service?

4. The HTW Corp., a Tucson company, is evaluating a cash management system proposal submitted by a large local bank. The proposal includes establishment of lockboxes in Dallas, Kansas City, San Francisco, and Tucson, which will serve as decentralized collection locations. Good funds in these accounts will be wired daily to the concentration bank in Tucson. The concentration bank will perform all posting of accounts receivable and will furnish a daily listing of all receivables transactions.

   The cost to the company for these services includes $102,000 for the four lockbox locations plus $25,000 for accounts receivable posting. It is believed that the system will reduce collection float by two days on annual credit sales of $250 million. Excess funds can be invested to earn 11%. Should the company use the cash management system? (Use a 365-day year.)

5. A firm with current sales of $1 million and a 45-day collection period is considering loosening its credit standards. The change is expected to increase sales by $500,000. However, the collection period is projected to be 50 days, and added investigation expenses may be $20,000. Bad debt expenses would probably be 3% of the

additional sales. The firm's contribution margin is 10%, and the before-tax cost of capital is 15%. (Use a 360-day year.)

a) What is the total marginal cost associated with a relaxation of the credit standards?

b) What is the marginal benefit of the policy change?

c) Should the change be implemented?

6. Because of recent increases in its outstanding accounts, Supplier Sales, Inc., is considering tightening credit standards and increasing collection efforts. Sales are $2 million a year, with accounts receivable averaging $250,000. Supplier Sales knows that such a move would hurt sales. Sales are expected to drop by $300,000, but it is believed that the new policy would enable the company to get accounts receivable down to 36 days, the industry norm, from its current level of 45 days.

   Investigation expenses would drop, but collection expenses would rise. The company estimates that the net effect would be a $10,000 increase in costs. This would be offset by a drop in bad debt expenses. Bad debts are currently 1.5% a year, but the new policy is estimated to cut this to 1%. Supplier Sales's variable cost ratio is 85%. They would like to make 25%, before taxes, on invested capital. Analyze the policy change. (Use a 360-day year.)

7. Berry's Computer Co. is considering changing its credit period from 30 to 45 days. It is believed that the change will increase credit sales by $250,000. The current credit sales level is $750,000. The company's variable cost percentage is 70%, and the before-tax cost of capital is 20%. If no other costs change, should Berry's change its credit period? (Use a 365-day year.)

8. Deer's Paints is considering changing its credit terms from net 30 to 2.5/10, net 30. It is believed that early payments motivated by the discount will reduce the average accounts receivable collection period from 35 to 24 days. Annual credit sales are expected to remain at $4,500,000. The profit margin of the firm is 20%, and the before-tax cost of capital is 15%. It has been estimated that 45% of all customers will take the discount. Should the credit terms be changed? (Use a 365-day year.)

9. Analysis establishes the following relations for inventory and storage costs:

a) Orders must be placed in multiples of 100 units.

b) Requirements for the 50-week year are 40,000 units.

c) Carrying cost per unit per year is $0.20.

d) Ordering cost per order per year is $10.

What is the EOQ? What is the optimal number of orders to be placed during the year?

10. Paige's Electric Co. produces a line of electric motors, with a volume of 50,000 units per year. Currently, it purchases the rotor shaft in quantities of 10,000 units per order. Inventory carrying costs amount to $0.50 per shaft per year, and it costs $45 to place an order. Find the EOQ and determine the yearly savings relative to the firm's current inventory system.

11. If the Quadruple-A Cleaning Supply Co. uses EOQ for inventory purchasing, how

many units of this particular item does the firm sell per year, according to the following information?

a) EOQ is 5,000 units.

b) Ordering cost per order is $12.50.

c) Carrying cost per unit per year is $0.10.

ADDITIONAL READINGS

Arnold, J., Jr. "Bankers Acceptance: A Low-Cost Financing Choice,' *Financial Executive* (July 1980), pp. 14–19.

Beranek, W. *Working Capital Management*. Belmont, Calif.: Wadsworth Publishers, 1966.

Carpenter, M. D., and J. E. Miller. "A Framework for Monitoring Accounts Receivable," *Financial Management* (Winter 1979), pp. 37–40.

"Cash Management: The New Art of Wringing More Profit from Corporate Funds," *Business Week* (March 13, 1978), pp. 62–68.

Cook, T., ed. *Instruments of the Money Market*, 4th ed. Richmond, Va.: Federal Reserve Bank of Richmond, 1977.

Dyl, E. "Another Look at the Evaluation of Investments in Accounts Receivable," *Financial Management* (Winter 1977), pp. 67–70.

Ferri, M. G., and J. P. Gaines. "A Study of Yield Spreads in the Money Market: 1971 to 1978," *Financial Management* (Autumn 1980), pp. 52–59.

Ferri, M. G., and H. D. Oberhelman. "A Study of the Management of Money Market Mutual Funds, 1975–1980," *Financial Management* (Autumn 1981), pp. 24–29.

Gitman, L. J., D. K. Forrester, and J. R. Forrester, Jr. "Maximizing Cash Disbursement Float," *Financial Management* (Summer 1976), pp. 15–24.

Gitman, L. J., and M. D. Goodwin. "An Assessment of Marketable Securities Management Practices," *Journal of Financial Research* (Fall 1979), pp. 161–69.

Levin, R. I., and C. A. Kirkpatrick. *Quantitative Approaches to Management*. New York: McGraw-Hill Book Company, 1975.

Lewellen, W. G., and R. W. Johnson. "Better Way to Monitor the Accounts Receivable," *Harvard Business Review* (May–June 1972), pp. 101–09.

Maier, S., and J. H. Vander Weide. "A Practical Approach to Short Run Financial Planning," *Financial Management* (Winter 1978), pp. 10–16.

Oh, J. "Opportunity Cost in the Evaluation of Investment in Accounts Receivable," *Financial Management* (Summer 1976), pp. 32–36.

Stone, B. K., and R. A. Wood. "Daily Cash Forecasting: A Simple Method for Implementing the Distribution Approach," *Financial Management* (Fall 1977), pp. 40–50.

Weston, J. F., and P. D. Tuan. "Comment on Analysis of Credit Policy Changes," *Financial Management* (Winter 1980), pp. 59–63.

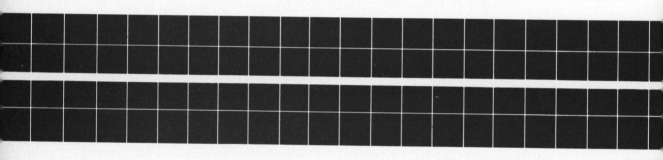

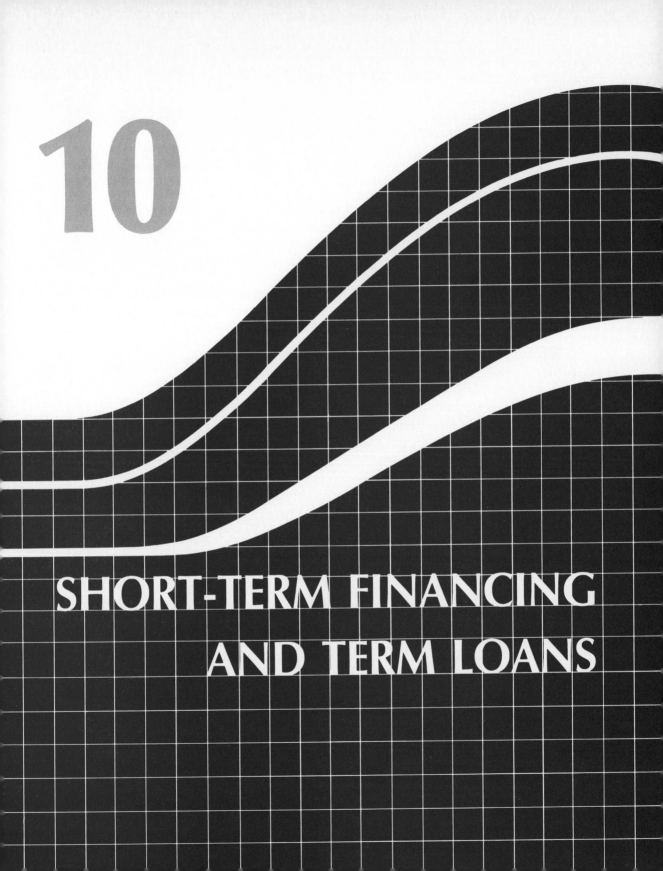

10

SHORT-TERM FINANCING AND TERM LOANS

Analysis of a firm's financing requirements should address three questions: (1) How much financing is needed? (2) For how long is it needed? (3) What sort of financing should the firm use? If a firm adopts the working capital management techniques presented in Chapter 9, it will reduce required financing to its lowest possible level. It can then determine the amount of financing needed using the cash budget as described in Chapter 7.

This chapter covers the third issue—the various types of short-term financing and term loans that most firms use. Common short-term financing opportunities include trade credit (which is an informal type of financing), bank loans, commercial paper, and pledging of working capital assets such as accounts receivable or inventory. Because almost all firms rely on commercial banks for at least some of their short-term financing, we have devoted a major portion of the chapter to a discussion of various commercial bank lending arrangements.

Term loans, which in many ways are similar to short-maturity loans, are borrowing arrangements with maturities of one to ten years. Commercial banks make term loans, as do other financial intermediaries, such as life insurance companies and pension funds.

Study of this chapter should enable you to

1. Describe the three types of trade credit arrangements commonly used, and evaluate the advantages and disadvantages of trade credit as a source of funds.

2. Define the following commercial bank lending terms:
   - Prime rate.
   - Compensating balances.
   - Line of credit.
   - Revolving credit.
   - Short-term, fixed-amount loans.
   - Simple interest loan.
   - Discounted loan.
   - Installment loan.

3. Evaluate the advantages and disadvantages of bank borrowing compared to other short-term sources of funds.

4. Be familiar with the reasons some firms issue commercial paper to obtain short-term financing.

5. Be familiar with ways to use inventory or accounts receivable to obtain funds, and the advantages and disadvantages of these arrangements.

6. Define the following terms related to the use of accounts receivable and inventory financing:

- Pledging receivables.
- Factoring receivables.
- Floating lien.
- Trust receipt.
- Warehouse receipt.
- Field warehousing.
- Terminal warehousing.

7. Know what is meant by a term loan and the sources from which term loans can be obtained.

SHORT-TERM FINANCING

Short-term financing generally is used to meet seasonal working capital requirements. The short-term financing requirements for the Clause Toy Co. shown on the *pro forma* balance sheets in Table 10.1 illustrate a normal situation faced by many companies.

Clause Toys, a manufacturer of children's toys and games, has been in business for over 40 years and carries a top credit rating from Dun & Bradstreet. The company produces a wide variety of plastic toys including trucks, cars, dolls, airplanes, and rockets. Most items have a one-day production run and are made with plastic using an injection molding process. Because toys are

TABLE 10.1
Clause Toy Co. Monthly *Pro Forma* Balance Sheets July to February (in 000s).

	July	Aug.	Sept.	Oct.	Nov.	Dec.	Jan.	Feb.
Assets								
Cash	$ 150	$ 150	$ 150	$ 150	$ 150	$ 150	$ 150	$ 150
Accounts receivable	100	100	450	625	1,250	1,450	1,650	1,225
Inventory	1,250	1,550	1,400	1,350	1,000	700	300	200
Net plant	400	400	400	400	400	400	400	400
Total assets	$1,900	$2,200	$2,400	$2,525	$2,800	$2,700	$2,500	$1,975
Liabilities and net worth								
Accounts payable	$ 725	$ 600	$ 550	$ 500	$ 350	$ 250	$ 200	$ 200
Short-term financing	50	450	675	825	1,100	900	650	50
Long-term debt	150	150	150	150	150	150	150	150
Equity	975	1,000	1,025	1,050	1,200	1,400	1,500	1,575
Total debt and net worth	$1,900	$2,200	$2,400	$2,525	$2,800	$2,700	$2,500	$1,975

highly susceptible to fads, the life of many products is very short. Customers of Clause Toys range from small dime stores to large discount chains, and sales are characterized by a large quantity of low-dollar-value invoices.

In June, Clause Toys constructed the *pro forma* statements shown in Table 10.1 to identify the financing required to carry the company through its seasonal production cycle. Because toy sales are concentrated in the December holiday season, inventory must start to expand in July in anticipation of holiday sales. Accounts receivable increase as sales are made to retail stores. The minimum cash balance needed each month will stay relatively constant at $150,000, and no additional plant investment over the current $400,000 is expected. On the liabilities side, accounts payable (trade credit) will provide some financing early in the expansion cycle, but other short-term financing must increase from $50,000 in July to a maximum of $1,100,000 in November and then decrease to a normal level of $50,000 by February.

Following the matching principle outlined in Chapter 8, the firm does not plan to increase long-term debt over the production period. Clause Toys is attempting to match short-term uses of funds with short-term sources. Any increase in long-term debt would require interest payments every month on funds that are needed only six months a year. Finally, equity will increase gradually over the period as earnings are retained by the firm, but most earnings growth occurs after the peak financing requirement in November.

The situation described by the *pro forma* balance sheets of Clause Toy Co. is not unusual. Many firms find it necessary to obtain short-term financing over a normal business cycle.

TRADE CREDIT

Trade credit is a form of short-term financing provided by the firm's suppliers. The most common form of trade credit is an open account, which is shown as accounts payable on the balance sheet. A firm that buys items from another business and is allowed a period of time before payment is due is using open account trade credit. Two other common forms of trade credit are promissory notes and acceptances, which are more formal and specific arrangements.

Open Account

In an **open account,** when a purchase is made on cash terms, payment is made after receipt of an invoice for the goods—usually within 10 days. The invoice usually accompanies the shipment. A buyer who has established a credit account with the supplier may be extended credit for 30 to 45 days or longer. In some industries, the normal credit period is 20 days or less, while in others it runs for several months. International credit terms are generally longer;

Japanese firms, for example, expect a credit period of at least six months when buying on an open account.

To promote early payment, many suppliers offer a discount if the bill is paid early and levy an interest charge if payment is not made by the end of the credit period. Payment terms of 2/10, net/30; $1\frac{1}{2}$% for over 30 days means that 2% may be deducted from the invoice amount if the bill is paid within 10 days; the total is due within 30 days, and an interest penalty of $1\frac{1}{2}$% per month applies if payment is not made within 30 days.

The cost of open account credit.   Trade credit may be considered costless if payment is remitted during the discount period or by the due date if no discount is given. If payment is made after the discount period, the cost of using trade credit is the difference between the invoice amount and the amount due after the discount. If payment is made after the due date, the direct interest penalty should be added as well. For most firms, it is advantageous to pay early and obtain the discount, even if other sources of financing must be obtained.

For example, assume that the suppliers of Clause Toys bill on a 2/10, net/30; $1\frac{1}{2}$% basis and that Clause Toys has purchased \$10,000 worth of goods from the HTW Corp. The cost of not taking the discount can be determined using Eq. (10.1):

$$\frac{\text{Cost of}}{\text{trade credit}} = \frac{\text{discount percent}}{(100 - \text{discount \%})} \times \frac{360 \text{ days}}{(\text{due date} - \text{discount period})} . \quad (10.1)$$

If payment is made by the tenth day only \$9,800 must be remitted. Keeping the \$9,800 another 20 days costs the firm \$200 in terms of the missed discount. Based on a 360-day year, the annualized interest cost is 36.73%:

$$\text{Cost of trade credit} = \frac{2\%}{(100\% - 2\%)} \times \frac{360 \text{ days}}{(30 \text{ days} - 10 \text{ days})}$$
$$= 36.73\%.$$

Other sources of funds, such as bank loans, generally will be cheaper on an annual basis than forgoing the discount, so most firms find that paying during the discount period is justified economically. If no discount is offered for early payments, however, or if the discount period has already passed, the firm should delay payment to the last day of the credit period.

To motivate prompt payment during the tight money periods of the late 1970s and early 1980s, many firms began adding an interest charge of 1 to 2% per month for payment beyond the credit period. While some businesses found this an effective means to motivate payment, others observed that their customers paid 15 to 30 days after the credit period, ignored the interest penalty, and still took the 2% discount.

Promissory Notes

In industries where the merchandise is of high unit value and readily identifiable, such as expensive watches or cameras, the buyer may be required to sign a **promissory note** (a note of indebtedness) to the selling firm. The purpose of this more formal arrangement is to avoid differences in case a dispute arises with regard to the debt. Open account trade credit also may be restructured as a promissory note when a buyer who is carrying a large balance on an open account encounters a period of economic difficulty. The promissory note arrangement can be designed to allow the seller the opportunity to receive complete payment while enabling the buyer to maintain solvency.

Acceptance

An **acceptance** is a time bill of exchange (essentially a check) drawn on a bank or purchaser by the selling firm to cover the cost of goods sold. When a bill of exchange is drawn on and accepted by a bank, it becomes a **bankers acceptance;** when it is drawn on and accepted by a business, it is called a **trade acceptance.** Acceptances are widely used to finance agricultural transactions and international trade. Here is how a trade acceptance works. Assume that an Arizona cotton gin sells several hundred cotton bales to a South Carolina fabric mill. On delivery of the cotton to the railroad, the gin receives an *order bill of lading* as a receipt. The gin then draws a sight draft on the mill for the purchase price of the cotton plus freight, insurance, and all other costs that it has prepaid, makes a commercial invoice, and endorses the bill of lading. It then mails the documents to a bank in South Carolina that has been specified by the mill. When the documents arrive, the bank notifies the mill so that arrangements for payment can be made and the mill can obtain the bill of lading needed to claim the goods from the railroad. The bank, acting merely as a collecting agent, obtains payment from the mill and remits it to the gin. Although this example is virtually a cash transaction, the seller has the advantage of retaining title to the goods until payment is made, and the buyer has the advantage of not paying for the goods until after receiving them.

Acceptances used as short-term financing usually are banker's acceptances; these are more secure than trade acceptances because both the firm and a bank have accepted responsibility for payment. Using the same example, a banker's acceptance could be created as follows. Before the South Carolina mill contracted with the Arizona gin, it would ask its own bank for a letter of credit. If the bank believes that the mill is creditworthy, it will provide a **letter of credit** specifying that it will extend a certain number of dollars of credit to the mill. The mill forwards the letter of credit to the gin, which completes the same documents previously described except that it uses a time draft (essentially a postdated check) instead of a sight draft, payable at some future date, say 60 days from the date it is accepted. When the bank receives the documentation, it observes its letter of credit, writes "accepted" on the face of the draft, and returns the draft to the Arizona gin. The gin may then hold the draft to maturity, sell it at a discount to obtain cash, or use it as security for a loan. If the acceptance is held to maturity, it is superior to an open account as evidence of a sale, and it is more acceptable than an account receivable as security for a bank loan.

Advantages of Trade Credit

Almost all firms use trade credit to some extent. The main advantage of an open account is its easy availability. It allows automatic financing of every purchase. Furthermore, because formal arrangements are not required when trading on an open account, the credit can be used when needed and is off the books when it is not required. Trade credit arrangements also enable the buyer to inspect the merchandise before making payment.

It costs the firm nothing to take full advantage of the discount period, and if no discount is offered, payment may be delayed for several weeks with no penalty. Prudent cash management dictates that all payments be made at the end of the discount period, or on the maturity date if no discount is allowed. However, trade credit can be relatively costly if discounts are not taken.

Clause Toy Co. wants to use trade credit as much as possible for financing working capital requirements in order to keep borrowing at a minimum. As their trade credit most likely will take the form of open account transactions with 30 days to pay, Clause cannot use trade credit to obtain all the funds it will need over its six-month production cycle. The accounts payable shown in Table 10.1 reflect the maximum financing available by trade credit, assuming that all accounts are paid within 30 days.

To obtain additional short-term financing, Clause Toys normally will turn to its local bank. The various financial arrangements available from most banks are discussed next.

SHORT-TERM BANK CREDIT

Typically, a bank loan made to a business firm is short-term, due in less than one year, and used primarily to finance working capital or other short-term assets. The magnitude of short-term bank credit is indicated by the fact that in August 1982 commercial banks were carrying over $384.5 billion in commercial and industrial short-term loans, with an average maturity of less than two months. Commercial paper, the second major source of short-term funds for business, amounted to only $173.4 billion in the same time period. Large, established firms with good credit ratings can obtain short-term bank loans on an unsecured basis, while small firms, especially those with short histories, will have to use accounts receivable, inventory, or real assets as collateral for the loan.

Normally, a firm applying for a loan will be asked to produce current audited balance sheets, income statements, and *pro formas* covering the next one to three years. Small businesses will be asked to include recent tax returns for either the corporation or the owner. The bank can then assess the quality of management and evaluate management's ability to produce the results shown on the *pro forma* statements. The factor most important to a bank in extending credit is whether the firm's projected *cash flows* are adequate to service the loan.

While bank loans can be tailored to meet almost any situation, three types of loan arrangements are the most prevalent: (1) line of credit, (2) revolving credit, (3) short-term fixed amount loans.

Line of Credit

The most flexible loan arrangement for most firms is an unsecured **line of credit,** which allows the firm to borrow funds up to the maximum limit specified in the agreement. Furthermore, the bank does not restrict the use of the funds to any specific purpose. When cash is required, the company merely notifies the bank to credit the appropriate amount to its checking account.

The line of credit usually is negotiated annually, with the maximum amount sufficient to cover the highest seasonal needs of the firm. A line of credit is not a contract; it is merely a statement that stipulates the maximum outstanding loan that a bank will allow the firm during the fiscal year. However, bankers generally feel obligated to live up to their line of credit authorizations in order to remain competitive.

According to the *pro forma* statements for the Clause Toy Co. shown in Table 10.1, the company requires a line of credit for at least $1,100,000, the maximum projected financing needed, which occurs during November. The company can draw down the credit from July through November as cash is required, and it can start to repay the borrowing in December. By February, borrowing will be reduced to its normal level. Clause Toys probably should ask for a credit line of $1,200,000 to $1,500,000 in order to provide a cushion for unforeseen cash requirements.

Costs for a line of credit.   The interest rate charged for a line of credit is stated in relation to the bank's prime rate and usually will change whenever the prime rate changes. The **prime rate** refers to the interest rate charged the most creditworthy, prime customers, AT&T or IBM, for example. As few businesses qualify for the prime rate, most firms will be charged an additional one to four points. Because the interest rate will vary with the prime, the company's cost of borrowing on the credit line may fluctuate significantly from month to month. Figure 10.1 illustrates the volatility in the prime rate during the late 1970s and early 1980s. During some periods, the prime rate changed weekly because of uncertain economic conditions.

In addition to charging direct interest, banks usually require a borrower to maintain a minimum checking account amount, called a **compensating balance,** which may represent 10 to 20% of the amount of the loan. The compensating balance required will be calculated as either an absolute minimum daily balance or an average daily amount determined by summing the account's daily good funds balance over the month and dividing by the number of days in the month. The compensating balance serves two purposes. First, it strengthens the bank's position in case the firm gets into financial difficulty. The bank can attach the firm's deposit in the bank and apply it against the firm's loan; this is called the *right of offset.* Second, it increases the cost of the loan to the borrower by requiring it to borrow more than is actually needed. For example, if Clause must keep a 20% compensating balance, it must borrow more than $1,100,000 at the time of peak fund requirements. Total borrowing is found by dividing the amount the firm needs by 1 minus the compensating balance percentage. Clause Toys must borrow $1,375,000, $1,100,000/(1 − .2), to obtain $1,100,000 in usable funds. During

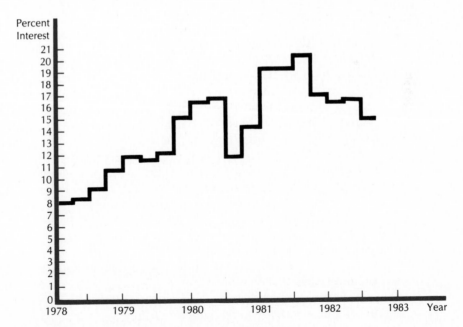

Figure 10.1 Average quarterly prime rate (1978–1982).

periods of tight money, banks stiffen their compensating balance requirements to earn a higher return and to provide more reserves for further lending.

To illustrate how to calculate the effective annual interest rate charged on a line of credit, we can determine the relevant costs for Clause Toys during its peak borrowing month of November. Assume that Clause Toys negotiates with its bank a $1,500,000 line of credit that calls for a compensating balance of 20% of the amount borrowed. The nominal interest rate for November is 12%, representing prime plus 2%. To determine the actual cost of the loan, it is first necessary to calculate the total loan required, including the compensating balance. As previously determined, Clause toys would have to borrow $1,375,000 to obtain $1,100,000 in available funds. The interest expense for November (one month) will be $13,750 [$1,375,000 × (12%/12 months)]. The effective interest rate can now be determined by using Eq. (10.2).

$$\text{Effective annual interest rate} = \frac{\text{interest expense}}{\text{usable funds}} \times \frac{360 \text{ days}}{\text{borrowing period}}. \quad (10.2)$$

The true rate of interest for Clause Toys is 15%, not the stated 12% nominal rate:

$$\begin{aligned}
\text{Effective annual interest rate} &= \frac{\$13,750}{\$1,100,000} \times \frac{360 \text{ days}}{30 \text{ days}} \\
&= .0125 \times 12 \\
&= .15.
\end{aligned}$$

Several factors will influence the nominal rate and compensating balance percentage that a bank quotes to a customer. A banker is more favorably disposed to lend at competitive rates to a good customer than to a total stranger. When evaluating a loan request, the banker will review the firm's checking account activity and daily good funds balance. If the good funds balance is sufficiently large, the bank may not require a further compensating balance for a loan. Often this may be true in the case of businesses that are not large enough to use sophisticated cash management procedures such as those described in Chapter 9. Larger firms that draw down and invest their good funds each day, on the other hand, will always be required to maintain a compensating balance or pay a fee to the bank.

The bank also evaluates the cost of servicing the account. A customer who demands many "free" services that the bank provides (e.g., credit reports, trust services, cash management advice) will pay more for a loan than one who does not. Finally, the bank's perceived risk of the loan will influence the premium required above the prime. A firm with a good history, adequate cash flow, and low debt-to-equity ratio will be able to borrow at more favorable rates. Bankers will not make loans that they believe will not be repaid at any interest rate, however high.

Revolving Credit Arrangements

A **revolving credit arrangement** is basically a line of credit agreement in which the bank is *legally committed* to provide funds to the business. To obtain the legal commitment from the bank, the borrower pays a commitment fee of .2 to .5% of the maximum amount of credit requested. Revolving credit agreements may extend for longer than the one-year maximum of a standard line of credit. One major reason for firms to obtain a revolving credit line is to provide backup funds to support commercial paper sales (a topic covered later in this chapter).

Equation (10.3) can be used to calculate the effective annual interest rate for a revolving credit arrangement. It differs from Eq. (10.2) only by the addition of the commitment fee to the cost of borrowing:

$$\frac{\text{Effective annual}}{\text{interest rate}} = \frac{\text{interest expense} + \text{commitment fee}}{\text{usable funds}} \times \frac{360\,\text{days}}{\text{credit period}}. \quad (10.3)$$

If Clause Toys prefers to obtain guaranteed, longer-term financing, it may request a revolving credit arrangement. Assume that the bank offers the company the same terms as before, except for adding a commitment fee of $5,000 per year plus .2% on the *unused* amount of the credit line. To determine the true cost of the loan arrangement, we calculate the financing required, the interest expense, and the commitment fee; we then use Eq. (10.3) to solve for the effective annual interest rate.

If the *pro forma* statements are accurate, average monthly borrowing for Clause Toys will be $408,333, calculated by assuming that borrowing for March through June is $50,000 and for the other months as shown under short-term financing in Table 10.1. Summing the monthly figures and dividing by 12 months yields $408,333. The compensating balance is 20%. Clause will have to borrow on average $510,417 [$408,333/(1 − .2)], resulting in a yearly interest expense of $61,250 (510,417 × .12). The commitment fee is $5,000, plus .002 of the difference between $1,500,000 and $510,417, or $1,979. Total commitment fee costs are $6,979 ($5,000 + $1,979). The effective annual interest rate for this revolving credit arrangement is 16.71%.

$$\text{Effective annual interest rate} = \frac{\$61,250 + \$6,979}{\$408,333} \times \frac{360\,\text{days}}{360\,\text{days}} = 16.71\%.$$

The higher borrowing cost can be attributed to the $5,000 fee and the charge levied on the unused credit line. The need for funds that peaks in November calls for a maximum credit requirement of $1,500,000, which is much greater than the monthly borrowing average and thereby increases commitment fee costs. Unless it considers a guaranteed loan to be an absolute necessity—for example, to back the sale of commercial paper—Clause Toys probably should avoid this type of arrangement because of its higher cost.

Short Term, Fixed-Amount Loans

A **short-term, fixed-amount loan** is one in which a specified amount is borrowed for a period of one year or less to be used for working capital purposes or to fund a specific asset. Obligations and terms of the arrangement are specified in a promissory note signed by the borrower. In the case of a small business, usually the owner as well as the corporation is liable for the loan. In addition, most short-term loans to small businesses are secured by assets of the business such as inventory, accounts receivable, or real property. Large firms with excellent credit ratings can obtain unsecured short-term loans. Repayment schedules and the manner in which interest is determined differ among the three common types of short-term business loans.

Simple interest loan.   For a **simple interest loan,** the firm signs a promissory note, agreeing to repay principle plus interest at the end of the borrowing period. Equation (10.2) can be used to determine the interest rate when a compensating balance is required. If no compensating balance is needed, the stated rate is the effective rate of interest.

Assume that Clause Toys borrows $1,100,000 to finance its working capital requirements on July 1 and repays the loan on February 28. If the bank quotes an interest rate of 12% and requires no compensating balance to be maintained, the effective annual interest rate is 12% as quoted ($88,000/1,100,000 × 360/240). Clause Toys probably would not choose this arrangement because it would obligate the company to pay for more funds than it requires during seven of the eight months in the borrowing period.

Discounted loan.   In a **discounted loan,** interest is deducted at the time the loan is established, thereby reducing the cash proceeds to the borrower and increasing the interest rate on the loan. Assume that Clause Toys is offered an eight-month discounted loan of $1,100,000 at 12%. The eight months worth of interest is deducted when the loan is made, providing Clause Toys with only $1,012,000. At maturity the company will repay $1,100,000 to the bank. Because Clause needs the full $1,100,000 now, it must borrow a greater amount to make up for the discounted interest. The required loan amount in this case can be determined by dividing 1 minus the period interest rate into the required amount of financing. The eight-month interest rate is 8% (which equals a 12% annual rate). Dividing (1 − .08) into $1,100,000 yields $1,195,652. Equation (10.2) can be used to show that the effective rate of interest charged on a discounted loan is always greater than the nominal rate.

Borrowing $1,195,652 for eight months requires discounted interest of $95,652 [$1,195,652 × (.12 × 240/360)], leaving $1,100,000 for Clause Toys. Equation (10.2) shows that the effective annual interest rate is 13.04%:

$$\text{Effective annual interest rate} = \frac{\$95,652}{\$1,100,000} \times \frac{360 \text{ days}}{240 \text{ days}} = .1304.$$

For Clause Toys, the discounted loan has the same drawbacks as a simple interest loan; in addition, it carries a higher interest rate.

Installment loan.   Under an **installment loan** agreement, the principal and interest are amortized over the life of the loan. We discussed amortized loans in Chapter 3 in presenting examples related to the time value of money.

Assume that Clause Toys wants to borrow $10,000 to buy a new injection molding machine. The Last National Bank might agree to finance the asset using a one-year installment loan with monthly payments, carrying a 12% **nominal interest rate.** First, we will show how the monthly payments generally are calculated by the bank. Then we will present the procedure for determining the **effective interest rate.**

On a one-year loan at a nominal rate of 12% the interest would amount to $1,200 ($10,000 × .12). The total to be paid the bank is $11,200, which is $933.33 per month for 12 months. It should be apparent that the effective interest rate on this type of loan is much greater than the nominal rate of 12%. The effective annual interest rate can be determined (using techniques presented in Chapter 3) by solving for the discount rate that equates the $10,000 to a 12-period annuity of $933.33.

$$\$10,000 = \$933.33 \times \text{PVIFA}$$

$$\frac{\$10,000}{\$933.33} = \text{PVIFA}$$

$$10.714 = \text{PVIFA}.$$

Looking up the interest factor of 10.714 in Table B "Present Value of an Annuity," in the 12-period row, we see that the monthly interest rate is between .0150 and .0200. Interpolation will yield a value of .018. Multiplying .018 by 12 to annualize the rate reveals an effective annual interest rate of 21.6%, far greater than the nominal interest rate of 12% quoted. The Consumer Protection Act of 1978 requires lenders to reveal the effective interest rate, usually called the *annual percentage rate (APR),* in addition to their quoted nominal interest rate. The reason for this law should be obvious.

Advantages and Disadvantages of Bank Financing

Bank loans can be designed to fit the needs of most businesses at interest rates that are competitive with those offered by almost any other source. In the situation facing Clause Toys, a general line of credit probably would be the best arrangement, because the company can borrow funds only when it needs them. Companies that require a fixed sum for a certain period may choose to use a promissory note and repay the loan in one of several ways. A disadvantage of bank borrowing is that legal covenants governing the loan agreement may restrict day-to-day firm operations. Banks frequently require a firm to maintain specified levels of working capital or to restrict future borrowing. The ultimate problem of any debt arrangement is that bankruptcy may result if the company cannot repay the debt as specified. However, the convenience and flexibility of bank loans make commercial banks the primary source of short-term business financing in this country.

COMMERCIAL PAPER

To finance short-term working capital requirements, large, well-known companies with impeccable credit ratings may sell unsecured promissory notes, called *commercial paper*, in the open market. Only several hundred firms consistently borrow using commercial paper, even though thousands of others could meet the credit standards. The growing importance of commercial paper as a source of business funds is illustrated in Table 10.2, which shows that the dollar value of commercial paper has almost tripled since 1977.

Issuers of commercial paper include industrial, transportation, and utility firms and large finance companies such as General Motors Acceptance Corporation (GMAC), Ford Motor Credit, and Beneficial Finance. The minimum denomination of commercial paper sold by nonfinancial firms is usually $100,000, with the average issue approaching several million dollars.

Maturity

Commercial paper may be sold with a maturity of as long as 270 days (a longer maturity would require registration with the Securities and Exchange Commission), but the average maturity of paper issued in 1982 was less than 30 days. Most firms prefer to borrow short-term to keep borrowing costs as low as possible. However, short average maturity means that most borrowers are in the market every month, **refunding** (rolling over) a maturing commercial paper issue with a new one. This procedure creates risk for the firm, as discussed in Chapter 8, because of uncertainty about the availability of funds and the interest rate that will be charged. To ensure that their commercial

TABLE 10.2	
Amount of Commercial Paper Outstanding (in Billions).	
December 1977	$ 65.1
December 1978	83.4
December 1979	112.8
December 1980	124.5
December 1981	165.5
August 1982	$173.8

Source: "Commercial Paper and Banker's Acceptances Outstanding," *Federal Reserve Bulletins,* pp. A-24/A-25.

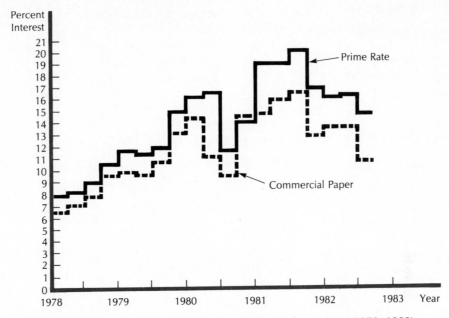

Figure 10.2 Commercial paper and prime rate, quarterly averages (1978–1982).

paper will be sold, all firms back their issues with a guaranteed line of credit from a bank. The commitment fee for the line of credit may be thought of as insurance for the commercial paper issue, because the firm seldom will have to draw down its credit line.

Yield

Most commercial paper is sold as discount paper (as are T-bills, as described in Chapter 9), with the difference between the maturity value and the price paid being the interest. Recently, more corporations have been issuing interest-bearing paper, primarily because it facilitates secondary trading of the paper. As Fig. 10.2 shows, a company's primary reason for selling commercial paper instead of borrowing from a bank is that commercial paper yields usually are below prime bank rates. Because the market determines the cost of borrowing, the interest rate of commercial paper is very sensitive to daily money market conditions.

Placement Procedure

Corporations issue commercial paper either through dealers or by direct placement. Most large investment banking firms such as Goldman Sachs, Salomon Brothers, and Merrill Lynch serve as commercial paper dealers.

Dealers either purchase the paper outright from the issuing firm or act as an agent to place the issue. The large dealer sales organizations are in daily contact with retail clients who usually are the end purchasers of each issue.

Direct placement is used primarily by the large finance companies such as GMAC, Ford Motor Credit, and Beneficial Finance, which issue such large quantities of paper that they find it cost effective to maintain an internal sales force. About 60% of all commercial paper is directly placed by the issuer.

Advantages and Disadvantages of Issuing Commercial Paper

Business firms with easy access to the credit markets may find it advantageous to issue commercial paper for the following reasons:

1. The sale of commercial paper can be used to supplement other short-term sources of funds, such as bank credit. Transactions in the commercial paper market are relatively large, and transaction fees are low.
2. Commercial paper usually carries a lower cost than bank borrowing, and no compensating balances are required.
3. Borrowing in the marketplace advertises the firm's name and financial soundness. Firms that finance in the open market may be able to borrow at more favorable terms from commercial banks.
4. Much larger sums can be borrowed using commercial paper than could be obtained directly from banks.

The major disadvantage of commercial paper lies in the risk inherent in continually rolling over maturing issues. While the commercial paper market is not as reliable a source of funds as banks for some issuers (such as GMAC), it is the only market where they can obtain adequate short-term financing. Clause Toys, at the other extreme, is probably too small to raise funds by selling commercial paper, even though it has a very high credit rating.

OBTAINING FUNDS BY USING CURRENT ASSETS

Current assets such as accounts receivable and inventory may provide acceptable collateral for short-term loans. Small businesses with little performance history often are unable to obtain loans unless the loans are secured by assets of the firm. Accounts receivable can be used as collateral for a loan, called pledging, or they may be sold outright to a third party, termed factoring. Inventory can also be used as collateral: It can be retained by the borrower under a floating lien or trust receipt, or held by a third party under a warehousing arrangement.

Pledging Accounts Receivable

When **pledging** receivables, a firm signs a promissory note, an agreement specifying the schedule of assigned accounts, and a record form for reporting collections. The agreement (1) defines the eligible accounts; (2) indicates the percentage loan value of pledged accounts, which may vary from less than 50% to a maximum of 95%; (3) permits the lender to examine the firm's records; and (4) authorizes the lender to notify the firm's customers that the receivables are being pledged even though the lender may never exercise authority over the accounts. Businesses prefer to establish a nonnotification agreement in which customers are *not* notified that the firm's receivables are being pledged, because it avoids disturbing the relationship between the firm and its customers.

After the agreement is executed, the borrower can obtain funds by preparing a schedule of accounts to be assigned and executing a demand note; the lender then stamps the assigned accounts in the borrower's ledger to indicate the lender's claim on the asset and advances the appropriate loan to the borrower. Pledging receivables does not diminish in any way the borrower's responsibility to repay the principal and interest of the loan, and the lender hopes that he does not have to obtain title to the borrower's accounts. Receivables merely provide greater security to the lender that the loan will be repaid.

The interest rates on receivable loans are tied to the prime and often are higher than those on unsecured loans because of the additional cost of monitoring the borrower's receivables and the greater loan risk perceived by the lender. If the lender will not make the loan without obtaining collateral, the firm is in a higher risk class than a business that can obtain unsecured financing. In addition to interest, the borrower usually pays a service charge of 1 to 2% of pledged receivables, based on the amount of supervision and bookkeeping required and the number of items handled.

The two principal issuers of financing against pledged receivables are banks and commercial finance companies (e.g., Beneficial and C.I.T. Financial Corp.). Banks prefer lending to local firms with a better credit rating than to businesses that borrow from finance companies.

Could Clause Toys obtain the necessary financing by pledging its receivables? Evaluating the relationship between accounts receivable and short-term financing in Table 10.1 reveals that Clause requires funds early in its production cycle to finance inventory, before accounts receivable expand. In August, accounts receivable are only $100,000, while short-term financing must equal $450,000. The highly seasonal nature of the toy business makes it impossible to obtain all the funds required by pledging receivables. Firms with more constant sales that are unable to obtain an unsecured bank loan, however, may find pledging receivables a viable way to raise short-term funds.

Factoring Accounts Receivable

In a **factoring** arrangement, the financial institution, called a *factor*, purchases the firm's accounts receivable and may assume the firm's risk of nonpayment, as well as performing credit and collection activities. The factoring agreement can be made with or without recourse to the business firm. *With recourse* means that the business must reimburse the factor for any accounts that prove uncollectible. *Without recourse* indicates that the factor bears the loss for uncollected accounts. In addition to purchasing the receivables, factors may make advances to supplement funds obtained by factoring accounts receivable and give advice on potential customers, market conditions, and other aspects of the firm's business.

Cost of factoring.   The cost of factoring is a function of the risk assumed and the work performed by the factor. The factoring company usually applies at least three types of charges:

1. A *service fee* on the face value of all receivables factored; this may vary from less than 1% to 2% or more. This fee is compensation for assuming the credit risk plus performing credit, collection, and record-keeping functions for the firm.

2. *Interest* if funds are advanced before the receivables are collected; the interest generally will be stated as prime plus 2 to 6%. The standard factoring arrangement calls for the factor to submit funds to the firm *after* the receivables are collected. If funds are needed earlier, the factor, like any other lender, will charge interest on the loan.

3. A *reserve* of 4 to 6% to cover uncollectible accounts. The reserve is released to the firm's account with the factor when the receivables are collected.

To evaluate the net cost of using a factor, the firm also should consider any savings realized from reducing credit and collection costs. However, the service fee usually makes factoring a more expensive source of funds than other credit arrangements. For example, assume that Clause Toys enters into a nonrecourse agreement with the Arizona Factor Co. that calls for (1) a service fee of 1.75% of the amount of receivables factored after consideration of any reserve requirement; (2) discounted interest at 12% annually (1% per month) for funds advanced before the receivables are collected; and (3) a reserve of 5% on funds advanced early. Clause Toys believes that use of a factor will save them $1,500 per month because of reduced credit and collection expenses.

Table 10.1 shows that on October 31, Clause Toys should have $625,000 in receivables (all of which are billed net 30 days). Assuming that all receivables are current and acceptable to the factor, the cost of obtaining $625,000 at 1.75% for one month by factoring the receivables is shown in column 3 of Table 10.3. The effects of service fees of .75 and 1% are shown in columns 1 and 2.

As Table 10.3 indicates, Clause Toys probably will pay more for funds obtained by factoring than from other sources, but the cost will be highly dependent on the negotiated service fee. Actually, a service fee of 1.75% is

TABLE 10.3
Cost of Funds Obtained by Factoring.

	Service Fee		
	Col. 1 .75%	Col. 2 1.00%	Col. 3 1.75%
Gross receivables	$625,000	$625,000	$625,000
Less: 5% reserve	31,250	31,250	31,250
	593,750	593,750	593,750
Service fee	4,453	5,938	10,391
Available for borrowing	589,297	587,812	583,359
Discounted interest (1%)	5,893	5,878	5,834
Usable funds	583,404	581,934	577,525
Annualized cost of borrowing			
Interest	4,453	5,938	10,391
Service fee	5,893	5,878	5,834
Less: Cost savings	(1,500)	(1,500)	(1,500)
Total	$ 8,846	$ 10,316	$ 14,725
Cost of factoring/funds received	8,846	10,316	14,725
	583,404	581,934	577,525
Annualized rate (monthly cost × 12 months)	18.20%	21.27%	30.60%

higher than the average factoring fee, and it would be charged because Clause Toys' receivables are characterized by many accounts of low average dollar value. Factoring rates of 1% or less are not uncommon when large per-order sales predominate, such as in the manufacturing and wholesaling businesses.

Even though accounts receivable are not sufficient to cover the short-term financing required for July through November, factoring arrangements probably can be used to obtain all the necessary financing for Clause Toys. Factors typically will make *overadvances* related to the anticipated accounts receivable from which they are repaid. Thus Clause Toys could request additional funds in November to obtain the necessary $1,100,000. If security is required for overadvances, inventory is commonly pledged. The factor also would assist the firm in drawing up the cash budget and planning other financing requirements.

Advantages and disadvantages of factoring.   Even though factoring is relatively expensive, it is considered an acceptable form of financing, especially by fast-growing firms with a large portion of working capital committed to accounts receivable. A firm using a factor expects sales to increase because (1) the factor may be willing to accept receivables of firms with credit ratings below the level acceptable to their clients; (2) the cost of the firm's credit operations can be reduced greatly; (3) the factor may be able to recommend new territories that can be developed, thus increasing sales; and (4) the advisory services of a factor may improve a firm's financial management capabilities.

Criticisms of factoring include (1) loss of personal contact with credit customers, (2) expense, and (3) loss of flexibility in handling the firm's receivables. Expansion by large banks into the factoring business, however, has increased competition among factors and reduced costs to client firms, making factoring a feasible source of short-term funds for many businesses.

Pledging Inventory

The most popular current asset to use as security for a loan is inventory. The most acceptable type of inventory is highly marketable, fully insured, non-perishable staples (such as farm commodities, oil and chemicals). Manufacturing firms find that raw materials or finished goods often will be acceptable to a lender, while work in process is of no value. In most instances, a firm pledging inventory to secure a loan will obtain the loan from a commercial bank. A floating lien, trust receipt, or warehouse receipt agreement will secure the bank's claim on the inventory.

Floating lien agreement. The most general form of inventory pledge is a **floating lien agreement,** which gives the lender a general claim on the firm's entire inventory. Inventory items of low unit value that are turned over rapidly are the best candidates for a floating lien agreement. Under the conditions of a floating lien, the inventory remains on the borrower's premises where it is maintained and controlled by the borrower. The lender will require continuous accounting of the inventory by the borrower and will also make periodic physical inspections. The loan amount, however, will be a great deal less than the book value of the inventory because (1) lenders exercise little control over pledged inventory items and (2) many items return only a fraction of their value when sold under distressed conditions.

Trust receipts. A **trust receipt** gives a lender title to goods that are held "in trust" by a borrower. While a trust receipt provides somewhat greater protection for the lender than a floating lien, holders of trust receipts may be classified as general creditors (in the event of borrower bankruptcy) unless they can prove that the specific goods covered by the trust receipts belong to them. Trust receipts are used for items such as automobiles, office equipment, and watches, which have high dollar value and can be identified easily by serial number. Clause Toys could not use a trust receipt arrangement because of the low unit value of its product and the obvious difficulty in identifying specific items to be held for collateral.

Warehouse receipts. The most secure legal protection for the lender who takes inventory for loan collateral is provided by a **warehouse receipt,** which is a legal document acknowledging storage of goods and specifying the terms on which they can be removed from the warehouse. When the receipt is nonnegotiable, goods will be delivered only to the person specified in the receipt; when it is negotiable, delivery may be made to the bearer or a person designated by the holder of the receipt. A warehouse receipt permits the lender to maintain title to stored goods while they are in the possession of a warehouse company. The borrower can obtain the inventory only through the lender or his agent. Typical warehousing arrangements use field warehouses and terminal warehouses.

With a **field warehousing arrangement,** goods are stored on the premises of the borrowing firm under conditions that permit them to be segregated, controlled, and supervised by the lender. The lender usually hires a field warehousing firm to control the pledged inventory. Even though the inventory is stored on the borrower's premises, the borrower cannot obtain possession of it without the lender's approval. Field warehousing is relatively simple to accomplish. It is necessary only to obtain space in the borrower's facility, a fence or partition, and a lock to segregate and secure the pledged items. Bulk commodities predominate among the types of goods that are field-warehoused.

A **terminal warehousing arrangement** calls for the collateral to be stored in a public warehouse under the control of a third party, rather than on the borrower's property. This is the most secure form of inventory financing from the lender's perspective, because the goods are completely removed from the borrower's premises. From the borrower's perspective, however, terminal warehousing usually is more expensive than field warehousing because of public warehouse charges. In addition, it is less convenient, because the inventory must be transported to and from the public warehouse.

Advantages and Disadvantages of Pledging Inventory

The advantages of pledging inventory are that (1) it may enable the firm to obtain a loan when an unsecured credit arrangement would not be granted, and (2) the borrower might be able to secure a lower interest rate on the loan, which would more than offset the additional expense and inconvenience of pledging inventory. This would be true when the inventory is of high quality and easily liquidated (such as an elevator of grain or a storage tank of oil).

Disadvantages include (1) expense, (2) loss of title and control of the inventory (under all conditions except those of a floating lien), and (3) inconvenience of maintaining additional inventory records.

While Clause Toys accumulates a significant amount of inventory from August to November, its collateral value will be very low because of the nature of the product. It is unlikely that Clause Toys could obtain a loan for more than 10 to 15% of its inventory value by using any type of inventory pledging arrangement.

TERM LOANS

A term loan differs from other short-term business financing in that its maturity is at least one year and may be greater than 20 years. Typical situations in which a term loan may be advantageously compared to short-term financing include (1) financing *permanent* working capital assets; (2) replacing short-term loans that have been renewed regularly; (3) obtaining relatively permanent financing at a time when it would be costly to float a new stock or bond issue because of high flotation costs or poor market conditions; (4) purchasing specific high-value assets (e.g., machinery or real property) that have a useful life greater than one year; and (5) refunding outstanding long-term debt. Term loans have two advantages over short-term financing: (1) the funds are available to the firm for a longer period, eliminating the need to obtain new financing every year, and (2) there is a great deal of flexibility regarding repayment of the loan.

CHARACTERISTICS OF TERM LOANS

The term loan agreement specifies the conditions and actions required by the borrower and lender. Important specifications are loan maturity, repayment schedule, interest rate, loan collateral, and covenants.

Loan Maturity

Maturities of term loans typically range from 1 to 10 years, with the majority of loans drawn for less than 5 years. Longer-maturity term loans of 20 years or more may be obtained if they are secured by real property. Maturities tend to lengthen when interest rates are low and to shorten when interest rates are high and funds are scarce. Firms can capitalize on the flexibility that a term loan arrangement affords by obtaining a maturity on the loan equal to the life of the asset being financed or the period for which the funds are required.

Repayment Schedule

The repayment schedule for term loans usually can be tailored to fit the needs of each borrower. The most common arrangement calls for amortizing the loan with equal annual, semiannual, quarterly, or monthly installment payments. After considering the cash flows available to repay the loan, though, a company may find it possible to negotiate a much different repayment schedule. For example, it might make regular payments of interest only during the life of the loan and repay the principal with a **balloon payment** at maturity; or the loan may be partially amortized with regular payments during the loan period, with a smaller balloon payment due at maturity. In addition, the borrower usually can retire the loan early, with no prepayment penalty, if the loan is from a bank. Lenders such as life insurance companies, however, may levy a prepayment penalty of 2 to 10% for early retirement.

Interest Rate

The interest rate on most term loans is variable and tied to the prime lending rate. The cost of the loan will fluctuate with changes in the prime or will be revised at specified intervals (monthly, quarterly, and so on). All else constant, a firm probably will have to pay .5 to 2% more for a term loan than for a short-term line of credit, because the lender is locked into the loan for a longer time and because the lender wants to make up for the higher costs incurred in administering installment loan contracts. Large firms can usually borrow at lower rates than small firms, probably because they have easier access to the capital markets, and banks must compete for their loans.

Loan Collateral

Many term loans are secured by assets, especially when borrowing is used to acquire specific high-value items (equipment, buildings, land, and machinery). The capital nature of these loans is illustrated by the types of businesses accounting for a large proportion of term loans—petroleum, coal, metal products, rubber, and transportation companies and public utilities all have heavy fixed capital requirements. If accounts receivable or inventory are pledged as collateral, legal arrangements described in the preceding section would be used to give the lender a claim on the assets.

Covenants

In addition to or in place of collateral, the lender may require the borrower to maintain certain financial relationships or may restrict the actions of the firm's management. These provisions are called *restrictive covenants* and typically relate to the following:

1. *Working capital.* For liquidity purposes, the borrower may be required to maintain a specified current or quick ratio or a certain dollar amount of net working capital.

2. *Debt/assets ratio*. The borrower may be prohibited from incurring additional debt or from pledging assets of the firm to obtain debt financing. Alternatively, the firm may be required to maintain a maximum debt/assets ratio.

3. *Dividends*. The firm may be prohibited from paying dividends while the loan is outstanding.

4. *Management personnel*. If the success of a small firm is highly dependent on a few individuals, the loan may become due and payable if one of these individuals changes employment or dies. The borrower may be required to insure the lives of these personnel, with the lender as beneficiary.

SOURCES OF TERM LOANS

While the majority of term loans are made by commercial banks, other financial institutions also engage in term loan lending, including pension funds, insurance companies, the Small Business Administration, and state and local economic development authorities.

Commercial Banks

Commercial banks prefer to make term loans of less than five years' maturity. The tendency for banks to make short-term rather than term loans is illustrated by the fact that commercial and industrial term loans made by major banks during the first week in November 1982 totaled only $4.0 billion compared to $37.8 billion in short-term financing. The average maturity of these term loans was 46.2 months compared to 1.2 months for the short-term loans.

Small businesses usually will be required to secure the loan with equipment or real property. Large firms may have to arrange a **syndicated** loan with a bank; with this arrangement, several banks and/or other lenders jointly assume responsibility for the loan. Syndication may be necessary for large loans, because a bank is prohibited from extending unsecured credit to a single customer in an amount exceeding 10% of the value of the bank's capital and surplus. In other cases, the lead bank in the syndicate may wish to share the risk of the loan with others in order to avoid heavy dependence on one customer. Generally, the borrower will deal with only the lead bank, and it will be that bank that receives a fee for the service.

Pension Funds

Pension funds are a growing financial intermediary created to fund retirement income for employees of various institutions. Because of their size and the predictability of their cash inflows and outflows, pension funds can make loans with a maturity of 10 to 20 years or longer having a value of over $1 million. Larger companies in need of significant financing, especially for real estate investment, which prefer not to sell bonds or stock in the capital market, are typical borrowers from pension funds.

Life Insurance Companies

Like pension funds, life insurance companies have a highly predictable flow of funds. Consequently, they also prefer long-term loan arrangements of 10 to 20 years or more. While insurance companies may make unsecured loans, they are a major source of funds for long-term real estate projects, securing the loans with a mortgage on the real property. At the end of 1980, the life insurance industry had over $131 billion in mortgage loans outstanding, representing over 27% of its investment activity.

The Small Business Administration

The Small Business Administration (SBA) was created in 1953 to assist small businesses in obtaining intermediate and long-term funds. To obtain funding assistance from the SBA, a small business must have sales of no more than $1 to $5 million annually or employ 250 to 1,500 people (depending on the industry). In addition, the firm must be unable to qualify for private commercial funding. Funds may be obtained from the SBA in one of three ways: (1) a *direct secured loan* of $100,000 or less, (2) a *bank participation loan* in which the SBA provides 75% of the funds, up to $150,000, and the local bank provides 25% or (3) an SBA *guaranteed loan* in which the SBA guarantees 90%, up to $350,000 of a loan, obtained from a commercial bank.

Further lending authority was provided the SBA in 1980, when it was allowed to guarantee bonds issued by *certified development companies*, local or regional corporations whose bond proceeds are used to make loans to small businesses. Loans from certified development companies are designed to provide long-term financing for fixed assets or land improvements and typically are for 40% of a project's costs up to a maximum of $500,000.

State and Local Economic Development Authorities

Economic development authorities (EDAs) have been established by many states or municipalities to promote industrial expansion and create jobs. Financial assistance provided by the EDA may take the form of low-cost leasing arrangements for equipment or facilities, guarantees, or participation loans with commercial banks. A leasing arrangement might involve a municipality constructing the physical plant and leasing it to a business firm on a long-term lease with attractive terms. For example, some fast food franchises have been constructed in depressed areas of major cities using this arrangement.

A loan guarantee calls for the EDA to guarantee the loan of a borrower who cannot obtain other adequate financing at reasonable rates. The maximum guarantee allowed on any project is usually $2 million. The participation loan is made in cooperation with a commercial bank that contributes 10% of the loan value, with the remaining funds supplied to the bank by the EDA. As a consequence, the bank has only 10% of the loan at risk. This arrangement allows small, speculative firms access to term loans that they would not otherwise have.

Funding for the EDA usually is provided by the sale of tax-free municipal bonds. Interest rates on the EDA leases or loans are below the market rates of term loans by private lenders. Missouri, California, Connecticut, and Indiana are some of the states that have established creative business financing alternatives using EDAs.

SUMMARY

Most firms find it necessary to procure short-term funds to finance seasonal working capital requirements and longer-term funds to finance fixed assets or permanent working capital. In this chapter, we have discussed the various sources of short-term borrowing and term loans.

Trade credit is an important component of working capital financing, with more than 90% of all wholesalers' and manufacturers' sales made on credit. Short-term bank credit is a very flexible and widely used form of financing that can be tailored to meet most borrowers' requirements. Large firms with top-quality credit may also obtain funds in the open market by selling commercial paper, an unsecured obligation. All commercial paper is backed by a bank line of credit to ensure marketplace acceptance of these unsecured notes.

Most small businesses may find it necessary to use current assets to obtain working capital financing. Accounts receivable may be pledged as collateral for a loan or may be sold outright to a factor, who typically assumes the credit risk and collection responsibilities. Inventory may be pledged using a floating lien or trust receipt in which the borrower maintains physical possession of the items, or with a warehouse receipt in which a third party controls the inventory.

When a firm requires financing for longer than one year, it usually seeks a term loan. Term loans can be structured with a great deal of flexibility regarding repayment schedules while at the same time giving the borrower access to financing for an extended period. Commercial banks typically provide term loan financing for less than five years, while life insurance companies and pension funds prefer to finance long-term real estate projects. For smaller businesses, the SBA is a viable source of financing as are EDAs now operating in many states and communities.

This chapter completes our discussion of working capital management. A significant proportion of any financial manager's time will involve working capital decisions that focus on the flow of cash through the firm. Budgeting, as described in Chapter 7, forms the foundation for making working capital decisions. Risk and return concepts described in Chapter 8 enable the financial manager to analyze how profitability and risk will be affected by changes in a firm's net working capital position. Techniques described in Chapter 9 allow the firm to minimize its investment in low-yielding working capital assets, and the financing arrangements described in this chapter show how the firm can obtain temporary, relatively inexpensive funds for fairly short periods. Part IV, which also deals with corporate financing, discusses sources of long-term capital for the firm.

QUESTIONS AND REVIEW ACTIVITIES

1. Distinguish among the three methods used today to extend trade credit.
2. Indicate why cash discounts are usually large when computed on an annual basis.
3. What are the advantages of financing in the open market with commercial paper?
4. The availability of bank loans is of greater importance to small firms than larger ones. Why?
5. The effective interest rate paid by corporations on loans is higher than the posted rate because banks generally require that some portion of a loan be kept on deposit, reducing funds available to the borrower. These compensating balances usually are 20% of the loan. If the prime rate were reduced from 8.5 to 8%, what would be the effective reduction in rate for a borrowing firm? Assume that no balances normally would be kept in that bank.
6. Identify (a) line of credit, (b) revolving credit arrangement, and (c) compensating balance.
7. When a bank discounts a note, how does this affect the cost of the loan?
8. What is the effect, if any, of a compensating balance on a bank loan?
9. How would the lending practices of two commercial banks differ if one bank has 60% time deposits and 40% demand deposits, while the other bank has the opposite deposit mix?
10. Distinguish between (a) short-term and long-term borrowing, and (b) secured and unsecured borrowing.
11. Consider using accounts receivable to obtain short-term financing:
    a) Define factor, and factoring.
    b) What are the chief characteristics of factoring?
12. What are the advantages and disadvantages of factoring?
13. Compare the risks to the borrowing firm of factoring versus obtaining loans made with receivables pledged as security.
14. Define (a) warehouse receipt, (b) trust receipt, (c) order bill of lading, (d) field warehousing.
15. Suggest an industry that might use each of the following forms of financing:
    a) Factoring.
    b) Pledging of accounts receivable.
    c) Warehouse receipts.

    d) Field warehouse receipts.

    e) Trust receipts.

    f) None of these.

    Explain your choices.

16. The popularity of term loans has increased greatly over the last 25 years.

    a) How do you account for the increased demand?

    b) Why have lending agencies shown an increased willingness to make such loans?

    c) Are term loans ordinarily self-liquidating in the sense that short-term loans are supposed to be self-liquidating?

17. What financial institutions are major suppliers of term loans? In what situations does the use of term loans appear to be a logical financial alternative?

PROBLEMS

1. On credit sales of $2 million, what would a firm sacrifice in before-tax profits if its credit terms were 2/10, net/30, and 30% of the customers took the cash discount? What would happen if the terms were 1/20, net/40, and 50% of the customers took the cash discount?

2. The sales of the Able Co. now amount to $300,000 per month; credit terms are 1/10, net/30. At the present time, half of its sales are on credit, and half of all credit customers take the cash discount (i.e., they pay by the tenth day).

    a) If you assume no past-due accounts, what is the average daily level of accounts receivable carried by the Able Co?

    b) Given the preceding data, what would be the level of receivables if all credit customers took the cash discount?

    c) What would be the result if credit terms were changed to 3/10, net/60, and as a result, all customers bought on credit and half of them paid by the tenth day?

3. Sandra's Silks has just received the invoices for $10,000 worth of merchandise purchased on terms of 2/10, net/30. Because of a temporary shortage of cash, the company will not take its discount on this purchase.

    a) When should the firm pay the bill?

    b) What is the cost of not taking the discount, stated on an annual basis?

    c) Do you think the decision to lose the discount is wise? Why or why not?

    d) Suppose that Sandra's Silks decided to borrow money from a bank for 30 days in order to take the discount. How high a rate of interest could they pay and still not be worse off in terms of dollars? (They can borrow only in multiples of $1,000.)

4. Aside from trade credit, the commercial bank is the major source of short-term credit.

    a) Why are the lending policies of banks more conservative than those of other lending institutions?

    b) How much will charging a discount and requiring a 20% compensating balance add to the actual interest cost on a loan of $10,000 at 5% for one year? (No balance is normally maintained at the bank.)

c) On the average, secured bank loans bear a higher rate of interest than unsecured loans. Explain.

5. The Tucson Hardware Co. is faced with borrowing money from its local bank to take advantage of a cash discount or forgoing the discount. The company is purchasing $10,000 worth of inventory on terms of 1/30, net/50. Currently, the bank is charging 12% interest. Should the company take out the loan?

6. The Mountain City Bank discounts its loans. What is the effective rate of interest for the following loans?

a) A $10,000 loan for six months at 10% interest.

b) A one-year loan of $40,000 at 12% interest.

c) A one-year loan of $75,000 at 14% interest.

7. The Midtown National Bank requires a 25% compensating balance of all firms that borrow over $2,000 per year. In return, the bank charges simple interest of 8% and does not discount its loans.

a) If a firm borrows $45,000, how much will the bank credit to its account?

b) How much will the firm have to borrow to obtain the immediate use of $45,000?

c) What is the effective rate of interest for the use of $45,000 in part (b)?

8. What is the effective interest rate a company must pay for the use of $8,000 if its bank is charging 8% to borrow funds and requires a 20% compensating balance?

9. The SKY Corp. is considering the use of a factor to handle all of its accounts receivable. The factor will charge the firm 12% on all advances (discounted) and 1% on the gross volume of receivables. SKY currently has annual credit sales of $5 million and an average accounts receivable balance of $500,000. If there is no change in sales or receivables, what will SKY pay annually for the services of the factor? What is the effective rate of interest for these services?

10. The Alligator Pool Co. has negotiated a revolving credit arrangement with the Death Valley Bank. The terms call for a maximum loan of $5 million during the next 12 months at an annual interest rate of 12%. A 10% compensating balance is required against all borrowed funds, and a commitment fee of $10,000 plus .015% interest on the unused balance will be charged. (Funds required to meet compensating balances are considered unused funds when calculating commitment fee costs.) Assuming that Alligator borrows the following amounts for the months specified, calculate the effective *annual* rate of interest on the loan.

Jan.	$ 75,000	July	$4,500,000
Feb.	75,000	Aug.	3,000,000
Mar.	3,000,000	Sept.	1,000,000
Apr.	4,000,000	Oct.	1,000,000
May	4,500,000	Nov.	75,000
June	$4,500,000	Dec.	75,000

11. The Last National Bank of Death Valley will make you an installment loan for $10,000 with the following terms: The simple interest rate is 8%; the term is one year, with 12 equal monthly payments required, calculated by dividing $10,800 by 12 months. What is the effective interest rate on the loan?

ADDITIONAL READINGS

Abraham, A. B. "Factoring: The New Frontier for Commercial Banks," *Journal of Commercial Bank Lending* (April 1971), pp. 32–43.

Adler, M. "Administration of Inventory Loans under the Uniform Commercial Code," *Journal of Commercial Bank Lending* (April 1970), pp. 55–60.

Bartter, B. J., and R. J. Rendleman, Jr. "Fee-Based Pricing of Fixed Rate Bank Loan Commitments," *Financial Management* (Spring 1979), pp. 13–20.

Bonker, K. "The Rule of 78," *Journal of Finance* (June 1976), pp. 877–88.

Daniels, F. L., S. C. Legg, and E. C. Yuille. "Accounts Receivable and Related Inventory Financing," *Journal of Commercial Bank Lending* (July 1970), pp. 38–53.

Denonn, L. E. "The Security Agreement," *Journal of Commercial Bank Lending* (February 1968), pp. 32–40.

Fisher, D. J. "Factoring—An Industry on the Move," *The Conference Board Record* (April 1972), pp. 42–45.

Gatti, J. F., J. R. Mills, and P. J. McTague. "The Feasibility of Small Denomination Consumer Note Issues as a Source of Funds for Non-Financial Borrowers," *Financial Management* (Autumn 1981), pp. 41–43.

Glasgo, P. W., W. Landes, and A. F. Thompson. "Bank Discount, Coupon Equivalent and Compound Yields," *Financial Management* (Autumn 1982), pp. 80–84.

Hayes, D. A. *Bank Lending Practices: Issues and Practices.* Ann Arbor, Mich.: Bureau of Business Research, University of Michigan, 1971.

Hungate, R. P. *Interbusiness Financing: Economic Implications for Small Business.* Washington, D.C.: Small Business Administration, 1962.

Hurley, E. M. "Commercial Paper Market," *Federal Reserve Bulletin* 63 (June 1977), pp. 525–36.

Nadler, P. S. "Compensating Balances and the Prime at Twilight," *Harvard Business Review* (January–February 1972), pp. 112–20.

Quarles, J. C. "The Floating Lien," *Journal of Commercial Bank Lending* (November 1970), pp. 51–58.

Quill, G. D., J. C. Cresci, and B. D. Shuter. "Some Considerations about Secured Lending," *Journal of Commercial Bank Lending* (April 1977), pp. 41–56.

Shadrack, F. C., Jr. "Demand and Supply in the Commercial Paper Market," *Journal of Finance* (September 1970), pp. 837–52.

Simione, P. A. "Positive Approach to Accounts Receivable Financing," *Journal of Commercial Bank Lending* (May 1973), pp. 13–17.

Stigum, M. *The Money Market: Myth, Reality, and Practice.* Homewood, Ill.: Dow-Jones, Irwin, Inc., 1978.

Stone, B. K. "Allocating Credit Lines, Planned Borrowing, and Tangible Services over a Company's Banking System," *Financial Management* (Summer 1975), pp. 65–78.

Stone, B. K. "How Secure Is Secured Financing under the Code?" *Burroughs Clearing House* (March 1965), pp. 302–12.

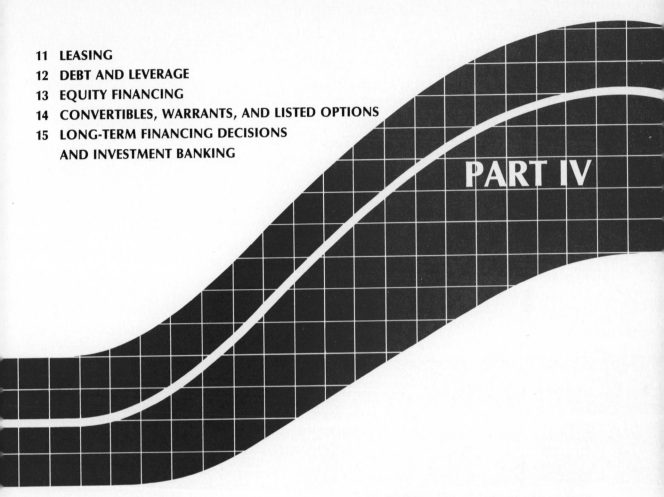

PART IV

CORPORATE
FINANCING

TYPES OF LEASES
SOURCES OF LEASE FINANCING
ACCOUNTING FOR LEASES
LEGAL CONSIDERATIONS
LEASING—PROS AND CONS
ANALYSIS OF LEASES

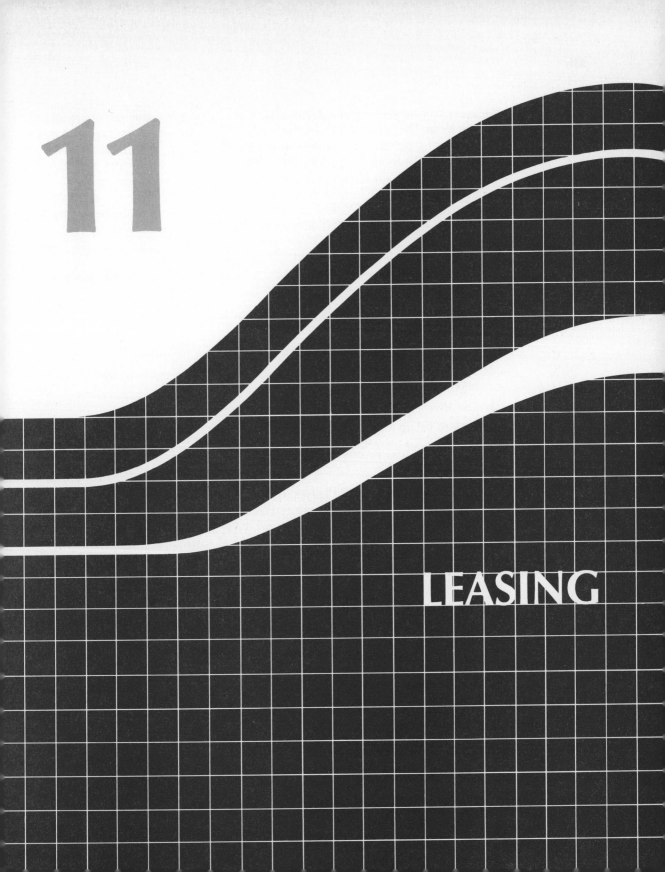

11

LEASING

A **lease** is an extended rental agreement. It is also a form of financing. It provides that the **lessee** (the renter who uses the asset) will pay the **lessor** (the owner of the asset) rent for a number of time periods in exchange for the right to use the asset. Leases have been around for a long time. Historical evidence indicates that Phoenician shipowners leased their crafts as long as 3,000 years ago. In the United States today, the lease as a form of financing is becoming more and more important; approximately 20% of all new equipment is leased. At the beginning of the 1980s, more than $100 billion worth of capital equipment was under lease.

This chapter covers a number of aspects of leasing. Through careful study of the chapter, you should learn

1. The different types of leases that a firm may use.
2. Who provides lease financing.
3. How leases are accounted for on a firm's financial statements.
4. Some legal aspects of lease financing, that is, how leases are treated by the Internal Revenue Service (IRS) and the courts.
5. The advantages and disadvantages of leasing.
6. How to set up the discounted cash flow analysis of leases.

TYPES OF LEASES

There are two main forms of leases: operating and financial. Operating leases (also referred to as service or maintenance leases) are for shorter periods of time, frequently provide for the lessor to maintain, or service, the asset, and generally are cancelable after some specified period of time. Normally, operating leases also spell out the terms under which they can be renewed or extended. Office equipment (typewriters, business machines, computers) is a good example of assets that are leased in this manner.

Financial leases are longer-term commitments with many of the same characteristics as installment loans; they are a more recent development. When a firm owns an asset, sells it to another party, and simultaneously agrees to lease that same asset from the buyer, the arrangement is called a sale and leaseback. Almost all sale and leasebacks are financial leases; that is, they are long-term. Many grocery stores are financed with sale and leasebacks.

Operating Leases

Operating leases have been around longest. The basic purpose of an operating lease is to transfer property from one company to another that uses it. The financial commitment is less binding than in the financial lease; it entails making rental payments in a total amount that is lower than the purchase price of the asset would be, with an option that permits a renewal of the lease or purchase of the asset at a specified price when the basic contract terminates. Because lessees may be less careful of leased property than their own, lease contracts normally require minimum standards of care and assess penalties for damage.

Operating leases embody all the provisions that make leasing attractive. When it leases instead of buys an asset, a lessee avoids large capital outlays and does not have to tie up funds in low-yielding capital assets for long periods. Leasing allows companies to conserve their limited capital funds for working capital and to avoid the cash down payment that is usually required when financing with chattel mortgages. Leasing may provide more financing than borrowing (the amount depends on the required down payment on the normal loan).

Rental or lease costs are deductible as expenses for income tax purposes, but the lessee, as it is not the owner, loses the depreciation deductions. Tax consequences have been a major factor promoting leasing, but accelerated depreciation has changed this situation somewhat.

The lessee, not being the owner of the leased property, may depend on the owner to provide maintenance and replacement services that the manufacturer or the leasing company usually can supply at a lower cost than the user could. Sometimes, business firms need additional fixed assets for short periods of time—to fulfill the terms of a government contract, for example. These equipment needs may be met by leasing rather than buying when buying would result in surplus assets at the end of the contract period.

Rental or lease payments may seem much higher than interest payments added to other financing charges, but frequently this difference is illusory. Which is cheaper—leasing or buying—can be determined only through discounted cash flow analysis.

If it leases an asset, the user loses the terminal value of the leased asset at the end of the lease period. This value may be considerable because of possible improvements made in the asset by the lessee, appreciation (e.g., in the case of land), and higher prices caused by inflation.

Financial Leases

A **financial lease** is a noncancelable contract that runs for a period that usually is shorter than the useful life of the asset being leased. During the life of the contract, the lessor recovers the entire cost of the property, plus financing and servicing charges, through periodic payments from the lessee.

Commercial, industrial, and mercantile firms are able to escape the burdens of ownership by leasing because others are willing to assume them. When the financial manager of a corporation finds it difficult to finance all the company's needs with funds generated by operations and from outside sources, he may turn to trusts, life insurance companies, other institutional investors, and banks that are willing either to buy the firm's assets and lease them back to it or to buy the new equipment needed and lease it to the company. The terms of such leases or leaseback arrangements may be tailored to fit the requirements of the particular business firm.

One of the first types of financial leasing occurred in merchandising, where large department stores, chain groceries, and supermarkets developed sale and leaseback techniques. As early as 1936, this type of financial leasing was used by Safeway Stores, Inc., and it has become standard procedure in financing land and equipment needed by major retailers, manufacturers, and transport carriers.†

Sale and Leaseback Financing

The basic procedure followed in **sale and leaseback** financing is for the business to purchase and develop business sites to meet its needs and then sell them to investors. The company leases the sites back for long periods, with a lease that permits the lessee to purchase the property at the end of the lease period. The repurchase price is set so that it will satisfy IRS requirements.

Sale and leaseback financing is used widely in the retail field, where there are many large firms with no ownership interest in the buildings and fixtures in selling their merchandise.‡ All the merchant's capital is tied up in working capital assets—cash, inventories, and receivables—which can be turned over rapidly and profitably. In shopping center leases, for example, the tenants agree to pay the owner a specified rental for an agreed-upon period and frequently an "override" related to their profits or sales volume.

Straight Financial Leases

A **straight financial lease** is identical to a sale and leaseback *except* that the lessee has not owned the property previously. The lessee-to-be negotiates with a seller and specifies what it needs with respect to the equipment or building. The lessee then negotiates with a financial institution to buy the property while simultaneously executing a lease agreement with the institution, which becomes the lessor.

A straight financial lease is essentially a loan agreement with minor modifications. However, because it is a lease instead of a loan, the transaction is entitled to different tax treatment, which may benefit the firm.

---

† In 1949, the Equitable Life Assurance Society of the United States announced its plan to purchase locomotives, freight cars, and other forms of equipment to lease to railroads. Rail equipment leasing is now common practice.

‡ Samuel J. Lee, *Introduction to Leasing* (San Marcos, Calif.: Anto Book Press, 1965), p. 16.

Lease financing and debt financing are similar. Each entails contractual obligations, with maturities that are long enough for the investor to recover its investment and the business firm to meet its obligations at specified times in the future. Both instruments provide a return to the investor and levy a cost on the user that can be measured fairly accurately in dollars. The soundness of both forms of financing depends on the general debt-paying ability of the business firm, whether it is a lessee or a debtor.

SOURCES OF LEASE FINANCING

Businesses may lease equipment from manufacturers or from independent lessors. The latter include insurance companies, banks, trusts, special leasing companies, and subsidiaries of manufacturing, commercial transportation, and financial corporations. Some manufacturers organize subsidiary corporations to lease their equipment to users. As manufacturers are interested primarily in profits from manufacturing, rather than from leasing equipment, such subsidiaries may offer more favorable terms than independent lessors. Lease or rental fees paid to such companies will replace payments from sales and often give the lessor a more stable income stream.

An independent lessor purchases the equipment or machinery it leases to users directly from the manufacturer, often having it delivered directly to the lessee. An independent lessor's profits are derived from leasing fees, agency or dealer discounts, and markups on the list price of the equipment. Much of the lessor's profit results from selling the equipment to the user at the end of the lease period, or from selling it in the open market as used equipment.

Banks have been permitted to engage in leasing since 1963, and their influence has been significant.† Unlike manufacturers and dealers, who use leasing as a merchandising device, banks and leasing companies make their profits from leasing rather than from manufacturing or markups. For this reason, they must take great care in dealing with both the manufacturers from whom they purchase the property and the firms to which they lease. They have a smaller margin for error.

Customarily, a lessee negotiates the purchase of the equipment according to its own specifications and then issues a purchase order in the name of the lessor. Ordinarily, the lessor pledges the lease as security for a loan. If the lessee pays the rentals and other obligations directly to the lessor, it may lose the equipment if the lessor defaults on a note that is secured by the leased property. Therefore, a company using leased property should secure the right, in the lease agreement, to make rental payments directly to the bank or any other lender, rather than to the lessor. Then, even if the leasing company should cease to operate, the lessee's right to the leased property would be

---

† Eugene F. Brigham, "The Impact of Bank Entry on Market Conditions in the Equipment Leasing Industry," *National Banking Review* (September 1964), p. 12.

protected. Another protective measure against repossession is a clause in the agreement that permits the lessee to take title to the property by paying off all remaining rentals at the time of any default by the lessor.†

Leasing as a Merchandising Method

Industries that have used leasing as a primary merchandising device probably account for some of the current popularity of leasing. In a few companies, for example, International Business Machines (IBM), products could be obtained only through leasing (until the federal courts forced them to offer their products for sale). Now many companies, no doubt influenced by the financial success of leasing manufacturers, offer to lease as well as sell their products. The use of leasing accelerated further when independent leasing firms entered the field, reducing users' dependence on manufacturers and making the leasing market more competitive. The manufacturing company that offers direct leasing benefits both from enlarging the market for its products and from spreading its rental income over the lease period, which may result in tax advantages. Furthermore, this mode of operation affords the lessor better control over the secondhand market for its products. (In order to maintain the market for the equipment, the manufacturer may scrap used equipment rather than sell it secondhand.)

ACCOUNTING FOR LEASES

Financial Accounting Standards Board (FASB) No. 13 represents the results of the accounting profession's continuing efforts to provide for accurate disclosure of the nature and impact of a firm's outstanding lease obligations. Accountants have been working on this issue since 1949, when the AIA‡ issued *Accounting Research Bulletin No. 38,* "Disclosure of Long-Term Leases in Financial Statements of Lessees." The current statement reconciles, to a large degree, the inconsistencies in the reporting requirements for lessors and lessees. It also serves to reconcile accounting requirements with those of the Securities and Exchange Commission.

Most of the financial community regards leases as a specialized form of debt. Current reporting requirements treat them exactly that way in order to result in consistent financial statements and to eliminate any incomparability that might result from use of this specialized form of financing. As of December 31, 1980, all new long-term leases are reported, in effect, as loans. A distinction, however, is made between financial and operating leases.

---

† Lee, *Introduction to Leasing,* p. 58.
‡ AIA was the forerunner of the American Institute of Certified Public Accountants (AICPA).

Classification of Leases

For reporting purposes, leases are of two types: *capital* and *operating*. **Capital leases** are what we have called *financial leases*. However, *FASB No. 13* definition is necessarily more precise. For accounting purposes, a lease is a capital lease if it meets any one of the following four requirements: (1) ownership of the leased property is transferred to the lessee at the end of the lease, (2) the lease contains a purchase option at such a low price that it is relatively certain that the lessee will exercise it, (3) the term of the lease equals 75% or more of the economic life of the asset,† or (4) the *present value* of the *minimum lease payments* (excluding that portion attributable to insurance, maintenance, and/or taxes) equals or exceeds 90% of the *fair value* of the asset (adjusted for any investment tax credit taken by the lessor).

All these provisions are straightforward except for the last. It requires explanation because it uses some uniquely defined terms. The *minimum lease payments* include minimum rental payments over the term of the lease, any residual value guaranteed by the lessee,‡ and any payment the lessee must make (or can be required to make) if it does not renew at the end of the current term. To calculate the *present value* of these payments, a discount rate must be defined. The prescribed rate is the lower of either the current loan rate the lessee would be charged to obtain funds for a similar transaction, or the implicit rate in that lease. (The "implicit rate" is the lessor's IRR—the discount rate that makes the present value of the rental portion of the payments equal the worth of the leased asset.)

The *fair value* of an asset is the price that would be arrived at in an arm's length transaction between independent parties. The fair value is the normal selling price of the asset reduced by the usual trade and/or quantity discounts.

Operating leases are defined by exclusion. Any lease that does not qualify as a capital lease is an operating lease.

Reporting of Leases

FASB No. 13 affects the reporting of all leases. For capital leases, the balance sheet shows an asset and a corresponding liability account for the leased asset. The amount of these accounts is the smaller of (1) the present value of the minimum lease payments (excluding the portion for insurance, maintenance, and taxes) or (2) the fair value of the asset, as previously defined.

The lessee's income statements treat the leased asset essentially as a loan-purchased asset. The asset account on the balance sheet is depreciated in a

---

† This provision does not apply if the lease starts in the last 25% of the economic life of the asset.

‡ If the lease contains a "bargain purchase option," as described in no. (2), the bargain purchase price is included here.

manner consistent with the firm's normal depreciation policy. If the lease contains a purchase requirement or a bargain purchase option, the depreciable life is the economic life of the asset. Otherwise, the asset is depreciated over the term of the lease.

Lease payments are treated as if they were loan payments. The interest rate, as previously described, is used to set up an amortization schedule. Each loan payment is considered to be part interest, which is reported as expense in the income statement, and part principal, which reduces the balance sheet liability.

The assets created by such accounting and their accumulated amortization, that is, depreciation, must be identified separately in the balance sheet (or its footnotes). The corresponding created liabilities must also be identified separately. The same is true of the income statement entries.

For capital leases, *FASB No. 13* requires that financial statements indicate

1. The gross amount of assets under the capital lease classified by nature or function.
2. Future minimum lease payments, in aggregate and for each of the next five years.
3. Sublease rentals.
4. Total contingent rentals.

FASB No. 13 does not change the reporting requirement for operating leases substantially, although it does call for more detailed disclosure. Rent is charged off as an expense when it becomes payable. If the payments are not all of equal amount, however, an adjustment may be required. Unless the firm can justify some other pattern, the expense must be recognized straight-line, that is, as if all lease payments were the same.

For operating leases, with remaining noncancellable terms exceeding one year, the firm must disclose

1. Future minimum rental payments, in aggregate and for each of the next five years.
2. Minimum rentals due in the future from noncancellable subleases.

For all operating leases, the firm must provide detailed breakdowns regarding rental expense and subleases.

Finally, the firm's financial statements must include a general description of the firm's leasing arrangements. At a minimum, this description must include

1. The basis for contingent rental payments.
2. The nature of any renewal, purchase, or escalation clauses in the leases.
3. Any restrictive covenants in the lease contracts.

In addition to these general provisions covering capital and operating leases, *FASB No. 13* contains specific requirements for leases involving real estate and leases based on sale and leaseback arrangements.

LEGAL CONSIDERATIONS

To be taxed as leases, contracts must conform to IRS requirements. Leases receive tax treatment different from that accorded to loans. They also have a different legal status that is important when a firm is forced into court under adverse conditions.

IRS Requirements

To be tax deductible as a rental expense, lease contracts must not be conditional sales contracts. "Rental or other payments required to be made as condition to the continued use or possession, for purposes of trade or business, of property to which the taxpayer has not taken or is not taking title or in which he has no equity"† are deductible for tax purposes.

Any lease that provides the lessee with the option to buy the asset at the end of the lease period can raise a potential tax problem. Specifically, a lease could be ruled a conditional sale, and lease payments disallowed as deductions, if the rental terms include any of the following: (1) rental payments are made applicable to any equity to be acquired by the lessee; (2) title passes to the lessee after a stated number of payments have been made; (3) required payments over a short period are inordinately large compared to the total sum needed to secure a transfer of title; (4) contracted rental payments materially exceed the current value, so that the payments include more than compensation for use of the property; (5) a purchase option specifies a nominal price relative to the value of the property at the time the option may be exercised, or a small amount relative to the total required payments; or (6) some portion of the periodic payments is designated or recognizable as the equivalent of interest.

While this issue may sound complicated, the idea is simple. If a company is essentially buying an asset, the IRS will not let it call the contract a lease so that it can deduct lease payments as expenses. If a lessee wants to buy the asset at the end of the lease, it must pay a price equal to what an independent third party would pay in an arm's length transaction; that is, it must pay the market value. A lessor and a lessee cannot reach an agreement to include part of the purchase price in the lease payments and have the lessee deduct it as rent.

---

† Internal Revenue Code, Section 162(a)(3).

Court Treatment of Leases

In reorganization and bankruptcy proceedings, rental agreements frequently receive more favorable treatment than debt obligations. Because the property leased does not belong to the business firm in financial difficulties, it cannot be seized by creditors. The receiver or trustee may decide to retain the leased asset and continue to pay rentals on it, or it may break the lease and return the leased property to its owner, accompanied by a payment of three years' rentals in cases of reorganization or bankruptcy.

In the case of debt obligations, however, the trustee or receiver may seize the property purchased with funds raised by borrowing. If the property is secured by a chattel mortgage, the lender has first claim to the pledged asset; if the receipts from the sale of the property are insufficient to satisfy the claims of the lender, the lender becomes a general creditor for the remainder of his claim. If leased assets cannot be distinguished from owned assets (because of the passage of time and/or sloppy identification procedures), leased assets may end up being held for the benefit of all creditors. It is therefore important for the lessor to make sure that such assets are properly identified and well marked.

LEASING—PROS AND CONS

Leasing is simply one more alternative that the firm must evaluate as a possible source of short-, intermediate-, and/or long-term financing. Some of the so-called advantages of leasing are illusory, evaporating when one considers them more closely. It is important to differentiate the advantages of operating leases and financial leases. One of the main benefits of short-term leases is their flexibility. This is not a characteristic of financial leases, which are generally as restrictive as their alternative—installment loans. Whether leasing or borrowing is cheaper can be determined only by detailed analysis, which we will demonstrate later.

Advantages of Operating Leases

Operating leases allow a firm to "own" part or all of an asset for part of its economic life. A company may want to have an office downtown and a store in the suburbs. To do so, it does not need to own a downtown office building and a suburban shopping center. The natural alternative is a lease. It can lease one office—a piece of the office building—and a single store—part of the shopping center.

Similarly, a firm may not need an asset year round. For example, a cannery may need extra forklifts and loading equipment only during the peak season, which would vary according to the nature of the commodity it was canning.

A company with its own fleet of trucks might own enough units for its normal needs and lease additional units for seasonal needs, for example back-to-school, Easter, and Christmas sales.

The ability to lease additional assets, or parts of assets, for only those times when they are needed is one of the most highly touted advantages of leases—flexibility. This advantage, though, is available only in operating, or maintenance, leases. Financial leases do not allow this sort of piecemeal "ownership."

Operational, or service, leases offer another possible advantage. Many service leases are direct leases; that is, the lessor is the manufacturer of the asset or a leasing subsidiary of the manufacturer. Many of these include maintenance as part of the lease package. Some suggest that direct leases provide the lessee with better maintenance at lower cost than would otherwise be available. (Examples of assets that may be leased in this manner include such diverse items as typewriters, office machines, duplicating machines, computers, forklifts, automobiles, tractor-trailer rigs, boxcars, and locomotives.)

In a direct lease, the lessor, the manufacturer, knows the product inside out. It holds title to the asset and therefore has an incentive to maintain it well; this keeps the lessee happy and increases the residual value of the asset. Further, the lessee benefits from an insurance effect. The manufacturer's cost of maintaining the more troublesome units would be offset by the savings on better-made units. Cynics might suggest that a manufacturer takes greater care in producing units that are to be leased rather than sold; a manufacturer-lessor would not knowingly sell itself a lemon.

Operating leases provide the lessee with another benefit—they allow the firm to continue to use the most up-to-date equipment or machinery available. Some service leases even make specific provisions for updating equipment whenever a new and improved version of the leased asset becomes available. Computer leases are common examples. A direct lease from IBM may provide for replacement of the original equipment with any updated versions that become available during the lease term.

Use of the most current equipment may have either tangible or intangible benefits. The tangible benefits come from using improved technology. Improved equipment can make jobs easier, quicker, or in some way less unpleasant (e.g., by providing improved job hazard protection).

Intangible benefits may be every bit as significant as tangible ones. Using new equipment can improve employee morale and therefore raise productivity. New equipment can also serve a marketing function. Businesses, like individuals, enjoy associating with those that are prospering. If leasing allows a company to use new equipment, or drive new cars or trucks, or be in a better location, the company's image may benefit. An improved appearance may well result in higher sales and profits.

Advantages of Financial Leases

Financial leases allow the firm to deduct costs that are otherwise nondeductible—primarily land. Land cannot be depreciated for tax purposes. If a business purchased a high-priced business site in a downtown financial district, for example, it would not be allowed to depreciate its investment in the land. If, on the other hand, the firm leased such sites, the lease payments would be tax deductible as rental expense.

Lease financing may be available when a firm is unable to borrow to buy an asset. This can happen for a number of reasons. First, the asset simply may not be for sale. Exclusive business locations are good examples. The firm may find itself unable to buy the location it wants—the owner will not sell (or at least not at an economically defensible price). There are other circumstances in which leasing may be possible when borrowing is not. If a firm has already borrowed heavily, lenders may be reluctant to advance any additional funds, believing that the firm's equity base is insufficient (that the firm is, in the lender's opinion, too highly leveraged).

A lessor may be better protected legally than a lender because of the court's treatment of leases. If an overextended firm goes bankrupt, the lessor simply reclaims its asset plus any rental payments the courts allow for the lessor's inconvenience. Alternatively, the receiver of the bankrupt firm may elect to honor the lease, in which case the lessor continues to receive its lease payments. If the lease is broken, the lessor may be inconvenienced by having to look for another lessee, but this is obviously better than being one of several claimants hoping to receive some compensation for loans made to the firm.

In some cases, leasing can offer the firm financing not otherwise available. For example, a firm's ability to borrow may be restricted by conditions of past loan contracts. One of the most onerous of such restrictions is the "after-acquired property" clause. Bond indentures of some extremely highly leveraged firms contain such clauses, as is the case in some railroad mortgage bonds. The clause says, in effect, that the mortgage securing the named bonds applies not only to existing property at the time of execution, but also to any real or other tangible property to be acquired in the future. Under such conditions, any lender financing an acquisition for such a company immediately subordinates its claims to those of the existing bondholders. The after-acquired property clause makes it nearly impossible for a company to obtain new debt financing. These clauses, however, normally do not cover leases. The result has been widespread use of lease financing for boxcars, locomotives, and other railroad equipment, which has allowed firms to acquire property without borrowing. Leases are also a popular form of financing in other sectors of the transportation industry, for example, trucking and barge transport.

Leases are often recommended as a way of allowing the firm to avoid the risk of equipment obsolescence; the lessor, not the lessee, is stuck with equipment when it becomes technologically outmoded. Such a view though, is myopic. When a lessor determines the amount of the lease payments to be charged, it takes account of the expected salvage value of the equipment in its calculations. If a lessor expects a piece of equipment to be outdated before the lease ends, it assumes a lower residual value for the asset, and it sets lease payments correspondingly higher.

Leases do not shift the *cost* of obsolescence; they do shift the *risk* of *unexpected* obsolescence. To the extent that the lessor underestimates the rate of technological change, it will overestimate the residual value of its equipment and not charge high enough lease payments. A lessee may benefit from this risk shifting when the lessor is *better* able to estimate, avoid, or forestall such obsolescence. For example, one would assume that IBM is better able to estimate the rate of technological advance in computers than the average user could be. In addition, IBM (or any other computer manufacturer-lessor) would be in a better position to update the lessee's older equipment or to lease it to another user who did not need the most recent equipment.

We have made some fairly fine semantic distinctions here, which it might be well to summarize. Leases do not allow lessees to avoid obsolescence costs (or risk). To the extent that an asset is expected to become obsolete, lease payments will be higher to compensate for that cost to the lessor. The greater the probability (risk) of such obsolescence, the more will be loaded into the lease charge. However, because a lessor may be better able to predict (or deal with) such risk than a user would be, leasing may be a relatively inexpensive form of insurance against unexpected obsolescence.

Disadvantages of Leasing

No financial decision is one-sided. While leases offer many benefits, they also have some disadvantages. The flexibility of leasing, its availability, and the shifting of technological risk are all attractive. Lessors know this, however, and can price accordingly. Leasing can be costly: For a lessor, the lease payments must include recapture of the original investment, interest, service costs (if maintenance is provided), an allowance for obsolescence, taxes, insurance, and any other costs associated with ownership.

Leasing allows the firm to expense the cost of a location (land), a deduction that otherwise would not be possible. However, when the lease runs out, the firm does not own the land. When it leases, a business forfeits any residual asset values.

Leasing may allow a firm to obtain the use of equipment it could not otherwise afford and get better maintenance in the bargain. The asset belongs to the lessor, though, and the lessor may resist any special-purpose modification of it. Such modification might help the lessee but reduce the market value (or lease potential) for the general market. The lessee must anticipate such restrictions when it leases equipment.

Lease payments are tax deductible. On the other side of the coin, however, are tax benefits that come with ownership, and a lessee is not entitled to these. The lessee forfeits the investment tax credit that the government allows purchasers of new capital equipment (unless the lease contract specifies that the tax credit will pass through to the lessee). In addition, a company cannot take depreciation on an asset it does not own—one that it leases.

The last disadvantage of leasing relates to its impact on the firm's ability to borrow. While firms can sometimes lease when debt financing is not reasonably available, this does not mean that lenders ignore the effect of outstanding leases. Financial leases are essentially long-term loans that are treated differently for tax purposes, and they are shown in published financial statements. A lender assessing the leverage position of a firm will give full weight to required lease payments. Every dollar due a lessor is one less dollar available to service outstanding loans. Firms have an overall limit on the amount of money they can borrow, and lease commitments reduce that loan capacity dollar for dollar.

In summary, leases have both advantages and disadvantages, which are outlined in Table 11.1. Operating leases enable piecemeal ownership, may make better maintenance available for the equipment, and allow the firm to use the latest equipment, which may have both functional and marketing benefits.

Financial leases allow business to write off location costs. Lease financing may be possible when the firm cannot borrow because of high leverage or restrictions in past loan contracts. Further, leasing shifts the risk of unexpected obsolescence to the lessor.

TABLE 11.1
Leasing: Advantages and Disadvantages.

Advantages	Disadvantages
Operating Leases	Cost
Piecemeal ownership	Loss of residual value
Better service	Difficulty in modifying assets
Latest equipment	Loss of ownership tax benefits
Financial Leases	Lowered debt capacity
Depreciation of land	
Availability	
Shift of unexpected risk of obsolescence	

These benefits are not free. Leasing can be costly. By leasing, the firm chooses not to acquire potentially valuable assets. The lessor's agreement must be obtained to modify leased equipment. A lessee foregoes any tax benefit that might come from ownership. And leasing is another form of borrowing; it diminishes the firm's debt capacity just as surely as if it were an installment loan. Detailed discounted cash flow analysis is the only way to determine whether leasing is cheaper than borrowing to buy.

ANALYSIS OF LEASES[†]

Analysis of a leasing decision involves two separate issues: (1) the acquisition (or investment) and (2) the type of financing. Investment decisions require comparison of the present value of the *operating* benefits to the cost of the asset; this is the analysis described in Chapter 5. In lease-or-borrow analysis, only the second issue, financing, is considered.

To do this, we compare the *present-value cost of the lease* under consideration to the *present-value cost of a comparable loan*. The important word here is *comparable*. Both the amount of the loan and the timing of the loan payments must be similar to those of the lease. If they are not, the analysis is biased.

Setting up a comparable hypothetical loan is trickier than it sounds. Generally, leases require beginning-of-the-year (BOY) payments[‡] Therefore, the comparable loan must require a down payment equal to the first lease payment and a last loan payment that coincides with the last lease payment. For example, a *10-year* lease with BOY payments is comparable to a *9-year* loan with a down payment equaling the first lease payment.

The biases introduced by using noncomparable loans are subtle, but it becomes clear that they exist when you remember that interest on loans is tax deductible (an advantage) and that the present value of costs is lower if the costs can be postponed. Consider the 10-year BOY payment lease as a basis for discussion. If the alternative loan does not have a down payment (equal to the first lease payment), the analysis assumes that greater financing is available through borrowing. The result is predictable: a larger loan with more interest deductions makes borrowing look relatively more attractive. Using a 10-year loan rather than a 9-year comparable loan works the same

---

[†] We are considering here only analysis of financial leases. For analysis of cancelable leases, see David O. Jenkins, "Purchase or Cancelable Lease: Which Is Better?" *Financial Executive* (April 1970), pp. 26–31.

[‡] Leases often require monthly payments, but assuming annual payments makes the analysis less tedious. Our purpose is to explain how to set up the analysis.

way—the longer you stretch out the loan, the greater the interest deductions and the lower the present value of the after-tax loan costs.

Another problem in comparing *present-value costs* is choosing the correct discount rates. Lease-or-borrow analysis is different from many capital budgeting problems in that most of the cash flows are highly predictable. The lease payments are known with certainty. The amount of alternative loan payments (and how much is interest and principal) is also certain. If the firm buys the asset, it can count on getting the depreciation deductions, whose amount can be figured out exactly. Given that all these cash flows are predictable, they should be discounted at a low-risk rate—the firm's cost of debt.†

It is sometimes suggested that the correct discount rate to use for this analysis is the after-tax cost of debt. That is wrong, for it is double counting. In lease-or-borrow analysis we adjust the comparable loan to take account of the interest tax shields. Lease payments are also calculated after tax. To use an after-tax riskless rate is to count the effect of interest deductibility twice. Using this rate (which would be too low) has a predictable effect—normally, it makes leasing look more attractive. The reason for this lies in the timing of the tax benefits of ownership. Ownership tax benefits come early in the life of the asset; interest is highest in the early years, accelerated depreciation puts the big deductions in the early years, and tax credits are immediate. Leasing provides deductions that are more uniform over the lease period. What leasing loses in the early years, it makes up for later. The lower the discount rate, the better the later-year benefits of leasing look.

Lease-or-borrow analysis entails only one obviously uncertain cash flow—the residual (salvage) value of the asset. If the firm buys an asset, it has something of value at the end of the investment period—the asset. The more the asset is worth, the better buying looks. Yet, the future worth of an asset is unpredictable. Therefore, we discount salvage values at the same rates as other risky cash flows—the firm's average cost of capital.

Before illustrating the analysis with an example, we will summarize what is necessary to carry it out:

1. Find the present-value cost of the lease. Compute the present value of the *after-tax* lease payments at the before-tax cost of debt.

2. Set up a comparable loan that involves the same amount of borrowing and the same payment timing as the lease.

3. Break the loan payments into interest and principal components (tax-deductible and nondeductible elements).

---

† One of the first suggestions that the pretax cost of debt be used in lease analysis was stated in Myron J. Gordon, "A General Solution to the Buy or Lease Decision: A Pedagogical Note," *Journal of Finance* (March 1974), pp. 245–50.

4. Find the present-value cost of borrowing: the purchase price of the asset, minus the present value of the tax shields from ownership (interest and depreciation), and minus the present worth of the asset's salvage value. The certain flows (the tax shields) are discounted at the before-tax cost of debt, and the uncertain one (salvage value) is discounted at the cost of capital.

5. Choose the cheaper method of financing—the one with the lower present-value cost.

Lease-or-borrow analysis—An example.   The information to use in the calculations is shown in Table 11.2. The company could lease the asset for $2,500 a year (BOY payments) on a six-year lease. The company could also buy the asset for $10,000. The estimated salvage value of the machine, six years from now, is $1,000. For this example, assume straight-line depreciation to the estimated salvage value. The firm's current loan rate (before tax) is 18% and its cost of capital is 22%.

With this information, we can do the analysis. Example calculations for each step are explained separately.

Present-Value Cost of a Lease

The present-value after-tax cost of a lease can be found in a number of ways. Comparison with the "borrow" analysis is facilitated if it is done in two steps. First, the present value of the payments is found by multiplying the value of a single payment by the factor for the present value of an *annuity due* for six years at 18% (the firm's pretax cost of debt). Then, we calculate and deduct the tax shields.

TABLE 11.2
Example for Analysis.

The Lease

Term: 6 years
Payments: $2,500 per year; BOY payments

Ownership

Asset cost: $10,000
Estimated salvage value in 6 years: $1,000
Depreciation: Straight-line, $1,000 salvage
Current loan rate: 18% per year
Firm's cost of capital: 22%
Corporate tax rate: 40%

Annuity due is a new term. An annuity due is different from a regular annuity; it has BOY payments instead of end-of-year ones; therefore its present value interest factor (PVIFAD) is different. Recall that the PVIFA for a regular annuity is simply the sum of the individual interest factors for that number of years. For example (see Table 11.3), the PVIFA$_{18\%,6}$ for a six-year, 18% annuity would be 3.498, the sum of the PVIFs for one, two, three, four, five, and six years.

For a six-year annuity due (see Table 11.4), the payments would occur at the beginning (time zero) and at years one, two, three, four, and five; therefore the PVIFAD$_{18\%,5}$ is 4.127.

TABLE 11.3
PVIFA for a Six-Year, 18% Annuity.

Year	0	1	2	3	4	5	6
Amount		$1	$1	$1	$1	$1	$1
PVIF	.847 ← .847						
	.718 ←	.718					
	.609 ←		.609				
	.516 ←			.516			
	.437 ←				.437		
	.371 ←						.371
	3.498						

TABLE 11.4
PVIFAD for a Six-Year, 18% Annuity Due.

Year	0	1	2	3	4	5
Amount	$1	$1	$1	$1	$1	$1
PVIF	1.000					
	.847 ← .847					
	.718 ←	.718				
	.609 ←		.609			
	.516 ←			.516		
	.437 ←				.437	
	4.127					

TABLE 11.5
Lease or Borrow: Analysis of Leasing.

Item	Before Tax	After Tax	Time	Discount Factor	Present Value
Payments	$ 2,500	—	0–5	4.127	$ 10,318
Less: Tax shields	(2,500)	(1,000)	0–5	4.127	(4,127)
					$ 6,191

To find the PVIFAD for an annuity due for any number of years, look up the factor in the table for *one less year* and add 1 to account for the time-zero payment. For a six-year, 18% annuity due, the factor is 4.127: the PVIFA for *five* years (3.127) + 1 = 4.127. Algebraically, $PVIFAD_{\%,n} = PVIFA_{\%,n-1} + 1$.

The present value of the lease payments (as shown in Table 11.5) would be $10,318. A firm that leases the $10,000 asset is paying more than the present-value cost of the asset. In other words, the implicit rate on the lease is higher than the company's normal loan rate of 18%.

However, we have yet to account for the effect of taxes. While only the interest portion of a loan payment is deductible, the entire lease payment is deductible as an expense. Each $2,500 lease payment saves the firm $1,000 in taxes—the amount of the lease payment times the tax rate ($2,500 × .4 = $1,000). The present value of these tax shields reduces the present-value cost of leasing to $6,191 (Table 11.5).

Comparable Loan

Our lease involves the immediate payment of $2,500 (BOY payments). To be comparable, a hypothetical loan must involve the same first payment. A loan comparable to this lease would require a $2,500 down payment and a loan of $7,500 ($10,000 − 2,500 = $7,500). The loan must be comparable not only in amount but also in terms. As the lease involves level payments over the next five years, the loan must also be for five years.

Knowing the amount and term of the loan, we can calculate the annual payments (as illustrated in Chapter 3) by dividing the loan amount by the PVIFA for five years at the firm's current loan rate of 18% as follows:

$$\text{Annual loan payment} = \frac{\$7,500}{3.127} = \$2,398.$$

Segmenting the Loan

Only the interest part of a loan payment is deductible, so we must identify the interest and principal components of each payment in an amortization schedule. One is provided for the comparable loan in Table 11.6.

Each row of the table separates the interest, which is deductible, from the principal, which is not. Since none of the down payment is interest, none of it is deductible. Of the next payment, $1,350 is interest—18% times the beginning loan balance of $7,500. The rest of the payment is principal ($2,398 − 1,350 = $1,048), which reduces the remaining balance to $6,452 ($7,500 − 1,048 = $6,452). Second-year interest is 18% of that amount: $1,611 = .18($6,452). The amortization continues over the life of the loan and demonstrates that the calculated payments would amortize the loan, that is, that the present value of the payments if $7,500. The sum of the down payment ($2,500) and the present value of the loan payments equals $10,000, the cost of the asset.

Present-Value Cost of Borrowing

The analysis of borrowing (Table 11.7) is similar to the lease analysis. The first entry is the present value of the payments, which equals the cost of the asset, $10,000.

Next, calculate the tax shields from interest. The before-tax amount comes directly from the amortization schedule in Table 11.6. To find the after-tax amount, multiply each of these entries by the firm's marginal tax rate, which is assumed to be 40%. The present value of the after-tax amount is calculated by multiplying this after-tax amount by the PVIF for the appropriate number of years at the before-tax cost of debt 18%.

TABLE 11.6
Amortization of a Comparable Loan.

Time	Payment	Principal	Interest	Balance
0	$2,500	$2,500	$ 0	$7,500
1	2,398	1,048	1,350	6,452
2	2,398	1,237	1,161	5,215
3	2,398	1,460	939	3,755
4	2,398	1,722	676	2,033
5	$2,398	$2,033	$ 366	$ 0

TABLE 11.7
Lease or Borrow: Analysis of Borrowing.

Item	Before Tax	After Tax	Time	Discount Factor	Present Value
Payments			0–5		$ 10,000
Less: Interest shields	$(1,350)	$ (540)	1	.847	(458)
	(1,161)	(464)	2	.718	(333)
	(939)	(376)	3	.609	(229)
	(676)	(270)	4	.516	(139)
	(366)	(146)	5	.437	(64)
Depreciation shields	(1,500)	(600)	1–6	3.498	(2,099)
Salvage	$(1,000)	$(1,000)	6	.303	(303)
					$ 6,375

Ownership also affords tax shields from depreciation. Writing off the $10,000 cost, straight-line to a $1,000 salvage, would yield deductions of $1,500 a year for six years:

$$\frac{\$10,000 - 1,000}{6} = \$1,500.$$

The after-tax amount is found by multiplying by the tax rate.

The discount factor for these flows would be a PVIFA for six years at the firm's before-tax cost of debt, 18%. From the tables, the factor is 3.498, making the present value of the depreciation-related tax shields $2,099.

Finally, we find the present value of the expected salvage. For this risky cash flow, we discount at the cost of capital (22%). The present value of the equipment's expected future worth ($1,000) is $303.

To calculate the cost of borrowing, subtract the present worth of all these elements from the present value of the loan payments, or the cost of the asset, $10,000. Our example reveals that the present-value cost of borrowing is $6,375.

Financing Choice

Our illustration shows that in the long run, leasing is cheaper than borrowing— $6,191 is less than $6,375. Note that this is true even though the firm paid a slight premium for leasing—the present value of the payments was more than the cost of the asset ($10,318 > $10,000). The key to this difference lies in the tax deductions. In this particular instance, the present value of the tax benefits from leasing was greater than that of the tax benefits and salvage that the firm would obtain from ownership. This result will not hold in all cases. Each analysis is different. Whether leasing or borrowing is better will depend on the amount of the lease payments, their timing, the firm's current borrowing rate, the tax benefits of ownership at the time, and the expected future worth of the asset in question. The DCF analysis will tell you which form of financing is cheaper.

This last point needs emphasis. As noted earlier, the analysis here considers only the financing problem. It does not address acquisition, or the investment issue. Whether the asset should be acquired depends on the present value of the *operating* flows. DCF lease-or-borrow analysis indicates only whether to lease or borrow *after* the firm decides that it is a worthwhile investment.

SUMMARY

A lease is an extended rental agreement. It is a financing arrangement that provides the firm with one way of obtaining the use of assets to produce goods and services for sale. Leases are of two types—operating and financial. Operating leases are short-term, renewable contracts; they allow the firm considerable flexibility in using part of an asset or using all of the asset for part of its useful life.

Financial leases are long-term contracts that are quite similar to installment loans. Over the life of a financial lease, the user will repay the full cost of the asset plus "interest." However, a lease payment does not consist of principal and interest; the entire payment is for the use of the asset and is therefore tax deductible to the lessee. The lessee does not own the asset at the end of the lease. Title remains with the lessor.

Lease financing is available from a number of sources. Most financial institutions that lend to businesses (banks, insurance companies, pension funds) also engage in financial leasing. Some manufacturing firms have their own leasing divisions, or subsidiaries, for leasing as a way to help market their products. There are also many independent lessors, firms or individuals, whose primary businesses is leasing.

FASB No. 13 has materially changed the accounting for leases, especially financial leases. Now a financial lease is capitalized, that is, the present value of the lease payments is shown in financial statements as a liability (just like a loan), and a corresponding account is shown as an asset. The asset account is amortized (depreciated) over time, just as if the firm had bought the asset outright.

For the lessee to be able to take advantage of its tax deductions, the lease contract must meet IRS requirements; it cannot be a disguised loan. Some shaky firms can lease when they cannot borrow, because the courts protect lessors better than lenders when a lessee (or borrower) runs into financial difficulty.

The advantages and disadvantages of leasing have been debated for years. Operating leases allow great flexibility. The same is not true of financial leases. If financial markets are efficient, which generally is conceded to be true, leasing cannot offer any advantage for which the firm does not pay.

Discounted cash flow analysis is necessary to compare financing choices. In each instance, the firm must evaluate the advantages and their cost, and then make a choice. The better form of financing is the one that offers the lowest present-value cost.

QUESTIONS AND REVIEW ACTIVITIES

1. Define, discuss, or explain
   a) Leasing.
   b) Operating leases.
   c) Financial leases.
   d) Sale and leaseback.
   e) Direct leases.
   f) *FASB No. 13.*
   g) Capital lease.
   h) IRS requirements for a lease.

2. Given the difference in the treatment of loans and leases by the courts, would you prefer to provide equipment to a financially shaky customer on an installment sales contract (loan) or a financial lease? Why?

3. Explain the use of leasing in financing stores, shopping centers, and large department stores.

4. Compare and contrast the provisions of a lease contract with the provisions of other debt instruments, such as conditional sales contracts.

5. Can a firm hedge against the risk of inflation by leasing?

6. Can a firm hedge against any technological change in its industry by leasing?

PROBLEMS

1. Rapid Photo Best Corp. (RPB) develops and prints photographs and slides. It also sells film, but its main business is processing. The firm's competitive advantages are convenience, speed, and cost. RPB outlets are primarily drive-up booths at convenience markets; it offers 24-hour service on most popular film sizes, and its prices are low.

   A recent technological development of a new film format requires the firm to acquire a new form of processor. The new size of film is designed for computer processing; this allows lower cost and faster processing, and has some other technical benefits.

   RPB has decided that it must acquire the new processors to remain competitive; market acceptance of the new format has been very good, and it looks as if the new film size will account for a lot of sales in the snapshot market. RPB can buy a processor outright from the sole producer for a cash price of $50,000, or it can lease the equipment at $16,000 a year, with end-of-year payments for five years. The equipment has a useful life of five years and no salvage value. RPB's tax rate is 40%, its current loan rate is 15%, and it uses straight-line depreciation.

Should RPB lease the equipment or borrow from its normal source? (Note that for simplicity, this lease assumes end-of-year payments; the comparable loan would be a $50,000 five-year loan, with no down payment and level annual installments.)

2. Fictional Corp. is considering the acquisition of a $100,000 piece of capital equipment. The equipment has an economic life of eight years. Depreciation would be straight-line (eight years, $4,000 salvage value). The company requires a 20% return on risky flows.

The company can borrow the money from the bank at 16% or lease from the manufacturer's leasing subsidiary for $18,000 a year. Using either plan, there would be BOY payments—a first payment plus seven equal annual installments. The tax rate is 40%. Prepare the lease-or-borrow analysis.

3. Whymzee, Inc., is evaluating the acquisition of some new electronic data processing equipment. It is estimated to have an economic life of five years. If purchased, the equipment would cost $17,500. It would be depreciated using the sum-of-the-years-digits method over a five-year life to a realistically estimated salvage value of $2,500. In addition, ownership would entitle Whymzee to an immediate $1,750 investment tax credit. If the firm borrows from the bank, it could receive 14% equipment-secured financing.

As an alternative, the manufacturer can lease the equipment for five years at $4,675 a year, with BOY payments. If the equipment is leased, the manufacturer will provide all necessary maintenance. If Whymzee buys the equipment, maintenance would cost the company $500 a year—a long-term maintenance contract with BOY payments. This type of contract is fairly common; it makes the payments certain, that is, riskless.

The company estimates that its cost of capital is 18%. The tax rate is 40%. Prepare the lease-or-borrow analysis.

ADDITIONAL READINGS

Bower, R. S. "Issues in Lease Financing," *Financial Management* (Winter 1973), pp. 25–34.

Gordon, M. J. "A General Solution to the Lease or Buy Decision: A Pedagogical Note," *Journal of Finance* (March 1974), pp. 245–50.

Henderson, G. V., Jr. "A Decision Format for Lease or Buy Analysis," *Review of Business and Economic Research* (Fall 1976), pp. 63–72.

———"A General Solution to the Lease or Buy Decision: A Pedagogical Note: Comment," *Journal of Finance* (March 1976), pp. 147–51.

Jenkins, D. O. "Purchase or Cancelable Lease: Which Is Better?" *Financial Executive* (April 1970), pp. 26–31.

Miller, M. H., and C. W. Upton. "Leasing, Buying, and the Cost of Capital Services," *Journal of Finance* (June 1976), pp. 761–86.

Statement of Financial Accounting Standards No. 13. Stanford, Calif.: Financial Accounting Standards Board, 1976.

Vancil, R. F. "Lease or Borrow—New Method of Analysis," *Harvard Business Review* (September–October 1961), pp. 122–36.

- **DEBT**
  INVESTMENT FEATURES OF BONDS
  ASSET CLAIM
  INCOME CLAIM
  VOTING PARTICIPATION
  DEBT RETIREMENT

- **LEVERAGE**
  OPERATING LEVERAGE
  FINANCIAL LEVERAGE
  CASH FLOW BREAK-EVEN
  LEVERAGE MEASUREMENT

12

DEBT AND LEVERAGE

Businesses in the United States make extensive use of debt financing. The calculations in Chapter 4 do much to explain why; debt is one of the cheapest forms of financing. The cost is lowered even further by the tax deductibility of interest.

The main reason bondholders will accept lower returns than equity investors is safety. Bondholders have a legally enforceable contractual claim against the firm. Their rights are enumerated in the bond contract called an *indenture*. Further, the federal law provides for a watchguard to protect bondholders' rights. In addition to their priority claim on income, bondholders have a prior claim on assets.

In addition to receiving interest, bondholders must be repaid the principal amount of the bond issue. Retirement provisions are spelled out in the indenture. To allow themselves additional flexibility, corporations often reserve the right to retire a bond issue before maturity (**call provision**). Whether a call is economically wise depends on the costs and benefits of such refunding.

Debt financing's low cost is not without penalty. Using such fixed-cost financing makes returns to shareholders more volatile, a phenomenon called **financial leverage**. The effects of financial leverage are more or less pronounced depending on the extent to which the firm has high fixed operating expenses (**operating leverage**). A financial manager must be able to analyze and quantify these leverage effects. The applicable techniques are financial break-even analysis and degree of leverage measures.

After careful study of this chapter, you should

1. Understand what debt financing is and identify those investment and safety features that make bonds (and notes) attractive to investors.

2. Know what an indenture is and how the Trust Indenture Act of 1939 serves to safeguard bondholders' rights.

3. Know how asset and income claim provisions serve to distinguish different types of bonds.

4. Recognize the different types of retirement provisions.

5. Know the purpose of a call provision, what a refunding is, and how to analyze a refunding.

6. Understand the concept of leverage and know the difference between operating and financial leverage.

7. Know how to analyze the choice between debt and equity financing using financial break-even analysis.

8. Be able to quantify the impact of leverage on earnings variability through the calculation of the degree of leverage measures.

DEBT

Corporations that need to raise long-term funds from outside sources frequently issue bonds or long-term notes to finance their requirements. Although they are the same in substance, bonds and long-term notes differ in form. Either may be secured by specific assets or unsecured, and both are issued under provisions designed to minimize the risks that are associated with long-term credit.

The present chapter discusses bonds; long-term notes are described in Chapter 15 in the section titled "Exemption and Private Placement." Both corporate issuers and potential investors have reason to be concerned with a bond's or note's maturity date, income and asset claims, and possible enforcement of rights for the investors.

INVESTMENT FEATURES OF BONDS

A **bond** is a written promise by the firm to pay the bond investor a specific sum of money one year or more after its issue. Customarily, corporations issue a bond as one of a series of similar credit instruments, all of which may or may not be of the same denomination and maturity. If a corporation borrows $10 million for 25 years, the resulting debt may be represented by 10,000 bonds of the standard $1,000 denomination. The aggregate is called a **bond issue,** and it is supported by the general credit of the debtor and by any security that may be specifically pledged. Most corporate bonds are in $1,000 denominations or multiples thereof, but $500 and $100 bonds, commonly called *baby bonds*, are issued occasionally. The major purchasers in the corporate bond market are institutional investors, such as banks, insurance companies, and pension funds.

Indenture Provisions

A document called a **trust indenture** describes the bondholders' rights and claims on the corporation's assets. The indenture contains a series of protective covenants and other contractual features that, taken together, create the bond contract. A *debenture*, a similar-sounding word sometimes confused with bond *indenture*, is a special type of bond that is discussed later. If the corporation issues a mortgage bond, a mortgage trust deed is drawn up and deposited with a trustee. Should the corporation pledge intangible property, such as stocks and bonds, the trustee may take physical possession of the collateral used as security. The indenture customarily contains a preamble giving the purpose of the indenture, the actions taken by the corporation to make the issue legal (such as a resolution by the board of directors), information on the nature of the bonds and bond coupons (if any), and other details. The indenture names the two parties of the contract—the debtor corporation (issuer) and the trustee—and also indicates the fees, commissions, and other payments to be received by the latter. The indenture states the conditions covering the issuance of the bonds, call features, right to convert into common stock, and other features.

A trust indenture contains a complete description of the pledged property and a statement as to whether or not property acquired in the future is to be included in the mortgage (after-acquired property clause). The debtor corporation agrees to keep mortgaged property in good repair, to insure it against loss from fire and other risks, to pay all assessments and taxes levied upon it, to defend the title and see that the mortgage is properly recorded, and possibly to make provisions for a sinking fund.

The corporation usually agrees to create no debt having priority over the claims of creditors covered in the indenture, to pay dividends only when earnings exceed interest and sinking fund requirements by a specified amount or percentage, not to permit net working capital to fall below a certain figure, and not to sell fixed assets unless the proceeds are used to retire the debt. Other restrictions cover the lease of property, consolidations, and mergers. The trust indenture also specifies the action that may be taken by trustees and bondholders in the event that the corporation defaults on any of its agreements. In case of default, the trust indenture may permit the trustee to take possession of the mortgaged property and to operate it for the benefit of the creditors, to sell the property to the highest bidder, to foreclose the mortgage and dispose of the property under judicial sale, to bring suit for specific performance of any agreement, to declare the principal due (the acceleration clause), and to take action to recover the unpaid portion of the debt. Without an acceleration clause, the trustee could bring suit for each missed payment but could not take action to recover the principal until the bond was due to mature. As the maturity date could be many years in the future, the bondholders' chances of recovering the principal are much poorer than they would be if legal action could begin immediately. The acceleration clause addresses this unfortunate possibility. As you may surmise, a trust indenture can be quite lengthy: One involving Pan American Airlines and several lenders (both domestic and international) exceeded 500 pages.

Trust Indenture Act of 1939

The Trust Indenture Act of 1939 requires corporations to select disinterested and competent trustees. To be considered disinterested, a trustee must have no financial or other interest in the issue that would conflict with the interests of investors. Trustees must provide the bondholders with periodic and special reports on the status of the trust, the condition of property held in trust, and other matters, and must notify bondholders of any default within 90 days. In case of default, the trustee must discharge his or her responsibilities with the same degree of care and skill that a prudent person would exercise under similar circumstances.

ASSET CLAIM

The claim on assets frequently is part of the description of the specific bond or note issue. A bond may be known as a *first mortgage bond, second mortgage bond, collateral trust bond,* or *debenture bond*. Generally, the name denotes the type of asset pledged; in the case of a debenture bond, it refers to lack of a specific asset. While the bondholders' claims to assets and income are interrelated, we will discuss them separately in order to emphasize each. We should stress that bondholders rely on the corporation's earnings to secure the payment of principal and interest. Pledging of specific assets is insurance in case the corporation is unable to fulfill its commitments.

Mortgage Bonds

A firm may give a **mortgage bond** on real property in order to obtain funds at a lower cost; however, if the earnings of the debtor are inadequate to meet interest and principal payments on the debt, the value of the assets pledged as security also may be inadequate to meet the same obligations in case of a foreclosure or liquidation sale. Nevertheless, holders of mortgage bonds have prospects of collecting something of value from the sale of the mortgaged assets. They also participate on the same basis as unsecured creditors in the distribution of the remaining assets of the corporation.

Another value of a first mortgage bond to creditors is that it gives them a prior claim on the earnings of the debtor corporation. Earnings must be available to retire debts and to meet interest obligations. A prior claim is important because it indicates the creditor's relative rank in any reorganization or liquidation, but earnings may be diverted to pay interest on mortgage bonds in order to forestall bankruptcy proceedings. Therefore, a prior claim on assets may ensure continuation of interest payments.

Collateral Trust Bonds

Collateral trust bonds are secured by pledges of stocks and bonds. As provided for in a collateral trust indenture, the corporation delivers the pledged property to a trustee to be held for the protection of bondholders. Stocks and registered bonds may remain in the name of the debtor or be transferred to the trustee. If a corporation defaults on interest or principal payments on collateral trust bonds, any pledged securities remaining in the name of the debtor corporation are transferred to the name of the trustee. As long as interest and principal payments on collateral trust bonds are being met, the income from the pledged securities will be turned over to the pledgor (debtor), but in case of default all interest and dividend payments on securities held as collateral will be retained by the trustee.

Debentures

In its broadest meaning, the term **debenture** can be used to describe all bonds issued by a corporation; in fact, the terms *debenture* and *bond* are sometimes used interchangeably, as both are promises by corporations to pay debts. In its more restricted meaning, a debenture is a direct obligation of the issuing corporation based solely on the general credit of the issuer without the assignment, mortgage, or pledge of property. But debenture bonds are more than general, unsecured promises to pay, because they are issued under trust indentures containing provisions that restrict the issuer for the protection of the creditors.

The fact that debenture bonds are unsecured by any specific lien on property is less important than their status with reference to other securities issued by the corporation. If the corporation has no secured obligations outstanding and no sizable amount of short-term debt, the status of its debentures is about the same as that of first mortgage bonds. In the event of bankruptcy, unsecured creditors, such as holders of debenture bonds, may sue, obtain judgments, and attach specific property to satisfy their claims. In practice, this protects debenture bondholders as much as the assigned property under a mortgage or other lien. Debenture bondholders, who are creditors, have a claim to earnings that comes before that of preferred stockholders.

Subordinated Debentures

Subordinated debenture bonds have received increasing attention in recent years. These debentures are usually issued under conditions making them subordinate to other specified creditors in regard to claims on earnings and assets. What constitutes senior debt must be clearly defined in every subordinated debenture issue. Bank loans generally are specified as senior debt, and outstanding bonds frequently are included as well. Of course, mortgage bonds still have a prior claim against the specific asset that has been pledged. Accounts payable are generally not defined as senior debt, and they probably would be on par with the subordinated debenture issue as general creditors of the firm. In the event of a corporation's insolvency, the advantage of the subordination agreement to the senior debt holders is that their claims will take precedence over those of the subordinated debt holders. After the senior debt is satisfied in full, any excess is then applied to the claims of the subordinated debenture holders.

	Amount of Claim	Without Subordination	With Subordination
TABLE 12.1			
Liquidating Payments (With and Without a Subordination Agreement).			
Senior debt	$ 400	$240	$400
Subordinated debt	300	180	20
Accounts payable	300	180	180
Net worth	1,000	0	0
Total claims	$2,000	$600	$600

This feature may be illustrated by the simple example shown in Table 12.1. The allocation of proceeds with and without subordination for the claims on the assets is shown. Total debt is $1,000, but it is assumed that only $600 was received from the liquidation of the assets. In the absence of a subordination agreement, each creditor would receive 60% of his or her claim, and the residual owners would receive nothing. However, the existence of subordinated debt results in payment in full of the senior debt, as shown by the following calculation:

$$\frac{\text{Senior debt ($\$400$) + subordinated debt ($\$300$)}}{\text{Total debt ($\$1,000$)}} \times \$600 = \$420.$$

The claims of the trade creditors are unaffected by the subordination feature. In either case, the equity holders would receive no share of the assets. The inclusion of a subordination agreement on notes or bonds gives valuable privileges to the senior debt. In addition, subordinated debt improves the borrowing power of the firm because it serves as a base upon which more senior debt may be superimposed.

The use of subordinated debentures or notes makes it possible for management to obtain cash without disturbing the priorities of the corporation's existing debt structure and without issuing common or preferred stock. In effect, it is a debt instrument that ranks immediately before preferred stock; but, unlike preferred stock, interest payments are treated as a fixed charge and are deductible for tax purposes. Subordinated debentures provide an attractive method of raising cash while retaining the corporation's borrowing power for future requirements.

INCOME CLAIM

The main advantage of financing with debt as compared to equity is its lower cost. In addition to saving on income taxes, debt financing avoids immediate dilution of the rights of common stockholders. When they lend funds to a corporation, creditors are entitled to a claim on its income that takes precedence over that of the owners. In a vast preponderance of cases, however, this prior claim on earnings is limited to a fixed sum. Hence, debt creates fixed interest charges and possible sinking fund obligations for repayment of the principal that drain cash regardless of the economic conditions confronting the industry and the firm. In order to minimize this potential cash shortage, management may issue income bonds. However, despite the advantages to the issuers of income bonds over preferred stock, corporations have not issued them voluntarily on a large scale. Most likely this is because historically many of the outstanding income bonds are the consequence of a corporate reorganization. One reason solvent corporations may not use income bonds may be this association.

Income Bonds

The indenture under which **income bonds** are issued specifies that interest is to be paid only when earned, thereby creating a contingent rather than a fixed obligation. Income bonds originate under two circumstances: those resulting from financial reorganizations due to bankruptcies and those issued by financially sound corporations.

Income bonds may be secured or unsecured, and cumulative or noncumulative. The trust indenture usually provides that interest payments must be declared by the corporation's board of directors when earned after certain specific deductions, but the decision on whether interest is paid if not earned is left to the discretion of the board of directors. If income bonds are cumulative, interest that has been passed becomes part of the amount that must be paid

TABLE 12.2 **Earnings Per Share of Common Stock Using Preferred Stock and Income Bonds.**		
Assumed level of earnings	$2,000,000	
Less: Federal corporate income taxes (40%)†	800,000	
Net after federal income taxes	1,200,000	
Less: Dividends on preferred stock (100,000 shares at $9)	900,000	
Available to common stock (100,000 shares)	300,000	
Earnings per share of common stock		$3.00
Assumed level of earnings	2,000,000	
Less: Interest ($10,000,000 in bonds at 9%)	900,000	
Earnings less interest	1,100,000	
Less: Federal corporate income taxes (40%)†	440,000	
Net after federal income taxes	$ 660,000	
Available to common stock (100,000 shares)	660,000	
Earnings per share of common stock		$6.60

† To simplify the illustration, use the same rate for all levels of income.

when the principal comes due (the cumulative period may be limited to a specific length of time, such as three years).

The main advantage of the issuing corporation in using income bonds in place of preferred stock lies in tax savings; interest paid on such bonds is deductible as an expense in computing taxable income, while dividends paid on preferred stock are not. The corporation must ensure, however, that the conditions under which the income bonds are issued are such that the courts will treat them as debt rather than as preferred stock. The difference in earnings per share of common stock when financing with preferred stock and income bonds is illustrated in Table 12.2.

VOTING PARTICIPATION

Ordinarily, bondholders have no voice in the management of the corporation, but under certain circumstances, income bondholders may be permitted to elect a given number of directors. Most often, this provision results from reorganization of the corporation and the replacement of other debts with income bonds. The reorganization under which the income bonds are issued may provide for bondholders' representation on the board of directors if interest is passed for a specific number of successive payment dates.

In general, bondholders have no control over management policies if interest is paid as agreed, and as long as other trust indenture covenants are not violated. If, however, interest or principal payments are in default, bondholders can pursue remedies that are more direct and effective than participation in the election of directors. Therefore, except in the case of income bonds, voting privileges for bondholders are not common.

DEBT RETIREMENT

Bonds are usually thought of as long-term credit instruments with maturities of five years or more. To some extent, there is a connection between maturity patterns and the industry of the issuer; railroad and public utility company bonds have longer maturities than those of other industries. Some corporations issue serial bonds, some coming due in 1 year, some in 2 years, and so on, with the result that maturities from 1 to 15 years may be included in a 15-year serial bond issue. Bonds with maturities of more than 40 years at the time of issue are distributed most commonly in connection with financial reorganizations.

Although it is unusual in the United States, bonds may be issued with no maturity dates (perpetual bonds, in which interest is paid in **perpetuity**). Without question there is a bias against perpetual bonds; therefore practically all bonds issued by U.S. corporations have a maturity date. What makes a maturity date important to the investor is that management must face the problem of paying off its debt on or before maturity. When bonds are convertible into common stock and bondholders use the conversion privilege, no repayment is necessary; however, management has no prior assurance that its stock will rise sufficiently so that conversion will take place.

Retirement of an issue may take place at various times; at maturity, when all the bonds come due; on a call date, as set in the bond indenture; periodically, as provided for in sinking fund or serial bond issues; piecemeal, by open-market purchases or direct negotiations with individual bondholders; or through the combined use of two or more of these methods.

Sinking Funds

A corporation may establish a **sinking fund** for debt retirement, which would require periodic deposits of cash to redeem the bonds or long-term notes before or at maturity. Existence of a sinking fund is considered to be beneficial to the investor. Sinking funds are provided for in the trust indenture or loan agreement, and usually a sinking fund for a bond issue is administered by the trustee who holds the trust indenture. Sometimes, in lieu of cash, a debtor corporation is permitted to deposit reacquired bonds of the issue being redeemed to fulfill sinking fund requirements. This provision is advantageous to the corporation if and when bonds can be acquired at less than face value (par) or less than their call price. The trustee administers bond redemptions according to the provisions set forth in the trust indenture. Contributions of a corporation to the sinking fund are usually compulsory. Therefore a corporation is technically insolvent when it fails to meet its sinking fund obligations, as well as when it fails to meet interest and principal payments when due.

Sinking fund contributions are usually invested in the bonds of the issue for which the sinking fund was created, but they may be invested in other securities or assets of the issuing corporation or in securities of other corporations. If the corporation invests in the bonds for which the sinking fund was created, the method whereby the sinking fund trustee may reacquire the bonds must be determined. Because open market purchases of bonds may drive up the market price, provision may be made at the time of issuing the bonds for calling the bonds by a lottery.

Serial Bonds

A **serial bond** or note issue is one made up of a series of bonds or notes with maturities arranged so that a specified number of them come due each year throughout the debt period. A firm may sell the bonds in a serial bond issue with a different coupon rate for each maturity or with the same coupon rate for all maturities. If bonds are sold so that the coupon rates reflect the yield curve in the market, all the bonds will sell at par, or face value. If the bonds have the same coupon rate, the market price of each maturity will reflect the yield curve in the market (see Table 12.3).

If the rates in the second column of Table 12.3 were charted, they would form an upward yield curve. This would show that, as of one date, the interest rate on each maturity of the same class of credit instrument increases with its maturity, with the lowest rate on 1-year obligations and the highest on 12-year obligations. Figure 12.1 shows the yield curve described in Table 12.3. A downward curve is just the opposite, with the highest rate being for the shortest maturity and the lowest rate being for the longest maturity. Yield curves are as of one time and are not a time series.

Market conditions, as reflected in yield curves, may be a factor in a corporation's decision to issue serial bonds or sinking fund bonds. When short-term interest rates are relatively low (an upward curve), investors prefer short-term obligations. Such conditions indicate a good market for a serial bond issue, which includes short-term and intermediate-term as well as long-term bonds. The total interest charges would be lower than for an equivalent issue of long-term bonds. As an alternative, if the corporation issues long-term sinking fund bonds, the higher interest paid may be offset by savings when the bonds are reacquired; for this to be true, however, the sinking fund trustee of the corporation would have to reacquire the bonds at a discount. This situation is possible if the sinking fund call price is set at or near the face value of the bonds. Call prices are explained in a later subsection.

TABLE 12.3
Yield curve, Coupon Rate, and Price of Serial Bonds.

Maturity Year	Price Constant Varying Coupon Rates			Coupon Rate Constant Varying Prices		
	Yield Curve	Coupon Rate	Price	Coupon Rate	Price	Yield Curve
1	10.00%	10.00%	$1,000	12%	$1,018.59	10.00%
2	10.50	10.50	1,000	12	1,026.44	10.50
3	11.00	11.00	1,000	12	1,024.98	11.00
4	11.25	11.25	1,000	12	1,023.64	11.25
5	11.50	11.50	1,000	12	1,018.62	11.50
6	11.75	11.75	1,000	12	1,010.56	11.75
7	12.00	12.00	1,000	12	1,000.00	12.00
8	12.10	12.10	1,000	12	994.97	12.10
9	12.20	12.20	1,000	12	989.26	12.20
10	12.30	12.30	1,000	12	983.00	12.30
11	12.40	12.40	1,000	12	976.33	12.40
12	12.50	12.50	1,000	12	969.33	12.50

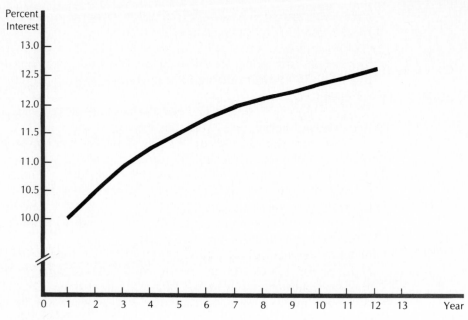

Figure 12.1 The yield curve.

Call Provisions

In the previous sections, we suggested that corporations make formal provisions for retirement of bonds by using either sinking fund or serial bonds. However, if market conditions are favorable (i.e., if interest rates have fallen since the bonds were sold), the corporation may wish to reacquire its outstanding bonds and to sell a new bond issue with a lower effective rate of interest. In order to accomplish this, the corporation must include a call feature when it sells a bond issue. Today practically all corporate bond issues are covered by trust indentures that permit the bond issues to be called and redeemed in whole or in part, either immediately or after a certain period of time, at the option of the issuing corporation. The call privilege permits the corporation to make adjustments in its capital structure. Corporations may use the call privilege for a number of reasons: to take advantage of a decline in interest rates, to eliminate bond issues with unfavorable indenture clauses, to reduce debt, and to replace long-term bonds with term loans or possibly short-term obligations.

Because interest rates fluctuate with the business cycle, the call option has been exercised most often during recessions to replace bonds bearing high interest rates with bonds bearing low interest rates. Over a period of years, a corporation may refinance its bond indebtedness several times in order to reduce interest charges.

When corporations finance with freely callable bonds, the issuers must anticipate a less favorable reaction from investors than when financing with deferred callable or noncallable bond issues. While a corporation gains from refunding at lower interest rates, investors lose. Buyers of callable bonds can anticipate having their bonds redeemed at a time when it is more difficult to obtain the same nominal rate of return on new investments.

Consequently, there are costs to the corporation in issuing freely callable bonds as compared to deferred callable bonds. This cost can be measured at the time the bond is issued by the difference in yield between what a company would be forced to pay if the bonds had a deferred call or were noncallable and what the company would have to pay with an immediate call feature.

The value of the call feature will depend upon investors' interest rate expectations. If interest rates are high and are expected to fall significantly, the call privilege should have a high value to the corporation. For the call feature to have a measurable value in the market, interest rate expectations must be such that investors believe that a freely callable bond might be called during the period of deferment of comparable deferred callable bonds. The immediate call privilege has the greatest value, and the greatest cost to the firm, when interest rates are relatively high and are expected to fall in the near term. This is so because investors prefer deferred callable bonds to hedge against a possible early call. The reluctance on the part of investors to purchase immediately callable bonds will cause yields to rise on these bonds compared to deferred callable bonds. In order to minimize this immediate cost, corporations frequently lengthen the period of deferment from 5 years to 10 years or more on new issues.

Call Price

The **call,** or redemption, **price** is negotiated when bonds are issued; and it will vary according to capital market conditions and the credit position and bargaining power of the issuing corporation. Frequently, the call price is equal to the principal amount plus one year's nominal interest. Thus, a 10% bond might have an initial call price of $1,100. It is not uncommon for the call privilege to be deferred for a period of time, with a declining schedule of call prices subsequent to the deferment period. For example, the call price might be $1,100 during the first three years, $1,080 during the next three years after deferment, and so on until face value is paid at the maturity date. This declining schedule of call prices increases the compensation to investors should the bond issue be called during its earlier years.

The influence of the call price on the market price of bonds depends upon the interest rates prevailing in the market. When the market rate is below the coupon rate, corporate management will consider refunding at a lower interest rate, but if the market rate is the same as the coupon rate, no savings in interest would result from refunding (retiring an existing issue with the proceeds of a new one). In the latter case, if the corporation decides to refund, it would be for reasons other than savings on interest charges.

If callable bonds are issued when interest rates are extremely low, there is less likelihood that the bonds will be called. (If and when the interest rate changes, it should move upward.) In such circumstances, a low call premium and an immediate call can be included because the terms will have little effect on the offering price of bonds. If interest rates are high and are expected to decline, the call feature will tend to depress the market price of the bonds, because investors will expect the debtor corporation to refinance when interest rates decline. In a new issue, the call price will have to be substantial and a deferred call period included to lower the effective interest rate (which in later years may be a serious deterrent to refinancing).

The call feature allows the issuing corporation the right to redeem bonds before maturity. This option is exercised at the discretion of the issuer. In contrast, some bonds have a put feature that allows the bondholder to sell the bond back to the issuing corporation at a predetermined price. The put feature may be attractive to investors interested in securing protection against loss of bond value due to possible increases in interest rates.

Refunding Analysis

Before deciding to call a bond issue, the issuing corporation will compare the savings in interest over the remaining life of the bonds with the costs of refinancing, including the call premium, underwriting fees, legal expenses, cost of engraving new bonds, routine expenses of retiring old bonds and issuing new ones, cost of preparing the registration statement, and extra interest payments. Refunding bonds necessitates overlapping interest payments because a corporation will not call an old issue until the new issue has been sold, and because old bondholders must be given 30 or 60 days' notice prior to the redemption date, which means that interest will be paid on both issues for the 30- or 60-day period. Managers making a refunding decision must compare the NPV of the interest savings with the cash outlay required for refunding to determine if the refunding is advantageous to the corporation.

The refunding decision is simply another capital budgeting decision. The NPV method of analysis is used. Analysis is not difficult because the cost and benefit estimates are virtually certain. At the time of refunding, the costs and benefits are calculated for the life of the "investment." Because of this certainty, a risk-free rate is used for the discounting. Work in this area suggests that the before-tax rate on the new bonds is the appropriate discount rate.†

---

† This rate was suggested by M. J. Gordon, "A Generalized Solution to the Buy-or-Lease Decision: A Pedagogical Note," *Journal of Finance* (March 1974), p. 249, and further analyzed in A. R. Ofer and R. A. Taggert, Jr., "Bond Refunding: A Clarifying Analysis," *Journal of Finance* (March 1977), pp. 21–31.

TABLE 12.4 Bond Issue Facts.		
	Old	**New**
Principal amount outstanding	$25,000,000	$25,000,000
Coupon rate	12%	10%
Years to maturity	20	20
Unamortized bond discount	$ 50,000	
Unamortized issue expense	$ 20,000	
Call premium	10%	
Issue expenses		$ 150,000
Duplicate interest (.10 × $25,000,000 × 45/360)		$ 312,500

The reasoning is similar to that explained in the analysis of leases (Chapter 11).

A detailed example will show how refunding calculations are made. Assume that a firm has a $25 million, 12% bond issue outstanding and that the issue still has 20 years to run before maturity. Interest rates have fallen sufficiently since the bond issue was sold so that the company can now sell a $25 million issue of 20-year bonds with an effective interest rate of 10%. These assumptions are summarized in Table 12.4. (An income tax rate of 40% is assumed.) Refunding analysis, being a specialized capital budgeting problem, can be organized in a worksheet similar to that used in Chapter 5.

For a refunding, the costs and benefits appear in Table 12.5: the call premium, issue expenses, and duplicate interest. Trading in a bond issue, like trading in old equipment, can create a tax loss. Any unamortized premiums, discounts, or expenses related to the old issue become immediately deductible.

In calling the old issue, the firm must pay a premium of 10%. This expense of $2.5 million (10% of $25 million) is tax deductible. The after-tax cost is then 60% (1 minus the 40% tax rate) of that amount. Issue expenses are not immediately deductible; they must be amortized. Therefore, the before-tax and after-tax amounts are the same. The example assumes that there is a 45-day overlap of interest payments on the two bond issues. Because of the refunding, the company will be paying interest on an extra $25 million for 45 days. The rate on this extra is the new issue's rate of 10%.†

As mentioned earlier, calling a bond issue accelerates the deduction of the related expenses. When the old issue is retired, the discount and issue expenses, which would otherwise be written off yearly, afford the company immediate tax savings, which reduces the cost of the refunding. The tax

---

† Some analysts use the rate on the old issue. We believe that the new interest is the incremental cost of changing over. The old interest would have been paid whether or not the bonds had been called.

TABLE 12.5
Analysis of Refunding.

	Before Tax	After Tax	Years	Discount Factor	Present Value
Costs					
Call premium	$ 2,500,000	$ 1,500,000	0	1	$ 1,500,000
Issue expense	150,000	150,000	0	1	150,000
Duplicate interest	312,500	187,500	0	1	187,500
Unamortized discount	(50,000)	(20,000)	0	1	(20,000)
Unamortized expense	(20,000)	(8,000)	0	1	(8,000)
					$ 1,809,500
Benefits					
Interest savings	$ 500,000	$ 300,000	1–20	8.514	$ 2,554,200
Tax shields	4,000	1,600	1–20	8.514	13,622
					$ 2,567,822

$$\text{NPV} = \text{present value of benefits} - \text{cost}$$
$$= \$2,567,822 - \$1,809,500 = \$758,322.$$

savings, or **shields,** would be the amount of these deductions times the tax rate.

There are two benefits that the firm normally receives from refunding. The first, and more important, is interest savings. Refunding in this case saves the company 2% (the difference between the old 12% and the new 10%) on $25 million each year for the next 20 years. The difference is $500,000 a year before taxes or $300,000 after taxes. The present value of these savings, discounted at 10%, is considerable.

The second benefit is the change in the firm's financing-related tax shields. Before, the firm's annual expenses were

$$
\begin{array}{lr}
\text{Discount} & \$50,000/20 = \$2,500 \\
\text{Expenses} & 20,000/20 = \underline{1,000} \\
& \$3,500
\end{array}
$$

The new deductible expenses are

$$\text{Issue expenses} \qquad \$150,000/20 = \$7,500.$$

The firm has $4,000 more in deductible expenses per year, which at a 40% tax rate provides added tax savings of $1,600 per year.

As is apparent, the refunding described in the example is very worthwhile. The example used a spread of 2% between the old issue and the new to make the calculations easier to understand. Actually, refunding is often financially desirable even when smaller interest rate differentials are involved.

Refunding is advantageous as long as the NPV is positive. If it is negative, the firm would not be justified in refunding an issue unless other considerations were of paramount importance to management, such as a desire to remove restrictive bond covenants.

Two additional points concerning the previous refunding example should be mentioned. First, this example assumes that the new bond issue has the same maturity as the old one. Frequently, a new issue will have a longer maturity than the old one; the analysis, however, should consider the cash benefits only up to the maturity of the old bond issue. Second, while it may be profitable to refund the bonds now, in the near future it may be even more profitable if interest rates were to decline further. Therefore the timing of refunding is of the utmost importance for the corporation to gain the maximum savings from the decline in interest rates subsequent to the time of the initial offering.

Refinancing at Maturity

When the corporation makes no formal provision for the retirement of its bonds, managers depend either on the ability of the corporation to refund them at maturity with a new issue or on the willingness of the bondholders to exchange their bonds for preferred or common stock at maturity. If a corporation refinances its bond issues at maturity, it may issue new securities to obtain cash with which to repay those outstanding, or it may offer new securities directly to bondholders in exchange for those they hold. In the latter case, bondholders who are unwilling to exchange their bonds are paid off in cash. Because refunding is debt replacement rather than debt liquidation, the problems of refunding differ from those of sinking fund and serial bond issues.

To meet maturing bond obligations, a corporation may issue new bonds, or preferred or common stock, or it may negotiate for a direct loan from insurance companies or banks. Bondholders may accept new bonds in exchange for old ones if they are offered one or more special inducements, such as a cash bonus, better security, a sinking fund, or a conversion privilege. As most corporate bonds are held by institutional investors, the debtor corporation may negotiate directly with these bondholders for a direct exchange. This practice doubtless would be more common were it not for the regulation requiring that new bond issues of certain regulated companies be sold to the highest bidder.

When a large bond issue matures, both the credit position of the issuer and conditions in the capital market will influence the method of refunding. It would be fortuitous if both of these factors happened to be favorable on the maturity date of the old debt. In the face of an unsettled capital market, a corporation would normally reappraise and postpone new financing plans, but this option does not exist when obligations mature. The maturing debt in this instance may be retired by issuing short-term notes in the capital market or obtaining loans from commercial banks or insurance companies.

LEVERAGE

Leverage is a process of conscious risk assumption. When a firm uses leverage, it intentionally takes on more risk in an effort to gain higher returns. There are two types of leverage, operating and financial leverage.

OPERATING LEVERAGE

Before considering total leverage—that is, the combined effect of operating and financial leverage—it seems appropriate to consider each of them separately. **Operating leverage** involves the use of fixed operating expenses instead of variable expenses in an effort to raise operating income, or earnings before interest and taxes.

To understand the effects of this substitution, consider a hypothetical example. There exists a company (Phoenix, Inc.) with no fixed costs and with variable costs that equal 90% of revenue regardless of the level of those revenues. At a sales level of $1 million, a partial income statement (down to the EBIT figure) would look like Table 12.6.

Phoenix, Inc., is considering a change in its operations that would involve incurring a fixed cost of $250,000 a year but would lower the variable costs at 60% of revenues. Assuming that these estimates are accurate, the income statement for the same sales volume, after the changeover, would look like Table 12.7.

This is the essence of operating leverage—substituting fixed costs for variable costs and raising operating income. Operating leverage not only increases expected profits at the current level, but it also magnifies the benefits of any increase in volume. Consider the effect of the change if the volume were to increase by 20% to $1.2 million. The impact is apparent in Table 12.8.

TABLE 12.6
Phoenix, Inc.: Operating Income Statement for the Year Ending December 31, 1983.

New sales		$1,000,000
Fixed expenses	0	
Variable expenses	$900,000	
Earnings before interest and taxes		$ 100,000

TABLE 12.7
Phoenix, Inc.: Operating Income Statement for a $1 Million Sales Level (After Operations Changeover).

Net sales		$1,000,000
Fixed expenses	$250,000	
Variable expenses	600,000	850,000
Earnings before interest and taxes		$ 150,000

TABLE 12.8
Phoenix, Inc.: Operating Income Statement for a $1.2 Million Sales Level.

	Without Leverage		With Operating Leverage	
Net sales		$1,200,000		$1,200,000
Fixed expenses	0		$250,000	
Variable expenses	$1,080,000	1,080,000	720,000	970,000
Earnings before interest and taxes		$ 120,000		$ 230,000

This example makes operating leverage appear extremely advantageous. The procedure raises expected operating income and magnifies the impact of any increases in sales. In this case, the leveraged EBIT increased from $150,000 to $230,000. The change amounts to a 53% increase in operating earnings as the result of a 20% rise in sales. However, such attempts to raise the expected return involve some risk. In the case of operating leverage, risk arises from the magnification effect we have just observed. Operating leverage magnifies not only the effect of increases in sales but also the effect of sales downturns. Table 12.9 illustrates how a 20% loss in sales volume would affect the company. In this case, leveraged EBIT drops by 53%.

The effect of operating leverage is now apparent. *Such leverage makes good times better and bad times worse.* Whether operating leverage is advisable depends upon the circumstances within a particular company at a specific time. The advisability of using operating leverage depends on how much variable costs can be cut by the substitution of fixed costs and on how likely the firm is to experience a reduction of sales (and by how much).

To evaluate these factors, financial managers must make some important and difficult estimates. After arriving at these estimates, they can evaluate the impact of the change using forecasted income statements, as was done in the example.

TABLE 12.9
Phoenix, Inc.: Operating Income Statement for a $800,000 Sales Level.

	Without Leverage		With Operating Leverage	
Net sales		$800,000		$800,000
Fixed expenses	0		$250,000	
Variable expenses	$720,000	720,000	480,000	730,000
Earnings before interest and taxes		$ 80,000		$ 70,000

FINANCIAL LEVERAGE

A corporation is said to be operating with **financial leverage** when it uses a fixed-cost form of financing, such as debt or preferred stock, instead of a variable-cost form of financing, such as common stock.

Debt, such as bonds and notes, is considered to be a fixed cost because the interest payments are set by the contract. Common stock, on the other hand, is a variable cost. Issuing stock dilutes the current shareholders' claims on future earnings. How much the current shareholder forfeits depends on how high those future earnings turn out to be.

To illustrate the effects of financial leverage, assume that a firm (Phoenix, Inc.) uses *no operating leverage* (no fixed operating expenses) and that operating earnings (EBIT) are 10% of sales at all sales levels. Assume that the firm is operating at a sales level of $1 million. Operating expenses are 90% of that figure and are all variable. Assume further that the firm pays taxes at a constant 40% rate. The firm is financed entirely with common stock—100,000 shares with a market value and a par value both at $10. An abbreviated income statement, including an earnings-per-share calculation, appears in Table 12.10.

Phoenix, Inc., is considering altering its capital structure and borrowing $500,000 to buy up half of the outstanding stock, leaving 50,000 shares. The firm will have to pay 9% interest on the borrowed money. This provides a clear-cut example of financial leverage. Although it may be unrealistic, the example illustrates a direct substitution of one form of fixed-cost capital (debt) for a variable-cost type (stock). The effects on net income and earnings-per-share (EPS) figures are illustrated in Table 12.11.

Like operating leverage, financial leverage, when successfully employed, benefits the shareholders by raising their expected return—earnings per share. This, in turn, should raise the value of their stock. Like operating leverage, financial leverage magnifies the benefits of any increase in volume, as illustrated in Table 12.12 for sales of $1.2 million and 50,000 shares.

TABLE 12.10
Phoenix, Inc.: Abbreviated Income Statement for a $1 Million Sales Level.

	Before Purchase of Stock
Net sales	$1,000,000
Earnings before interest and taxes	100,000
Less: Interest	0
Earnings before taxes	100,000
Less: Taxes	40,000
Net income	$ 60,000
Earnings per share (100,000 shares)	$0.60

TABLE 12.11
Phoenix, Inc.: Abbreviated Income Statement for a $1 Million Sales Level (After Financing Change).

	After Purchase of Stock
Earnings before interest and taxes	$100,000
Less: Interest	45,000
Income before taxes	55,000
Less: Taxes	22,000
New income	$ 33,000
Earnings per share (50,000 shares)	$0.66

TABLE 12.12
Phoenix, Inc.: Abbreviated Income Statement for a $1.2 Million Sales Level.

	Without Leverage	With Financial Leverage
Earnings before interest and taxes	$120,000	$120,000
Less: Interest	0	45,000
Income before taxes	120,000	75,000
Less: Taxes	48,000	30,000
Net income	$ 72,000	$ 45,000
Earnings per share	$0.72	$0.90

TABLE 12.13
Phoenix, Inc.: Abbreviated Income Statement for a $800,000 Sales Level.

	Without Leverage	With Financial Leverage
Earnings before interest and taxes	$80,000	$80,000
Less: Interest	0	45,000
Income before taxes	80,000	35,000
Less: Taxes	32,000	14,000
Net income	$48,000	$21,000
Earnings per share	$0.48	$0.42

Notice that the spread between the EPS figures is even greater than at the former sales level of $1 million. Without leverage the EPS figure increased by the same amount as sales did—20%. Leveraged earnings increased more rapidly, from $0.66 to $0.90— a rise of over 36%. Again, leverage made good times better.

Unfortunately, financial leverage can also make bad times worse. The amount of interest expense does not decrease when the sales volume declines. The result is a more severe erosion of the EPS, as illustrated in Table 12.13.

Financial leverage is simply the use of fixed-cost capital such as debt. If the money raised is successfully employed, it increases the EPS. The impact is magnified further because interest changes on debt are tax deductible. However, the money must be used advantageously; otherwise, the interest expense can reduce shareholders' returns.

Whether or not the use of financial leverage benefits stockholders is a complex issue that has been subject to extensive debate and empirical investigation. Greater use of financial leverage can increase the average EPS but may not maximize the value of the firm and the value of the security holders' wealth. The higher EPS may be accompanied by higher financial risk and might not be worth the higher returns. The issue is further complicated by the deductibility of interest payments in calculating the corporate income tax liability and the costly nature of bankruptcy proceedings.

Financial Break-even Analysis

Analysis of financial break-even permits the financial manager to explore the relationship between the type of financing used and its effect on EPS. Although the effects of both financial and operating leverage can be included in the analysis, it is less confusing to introduce the topic with a simplified example— Phoenix, Inc., without operating leverage.

When simple capital structures are involved, the analysis is relatively easy. First, plot EPS as a function of sales for each financing alternative. The illustration in Fig. 12.2 uses the figures derived in Tables 12.10 through 12.13.

In Fig. 12.2(a), the EPS-sales graph for the unleveraged firm is depicted. The Xs mark the EPS figures that were calculated in Tables 12.10 and 12.13. Note that only two points were necessary to determine the line. In this instance, the line could have been graphed with only one point because, for a firm with *absolutely no leverage*, the line will come out of the origin. If the firm had any leverage, either operating or financial, that would not be the case.

Figure 12.2(b) depicts the relationship that would exist if the firm had financed with debt in the manner suggested in the examples. Again, two points determine the line. The sales intercept of this line also provides some insight. EPS will be zero at the sales level at which operating earnings equal the interest charges. In this case, the contribution margin was 10% (variable costs were 90%). At a sales level of $450,000, operating income equals interest expenses, both being $45,000.

In Fig. 12.2(c), the two graphs are combined to determine the financial break-even point. In this case, with no operating leverage, financial break-even is at a sales level of $900,000. At that sales level, either method of financing will produce EPS of $0.54. The financial manager must next estimate what sales will be and decide whether it is likely that sales will fall below $900,000.

If the financing alternatives are more complicated, that is, if they involve the use of more than one type of debt, multiple interest rates, and possible

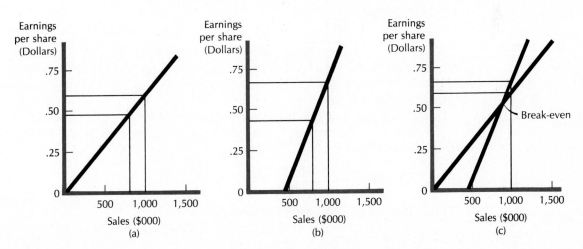

Figure 12.2 Construction of financial break-even chart: (a) All equity, (b) with debt, and (c) financial break-even point.

preferred stock and/or convertible issues, developing the EPS estimates becomes more difficult and the EPS-sales line may be nonlinear or even discontinuous. However, the technique remains valid. Simply calculate a number of EPS points, graph them for each financial plan, and combine the graphs to determine the break-even point.

In some cases, it is possible to calculate the break-even points algebraically. To do this, derive an expression for calculating EPS for each alternative. For the example just reviewed, the expressions would be

$$EPS_{stock} = \frac{[(\text{contribution margin}) \times \text{sales} - \text{fixed cost}](1 - \text{tax rate})}{\text{shares outstanding}}$$

$$= \frac{(.1 \text{ sales} - 0)(1 - .4)}{100,000}$$

$$= \frac{(.1 \text{ sales})(.6)}{100,000}$$

$$= \frac{.06 \text{ sales}}{100,000}.$$

$$EPS_{leveraged} = \frac{[(\text{contribution margin} \times \text{sales}) - \text{fixed cost} - \text{interest}](1 - \text{tax rate})}{\text{shares outstanding}}$$

$$= \frac{(.1 \text{ sales} - 0 - 45,000)(1 - .4)}{50,000}$$

$$= \frac{(.1 \text{ sales} - 45,000)(.6)}{50,000}$$

$$= \frac{.06 \text{ sales} - 27,000}{50,000}.$$

In these expressions, the contribution margin can be defined as the percentage difference between the sales volume and the variable cost. In the example, the contribution margin was 10%; that is, variable expenses were 90% of the sales revenue.

To solve for the financial break-even point, set the two expressions equal to each other, which they would be at the break-even point, and solve for the break-even sales level.

$$\frac{.06 \text{ sales}}{100,000} = \frac{.06 \text{ sales} - \$27,000}{50,000}$$

$$.06 \text{ sales} = 2(.06 \text{ sales} - 27,000)$$

$$= .12 \text{ sales} - 54,000$$

$$= 54,000$$

$$\text{Sales} = \$900,000.$$

Developing the equation serves to validate the result found graphically and to amplify the logic of the charts. For more complex financial structures the algebra can be tedious, and the charts are generally easier to follow.

CASH FLOW BREAK-EVEN

In the preceding section, the break-even point was calculated in terms of operating leverage and financial leverage. Another useful concept is that of cash flow break-even. The procedure is the same except that the break-even point is calculated in terms of cash flows rather than accrual accounting procedures.

LEVERAGE MEASUREMENT

The principal effect of leverage is to increase the volatility of a firm's earnings. Operating leverage magnifies the impact of sales volume changes on operating earnings. Financial leverage magnifies the impact of any changes in operating earnings on EPS. Useful measures should indicate to what degree these changes are magnified.

Degree of Operating Leverage

The **degree of operating leverage (DOL)** is logically analogous to the power marking on a telescope or a pair of binoculars. A seven-power pair of binoculars magnifies the image of distant objects seven times. A firm's DOL indicates the degree of magnification within the firm.

The DOL can be defined more precisely as the percentage change in operating earnings (EBIT) for a 1% change in sales volume at a given level of operations. A firm's DOL is not constant. It is a point measure, meaning that it is valid only at one point, the sales level for which it is calculated.

The DOL can be calculated by using the following formula:

$$\text{DOL} = \frac{\text{sales} - \text{variable expenses}}{\text{EBIT}}.$$

Returning to the example for a $1 million sales level, Phoenix's DOL would be 2.67 if operating leverage were used. Substituting the figures from Table 12.7, the calculation is

$$\text{DOL} = \frac{400,000}{150,000} = 2.67.$$

Thus, if sales increased by 1%, operating earnings should rise by 2.67%. The result can be checked very easily. A 1% change in sales is $10,000. The operating income statement would then be as illustrated in Table 12.14. As

> **TABLE 12.14**
> **Phoenix, Inc.: Operating Income Statement for a $1,010,000 Sales Level (With Operating Leverage).**

Net sales		$1,010,000
Fixed expenses	$250,000	
Variable expenses	606,000	856,000
Earnings before interest and taxes		$ 154,000

can be seen, the operating income would rise by $4,000, or 2.67% of the previous level of $150,000.

Another formula for calculating the DOL is as follows:

$$DOL = \frac{\text{percentage change in EBIT}}{\text{percentage change in sales}}.$$

Using the same example, Table 12.14 shows that a 1% increase in sales increases the operating income by $4,000, or 2.67%. Applying the formula gives these results:

$$DOL = \frac{2.67\%}{1\%} = 2.67.$$

Degree of Financial Leverage

The DOL indicates the degree of magnification between sales and EBIT. The **degree of financial leverage (DFL)** quantifies the relative volatility of EPS with respect to EBIT. More precisely, the DFL is the percentage change in earnings per share for a 1% change in operating earnings at a given level of volume. It can be calculated using the formula

$$DFL = \frac{EBIT}{EBIT - \text{interest expense}}.$$

In continuing the example used in the discussion of DOL, assume that Phoenix is to use both types of leverage, operating and financial. At a $150,000 level of operating earnings, the firm's DFL would be

$$DFL = \frac{150,000}{150,000 - 45,000} = 1.43.$$

A 1% increase in EBIT, to $151,500, would raise EPS by 1.43%. Again, the result can be easily validated, as shown in Table 12.15.

TABLE 12.15 Phoenix, Inc.: Abbreviated Income Statement.		
Earnings before interest and taxes	$150,000	$151,500
Less: Interest	45,000	45,000
Income before taxes	105,000	106,500
Less: Taxes	42,000	42,600
Net income	$ 63,000	$ 63,900
Earnings per share	$1.26	$1.278

Degree of Total Leverage

If DOL quantifies the magnification between sales and operating earnings, and DFL measures the magnification between EBIT and EPS, the total magnification between sales and EPS should be the product of the two. The **degree of total leverage (DTL)** is the percentage change in earnings per share for a 1% change in sales at a given level of volume.

The DTL can be calculated in either of two ways:

$$DTL = DOL \times DFL;$$

$$DTL = \frac{\text{sales} - \text{variable expenses}}{\text{EBIT} - \text{interest expense}}.$$

As you would expect, both calculations yield the same result. For the previous example,

$$DTL = 2.67 \times 1.43 = 3.81;$$

$$DTL = \frac{1,000,000 - 600,000}{150,000 - 45,000} = 3.81.$$

Again, the result can be validated, as shown in Table 12.16. With a 1% sales increase, EPS increased by just under a nickel, or exactly 3.81%.

Simple as they are, these measures allow a manager to anticipate the effect of changes in volume, both upward and downward. Further, the measures pinpoint the source of the firm's earnings volatility. That is, they indicate whether volatility is due to the nature of the firm's operations or to the way in which the firm is financed.

More importantly, the measures allow the managers to assess the impact of any proposed changes on either operations or financing. One other point should be made clear—the effects of leverage are multiplicative. There are policy implications for the managers. Managers should be aware that the nature of the firm's operations limits the financing alternatives. If operations cause highly volatile operating income, the method of financing should be

TABLE 12.16 Phoenix, Inc.: Comparative Income Statements.				
New sales		$1,000,000		$1,010,000
Fixed expenses	$250,000		$250,000	
Variable expenses	600,000	850,000	606,000	856,000
Earnings before interest and taxes		150,000		154,000
Less: Interest		45,000		45,000
Income before taxes		105,000		109,000
Less: Taxes		42,000		43,600
Net income		$ 63,000		$ 65,400
Earnings per share		$1.26		$1.308

conservative. Conversely, if operations result in stable operating income, the financing pattern can be less conservative. The electric public utility industry is an excellent example of the latter observation.

SUMMARY

A bond is one instrument whereby a corporation can raise funds. A bond contains a promise to pay interest on stated dates. An exception is the income bond, on which interest is paid only when earned.

A mortgage bond includes a lien on real property and is issued so that the corporation can obtain funds at a lower cost. Collateral trust bonds are secured by pledges of stocks or bonds. A debenture bond is a direct obligation based upon the general credit of the borrower.

The issuance of bonds with maturity dates necessitates making plans for their extinction. Such plans may provide for redemption, or refunding. Redemption or retirement of a bond issue may take place when all bonds come due; on a call date, as provided in the trust indenture; periodically, over the life of the issue when serial bonds are issued; or piecemeal, by repurchase of bonds in the open market or by negotiation with individual bondholders. Sinking funds may be set up to redeem bonds, or other debt obligations may be created to obtain funds with which to retire the original issue (refunding).

The call feature in bonds permits corporations to (1) reduce interest charges by replacing high-interest-bearing bonds with obligations carrying a lower interest rate, (2) eliminate bond issues with unfavorable indenture clauses, and (3) expedite conversion when bonds have the conversion feature. A sinking fund for debt retirement provides for periodic appropriations of cash for redeeming bonds on or before maturity. When bonds are refunded before maturity, the corporation will issue new securities, which are sold to obtain cash to redeem those outstanding. A corporation may contemplate refunding when there is a decline in market interest rates large enough to provide net cash savings to the firm if the old bond issue is called and replaced with a new issue at a lower interest rate. Refunding analysis is treated as a riskless capital budgeting problem.

The second part of this chapter analyzes two important concepts—operating and financial leverage. Operating leverage is present when a firm has fixed costs that do not vary with changes in output.

Financial leverage is present when the firm uses fixed-cost financing such as debt. Whether this is beneficial depends on how successfully the funds are employed. Both graphic and algebraic methods of analyzing the use of financial leverage are available.

Both types of leverage increase the volatility of the firm's earnings. Measures of earnings volatility such as DOL, DFL, and DTL can help a financial decision maker assess whether a particular plan of operations or form of financing is advisable, given the nature of the firm. Review of these measures also illustrates the multiplicative nature of the two types of leverage.

QUESTIONS AND REVIEW ACTIVITIES

1. Large business firms that raise funds by public financing usually depend more on bond issues than on sales of common or preferred stock. Why?

2. What provisions are usually found in a trust indenture?

3. What are the functions of a trustee under the provisions of a trust indenture?

4. "Refunding is debt replacement rather than debt liquidation." Explain.

5. Discuss the advantages of a firm's mortgage lien over an unsecured loan from the creditor's viewpoint.

6. What is a subordinated debenture bond?

7. Identify the following:

   a) Call privilege.

   b) Deferred call.

   c) Immediate call.

8. "Investors should place a value on a deferred call only if they expect interest rates to fall during the deferment period." Discuss.

9. If an investor purchases a bond at $1,040, and it is called for sinking fund purposes as $1,020, he loses $20. How can this be reconciled with the statement that bondholders are benefited by a sinking fund provision?

10. Define the concept of leverage.

11. Within the context of a firm, define and distinguish between operating and financial leverage.

12. Define DOL, DFL, and DTL in your own words.

PROBLEMS

1. In 1984, the Coast-to-Coast Railroad exchanged new 10% income bonds due in 2019 for its outstanding 10% preferred stock in order to retire the latter. The new income bonds were junior in rank and matured subsequent to all other Coast-to-Coast bonds. Describe how this change affected

   a) Coast-to-Coast's federal income tax liability.

   b) The position of the common stockholders.

   c) The position of Coast-to-Coast's other bonds.

   d) The position of the preferred stockholders who accepted the new bonds.

   e) The position of the preferred stockholders who did not accept the new bonds.

2. You bought a high-grade corporate bond bearing a 10% coupon rate and due in 25 years, at par, to yield 10%. Suppose that the market yields on such obligations decline to 8% within six months. Reverse the supposition and assume that, in six months, interest rates rise, and your bond now sells on a 12% yield basis.

   a) How much is your bond worth in each instance?

   b) What factors may have caused the shift in rates?

   c) Would the answer be the same in part (a) if the bonds were callable?

3. Given the following facts, analyze the indicated refunding decision. Assume that the firm has a 40% tax rate. The PVIFA for 15 years at 7% is 9.108.

Bond Issue Facts	Old	New
Principal amount outstanding	$10,000,000	$10,000,000
Coupon rate	8%	7%
Years to maturity	15	15
Unamortized bond discount	$ 90,000	
Unamortized issue expense	$ 150,000	
Call premium	8%	
Issue expenses		$ 300,000
Duplicate interest†		
(.07 × $10,000,000 × 60/360)		$ 116,670

† Assumes a 60-day overlap.

4. The RPB Corp. has pretax earnings of $4 million. Its present capitalization includes 100,000 shares of $10 preferred stock, par value $100, and 1 million shares of no-par common stock. The corporation plans to retire its preferred issue and to offer $10 million worth of 10% income bonds to the preferred shareholders. Determine the effect of the proposed change on the EPS available to common stockholders, assuming a marginal tax rate of 50%.

5. During the tight money period of 1981 and the resultant upheaval in the money and capital markets, you purchased at par a corporate bond with a 14% coupon.

Assume that presently the market rate of interest for similar-quality bonds is (a) 16%, (b) 14%, or (c) 10%. Assume that 20 years remain until maturity. Calculate how much your bond is worth under each rate of interest. (Assume annual interest payments.)

6. What price would investors be willing to pay for each of the following:

   a) A 20-year $1,000 par value bond with a nominal annual interest rate of 9%, and, a current yield of 8%.

   b) A 15-year, $1,000 par value bond, five years after issuance, with a nominal annual interest rate of 6% and a current yield of 9%.

7. Ajax, Inc., has issued $100,000 in mortgage bonds. The bonds have a life of 20 years. The indenture requires that a sinking fund be established that, through equal annual contributions, will be sufficient to redeem the entire bond issue on the maturity date.

   a) What is the annual sinking fund deposit if the fund earns no interest?

   b) How much must each annual contribution be if the fund can earn 10% compounded annually?

8. Phoenix, Inc., plans to refund an outstanding issue of 12% bonds. The terms of the current issue are as follows:

Amount outstanding	$100,000,000
Coupon rate	12%
Call price	$1,120
Years to maturity	20
Unamortized bond discount	$100,000
Unamortized issue expense	$150,000

The terms of the new issue are as follows:

Principal amount	$100,000,000
Coupon rate	9%
Years to maturity	25
Proceeds to corporation	Par
Bond issue expense	$250,000
Duplicate interest expense	60 days
Weighted average cost of capital	14%
Corporate tax rate	40%

   a) Determine the cash outlay.

   b) Determine the cash benefits.

   c) Would you go ahead with the refunding?

9. Handy-Dandy Manufacturing, Inc., maker of Handy-Dandy Indispensables, is considering how to finance a plant expansion. After the expansion, fixed costs will be $325,000, and variable costs will be 40% of net sales.

The company currently has 25,000 shares of stock outstanding. The expansion can be financed by selling an additional 25,000 shares or by issuing $300,000 worth of 8% debt. Assume a 40% tax rate.

a) Graphically determine the financial breakdown.

b) What is the sales level and what are EPS?

(Using sales figures of $1 million and $600,000 is convenient, although not essential.)

10. N. Welsh, Inc. is considering a change in its financing. The current income statement follows below. The company is considering borrowing $165,000 at 9%. The proceeds would be used to buy half of the outstanding stock.

a) What would be the new earnings per share?

b) What are the DOL, DFL, and DTL now?

c) What would they be after the change in financing?

d) Discuss the implications of your findings.

Net sales		$500,000
Fixed expense	$125,000	
Variable expense	250,000	375,000
Earnings before Interest and taxes		$125,000
Less: Interest		15,000
Earnings before taxes		$110,000
Less: Taxes (40% rate)		44,000
Net income		$ 66,000
Earnings per share (30,000 shares outstanding)		$2.20

ADDITIONAL READINGS

Bowlin, O. D. "The Refunding Decision: Another Special Case in Capital Budgeting," *Journal of Finance* (March 1966), pp. 55–68.

Fraine, H. G., and R. H. Mills. "Effect of Defaults and Credit Deterioration on Yields of Corporate Bonds," *Journal of Finance* (September 1961), pp. 423–34.

Gordon, M. J. "A Generalized Solution to the Buy or Lease Decision: A Pedagogical Note," *Journal of Finance* (March 1974), pp. 245–50.

Gritta, R. "The Effect of Financial Leverage on Air Carrier Earnings—A Break-even Analysis," *Financial Management* (Summer 1979), pp. 53–60.

Halford, F. A. "Income Bonds," *Financial Analysts Journal* (January–February 1964), pp. 73–79.

Jen, F. C., and J. E. Wert. "The Effects of Call Risk on Corporate Bond Yields," *Journal of Finance* (December 1967), pp. 637–52.

———. "The Value of the Deferred Call Privilege," *National Banking Review* (March 1966), pp. 369–78.

Kalotay, A. "Sinking Funds and the Realized Cost of Debt," *Financial Management* (Spring 1982), pp. 43–54.

Laber, G. "Implications of Discount Rates and Financing Assumptions for Bond Refunding Decisions," *Financial Management* (Spring 1979), pp. 7–12.

Mayor, T. H., and K. G. McCoin. "The Rate of Discount in Bond Refunding," *Financial Management* (Autumn 1974), pp. 54–58.

Ofer, A. R., and R. A. Taggert. "Bond Refunding: A Clarifying Analysis," *Journal of Finance* (March 1977), pp. 21–30.

Winn, W. J., and A. Hess, Jr. "The Value of the Call Privilege," *Journal of Finance* (May 1959), pp. 182–95.

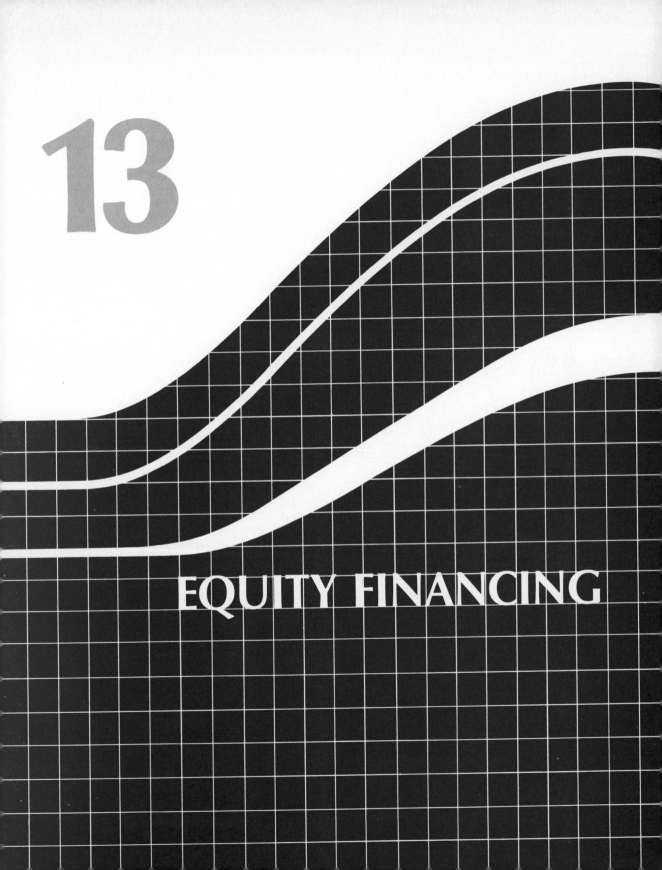

13

EQUITY FINANCING

There are three main sources of equity capital for a corporation: common stock, retained earnings, and preferred stock. A corporation's existence starts with the sale of common stock. After the initial sale of stock, most corporate equity comes from retention of earnings. Earnings retained are dividends not paid, making dividend policy one of the toughest tasks of financial managers. There are no clear-cut solutions.

There is another source of equity financing—preferred stock. Because of its claims on assets and income, preferred stock is much like debt. However, in some ways it is markedly inferior to debt as a form of corporate financing. Preferred stock continues to exist for a number of reasons. It was issued long ago when the economic environment was different. Eighty-five percent of its dividends are nontaxable when received by another tax-paying corporation. Further, preferred stock can serve certain purposes in creating mergers.

After careful study of this chapter, you will

1. Understand what is meant by equity capital and how equity differs from debt with regard to (a) claim on assets, (b) claim on income, and (c) voting rights.
2. Know how common stock controls a corporation and the procedures involved in voting common stock.
3. Know what is meant by the preemptive right and what a privileged subscription is; how privileged subscriptions give rise to rights and how to determine the value of a right.
4. Understand the major issue in setting dividend policy.
5. Know what corporations have done historically with regard to distribution of earnings, that is, paying dividends.
6. Understand the bases for dividend policy decisions as indicated by corporate directors.
7. Know what stock dividends and stock splits are, and learn what statistical studies have found to be the benefits of such "distributions."
8. Learn why preferred stock is so called and why corporations generally do not prefer it.
9. Learn about the dividend and voting provisions pertaining to preferred stock.
10. Understand how preferred stock can be useful in arranging a merger.

COMMON STOCK

All business enterprises, incorporated and unincorporated, must have equity capital. Owner's equity constitutes the initial source of capital for any firm. As time passes, this initial contribution is supplemented by additional capital inflows by the current owners and by retention of earnings. Therefore common equity becomes the basis of the use of debt or preferred stock in the ongoing search for an optimal capital structure.

Common stock equity represents the ultimate ownership of the firm. As such, stockholders differ from bondholders and preferred stockholders with respect to claim on assets, claim on income, voting rights, and the protection of their position as corporate owners. It is the position of the claims on assets and income that gives rise to the use of the term *residual owner* when referring to common stock.

CLAIM ON ASSETS

Dissolution of a corporation can be either voluntary or involuntary. In the former case, the owners may decide to terminate the corporation's existence by selling off its assets. In the latter case, it may be dissolved as a consequence of merging with another corporation when its stock is purchased. In either alternative, the common stockholders are the residual claimants to the firm's assets. All other claimants, whether holders of debt or preferred stock, have prior claims on the firm's assets. When a business is terminated voluntarily, the stockholders typically receive proceeds from the liquidation of the firm's assets. However, this is not usually so when a firm goes bankrupt. The equity holders assume the greater risk; the residual nature of common stock means that stockholders normally receive nothing in a bankruptcy proceeding. Presumably, the equity holders make permanent investments in the firm. Shareholders may sell their ownership interest to others, or the firm may be liquidated and the proceeds divided among the owners after prior claims have been paid off, but neither of these possibilities is prearranged. Thus, in regard to their claim on the firm's assets, the equity holders are the greatest risk bearers.

The amount of the residual claim of the common stockholders is shown in the net worth section of the balance sheet. To arrive at common stock equity, it is first necessary to subtract the preferred stock value from the total net worth. Common stock equity divided by the number of common shares results in the book value per share.

It would be strictly coincidental if book and market share values were the same. Market value is derived in a manner entirely different from that used to calculate book value. In Chapter 4 we noted that the value of a stock is the present value of the benefits that are expected to be generated. In equity investments, the purpose of investing is to participate in the earnings of the firm through dividends when (and if) they are distributed. Therefore the real or intrinsic value of a stock is the present value of the cash dividends using an appropriate RADR. In an efficient market, this intrinsic value is translated into an equivalent market price.

The book value of common stock is derived from balance sheet data, not cash flows, which explains why little attention is paid to book value in liquidations, either forced or voluntary. In most bankruptcies, the assets are usually disposed of for considerably less than book value. As prior claims must be satisfied first, it is not unusual for common stockholders to receive little or nothing.

Should the market price of the common stock fall too low in relation to book value, a speculator may seek to acquire the stock either through open market purchases or by a formal tender offer. Before doing so, however, such a purchaser seeks to determine the underlying market value of the assets. If this value is significantly above the going concern value, the speculator may purchase the stock for the purpose of liquidating the firm voluntarily. The point to note here is that the purchaser's attention was directed to the firm by the large divergence between the book and market values of the stock. In many cases in the early 1980s, mergers were initiated because purchasers found the underlying asset value of natural resource companies to be considerably in excess of both book and market value. Therefore the mergers allowed the purchasers to acquire natural resource assets at a lower cost than would be possible in searching for them. Further, many of these mergers utilized borrowed funds, thereby giving the acquiring firm the additional benefit of employing financial leverage in a period of sustained rising prices.

CLAIM ON INCOME

The owners of equity capital are entitled to net earnings after taxes and interest are paid and all other obligations of the firm are met. They are the residual claimants to the income of a business enterprise, which may be much, little, or nothing. Net earnings also may be retained in the business rather than paid out to the owners; despite large earnings, it is possible that their dividends may lag for long periods of time, depending upon the investment opportunities available to the firm.

Since World War II, inflation has been a powerful factor in the price appreciation of common stocks, although appreciation has not been continuous, as the stock market has suffered several rather severe reversals throughout the period. Inflation tends to reallocate the value of the assets of corporations among their security holders by reducing the real value of fixed-income securities and by increasing the real value of variable-income securities. If a firm with assets of $1 million has creditors' claims against it for $500,000, its stockholders' share in assets is $500,000. Assuming inflation of 100%, the corporation's assets will have a value of $2 million, the creditors' claims still will be $500,000, and the stockholders' share in the assets will be $1.5 million. If net earnings maintain the same ratio to assets after inflation as before, net earnings available for dividends will increase 300% even though the corporation's assets increase only 100%. Therefore the disproportionate rise in net earnings on common stock equity will support further price appreciation in the common stock. Any such increase cannot be calculated with great precision because, as market conditions change, the PE ratios adjust to the constantly changing environment.

CONTROL OF THE CORPORATION

The final authority for managing a corporation resides with the common stockholders. In large corporations this control is indirect; that is, the stockholders elect members of the board of directors. Election of directors typically takes place at the annual stockholders' meeting. Because most stockholders find it impractical to attend the annual meeting, there is widespread use of **proxies** solicited by management. The election of directors is usually the most important business to be transacted at the annual meeting of the stockholders.

Stockholders of a corporation usually permit their elected representatives, the members of the board of directors, to select officers and other agents to manage the corporation's affairs. This does not invalidate owner control so long as the owners of equity capital do not surrender their right to exercise control over election of the directors. Two common methods of voting in use today are majority and cumulative voting.

Majority Voting

Under **majority voting,** a stockholder may cast no more votes for any director than the number of shares he or she owns or controls through proxies. Thus if a stockholder controls 100 shares, only 100 votes may be cast for any one director. This method of voting has the effect of preventing minority representation on the board of directors, because a group owning or controlling 50% of the voting shares plus one can elect its slate of candidates for directors. Majority voting is the typical method of voting.

Cumulative Voting

The alternative method of voting is called **cumulative voting.** In some states, statutory provisions are made for cumulative voting (as well as by the federal government for national banks) in order to make it possible for minority stockholders to influence representation on boards of directors. In cumulative voting, a stockholder may cast votes equal to the number of shares held (assume 100) times the number of directors to be elected (assume 10) for any one candidate (thus 1,000 votes). All 1,000 votes may be cast for one candidate, or the stockholder may distribute the 1,000 votes in any way desired among the candidates.

The formula for cumulative voting is as follows:

$$r = \frac{S \times d}{D + 1} + 1,$$

where

r = the number of shares required to elect a desired number of directors,

S = the number of voting shares,

d = the number of directors desired, and

D = the number of directors to be elected.

If 1,000 shares are to be voted and 10 directors are to be elected, a minimum of 91 shares or 910 votes will be needed to elect one director.

$$91 = \frac{1,000 \times 1}{10 + 1} + 1.$$

Therefore a stockholder owning 100 shares can be assured of electing one director.

By using **classified boards** (a term of office for directors of more than one year), a corporation can nullify much of the impact of cumulative voting because the denominator in the previous equation is lower than it would be if all directors are elected every year.

If a group controls a given number of shares before an election (e.g., 200 shares), it is possible to arrive at the number of directors it can elect by rearranging the previous formula:

$$d = \frac{(r - 1)(D + 1)}{S}$$

$$= \frac{(200 - 1)(10 + 1)}{1,000}$$

$$= \frac{199(11)}{1,000}$$

$$= \frac{2,189}{1,000} = 2.189 \quad \text{directors.}$$

Therefore, if a group owns 200 shares, it can elect two directors to the board.

In order to accumulate votes intelligently, a group must have an estimate of (1) the number of shares that will be voted (in person or by proxy), (2) how the nonmanagement shareholders will vote, and (3) how many shares the potential opposition controls. It is possible, under cumulative voting, to give certain candidates so many votes beyond those required for election that an additional director might have been elected.

Foreknowledge of the extent to which shareholders will vote might permit diversion of votes to other more desirable candidates. If no prior list of candidates is proposed and there is no knowledge that some shareholders plan to cumulate their votes, management may find itself spreading its votes over the entire slate of candidates and ending up with minority representation on the board of directors.

Cumulative voting is not the usual procedure, and the wisdom of authorizing it has been questioned. While diversified representation is considered desirable, it is not necessarily assured by selecting board members by means of cumulative voting. Some minority-stockholder directors elected through cumulative voting have been known to take the position that they were obliged to disagree with management, regardless of the merits of the issues. Cumulative voting does favor special groups who may not represent the interests of all stockholders equally.

THE PREEMPTIVE RIGHT

The **preemptive right** is the right of stockholders, under corporate charters or state laws, to subscribe to additional shares of corporate stock before it is offered for sale to nonstockholders. The preemptive right of common stockholders permits them to participate proportionately in any increase in the amount of capital stock of their company. Hence, they are given the opportunity to maintain their percentage interest in their company, and by using this privilege to buy new stock when offered, they protect their interest in the company from being diluted.

The first argument in support of the common law preemptive right principle is that it permits existing common stockholders to protect their voting positions. Assume that an individual owns 10%, or 2,000 shares, of the 20,000 shares of voting stock of a corporation. If a new issue of stock is sold to outsiders in an amount equal to the number of shares outstanding, the voting rights of the original stockholder would be reduced from 10 to 5%. If the shareholder were given the right to subscribe to an additional 2,000 shares before they were offered to others, he or she would have the opportunity to protect the 10% voting position.

A second argument in support of the preemptive right principle is that it permits shareholders to retain their proportionate share in the retained earnings of their corporation. If we assume that this value is $100, and that the par value is the same, each share of common stock outstanding has a book value of $200 ($2,000,000 capital stock + $2,000,000 retained earnings ÷ 20,000 shares outstanding = book value of $200 per share). If we assume that 20,000 shares of a new issue are sold at the par value of $100, the book value of each share of outstanding common stock would be reduced from $200 to $150 ($4,000,000 in capital stock + $2,000,000 in retained earnings ÷ 40,000 shares outstanding = $150). In effect, selling new shares at par value transfers $50 "on the books" from old stockholders to new ones.

A third argument in support of the common law preemptive right principle is that the old stockholders must be permitted to retain their proportionate interest in the earnings of their corporation. If the corporation is earning $320,000, or 8% after taxes, on a net worth of $4 million ($320,000 ÷ $4,000,000 = 0.08), this would amount to $16 per share ($320,000 ÷ 20,000 = $16). If 20,000 new shares are sold for $100 per share, the new worth of the corporation would be increased by $2 million, which would earn $160,000 at the rate of 8% after taxes, thereby increasing total earnings to $480,000. When these earnings are divided by the number of shares outstanding, EPS would be $12 ($480,000 ÷ 40,000 = $12). In effect, the old stockholders' interest in earnings would be reduced from $16 to $12 per share, and the new stockholders' interest in earnings would be increased from $8 to $12 per share. In other words, issuing of new shares without preemptive rights would transfer future EPS from the old stockholders to the new ones.

If the common law principle pertaining to the preemptive right of old stockholders to buy new common stock is justified, it is equally applicable to any new issues of preferred stock, bonds, or other notes that are convertible into common stock. If the right to exchange preferred stocks, bonds, or other securities for common stock has any value, the right of old common stockholders in regard to voting, equity, and earnings of the corporation will be diluted at the time of conversion in the same way as noted in the case of new common stock sales to new stockholders.

Preemptive rights are based only on common law, and they may be withdrawn by statutory law. Statutes in some states make provisions for waiving preemptive rights in the articles of incorporation of firms incorporated in those states.

Preemptive Rights Offerings

The market for securities sold under preemptive rights is assumed to be limited to old stockholders, but the rights are transferable and they may be sold. The size of a new issue is an important factor in the success of a rights offering in that old stockholders are in a better position to absorb all the shares offered when the ratio of new to old securities is small—assume 1:20 as compared to 1:1. In the first case, stockholders would be asked to increase their investment by only 5%; in the second case, they would be asked to approximately double their investment. It is important that management make a careful analysis of the distribution of existing shares in order to decide the size of the issue that could be absorbed by existing stockholders. The stock may be owned by a few large stockholders who are unable to purchase more shares or who would be unwilling to do so because they want to diversify their investment portfolios. On the other hand, existing stock may be owned by a small number of institutional investors, including investment companies, which are both willing and able to acquire new shares at bargain prices.

Generally speaking, the best market for privileged subscriptions exists when there is a large number of satisfied shareholders. Previous sales of new securities by privileged subscription may have demonstrated to stockholders that the degree of dilution of each share was negligible and that any possible reduction in the market price of the stock was only temporary.

Given the assumption that everyone is interested in purchasing at bargain prices, the key to successful financing is the spread between the **subscription price** and the **market price.** In other words, a new issue should be a success if the subscription price is sufficiently below the market price. If we assume a market price of $150 and a subscription price of $125, we would expect an offering of new stock to old stockholders to be successful. Of course, the lower the subscription price, the smaller will be the return to the company for each share sold, and a greater number of new shares will have to be sold to raise a given amount of funds. The more new shares sold, the greater will be the dilution in the earnings of each old share; this, in turn, may depress the market price of each share.

Management may set an unusually low subscription price purposely to adjust the market price of the stock downward; in such cases, management may be guided in part by the same motives that lead a corporation to declare a stock dividend or stock split. In fact, if the corporation perceives no objection to a reduction in the market price of the stock and no pressure to maintain its old dividend rate, there is no reason why the subscription price for a new issue may not be at a substantial discount from market.

Value of a Right

A **subscription warrant** is a certificate issued by a corporation specifying the conditions under which shareholders of record are entitled to purchase additional new stock that the corporation plans to issue imminently. It should be distinguished from a long-term stock purchase *warrant* giving the holder the right to purchase a certain number of shares at a specified price within a specified time. (The long-term stock purchase warrant is discussed in Chapter 14.)

The theoretical value of a **right** can be calculated readily. However, it is first necessary to determine whether the stock is selling **rights on** (with rights) or **ex-rights** (separately from rights). The procedures for handling rights are similar to those for handling dividends on stock. Dividends go with the stock until the **ex-dividend** date, which is four business days before the **stock-of-record** date. Rights are generally traded in the same manner.

Thus on January 15 the board of directors might announce that rights will be mailed out March 1 to stockholders of record as of February 15, the **holder of record date.** Any investor purchasing the stock between January 15 and February 10 would receive the rights; hence, the stock would be selling rights-on. From February 11 until the end of the subscription period, the stock would be selling ex-rights, or separately from the rights. Using $200 as the market price of the stock, $175 as the subscription price, and five rights necessary to purchase one share, it is possible to calculate the theoretical value of the rights.

When the stock is selling rights-on, the following formula can be used to determine the market price of each right:

$$R = \frac{M - S}{N + 1},$$

where

R = the value of the right,
M = market price of the stock,
S = the subscription price of the stock, and
N = the number of rights needed to buy one share.

Given the assumptions noted previously, the value of the right would be $4.17:

$$R = \frac{\$200 - \$175}{5 + 1} = \$4.17.$$

Another way of viewing the problem is as follows: To become entitled to an additional share at $175, a stockholder would have to own five shares worth $200 each. Exercising the right at $175 would result in six shares having a total value of $1,175 [5($200) + $175]. The average price of the six shares would be $195.83 ($200 − $4.17).

Any investor not choosing to exercise the privilege would find that the investment would depreciate if no provision was made to sell the rights before the expiration date. This decline would occur because the new shares can be purchased at a bargain price of $175. Therefore an active market usually develops for the rights as soon as they are separated from the stock.

At the ex-rights date, the purchaser of the stock does not receive the rights. At that time the market price of the stock should fall by the value of the right, or to $195.83 in our example. This decline in price can be confirmed by the use of the ex-rights formula:

$$R = \frac{M_e - S}{N}$$

$$= \frac{\$195.83 - \$175}{5} = \$4.17,$$

where M_e is the market value of the stock ex-rights.

Rights offerings have considerable speculative appeal. For example, an investor with $195.83 to invest could purchase one share of stock or 47 rights. If the stock rises from $195.83 to $215.83, the value of the rights would climb to $8.17. The gain on the rights would be $188 (47 × $4) versus $20 if the stock were purchased outright. This result is possible because 47 rights would have purchased 9.4 shares of stock at $175 a share.

While the purchaser of 47 rights would have had a claim on 9.4 shares, thereby magnifying the potential gain if the stock price rises, it should be remembered that the opposite may also occur. If the price of the stock falls $20, from $195.83 to $175.83, the value of a right would decline to $0.17 (47 times × $0.17 = $7.99). In the first instance, when the stock rose $20 a share, a profit of $188 would be realized; in the second, a loss of $188 would be incurred if the stock price falls by the same amount. This example illustrates why rights offerings may give rise to speculation if the price of the common stock shows a substantial movement in either direction during the rights period.

Standby Underwriting

Firms may arrange for **standby underwriting;** that is, they may negotiate a contract with an investment banking syndicate to purchase the unsold portion of an issue to be offered to its stockholders. Under such an arrangement, the corporation may pay either a flat commission on the entire issue or a smaller commission on the issue plus a higher one on the unsubscribed convertible bond or share portion. When it plans to offer an issue under subscription rights, a corporation generally uses the services of an investment banker to prepare forms, price the stock and register it with the Securities and Exchange Commission, prepare the prospectus, and handle other details associated with distribution of the securities.

COMMON STOCK—SUMMARY

There are two main sources of capital funds: owners and lenders. Equity or proprietary capital refers to that provided by owners. It is distinguished by the following characteristics: The firm is under no contractual obligation to pay a return on the investment; there is no stated date on which the funds must be returned to the investor; and those who provide funds are responsible for the management and control of the firm. Sometimes the term *risk capital* is used; this emphasizes the fact that owners of common stock assume risks to a greater degree than do lenders. Even though owners must assume risks in owning stock, these risks may be more than offset by the prospect of high returns.

Corporation law usually states that each outstanding share of stock is entitled to one vote if it is not of a class of stock that is denied the right to vote by the articles of incorporation. Directors may be elected either by majority or cumulative voting. In the former instance, one vote is cast for each director to be elected. In the latter, a stockholder (or a proxy) may cast votes for any one candidate equal to the number of shares he or she owns or controls times the number of directors to be elected, or the stockholder may split them up between two or among three or more candidates.

The common law preemptive right principle holds that existing stock-holders should be given the right to protect their proportionate voting power and commensurate share in the net worth and earnings of their company. As a financing device, a preemptive rights offering is most important to existing stockholders when the value of subscription rights is substantial. For rights to have value, the market price must be above the subscription price.

DIVIDEND POLICY AND RETAINED EARNINGS

A **dividend** is a periodic payment made to stockholders to compensate them for the use of and risk to their investment funds. Most commonly, dividends are declared out of current earnings. The firm's board of directors determines the type, size, and time of dividend payments. The firm may declare one dividend each year, or several interim (usually quarterly) and a final (year-end) dividend instead. The two most common types of dividends are (1) those that reduce the assets of a corporation, such as cash dividends; and (2) those that neither decrease assets nor increase liabilities, such as stock dividends. Of the two types, those payable in cash are the most common and most important; when the term *dividend* is used without qualification, we are referring to a **cash dividend.**

Dividend policy, which determines the amount of earnings to be retained or paid out by the firm, is one of the key decision areas of financial management. A corporation's board of directors is under no contractual obligation to pay dividends on common stock. A firm's dividend policy determines how much of its earnings it retains. At the same time, dividends may affect stock prices.

The question is whether it is better to retain earnings, providing necessary equity, or to pay dividends and be able to raise equity by selling stock at higher prices due to the attraction of the dividends. Although the question is well understood, the answer is unknown. Academicians have analyzed and debated the issue for decades. The issue remains unresolved. Rather than get involved in the debate, we will concentrate on the known: what firms have done historically with regard to dividends, the bases on which they supposedly make such decisions, cash dividend payment procedures, the procedures and effects of stock dividends (and splits).

CORPORATE DIVIDEND HISTORY

Extensive long-term data exist on total dividends and earnings of U.S. corporations. By using these data, one can calculate overall **divided payout ratios.** Table 13.1 shows these payout ratios from 1950 through 1982. The payout percentages range from 30 to 63% during the period, with an overall average of 43%. In general, low payout rates occurred in years when earnings grew rapidly and high payout rates occurred when growth was low or earnings declined.

In 1951 corporate earnings declined, and the proportion distributed increased. From 1952 to 1954 earnings were fairly stable, as was the payout rate. In 1955 earnings rose markedly. Dividends lagged, resulting in a low payout ratio. Next year's earnings (1956) were little changed, and the payout percentage edged back toward the previous average. When 1957–1958 earnings were down, the proportional payout increased. In 1959 earnings jumped and the payout rate dropped. In 1960–1961 earnings were down. When dividends rose slightly, the payout ratio increased markedly. In 1962 and 1963 earnings were up modestly, and the payout rate dropped slightly. From 1964 through 1967, earnings soared and payout rates dropped. When earnings moderated in 1967–1968, the payout rates crept back toward 50%. When earnings dropped in 1969–1970, payout rates went to historic highs as corporations resisted cutting dividends. In 1971–1973, as earnings rose sharply, payout rates receded to the 41% level.

From 1975, when corporate profits jumped markedly, to 1980, payout ratios hovered at the lower end of the range, but returned to the mean when earnings dropped in 1981. Corporations appear to be reluctant to raise dividends until they are assured that the new profit levels can be sustained.

There is an alternative explanation for the recent low payouts. High profits in recent years have been partly due to inflation; that is, higher prices with the same margins generate higher dollar profits. During this period, external financing has been relatively unattractive. Interest rates have been high, and

TABLE 13.1
Corporate After-Tax Profits and Dividends, 1950–1982 (in billions of dollars).

Year	Profits after Taxes	Dividends	· Payout % (Dividends/Profits)
1950	$ 24.9	$ 8.8	35%
1951	21.6	8.6	40
1952	19.6	8.6	44
1953	20.4	8.9	44
1954	20.6	9.3	45
1955	27.0	10.5	39
1956	27.2	11.3	42
1957	26.0	11.7	45
1958	22.3	11.6	52
1959	28.5	12.6	44
1960	26.7	13.4	50
1961	27.2	13.8	51
1962	31.2	15.2	49
1963	33.1	16.5	49
1964	38.4	17.8	46
1965	46.5	19.8	43
1966	49.9	20.8	42
1967	46.6	21.4	46
1968	47.8	23.6	49
1969	44.8	24.3	54
1970	39.3	24.7	63
1971	47.6	25.1	53
1972	55.4	26.0	47
1973	72.9	29.6	41
1974	74.5	31.0	42
1975	73.3	32.4	44
1976	92.2	35.8	39
1977	104.5	42.1	40
1978	121.5	47.2	39
1979	167.7	50.1	30
1980	157.8	58.1	37
1981	150.9	65.1	43
1982	117.5	70.3	60
	$1,905.4	$826.0	43%

Sources: *Economic Report of the President* 1973 (Washington, D:C.: U.S. Government Printing Office, 1973), p. 273. *Federal Reserve Bulletin*, February 1974, p. A48; November 1974, p. A43; December 1977, p. A38; April 1983, p. A37.

stock prices generally have been depressed. However, the need for capital assets persists, and at higher prices the problem is compounded. Greater internal financing may be a result of this squeeze play.

While many business firms may follow a policy of using profits to provide for anticipated needs, the payment of cash dividends appears to take precedence over retention of earnings, with dividend stability and growth being of prime importance. Cash dividends have been more stable than either corporate income after taxes or income retained in the businesses. Figure 13.1 illustrates this point. It can be seen that undistributed profits, not dividends, have borne the brunt of annual variations in profits.

That dividends to stockholders sometimes come first can be illustrated by the fact that, from 1931 to 1933, when most corporations were operating at a loss, dividends were being paid. Also, there has been a steady, virtually uninterrupted rise in dividend payments since 1950.

Residual Theory of Dividends

In the previous discussion, the data seem to indicate that undistributed profits, not dividends, have borne the brunt of the variations in profits. However,

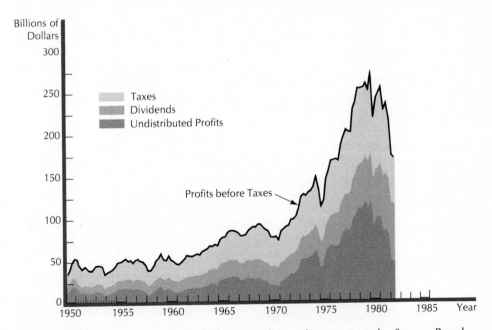

Figure 13.1 Corporate profits: Seasonally adjusted annual rates, quarterly. *Source:* Board of Governors of the Federal Reserve System, 1982 *Historical Chart Book* (Washington, D.C.: 1982), p. 60.

theoretical prescriptions for dividend policy frequently treat dividends as a leftover by-product of investment policy. In order for dividends to be a residual, the management of the firm must determine the (1) desired capital budget, (2) amount of equity capital necessary to finance the planned capital budget, (3) amount of earnings that will be available, and (4) amount of earnings that may be paid out as dividends, if all earnings are not required to finance the capital budget. Corporate management should retain earnings if the funds can be put to good use. Any unused remainder can be distributed to the shareholders. The theory implies that investors prefer to have the firm retain earnings as long as the firm can earn more than the investors can earn themselves. It has been suggested that such a policy would maximize shareholder wealth.

Management has greater freedom in spending funds generated internally compared to funds obtained from outside sources, because the latter are usually borrowed for specific purposes and the terms under which they are obtained may contain provisions that limit their use. Thus, when financing with internally generated funds, the advantages to the stockholders of close scrutiny by creditors are lost. This absence of scrutiny of retained earnings has bothered some financial analysts because of the inherent possibility that the funds will not be employed advantageously by the firm. It is argued that dividend policies should direct funds from the less profitable firms to the more profitable ones. Perhaps this concern is a bit overstated, because a firm that depends upon the money and capital markets for part of its marginal need for funds does not lose the advantage of outside review of its financial policy.

Do stock prices react favorably to certain types of dividend policies? The statistical information does not provide a clear-cut answer to this question. However, the evidence does seem to establish discernible patterns of corporate dividend policy. Whether corporations *should* adopt particular types of dividend policies is unclear, but it can be suggested that they *seem* to do just that. The next section examines the bases for dividend policies of domestic corporations.

BASES FOR DIVIDEND POLICIES

The primary basis for corporate dividends is earnings. Dividends are distributed on the basis of current earnings and the relationship of those earnings to expected future earnings. Firms strive for the appearance of stability in such policies. However, the firm must consider more than the current level of earnings in setting policy. Some additional considerations are discussed briefly.

Legal Restrictions

Before declaring dividends, management must be sure that realized earnings are available for distribution and that dividend payment will not threaten the paid-in capital of the firm. Payment of cash dividends when a corporation is insolvent or would be made insolvent by such payment is illegal. (The concept of insolvency will be discussed in some detail in Chapter 18.) A firm can be insolvent in basically two ways: (1) liabilities exceed assets, or (2) there is insufficient cash to meet current obligations. Directors are responsible, jointly and severally, for such illegal dividend payments. Legal phraseology varies from state to state, and a corporation's board of directors must be sure that a proposed cash dividend payment is legal under the statutes of the state of incorporation. More specifically, management must be sure that, even under the most critical court review, negative answers would be given to the following four questions regarding payment of a cash dividend: (1) Would it threaten the corporation's capital? (2) Would it threaten the claims of creditors? (3) Is the corporation insolvent? (4) Would the payment cause insolvency?

Contract Restrictions

Before declaring a cash dividend, a corporation's board of directors must be careful to comply with any restrictions on payment of dividends that apply in current debt contracts. Most frequently, such restrictions are present in long-term debt contracts, but they may also exist in intermediate- and short-term debt contracts, such as term-loan agreements and short-term debt agreements.

A corporation's board of directors could also be denied the right to declare dividends on common stock when there are preferred stockholders, whose rights are prior to those of common stockholders. In some cases, clauses in a corporation's charter or bylaws may make it illegal to pay dividends on common stock unless certain financial standards have been met and are maintained. An example would be a requirement that net current assets be 150 or 200% of the par value of the outstanding preferred stock before dividends may be paid. In other cases, compliance with a sinking fund requirement for retirement of debt or preferred stock may prevent the declaration of dividends. Such restrictions serve to ensure the maintenance of a corporation's liquidity and solvency; hence a policy of keeping cash and increasing retained earnings is desirable.

Working Capital Position

Two factors are important in determining the effects of divided payments on the working capital position: the firm's cash position and its debt-servicing requirements (or need to repay debt). In voting a cash dividend, a board of directors creates a current liability; when these dividends are paid, there will be a loss of working capital assets. Because other current liabilities may be coming due at the same time, the need for cash and other assets must be projected.

Access to Capital Markets

A factor that is important to many firms in the determination of their dividend policies is the availability of capital funds from outside sources. If a firm has access to capital markets at reasonable costs, it follows that it would have less need to rely on internally generated funds as a source of capital than a company that has not established itself in the marketplace. In effect, when a firm has established alternative sources of funds, it has greater latitude in determining its dividend policy and can establish a stable dividend payout more readily. Thus a well-established firm is more likely to have a stable rate than a new or small firm, not only because it may have fewer expansionary needs but also because it has greater access to capital markets.

The Human Element

Although we can discuss dividend payments in legal, financial, or economic terms, in practice it is not possible to keep the human element out of decisions made by directors. A corporation is regarded as a continuing business enterprise, but individual stockholders may end ownership by selling their interest to others if they are dissatisfied with current or anticipated dividend policies. A board of directors must safeguard the interest of both stockholders and creditors; therefore protection of capital assets must come before dividend payments. Yet, if stockholders are to be induced to provide venture capital, in the long run the return on their investment in stock must be equal to a normal interest payment plus enough to compensate them for the risks assumed.

The decision as to when and under what circumstances stockholders are to share in the earnings of their corporation is left to the board of directors; once a cash dividend has been declared, it becomes a liability of the corporation. Although stockholders do have the power to force a change in management if they act collectively, they have met with little success in attempting to force directors to vote dividends through court proceedings. An exception to this general rule was a 1916 suit brought by stockholders of the Ford Motor Company in a Michigan state court, which resulted in an order that the Board of directors declare a dividend totaling $19 million.

DIVIDEND PAYMENT PROCEDURES

A cash dividend declaration is effected by majority resolution of the directors at a regular or special meeting. The declaration gives the name of the stock on which the dividend is to be paid, the amount per share, the date and time when the names of stockholders are to be determined for dividend purposes (such as at the close of business on December 15, 1983), and the date on which the dividend checks are to be dated and mailed to stockholders.

Cash dividends may be called *regular, irregular, extra* or *special, interim, final* or *liquidating* (or they may have no label attached). Regular dividends may be made quarterly, semiannually, or annually (in rare cases, even monthly). If a board of directors designates a dividend as the "regular quarterly dividend of $1 per share of common stock," it indicates that management's policy is to maintain that rate. The term *regular* dividends is most frequently used to describe dividends payable on preferred stock; however, when a corporation has a long record of paying a specified dividend on common stock at regular intervals, it may also be known as a regular dividend. One of the best illustrations of this is the $2.25 quarterly common stock dividend that the American Telephone and Telegraph Company paid from 1922 to 1959, when the stock was split three for one and the quarterly rate per share was fixed at 82.5 cents. Companies that have paid at least one dividend a year for long periods of time include National City Bank of New York (now Citicorp) since 1813; Scovill, Inc., since 1835; Hartford Fire Insurance Company since 1873; American Telephone and Telegraph Company since 1881; General Electric Company since 1899; and many other major companies going back more than 50 years.

Irregular dividends are those paid in varying amounts, usually by companies whose earnings fluctuate widely (high earnings, high dividends—low earnings, small or no dividends). Irregular dividend policies are usually unpopular with shareholders.

A corporation may share higher profits with stockholders by declaring an *extra* dividend rather than by increasing the regular dividend. This practice does not commit the board of directors to a future increase in the dividend rate, and it places stockholders on notice that they should not assume that the extra dividend will be declared again on the next dividend date. When an extra dividend is paid, it is usually distributed along with the regular dividend as a year-end payment.

Some U.S. corporations have adopted the English terminology, calling all dividends paid during the year *interim* dividends. Such payments may be paid as often as seems appropriate throughout the fiscal year.

When a cash dividend represents a return of capital, it may be termed a *liquidating* dividend. Liquidating cash dividends may be paid when a natural resource corporation pays a cash dividend (part of the payment may represent profits and part a return of capital), or when a firm is being liquidated under supervision of the federal bankruptcy court.

COMMON STOCK REPURCHASE

Common stock that has been issued and subsequently acquired by the issuing firm is called **treasury stock.** Such stock is then treated as a deduction from the stockholders' equity. The repurchase of stock represents an alternative to the payment of cash dividends.

Many firms repurchase their common stock. Most repurchases amount to a few million dollars, but occasionally they can be substantial. For example, International Business Machines (IBM), in the largest repurchase on record, offered to purchase 4 million shares of its own common stock at a price of $280 beginning on February 22, 1977, and continuing through March 7, 1977. It retained the option to purchase up to a total of 5.5 million shares. The offer to purchase was extended to March 9, 1977. At the close of the tender offer on the latter date, IBM reacquired 2,546,000 shares at a cost of $713 million.

Stock can be repurchased by either a *tender offer* to the existing stockholders or by purchases in the open market. If a tender offer is made, all stockholders must be given an equal opportunity to tender their shares. If more shares are tendered than the firm agrees to purchase, the tendered stock is prorated. For example, if a firm agrees to purchase 100,000 shares and 200,000 are tendered, each tender offer would be allocated 50%.

With an alternative method used less frequently in tender offers, the stockholders set the price at which they are willing to sell. The company then purchases the least expensive shares and continues until the 100,000 shares are acquired. As a rule, a firm will specify the maximum price that it will pay.

Reasons for Repurchases

A number of reasons have been advanced for the repurchase of a firm's stock. When the price of its common stock is relatively low, a firm may reacquire outstanding shares and justify the action in various ways. These include the desire to

1. Reduce future dividend requirements.
2. Lower the amount of invested capital to conform to changed business conditions.
3. Find a profitable outlet for funds on hand.
4. Support the market price of the stock.
5. Reacquire stock for future corporate needs, such as executive and employee stock options.
6. Increase the EPS because of the smaller number of outstanding shares remaining.

The effect of the repurchase of shares on the EPS and the subsequent market price of the stock is illustrated in the following example. Assume that a firm has 1 million shares outstanding and earnings after taxes of $2 million. Therefore, the EPS is $2. If the PE ratio is 10, the market price of the stock would be $20. If the firm repurchases 50,000 of its shares in lieu of paying a cash dividend of $1 per share and earnings do not change, the EPS would rise to $2.10:

$$\frac{\text{Earnings after taxes}}{\text{Shares after repurchase}} = \text{EPS after repurchase}$$

$$\frac{\$2,000,000}{950,000} = \$2.10.$$

The market price after repurchase should rise to $21 ($2.10 × 10). It should be kept in mind that for this result to hold, the stock must be purchased at precisely $20. In either case, the stockholders receive the benefit of the $1 per share dividend.

For income tax purposes, the $1 per share dividend is treated differently. Cash dividends are taxed at ordinary income tax rates, and stock repurchases qualify for capital gains rates. At 1983 tax rates, the maximum marginal tax rate on ordinary income is 50% and the maximum for capital gains is 20%. The tax advantage favoring repurchases appears to be a strong motivation for the action of some managements.

Criticism of Repurchases

A number of criticisms have been raised against repurchases.

1. A repurchase of common stock implies that this is the best opportunity available to the firm. In other words, a firm lacks investment opportunities that have returns equal to or greater than its cost of capital. It is argued that the repurchase of stock is bad advertising and therefore should be avoided.

2. A repurchase of stock weakens protection for the firm's creditors. However, bond indentures usually prohibit the use of corporate assets to reacquire the firm's stock except under special conditions that give adequate protection to the bondholders. Therefore if the criticism has merit, it would seem to imply that the firm has a substantial amount of unsecured short-term debt.

3. A firm might pay too much to reacquire its stock. If it does, the interests of the remaining stockholders have been harmed. This situation is most likely to occur if there is an impending proxy fight. For example, if Firm X makes a tender offer to the stockholders of Firm Y, the management of Firm Y can counter with a tender offer above the price of Firm X's bid. The probable outcome will be that the stockholders will tender their stock to the higher bidder. The takeover attempt may be thwarted, or at least temporarily sidetracked. But in the process, the firm may be forced to pay a substantial premium over its former market price.

STOCK DIVIDENDS AND STOCK SPLITS

Readjustments in the owner's equity section of the balance sheet are necessary when either a stock dividend or a stock split occurs. For a stock dividend, journal entries are required to reflect changes in value of common stock, capital in excess of par (paid-in capital), and retained earnings. A stock split needs only a journal notation changing the number of shares and the par value.

Stock Dividends

A **stock dividend** is one distributed in the same kind of stock as the one on which the dividend is declared. When stockholders receive a stock dividend, there is no change in their proportional equity. The number of shares has been increased, but the book value of the corporation's assets represented by the owners' holdings has remained unchanged. If a stockholder who owns 100 shares, representing 1% of the corporation's capital, receives a stock dividend of 10%, he or she still owns 1% of the capital stock. The shareholder will have more shares, but each share will represent proportionately less equity; the total proportional interest will be unchanged.

Tempe Corp.'s partial balance sheet in Table 13.2 illustrates this point. The firm has just recorded a 20% stock dividend entry on its books. At the time of the stock dividend declaration, the market price of $2 per share formed the basis for the journal entry capitalizing the market value of the shares. Therefore of the $4 million market value of the new shares (2,000,000 shares × $2), $1 million was placed in the capital account and $3 million was

---

TABLE 13.2
Tempe Corp.: Partial Balance Sheet Showing Effects of a 20% Stock Dividend.

Before

Common stock (10 million shares at $0.50 par)	$ 5,000,000
Capital in excess of par	1,000,000
Retained earnings	12,000,000
	$18,000,000

After

Common stock (12 million shares at $0.50 par)	$ 6,000,000
Capital in excess of par	4,000,000
Retained earnings	8,000,000
	$18,000,000

allocated to the capital in excess of par account. The holder of 1% of the shares (100,000) before the split owned shares with a total book value of $180,000, or $1.80 per share. After the stock dividend, the book value of 120,000 shares would still be $180,000 or $1.50 per share. Thus there has been no increase in the stockholder's overall position.

Although stock dividends give stockholders nothing they did not already have, the dividends amount to extra shares that may be sold; therefore stockholders may consider a stock dividend preferable to no dividend at all. Yet stockholders must pay brokerage fees when they sell stock, and selling may be an expensive way to obtain cash if their holdings are small.

The chief justification for a regular stock dividend by a corporation is that it recognizes financing with retained earnings. Frequently a corporation continues to pay the same cash dividend rate on its stock after a stock dividend distribution; thus it has a larger cash outlay because the number of shares has increased. In this case, if the intent of management is to increase the return to its shareholders, it can do so merely by increasing the cash dividend rate.

Proceeds from the sale of stock dividends by stockholders are taxed at the rate for capital gains, which is below that on ordinary income for long-term gains, a factor that is important for those in higher income brackets. Of course, if dividends were omitted entirely, stockholders would have the same tax advantage if they sold some of their shares for income. If stockholders retain their stock dividends, and if the corporation resumes payment of regular cash dividends, shareholders' dividend receipts will increase. In addition, retention of earnings that might have been distributed as cash dividends should have a favorable effect on the market price of the stock in the future, perhaps then permitting larger cash dividends than otherwise would have been possible.

Stock Splits

A stock **split** is not a dividend. A split changes the par value of the stock. Again, the stockholders have no change in their proportional equity, but in this case there is no shifting of funds from the retained earnings account into common stock, as is done with stock dividends. Using the same data as in Table 13.2 for the Tempe Corp., a two-for-one stock split would have only a modest effect on the balance sheet. Table 13.3 shows that the common stock account would show 20 million shares at $0.25 par value instead of the former 10 million shares at $0.50. There are no adjustments required in any other accounts.

Market Effects

There is general consensus in the academic literature on the merits of stock dividends and stock splits. They are of questionable importance. Stockholders receive nothing of value; their proportionate ownership is unchanged. Unless

TABLE 13.3
Tempe Corp.: Partial Balance Showing Effects of a Two-for-One Stock Split.

Before

Common stock (10 million shares at $0.50 par)	$ 5,000,000
Capital in excess of par	1,000,000
Retained earnings	12,000,000
	$18,000,000

After

Common stock (20 million shares at $0.25 par)	$ 5,000,000
Capital in excess of par	1,000,000
Retained earnings	12,000,000
	$18,000,000

something else about the firm changes, the total value of the stockholders' shares will remain the same. The stock price should change to make the value of the holdings of all investors the same as they were before the split or dividend. For example, if a stockholder owned 100 shares selling at $100 and the stock split two for one, the investor would end up owning 200 shares of $50 stock. A 25% stock dividend would create 125 shares of $80 stock. There would be no net benefit in either case. Extra pieces of paper do not add to real value.

Empirical work supports this position. One study found that unless the total cash dividends on the after-split shares exceeded the total dividends before the split, the price increases generated by the split generally dissipate.† Another paper, which may be the best-known work on this topic, suggests that stock splits per se have no effect on price. In most split stocks, unusual return activity can be detected far in advance of the split announcement, which might mean that any observed effect of a split actually resulted from a reduction in uncertainty. That is, a split serves to formalize information already in the market, making the stock less risky and therefore more valuable.‡ The results of this study paralleled those of the earlier one with regards to cash dividends; where an increase was not forthcoming, the returns deteriorated.

---

† C. Barker, "Effective Stock Splits," *Harvard Business Review* (January–February 1956), pp. 101–106.

‡ E. F. Fama, L. Fisher, M. C. Jensen, and R. Roll, "The Adjustment of Stock Prices to New Information," *International Economic Review* (February 1969, pp. 1–21.

This suggests that stock dividends and splits are nothing more than advertising. They are a way of calling the market's attention to the stock. Like cash dividend increases, stock dividends and splits reflect optimism on the part of management. If that optimism is not backed by performance, though, any short-run price effect will quickly fade.

DIVIDEND POLICY AND RETAINED EARNINGS—SUMMARY

Dividend policy and retained earnings are really two parts of the same problem. Both are influenced by the firm's present and future financial requirements.

A firm must establish guidelines regarding its distribution of corporate earnings. Periodic dividend decisions are made within the framework set by dividend policy. The purpose of such a policy should be to work for the best interests of the shareholders, that is, to maximize the market value of the common stock.

Decisions on dividend payments may be influenced by a number of factors. Some of the more important considerations are legal and contract restrictions, working capital position, access to capital markets, and the human element. Cash dividends may be regular, with the rate and the dividend date uniform over a period of time; extra, and paid with a regular dividend (usually at the end of a corporation's fiscal year); or liquidating, representing a return of capital.

PREFERRED STOCK

When the objective of the organizers of a corporation is to give management considerable latitude in financing the corporation, the articles of incorporation may contain provisions authorizing the issuance of one or more classes of preferred stock in addition to common stock. Both preferred stock and common stock represent owners' equity on the balance sheet. Since World War II, practically all U.S. corporations have relied less and less on equity funds provided by preferred stock when compared to the sum provided by common stock equity. The main disadvantage of financing with preferred stock instead of bonds is that stock dividends are not deductible for federal income tax purposes. Until World War II, when corporate income rose sharply, such nondeductibility was not great enough to offset the advantages of financing with preferred stock.

Preferred stockholders' claims on assets and income are subordinate to those of debtors. However, their claims are senior to those of common stockholders. Unless otherwise specified, which is normally the case, preferred stockholders are entitled to vote. In general, the preferences given preferred stockholders are detrimental to common stockholders' interests. This fact, added to the nondeductibility of the dividend, makes preferred stock financing unattractive. Very little new preferred is being issued, and most of that arises in connection with mergers. Because of its disadvantages, corporations generally arrange to retire preferred stock.

RETIRING PREFERRED STOCK

Retirement of preferred stock may be provided for at the time of issuance by including a call feature or a sinking fund. The call price is of concern to preferred stockholders, because management tends to exercise the **call option** when it is to their advantage to do so. In order to refinance economically, management must keep the call price as low as possible without seriously jeopardizing the salability of the preferred stock. The call price is higher than the par or stated value of the stock; the amount above par or stated value—the call premium—will be highest when financing in the capital market is most difficult, and vice versa.

When issuing preferred stock, a corporation may make provisions for its retirement instead of planning to refinance the issue if and when market conditions are favorable. The corporation may redeem a specified amount of the stock each year or to set aside a definite sum for this purpose. The pool of assets earmarked to retire preferred stock is called a *sinking fund*. Usually, funds required for such redemption must be set aside before dividends are paid on common stock.

As with callable preferred stock, the sinking fund redemption price is customarily above the par or stated value of the shares. This price may be adjusted downward with the passage of time, because the preferred stockholder's cost of investing will gradually have been amortized out of dividends on the preferred stock. The justification for the downward adjustment in the redemption price is that the higher premium paid during the early life of the stock is a compensation to the investor for reinvesting; the investors who hold preferred stock for 10 years have less claim to compensation than those who hold it for only one year.

CLAIM ON ASSETS

In case of liquidation or dissolution of a corporation, corporate charters usually give preferred stockholders priority over common stockholders in the distribution of assets as well as dividends. But when the articles of incorporation give them preference as to dividends only (being silent on priority in regard to assets), preferred stockholders share pro rata with common stockholders in case of liquidation or dissolution. The purpose of giving preferred stockholders priority in terms of assets is to facilitate financing by making the stock more salable, in the same way that pledges of property make bonds more salable.

The preferred stockholders' preference in the distribution of assets, as with dividends, is subject to limitations. In the case of involuntary liquidation or dissolution, the priority of assets of preferred stock is limited to the par value, or to the stated value if there is no par. If the corporation is liquidated, preferred stockholders have the first claim to any cash remaining after taxes and debts have been paid.

Sometimes the corporate charter will make a distinction between voluntary or involuntary dissolution and the right to assets of preferred stock. Preferred stock's claim on assets is usually greater when the dissolution is voluntary. The general rule seems to be that, if there is any uncertainty, preferred stock is entitled to a fair return on investment value, which may be more than the par or stated value. But if there is a statement that preferred stock has a prior claim on assets in an amount equal to par value or some other specified amount, a contract exists that limits the claims of preferred stockholders to that amount.

It is not unusual to issue preferred stock that has special features that provide additional protection for investors. For example, the terms under which preferred stock is issued may make it obligatory for a corporation to limit long-term borrowing, forgo expenditures that would reduce working capital, and refrain from additional issues of preferred stock. The purpose of these restrictions is to preserve the preferred stockholders' claim on assets by limiting the firm's ability to issue new securities with higher claims.

CLAIM ON INCOME

Customarily, the dividend rate on preferred stock is specifically stated in the corporate charter, where management sets a rate that will assure the sale of the stock at the time of issue. When preferred stock has par value, the dividend rate is expressed as a percentage; when it is no-par stock, the rate is expressed as a specific amount per share. The name of a no-par preferred stock includes the dollar amount: for example, General Motors Corporation, $5 cumulative preferred stock with no par value.

Cumulative Dividends

The often-stated advantage to the issuer of financing with preferred stock—that dividends may be not paid and cash may be retained—is a technical rather than a practical advantage. While financing with preferred stock permits the use of leverage without incurring legally binding fixed charges, usually the corporation will find it necessary to meet dividend payments on preferred stock in order to avoid harming its credit standing. When preferred stock is cumulative—a common feature—the pressure to pay dividends is magnified because unpaid dividends *accumulate as claims* against future earnings of the corporation that must be met before dividends can be paid on common stock—**cumulative dividends.** When dividends have not been paid on cumulative preferred stock, this situation is referred to as **arrearage.** Corporations try to avoid dividend arrearages on preferred stock issues, because they impair the corporation's credit and depress the market price of its common stock as well as its preferred stock. The amount of preferred stock outstanding is usually small compared to the amount of common stock, and it is more important to maintain the market value of the common stock than to pass dividends on preferred stock just to prevent a cash drain.

If preferred stock dividends are postponed for any length of time, the amount in arrears may be so great as to make it almost impossible for earnings to catch up. In this case, the board of directors may propose a settlement, such as giving some cash and preferred stock for the dividends in arrears.

Noncumulative Dividends

The articles of incorporation may permit the avoidance of the risk of preferred stock dividend arrearages by specifying that a preferred stock issue has **noncumulative dividends.** During periods of low earnings, dividends on noncumulative preferred stock may be passed on freely, as on common stock, without creating any future claims that are prior to the claims to dividends on common stock. Many of the preferred stock issues outstanding that include a noncumulative feature have resulted from involuntary reorganizations of corporations in which bondholders were required to exchange bonds for preferred stock of this class. When noncumulative preferred stock is sold, it customarily has a higher dividend rate than would otherwise be necessary. However, the great majority of preferred stock outstanding today includes the cumulative feature.

Participating Dividends

As we noted earlier, the typical preferred stockholder is not entitled to receive dividends over or above the rate specified on the stock certificate. However, in some cases, in order to make a preferred stock more attractive to investors, the corporation may make specific provisions for eligibility to dividends beyond the stated rate. Typically, **participating dividends** would not be offered unless it was necessary to sell the stock. Most exceptions to this generalization would probably occur in closely held corporations in which participating preferred stock is granted to a particular stockholder because of some key relationship (past or present) with the corporation. If a participation feature exists, its extent must be spelled out precisely in the contract in order to remove any uncertainty regarding interpretation.

VOTING RIGHTS OF PREFERRED STOCKHOLDERS

Voting rights refer to the privilege of voting for directors, as well as on policies and other matters brought before annual and special meetings of stockholders. Unless it is specifically stated to the contrary in the articles of incorporation, preferred stockholders have the same voting rights as common stockholders. There may be a number of limitations on preferred voting rights, all of which will be discussed. Since the right to vote is a fundamental one, any voting limitations placed on preferred stockholders must be permitted by state statute as well as included in the articles of incorporation and printed on the preferred stock certificate. However, complete disenfranchisement is unusual.

Consent Voting

When the distribution of assets of the corporation is considered, or changes in the rights and privileges of preferred stockholders are proposed, the preferred stockholders must agree before management can take any such action. This process is called **consent voting.** Since preferred stockholders vote as a class on proposals affecting their rights and privileges, they can defeat a proposal by voting in the required percentage, even though a much larger number of common stockholders favors the proposal. If management wants to pursue a proposal in spite of its rejection, it may have to acquire the preferred shares, obtain a court ruling to permit the corporation to proceed with it plans, or amend its proposal to make it acceptable to preferred stockholders. Thus the existence of preferred stock may be a serious obstacle to management in obtaining new financing if any proposed new shares have rights and preferences superior or equal to those of existing preferred shareholders.

Variation in Voting Strength

If and when preferred stock is given a temporary or permanent voting right for the election of directors and on other matters, the effect of this right is determined by the relative voting strength of preferred stockholders. The number of shares of preferred stock relative to common stock may be such that the preferred stockholders are able to select all or none of the directors. If cumulative voting for directors is permitted, the minority group may obtain representation. In all cases, shareholders must vote in person or by proxy. If the voting arrangement is "one share, one vote" (majority voting), preferred stock is usually outnumbered, and so special charter provisions may be made to give preferred stock representation on the board of directors. Preferred stockholders may be given two or three votes per share; most commonly, the principle of class voting is applied to the selection of directors, with preferred stockholders being permitted to select a given number or a given percentage of directors.

As provided for in the articles of incorporation, preferred stockholders' right to vote may be temporary or permanent. To the extent that preferred stock dividends are being paid regularly, as provided for in the corporate charter, the status of preferred stockholders is different from that of common stockholders. But if preferred stock dividends are passed, preferred stockholders are in the same relative position as common stockholders and thus should have a share in management. Customarily, preferred stockholders are entitled to vote if dividends on preferred stock are passed a specified number of times (usually four consecutive quarters). In some cases, when dividends on preferred stock are in default in an amount equivalent to four full quarterly dividend payments, the preferred stockholders may be authorized to elect a majority of the board of directors until all the arrearages have been paid.

Class Voting

Class voting is required on proposals to increase or decrease the authorized number of preferred shares, to permit an exchange whereby another class of stock may be converted into the preferred class, to create a new class of shares having rights or preferences prior to those of existing preferred shares, to increase the rights and preferences of any class that has inferior rights so that they become equal or prior to those of the preferred shares, and to cancel or otherwise affect dividends that have accrued but have not been declared. While this list is not complete, it suggests the difficulties a corporation may encounter in financing with a second issue of preferred stock.

MERGER FINANCING WITH CONVERTIBLE PREFERRED STOCK

Since World War II, while preferred stock has played a minor role in new corporate financing, **convertible preferred stock** has been used in the financing of corporate mergers and acquisitions. A convertible security permits the holders, at their option, to exchange such a security for another of the same company under certain specified conditions. The securities that may be exchanged are usually bonds, but convertible preferred stock enjoys a peculiar advantage over bonds when used in mergers and acquisitions. While the discussion of convertibles is reserved for the following chapter, we will explain the reasons for the use of convertible preferred stock in mergers here.

Advantages to the Acquiring Firm

There are two important reasons for using convertible preferred stock over common stock in mergers and acquisitions. First, it enables the acquiring firm to obtain immediate earnings leverage. If the after-tax net earnings of the acquired firm are larger than the dividend requirements on the newly issued preferred stock, the surviving firm will show increased EPS on its common stock. To illustrate this point, assume that Corporation A is to be merged into Corporation B using preferred stock of B as the means of payment to A's stockholders. The premerger net earnings after taxes of Corporations A and B are $20,000 and $50,000, respectively. Now, assume the following postmerger facts in regard to Corporation B:

Net earnings after taxes ($20,000 + $50,000)	$70,000
Number of new preferred shares issued by Corporation B	5,000
Dividend rate on new preferred shares	$3.00
Number of common shares of Corporation B outstanding	10,000
Net earnings per share before merger of Corporation B ($50,000 ÷ 10,000)	$5.00
Net earnings per share after merger of Corporation B ($70,000 − 15,000 = 55,000 ÷ 10,000)	$5.50

The postmerger earnings per common share are $5.50 as compared with the premerger per-share earnings of $5.00. However, in order to get the stockholders of Corporation A to agree to a merger, it probably would be necessary to offer them dividends on the preferred stock that are higher than those received on the common stock of Corporation A, or perhaps to make the preferred stock convertible into Corporation B's common stock. It might even be necessary to offer them both inducements.

The second advantage of convertible preferred stock in contrast to common stock is that it enables the acquiring and acquired firms to reconcile divergent cash dividend policies. The use of preferred stock permits the acquiring firm to maintain its existing cash dividend policy on its common stock and still pay the acquired firm's stockholders their former dividends. If the acquiring firm pays no dividends at all on its common stock, issuing preferred stock will enable the firm to pay dividends to the stockholders of the merged firm.

Advantages to the Sellers

A merger financed with convertibles is also advantageous to the selling shareholders. If bonds are issued to Corporation A's stockholders, capital gains rates apply on the proceeds stockholders receive over and above their original cost. This is not the case when convertible preferred stock is used. In the latter case, the cost basis of the acquired convertible preferred stock is the same as the basis of the original common shares. This means that the capital gains tax payment can be postponed until the convertible preferred (or the common stock into which it can be converted) is sold.

FUTURE ROLE OF PREFERRED STOCK

Corporate financing in the post-World War II years has emphasized internal financing, along with the use of debt rather than equity when external funds are sought. Management has all but ignored preferred stock issues as a source of new corporate funds. This unpopularity of preferred stock basically stems from the fact that preferred stock dividends are not deductible for corporate income tax purposes, whereas interest charges on bonds are. For a company paying dividends on its common stock, the prior claim on income of preferred stock becomes an unavoidable fixed charge on income; hence, a company is further ahead if it pays interest on a bond issue that does have the advantage of deductibility.

Preferred stock is not destined to disappear completely from corporate balance sheets. As long as convertible preferred stock can be used advantageously in corporate acquisitions and mergers, and as long as public utilities require large sums of outside capital, preferred stocks will continue to be issued in these special instances. In capital-intensive industries such as public utility enterprises, the use of tax credits by the federal government to stimulate economic growth may make preferred stocks more attractive. Income tax credits will lower the effective after-tax cost of preferred stock by lowering the corporation income taxes payable by such firms. However, a drastic change in corporate tax laws will be required before preferred stocks become a significant factor in the new corporate funds market. For example, if the corporate tax laws were changed to permit the partial or full deductibility of dividend payments, preferred stock again would become an important alternative to bond financing.

PREFERRED STOCK—SUMMARY

Preferred stock has priority over common stock regarding dividends and, usually, assets in case of liquidation; in return, the firm customarily places limitations on preferred dividend rates and on the right to vote for directors.

Preferred stock may be cumulative or noncumulative; that is, when dividends are not paid, they may or may not accumulate as claims to future earnings that will have to be paid before dividends may be paid on common stock. Preferred stock may be entitled to receive dividends beyond the rate specified on the stock certificate, but usually it is not.

Redemption or retirement of preferred stock issues may become desirable at some future time, a situation that can be anticipated by making the preferred stock callable. The most important advantage in issuing callable preferred stock is that the corporation can replace an issue carrying a high dividend rate with one carrying a lower rate. The corporate charter may also provide for issuance of various series of preferred stocks differing in the rate of dividends, price, and terms under which shares may be redeemed; the amount payable in case of liquidation; sinking fund provisions; and the terms and conditions under which shares may be converted.

Although there are usually some limitations on voting rights, complete disenfranchisement is rare. Preferred stockholders have the right to vote on any proposals that affect their rights and privileges, and it is not uncommon for them to have a temporary or permanent right to vote for specific representation on the board of directors.

The main disadvantage of preferred stock to the firm, as compared to bonds, is that dividends are not deductible as expenses for federal income taxes. Bond interest is deductible, which is probably the single most important factor accounting for the decline in issuance of preferred stock since World War II.

SUMMARY

This chapter discusses three important aspects of equity capital: common stock, retained earnings, and preferred stock. Table 13.1 shows that the traditional method of acquiring additional equity capital is the retention of earnings. New common and preferred stock issues are used sparingly except in the public utility industry. Convertible preferred stock is particularly important in merger negotiations because of its flexibility.

A firm's dividend policy determines how much of its earnings will be available for expansion. At the same time, dividends affect stock prices. The question is whether it is better to retain earnings, providing necessary equity capital, or to pay dividends and raise common stock equity by selling stock at higher prices due to the attraction of the dividends. U.S. corporations have taken the approach of retaining substantial amounts of their earnings.

When new outside capital is required, the typical firm resorts to bond financing. This behavior is consistent with the position taken in Chapters 4 and 12, which advocates that to maximize its value, the firm should strive to minimize the cost of capital by the judicious use of debt and equity.

There are still two areas of equity financing that require special coverage: convertibles and warrants. Both provide common stock equity to the firm, but only if certain conditions are met. These topics are discussed in Chapter 14.

QUESTIONS AND REVIEW ACTIVITIES

1. What is the chief disadvantage of financing with common stock in comparison with debt?

2. What are the most important characteristics of equity capital?

3. From the viewpoint of the investor in common stock, what justification is there for calling common stock *risk capital*?

4. Why does a relatively unknown company have a lower PE ratio than a better known one?

5. Discuss and analyze the reasons supporting the preemptive rights principle.

6. Why is there usually a discrepancy between the calculated price of a right and the actual market price?

7. How would you respond to stockholders' complaint that the subscription price of a recent stock offering was too low, thereby unduly depressing its market price?

8. What are the advantages to a corporation of having a classified board of directors (one in which the terms of office are staggered and only a portion of the board is elected annually)?

9. As a stockholder, would you favor cumulative voting?

10. How important are funds accounted for as retained earnings in explaining the growth of U.S. business enterprises?

11. Retention of earnings, it has been said, represents an involuntary form of investment by stockholders. In what way do stockholders benefit from retained earnings?

12. Earnings should be retained to the point where they contribute more to stockholders' wealth than to the payment of dividends. Explain.

13. How does a firm's access to capital markets affect its dividend policy?

14. Define the following types of dividends: (a) cash, (b) regular, (c) interim, (d) stock, and (e) liquidating.

15. Distinguish between stock dividends and stock splits and analyze what effects, if any, they have on the market price of a company's common stock.

16. Is one justified in calling the typical preferred stock a *hybrid security* that possesses certain characteristics of common stock and certain characteristics of a long-term bond? Explain.

17. May the covenants for a preferred stock issue be drawn so that the securities will have more of the characteristics of a bond than a common stock? Explain. May the opposite be true?

18. Assume that financing is difficult and that it is necessary to offer attractive terms to investors. What features would you include in order to make preferred stock

attractive and still keep the dividend rate in line with those of outstanding preferred stock issues? Explain. Assume that financing is easy and that it is possible to negotiate favorable terms. Would your answer differ?

19. Discuss the advantages and disadvantages of a preferred stock sinking fund from both the issuing corporation's and the stockholder's viewpoints.

20. There is *no* difference between the investor's or the issuing corporation's preference as to whether a preferred stock has a low or a high call price. Discuss.

21. Should preferred stock be considered as debt or equity when measuring a firm's financial leverage?

PROBLEMS

1. The common stock of KLS Inc. is selling at $40 per share, rights-on. Find the value of the right if the stockholders are offered one new share at a subscription price of $30 for every four shares held.

2. Table 13.4 is the Southwest Co. balance sheet and income statement for the year 1983. The firm is contemplating a stock rights offering.

TABLE 13.4
Southwest Co.: Balance Sheet before Rights Offering for the Year Ending December 31, 1983.

Total assets	$900,000	Bonds (8%)	$400,000
		Common stock (par value $1)	100,000
		Retained earnings	400,000
Total assets	$900,000	Total liabilities and capital	$900,000

Earning rate, 10% on total assets	
Total earnings	$90,000
Interest on bonds	32,000
Earnings before income taxes	$58,000
Income taxes (40% rate assumed)	23,200
Earnings after taxes	$34,800
Earnings per share	$ .348
Dividends per share	0.20
Price-earnings ratio	13 times
Market price per share	$ 4.52

It wants to raise an additional $200,000 by a rights offering. The new funds will earn 15% of assets. The PE ratio will probably rise to 14 because of improved market conditions. Dividends are not expected to change. Assume that the subscription price will be set at $4 per share.

a) How many additional shares of stock will be sold?

b) How many rights will be needed to purchase one new share?

c) What will be the new EPS?

d) What will be the new market price per share?

e) Why did the EPS increase slightly?

f) Is this rights offering likely to succeed?

3. Gas Lite, Inc., is preparing a new issue of common stock. It has 1 million shares currently outstanding and will issue 100,000 new shares.

a) How many rights must be issued?

b) How many shares is each right entitled to?

c) If the current market price of Gas Lite is $50 and the subscription price is $44.50, what is the value of each right?

d) What is the value of each right when the stock is traded ex-rights? (Assume that the price of the stock remains at $50.)

4. On June 1, Corporation D announced that it was offering subscription rights to its stockholders of record as of June 15 to purchase new shares in the ratio of one new share for each five held. The subscription price of this stock was $55 a share, and the rights were to expire June 30. From May 20 until June 24 the price remained stationary at $60 a share. On June 25 it declined to $58 a share and remained there through June 27.

a) What would be the probable market value of a right on June 27?

b) Why is there said to be a strong element of compulsion in most rights offerings?

c) Is this one likely to succeed?

5. The Columbia Corp. will hold its annual meeting next week.

a) If cumulative voting exists in the corporation, how many shares must a minority group have or obtain to assure themselves the election of 4 directors if 19 are to be elected and 100,000 shares are outstanding and entitled to vote?

b) How many cumulative votes must the minority have in the preceding problem?

6. If a group holds 40,000 of the 200,000 shares outstanding, how many directors can it elect if nine are going to be elected?

7. Assuming that there are 6,000 shares of stock in a corporation, the stockholders have the right of cumulative voting, and seven directors are to be elected.

a) How many shares are needed to elect two directors? All the directors?

b) Assuming majority voting, how many shares could unquestionably elect a single director? All the directors? (Give the minimum number.)

8. Assuming that there are 1,000 shares of stock in a corporation, the stockholders have the right of cumulative voting, and 10 directors are to be elected.

a) How many shares are needed to elect a single director? A majority of the directors? All the directors?

b) If you had 170 shares of stock, how many directors could you be sure of electing?

c) Do you think cumulative voting permits a greater degree of democracy in the control of a corporation?

9. The management of JBW, Inc., is contemplating the sale of a common stock issue as a means of financing the firm's capital requirements. Its current financial position is as follows:

Net profit after taxes	$20,000,000
Number of shares outstanding	5,000,000
Market price	$80

If the firm uses common stock as a means of raising money, management estimates that it will have to issue 500,000 new shares and that the use of funds should result in a $4 million after-tax increase in profits. The firm will go ahead with the stock issue only if it does not reduce the market price of the stock. Assuming that the PE ratio remains the same after the stock issue (and the increase in profits), should JBW issue the new common stock?

10. The Waldon Corp. is determining whether to pay dividends or to retain the earnings. The firm's cost of capital is 15%. The company has $2 million in current earnings. It has sufficient liquidity to pay any dividends that might be declared. It can also invest in any or all of the following projects:

a) $300,000—New machinery that will yield a 22% return.

b) $500,000—Inventory that will improve customer service and consequently profit. The return from such an investment is estimated to be 18%.

c) $400,000—Plant expansion, generating an annual net return of 14% on invested capital.

d) $800,000—Purchase of raw land for future expansion; land prices are increasing at 8% a year.

If the firm used the residual theory of dividend policy and had 600,000 shares outstanding, what per-share dividend would it pay?

11. Selected items from the balance sheet of the Tempe Co. are shown below (in 000s):

Cash	$ 3,000	Bonds payable	$2,000
Investments	1,000	Retained earnings	9,000
Fixed assets	11,000	Common stock (100,000	
Patents	2,000	shares at $50 par)	5,000

The board of directors is considering four separate possibilities:

a) A cash dividend of $5 a share.

b) A 50% stock split.

c) A four-for-one split.

d) A dividend consisting of the Tempe Co.'s investments.

Prepare a tabulation for the board showing the effect of each possibility on the selected items from the balance sheet.

12. The Tucson Clothing Co. has 10,000 shares of cumulative preferred stock outstanding; it pays annual dividends of $8 per share. In 1983, the company could pay only $4 per share to preferred stockholders because of poor earnings.

    a) What will be the total payment in 1984 if the company becomes current on the dividend payments?

    b) Would it make any difference if the preferred stock were participating but noncumulative, if only $4 is paid in 1983?

13. The board of directors of the SMW Corp. is discussing the possibility of making a $500,000 investment in one of the following alternatives:

    a) Corporate bonds paying 10%.

    b) Common stock at $40 per share, which is currently paying a dividend of $1.50.

    c) Five thousand shares of 8% preferred stock with a par value of $100.

    Which investment should they make? Assume a 40% tax bracket for the firm. Disregard possible capital gains on each investment.

14. The executive committee of JW, Inc., is considering three financing proposals. The proposals are as follows:

    Proposal X: Corporate bonds paying 9%.

    Proposal Y: Common stock paying a dividend of $3 annually, with a market value of $40 a share.

    Proposal Z: Convertible preferred stock paying $5.50, with a par value of $100.

    Assuming a marginal tax rate of 40%, determine the after-tax interest or dividend cost to the firm of each proposal. Which proposal minimizes this cost? Assume that there are no flotation costs.

ADDITIONAL READINGS

Bacon, P. W. "The Subscription Price in Rights Offerings," *Financial Management* (Summer 1972), pp. 59–64.

Barker, C. A. "Evaluation of Stock Dividends," *Harvard Business Review* (July–August 1958), pp. 99–113.

———— "Effective Stock Splits," *Harvard Business Review* (January–February 1956), pp. 101–06.

Donaldson, G. "In Defense of Preferred Stock," *Harvard Business Review* (July–August 1962), pp. 123–36.

Fischer, D. E., and G. A. Wilt, Jr. "Non-Convertible Preferred Stock as a Financing Instrument, 1950–1965," *Journal of Finance* (September 1968), pp. 611–24.

Harkavy, O. "The Relation between Retained Earnings and Common Stock Prices for Large Listed Corporations," *Journal of Finance* (September 1953), pp. 283–97.

Henderson, G. V., Jr. "Shareholder Taxes and the Required Rate of Return on Internally Generated Funds," *Financial Management* (Summer 1976), pp. 25–31.

Hubbard, P. M., Jr. "The Many Aspects of Dilution," *Financial Analysts Journal* (May–June 1963), pp. 33, 36–40.

Miller, M. H., and F. Modigliani. "Dividend Policy and Market Valuation: A Reply," *Journal of Business* (January 1963).

——— "Dividend Policy, Growth, and the Valuation of Shares," *Journal of Business* (October 1961), pp. 411–33.

Nelson, J. R. "Price Effects in Rights Offerings," *Journal of Finance* (December 1965), pp. 647–50.

Reilly, F. K., and E. F. Drzycimski. "Short-Run Profits from Stock Splits," *Financial Management* (Summer 1981), pp. 64–74.

Stevenson, R. A. "Retirement of Non-Callable Preferred Stock," *Journal of Finance* (December 1970), pp. 1143–52.

Van Horne, J. C., and J. G. McDonald. "Dividend Policy and Equity Financing," *Journal of Finance* (May 1971), pp. 507–19.

- **CONVERTIBLE SECURITIES**
  DEFINITIONS
  WHY FIRMS ISSUE CONVERTIBLE SECURITIES
  VALUATION OF CONVERTIBLE SECURITIES
  TIMING OF CONVERSION

- **WARRANTS**
  DEFINITIONS
  THE EXERCISE PROCESS
  REASONS FOR ISSUING WARRANTS
  VALUATION OF WARRANTS
  FINANCING WITH WARRANTS COMPARED TO CONVERTIBLE SECURITIES

- **LISTED OPTIONS**
  DEFINITIONS
  REASONS TO BUY AND SELL OPTIONS
  VALUATION OF OPTIONS

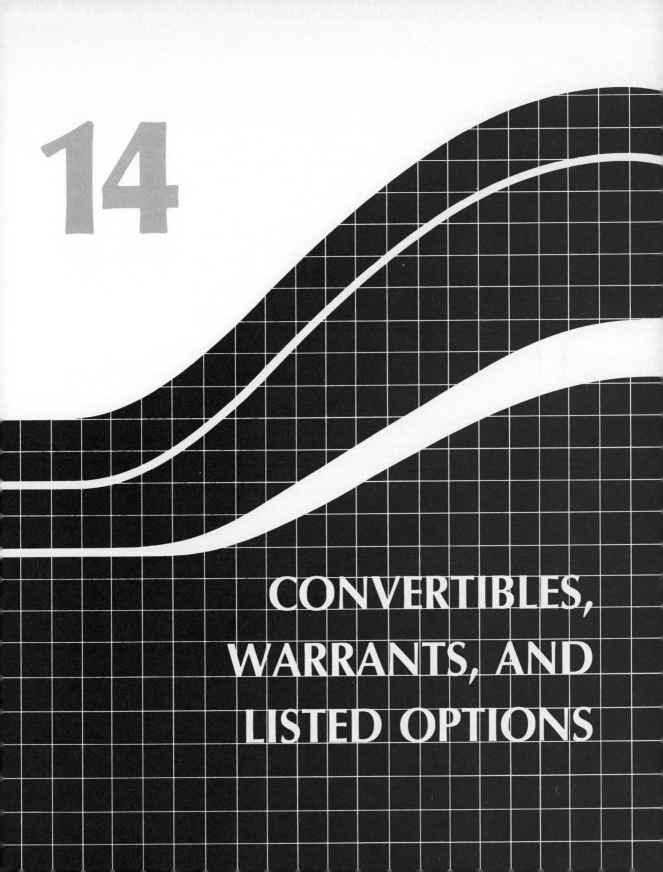

14

CONVERTIBLES,
WARRANTS, AND
LISTED OPTIONS

In addition to bonds, preferred stock, and common stock, firms frequently use hybrid securities to raise capital. Convertible securities and warrants possess characteristics of both stocks and bonds, and when the firm uses them at the proper time, they can provide advantageous financing.

Topics in this chapter include convertible securities, warrants, and listed options. Convertible securities are either bonds or preferred stock that can be converted into the common stock of the issuing corporation. (In a few cases firms have sold bonds that are convertible into preferred stock, but the most usual arrangement calls for conversion into common stock.) Most of our discussion is about convertible bonds, but the comments are equally applicable to convertible preferred stock.

A warrant is a certificate that allows the holder to buy the common stock of a company at a specified price during a specified period of time. Warrants usually are attached to a senior security (a bond or preferred stock) and sold to investors as a package. We will discuss convertibles and warrants together because they are used for the same reasons.

Listed options are contracts to purchase common stock at a predetermined price during a specified time period. Options, however, are not issued by the corporation. Instead, they are created by individual investors. We include a discussion of them in this chapter because, to an investor, their characteristics are similar to those of warrants. Also, the valuation theory developed for options will help you understand the valuation of warrants and convertible securities.

After careful study of this chapter, you should know

1. The following terms:
   - Convertible bond.
   - Convertible security.
   - Conversion price.
   - Conversion ratio.
   - Speculative premium.
   - Overhanging issue.
   - Warrant.
   - Exercise price.
   - Expiration date.
   - Intrinsic value.
   - Primary earnings per share.
   - Fully diluted earnings per share.
   - Listed options.
   - Call option.

- Put option.
- Striking price.

2. Why corporations issue convertible securities and warrants.

3. The three components determining the value of a convertible bond (or convertible preferred stock).

4. The five factors affecting the value of warrants and options.

5. The similarities and differences between financing with convertibles versus warrants.

6. Why investors trade options and warrants.

Financing with convertibles—An example.   In the fall of 1981, Wang Laboratories Inc. a leading producer of multiterminal, display-type word-processing systems, needed $100 million in new capital. The sale of common stock was not attractive, because the market price of the company's stock was depressed. Also, a new stock issue would dilute EPS, which would exert further downward pressure on the stock price. Interest rates on bonds at the time were relatively high, deterring the issuance of long-term bonds at a fixed rate. In addition, investors seemed to be attracted only to high-quality debt issues because of uncertain economic conditions.

To raise the necessary capital, Wang's management decided to issue **convertible bonds,** securities that have fixed interest payments and a specified maturity just like an ordinary bond, but that provide the bondholders an opportunity to speculate on a price rise in the underlying stock of the company.

On November 13, 1981, $100 million worth of 10% convertible bonds were offered for sale. The maturity date is November 15, 2006, and the bonds are callable at $1,100 any time during the period, with 30 to 60 days' notice. The bonds are convertible into common stock at $40¼ any time before maturity. (Wang stock was selling for $33 at the time of issue.) The bonds were rated Ba (medium grade—speculative) by Moody's when issued. Although ordinary bonds of this grade might have been hard to sell in that economic environment, the convertible issue sold quickly, because it offered investors a large gain if Wang's stock appreciated in value.

The following section describes convertible securities, outlines the reasons corporations issue convertibles, and discusses the factors that determine the value of convertible bonds. Study of this section will enable you to better understand why Wang chose to raise capital by the sale of convertible bonds.

CONVERTIBLE SECURITIES

DEFINITIONS

A **convertible security** is a bond or convertible preferred stock that can be exchanged *at the discretion of the holder* for a specified number of shares of common stock during a defined time period. The bond indenture that contains legal details about the issue defines the conversion factor in terms of either a conversion price or a conversion ratio.

In the case of Wang Laboratories Inc., the **conversion price** was specified as $40¼, meaning that the bondholder can use the bond at par value ($1,000) to purchase common stock from Wang for $40.25 per share. The **conversion ratio** is the number of shares of common stock that each bond will purchase. It can be calculated from the conversion price as follows:

$$\text{Conversion ratio} = \frac{\text{par value of convertible}}{\text{conversion price}}.$$

For the Wang bonds the conversion ratio is 24.84 ($1,000/40.25).

The conversion ratio or price that is fixed at the time of issue is usually 10 to 20% above the stock's current market price. Convertible bondholders must wait until the market price rises to make conversion profitable. In the example of Wang, the common stock price was $33 when the convertibles were offered. The stock would have to appreciate almost 22% [(40.25 − 33.00)/ 33.00] for conversion to be economically justified.

The **conversion period** is the time during which the holder may exercise the right to convert. For the Wang Labs bonds, it extends from the time of issue to the maturity date, November 15, 2006. The conversion period is specified in the indenture and usually extends for the life of the bond. However, in some cases it may not become effective until several months or years have elapsed, or it may expire several years before bond maturity.

Holders of convertible securities are protected in case of stock splits or extraordinary stock dividends during the conversion period. In the Spring of 1983 Wang Labs stock had appreciated to $65 and the company split their common stock two for one. The conversion ratio increased to 49.68 (24.84 × 2) shares per bond.

WHY FIRMS ISSUE CONVERTIBLE SECURITIES

The arguments favoring the use of convertible securities include (1) availability of delayed equity financing at a price higher than the stock's current market price; (2) increased marketability of debt securities at a lower interest rate than that of a straight debt issue; and (3) the possibility of raising short-term, inexpensive funds.

Delayed Equity Financing

Most companies that issue convertible securities would prefer to sell straight equity. However, to raise a great deal of capital under conditions of depressed stock prices would require issuing a large number of shares. Reported EPS would be reduced, and downward pressure would be exerted on the stock price. When it issues a convertible bond, Wang Labs hopes that at some future time the common stock price will appreciate above the $40\frac{1}{4}$ conversion price from its current value of $33. Selling convertible bonds allows the firm eventually to issue fewer shares than would be necessary if it sold common stock at present. If Wang were to issue straight common stock, it would have to be sold at slightly below the market price to make it attractive. Because the conversion price is above the stock's market price, fewer shares of common stock will have to be issued when the convertibles are exchanged. In addition the debt/equity ratio of the corporation will be reduced, fixed interest charges will be lowered, and the way will be cleared for future debt financing. If the stock price does not rise far enough for conversion, the firm simply has debt financing, and at a lower interest rate than would have been available on straight debt. A convertible whose market price stays below the conversion price is called a *hung convertible*.

Increased Marketability of Debt

A second reason for using convertible securities is to improve the chances that the debt issue will be accepted in the marketplace at a reasonable interest rate. For firms with good credit ratings, this means that the effective interest rate will be 2 to 5% *below* that of comparable nonconvertible issues. Some speculative firms may find that their debt securities will not be purchased at all unless the convertibility feature is offered. The Wang Laboratories convertible bonds previously discussed were rated Ba and sold at an effective yield of 10.1%. At the same time, market rates for long-term Baa (one higher grade) bonds were above 16%. Investors sacrificed over 6% for the opportunity to speculate on Wang's common stock.

Ability to Raise Short-Term Funds

A significant period of time may be required before new capital funds received by the firm are translated into increased EPS. Use of convertible debt provides relatively inexpensive funds during the capital expansion period because the explicit after-tax cost of debt is much lower than the cost of equity. Reduction in reported EPS during this period is also avoided. If the expansion is profitable, EPS will increase, the stock price will rise, and conversion of bonds to stock will occur.

VALUATION OF CONVERTIBLE SECURITIES

Investors' reasons for buying convertible securities suggest three factors that determine the securities' value: (1) the fixed-income interest stream provided by the bond; (2) the value of the securities as common stock; and (3) a speculative premium that investors are willing to pay for potential price appreciation in the underlying stock. Figure 14.1 illustrates these concepts.

Value as a Bond

Because a convertible bond possesses all the characteristics of a bond (fixed interest payments and repayment of principal at maturity), it will sell for *no less* than a straight bond of comparable risk. As we showed in Chapter 4, the value of a bond is found by discounting interest payments and principal at the appropriate market interest rate, i:

$$\text{Bond value} = \sum_{t=1}^{n}\frac{\text{interest}}{(1+i)^n} + \frac{\text{principal}}{(1+i)^n}.$$

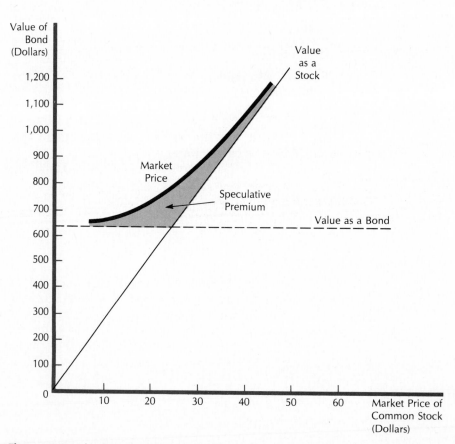

Figure 14.1 Valuation of a 10% Wang Laboratories Inc. convertible bond. Maturity is 25 years; market interest rate is 16%.

For the Wang Labs 10%, 25-year convertible issue, where market interest rates are 16% and the interest payments are semiannual, the security's value as a bond is calculated as follows (interest factors from the tables are for $16\%/2 = 8\%$ and 25 years $\times 2 = 50$ periods):

$$\begin{aligned} \text{Bond value} &= \$50\,(\text{PVIFA}) + \$1,000\,(\text{PVIF}) \\ &= \$50\,(12.23) + \$1,000\,(.021) \\ &= \$611 + \$21 \\ &= \$632 \end{aligned}$$

Value as Common Stock (Conversion Value)

Conversion value represents the market value of the common stock obtainable if the convertible security is changed into common stock. It is determined by multiplying the market price of the common stock by the conversion ratio. For Wang Labs bonds, the conversion value is

$$\begin{aligned} \text{Conversion value} &= \text{market price of common stock} \times \text{conversion ratio} \\ &= \$33 \times 24.84 \\ &= \$819.72. \end{aligned}$$

The Wang Labs convertible bonds will not sell for less than $819.72 if the common stock sells for $33 a share. To understand why, assume that you could obtain the bond for less than $819.72, say $800. By immediately converting it to 24.84 common shares and then selling the stock, you receive $819.72, thereby earning a riskless profit of $19.72 ($819.72 − $800.00), less commissions. Enough market participants trade without commissions to ensure that a price near $819.72 will be maintained.

Speculative Premium

Comparison of the market price of convertible securities to their bond or conversion values reveals that investors usually are willing to pay more for the convertible compared to its value as a straight bond or its worth as common stock. The Wang Labs convertible sold for $990 at a time when its conversion value was $819.72 and its value as a bond was $632. This positive difference is referred to as the **speculative premium.** It exists because of the unique features offered by the convertible security. The investor has the safety of a bond while awaiting the anticipated increase in the stock price. He or she accepts a lower yield on the bond in exchange for the future opportunity to purchase common stock at a prearranged price, even though that price is above the current market value.

Figure 14.1 illustrates how the three valuation components of a convertible bond interact to determine the security's market price. The horizontal line labeled "Value as a Bond" depicts the bond value component. While it remains horizontal, its position on the graph rises or falls as market interest rates change. A decrease in market rates from 16 to 10% would cause the bond value line to rise to the $1,000 level.

In Fig. 14.1 the line representing the convertible security's value as a stock, labeled "Value as a Stock," passes through the origin and has a slope equal to the conversion ratio of the bond. A $1 price rise in the stock results in a $24.84 rise in the value of the convertible security. Unlike the bond value line, which moves up or down as market interest rates change, the "Value as a Stock" line remains fixed as long as the conversion price is constant. Changes in the market price of the common stock represent movement along this line. For example, if the common stock appreciates to $45, the conversion value of the bond becomes $45 × 24.84 = $1,117.80.

The speculative premium is represented by the colored area of the figure. When the stock price is low relative to the conversion price, say $10 for Wang stock, only a small speculative premium exists, since the probability of the stock price exceeding the conversion price is low. As conversion value approaches bond value (i.e., as the stock price increases), the speculative premium increases to its greatest relative amount because a greater probability exists that the market price of the common stock will rise above the conversion price. (Note that the value as a stock and value as a bond lines in Fig. 14.1 are not required to intersect at the conversion price for the convertible.) Given a market interest rate of 16%, the largest speculative premium on the Wang convertible will exist when the market price of the common stock is slightly above $29 (Value as a stock = bond value). Finally, the conversion premium shrinks as the common stock price appreciates above the conversion price. Since the company may call the bond and thus force conversion (as described subsequently), an investor is less willing to pay a premium for the bond above its conversion value. The higher the common stock price, the greater the likelihood that a forced conversion will occur.

Our discussion indicates that the market price of a convertible security is dependent upon three factors: its bond value, its conversion value, and the speculative premium that market participants are willing to pay. In an efficient market, the minimum value for the convertible will be the *higher* of its bond or conversion value. High interest rates in 1981 and low bond prices cause the floor value of our Wang Labs convertible to be determined by its conversion value of $819.72. If interest rates fall to 10% and the common stock remains at $33, the floor value will be the $1,000 bond value. Arbitrage activity by market participants should keep a convertible from falling below its minimum price. The convertible probably will sell somewhat above its minimum value because of the speculative premium investors are willing to pay for these securities.

TIMING OF CONVERSION

While conversion of a convertible security occurs at the discretion of the owner, actual conversion either may occur *voluntarily* by the bond holder or may be *forced* by the issuing corporation.

Voluntary Conversion

Voluntary conversion may take place if

1. *The market price of the common stock rises significantly.* If the stock appreciates as the investor hoped when the convertible was purchased, a profit can be earned by converting the bond and selling the common stock. The holder of our Wang Labs convertible bond would earn a profit by converting when the common stock appreciated above $39\frac{7}{8}$ if the bond was purchased at issue for $990 ($39.875 × 24.84 = $990). Note that the stock price does not have to surpass the conversion price for conversion to be profitable. However, if the stock appreciates above the conversion value, a greater likelihood exists that the company will call the issue and force conversion, as described subsequently.

2. *Dividends on the common stock are increased.* Bondholders may become willing to give up their more secure position as creditors to obtain the increased dividend. One way some corporations have encouraged conversion is to declare an extra dividend on common stock and notify holders of convertible securities so that they may participate in the extra dividend by converting before a specified date.

Forced Conversion

When companies issue convertible securities, they expect that at some future date the securities will be converted into common stock. While companies cannot require security holders to convert, they may be able to use the call provision or reduced conversion ratio to cause conversion. This is called a **forced conversion.** An **overhanging issue** results if the convertibles cannot be forced into conversion.

In October 1981, Storage Technology, a maker of magnetic tape and disk data subsystems for computers, called their 10.25% convertible bonds, due in the year 2000, for redemption on November 27, 1981, at $1,092.25. The conversion price was $25.25, and the common stock was selling for $37\frac{1}{4}$, providing a conversion value of $1,475. Any rational investor would convert the bond into common stock before November 27, instead of allowing the bond to be redeemed by the company for $1,092.25.

Most companies will wait until the market price of the company's stock exceeds the conversion price by at least 10 to 15% before attempting a forced conversion. If the call notice is given when the stock is selling at only slightly above the conversion value, the sale of stock received from converting the bonds might drive the market price below the conversion price. Conversion activity then would terminate.

A second means of forcing conversion is a scheduled drop in the conversion ratio. Some issues contain a provision for the conversion ratio to decrease (conversion price to rise) at specific dates during the conversion period. Consequently, the investor may find it necessary to convert the security to avoid a capital loss. For example, if the conversion ratio of the Wang Labs bond is scheduled to fall from 24.84 to 20 on July 1 and the common stock is selling for $40, the conversion value of the bond would drop from $993 to $800. Most investors would convert instead of holding a security that will lose $192.60 in value overnight. (This example assumes that the straight bond value is below $800, which will be true if market interest rates are above 15%.) This circumstance is slightly different from that of a conversion induced by a call, as the timing of the call is uncertain, while changes in the conversion ratio are specified in the indenture when the securities are issued.

If the common stock price is not high enough to force conversion, the overhanging issue may hamper the sale of additional debt securities and create uncertainty about the direction of future financing by the firm. The sale of common stock will not be attractive since the price is still depressed. Investors may be reluctant to purchase additional debt that increases the financial risk of the company. Companies do not want to be in the position of having a convertible issue overhanging the market.

The Storage Technology conversion is not an overhanging issue. It is an excellent illustration of what a company wants to happen when convertible securities are sold. The issue came to market in August 1980, when the common stock was around $15. The 10.25% interest rate on the convertible was 5% below the market rate. In just 15 months, the common stock price had appreciated to 37\frac{1}{4}$, and conversion of the debt into common stock was assured.

WARRANTS

DEFINITIONS

A **warrant** is an option to buy a specific number of shares of common stock of the issuing company within a given time period at a predetermined price. Warrants usually are attached to a senior security (bond or preferred stock) at the time of the sale. The warrant serves as a "sweetener" to motivate purchase of the bonds or preferred stock. The investor receives not only the fixed income return from the debt or preferred stock but also an opportunity to purchase common stock at a prearranged price. If a company's stock price appreciates, the warrant will become valuable; if it does not, the warrant may be worthless. Companies issue warrants for many of the same reasons they issue convertible securities, but the mechanics of exercise and the impact on the firm are quite different.

The **exercise price** of the warrant is the price per share at which the holder can obtain the common stock. As with convertibles, the exercise price usually is set at least 10 to 20% above the market price of the common at the time of issue. The common stock must increase in price before the expiration date if the warrants are to have more than a speculative appeal to investors.

The exercise price may be either fixed or variable. If it is fixed, the holder can purchase the common stock at a certain price any time before the warrant expires. If the price is variable, it increases periodically until the warrant expires. As with convertible securities, the exercise price of the warrant is adjusted for stock splits or significant stock dividends.

The **expiration date** is the time at which the privilege of obtaining common stock with the warrant ceases. The extreme case is perpetual warrants such as those issued by the Allegheny Corp., which will be outstanding as long as the corporation exists. Normally, warrants are issued with a life of 5 to 10 years, during which time the company expects the common stock to appreciate sufficiently for exercise to occur. No mechanism exists for a company to force exercise of a warrant; in other words, warrants do not include anything like the call feature used with convertible securities. If the exercise price exceeds the market price of the common stock immediately before expiration, the warrants will be exercised; otherwise they will expire worthless.

A *detachable* warrant can be separated from the bond and traded independently. If the owner does not wish to exercise the warrant, it may be removed from the senior security and sold to another investor through normal brokerage channels. In the case of a *nondetachable* warrant, only the owner of the bond can exercise the warrant. Thus, a nondetachable warrant cannot trade in the marketplace independent of the senior security. As you might guess, most warrants are detachable since these have the greatest appeal to investors.

THE EXERCISE PROCESS

If the price of the common stock goes above the exercise price of the warrant, the holder may elect to exercise the warrant. (A warrant is not exercised if the stock price is below the exercise price, because the stock could be obtained more cheaply in the marketplace.) Individuals who pay standard commissions on stock transactions may exercise the warrant when the stock price is slightly below the exercise value, because, when the warrant is exercised, stock is obtained from the issuing company with no commission charge. To exercise, the investor merely sends the appropriate number of warrants needed to obtain each share of stock, plus the exercise price per share, to the issuing company (or its transfer agent). Frequently, one warrant can be used to buy one share of stock, but no conventional practice exists. In some instances, several warrants are needed for each share, while in others more than one share can be obtained with each warrant. Since the investor deals directly with the company issuing the stock, no brokerage fees are involved.

REASONS FOR ISSUING WARRANTS

Companies issue warrants for many of the same reasons they issue convertible securities. These reasons include the following:

1. Warrants attached to a bond or preferred stock usually enable the company to pay a lower interest rate on the fixed income security. Investors are willing to sacrifice current return to speculate on future price appreciation in the common stock.

2. Warrants are used to promote the sale of an otherwise unattractive issue, which might not be marketable on reasonable terms without warrants attached. Warrants are therefore a sweetener for the bond or preferred stock issue.

3. Warrants provide for deferred equity financing above the current common stock price.

Before 1970, warrants were viewed skeptically by many investors as speculative securities issued only by low- to medium-quality firms. However, they gained respectability in November 1970, when American Telephone and Telegraph (AT&T) came to market with 31.1 million warrants attached to a new bond issue. Each warrant could be used to purchase one share of common stock at $52 any time before May 15, 1975. The market price of the stock was $47 at the time of issue. In 1972 and 1973 the stock climbed to the mid-$50s range, but it dropped to $48 a share one month prior to expiration.

Events during the month prior to expiration served to tarnish the warrants' newfound respectability. On May 19, 1975, a few days after expiration, the *Wall Street Journal* reported that the Securities and Exchange Commission had begun an investigation into recent heavy trading of AT&T shares and warrants. Concern was expressed because the market price of the common stock had appreciated from $48 a month earlier to $51\frac{7}{8} on the expiration date. On May 20, 1975, the *Journal* reported that AT&T and its investment banking firm were being sued by an investor who charged that a conspiracy existed to manipulate AT&T stock and warrants for the purpose of personal gain.

VALUATION OF WARRANTS

The value of a warrant is based on two factors: its value for conversion to common stock (sometimes called **intrinsic value**), and the speculative premium that investors are willing to pay to share in the price appreciation of the underlying stock.

To understand warrant valuation, consider the warrants issued by Mattel, Inc., the well-known maker of toys, dolls, and games. Each warrant allows the holder to buy one share of common stock at $4 until April 5, 1986. The stock is selling at $6\frac{1}{2}$, and the warrant is trading for $4\frac{5}{8}$. If the stock's market price is above the exercise price, the warrant's intrinsic value is the difference between the exercise price, X, and the stock price, P, times the number of shares each warrant will purchase, S, or $(P - X)S$. It represents the profit possible from exercising the warrant and selling the stock received at market value.

If the stock price is below the exercise price, intrinsic value is zero. This can be expressed mathematically as

$$\text{Intrinsic value} = \text{Max} \ [0; \ (P - X)S].$$

The intrinsic value of the Mattel warrants is calculated as follows:

$$\text{Intrinsic value} = \max \ [0; \ \ (\$6\tfrac{1}{2} - 4)(1)]$$
$$= \$2\tfrac{1}{2}.$$

In Figure 14.2 the intrinsic value of the warrant at various common stock prices is shown by the heavy horizontal line from the origin to the exercise price and the upward-sloping 45-degree line as the stock price exceeds the warrant's exercise price.

It is reasonable to ask why the warrant is selling for $4\frac{5}{8}$ when its intrinsic value is only $2\frac{1}{2}$. The additional $2\frac{1}{8}$ ($4\frac{5}{8} - $2\frac{1}{2}$) is the speculative premium, or nonintrinsic value, and represents what investors are willing to pay to speculate on the price appreciation of Mattel stock. The speculative, or nonintrinsic, premium is shown in Fig. 14.2 as the distance from the intrinsic value to the curved line labeled "Market Price." The speculative premium is small when the stock price is well below the exercise price, because the probability that the stock will appreciate above the exercise price is low. When the stock's market price equals the exercise price, the speculative premium is at its greatest level and contributes 100% of the warrant's value. As the stock's price exceeds the exercise price, the speculative premium shrinks, but the warrant increases in value because the intrinsic value is increasing.

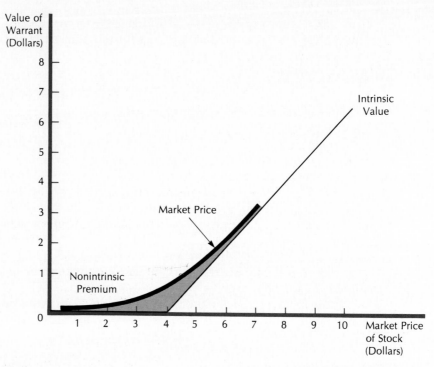

Figure 14.2 Valuation of Mattel Inc. warrants. Maturity is 1986; exercise price is $4.

The size of the speculative premium for any particular warrant is a function of five factors:

1. *The stock price*—the higher the stock price the greater the warrant's value.
2. *The exercise price*—the lower the exercise price, the greater the warrant's value.
3. *Time to expiration*—the longer the time remaining to expiration, the greater the warrant's value.
4. *Volatility of the underlying stock*—more volatile stocks will have higher-priced warrants.
5. *Level of interest rates in the economy*—higher interest rates cause speculative premiums to rise.

Investors are willing to pay a speculative premium when purchasing warrants primarily because of leverage and the limited dollar risk present in warrant positions. For example, if you believe that Greyhound stock will perform well over the next two years, you could speculate by purchasing either Greyhound common stock selling for $15½ or by buying a warrant for $1⅞. The warrant allows you to purchase the common stock at $24.

Assume that Greyhound common stock climbs to $30 between now and the month prior to expiration. Comparison of the returns for the stock and the warrant will reveal which is the more profitable. To calculate the returns, we need to know that Greyhound pays $1.20 a year in dividends to common stockholders and that the warrant will sell for very close to its intrinsic value of $6 ($30 − $24) as expiration approaches. (Warrant holders do not receive dividends.)

$$\text{Holding period yield (HPY)} = \frac{\begin{array}{c}\text{price of} \\ \text{security at} \\ \text{end of period}\end{array} + \text{dividends} - \begin{array}{c}\text{price of security} \\ \text{at beginning} \\ \text{of period}\end{array}}{\text{price of security at beginning of period}}$$

$$\text{HPY from stock} = \frac{30 + 2.40\dagger - 15.5}{15.5}$$

$$= \frac{16.9}{15.5} = 109\%.$$

$$\text{HPY from warrant} = \frac{6 + 0 - 1.875}{1.875}$$

$$= \frac{4.125}{1.875} = 220\%.$$

The much higher rate of return earned on the warrant compared to the stock is an example of the leverage available from this type of security. On the other hand, if the stock does not appreciate, the most you could lose by buying Greyhound warrants is $1⅞ per share, while the stock theoretically could decline to $0. Thus a much smaller *dollar risk* is present with warrant positions.

FINANCING WITH WARRANTS COMPARED TO CONVERTIBLE SECURITIES

While warrants and convertible securities appear to be similar, the impact they can have on a firm's capital structure is quite different. The similarities and differences are summarized here.

---

† The $2.40 represents two years of dividends at $1.20 per year.

The *similarities* between financing by convertibles and warrants are as follows:

1. Both securities are issued with the expectation that they will be exchanged for common stock in the future. Thus both are a form of *deferred* equity financing.

2. Warrants and conversion features are used to make debt or preferred stock issues more marketable and to reduce the cost to the firm of debt or preferred stock financing.

3. Both securities enable the firm to use cheaper funds during the period when new capital is being assimilated into the firm.

4. Current accounting standards require that EPS be reported on a primary and a fully diluted basis. **Primary earnings per share** is determined by dividing earnings available to common stockholders (EACS) by the number of shares of common stock outstanding. **Fully diluted earnings per share** assumes that all warrants or convertible issues are exchanged for the appropriate number of common shares. The lower fully diluted EPS value may give a better indication of the earnings potential of the firm.

The differences between convertibles and warrants are as follows:

1. When convertibles are exchanged for common stock, debt is removed from the balance sheet. The firm becomes less financially risky. When warrants are exercised, the debt remains on the balance sheet and the total capital increases. However, the firm will possess a higher debt/equity ratio.

   This concept is illustrated in Table 14.1. In panel A, $2,000,000 worth of convertible bonds with a conversion ratio of 50:1 are exchanged for common stock. The debt/equity ratio declines from 1.0 to .43. In panel B, it is assumed that the company had issued $2,000,000 worth of bonds with warrants attached that allow the warrant holder to purchase 50 shares of common stock at $20 per share. In this case, the bonds remain on the balance sheet and common equity increases by $2,000,000. The debt/equity ratio declines to only .71.

2. Exercise of warrants produces a cash inflow to the firm from the sale of new stock. Exchange of convertible securities merely results in transfer of balances between accounts.

3. The firm has little control over the conversion of warrants, while a call feature may be used to force conversion of convertible bonds or preferred stock.

While the reasons for issuing warrants are very similar to those for selling convertible securities, many more firms issue convertibles than warrants. It appears that firms prefer convertibles because of the greater control they offer

TABLE 14.1
Effect on the Balance Sheet of Conversion of Convertible Bonds versus Exercise of Warrants.

A. Exchanging $2,000,000 worth of convertible bonds

Capital Structure	Before Conversion	After Conversion
Bonds	$ 3,000,000	$ 3,000,000
Convertible bonds	2,000,000	0
Common equity	5,000,000	7,000,000
Total capital	$10,000,000	$10,000,000
Debt/equity ratio	1.0	.43

B. Exercise of warrants

Capital Structure	Before Exercise	After Exercise
Bonds	$ 3,000,000	$ 3,000,000
Bonds sold with warrants attached	2,000,000	2,000,000
Common equity	5,000,000	7,000,000
Total capital	$10,000,000	$12,000,000
Debt/equity ratio	1.0	.71

over the conversion process and the elimination of debt on the balance sheet due to conversion.

The following section is devoted to the study of options, securities that have characteristics similar to those of warrants but that are created by individuals rather than corporations. Examination of the valuation process for options will further your understanding of warrants and convertible securities.

LISTED OPTIONS

Listed options are securities created by individual investors and are an important subject in investment management courses. They are not issued by the firm and are not a source of capital for corporations. We discuss them in the context of financial management because the theory underlying option valuation provides greater understanding of the valuation process for warrants and convertibles and even for the firm itself. Also the widespread popularity of listed options compels students of finance to be familiar with the characteristics and uses of these securities.

The listed option market began in April 1973, when the Chicago Board Options Exchange (CBOE) offered option trading on 16 securities. This exchange provides the facilities for trading options as the option contracts are created by individual investors. Growth of investor interest in this market has been phenomenal. Today more than 200 stocks have listed options available on four different option trading exchanges.

The terminology of options is presented first. Afterward, we will discuss reasons for buying and selling options and deal with option valuation.

DEFINITIONS

Options are of two types. A listed **call option** is a contract allowing the holder to buy from the option seller 100 shares of a specified security at a predetermined exercise price anytime during the option contract period. (The term *listed option* is used to distinguish these securities from stock options, which are frequently used by corporations as part of an executive compensation package. While both types of options allow future purchase of stock at a predetermined price, the impact on the firm and the trading mechanism for the two securities are vastly different.) A listed **put option** allows the option buyer to sell specified stock to the option seller any time during the contract period. Note that for each option contract there exists a seller and a buyer.

The seller is also termed the option *writer,* and the amount the option writer receives from the buyer is the *option premium.* Whether or not the option is exercised is at the discretion of the buyer of the contract.

If the writer of a listed call option owns the underlying stock, a *covered* option position results. If the underlying stock is not possessed, the writer has a *naked* option contract.

The price at which a call buyer can "call the stock" from the seller is termed the **striking price.** If the striking price is above the market price of the underlying stock, the option is termed *out-of-the money.* Conversely, a striking price below the current stock value is an *in-the-money* option. An *at-the money* option has a striking price equal to the price of the stock.

It should be apparent that listed call options are very similar to warrants. However, there are two important differences:

1. Option contracts are created by individual investors who deliver stock from their own portfolios if the option is exercised. Warrants are issued by a company that stands ready to sell new shares of the company's stock if the warrants are exercised. A firm whose stock has listed options available is totally independent of the option market and the trading in those options.

2. The longest maturity for a listed option is 9 months, while warrants generally are issued with maturities of 5 to 10 years.

TABLE 14.2
Call Option Premium Quotations of January 15, 1982.

(1) Stock and NY Close		(2) Strike Price	(3) Calls			(4) Puts		
			Jan.	Apr.	July	Jan.	Apr.	July
Am Tel	$58\frac{1}{4}$	50	$8\frac{1}{4}$	—	—	—	$\frac{1}{16}$	$\frac{1}{8}$
	$58\frac{1}{4}$	55	$3\frac{1}{2}$	$4\frac{3}{8}$	5	$\frac{1}{16}$	$\frac{5}{8}$	$1\frac{1}{4}$
	$58\frac{1}{4}$	60	$\frac{1}{16}$	$1\frac{1}{4}$	2	$1\frac{3}{4}$	$3\frac{1}{4}$	$3\frac{1}{2}$
	$58\frac{1}{4}$	65	—	$\frac{1}{4}$	$\frac{3}{4}$	—	—	—
Motorola	55	55	$1\frac{1}{2}$	$4\frac{3}{4}$	$6\frac{3}{4}$	$1\frac{1}{2}$	$3\frac{5}{8}$	—
	55	60	$\frac{1}{8}$	$2\frac{5}{8}$	$4\frac{3}{4}$	$5\frac{1}{2}$	$6\frac{1}{2}$	7
	55	65	—	$1\frac{1}{2}$	$3\frac{1}{4}$	$10\frac{1}{2}$	$10\frac{3}{4}$	—
	55	70	—	$\frac{9}{16}$	2	$15\frac{1}{2}$	16	—
Storage Tech	35	25	$9\frac{3}{8}$	$10\frac{1}{8}$	—	$\frac{1}{16}$	$\frac{1}{4}$	—
	35	30	$5\frac{3}{8}$	$6\frac{1}{4}$	$7\frac{1}{8}$	$\frac{1}{16}$	$\frac{3}{4}$	$1\frac{1}{2}$
	35	35	$\frac{1}{2}$	3	$4\frac{3}{8}$	$1\frac{1}{8}$	$2\frac{3}{4}$	4
	35	40	$\frac{1}{16}$	$1\frac{1}{4}$	$2\frac{3}{4}$	—	—	$11\frac{1}{2}$

The reasons for investing in options can be illustrated by using the option premium quotations presented in Table 14.2. After the name of each stock, the data presented include (1) the stock closing price on the New York Stock Exchange (35 in the case of Storage Technology); (2) the option's striking price; and (3) the premiums of the last option traded with an expiration date in January, April, and July. (October is also an expiration month for these options. Since the longest maturity for a listed option is nine months, only three expiration dates will be available at any time.) For example, the *Storage Technology January 30 calls* sold for $5⅜, whereas the *January 40 calls* sold for $$\frac{1}{16}$. We will use information about the Storage Technology options to illustrate reasons for buying and selling options.

REASONS TO BUY AND SELL OPTIONS

Investors purchase options for two of the same reasons they buy warrants: (1) to use leverage in speculating on a security and (2) to expose themselves to a minimal dollar risk. Investors sell options to (1) reduce the risk of equity positions and (2) increase current income. In addition, they can be used in various hedging strategies to be discussed.

Reasons for Buying Options

Buying a call is an alternative to buying the stock, since a profit is made if the stock appreciates. One hundred shares of Storage Technology would cost $3,500. A similar position in an April 35 contract on 100 shares would cost $300. Compare the holding period returns that would be earned assuming that Storage Technology stock appreciates to $40 by the third week in April if we (1) bought the stock for $3,500 or (2) bought an April 35 call contract for $300. Important in our analysis is that Storage Technology pays no dividend on its common stock. Immediately prior to expiration, the April 35 call will sell for $5 since the stock's market price is $40 and the call allows purchase of the stock for $35. Realize, however, that the option holder will not exercise the option to earn the $5 per share profit, but will sell the option just before it expires, since commissions for options are much lower than those for stocks. In most cases, the option would be purchased by a floor trader on an options exchange who deals without commissions and who ultimately will exercise the option. Holding period yield calculations from the stock and option positions are shown in Table 14.3. If Storage Technology appreciates to $40 over the next three months, buying the option and earning a 66.67% return is preferable to earning only 14% on the stock itself.

In addition, dollar losses are limited for the call buyer if Storage Technology declines in price. In our example, $300 is the most that the option buyer will lose since the option will expire worthless if the stock is below $35 at expiration. The buyer of the stock could lose $3,500 if Storage Technology went bankrupt (even though bankruptcy is highly unlikely).

Purchase of put options is motivated by the belief that the stock will fall in value, since a put permits sale of the specified stock at a predetermined striking price. Buying a put is an alternative to selling a stock *short*, just as buying a call is an alternative to buying a stock. Reasons for buying a put are also based on leverage and limited dollar loss.

TABLE 14.3
Return from Buying Storage Technology Stock versus Buying the April 35 Option.

Strategy	Holding Period Yield
Buy stock	$\dfrac{\$4,000 - 3,500}{\$3,500} = 14.29\%$
Buy April 35 option	$\dfrac{\$500 - 300}{\$300} = 66.67\%$

It should be apparent that the purchase of a call, put, or warrant is a highly leveraged method of speculating on the price change of a security. The option or warrant buyer's position promises either very high returns or total loss of principal.

Reasons for Selling Options

Option writing is a conservative investment strategy used to (1) reduce risk in common stock investments and (2) generate current income for the option writer. To illustrate, consider creating a covered option position by buying Storage Technology common stock at $35 and writing the Storage Technology April 35 option for $3. Sale of the option contract on 100 shares of stock produces current income to the writer of $300, which in effect reduces the cost of the stock to $32 per share ($35 − $3). Risk is reduced because the stock price must decline below $32 per share before a loss occurs.

If we assume that Storage Technology appreciated to $40 by mid-April, the option holder could call the stock and purchase it for $35 instead of paying $40 in the marketplace. The holding period yield for the option writer of 9.38%, or ($35 − $32)/$32. is the maximum return possible because, regardless of how much Storage Technology appreciates, the stock will be called by the option buyer for $35. However, many investors prefer the more certain but lower return promised by covered option positions to the more uncertain but potentially greater return possible from holding only the stock.

Naked option writing (selling calls on stock that the writer does not own) is a seldom used option trading strategy for the average investor. Profits from a naked call are limited to the option premium if the stock falls in price, while losses are theoretically unlimited if the stock appreciates rapidly.

Investors generally write put options in combination with stock and call options to create hedged positions. For example, an individual who believes that Storage Technology will not change significantly in price over the next three months might buy the stock for $35 and sell both a put and a call with a striking price of $35 that mature in April. (This is called a *straddle*.) Premiums received would total 5\frac{3}{4}$ per share ($3 + 2$\frac{3}{4}$). A profit results if the stock stays above 29\frac{1}{4}$ ($35 − 5\frac{3}{4}$) or below 40\frac{3}{4}$ ($35 + 5\frac{3}{4}$), because one of the options will have value at maturity and the other will expire worthless. (For example, if the stock is worth $40 at maturity, it will be called away by the call holder, but the put will have no value.) The ability to modify risk and return positions using options is the primary reason for the great popularity of these securities.

VALUATION OF OPTIONS

The factors contributing to the value of *call options*—time to maturity, striking price, stock price, stock volatility, and interest rates—are identical to those listed earlier for warrants. The behavior of option premiums in relation to these variables can be illustrated by the data in Table 14.2.

Notice that as the *time* to expiration lengthens, the options for all stocks increase in value, for a greater probability exists that the stock will appreciate. Conversely, *striking price* is inversely related to option value. The Storage Technology calls with a $25 striking price maturing in April sell for $10⅛, while the April 40s sell for $1¼.

Stocks with a higher *price* will have options with higher premiums, all else constant. Compare the Motorola at-the-money April 55s, selling for $4¾, to the Storage Technology at-the-money 35s selling for $3. If less *variability* is expected in stock price, a lower option premium will result. The options of AT&T, a relatively stable security, are generally less expensive than those of Storage Technology, a more volatile stock.

The reason *interest rates* affect option (or warrant) premiums is not readily apparent, but it has to do with the fact that stocks can be combined with options to create a "riskless hedge," meaning that regardless of the movement in stock price, no gain or loss will result for the investor. For example, the writer of a naked option loses money if the stock appreciates, because the stock that must be delivered becomes more costly. Conversely, the holder of only the stock earns profits from a rise in the security's price. Combining the proper number of options written against each share of stock owned will produce a riskless hedge. The loss from the options will exactly offset the gain resulting from the increased value of the security. The reverse holds for a small decline in stock price. The rate of return that should be earned from this riskless hedge is the risk-free rate of interest. T-bills or commercial paper typically are used as a measure of the risk-free rate. Consequently, as interest rates rise, option premiums increase; and as interest rates fall, option prices decline.

The five variables just described have been combined into a mathematical equation for valuing options called the *Black-Scholes Option Pricing Model* (OPM). It has been shown to be reliable in predicting option premiums, and it is widely used by investors attempting to identify mispriced options.

Derivation of the OPM has far-reaching implications for corporate finance. Theory currently is being developed to use the OPM for pricing corporate stock and other risky assets. In the future, it may provide an alternative to the widely accepted CAPM for determining the value of the firm and the cost of equity capital.

SUMMARY

Convertible securities are bonds or preferred stock that can be exchanged for common stock at a specified conversion ratio or price. They are used by the firm to increase the marketability of the debt or preferred stock; to obtain short-term, inexpensive funds; and in the hope that their issue will result in future equity financing at a higher stock price. The value of a convertible security is a function of its value as a straight bond, its conversion value, and the speculative premium that the buyer is willing to pay.

A warrant is a security that allows purchase of the company's common stock at a specified price any time during the exercise period. Warrants usually are attached to a bond or preferred stock. The reasons a firm sells warrants are the same as those for issuing convertible securities, but exercise of warrants affects the firm differently from conversion of convertible securities. Exercise of warrants produces a cash flow to the firm and increases the firm's equity. Conversion of convertible securities removes debt from the balance sheet and increases equity, thus reducing the financial risk of the firm.

Listed options are either calls or puts. They are created by individual buyers and sellers in the security market and are totally independent of the firm. Investors buy options because of leverage, lower dollar risk, and the hedging opportunities they provide. Investors sell options to reduce risk, increase current income, and create a hedge. Options are discussed in this chapter because valuation theory for options can also be used to value convertible securities, warrants, and the firm itself.

QUESTIONS AND REVIEW ACTIVITIES

1. Define
   a) Convertible securities.
   b) Warrant.
   c) Call option.
   d) Put option.
2. Debts may be eliminated by conversion into stock, but the option lies with the bondholder. Does the time when bondholders tend to use the conversion privilege coincide with the time when doing so would be most beneficial to the corporation? Explain.
3. Explain what is implied by the statement that a purchaser of a convertible bond pays more for the bond than it's really worth.
4. Explain the different effects on the balance sheet of the conversion of a bond into stock and the exercise of a warrant.
5. Why do warrants frequently sell at prices above their theoretical value?
6. Why do convertible bonds frequently sell at prices above their theoretical values both as converted stock and as straight debt?
7. What is the purpose of an antidilution clause?
8. Why will the warrant have a market value even though the market price of the stock is substantially below the exercise price of the warrant?
9. Why does a speculator prefer trading in warrants to purchasing the stock directly?
10. For what reasons do companies issue convertible securities or warrants? Why do they appeal to investors?

11. Compare the position of the writer of a call option to that of a firm that has issued warrants. How are they the same? How are they different?

12. Why would an investor buy a call option? Buy a put option?

13. Why would an investor sell a call option? Sell a put option?

14. Discuss the factors that affect the value of a call option.

PROBLEMS

1. Speculation Unlimited decides to finance a $5 million expansion with a convertible bond issue, which it is able to sell at par. The bonds will be convertible at $40 a share or 25 shares per bond. The market value of the corporation's stock at present is $36. The firm's balance sheet (in millions) is as follows:

Assets	$50	Liabilities	$15
		Capital stock:	
		1 million shares	10
		Paid-in surplus	5
		Retailed earnings	20
Total	$50	Total claims	$50

a) If conversion is forced when the stock price rises to $50, what is the effect on the book value of the common stock?

b) By what means can Speculation Unlimited, or any corporation, force conversion?

2. The Colonel Tire Corp. has an issue of $2 million in 10% subordinated convertible debentures outstanding. These bonds have a par value of $1,000 and can be converted at any time into 30 shares of common stock with a par value of $250. The bonds are callable at $1,100 at any time.

a) Will conversion take place if the price of the stock goes to $28 a share? If it goes to $40 a share?

b) Can the call provision bring about the conversion of these bonds in each instance in part a?

c) Assume interest rates are 10%. Approximately what price must the debentures have been selling for in each instance in part a?

d) If the dividend per share of common stock is increased from $1.50 to $1.75, causing the market price to increase from $28 to $34, will all the subordinated convertible debentures be converted?

e) In relation to the market price of common stock, where would you expect the conversion price of a typical convertible security to be placed at the time of issuance?

3. Company G has an issue of $2 million in 12% subordinated convertible debentures outstanding. These bonds have a par value of $1,000 and can be converted at any

time into 20 shares of common stock with a par value of $5. They are callable at $1,050 at any time.

a) Will conversion take place if the price of the stock goes to $25 a share? If it goes to $55 a share?

b) Can the call provision of bonds affect their conversion in each instance in part a?

c) Assume interest rates are 12%. Approximately what price must the debentures have been selling for in each instance in (a) above?

d) Could conversion take place in some instances because of a decrease in the market value of the bonds rather than an increase in the price of the common stock?

e) Is the conversion price of a stock always higher than its market price at the time the convertible securities are issued?

f) Why do companies issue convertible bonds?

4. One of the owners of TRE Corp.'s warrants wonders whether it is now advantageous for her to exercise her warrant. The warrant allows her to purchase 3.2 shares of common stock at $30 per share.

a) Should she exercise her warrant if the market price of the common stock is $35?

b) What is the market value of her warrant when the stock price is $35?

c) Would you pay $18.50 for the warrant in part b?

5. The common stock of ECC sells at a PE ratio of 20. The firm earns $2.50 per share after taxes and has a dividend payout ratio of 40%. ECC plans to issue $5 million worth of 10%, 10-year convertible debentures with a call price of 108 and an initial conversion premium of 25%. ECC's capitalization presently is 1 million shares. Determine

a) The conversion price in dollars.

b) The conversion ratio per $1,000 par value bond.

c) The initial conversion value of each bond.

d) How many new shares of equity must be issued if all the debentures are converted.

6. The Great American Corp. sold a bond issue that included detachable warrants to purchase company stock. If each warrant entitles the holder to buy two shares of common stock at $11 a share and the current market price is $15 a share, calculate the theoretical value of the warrant. Calculate the value if the stock market price of the stock is $10.

7. Jackie Jones is debating whether to invest $500 in warrants or in common stock of the WYX Corp. The current market price of its stock is $22. Jones could purchase warrants that entitle the holder to buy one share of stock per warrant at a price of $20. These warrants have a market price of $2.

Evaluate the following investments:

- 23 shares of stock for $506.
- 250 warrants for $500 (ignore transaction costs).

Assume that one year afterward,

a) The market price of the stock has risen to $28 a share.

b) The market price of the stock has fallen to $18 a share.

Why are the results of the stock and warrant purchases so dissimilar? What do you advise Jones to do?

8. Adrienne Amanda believes that AT&T stock will appreciate to at least $68 over the next six months. She is evaluating the return possible from buying the stock or buying a July call option.

a) Calculate the six-month holding period yield from buying the stock today for $58.25. (Dividends would be $2.70 over this period.)

b) Calculate the return from buying the July 60 call for $2 and the July 65 for $¾.

c) Which purchase would you recommend to Amanda—the stock, the July 60 option, or the July 65 option? Evalute the risk of each purchase.

ADDITIONAL READINGS

Ayers, H. F. "Risk Aversion in the Warrants Market," *Industrial Management Review* (Fall 1963), pp. 45–53.

Black, F., and M. Scholes. "The Pricing of Options and Corporate Liabilities," *Journal of Political Economy* (May–June 1973), pp. 637–54.

Brigham, E. F. "An Analysis of Convertible Debentures," *Journal of Finance* (March 1966), pp. 25–54.

Broman, K. L. "The Use of Convertible Subordinated Debentures by Industrial Firms, 1949–1959," *Quarterly Review of Economics and Business* (Spring 1963), pp. 65–76.

Hayes, S. L., and H. B. Reiling. "Sophisticated Financing Tool: The Warrant," *Harvard Business Review* (January–February 1969), pp. 137–50.

Nelson, J. R. "Price Effects in Rights Offerings," *Journal of Finance* (December 1965), pp. 747–50.

Officer, D., and G. L. Trennepohl. "Price Behavior of Corporate Equities Near Option Expiration Dates," *Financial Management* (Summer 1981), pp. 75–80.

Pease, F. "The Warrant—Its Power and Its Hazards," *Financial Analysts Journal* (January–February 1963), pp. 25–32.

Shelton, J. P. "The Relation of the Price of a Warrant to the Price of Its Associated Stock," *Financial Analysts Journal* (May–June and July–August 1967), pp. 143–51 and 88–99.

Smith, C. W. "Option Pricing: A Review," *Journal of Financial Economics* (January–March 1976), pp. 2–51.

Thorp, E. O., and S. T. Kassouf. *Beat the Market.* New York: Random House, 1967.

Trennepohl, G. L., "A Comparison of Listed Option Premiums and Black and Scholes Model Prices: 1973–1979," *Journal of Financial Research* (Summer 1981), pp. 11–20.

Trennepohl, G. L., and W. P. Dukes. "Return and Risk for Listed Option Contracts," *Journal of Financial Research* (Spring 1979), pp. 37–49.

Vinson, C. E. "Rates of Return on Convertibles," *Financial Analysts Journal* (March–April 1970), pp. 81–85.

Walter, J. E., and A. V. Que. "The Valuation of Convertible Bonds," *Journal of Finance* (June 1973), pp. 713–32.

Weil, R. L., Jr., J. E. Segall, and D. Green, Jr. "Premiums on Convertible Bonds," *Journal of Finance* (June 1968), pp. 445–63.

- **LONG-TERM FINANCING**
  THE CAPITAL STRUCTURE PROBLEM
  DECISION CRITERIA FOR LONG-TERM FINANCING DECISIONS

- **INVESTMENT BANKING**
  FUNCTIONS
  ORIGIN OF PUBLIC ISSUES
  DISTRIBUTION OF THE ISSUE

- **REGULATION OF SECURITIES**
  FEDERAL SECURITIES LAWS
  REGULATION OF OUTSTANDING SECURITIES ISSUES

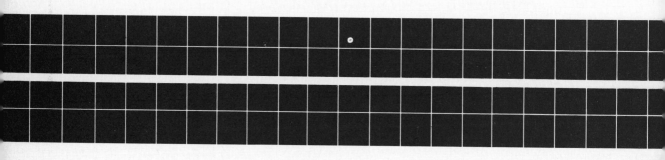

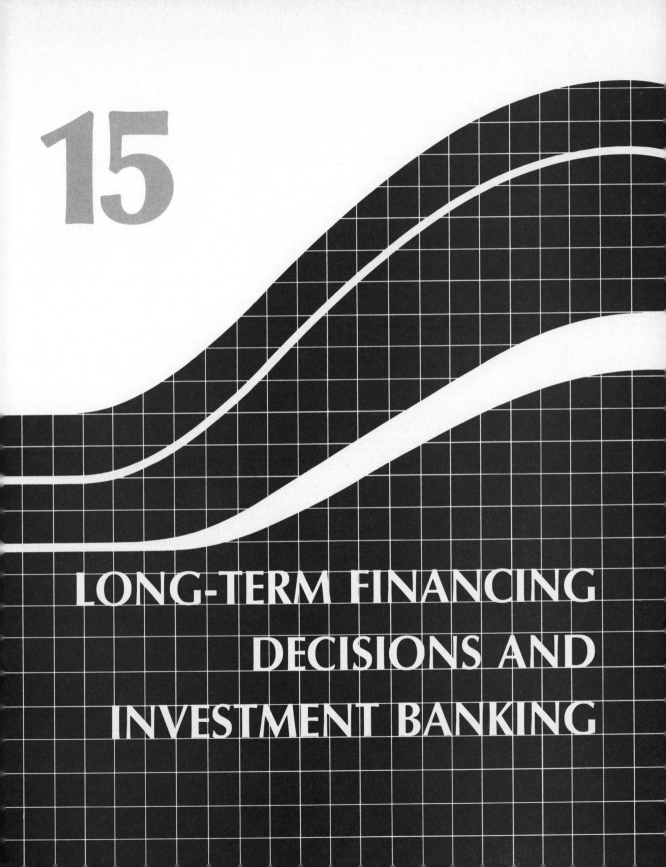

15

LONG-TERM FINANCING DECISIONS AND INVESTMENT BANKING

A firm's financial managers face two types of problems with regard to long-term financing. The firm first needs overall guidelines on the appropriate mix of debt and equity to be used over time. This raises the question of whether a best combination exists and, if so, what factors affect its composition. A long-run goal for the use of debt and equity constitutes a policy.

A second recurring problem centers on how to finance the firm at specific points in time. A basic tenet of this book is that there is a best combination of debt and equity, that is, an optimal capital structure. As stated in Chapter 1, the generally accepted objective of all financial decisions is the maximization of the value of the firm. However, a firm is not likely to finance with the best combination of debt and equity when raising funds on any given occasion. A number of reasons account for this, one being flotation costs. Long-term financing decisions—the problem of exactly how to raise needed funds at a given point in time—generally require a cost-benefit analysis that evaluates a number of factors. Capital structure policy is only *one* consideration, albeit a very important one.

After careful study of this chapter, you should

1. Know how the firm determines its capital structure in order to maximize the value of the firm.

2. Know what factors are considered at any specific point in time when additional financing is required.

3. Know what services are provided by investment banking firms.

4. Understand the advantages and disadvantages of financing with public offerings and private placements.

5. Understand how public issues are originated, underwritten, and distributed to investors.

6. Be aware of the difference between investment banking firms underwriting an issue or selling it on a best efforts basis.

7. Know how the Securities and Exchange Commission regulates new security issues under the Securities Act of 1933 and outstanding security issues under the Securities Exchange Act of 1934.

8. Know what recent changes have been promulgated by the Securities and Exchange Commission to shorten the time and lower the cost required to float a new security issue.

LONG-TERM FINANCING

Capital structure is defined as the composition of a firm's long-term financing represented by its long-term debt, preferred stock, and common stock. When current liabilities are included, the total generally is called **financial structure.**

THE CAPITAL STRUCTURE PROBLEM

The capital structure problem is to derive a policy that provides guidance on its appropriate composition—how much debt and how much equity should exist. Attempting to determine a best capital structure implies that such an optimal policy exists. For many years, financial theorists took the existence of such an optimum for granted. For such an optimum structure to exist, institutional factors must create incentives for the use of different types of capital.

A 1958 study by Modigliani and Miller (MM)† considered the problem using the theory of equilibrium economics. The MM work caused reevaluation of all existing theories of valuation and the cost of capital. The controversial paper caused heated exchanges and occasioned a great deal of rethinking of the issues. The results were a better understanding of the factors that influence capital structure, a clearer definition of the relationship between capital structure policy and the cost of capital, and some important guidance for capital budgeting.

The chief point of contention between MM and the traditionalists that should concern us here is whether there is a range of capital structures over which there is freedom for financial decision making. The question is whether counterbalancing factors exist that offset the tax benefit of deductible interest payments on debt. Some of the unfavorable factors involved in increased use of debt are increased bankruptcy risks, increased earnings variability, and higher covariability with market returns, which can cause diversification difficulties for stock investors.

Long-Term Financing Constraints

The capital structure problem remains an unresolved theoretical issue. Even if it was completely resolved, theory will not solve all the front-line financial manager's long-term financing problems. Capital structure policy, even imperfectly derived, must often be ignored because of short-run considerations. The financial manager must raise funds now, and what is expedient may not always be consistent with a policy that would be best in the long run.

There are numerous occasions when policy and short-run tactics can conflict. Two examples will suffice here. Small proprietors often prefer to run a debt-free enterprise. When they wish to expand, however, they generally do use debt capital because they prefer not to or are unable to raise outside equity capital. In the fairly recent past, quite a few large firms wrestled with this dilemma. Although they desperately needed long-term capital and their financing policy dictated that they should sell bonds, they actually used other means to raise funds. These firms financed with short- and intermediate-term

† F. Modigliani and M. H. Miller. "The Cost of Capital, Corporation Finance, and the Theory of Investment," *American Economic Review* (June 1958), pp. 261–97.

debt or, in a few cases, even sold equity issues despite the fact that the equity market was not very hospitable. High interest rates on long-term debt dictated this behavior.

These examples indicate two factors that may override policy dictates: control and timing. There are other such considerations. Different forms of financing are desirable for different reasons, depending on their unique legal characteristics. Chapters 12 through 14 have described these features in some detail. For now, we can review them in passing before showing how their characteristics can make them a desirable means of financing at a particular time.

We will discuss here only pure debt and common stock. Other securities are hybrids, with some of the traits of bonds and some of those of common stock. Convertible bonds are bonds when issued, but they may, at some later time, be converted into stock. Preferred stock is equity by definition, but it is more like debt in that generally it receives a limited preferential payment, a preferred dividend. Securities such as these are appropriate forms of financing when a blend of debt and equity characteristics is desirable. This is why they were developed. For current purposes, however, concentration on the simpler forms is more enlightening.

Legal Characteristics of Debt and Equity

The security owner's rights with debt and equity differ with respect to four important features: right to recovery of the original investment, claim on income, claim on assets, and representation. Debt holders, or bondholders, are not investors; they are lenders. Lenders are entitled to added safeguards to ensure recovery of their investment and payment for its use. However, they have no right to representation unless their preferential position with regard to principal and income appears to be in jeopardy.

Bondholders are guaranteed by contract that they will receive their original investment. Bonds mature; they come due just like promisory notes. At the time of maturity, the issuer is legally bound to repay the face value of the bonds or to suffer the legal consequences. If the firm has financial difficulties, the bondholders are in a preferential position with regard to participation in assets. They have a prior claim over residual owners (common stockholders), with the amount limited to their original investment. (This provision is seldom significant because the assets of a failed firm are generally insufficient to cover court costs, attorneys' fees, and creditors' claims. If anything remains, it belongs to the stockholders.)

Bondholders are contractually assured not only of a return of their invested capital but also of receiving payment for the use of that capital in the form of interest. Bondholders have a preferential claim on income; that is, interest must be paid them before stockholders receive any distribution. Except in rare cases (income bonds), interest must be paid even if there is no income. Nonpayment of interest constitutes default, and the bondholders, or their representatives, can sue.

Stocks, on the other hand, never mature. They do not come due. The buyer is in no way assured that the original investment will ever be repaid. The investor surrenders capital to the company and then hopes for the best.

Stockholders also receive no guarantee of payment for the use of their invested capital. However, they do hope to receive dividends. While the contractually agreed-upon interest payment limits the bondholders' claim on income, common stockholders are not subject to such limitations. They have the right to unlimited participation in earnings to the extent that the corporation declares dividends. Even when common dividends are not paid, the shareholders generally benefit. Higher retained earnings will normally increase the value of the stock, and the investors can realize the benefit when they sell part or all of the stock.

Because they have invested in the firm (surrendered their capital to it), the shareholders have a right to a voice in its management. Through their collective vote, they elect the board of directors, which in turn appoints the management. Some believe that such a representative process severely reduces the average shareholder's clout. However, contests for control of firms through the election of directors are far from uncommon. The threat of such struggles no doubt makes management more responsive to the perceived desires of the stockholders.

While bondholders do not vote under normal circumstances, it is not strictly correct to say that they have no voice. The restrictive provisions (covenants) of bond contracts can restrain management. Because these restrictions are contingent only upon default of principal or interest (or of both), it is common to speak of bondholders as not having a voice in management.

These legal characteristics (maturity, claim on income and assets, and voice) affect the desirability of the different forms of financing in any given situation. Because the firm can choose the maturity of the debt it issues, it can choose a financing period that is suitable to its needs. As you know, the two securities (stocks and bonds) have different rights regarding representation, so control is often an issue. Debt has a limited, enforceable, preferential claim on income as compared to equity's residual, but unlimited, claim. Because of the differences in these claims, issuing stocks or selling bonds will have different effects on EPS, riskiness, and the flexibility of the firm in making future financing decisions. Recognizing that the firm will need financing again in the future raises the question of which type of financing to use now and which to issue later. This last issue, timing, is often the key to success in long-term financing decicions.

DECISION CRITERIA FOR LONG-TERM FINANCING DECISIONS

Because of their legal characteristics, debt and equity capital affect the firm differently. Here we will weigh some of the consequences of a long-term financing decision that a financial manager should consider in making a choice. The discussion of individual factors will often refer to analytical techniques discussed in earlier chapters. You may need to review these chapters to recall the mechanics of the techniques. (Throughout the discussion, we will note where review may be helpful.)

Consider one additional point: There is no simple way to combine the analysis of the individual factors into one precise summary measure. The analyses of the individual factors cannot simply be summed, nor can they be strictly averaged. A manager making a financing decision must examine the total consequences of the different alternatives and choose the one that represents the best compromise solution. On rare occasions, one type of financing will appear to be preferable in all respects. More frequently, though, decision making involves selecting the best of a number of less-than-perfect choices.

Suitability

Suitability refers to how well the financing alternative fits the need. If the firm needs financing for only a short period of time, long-term bonds or common stock are unsuitable. The firm is still saddled with them after the need for capital has ended.

Debt is more flexible in this regard than equity. The firm can choose to issue debt that is scheduled to retire when the need for funds is over. The firm can use short-term debt to finance seasonal working capital, intermediate-term debt for equipment, and long-term debt for financing plant expansion.

Equity, on the other hand, is often suitable for financing the same assets if there is a permanent need. For example, equity funds might logically finance permanent increases in working capital, equipment, or plant.

The idea is to use funds in such a way as to provide the company with a firm foundation, but not to burden it with unnecessary financing and its associated costs. The firm does not want insufficient or excess financing at any time, now or in the future.

Control

Relatively small holdings of common stock often control companies. Although the percentage of the outstanding shares held may be small, the dollar amount of the controlling block is generally substantial. If the firm sells new shares, the controlling shareholders must buy a proportionate amount of the new stock if they wish to maintain their percentage control. Because of the large dollar amounts involved, such purchases may not be feasible.

Because they do control the company, such shareholders may prefer the sale of bonds to the issue of additional stock. Bondholders would have no voice in management unless the company defaulted on interest or principal payments. Actually, since in such cases the bondholders might well end up with total control, control is an issue even with the sale of bonds.

Earnings per Share (EPS)

Chapter 12 described the different effects of debt and equity on EPS. If debt financing is used successfully, EPS will increase. Should volume fall, however, the added burden of the interest charges compounds the problem, a phenomenon referred to as *financial leverage*. Equity financing does not magnify the effect of changes in volume. It does not provide leverage.

Methods for analyzing the effect on EPS of different financing alternatives were described in detail in Chapter 12. If the analyst wished to know EPS at a particular sales level, a *pro forma* income statement would provide the answer. A financial break-even chart, such as the one in Fig. 12.2, provides that information for a wide range of volume levels. Such a chart would help the manager to evaluate the EPS consideration.

Riskiness

The financial break-even chart does more than indicate the EPS forecasts for various financing alternatives. It highlights another aspect of the problem. Although debt capital can provide favorable leverage and raise EPS, it can also increase the vulnerability of EPS to changes in volume. This is one aspect of riskiness: earnings volatility.

With debt financing, EPS are more volatile, that is, subject to wider variations with changes in the economic environment. The leverage measures (DOL, DFL, DTL) described in Chapter 12 are efficient ways of describing, and are therefore helpful in assessing, this aspect of choosing among financing alternatives.

Earnings volatility is only one feature of the greater riskiness of debt. Debt also carries a risk that stems from fixed interest payments. If the firm misses a payment, there are severe legal repercussions, including the possibility of bankruptcy.

One way of measuring such a default risk is by using the coverage ratios explained in Chapter 2. In many cases, however, the ratios are calculated on a *pro forma* basis, that is, on the basis of forecasted income statements. Because the penalties for default are so severe, firms generally are very conservative with regard to default risk.

Flexibility

Flexibility refers to the firm's ability to adapt to a changing economic environment. The firm would like to have some flexibility with regard to future financing decisions. If a firm issues too much debt capital, it may find itself forced to use equity financing at a time when the sale of stock is particularly unattractive. Firms are reluctant to sell stock in poor markets. However, they may have to choose some other equally unattractive strategy, a number of which have been observed in recent years. These include selling callable bonds (bonds subject to accelerated retirement) at high interest rates, with the hope of rearranging the firm's capital structure when the economic environment improves; selling short-term debt or postponing the decision in the hope that the situation will change; selling convertible bonds so that the indebtedness may be extinguished through conversion when times are better; and finally, severely curtailing capital expenditures.

A similar problem arises if too much equity financing is used. If a firm wants to contract operations (i.e., become smaller by selling assets or possibly even an entire operating division), excess equity is often troublesome. With debt, management can wait until the bonds mature and retire them. Management may even reserve the right to retire the debt early through a call provision. With stock, management is put in the delicate situation of bargaining with the stockholders in order to persuade them to sell their ownership rights.

To be flexible, the firm must maintain its options. Then if it wishes to expand, it can do so using the most attractive form of financing available *at the time*. To be truly flexible, the firm needs to maintain its choices for either expansion or contraction, though generally the emphasis is on the former.

Timing

In discussing flexibility, we made frequent reference to time. In making any financing decision, financial managers must consider both the current market environment and the conditions that might exist the next time the firm enters the market.

Generalizations regarding the correct tactics for corporate financing decisions are difficult. Any prescription for such decisions will seem oversimplified in light of the complexities of modern capital markets and the volatile, ever-changing nature of market behavior. However, there are observable patterns in the relationship between security returns and general economic conditions that suggest guides to the timing of corporate issues.

In the past, interest rates generally were lower during recessions. This suggests that debt financing should be undertaken during such periods. Such action, though, requires considerable courage on the part of management. Managers would have to add fixed interest expenses during periods when the outlook is gloomiest.

Generally, interest rates reach their highest level at or near the peak of expansionary periods. This occurs when the government applies restraints to reduce the inflationary pressures that mount during such a boom. These high interest rates will have a negative effect on stock prices, which will have risen during the economic expansion, because of improving profits and higher EPS expectations.

At the height of the boom, productive capacity is fully utilized, or nearly so, and increased demand results in higher prices for goods and services rather than in increased production. Unusually high prices are socially undesirable, and the government acts to keep inflation under control. Government agencies do this primarily through the management of the cost and supply of loanable funds. Monetary restraint will push interest rates even higher and cause stock prices to moderate. High yield makes bonds more attractive alternative investments and thus serves to restrain stock prices.

The government will attempt to keep the economy running at or near peak capacity. If the effects of its monetary management are too severe, that is, if interest rates climb too high, too fast, a recession may occur. The same thing can happen if the business community becomes pessimistic about the economic future and cuts back on production. Reductions in production can snowball the same way increases do in times of expansion. Economic slumps occasionally occur out of all proportion to the economic restraint applied by the government. The economy is not a perfectly manageable system.

This stylized scenario of economy and market behavior should give you some insight into the timing problem. During recessions, interest rates are relatively low. Cheaper and more readily available funds induce firms to make new investments, providing the base for subsequent economic recovery. As the recovery begins, other firms are encouraged to borrow and to increase production. Increased borrowing will push interest rates upward. The pattern repeats itself and is magnified until boom conditions are reached. Because of their profits, the firms' stock prices rise.

Financial Manager's Dilemma

The prescription for the financial manager is as follows: Acquire debt capital during a recession when interest rates are low, and sell stock just before the peak of an expansion. To accomplish this, however, the manager must forecast when the recessions and booms will occur. Further, the decision maker is continually exposed to ultimate financial embarrassment. Proper timing will have the firm issuing debt when profits are lowest, during recessions. During expansions, when the benefits from leverage are greatest, the financial manager will be advocating the sale of equity securities and the consequent possible short-term dilution of earnings.

This highlights a central problem in long-term financial decision making. Accurate forecasts are the key to good timing. In addition to forecasting the firm's need for funds during the different phases of the business cycle, the manager must predict what market conditions will exist when these needs arise. This involves guessing how and when the economy will expand and what the government's response to the resulting economic conditions will be. The manager also assesses the economy's reaction to governmental tinkering. The magnitude of this forecasting problem does much to explain why financial managers attempt to stay constantly attuned to economic conditions and predictions. They read the financial press, listen to government announcements, make economic consulting arrangements, and try anything they can to stay in touch with tomorrow's financial market environment. With the dollar amounts involved, an astute financial manager can save the firm millions of dollars by properly timing the various issues of the firm's securities.

INVESTMENT BANKING

In the course of reviewing the firm's financial requirements to carry out desirable investment projects, management may conclude that the use of retained earnings or short-term bank loans is not appropriate, or even that the amounts available are not sufficient. The company may decide to sell either stocks or bonds in the capital markets, assuming that the firm is large enough to have this alternative available. The use of the capital markets requires a type of financial intermediary not yet discussed, the investment banking firm.

A corporation raising funds in the capital market may sell either stocks or bonds. In either case, it has two options—to sell the issue by private placement or through a public offering. The corporation may negotiate with an insurance company or another institutional investor for the private placement of a long-term loan or bond issue. When two or more lenders participate in a capital loan or in buying a bond issue, the promissory notes or bonds seldom reappear in the public capital market, but when stocks or bonds are sold through investment bankers as a public offering, they may change ownership many times. Investment bankers and other advisors who aid firms in placing long-term obligations and equities, and dealers and brokers who make a secondary market for the securities already outstanding, play an important role in macroeconomic development by channeling funds from investors to firms that need external capital.

FUNCTIONS

The primary economic function of investment banking firms is to provide long-term capital funds for business enterprises and governments. They do this by purchasing issues of securities from business corporations and governments and then selling the securities to institutional and individual investors. They assume the risk of being unable to sell the securities at a price that will provide them a net return large enough to meet expenses and yield a profit. Investment bankers are middlemen between sellers and buyers of securities; but, because of the nature of the merchandise they handle, they often must act as financial advisors not only to the business firms whose securities they originate and distribute but also to the investors to whom they sell the securities.

While investment bankers are primarily interested in purchasing and selling entire issues of new securities, they also contract with corporations to assist in selling new issues of stock or convertible bonds. These firms offer them first to old stockholders through subscription rights. Under a contract called a *standby agreement*, investment bankers help corporations by buying the portion of the issue for which old shareholders have not subscribed.

Giving Advice

When investment bankers assist in raising new capital for a business corporation, they advise the corporation on the type and form of securities it should offer: whether to issue preferred or common stock in the case of a stock offering, and whether to issue convertible or nonconvertible bonds. Because the methods used to raise capital funds may vary and because market conditions are subject to change, the advice of investment bankers will depend not only on the requirements of the corporation and on its capital structure but also on conditions prevailing in the capital market. In some situations, a public offering may be preferred over private placement; other cases may call for a private placement with a small number of institutional investors.

Safeguarding the Interests of Buyers and Issuers

Investment bankers must consider the interests of both buyers (investors) and issuers (corporations). In order to safeguard the interest of buyers, the investment banker supplies them with information on conditions in the industry as well as on the characteristics of the securities offered. Historically, the interests of issuers may have been represented more adequately than those of the thousands of widely scattered investors; as a result, federal and state governments found it necessary to regulate new security issues in order to protect investors. However, in recent years there has been a tendency to question the efficacy of extensive government regulation in the securities industry. In 1981, the Securities and Exchange Commission (SEC) began to consider relaxing the reporting requirements of large firms that use the capital markets on a recurring basis.

ORIGIN OF PUBLIC ISSUES

Investment bankers are sometimes classified according to the nature of their merchandising business, such as (1) originators of issues, (2) underwriters, and (3) retailers. While no investment banking organization necessarily limits itself to only one of these phases of the business, some investment banking firms originate and participate in underwriting new securities but do practically no retail selling. Such investment bankers may act as managers of underwriting syndicates and also as dealers in placing large blocks of securities with other dealers, retailers, and large institutional investors. A few such organizations may also have sales representatives who sell some securities at retail, but this is usually not a significant phase of their business.

Most financial managers who use the capital markets regularly have established contacts with originating investment banking firms; a proposal for a new issue may come from either the investment banker or the corporation. There is a tendency for investment banking firms to become specialists in **originating** issues in certain fields, for example, in the energy, technology, transportation, and utility industries. After acquiring the techniques and skills essential for handling an issue of a certain industry, the investment banking firm may offer its services to others in the same industry. Other investment bankers may solicit the services of such a firm to originate an issue; to manage the underwriting syndicate, either alone or with a second banker; or to be a member of an underwriting or selling syndicate. A firm that has successfully underwritten an issue of a corporation often becomes its permanent investment banker. And once an investment banking firm has established a reputation in a certain field, its clientele may include not only business corporations in this field but also investors interested in these types of securities (which would facilitate retail sales of new securities).

Negotiated Issues

The oldest and most common method whereby investment bankers obtain new issues is direct negotiation with financial managers of firms. With **negotiated issues,** the financial officers of a corporation meet with the investment banker (with whom the firm probably has done business previously) to discuss the terms of the tentative issue. If the prospects appear to be favorable, the officers make the necessary preparations, including drawing up the prospectus, trust indenture, financial statements, and other documents necessary for registration with the SEC.

After reaching an agreement on the terms of sale, the parties sign a detailed formal purchase contract. The investment banker arranges for the engraving of the security certificates. The corporation contracts for the services of a trustee, usually with the advice of the investment banker. The purchase agreement sets forth the plan, time, and method of payment, along with provisions for delivery of the securities.

Often the corporation considers several plans for financing, and conditions in the capital market will affect both the details of the plan selected and the actual timing of the issue. While market conditions may be unsatisfactory for a short-term issue, they may be favorable for a long-term one. At any particular time, there is a best plan for financing a specific company's capital needs, but there is no specific plan that is best for financing the company's needs at all times.

In the final stages of negotiation, the corporation and the investment banker will agree upon the **offering price** (the price at which the securities are to be offered to the general public) and the price to be paid to the corporation by the investment bankers. The difference between the two prices is the **gross spread.** The offering price must be selected to meet anticipated market conditions. It will be influenced by the market prices of the corporation's outstanding securities and those of similar securities of other corporations in the same industry, as well as by general market conditions. The gross spread is the underwriter's compensation; however, when the issuer is a new corporation, the underwriters often receive an allotment of common stock in addition.

Competitive Bidding

The high quality of the securities of some very large corporations makes it possible to sell them at public auction rather than through investment banking firms using direct negotiation. State and local governments have also followed this method for many years to sell their issues. In 1941, the SEC adopted Rule U-50, which, with certain exceptions, requires that securities of corporations subject to the Public Utility Holding Company Act of 1935 be sold by **competitive bidding.**† In 1944, the Interstate Commerce Commission adopted a somewhat similar position in regard to the sale of railroad debt issues.

In the published invitation for bids, a corporation indicates the time, place, and other conditions. Typically, investment bankers withhold their bids until the deadline in order to set **bid prices** that are in accordance with the latest prevailing market prices. At closing time, the investment bankers exchange information about their bid prices, and those on Wall Street may know who is the successful bidder even before the vendor can open the bids, determine the highest bidder, and make the announcement.

Competitive bidding probably is best suited for use in regulated industries. Such firms must report financial information to their respective regulatory

---

† Competitive bidding in accordance with the provisions of Rule U-50 became effective on May 7, 1941. The SEC retains the right to grant exemptions by order when it appears that competitive bidding is not necessary or appropriate to carry out the provisions of the Public Utility Holding Company Act. For a summary statement of financing pursuant to Rule U-50, see Securities and Exchange Commission, *19th Annual Report for the Fiscal Year Ended June 30, 1953* (Washington, D.C.: U.S. Government Printing Office, 1954), pp. 79–80.

authorities on a fairly uniform basis, and their activities are not usually as diverse as those of nonregulated firms. These conditions enhance the likelihood of attracting a larger number of bids.

This is not to say that there is no competition involved in negotiated issues. The issuing firm is always free to listen to alternative proposals of competing investment banking firms before deciding with whom to sign the underwriting agreement. This potential competition tends to keep the terms and costs of a prospective issue relatively competitive, even though a firm does not use or even contemplate using competitive bidding. The opportunity to replace a banking firm is always present even though a long-term friendly relationship has existed. In other words, even in circumstances of direct negotiation, the investment banker must still meet the test of the marketplace.

Even when selling an issue through competitive bidding, the issuer customarily uses the advisory services of an investment banking firm during the preoffering phase. Investment bankers help to prepare bond indentures and select trustees, secure approval of the appropriate regulatory agencies when required, and prepare registration statements and other documents required by the SEC and state agencies.

DISTRIBUTION OF THE ISSUE

In the preceding section, the relationships between the issuers and the investment banking firms were the main focus; here the emphasis is on the relationship among the investment banking firms in the distribution of an issue. In a typical issue, there are three levels of participation; these involve the originator and the underwriting and selling groups. Figure 15.1 shows the usual pattern. Underwriting syndicates for large issues may include up to 50 firms; for the same size issue, the selling group may range from 100 to 500 firms.

Underwriting the Issue

In investment banking, **underwriting** refers to an investment banking firm's guarantee to an issuing corporation of a definite sum of money on a specified date in return for the corporation's issue of stocks or bonds. Because such issues are usually for large amounts, two or more investment banking firms may form underwriting **syndicates** to handle them. The number of participants in such a syndicate varies with the size of the issue, the resources of the investment bankers, the riskiness of the issue, and the condition of the retail market for the securities.

As there are several days between the date the money is paid to the corporation and the date when payment for the securities by the ultimate purchasers is received, the underwriting syndicate arranges for a short-term

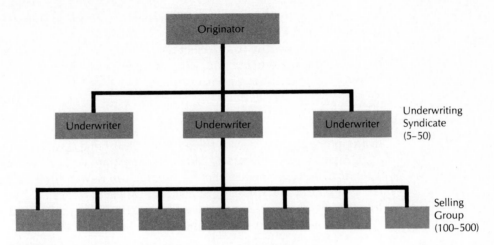

Figure 15.1 Participating groups in a typical underwritten security.

bank loan as interim financing. During this period, the syndicate bears the risk of adverse price fluctuations of the securities. If the market price of the stock or bond issue declines in this interim period, the syndicate carries the entire risk of loss on the sale.

Assume that the issuing corporation and the originating firm are ready to sign a purchase agreement. At this point, the investment banking firms joining in the underwriting participate formally by signing the purchase agreement. According to the terms of the contract, each member of the syndicate participates separately in the purchase of the issue. If an investment firm agrees to take $10 million worth of bonds in an issue totaling $100 million, it is liable to the issuer for a limit of $10 million. In other words, an issuer cannot hold the investment firm liable for the purchase of the remaining $90 million in bonds.

When registering securities with the SEC the underwriters must depend on the issuing corporation to make sure that certain provisions of the law and regulations of the Commission are met. Therefore, the syndicate manager requires the corporation to covenant to do certain things, such as prepare and file a registration statement and a prospectus that meet the requirements of the law and the regulations of the Commission; provide properly certified copies of the corporation's most recent financial statements; assert that there has been no adverse change in the corporation's affairs since the date of the last balance sheet; use the net proceeds of the issue for the purpose stated in the registration statement; and attest that there are no pending lawsuits against the corporation except as specifically stated. The corporation also agrees to indemnify the underwriters against liability because of any untrue, misleading, or incomplete statements in registration statements or in the prospectus (under provision of the Securities Act of 1933). Actually, the corporation draws up the essential documents used in financing prior to signing the underwriting contract, and it will have worked closely with the originating firm in their preparation.

Underwriting Spread

In the previous example of the $100 million bond issue to be sold at par, or $1,000 per bond, the gross spread is negotiated to be 1% or $1 million. Therefore the proceeds to the corporation are $99 million, or $990 per bond. On a one-point **underwriting spread,** the proceeds might be divided as follows: .125% to the originator or **syndicate manager,** .375% to the entire underwriting syndicate, and .5% to the members of the selling group. Table 15.1 shows the proceeds for each group.

The allocation of the underwriting spread depends upon the relative contribution of each group. Logically, the division is based upon the difficulty in selling and, therefore, the risk inherent in each specific issue.

Stabilization Period

During the period between the offering of the security to the public and the final distribution, the underwriting group typically stabilizes the price. This price support, or **stabilization period**, lasts until the issue is completely sold, or the underwriting group is disbanded if the issue is not completely sold. It is unusual for such stabilization periods to last for more than 30 days. The purchase of the underwritten security is designed to maintain the market price at the offering price so as to forestall a fall in the price that would endanger the success of the entire operation. At the end of the stabilization period, the security may seek its own market level. From a social viewpoint, if the underwriting syndicate cannot engage in what amounts to short-run price fixing, the only alternative is to increase the underwriting spread, and thereby raise the flotation cost to the issuing corporation.

TABLE 15.1
Allocation of the Gross Spread on a $100 Million Bond Issue.

Group	Amount
Originating	$ 125,000
Underwriting	375,000
Selling	500,000
	$1,000,000

Best Efforts Basis

Investment banking firms may on occasion contract with issuing corporations to sell new issues on a **best efforts basis.** Under this arrangement, an investment banker acts as an agent for the issuing corporation, receiving a commission based upon the number of shares actually sold. The investment banking firm does not take title to the securities; that is, it signs no underwriting or purchasing agreement. Because there is less risk involved in such an arrangement, commissions are smaller than they would be if the securities had been underwritten. Because of its established clientele, an investment banking firm can usually distribute securities more effectively than the issuing corporation.

The best efforts basis is used by two types of corporations, the strongest financially and the weakest. The strongest firms' securities are so well established in the financial markets that the firm does not need to pay an underwriting commission. At the other end of the spectrum, the weakest firms can either find no investment banking organization willing to underwrite their issues or find the cost excessive. Therefore the investment bankers in either case are instructed to do the best that they can. In any event, the issuing firm, not the investment banking firm, must take the risk of not being able to attract the funds it desires. In general, agreements on such issues state that if a minimum amount of capital is not raised, all payments by those who have subscribed for the securities will be returned to the prospective purchasers.

Table 15.2 shows the method of distribution of securities for the years 1979–1982 in dollar amounts and numbers of issues. If measured in dollar amounts, underwritten debt issues are clearly the dominant method of distribution. This dominance, however, does not apply to the actual number of issues. A significant number of common stock offerings are issued on the best efforts basis. Debt is more likely to be underwritten than common stock because it is possible to minimize the risk, for instance, by pledging specific assets. This is not possible for common stock; therefore if the firm needs additional equity, the best efforts basis may be the only choice available to it. Supporting this further is the fact that, if a firm attempts to distribute an issue directly, it is most likely to be a common stock issue.

Selling the Issue

Many investment banking firms primarily sell securities, but they also participate in underwriting activities and may on occasion act as originators of new issues. For the most part, however, they obtain their securities to sell by participating in **selling groups.** This is so because their financial resources are limited and their staffs small, restricting their ability to assume the risks of underwriting.

TABLE 15.2
Corporate Securities Issues by Method of Distribution and by Type of Security, 1979–1982 (in millions).

Year	Underwritten				Agency Best Efforts				Direct by Issuer			
	Total	Debt	Preferred	Common	Total	Debt	Preferred	Common	Total	Debt	Preferred	Common
1979	$ 29,859	$ 22,957	$ 1,897	$ 5,007	$ 3,212	$ 990	$50	$ 2,173	$ 2,413	$ 889	$16	$ 1,500
1980	51,446	36,904	3,270	11,272	5,358	1,685	0	3,675	7,779	3,604	14	4,163
1981	47,921	33,581	1,679	12,660	9,537	1,266	4	8,267	6,946	3,307	29	3,609
1982	40,147	23,974	4,978	11,193	12,030	2,793	11	9,229	4,489	2,821	7	1,661
1979–1982	$169,373	$117,416	$11,824	$40,132	$30,137	$6,734	$65	$23,344	$21,627	$10,631	$66	$10,933
Number of Issues												
1979	554	249	50	245	185	27	1	157	149	43	4	102
1980	1,067	448	74	545	353	32	0	321	228	75	5	148
1981	1,261	407	42	812	530	20	1	509	245	56	6	183
1982	911	374	85	452	542	45	3	494	225	39	5	181
1979–1982	3,783	1,478	251	2,504	1,610	124	5	1,481	847	213	20	614

Source: Securities and Exchange Commission, *Monthly Statistical Review* (Washington, D.C.: U.S. Government Printing Office, May 1983), p. 35–36.

The underwriting group usually offers other firms an opportunity to participate in selling the issue. Among the companies contacted are those with well-known distributing abilities. The underwriting syndicate may on occasion sell small issues without help from other dealers, but selling groups usually handle large issues. The selling group agreement covers the terms of public offerings, the dealers' commission (a portion of the spread between the price to the issuer and the offering price), and the provisions for terminating the selling group's existence.

REGULATION OF SECURITIES

When business corporations obtain capital from investors, they must abide by the rules of both state and federal securities markets. All states except Nevada regulate some aspects of securities offerings within their boundaries, and since 1933 the federal government has also regulated interstate transactions, mainly through the SEC.

FEDERAL SECURITIES LAWS

The securities laws are in large part a reaction to the chaotic securities markets of the 1920s, when stocks and bonds were often sold on the basis of unfounded promises of fantastic profits and without disclosure of important information to investors. Many believed that these conditions were major factors contributing to the stock market crash of 1929. In response, Congress passed the Securities Act of 1933 (The Act of 1933) and the Securities Exchange Act of 1934 (The Act of 1934) and established the Securities and Exchange Commission (SEC) to administer those laws. Between 1935 and the present, Congress has passed five additional acts that effectively regulate all aspects of interstate securities transactions. All these acts are revised or amended from time to time. Further, the SEC has the authority to issue interpretations of the acts, as well as rules or regulations that define procedures to be followed by firms and individuals to comply with the provisions of the acts.

Disclosure Principles

The Securities Act of 1933 requires that companies wishing to sell their securities to the public in interstate commerce or by the use of the mails must **register** their securities with the SEC by issuing a **prospectus** (see Exhibit 15.1) and a **registration statement.** The purpose of both documents is to provide full **disclosure** of all material facts concerning the securities to be offered. Full disclosure is the cornerstone of the Act of 1933, as well as of all

Exhibit 15.1

P R O S P E C T U S

2,000,000 Shares

Chemical New York Corporation

Adjustable Rate Cumulative Preferred Stock, Series B

(Stated Value $50 Per Share)

The dividend rate on the Adjustable Rate Cumulative Preferred Stock, Series B (the "Adjustable Rate Preferred Stock") for the initial dividend period ending December 31, 1982 will be 13.36% per annum. Thereafter, dividends will be at the "Applicable Rate" in effect from time to time. The "Applicable Rate" for any quarterly dividend period will be (a) .65 of 1% less than (b) the highest of the "Treasury Bill Rate", the "Ten Year Constant Maturity Rate" and the "Twenty Year Constant Maturity Rate" determined in advance of such dividend period. However, the Applicable Rate for any dividend period will not be less than 7½% per annum nor greater than 15¼% per annum. See "Description of Adjustable Rate Preferred Stock—Adjustable Rate Dividends".

The Adjustable Rate Preferred Stock is redeemable, in whole or in part, at the option of the Company on or after August 15, 1987 and prior to August 15, 1992 at a price of $51.50 per share and thereafter at $50.00 per share plus, in each case, dividends accrued to the redemption date. See "Description of Adjustable Rate Preferred Stock".

Application will be made to list the Adjustable Rate Preferred Stock on the New York Stock Exchange. Listing will be subject to meeting the requirements of the Exchange, including those relating to distribution.

THESE SECURITIES HAVE NOT BEEN APPROVED OR DISAPPROVED BY THE SECURITIES AND EXCHANGE COMMISSION NOR HAS THE COMMISSION PASSED UPON THE ACCURACY OR ADEQUACY OF THIS PROSPECTUS. ANY REPRE-SENTATION TO THE CONTRARY IS A CRIMINAL OFFENSE.

	Price to Public(1)	Underwriting Discounts and Commissions(2)	Proceeds to Company(2)(3)
Per Share	$50.00	$1.20	$48.80
Total	$100,000,000	$1,800,000	$98,200,000

(1) Plus accrued dividends, if any, from date of original issue.
(2) No underwriting discounts or commissions will be payable on 500,000 shares offered hereby which are expected to be sold by the Underwriters to an institutional investor; the per share proceeds to the Company of such sale will thus be $50.00. For additional information regarding this sale, see "Underwriting".
(3) Before deduction of expenses payable by the Company estimated at $220,100.

The shares of Adjustable Rate Preferred Stock are offered by the several Underwriters when, as and if issued by the Company and accepted by the Underwriters and subject to their right to reject orders in whole or in part. It is expected that the certificates representing the shares of the Adjustable Rate Preferred Stock will be ready for delivery on or about August 19, 1982.

The First Boston Corporation

Merrill Lynch White Weld Capital Markets Group
Merrill Lynch, Pierce, Fenner & Smith Incorporated

Goldman, Sachs & Co.

Salomon Brothers Inc

The date of this Prospectus is August 12, 1982.

Exhibit 15.1 *(Cont.)*

IN CONNECTION WITH THIS OFFERING, THE UNDERWRITERS MAY OVER-ALLOT OR EFFECT TRANSACTIONS WHICH STABILIZE OR MAINTAIN THE MARKET PRICES OF THE SECURITIES OFFERED HEREBY AT LEVELS ABOVE THOSE WHICH MIGHT OTHERWISE PREVAIL IN THE OPEN MARKET. SUCH TRANSACTIONS MAY BE EFFECTED ON THE NEW YORK STOCK EXCHANGE, IN THE OVER THE COUNTER MARKET OR OTHERWISE. SUCH STABILIZING, IF COMMENCED, MAY BE DISCONTINUED AT ANY TIME.

AVAILABLE INFORMATION

The Company is subject to the informational requirements of the Securities Exchange Act of 1934 (the "Exchange Act") and in accordance therewith files reports and other information with the Securities and Exchange Commission. Information, as of particular dates, concerning directors and officers, their remuneration, options granted to them, the principal holders of securities of the Company and any material interest of such persons in transactions with the Company, is disclosed in proxy statements distributed to stockholders of the Company and filed with the Commission. Such reports, proxy statements and other information can be inspected and copied at the offices of the Commission, at Room 1024, 450 Fifth Street, N.W., Washington, D. C.; Room 1228, Everett McKinley Dirksen Building, 219 South Dearborn Street, Chicago, Illinois; Room 1100, Federal Building, 26 Federal Plaza, New York, New York; and Suite 1710 Tishman Building, 10960 Wilshire Boulevard, Los Angeles, California. Copies of such material can be obtained from the public reference section of the Commission at 450 Fifth Street, N.W., Washington, D. C. 20549 at prescribed rates. Reports, proxy material and other information concerning the Company also may be inspected at the offices of the New York Stock Exchange. This Prospectus does not contain all information set forth in the Registration Statement and exhibits thereto which the Company has filed with the Commission under the Securities Act of 1933 and to which reference is hereby made.

INCORPORATION OF CERTAIN DOCUMENTS BY REFERENCE

There are incorporated herein by reference the following documents of the Company heretofore filed by it with the Securities and Exchange Commission:

(a) Annual Report on Form 10-K for the year ended December 31, 1981 (which incorporates by reference certain portions of the 1981 Annual Report to Stockholders and the Definitive Proxy Statement for the Annual Meeting of Stockholders held on April 28, 1982), filed pursuant to Section 13 of the Exchange Act.

(b) Quarterly Report on Form 10-Q for the three months ended March 31, 1982, filed pursuant to Section 13 of the Exchange Act.

(c) Quarterly Report on Form 10-Q for the three months ended June 30, 1982, filed pursuant to Section 13 of the Exchange Act.

All reports filed pursuant to Sections 13(a), 13(c), 14 and 15(d) of the Exchange Act subsequent to the date of this Prospectus, in each case filed by the Company prior to the termination of the offering of the shares of Adjustable Rate Preferred Stock offered hereby, are hereby incorporated herein by reference and such documents shall be deemed to be a part hereof from the date of filing of such documents. Any statement contained in a document incorporated or deemed to be incorporated by reference herein shall be deemed to be modified or superseded for purposes of this Prospectus to the extent that a statement contained herein or in any other subsequently filed document which also is or is deemed to be incorporated by reference herein modifies or supersedes such statement. Any statement so modified or superseded shall not be deemed, except as so modified or superseded, to constitute a part of this Prospectus.

The Company will provide without charge to each person to whom this Prospectus is delivered, on the request of any such person, a copy of any or all of the foregoing documents incorporated herein by reference (other than exhibits to such documents). Requests should be directed to:

Chemical New York Corporation
277 Park Avenue
New York, New York 10172
Attention: Office of the Secretary
Telephone: 212—310-6489.

2

subsequent federal securities regulation. Disclosure of information is classified as transactional (providing for the registration statement and prospectus, specified by the Act of 1933) or periodic (specified by the Act of 1934). Periodic disclosure includes, for example, the annual Form 10-K.

In 1981 the SEC proposed an "Integrated Disclosure System" to streamline existing disclosure requirements. The express purpose of the proposed system is to integrate disclosure requirements under the two acts "so that investors and the marketplace are provided meaningful, nonduplicative information, both periodically and when securities distributions are made to the public, while the costs of compliance for public companies are decreased."[†] Under the integrated system, issuers of securities are classified into one of three categories:

1. Companies that are widely followed by professional securities analysts.
2. Companies that have been subject to the periodic reporting system of the Act of 1934 for three or more years but are not widely followed by professional analysts.
3. Companies that have been subject to the periodic reporting system of the Act of 1934 for less than three years, or companies that are offering securities to the public for the first time.

Firms that qualify for the first group are required to make limited disclosure in the prospectus for an offering by virtue of "incorporation by reference" to the firm's filings under the Act of 1934. That is, such a firm simply needs to give information in the prospectus that would allow a prospective shareholder to obtain the firm's periodic disclosures, such as its forms 10-K and 10-Q. Exhibit 15.1 shows this under "Incorporation of Certain Documents by Reference." Firms in the second group can satisfy most of their disclosure obligations by integrating the firm's annual report into the prospectus. Only firms in the last group are required to include "full presentation of disclosure" in the prospectus, without outside references.

Exemption and Private Placement

The Act of 1933 provides for the exemption from registration of certain types of issues. The most important of these are issues that are privately offered and those that are issued by common carriers, which are subject to regulation by the Interstate Commerce Commission. In March 1982, the SEC adopted new **private placement** standards in Rules 504, 505, and 506. Rule 504 offers exemption from registration of offerings of $500,000 or less. The offering may be to an unlimited number of investors, but no general solicitation of the

---

† Securities Act Release No. 33-6331; 34-18007, August 18, 1981, in *Federal Register* 46, No. 159, p. 40902.

public may be made, and resale of the securities is restricted unless they are later registered. Rule 505 allows sales of up to $5 million to 35 or fewer investors, with the same restriction on public solicitation and resale. Rule 506, the so-called safe harbor rule, allows exemption for sales of an unlimited dollar amount to up to 35 investors, so long as the purchasers are sophisticated investors and able to assess the merits and risks of the investment. Under all these exemptions, the issuer remains subject to the antifraud and civil liability provisions of the federal securities laws and must also comply with any state requirements that might be placed on the issue.

Other issues exempt from registration are (1) direct and guaranteed obligations of the United States government or any state, territory, city, or other political subdivision; (2) securities issued by national and state chartered banks; (3) those of nonprofit organizations such as churches; (4) short-term commercial paper; (5) insurance policies and contracts; and (6) receivers' and trustees' certificates such as those used to finance railroad equipment.

Shelf Registration

Another recent alteration of disclosure in practice was the enactment in 1981 of SEC Rule 415, the **shelf registration** rule. Rule 415 allows companies to register all the securities they plan to issue over the following two years and then sell some or all of them whenever they choose. Shelf registration enhances the flexibility of issuers in several critical ways. First, once its registration statement has been filed and cleared, a company can make offerings instantaneously, without taking time for the registration process. When interest rates are volatile, this can be very valuable in keeping interest costs down on bond issues; when stock prices are volatile, the practice allows issuers to receive higher prices for their stock offerings. Second, a company no longer has to settle on an underwriter for its securities before it registers an offering. Rather, it simply lists the investment bankers and brokers whom it would be willing to accept. The investment bankers and brokers then make competing offers for the securities. This competition is expected to sharply reduce underwriters' fees and discounts—the underwriter's spread.

Shelf registration has the potential to radically reshape the new-issue market and the relationship between firms issuing securities and underwriting firms. Under Rule 415, companies may sell securities directly to investors without using underwriters at all. Investment bankers, who in the past received as much as 3% of the total proceeds of an offering, may find that many offerings are sold without their participation.

Due Diligence

The Securities Act of 1933 makes the sponsors of registered securities accountable for misrepresentations, omissions, and untrue statements of material facts. Persons who may be held accountable include directors, officers, and partners of the issuer, underwriters, brokers, accountants, engineers, appraisers, lawyers, and others who act as experts, and any other professional persons who have been named in the preparation or certification of any part of the registration statement. It should be noted that, while the SEC either permits or refuses to permit registration to become effective, it does not pass on the merits of the securities, and any representation to the contrary by an issuer or seller is a criminal offense. All the accountable persons must exercise **due diligence** in making sure that all required information in the registration statement and prospectus is disclosed and *factual*. Civil or criminal liabilities are prescribed, therefore, for sins of omission as well as for fraud or misrepresentation.

REGULATION OF OUTSTANDING SECURITIES ISSUES

The common perception of the stock market is not of a group that issues new securities, but rather of a place where stock is traded by individual investors on organized exchanges such as the New York Stock Exchange or the over-the-counter (OTC) market. Since 1934, securities exchanges whose business is predominantly interstate have been under the regulation of the SEC through the Securities Exchange Act of 1934.

The purpose of the Act of 1934 is to ensure fairness and honesty in securities transactions on the organized exchanges and in the OTC market. The act forbids trading in a security unless it is registered under the provisions of the Act of 1933. In order for a registered security to be traded on an exchange, it must first be accepted for **listing** by the exchange. An application for listing is usually refused if anticipated trading in the issue is small. To be accepted for listing on the New York Stock Exchange, a company is expected to have the following: annual earnings of at least $2.5 million before income taxes, pretax earnings averaging $2 million for the preceding two years, and an aggregate market value of publicly held shares equal to $16 million; at least 2,000 common stockholders who hold 1 million shares exclusive of centralized or family holdings; and the existence of a broad national interest in the security so that adequate liquidity can be expected. Standards on other exchanges are less stringent; therefore firms often first list their stock on the Pacific Exchange or the American Stock Exchange, for example, and then later list on the New York Stock Exchange. Frequently, a company will continue to maintain its listing on the smaller exchange; in this case, the stock is said to have *dual listing*.

There are several perceived advantages to listing. First, it is believed that there is some advertising value in listing. That is, the stock and thereby the firm itself, is more widely known and therefore more readily accepted by the investing public. Second, listed stocks tend to have broad distribution, which prevents excessive concentration of ownership. Finally, listing makes it easier to sell new issues of stock and to trade at better prices, which saves financing costs.

Securities may be *delisted* either on the request of the securities exchange, the corporation issuing the securities, or the SEC. The chief reason for delisting is a decline in trading volume, because of either a decrease in the number of securities outstanding due to retirement or redemption, or concentration of ownership due to merger.

Much of the direct regulation of the securities markets has been left to the industry, which operates under its own rules that interpret and expand those of the SEC. The managers of the exchanges police their own organizations, and the National Association of Securities Dealers (NASD) oversees both the members of the exchanges and those brokers and dealers engaged in the OTC market. Penalties for violating rules of conduct or ethics may include revocation of exchange membership or expulsion from the NASD, which would effectively put a broker or dealer out of business.

State Securities Laws

The right of states to regulate securities transactions occurring within their borders was specifically reserved in the federal securities laws. State securities laws are commonly referred to as **Blue Sky laws.** These laws generally provide for the regulation and registration of securities and securities transactions in the state, and for the regulation of brokers, dealers, investment advisors, and agents. The substance of the Blue Sky laws varies from state to state, but more than 35 states have adopted the Uniform Securities Act or a variation of it. Many of the provisions of the federal regulations are incorporated in the Uniform Act. Specifically, it provides for *registration by coordination*, which permits state registration to become effective if and when federal registration is allowed. If a security will be sold only within the state, and no SEC registration is undertaken, then registration with the state is made by *qualification*.

The Uniform Act relies on the doctrine of disclosure, as does the SEC; however, some states rely on the "fair and equitable" doctrine and can deny registration on the basis of the state's opinion of the merits of the offering. As exemplified by the wide acceptance of the Uniform Act, the trend in regulatory philosophy appears to be in the direction of disclosure. In any securities offering, or in the regulation of brokers or dealers, the Blue Sky laws of a state are senior to the federal regulations; in order to conduct business in a state, the firm must obey all state laws. Therefore, it would not be unusual for a security to be sold in Colorado and in Arizona, for example, but not in California, because the issuer was either unable or unwilling to conform to California's particular regulations.

SUMMARY

This chapter has considered the long-term financing decision from two perspectives. Capital structure policy prescribes guidelines on the appropriate mix of debt and equity for a firm to use as a target over time. However, financing decisions are not made over time; they are made at particular times. Tactical decisions of this nature involve multiple considerations that must be weighed simultaneously.

The desirability of debt or equity at a specific time depends on the legal characteristics of the securities: the right to a return of invested capital, claims on assets and income, and voting rights. The different attributes of debt or equity financing must be considered in terms of the securities' suitability for the financing need. There are limits on the amount of debt a firm can use. To maintain flexibility, a firm must operate below that limit. The salability of the two forms of capital varies with prevailing economic conditions. Forecasting the firm's needs and the probable economic environment at the time of these needs is one of the most troublesome aspects of the financing problem. These forecasts are the key to timing, which is central in handling the firm's recurring financing decisions.

Management's deliberations may lead to a decision to sell either stocks or bonds in the capital markets. This means of financing will require the issuing corporation to use the services of an investment banker.

Investment bankers are intermediaries between issuers and investors; in this capacity, they are advisors of both. While some investment bankers are primarily underwriters, others primarily retailers, and still others participants in originating, underwriting syndicates, and selling groups, there is considerable overlap in their operations. Investment bankers customarily assist in financing business firms by advising the corporation on its financing problems and helping to solve them. The investment banking firm may purchase an issue from the corporation through negotiation or competitive bidding, make a standby commitment that involves purchasing any part of an issue not sold by the issuers, or agree to use its best efforts to sell a new issue of securities. Certain classes of securities require competitive bidding, and other firms may use this method when the quality of securities is high enough to warrant this method of selling. In some cases, corporations place entire issues privately, thereby bypassing the investment banker and avoiding the expense and delay that are inevitable when registering the issue with the SEC.

Underwriting and distributing corporate securities calls for cooperation among investment bankers and usually entails three distinct agreements: one between the issuer and members of the underwriting syndicate, a second among the members of the underwriting syndicate, and a third between the purchasing or underwriting syndicate and the selling firms.

Most new corporate issues are subject to registration by state or federal agencies. The Securities Act of 1933, as amended, requires full, fair, and accurate disclosure of the character of securities offered publicly for sale in interstate commerce or through the mail. According to this act, a registration statement and a prospectus must be filed with the SEC. The Commission either permits or refuses to permit the registration to become effective, but it does not pass on the quality of the securities. The Securities Act of 1933 allows for the exemption of certain transactions, including those privately placed and certain issues such as those of railroads and state and local governments.

After the primary distribution of a security issue, the securities may be traded on one of the secondary markets—securities exchanges or OTC markets. Of the national exchanges, the New York Stock Exchange is the most important. Listing the securities of a corporation on a stock exchange necessitates registering the issue, meeting the standards set by the exchange, and fulfilling the requirements of the SEC.

In 1981, the SEC proposed regulations to streamline disclosure requirements by integrating disclosure requirements under the 1933 and 1934 acts so that investors are provided meaningful, nonduplicative information periodically and when securities are offered to the public. Another important alteration in disclosure requirements allows shelf registration, which permits a corporation to register all the securities it plans to issue over the following two years and then sell some or all of them as necessary. Shelf registration gives issuers added flexibility.

QUESTIONS AND REVIEW ACTIVITIES

1. Distinguish between the capital structure issue and the long-term financing problem.
2. Review each of the decision criteria for long-term financing decisions discussed in the chapter. For each of these considerations, describe a method of analysis.
3. Would inflation benefit a firm with a high debt/total capitalization ratio more than a firm in the same industry with a lower ratio? Explain.
4. Considering the current economic climate, what type of financing do you consider appropriate? Consult the financial press to see if your answer is consistent with what is going on in the market.
5. Explain the following statement: "The machinery for distribution of new securities is complex, but it is fundamentally only merchandising on a broad scale."
6. Classify investment bankers by their functions. Explain.
7. Why must the investment banker consider the wishes of investors?
8. Identify (a) underwriting, (b) standby underwriting, and (c) best efforts commitment.
9. In what ways does a corporation benefit from the sale of its securities by competitive bidding?
10. When a large corporate issue of bonds is handled, what three types of contracts or agreements are involved? Why?
11. Why is the size of the issue an important determinant of the spread of the underwriting group?
12. Do you believe that nonregulated corporations should be required to sell their securities by competitive bidding, as is currently required of some regulated firms? Why or why not?
13. Investment bankers price *new* securities relative to outstanding securities. Why does a spread exist between the yields of new and outstanding securities?
14. Do you believe that investors are benefited by the price-support practices of underwriting syndicates? Explain.

PROBLEMS

1. Two small shoe manufacturers, Fast Service Shoe Co. and Comfort-Last, generate identical operating earnings of $100,000 a year. Both companies have been offered to you as potential investments. Fast Service has $300,000 of 8% debt outstanding. The owners offer to sell the company for $550,000 if the buyer assumes the liabilities. This would give almost a 14% rate of return. The owners of Comfort-Last offer to sell their operation, debt free, for $800,000. Even though the return would be only 12.5%, the owners are certain that they are offering a better deal. Assuming that up to $300,000 could be borrowed at 8% and ignoring taxes, evaluate the two alternatives.

	Fast	Last
Operating earnings	$100,000	$100,000
Interest expense	24,000	0
Net income	76,000	100,000
Offering price	$550,000	$800,000
Return on investment	13.8%	12.5%

2. The Equity Corp. has a capital structure composed entirely of equity (200,000 shares of common stock). The firm desires to raise additional capital of $3 million. The controller is considering three alternatives:

a) An unsecured bond issue paying 12%.

b) A preferred stock issue paying 10%.

c) The sale of 100,000 shares of additional common stock.

Future earnings before interest and taxes have been estimated at $1 million. Determine the net effect of the proposed alternatives. (Assume a 40% tax rate.)

3. The XYZ Corp. has the following capital structure:

Debt issues (6%)	$200,000
Preferred stock (5%)	100,000
Common stock equity (30,000 shares)	300,000
	$600,000

The planning department projects earnings before interest and taxes of $80,000 for the next three years. (Assume a 40% tax rate.) Should the corporation raise $100,000 of additional capital through the sale of 10,000 shares of common stock or through the use of a 10% bond issue?

4. The Superior Corp. has a capital structure composed entirely of equity (100,000 shares of common stock totaling $3 million). The financial manager is determining which of the following three methods would be most advantageous (from the

stockholders' viewpoint) for raising an additional $2 million:

a) Debentures paying 12%.

b) Preferred stock paying 14%.

c) The sale of 50,000 share of common stock.

The forecast of earnings before interest and taxes for the next year is $600,000. Assuming a 40% tax rate, find the EPS for each alternative.

5. The comptroller of J. W., Inc., recently pulled off a major coup. The company recently issued $400 million of 30-year bonds with an effective yield of 12%. Less than two months ago, it withdrew the issue when the rate climbed to 12.75%. By waiting less than 60 days, the comptroller saved considerable interest expense.

a) What is the annual difference in interest expense?

b) If you assume that the firm is in a 40% tax bracket and discount the interest savings at 12%, what is the present value of the savings?

6. Plasto Enviro Products, Inc. (PEP), is considering how to finance a major plant expansion of $200 million. The two alternatives being considered are (a) issuing $200 million in mortgage bonds secured by the new plant, with an anticipated interest cost of 9%, or (b) selling 4 million additional shares of common stock at $50 each. The firm's current balance sheet and income statement are shown in Tables 15.3 and 15.4.

TABLE 15.3
PEP, Inc.: Balance Sheet of December 31, 1983 (in millions).

Cash	$ 150	Current liabilities		$ 400
Accounts receivable	570	Long-term debt		500
Inventories	560	Stock		
Total current assets	1,280	(20-million shares)	$500	
Net plant and equipment	720	Retained earnings	600	
		Net worth		1,100
Total assets	$2,000	Total claims		$2,000

TABLE 15.4
PEP, Inc.: Income Statement for the Period Ending December 31, 1983 (in millions).

Net sales	$5,500
Fixed cost	1,650
Variable costs (65%)	3,575
Operating income	275
Less: Interest	35
Income before taxes	240
Less: Taxes (40%)	96
Net income	$ 144
Earnings per share	$ 7.20

TABLE 15.5
PEP, Inc.: *Pro Forma* Operating Income Statement for the Period Ending December 31, 1984 (in millions).

Net sales	$5,660
Fixed costs	1,680
Variable costs (65%)	3,679
Operating income	$ 301

By undertaking the expansion, the company can increase sales by $160 million. Variable costs will remain at 65%, and fixed costs will rise by $30 million. As indicated in Table 15.5, operating earnings will increase by $26 million. In addition, the company has made plans to enter a new market area that it believes has good potential.

a) Discuss the suitability of the two financing alternatives.

b) A major shareholder group currently owns 40% of the outstanding common stock and believes that it needs to maintain 33% ownership for control.

   i) If these shareholders wished to maintain 40% ownership, how much of the new issue would they be forced to buy?

   ii) What must they spend to maintain control if 33% percent ownership is sufficient?

c) To assess riskiness, calculate

   i) DOL, DFL, and DTL for current operations.

   ii) The same measures for both financing alternatives if the project is undertaken and the forecasted sales level is achieved.

   iii) Times-interest-earned figures for current operations (the industry average is six times).

   iv) Times-interest-earned figures for both alternatives if the expansion is undertaken.

d) In this industry, the average debt-to-total assets ratio is 47%. Using *pro forma* balance sheets and ratios, evaluate the financing alternatives with regard to their effect on the firm's flexibility.

e) PEP, Inc., manufactures environmental protection devices and is attempting to develop biodegradable plastic containers. Currently, the economic environment is best described as being at "mid-cycle." Interest rates, although far from being a bargain, are much lower than they were in the recent past. Although there have been favorable announcements by numerous government sources regarding the economic indicators, the stock market and the sale of new issues have been somewhat sluggish. PEP believes that its shares might be received somewhat more enthusiastically because of a future potential for environmental products derived from the current concern about environmental issues. Discuss the implications for the timing of the two alternatives.

7. The Allied Manufacturing Co. is issuing 200,000 new shares of its common stock through an underwriter. The stock will be sold at $45 per share to the existing

stockholders. When 180,000 shares have been sold, what would the company receive had the issue been underwritten on a standby basis? What would the company receive had the stock been issued with no underwriting agreement? (Ignore commissions and fees.)

8. Selected data for a pending bond issue are as follows: The issue is for $5 million with a 10-year maturity. The investment banker states that the bonds can be sold publicly with a 9% coupon and a $120,000 gross spread, the company to net $4.88 million. Alternatively, the company can place a 9.5% note privately, with a $20,000 investment banking advisory fee. If the firm does not repay either loan arrangement before maturity, it will make annual interest payments, and it has an after-tax cost of capital of 10% (assume a 40% tax rate). Which form of financing should the firm choose? Why?

9. The Tri-State Utility Co. is issuing $50 million of 12%, 10-year bonds. The bid of the investment firm of Market Timer of $985 was accepted.

a) Compute the proceeds to Tri-State.

b) Compute the approximate effective cost to Tri-State for a $1,000 bond.

c) What is the gross profit to the investment firm if the bonds are sold to the public to yield 12%?

ADDITIONAL READINGS

Block, E. "Pricing a Corporate Bond Issue: A Look Behind the Scenes," in *Essays on Money and Credit.* New York: Federal Reserve Bank of New York, 1964, pp. 72–76.

Cates, D. C. "Bank Capital Management: Investment Banker Selection," *The Bankers Magazine* (Winter 1974), pp. 11–12.

Dyl, E. A., and M. D. Joehnk. "Competitive versus Negotiated Underwriting of Public Utility Debt," *Bell Journal of Economics* (Autumn 1976), pp. 680–89.

Ederington, L. H. "Negotiated versus Competitive Underwritings of Corporate Bonds," *Journal of Finance* (March 1976), pp. 17–28.

Hayes, S. L., III. "The Transformation of Investment Banking," *Harvard Business Review* (January–February 1979), pp. 153–70.

Miller, G. R. "Long-Term Business Financing from the Underwriter's Point of View," *Journal of Finance* (May 1961), pp. 280–90.

Scott, D. F., Jr., and D. L. Johnson. "Financing Policies and Practices in Large Corporations," *Financial Management* (Summer 1982), pp. 51–59.

Sorensen, E. "On the Seasoning Process of New Bonds: Some Are More Seasoned Than Others," *Journal of Financial and Quantitative Analysis* (June 1982), pp. 195–208.

———. "The Impact of Underwriting Method and Bidder Competition upon Corporate Bond Interest Cost," *Journal of Finance* (September 1979), pp. 863–69.

Sorensen, E., and J. Wert. "Estimating New Issue Bond Yields: A New Tool," *Journal of Portfolio Management* (Spring 1981), pp. 42–45.

Wyndham, R. "The Underwriters Have to Offer Even More," *Fortune* (January 1973), pp. 116ff.

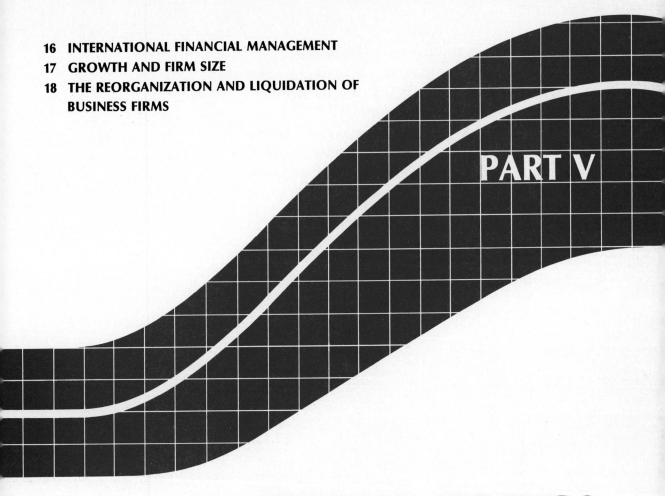

PART V

SPECIAL TOPICS

RISKS IN INTERNATIONAL TRADE
TYPES OF INTERNATIONAL OPERATIONS
THE FOREIGN TRADE TRANSACTION
EXCHANGE OF CURRENCY
THE INTERNATIONAL MONETARY SYSTEM
EXCHANGE RATE RISK FOR MULTINATIONAL COMPANIES
OBTAINING FUNDS FOR FOREIGN INVESTMENTS

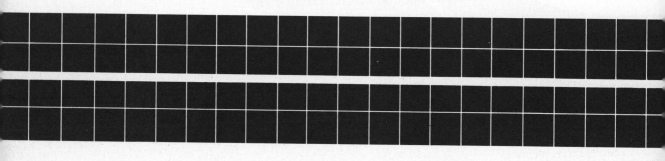

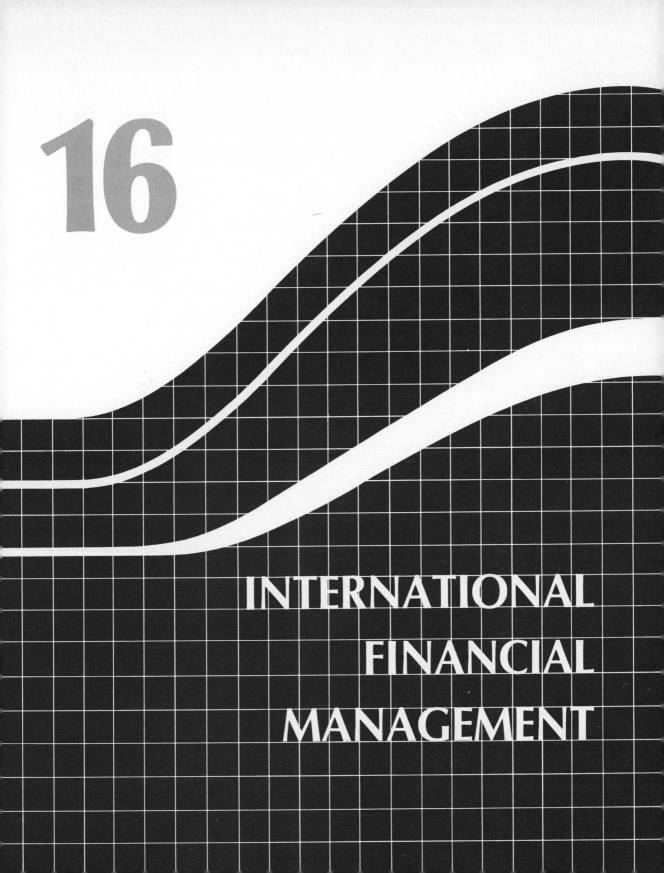

16

INTERNATIONAL FINANCIAL MANAGEMENT

The volume of international trade has increased dramatically during the past two decades, as Fig. 16.1 shows. U.S. businesses of all sizes routinely buy or sell products abroad, and many large corporations own production facilities in foreign countries. Companies operating in more than one country are called **multinational corporations.**

As businesses expand internationally, they become increasingly complex and expose themselves to greater risk in financial transactions. Because international trade requires exchange of currencies to buy or sell foreign products, a major part of this chapter discusses exchange rates between currencies, the spot and forward markets for foreign exchange, and the international monetary system.

Careful study of this chapter should enable you to

1. Describe four common types of international business operations.
2. Define and list the documents required for a typical international transaction.
3. Understand what is meant by translation of currency and the spot and forward markets for foreign exchange.
4. Be familiar with factors affecting exchange rates between currencies.

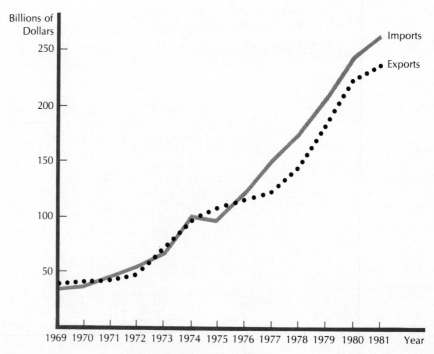

Figure 16.1 U.S. exports and imports, 1969–1981.

5. Differentiate between fixed and floating exchange rate systems.

6. Understand what is meant by an exposed foreign currency position and the procedures used to hedge an exposed position.

7. Be familiar with sources of funds for international investments.

RISKS IN INTERNATIONAL TRADE

International transactions are exposed to exchange rate risk, collection risk, and political risk not present in domestic transactions. All these risks are in addition to the standard business risks companies face.

Exchange Rate Risk

The **exchange rate** is the price of one currency in terms of another. For a U.S. business, **exchange rate risk** refers to uncertainty regarding the number of dollars involved in a foreign transaction when future cash flows are denominated in a foreign currency. Exchange rates for currencies of major industrialized nations change continuously in response to supply and demand forces. Many smaller countries fix the exchange rate for their currency in terms of dollars and change the rate periodically in response to international monetary conditions. Consequently, the revenue received from or the cost of a foreign transaction is uncertain until the foreign currency is exchanged for dollars. A significant portion of the international financial manager's time is spent hedging exchange rate risk.

Collection Risk

Collection risk refers to uncertainty about collection of payment for goods sold on credit. Collection risk increases with foreign transactions because international trade laws are less consistent than domestic laws, and they may be more difficult to enforce. Collection risk is greatest when the transaction is on an open account credit basis, but it exists to some degree in any sale if cash is not received before shipment is made. Numerous legal documents exist to reduce collection risk, support international currency exchange, and facilitate legal action when necessary.

Political Risk

Political risks exist because there is always the danger that governmental actions may impede the foreign business transaction. Restrictions may take the form of import or export licenses and quotas; limitations on transfer or repatriation of currencies; confiscation of property; or war, rebellion, or insurrection. Instability in government caused by internal strife is the source of severe political risk, but problems can arise even in countries with stable political climates. For example, in 1982 France became dissatisfied with Japanese trade policy. To make its opinion evident, France required all imported Japanese videotape recorders, a very popular item, to pass through a small, remote customs house staffed only two hours a day. Thousands of Japanese recorders quickly accumulated, awaiting customs inspection and delaying sales.

TYPES OF INTERNATIONAL OPERATIONS

Most businesses engaging in foreign sales do so only after establishing their reputation as successful domestic firms. A company considers exporting as a way to expand sales and increase profits, not as an escape from failure to meet domestic competition. International operations may be carried on through one of four basic forms of organization—direct exporting or importing, licensing, joint venture, or a wholly owned subsidiary. The various forms that foreign trade may take require different levels of expertise in international finance.

Direct Exporting or Importing

For most firms, establishing direct foreign trade is the first step in entering the international marketplace. Direct sales to importers in foreign countries may be profitable because of the company's cost or quality advantages, or when a company is in a monopolistic position because of supply or technological dominance. The investment needed to begin exporting or importing is low, requiring at most employment of company representatives who call on foreign customers. Some expertise in international shipping and currency flows will also be needed to facilitate the sales efforts. The disadvantages of direct foreign trade are that (1) it is highly competitive, and pricing is a major factor in sales, and (2) long-term sales relationships can be difficult to maintain.

Licensing

A **licensing** arrangement allows a foreign company to manufacture the domestic firm's product in its own country. Licensing may be attractive in the presence of significant domestic or foreign restrictions on foreign investment. In addition, the domestic firm needs to make only a minimal investment, and it may earn substantial income from royalty fees. Because all production and sales are carried out by the foreign firm in its own country, the possibility of cultural conflicts can be minimized. Problems with licensing include loss of direct quality control, possible difficulty in the manufacturing process if the technology is advanced, and the creation of a potential future competitor.

Joint Venture

Many countries require a certain proportion of local ownership in any investment by a foreign firm. One method of meeting this requirement is by forming a **joint venture** with a local company. Under a joint venture arrangement, both the foreign and domestic firms contribute equity capital and earn a pro rata share of the profits. A joint venture also may be used to obtain an established local partner who knows the culture and customs of the foreign country. The disadvantages of joint ventures include potential conflicts of objectives between the domestic and foreign partners and the danger of losing control entirely if the foreign firm maintains a majority interest.

Wholly Owned Subsidiary

The most complex form of foreign investment involves establishment of a **wholly owned foreign subsidiary** that is responsible for the production and sale of the firm's products. The advantages of a wholly owned subsidiary include complete management control, greater ability to produce technically advanced products, avoidance of import restrictions, and certain tax benefits. The disadvantages include difficulty in establishing a relationship with the local business community and government, danger of expropriation of assets, and restrictions on repatriation of profits to the domestic firm.

THE FOREIGN TRADE TRANSACTION

A foreign sale by a direct exporter is the simplest example of a foreign trade transaction. The HTW Corp. of Tucson develops and produces computer software for personal computers. Assume that in December 1982 it agrees to supply a financial planning program to Sinclair Ltd., a British computer manufacturer. The contract calls for air shipment on January 8, 1983, of 5,000 floppy disks containing the programs and 5,000 instruction manuals from Tucson to Gatwick Airport south of London. Sinclair Ltd. has agreed to pay £14 (English pounds) per disk 60 days after receipt of the goods. The total contract value is £70,000 plus air freight charges and insurance. On December 10, £1 was worth $1.65. HTW will earn a normal profit on the transaction if it receives at least $111,000. The standard documents required to complete the transaction include a commercial letter of credit, a bill of lading, and a bill of exchange.

Letter of Credit

Once HTW and Sinclair have agreed to the terms of the sale, Sinclair normally will apply for a commercial *letter of credit*, from its bank, Barclays of London (see Fig. 16.2). A letter of credit is a document issued by a bank in which the

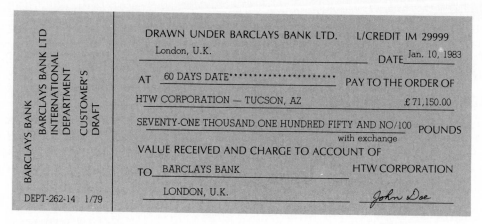

Figure 16.2 Time draft.

bank agrees to extend credit to the buying firm for the purpose specified in the letter. The letter of credit from Barclays will define the goods, the terms of sale, and the documentation required. The letter of credit may be *irrevocable*, meaning that Barclays guarantees payment if all terms in the letter are met, or *revocable*, which allows the issuing bank and the buyer to withdraw from the agreement before the documents of the sale are presented to HTW's bank. Sinclair Ltd. will pay a fee to Barclays for preparation of the letter of credit.

Barclays, the issuing bank, will then forward the letter of credit to a U.S. correspondent bank, such as Citicorp in New York, which forwards it to HTW's Tucson bank, Valley National Bank. Valley National, the advising bank, forwards the letter of credit to HTW. If Valley National adds its obligation to pay, the document becomes a *confirmed*, irrevocable letter of credit, and Valley National becomes the confirming bank.

Bill of Lading

Upon receipt of the confirmed, irrevocable letter of credit, HTW will ship the goods to London. A **bill of lading** will be signed by the transportation company in Tucson and given to HTW as a receipt for the shipment. It specifies the party (consignee) to whom the goods will be delivered. The bill of lading controls the right to the goods. HTW will attach it to the letter of credit and send all documentation to Barclays Bank. The bill of lading will be used to claim the goods on their arrival. If goods are shipped FOB (free on board) the importer, Sinclair Ltd., will pay all transportation costs and receive title to the goods at the point of export. However, HTW probably will pay the transportation charges and ship the goods CIF (cost, insurance, and freight), in which case it retains title until the goods are claimed by Sinclair in London. If the bill of lading is made out "to order," it is negotiable and can be used by the bearer to claim the goods. A "straight" bill of lading is nonnegotiable and specifies that the goods can be delivered only to the person (consignee) named on the document.

Bill of Exchange

A **bill of exchange** is a document ordering the party to whom it is addressed to pay a specified sum "to the order of" or "to the bearer." A personal check that you write is a bill of exchange requesting your bank to pay a certain number of dollars to the order of the payee. Sight or time drafts used in international trade transactions also are bills of exchange. Using the letter of credit as authority, HTW will create a time draft (bill of exchange) "under the letter of credit No. IM29999" drawn against Barclays Bank for £70,000 plus £1,150 for shipping and insurance.

HTW will forward the time draft, the bill of lading, and other required instruments to Valley National Bank, which sends the documentation to the issuing bank in London. Barclays will notify Sinclair Ltd. when the documents arrive and Sinclair will accept the documents, thereby taking title to the goods and assuming an obligation to pay Barclays in 60 days. The flow of goods and documents is depicted in Fig. 16.3.

At the same time, Barclays will verify that the documents conform to its letter of credit and write "accepted" on the time draft, which then becomes a bankers' acceptance. By agreeing to use a time draft, HTW is providing short-term credit to Sinclair to allow the purchase of its product (see Chapter 10). HTW may request Barclays to send the bankers' acceptance back to them, in which case the acceptance may be held by HTW for 60 days and then presented to Barclays for payment of £71,150. In most cases, HTW will instruct Barclays to discount the bankers' acceptance and forward the proceeds. If the discount rate is 12%, the proceeds to HTW will be £69,727 [£71,150 − (71,150 × .12 × 60 days/360 days)]. More than likely, Barclays will sell the acceptance in the money market. Sixty days later, the holder of the acceptance will present it to Barclays for payment, and Sinclair will pay Barclays £71,150.

Use of a bankers' acceptance benefits the buyer, the seller, and the issuing bank. Sinclair receives financing for its receivables, HTW immediately obtains cash from the sale of the bankers acceptance, and Barclays earns a fee for its services.

HTW has minimized its collection risk by requiring a bank's confirmed, irrevocable letter of credit from Sinclair. Only by requiring payment before shipment could HTW have eliminated the collection risk. Exchange risk, though, still exists because the contract is denominated in pounds.

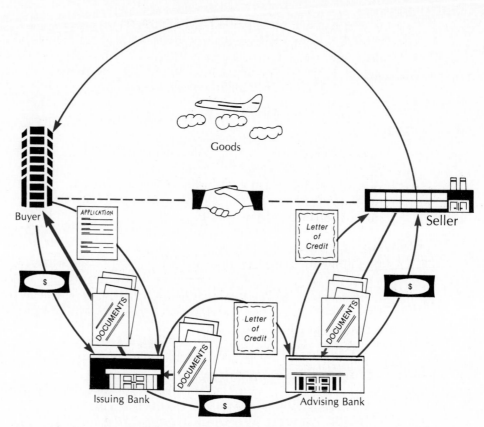

Figure 16.3 Documents required in an international transaction.

EXCHANGE OF CURRENCY

Foreign exchange refers to the currency of another country, and the exchange rate, as mentioned previously, is the cost of one currency in terms of another. Figure 16.4 presents the Foreign Exchange table from the *Wall Street Journal* for selected currencies. Column 1 lists the number of dollars required to purchase one unit of the foreign currency (FC; direct quotation), and column 2 shows the amount of foreign currency that can be purchased for one U.S. dollar (indirect quotation). The indirect quotation is the reciprocal of the direct quotation (i.e., \$/FC = 1 ÷ FC/\$).

On January 10, 1983, one British pound was worth \$1.5902 (column 1), or stated differently, one dollar would buy £.6289 (column 2.) Prices quoted in Fig. 16.4 reflect actual rates for transactions between banks in amounts of \$1 million or more. Individuals buying smaller amounts of foreign exchange will pay more than the quoted rate, as the table notes.

Two types of exchange rates are given in Fig. 16.4: the spot market rate, which is shown for all currencies, and the forward market of 30, 90, and 180 days given for currencies of major U.S. trading partners. Belgium is the only major trading country that maintains two different exchange rates. The commercial rate applies to currency for the sale or purchase of goods, and the financial rate is used for currency to be invested in financial assets.

Spot Market

The **spot market** is not a physical location. It refers to a currency transaction for immediate exchange. Assuming that HTW requested Barclays to discount the acceptance and send payment, Barclays would exchange pounds for dollars

Foreign Exchange

Monday, January 10, 1983

The New York foreign exchange selling rates below apply to trading among banks in amounts of $1 million and more, as quoted at 3 p.m. Eastern time by Bankers Trust Co.   Retail transactions provide fewer units of foreign currency per dollar.

Country	U.S. $ equiv. Monday	U.S. $ equiv. Friday	Currency per U.S. $ Monday	Currency per U.S. $ Friday
Argentina (Peso) ..	.000021	.000021	46465	46465
Australia (Dollar)	.9901	.9887	1.0100	1.0114
Austria (Schilling)	.06105	.06085	16.3800	16.4350
Belgium (Franc)				
Commercial rate	.02181	.02171	45.86	46.07
Financial rate	.02078	.02077	48.13	48.15
Brazil (Cruzeiro)	.004029	.004029	248.20	248.20
Britain (Pound) 1.5902		1.6085	.6289	.6217
30-Day Forward 1.5881		1.6065	.6297	.6225
90-Day Forward 1.5833		1.6020	.6316	.6242
180-Day Forward 1.5777		1.5975	.6338	.6260
Canada (Dollar)	.8166	.8158	1.2246	1.2258
30-Day Forward	.8157	.8165	1.2259	1.2247
90-Day Forward	.8146	.8175	1.2276	1.2232
180-Day Forward	.8129	.8191	1.2301	1.2208
Chile (Official-Rate)	.01333	.01333	75.00	75.00
China (Yuan)	.5277	.5277	1.8950	1.8950
Colombia (Peso)	.01434	.01434	69.73	69.73
Denmark (Krone)	.1215	.1205	8.2300	8.2980
Ecuador (Sucre)	.03017	.03017	33.15	33.15
Finland (Markka)	.1909	.1900	5.2390	5.2620
France (Franc)	.1514	.1509	6.6040	6.6250
30-Day Forward	.1498	.1495	6.6765	6.6900
90-Day Forward	.1468	.1465	6.8140	6.8250
180-Day Forward	.1434	.1432	6.9740	6.9850
Greece (Drachma)	.01200	.01389	83.35	72.00
Hong Kong (Dollar) ...	.1538	.1538	6.5000	6.5000
India (Rupee)	.1031	.1030	9.70	9.71
Indonesia (Rupiah)	.001456	.001456	687.00	687.00
Ireland (Punt) 1.4235		1.4205	.7025	.7040
Israel (Shekel)	.03028	.03028	33.03	33.03
Italy (Lira)	.0007449	.0007407	1342.50	1350.00
Japan (Yen)	.004414	.004364	226.55	229.15
30-Day Forward	.004425	.004375	226.00	228.57
90-Day Forward	.004442	.004392	225.13	227.67
180-Day Forward	.004470	.004420	223.73	226.25

Country	U.S. $ equiv. Monday	U.S. $ equiv. Friday	Currency per U.S. $ Monday	Currency per U.S. $ Friday
Lebanon (Pound)	.2566	.2566	3.8975	3.8975
Malaysia (Ringgit)	.4209	.4370	2.3760	2.2885
Mexico (Peso)	z	z	z	z
Netherlands (Guilder) .	.3886	.3880	2.5735	2.5770
New Zealand (Dollar) .	.7365	.7345	1.3578	1.3615
Norway (Krone)	.1441	.1431	6.9415	6.9905
Pakistan (Rupee)	.07711	.07711	12.9678	12.9678
Peru (Sol)	.001149	.001149	870.05	870.05
Philippines (Peso)	.1100	.1100	9.089	9.089
Portugal (Escudo)	.01105	.01099	90.50	91.00
Saudi Arabia (Riyal) .	.2908	.2908	3.4390	3.4385
Singapore (Dollar)	.4840	.4804	2.0660	2.0815
South Africa (Rand) ..	.9392	.9370	1.0647	1.0672
South Korea (Won)	.001342	.001342	745.20	745.20
Spain (Peseta)	.008045	.008006	124.30	124.90
Sweden (Krona)	.1387	.1381	7.2100	7.2430
Switzerland (Franc)	.5216	.5171	1.9170	1.9340
30-Day Forward	.5249	.5202	1.9050	1.9225
90-Day Forward	.5295	.5248	1.8885	1.9055
180-Day Forward	.5366	.5321	1.8635	1.8795
Taiwan (Dollar)	.02464	.02464	40.58	40.58
Thailand (Baht)	.04348	.04348	23.00	23.0
Uruguay (New Peso)				
Financial	z	z	z	z
Venezuela (Bolivar) ...	.2329	.2329	4.2930	4.2930
W. Germany (Mark) ..	.4290	.4283	2.3310	2.3350
30-Day Forward	.4303	.4296	2.3240	2.3280
90-Day Forward	.4326	.4320	2.3115	2.3150
180-Day Forward	.4363	.4354	2.2920	2.2967

SDR .... 1.11281   1.10873   .898625   .901933

Special Drawing Rights are based on exchange rates for the U.S., West German, British, French and Japanese currencies. Source: International Monetary Fund.

z-Not quoted.

Figure 16.4 Foreign exchange rates.

and remit \$110,880 to HTW. The value of the £69,727 check in U.S. dollars can be calculated using either (16.1) or 16.2) with the spot rates given in Fig. 16.4:

$$\text{U.S. dollars} = \text{foreign currency} \times \text{dollars/foreign currency}$$
$$= £69{,}727 \times 1.5902 \text{ dollars per pound} \tag{16.1}$$
$$= \$110{,}880$$

or

$$\text{U.S. dollars} = \frac{\text{foreign currency}}{\text{foreign currency per dollar}}$$
$$= \frac{£69{,}727}{£.6289 \text{ per dollar}} \tag{16.2}$$
$$= \$110{,}871.$$

(The difference between the two calculations is due to rounding.)

Forward Market

The **forward market** in foreign currencies refers to the creation of a contract calling for exchange of currencies at a specified future date and a specified exchange rate. On January 10, major currencies could be traded for delivery 30, 90, or 180 days forward to the rates shown in Fig. 16.4. Forward currency markets exist so that companies can hedge exchange rate risk. For example, on January 10 International Business Machines (IBM), anticipating receipt of £10,000,000 in one month from a British subsidiary, could sell that amount forward 30 days to Chase Manhattan Bank at the 30-day forward exchange rate of 1.5881 \$/£. On February 8, IBM will be required to deliver £10,000,000 to Chase, which will give IBM \$15,881,000 *regardless of the spot rate on that date.*

On January 10, 1983, all forward rates for pounds were below the spot rate, meaning that the pound was expected to depreciate relative to the dollar (fewer dollars, were required to purchase £1). Conversely, forward rates for the Japanese yen were above the spot rate, indicating an expectation that the yen would appreciate relative to the dollar. Factors affecting the spot and forward rates include relative inflation and interest rates, the relationship between the volume of imports and exports, and the supply and demand of the relative currencies.

The forward rate data in Fig. 16.4 are derived from transactions between major banks and their customers. The customers may either buy or sell the currency forward, depending on whether they have a short position (need the foreign exchange) or a long position (want to convert the foreign exchange to dollars); the bank will take the opposite side of the transaction. The rates quoted in Fig. 16.4 represent **bid rates,** the exchange rate for *selling* foreign currency to the bank. **Asked rates,** the exchange rate for *buying* the foreign currency from the bank, are slightly higher. The difference between bid and asked rates represents the fee the bank earns for making a market in foreign exchange. Major currencies are traded under a **floating exchange rate system,** meaning that exchange rates can adjust daily to economic factors influencing their values. Because rates float, the value of one currency against another at any future date is uncertain.

Consider again the HTW–Sinclair example. HTW is exposed to exchange rate risk until the pounds it receives are converted into dollars. For example, if Barclays' payment for the Sinclair sale had arrived on January 5 when the dollar/pound exchange rate was $1.6255, HTW would have received $113,341 (£69,727 × 1.6255) instead of $110,924. The difference of $2,461 will determine whether HTW makes a normal profit on this transaction. The forward market allows a firm to hedge exchange rate risk before the foreign currency is received.

Hedging Exchange Rate Risk

HTW could use the forward market to hedge its foreign currency exposure in the following way. On December 10, when the agreement with Sinclair was signed, HTW could have *sold* £69,727 30 days forward at the 30-day forward rate of $1.6321 per pound. The forward sale will lock in a dollar return on the contract of $113,801 (£69,727 × 1.6321). Since the pound is expected to depreciate relative to the dollar, the sooner HTW converts pounds to dollars, the more dollars it will obtain. HTW cannot use the spot market on December 10 because it will not receive pounds until January 10. HTW *sells* the pounds forward because it will be *receiving* pounds in 30 days. (If HTW had been *purchasing* products in January whose price was denominated in pounds, it would have *bought* pounds forward to hedge.) On January 10, HTW will receive pounds from Barclays Bank, which it would deliver in exchange for dollars. Selling pounds forward creates a hedged exchange rate position for HTW and removes the exchange rate uncertainty. Because the pound is depreciating against the dollar, the forward sale in December produces a greater dollar return from the contract than the spot market sale in January.

Many firms will hedge their foreign currency positions to remove uncertainty even when forward rates are above spot rates. Consider a sale by HTW to Sukari of Japan for ¥26,053,250 (Japanese yen), for which payment is due on February 8. Figure 16.4 gives the dollar/yen spot exchange rate on January 10 as .004414, with the 30-day forward rate at .004425. A spot market sale yields only $114,999 (¥26,053,250 × .004414), while selling a 30-day forward contract returns $115,286. If the spot rate for the yen continues to appreciate, HTW might receive more than $115,286 by waiting until February 8 and converting the yen to dollars in the spot market. However, if unforeseen economic factors cause the yen to depreciate, HTW might receive less than $115,286. Many financial managers prefer to remove any uncertainty about the currency translation and always use the forward market to hedge exchange rate risk, regardless of the expected changes in exchange rates.

THE INTERNATIONAL MONETARY SYSTEM

Because the exchange rate is the price of one currency in terms of another, every international trade involves two prices: the stated price of the good and the price of the currency needed to purchase it. The process for determining exchange rates is important because exchange rates affect the price of a country's products. When the exchange rate of one country is appreciating relative to other currencies, its goods are becoming more expensive in world markets and foreign products are becoming cheaper domestically. Exports should decline, while the cheaper imports should rise.

Consider the sales by HTW to English and Japanese firms described earlier. Forward rates for yen and pounds reveal the expectation that the yen will rise and the pound will fall relative to the dollar. Assuming that the spot rates 30 and 90 days from January 10 equal the forward rates shown in Fig. 16.4, the prices of HTW's products will decline in Japan and rise in England, as shown in Table 16.1.

Without mechanisms to exchange one currency for another and to hedge exchange rate risk, international trade as we know it would cease. For example, trade today between less developed countries often is based on a barter system because no procedure exists to translate their currencies. For industrialized countries, the international monetary system provides the framework for currency exchange. Key elements of this system are the procedures for determining exchange rates and the role of banks in facilitating currency transfers.

TABLE 16.1
Relative Purchasing Power of the Yen and the Pound.

Date	Dollar Cost of Product	Yen per Dollar	Yen cost of Product	Pounds per Dollar	Pound Cost of Product
Jan. 10	$70	226.55	15,858.50	.6289	44.02
Feb. 8	70	226.00	15,820.00	.6297	44.08
Apr. 8	70	225.13	15,759.10	.6316	44.21

Factors Affecting Exchange Rates

As with any commodity, the supply of and demand for a country's currency are the factors that determine its value. Factors affecting supply and demand include (1) the balance of trade between countries, (2) the movement of funds for investment, and (3) relative inflation and interest rates.

Balance of trade. The difference between the imports and exports of a country is called its balance of trade. Purchase of foreign goods usually requires obtaining that country's currency. If exports and imports are unequal, the changing supply and demand for the currency will cause changes in the exchange rate. A country that continually runs balance-of-trade deficits (more imports than exports) will be supplying more currency to foreigners than they require to purchase domestic goods. If everything else is constant, the price of the currency will depreciate relative to most other currencies.

Movement of funds for investment. A U.S. company building a plant abroad will be required to invest capital in that facility. Funds are obtained by exchanging U.S. dollars for the required foreign currency, which increases the supply of dollars for foreigners. If the investments of U.S. companies and individuals abroad exceed those of foreigners in the United States, the supply of dollars will be greater than the demand, and downward pressure will be exerted on the dollar's exchange rate. Since World War II, U.S. foreign investments have exceeded those of foreigners here. This difference may be narrowing, as Japanese and German auto and steel manufacturers begin investing in U.S. plants.

Besides investment in physical assets, currency flows between countries for purchase of financial assets (money market securities, stocks, and bonds). Bankers refer to these funds as *hot* money because they are investments in liquid assets that can and will be transferred quickly to another country depending on relative changes in interest rates and investment opportunities that may make such a shift desirable. For example, in 1982 short-term U.S. interest rates were at a record 15–16% for T-bills, and foreign investors exchanged their currency for dollars to invest in the United States at these high rates. The result was an appreciation in the dollar and a reduction in U.S. exports.

Inflation and interest rates. Relative inflation rates also affect foreign exchange because of the principle of **purchasing power parity.** This principle states that a "market basket" of comparable goods should sell for equivalent prices regardless of the currency used to price the goods. A bushel of wheat priced at $4.00 in the United States and £2.00 in the United Kingdom implies a dollar/pound exchange rate of $2.00. While purchasing power parity will not hold precisely on a daily basis, it will affect exchange rates over the long run.

For example, if inflation is 10% in the United Kingdom and 0% in the United States, the pound must depreciate relative to the dollar to maintain purchasing power parity. The £2.00 bushel of wheat will sell for £2.20 at year end, while U.S. wheat still costs $4. The dollar/pound exchange rate will fall to $1.82.

Because expected inflation is impounded in interest rates, it is more correct to evaluate how relative interest rates affect supply and demand for currencies. The theory underlying the relationship is called the **interest rate parity theorem.** Interest rate parity implies that differences in the spot and forward rates for currencies are due solely to differentials in interest rates. For example, assume that one-year interest rates are 5% in the United States and 10% in the United Kingdom. The current spot exchange rate is $2.00. If interest rate parity holds exactly, the one-year *forward* rate will be $1.91. The 5% interest rate advantage that could be obtained by investing in the United Kingdom will be offset by a 5% depreciation in the value of the pound. The activity of foreign exchange traders engaging in **covered interest arbitrage** causes spot and forward rates to conform closely to the interest rate parity theorem. **Arbitrage** is the attempt to earn riskless profits from simultaneously buying and selling the same security at two different prices.

To illustrate covered interest arbitrage, we will analyze a covered interest position for a U.S. investor choosing between investing $100,000 in the United States or Great Britain. Assume the interest rates and exchange rates shown in Table 16.2.

To invest in pounds earning 18% the U.S. investor must (1) convert dollars to pounds, (2) hold pounds for 90 days, and (3) translate the interest and principal back to dollars. Exchange risk exists during the investment period, but the risk can be hedged by *selling* pounds 90 days forward at the rate shown in Table 16.2, hence the term *covered interest arbitrage*. Interest rate parity implies that the dollar/pound difference between spot and forward rates will exactly offset the interest rate differential between the two countries. If interest rate parity holds, Eq. (16.3) will equal zero.

$$\frac{\$/FC \text{ forward} - \$/FC \text{ spot}}{\text{Spot rate } \$/FC}$$

$$- \left(\frac{\text{domestic interest rate} - \text{foreign interest rate}}{1 + \text{foreign interest rate}} \times \frac{\text{holding period}}{360 \text{ days}} \right). \quad (16.3)$$

TABLE 16.2				
Data for Example of Covered Interest Arbitrage.				
	Interest Rate (Annualized 90-Day Rate)		**Exchange Rate**	
United States	12%		Spot	$2.00
United Kingdom	18%		90-day forward	1.98

> **TABLE 16.3**
> **Covered Interest Arbitrage.**
>
> Spot rates $/£ = 2.00   90-day forward rates $/£ = 1.98
>   £/$ = .5000   £/$ = .5051
>
> **Available for investment: $100,000†**
>
> *Today*
>
> 1. Exchange dollars for pounds and invest the proceeds at Barclays in London:
>
> $100,000 × .5000 $/£ = £50,000.
>
> 2. Sell pounds forward at Chase Manhattan Bank of New York equal to the principal plus interest:
>
> | | |
> |---|---|
> | Principal | £50,000 |
> | 90 days' interest (18% × 90/360) | 2,250 |
> | Total | £52,250 |
>
>   The rate today on a 90-day forward contract is 1.98 $/£.
>
> *In 90 days*
>
> 1. Receive £52,250 from Barclays.
> 2. Deliver the £52.250 to Chase and receive dollars:
>
>   £52,250 × $1.98 $/£ = $103,455.

†In the strictest sense of riskless arbitrage, the U.S. investor would not have personal capital at stake but would borrow $100,000 in the United States at 12%. At the end of three months, the U.S. loan of $103,000 (principal plus interest) would be repaid from the $103,455 proceeds, yielding a riskless profit of $455.

If Eq. (16.3) yields a positive result, there is an advantage to investing in the foreign country. If the result is negative, the investor should invest domestically, because the higher foreign interest rate is more than offset by the depreciation in the foreign currency.

Using exchange rate and interest rate data from Table 16.2 in Eq. (16.3) results in a positive value of .00271. In this case, an investor can earn a riskless return by creating a covered interest position in the foreign currency:

$$\frac{1.98 - 2.00}{2.00} - \left(\frac{.12 - .18}{1.18} \times \frac{90}{360}\right) = \text{riskless return}$$

$$-.01000 + .01271 = \text{riskless return}$$

$$.00271 = \text{riskless return}.$$

The sequence is summarized in Table 16.3.

Interest arbitrage activities will affect exchange rates and interest rates in the following manner if all other factors are held constant. Funds flowing from the United States to London will cause interest rates in London to fall and U.S. rates to rise, making the interest rate differential narrower (the .01271 value becomes smaller). The spot supply of dollars will increase as investors attempt to exchange dollars for pounds, causing the $2.00 exchange rate to rise. At the same time, the 90-day forward rate of $1.98 should fall as more pounds are offered for forward sale. The current differential between the spot and 90-day forward rates of $-.01$ will become more negative. The adjustment process will continue until the relationship specified by Eq. (16.3) equals zero.

Three participants in foreign exchange markets will cause spot and forward rates to conform closely to interest rate parity. These include (1) businesses that require foreign exchange for transactions, (2) speculators willing to risk money betting on the change in a currency's value, and (3) arbitrageurs attempting to earn profits through covered interest arbitrage activities.

A History of Exchange Rates

Today, most major trading nations are operating under a floating exchange rate system that allows supply and demand factors to be reflected daily in the currency's value. Large banks, corporations, and central banks buy and sell foreign currencies to facilitate international fund transfers. Before 1973, foreign currency transactions generally were made under fixed exchange rate systems. Only since 1973 have the more industrialized countries used a floating system to establish exchange rates. The same factors will influence exchange rates whether they are determined by a fixed or floating rate system. Under a floating rate arrangement small adjustments occur daily in reaction to market forces. Under a fixed rate system changes in exchange rates occur infrequently, but when they do, changes are usually of large magnitude.

From the early 1900s until World War I, all major countries operated under a **fixed exchange rate system.** Currencies were backed by gold, and each unit of paper money could be exchanged for gold at a ratio set by the country's central bank. The exchange rate between currencies was a function of their purchasing power in gold. For example, if Britain exchanged one pound for one ounce of gold while France set the price of one franc at half an ounce of gold, the exchange rate would be one pound for two francs, because each is equivalent to one ounce of gold.

The international monetary system collapsed during World War I, and it was not until the late 1920s that fixed rates were restored. The worldwide Depression of the 1930s caused the system to fail again as many countries devalued their currencies in an attempt to generate exports, reduce imports, and create jobs. World War II brought a pegging of exchange rates and suspension of all dealing in foreign trade.

In 1944 the Allies met in Bretton Woods, New Hampshire, to create a new fixed rate international monetary system, which remained in effect until 1971. Under the *Bretton Woods Agreement,* all exchange rates were fixed in terms of the U.S. dollar, and each country was responsible for keeping the rate within 1% of the fixed value. The U.S. dollar served as an international currency, and most international transactions were paid in dollars. The United States agreed to run trade deficits (imports greater than exports) with the rest of the world, so that foreigners could collect dollars, and to guarantee the redemption of dollars for gold at $35 an ounce. (In 1944 the United States had $23 billion in gold, three-fourths of the world's gold supply.)

The International Monetary Fund (IMF) was created to oversee the international monetary system. Its functions were (1) to promote cooperation in international monetary matters, (2) to facilitate the expansion of world trade, and (3) to maintain exchange rate stability and monetary agreements. Devaluation or revaluation of exchange rates could occur only after consultation with the IMF, and relatively few changes occurred between 1950 and 1971.

The demise of the Bretton Woods system in 1971 was brought about by U.S. inflation and the continuous U.S. balance-of-payments deficits. In August 1971, the United States halted conversion of dollars to gold when its gold supply reached $10 billion. This action, in effect, terminated the Bretton Woods Agreement.

Following a four-month period of floating exchange rates, the *Smithsonian Agreement* was signed by the major trading nations. Another fixed rate system, it allowed for wider fluctuation around the fixed rates. In February 1973, the foreign exchange markets in London, Tokyo, and Paris closed because of pressure on the U.S. dollar. Upon their reopening the following week, major currencies were allowed to float against the dollar and each other.

The Current Exchange Rate System

After February 1973, the exchange rates between the currencies of the major industrial nations (e.g., France, Japan, West Germany, the United Kingdom) have been determined under a floating rate system. However, many smaller countries still fix the value of their currency to the U.S. dollar or to a collection of currencies of other countries. Many developing countries maintain strict control over their currency and exchange rates. Korea, for example, has a totally controlled foreign exchange system. Exchange rates are set by the central bank, and anyone wanting Korean currency (e.g., an importer) must obtain it from the central bank at a government-determined exchange rate.

The floating system for major currencies is more properly called a **dirty float** because of daily intervention in foreign exchange markets by central banks. In the short run, exchange rates can be affected by a country's central bank (e.g., the Federal Reserve Bank in the United States) that is buying and selling foreign exchange. For example, if the Japanese yen is appreciating relative to the dollar, making Japanese goods more expensive in the United States, the Japanese Central Bank can sell yen and buy dollars to moderate the rise. If the yen is expected to fall relative to the dollar and Japan believes that this is not in its national interests, the Japanese Central Bank can buy yen with gold or other foreign exchange to support the yen. A country's ability to prop up a falling currency, however, is limited by the gold and foreign currency reserves that it possesses. The term *dirty* is sometimes used because many countries will work to influence their exchange rates to achieve economic gain at the expense of other nations (e.g., artificially depressing a currency's price to stimulate exports).

Role of the Banking System in International Fund Transfers

To make international trade possible, there must be a regular process for obtaining and moving foreign exchange between countries. This is provided by the commercial banking system. As an illustration of transfer of currencies, recall the previous example of HTW and Sinclair, in which HTW instructs Barclays to discount the banker's acceptance and forward £69,727. Assume instead that the contract was specified in dollars rather than in pounds. Sinclair would instruct Barclays to obtain dollars by exchanging pounds with an institution willing to sell dollars, such as Barclays or another British bank, the Bank of England, or a U.S. bank that might have a customer buying British goods. Assume that Citicorp of New York is willing to exchange dollars for pounds with Barclays. The journal entries required to effect this transaction (T-account) are shown in Fig. 16.5 (assuming an exchange rate of $1.5902 per pound). Observe that no physical transfer of currency takes place; journal entries on the two banks' books will reflect the exchange. Barclays will then instruct Citicorp to transfer the funds to Valley National Bank, which will credit HTW's demand deposit account with $110,880.

Transfer of currencies between individuals and businesses in different countries in this manner is achieved through international banking relationships. References to "dollars in the hands of foreigners" are somewhat misleading. It would be more appropriate to refer to demand deposits in U.S. banks owned by foreign banks, corporations, and individuals.

BARCLAYS BANK		CITICORP	
Assets	**Liabilities**	**Assets**	**Liabilities**
	Demand Deposits Citicorp £69,727		Demand Deposits Barclays $110,880
Due from Foreign Exchange + £69,727		Due from Foreign Exchange + $110,880	

Figure 16.5 Bank-to-bank currency exchange.

EXCHANGE RATE RISK FOR MULTINATIONAL COMPANIES

Exchange rate risk becomes more complex when firms establish wholly owned subsidiaries in foreign countries. The previous example of a direct foreign sale by the HTW Corp. illustrated exchange rate risk caused by translation of pounds to dollars. For companies owning foreign subsidiaries, exchange rate risk also affects that net value of assets held by the foreign subsidiary. The dollar value of financial assets such as cash and accounts receivable held in foreign currencies will change if the foreign currency's value fluctuates relative to the dollar. The dollar value of liabilities such as accounts payable or debt will also vary with changes in the exchange rate. **Devaluation** of a foreign currency will cause the dollar value of both foreign financial assets and liabilities to fall, while **revaluation** will produce the opposite effect.

The balance sheet for Pyrenees Electronics Co., a wholly owned French subsidiary of the HTW Corp., is shown in Table 16.4. Columns 1 and 2 reflect the balance sheets in French francs and U.S. dollars, assuming a dollar/franc exchange rate of $0.20. Columns 3 and 4 show the effect of a devaluation of the franc to $0.15. The balance sheet denominated in francs does not change, while the dollar-denominated balance sheet declines by 25%. To protect foreign investments from depreciating in dollar terms, multinational compa-

---

TABLE 16.4
Effect of Exchange Rate Changes on the Dollar Value of a Foreign Subsidary: Pyrenees Electronics Balance Sheet (000s of Dollars or Francs).

Exchange rate =	.20 (dollars/franc)		.15 (dollars/franc)	
	Franc	Dollars	Franc	Dollars
Assets				
Cash	7,000	1,400	7,000	1,050
Accounts receivable	14,000	2,800	14,000	2,100
Inventory	20,000	4,000	20,000	3,000
Net fixed assets	110,000	22,000	110,000	16,500
Total assets	151,000	30,200	151,000	22,650
Liabilities				
Notes payable	20,000	4,000	20,000	3,000
Accounts payable	12,000	2,400	12,000	1,800
Long-term debt	30,000	6,000	30,000	4,500
Equity	89,000	17,800	89,000	13,350
Total liabilities plus equity	151,000	30,200	151,000	22,650

nies assess the exposure of foreign assets to exchange rate risk and design hedging strategies to reduce net financial asset exposure.

Net Financial Asset Exposure

A firm's **net financial asset exposure** is the difference between its financial assets and its liabilities, which can vary in value because of exchange rate fluctuations. The dollar value of cash and accounts receivable denominated in the foreign currency will be changed immediately by any variation in the exchange rate. Inventory may or may not be affected. If the foreign currency is depreciating because of inflation, it may be possible to increase the price of the finished product, leaving the dollar value of the inventory unchanged. However, if the inventory is for export or if its sale is restricted by government price controls, it will be exposed to exchange rate risk.

Fixed assets usually are not included in the calculation because their value typically moves in an opposite direction to the exchange rate. For example, factors causing the exchange rate to fall (inflation or rising interest rates) will lead to an appreciation in the value of real assets. All financial liabilities are subtracted from financial assets to determine the net exposure to exchange rate fluctuations. Equity representing the book value of the owner's position is not included. The format for determining net financial asset exposure is given in Table 16.5.

If the company possesses a positive net financial asset position, and the foreign currency depreciates relative to the dollar, the amount of the parent company's wealth that is contributed by the foreign subsidiary will fall. Subsidiaries with a negative net financial asset position will benefit from a

---

TABLE 16.5
Net Financial Asset Exposure.

Financial assets

Cash
Accounts receivable
Inventory?
Other local currency claims

Financial liabilities

Notes payable
Accounts payable
Taxes payable
Long-term debt

Net financial asset exposure = financial assets − financial liabilities.

depreciating foreign currency. A zero net financial asset position implies that the subsidiary is perfectly hedged and that the dollar value of the foreign subsidiary will not change with fluctuations in the exchange rate.

The net financial asset position of Pyrenees Electronics is calculated as follows, assuming that any price changes in the French franc can be passed on to customers so that inventory is not exposed to exchange rate risk:

Financial assets		
Cash	7,000	
Accounts receivable	14,000	21,000
Financial liabilities		
Notes payable	20,000	
Accounts payable	12,000	
Long-term debt	30,000	
		−62,000
Net financial asset exposure	(FF) =	−41,000

If HTW believes that the franc is likely to depreciate relative to the dollar, it is appropriate to maintain a negative exposure. However, if HTW wishes to reduce exchange risk exposure because it does not know which way rates may move, it has a number of options.

Hedging Net Asset Exposure

Companies should maintain positive net asset positions in strong currencies and negative positions in weak currencies. If exchange rate prospects are highly uncertain, a company should reduce exchange rate exposure to zero if possible. The following techniques can be used to alter net financial asset exposure.

Leads and lags of payments refers to timing payment flows between subsidiaries or between the parent and the subsidiary so as to take advantage of exchange rate movements. Payments are made quickly into strong currencies (leading payment) and delayed when made into weaker ones (lagging). Accounts best suited to timing strategies are cash, accounts payable, and accounts receivable. Since the floating rate system began in 1973, multinational companies have paid considerable attention to the timing of cash flows so as to reduce exchange rate risk.

Another way to change net financial asset exposure is by *restructuring assets and liabilities*. This is accomplished by borrowing or lending in the foreign currency. If HTW believes that the dollar/franc exchange rate is highly uncertain and wants to maintain a new financial asset exposure of zero, it can contribute more equity to the firm and use the cash proceeds to reduce long-term debt.

To maintain a hedged position over the long run, companies often follow the policy of matching increases (or decreases) in assets with offsetting complementary changes in foreign currency liabilities. Thus the effect of exchange rate fluctuations will be zero. Short-term loans in francs, for example, would be used to finance working capital increases of a French subsidiary.

Intracompany transactions also can be used by multinational corporations to manage exchange rate exposure. Two common procedures are transfer pricing and funds management. *Transfer pricing* refers to costs charged one subsidiary by another. Companies can move funds into a country whose currency is appreciating by charging higher prices for products from that subsidiary. The same effect may be achieved by including a royalty fee or surcharge in the price.

Funds management refers to moving cash balances between subsidiaries in different countries to take advantage of expected currency fluctuations or to create hedged positions. Subsidiaries in countries with weak currencies would make loans or accelerate payments to subsidiaries holding appreciating currencies.

Transfer pricing and funds management combined with leading and lagging techniques enable the multinational corporation to balance exposed positions among foreign operating locations. The overall goal is to ensure that funds are not owed in an appreciating currency and that cash and receivables are not held in a depreciating currency.

OBTAINING FUNDS FOR FOREIGN INVESTMENTS

International financial markets are used to finance investments in foreign countries. In addition, the World Bank and the International Development Association play an active role in international finance. Multinational companies frequently use Eurodollars, foreign bonds, and Eurobonds to finance international investments.

World Bank

The **World Bank,** also known as the International Bank for Reconstruction and Development, was established to provide long-term credit to underdeveloped countries or private firms in these countries. While the bank does not give outright grants, it can make loans at below-market rates to finance socially beneficial projects. Capital is obtained through the sale of bonds issued by the World Bank. The government of the country receiving the loan guarantees repayment. As of December 1982, 135 countries belonged to the World Bank.

International Development Association

An affiliate of the World Bank, the IDA was established in 1960 to provide credit to the least-developed nations. Loans from the **International Development Association (IDA)** are long-term and carry no interest, but yearly payments are required that amortize the loan by maturity. A minimal service charge is levied each year.

Eurodollars

Eurodollars represent dollar deposits accepted by banks outside the United States. Firms can deposit dollars into interest-bearing time accounts instead of transferring the dollars to a U.S. bank. Other firms may borrow dollar balances instead of borrowing in the United States. While the distinction may appear trivial, banks usually do not carry deposits in a foreign currency. Suppose you deposit a Mexican peso check at Valley Bank in Tucson. Valley Bank processes the check and clears it through the Mexican bank upon which it is drawn. Dollars would be credited to your account based on the dollar/peso exchange rate on the clearing date. U.S. banks denominate all deposits in dollars, and foreign banks typically denominate deposits in their own currency. Eurodollar deposits are unique because they represent dollar deposits in non-U.S. banks.

The Eurodollar market developed in the early 1950s when banks in London began holding deposits denominated in U.S. dollars. At that time, it was the international currency role of the dollar that motivated foreign countries to hold substantial dollar balances for transaction purposes. Multinational companies began borrowing and lending in the Eurodollar market instead of transferring dollars back to the United States.

Operation of the Eurodollar market—An example.   Assume that Pyrenees Electronics agrees to accept $200,000 as payment for a sale to a West German manufacturer. Instead of converting the dollars to francs or repatriating the dollars to the parent, HTW, Pyrenees could deposit the dollars to Barclays Bank in London in a Eurodollar account. Barclays would pay Pyrenees an interest rate close to the short-term U.S. rates (arbitrage keeps U.S. and Eurodollar rates very similar). Barclays can then lend the dollars to another firm, say Sinclair Ltd., in London, which wants to hold dollar balances instead of pounds. The T-accounts reflecting these transactions are shown in Fig. 16.6 (assuming that Citicorp is the U.S. bank of all participants).

1. West German firm pays Pyrenees in dollars, and Pyrenees opens a Eurodollar account at Barclays Bank.

NEW YORK: CITICORP		LONDON: BARCLAYS BANK	
Assets	Liabilities	Assets	Liabilities
	Demand Deposits		Demand Deposits
	West German Firm −$200,000 Barclays Bank +$200,000		
		Due from Foreign Exchange +$200,000	Time Deposits Pyrenees +$200,000

2. Barclays lends $100,000 to Sinclair Ltd.

NEW YORK: CITICORP		LONDON: BARCLAYS BANK	
Assets	Liabilities	Assets	Liabilities
	Demand Deposits	Loan Sinclair Ltd. +$100,000	Demand Deposits
	Barclays Bank: $ 200,000 −100,000 ‾‾‾‾‾‾‾ $ 100,000 Sinclair Ltd. +$100,000		
		Due from Foreign Exchange $100,000	Time Deposits Pyrenees $200,000

Figure 16.6 Eurodollar deposit chain.

Total U.S. demand deposits do not change because of Eurodollar accounts, but ownership of the demand deposits at Citicorp is changed to reflect currency transfers. Barclays is obliged to deliver $200,000 to Pyrenees when the time deposit comes due even though Barclays, at present, does not possess $200,000. Also, as in previous examples of international currency translations, the dollars never leave the United States but merely are reflected as accounting entries at the appropriate U.S. banks.

U.S. firms using Eurodollar deposits or loans incur no foreign exchange rate risk. Thus foreign subsidiaries of U.S. firms may use the Eurodollar market as a convenient means of hedging net asset exposure in a foreign currency. Some, though, view the Eurodollar market as more risky than dollar accounts in the United States, because Eurodollar banks are not governed by U.S. reserve requirements or other banking regulations. However, as of 1983, no Eurodollar institution had declared bankruptcy or defaulted on a Eurodollar obligation.

Foreign Bonds

In countries with an organized financial market, a foreign borrower can obtain debt financing by issuing bonds denominated in the local currency. Principal and interest payments must be made in the local currency. Firms with large capital requirements in a country with a weak currency usually will sell **foreign bonds** to hedge their net asset exposure. The United States, Switzerland, and Germany are the major markets for foreign bonds. Generally, a secondary market for foreign bonds exists only in the country in which they are issued.

Eurobonds

Eurobonds are bonds denominated in a currency not of the country in which they are sold. For example, HTW might sell bonds denominated in francs in Great Britain to raise capital for its Pyrenees subsidiary, or Sinclair Ltd. might sell bonds denominated in pounds in France to raise capital. Interest and principal of the Eurobond are paid in the denominated currency, not in the currency of the country in which the bond was issued. Eurobonds typically are traded in the markets of more than one country and are sometimes called *international bonds*. The sale of Eurobonds and foreign bonds is another technique by which multinational companies can adjust their exposure to exchange rate risk while at the same time raising funds needed for investment.

SUMMARY

As the world becomes more and more economically interdependent, more businesses will engage in international transactions. Financial management is more complex in the face of increased collection risk, political uncertainties, and the need to use and hold different currencies. Even in the simplest situation—a direct sale abroad—a large number of documents are required to reduce collection risk. Exchange risk is present unless the company hedges its exposure in the foreign currency. Spot and forward markets in foreign currencies exist to facilitate foreign trade; they also make currency hedging strategies possible.

International operations require the financial manager to become familiar with factors influencing exchange rates. Balance of trade, movement of investment funds, and interest rates cause exchange rates to fluctuate. The foreign currency can be floating or fixed relative to the dollar.

Financial managers in multinational companies must be concerned about the net financial exposure of foreign subsidiaries. Funds can be moved among foreign subsidiaries in an attempt to hold a positive net asset position in currencies that are appreciating relative to the dollar and a net liability position in depreciating currencies.

To facilitate international trade and investment, the World Bank and the IDA make loans to firms in developing countries. Most U.S.-based multinational companies will use the Eurodollar market to obtain short-term loans or invest excess cash balances. Also, foreign capital markets allow firms to issue debt instruments denominated in various currencies.

International trade has developed since World War II to become an important part of world economic activity. Its significance can only be expected to increase in the coming years.

QUESTIONS AND REVIEW ACTIVITIES

1. How do international transactions complicate the financial manager's job?

2. List and describe the three risks incurred in international operations.

3. What organizational forms may be used to conduct international operations? Describe the advantages and disadvantages of each operation.

4. Describe the use of a letter of credit, bill of exchange, and bill of lading in an international transaction.

5. Explain the difference between a revocable and an irrevocable letter of credit, and a confirmed or ordinary letter of credit.

6. What is foreign exchange?

7. What is the foreign exchange rate? Explain the difference between a direct and an indirect exchange rate quotation.

8. Define the terms *spot market* and *forward market* for foreign exchange. Why would a firm use the spot market? The forward market?

9. What is meant by a country's balance of trade? Why does the balance of trade affect the exchange rate of a country's currency?

10. What are the four factors affecting the exchange rate of a currency? How does each factor influence the exchange rate?

11. What is meant by purchasing power parity?

12. What is the interest rate parity theorem, and what implications does it have for forward exchange rates?

13. Distinguish between fixed and floating exchange rate systems.

14. Describe the current international monetary system and the manner in which exchange rates are determined.

15. Describe the major components of the Bretton Woods Agreement regarding the international monetary system.

16. What is net financial asset exposure, and why is the financial manager of a multinational firm concerned about the net exposed position?

17. What techniques can be used to hedge net financial asset exposure?

18. Draw T-accounts to show how Eurodollars are created. Where are Eurodollars located? How can the financial manager use Eurodollars?

19. Distinguish between Eurobonds and foreign bonds.

PROBLEMS

1. Convert the following pound/dollar (indirect) exchange rates into direct exchange rates (dollars/pounds): .6500, .9500, 1.1000, 1.5000.

2. The following exchange rates are given:

Dollar/pound (£)	1.75	Pound/dollar	.5714
Dollar/German mark (DM)	.25	German mark/dollar	4.0000
Dollar/French franc (FF)	.15	French franc/dollar	6.6667

a) You are offered £15. How many dollars is that worth?

b) You are offered DM 112. How many dollars can you get in exchange?

c) A Porsche costs DM 72,000. How many dollars are required to buy it?

d) A find French wine sells for FF 166.67. What will you have to pay in marks?

3. The following exchange rates are given:

	Dollar/Pound	Pound/Dollar
Spot	1.90	.5263
30-day forward	1.88	.5319
90-day forward	1.84	.5435

Emery's Accessories exports men's hats to Bedford, England. The latest shipment was billed at £30,000; payment is due in three months.

a) If payment were received today, how many dollars would Emery get?

b) If payment is made in 90 days and the spot rate at that time equals today's 90-day forward rate, what will Emery receive in dollars?

c) Assume that Emery wants to hedge its exposure to exchange risk. How can it do so? If the spot rate in 90 days is $1.80, does Emery gain or lose by hedging? What if the spot rate is $1.86 in 90 days?

4. The following exchange rates are given:

	Dollar/Swiss Franc	Swiss Franc/Dollar
Spot	.5035	1.9860
30-day forward	.5066	1.9740
90-day forward	.5166	1.9357

Harold's Camping Gear in Arizona is buying mountain-climbing equipment from a Swiss firm. Harold has provided a letter of credit to the Swiss firm, which shipped the gear to Tempe, Arizona. Valley Bank has received a time draft drawn on Harold's account for SF 139,418, payable in 90 days.

a) What will Harold have to pay in dollars if it pays the full value of the draft to the Swiss firm immediately?

b) What will Harold pay in dollars by waiting 90 days?

c) How can Harold eliminate exchange risk in this transaction? Be sure to show all required transactions.

5. The following prices exist in the spot and forward markets:

	Dollar/Pound	**Pound/Dollar**
Spot	1.70	.5882
30-day forward	1.68	.5952
180-day forward	1.58	.6329

Interest rates are 8% in the United States and 12% in Great Britain. You are the treasurer of a U.S. corporation with $1 million to invest for six months, after which time you will again need dollars for operations.

a) In which country should you invest the $1 million?

b) What actions will be taken by domestic and foreign investors to bring interest rates and exchange rates into parity?

c) What British interest rate would be required to neutralize any investment advantage?

6. The following exchange rate information is given:

	Dollar/German Mark	**German Mark/Dollar**
Spot	4.00	.25
180-day forward	4.35	.23

You are the treasurer of a U.S. subsidiary in Germany. All of your transactions are in German marks. You have DM 1 million to invest for six months. German interest rates are 11.3%, and U.S. rates are 20%. At the end of six months, you require German marks for transactions purposes.

a) In which country should you invest your DM 1 million?

b) At what U.S. interest rate would there be no difference between investing in the two countries?

7. A German subsidiary of a U.S. firm takes out a DM 1,000,000 simple interest

loan to be repaid in one year. The interest rate is 10%, and the current exchange is .25 DM/$.

a) What is the dollar value of the loan today?

b) Assume that the exchange rate is .2750 at year end. How many dollars are required to repay the interest and principal?

c) What action could the German subsidiary take to hedge the exchange risk in this situation?

8. A French subsidiary has FF 200,000 in accounts receivable that it expects to collect in 30 days. Exchange rates (in dollars per French franc) are as follows:

Spot	.20
30 days forward	.18
90 days forward	.14

a) What is the value in dollars today of the receivables?

b) What will be the value in dollars when they are collected if the spot rate in thirty days equals today's 30-day forward rate?

c) What actions could the subsidiary take to hedge its exposure to exchange risk?

d) If the spot exchange rate is .16 in 30 days, would hedging the risk have been profitable or not? What if the rate is .22 in 30 days?

9. Table 16.6 is the balance sheet for Adrienne's Apparel in Bern, Switzerland, a wholly owned U.S. subsidiary of the Paige Manufacturing Co. The current dollar/Swiss franc exchange rate is .5000, and the Swiss franc/dollar rate is 2.00.

a) Translate the balance sheet of Adrienne's Apparel into dollars. Assume that any price changes in the Swiss economy cannot be passed along by adjusting the price of the product.

TABLE 16.6
Adrienne's Apparel: Balance Sheet as of December 31, 1983
(000s of Swiss Francs)

Assets		Liabilities	
Cash	75	Notes payable	40
Accounts receivables	150	Accounts payable	110
Inventory	90	Accrued taxes	40
Other assets	10	Other liabilities	10
Total current assets	325	Total current liabilities	200
		Long-term debt	825
Net plant	1,500	Equity	800
Total assets	1,825	Liabilities plus equity	1,825

b) Calculate the net financial asset exposure of the company.

c) Assuming that the parent firm, Paige Manufacturing, is not restricted in transactions, what alternatives would you suggest to them that could reduce exchange risk exposure to zero?

ADDITIONAL READINGS

Cornell, B. "Inflation, Relative Price Changes and Exchange Risk," *Financial Management* (Autumn 1980), pp. 30–34.

———. "Spot Rates, Forward Rates and Market Efficiency," *Journal of Financial Economics* (August 1977), pp, 55–65.

Dufey, G. and I. H. Giddy, *The International Money Market.* Englewood Cliffs, N.J.: Prentice-Hall, Inc., 1978.

Eaker, M. R. "Covered Interest Arbitrage: New Measurement and Empirical Results," *Journal of Economics and Business* (Spring–Summer 1980), pp. 249–53.

Eiteman, D. K., and A. I. Stonehill. *Multinational Business Finance.* Reading, Mass.: Addison-Wesley Publishing Company, 1982.

Evans, T. G. *The Currency Carousel.* Princeton, N.J.: Dow Jones, Inc. 1977.

Finnerty, J. E., T. Schneeweis, and S. P. Hegde, "Interest Rates in the $Eurobond Market," *Journal of Financial and Quantitative Analysis* (September 1980), pp. 743–755.

Folks, W. R., and R. A. Advani. "Raising Funds with Foreign Currency," *Financial Executive* (February 1980), pp. 44–49.

Frenkel, J. A. "Efficiency and Volatility of Exchange Rates and Prices in the 1970's," *Columbia Journal of World Business* (Winter 1979), pp. 15–27.

Friedman, M. F., and R. Roosa. *The Balance of Payments: Free versus Fixed Exchange Rates.* Washington, D.C.: American Enterprise Institute, 1967.

Katz, S. I. "Exchange Risk under Fixed and Flexible Exchange Rates," *The Bulletin,* New York University Graduate School of Business (June 1972).

Lietaer, B. A. "Managing Risks in Foreign Exchange," *Harvard Business Review* (March–April 1970), pp. 127–38.

Meier, G. M. *Problems of a World Monetary Order.* New York: Oxford University Press, 1974.

Rodriguez, R. M., and E. E. Carter. *International Financial Management.* Englewood Cliffs, N.J.: Prentice-Hall, Inc., 1979.

Severn, A. K., and D. R. Meinster. "The Use of Multi-currency Financing by the Financial Manager," *Financial Management* (Winter 1978), pp. 45–53.

Shapiro, A. C., and D. P. Rutenberg. "Managing Exchange Risks in a Floating World," *Financial Management* (Summer 1976), pp. 48–58.

Tech, A. "Control Your Exposure to Foreign Exchange," *Harvard Business Review* (January–February 1974), pp. 66–75.

Weston, J. F., and B. W. Sorge. *International Financial Management*. New York: McGraw-Hill Book Company, 1979.

Zenoff, D. B., and J. Zwick. *International Financial Management*. Englewood Cliffs, N.J.: Prentice-Hall, Inc., 1969.

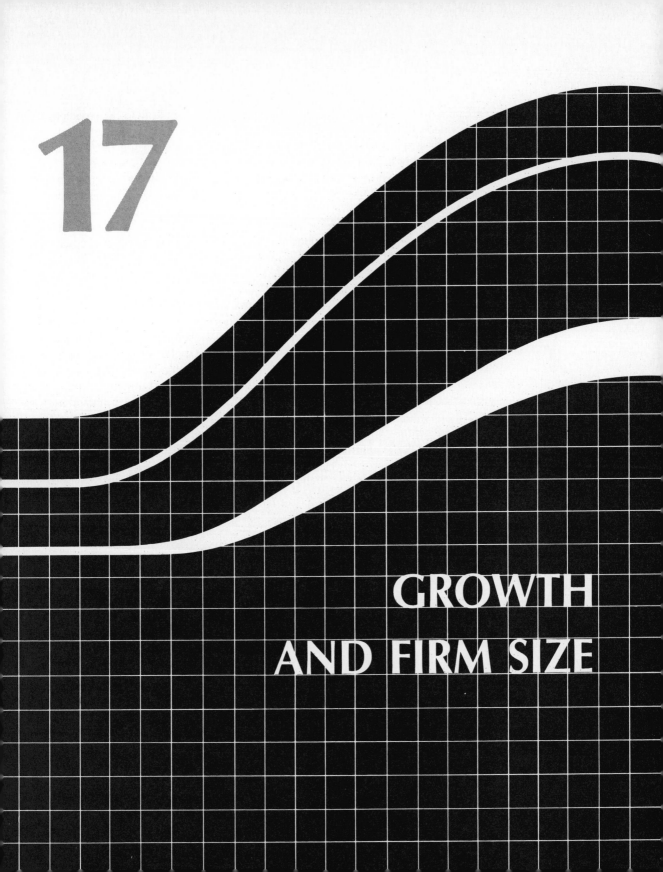

17

GROWTH
AND FIRM SIZE

In a healthy, free economy, growth of business firms is not only to be expected, it is demanded to accommodate the social goal of improvement of the quality of life. Growth in the ability to provide more goods and services is necessary in a modern economy to accommodate increases in population, income, and the standard of living. Further, the advances made in a growing economy in communications, transportation, and technology, for example, themselves motivate further expansion.

While growth in the entire economy is therefore almost universally considered to be good, there are a number of reasons why the growth of a particular firm may or may not serve the goal of maximizing the value of that firm. In general, a firm should seek to grow only to that size that is optimal for its particular business and organizations.

This chapter is concerned with the determinants of the optimal size of a firm and with internal expansion, or expansion that does not involve the absorption of other business units. The remainder of the discussion is concerned with external expansion. The types of expansion are defined as horizontal, vertical, and conglomerate. Next, the history of expansion and merger in the United States is discussed, for it is important to realize that the present interest in merger and business acquisition is part of an ongoing trend in American business organization. The next topics in our discussion are the financial consequences and effects of mergers: synergy, increased EPS, and risk reduction through diversification. The final topic is the alternative structures that business combinations can take.

After careful study of this chapter, you should know

1. Definitions of the following terms:
   - Horizontal combination.
   - Vertical combination.
   - Product extension combination.
   - Market extension combination.
   - Diversified activity combination.
   - Synergy.
   - Q-ratio.
   - Holding company.
   - Consolidation.
2. The determinants of optimum firm size.
3. The advantages and disadvantages of internal expansion.
4. The advantages and disadvantages of external expansion.
5. The history of merger activity in the United States.
6. The financial effects of mergers.
7. The various types of business combination.

DEFINITION OF REAL GROWTH

This chapter is concerned with growth in the *size* of a firm, that is, growth in the productive *assets* that the firm uses to generate returns to its owners. It is important to keep in mind that growth in asset size, however, does not itself ensure growth in profits. It is possible, in an inflationary economy, for growth in a firm's size to come about merely through the effects of inflation: New investment projects, for example, cost more, even though their *real* contributions to the productive base of the firm are not increased; current assets, as well, will tend to grow in size due to inflation, as nominal increases occur in the levels of inventory, accounts receivable, and even cash balances.

What a firm seeks, therefore, is *real* growth. Real growth of business firms has two facets. First, real growth occurs only when the productive value of the firm is increased by acquiring new means of production. The reason for this is that the determinants of optimum firm size, which are discussed next, are implicit in real terms. In other words, the microeconomic bases of the determinants of firm size, such as economy of scale, are meaningful only when "deflated," or adjusted for inflation. Second, real growth can only be that which increases the rate of return to the stockholders. We noted in Chapter 5 that the capital budgeting procedures of the firm ensure that *no* expansion will be undertaken that does not meet the requirement of increased rate of return, so long as the discount rate applied to expansion projects really reflects both inflation and a real rate of return.

These two facets can be combined into the following definition: Real growth is the acquisition of assets that increase the economic efficiency and competitive position of the firm and thereby increase the rate of return to the present stockholders.

DETERMINANTS OF OPTIMUM FIRM SIZE

The **optimum size** of a business firm is the size that enables it to produce most efficiently and at the lowest possible unit cost. The firm will then be able to sell its products at the lowest possible price and still meet its competition in the market. The optimum size of a particular firm is determined largely by the value of the firm's final product and by technological, managerial, marketing, and financial factors.

Value of the Final Product

Other things being equal, the optimum size of a production unit tends to increase as the value of the final product increases. A firm that produces a complex or expensive final product, such as ships, aircraft, or automobiles, cannot be small. The amount of capital required to produce such products may run into millions or even billions of dollars, and the labor costs required for specialized skills and efficient production put such products out of the range of the small enterprise. Small firms generally produce lower-valued consumer goods and services. Of course, the relationship between size and value is not an exact one; lower-priced consumer goods can be produced by the largest firms.

Technological Factors

If a firm's production process can employ labor-saving machinery and division of labor to advantage, the optimum size of a business unit will tend to increase. This relationship is rooted in the concept of operating leverage: Once a capital expenditure has been made for machinery, the firm is motivated to expand production to the point where the machinery is used to capacity, thereby minimizing the cost of the machinery on a per-unit-produced basis. Hence, the optimum size of a firm whose production activities are very capital intensive will depend to a great degree on full-capacity utilization of the capital goods and technology.

Marketing Factors

In certain lines of business, such as brand-name consumer items, the costs of marketing may be the most significant single component of the full unit cost of production. In these cases, the costs of marketing, and not necessarily the value of the final product, will tend to encourage expansion of the firm. Once again, this relationship is rooted in operating leverage: The costs of marketing a brand-name product are reduced on a per-unit-produced basis as production increases, which makes the total cost of production fall. This effect can keep small producers from entering the marketplace. For example, a small firm could produce a simple item such as a cigarette or even a complex item such as a small computer. Success in the marketplace, though, would necessitate marketing outlays that would increase the full cost per unit beyond those of the major competing companies, which can allocate those outlays over large volumes of sales.

By-products

In the tradition of the meat-packing firms that were said to use "everything from the hog but the squeal," manufacturing firms seek to use or sell the by-products of primary production. Use or sale of by-products cuts waste in the primary production, thereby reducing the full unit cost. Further, the production of the by-product itself can make plant utilization more efficient. It is likely, however, that full-scale production of the by-product would require the addition of facilities, thereby tending to increase firm size. There may also be motivation to expand the primary operations to ensure a sufficient supply of the by-products needed to make those operations profitable.

Capital Costs

All firms, regardless of size, must face the problem of obtaining sufficient capital to finance growth. Large, well-known firms may have access to sources of capital that are not available to small firms: They may be able to issue equity or debt securities publicly and privately, and thereby obtain capital at lower costs than would be incurred if they had to borrow from banks or other lenders. More important, in times of tight money, a large firm's easier access to the capital markets may allow it to gain funds when small firms find it difficult or impossible to obtain capital at any price. Availability of external capital, of course, does not necessarily imply that the firm should utilize all available funds. As always, the decision regarding growth is basically one of capital budgeting, and only those projects that have positive NPVs should be considered.

Management's Perception of Optimum Size

A firm's management must continuously evaluate all factors to arrive at a strategy of optimum firm growth and size. Failure to do so could result in the stagnation or even failure of the business. The problem is a challenging and continuing one because of fluctuations in a firm's position caused by changes in prices, consumer tastes or perceptions, technology, taxes, or public policy. The ability of top management to formulate a workable strategy for reaching an optimum size may be the most important factor in explaining expansion of a business firm and the direction that expansion takes.

INTERNAL VERSUS EXTERNAL GROWTH

If top management's perception of the firm's position suggests that growth is desirable and profitable, then management can embark on a strategy of expansion either through internal or external growth. Assume that the firm has decided to expand. The first strategic decision facing management is whether to achieve that expansion internally or to seek growth in the size or scope of the firm through acquisition of other enterprises.

Internal Growth

Internal growth is defined as expansion of the size or scope of the activities of the firm by the application of retained earnings—the traditional plowing back of profits—or by the use of outside funds. These latter funds can come from the sale of new common stock, preferred stock, bonds or debentures, or from long-term financing through banks or other financial institutions. In other words, internal growth is not defined by the use of internally generated funds alone; rather, it includes all expansion *except* that resulting from the complete or partial absorption of other business units.

Internal expansion has a variety of advantages over external expansion.

1. It avoids valuation problems and alteration costs incurred in remodeling acquired facilities. By creating new facilities and employing the most modern equipment, the firm can take advantage of new technology and possibly strengthen the firm's competitive position.

2. Internal expansion avoids potential problems with an acquired firm's management and labor force.

3. New facilities can be located, or existing facilities can be relocated, to take advantage of favorable labor markets, raw material supplies, or a better business environment.

4. It avoids the need to seek approval of the firm's own stockholders, as well as the stockholders of the firm or firms to be acquired.

There are some drawbacks to internal expansion, however. The most serious drawback is that internal expansion takes time. From the moment the decision to expand is made to the time that the new production facilities are running profitably may be years. If the firm's cost of capital is high, and if it has to wait a long time before positive cash flows are realized from an expansion project, the NPV of the project may be reduced to the point where it cannot be (or should not have been) undertaken.

Another disadvantage of internal expansion in some industries is that it adds to the total capacity of the industry. The size of an expansion project, such as a new plant, may have to be quite large in order to be profitable. Adding a new plant to the firm's existing capacity, as well as to the total capacity of the other firms in the industry, could possibly result in an excess supply of the product in the marketplace. This consideration, along with the problem of start-up time, makes large expansion projects difficult to justify in many industries.

External Growth

External growth, commonly referred to as **merger** or acquisition of existing firms, overcomes the drawbacks of internal growth. Start-up time and costs can be markedly reduced. In the absence of strong opposition to an acquisition by stockholders or regulatory agencies, delay is limited to the time it takes a firm to search for the best acquisition candidates, to consummate the acquisition, and to integrate the new activities into the firm's internal organization. All these activities typically do not involve significant capital outlays prior to the realization of cash flows from the new acquisition. Once an acquisition has been made and the productive assets integrated into the firm, any increase in the capacity of the industry caused by the acquisition is the result of economics realized from the merger of the two firms' activities; there may actually be a decrease in competition.

A decided advantage of external growth is that it allows the firm broader scope than internal expansion can provide. That is, internal expansion is normally limited to activities that are very similar in nature to the original ones of the firm, because the production experience, line expertise, technology, and marketing techniques of a particular product or service may not be fully transferable to a different type of activity. This is much less of a concern in external expansion; in fact, the possibility of expanding the scope of activity into unrelated businesses may be a central motivation for seeking acquisitions.

CHARACTERIZING TYPES OF EXPANSION

The most familiar way to characterize the ways in which firms can expand is by the relationship between the activities of the acquiring and acquired firms. Five distinct types of external expansion can be defined: horizontal, vertical, product extension, market extension, and activity diversified. The last three terms are frequently aggregated into the term *conglomerate merger*.

Horizontal Combination

A **horizontal combination** involves merger of two firms that produce one or more of the same or closely related products in the same geographic area. For example, the Southland Corp., which operates the 7-Eleven convenience stores, acquired Lavicio's convenience stores in Arizona, even though their stores in some places are less than one block apart. Horizontal expansion is usually motivated by economies of scale in marketing, production, or sales. It also, of course, reduces competition for the final product. In the case of 7-Eleven and Lavicio, the stores may complement each other by serving traffic moving in different directions when turning across traffic is not possible, thereby effectively expanding the firm's markets even in the same geographic area.

Vertical Combination

A **vertical combination** occurs when two or more successive stages of production are brought together, usually when the companies involved have or could have a buyer–seller relationship prior to the merger. For example, in the steel industry, a complete vertical combination would include iron ore mining, transportation and refining of the ore, converting the ore into steel, and distributing steel and steel products. Vertical combinations offer the advantages of stabilizing the supply and production of raw materials at all stages of the production process. Further, vertical combination provides a firm's management with better control over the accumulated costs and values added by materials in all stages of production.

The last three forms of expansion describe conglomerate mergers. However, the reasons why a firm would pursue one or the other of the following types of expansion are quite different; only the last of the three forms is a conglomerate combination in the sense of the conglomerate movement of the late 1960s and 1970s.

Product Extension Combination

A **product extension combination** occurs when the acquiring and acquired companies have related production and/or distribution activities but products that do not compete directly with one another. An example of a product extension merger was the acquisition in 1979 of the Western Publishing Company, a publisher of children's books and comic books and holder of a number of Disney cartoon character licenses, by Mattel, the toy and electronic game manufacturer. Clearly, the target market of these companies is the same, but the products themselves complement rather than compete with one another. Another example of product extension merger was the acquisition by Phillip-Morris of the Miller Brewing Company. In this case, the expertise in name marketing of Phillip-Morris was directly extended to Miller's beer products.

Market Extension Combination

A **market extension combination** occurs when the acquiring and acquired firms produce the same products but sell them in different geographic markets. An example of market extension expansion strategy involves the Dayton-Hudson Corp., a Minneapolis-based department store retailer. Rather than attempt to extend its own stores beyond the upper Midwest, Dayton-Hudson acquired the Diamond's chain, among others, in the West. An advantage of market extension mergers is that the management skills, production, and marketing systems of the acquiring firm are usually completely transferable to the acquired firm. Further, name or brand identification, and goodwill in general, are also acquired.

Diversified Activity Combination

A **diversified activity combination** is a conglomerate merger in the popular sense of the word. Such a merger involves the consolidation of two essentially unrelated firms. In virtually all of the four other forms of combination, production line activity, expertise, or technology are transferable to or from the acquired firm. In a conglomerate merger, any such exchange between the acquiring and acquired firms is limited to managerial skills and philosophy, other staff activities, and enhancement of the resulting firm's financial base. In fact, the management of an acquiring firm is often not at all interested in running the acquired company.

As an example, had Seagram Brothers, the world's largest distilling business, successfully acquired the Conoco oil company, the combination clearly would have been a conglomerate. After Seagram lost its bid for Conoco to DuPont, it ended up with 20% of the common stock of DuPont when its Conoco shares were converted. Later, DuPont announced that it wished to divest itself of some of Conoco's coal and oil properties. Seagram's chief financial officer ended speculation that Seagram might be interested in trading some of its DuPont stock for some of those properties by saying, "You can categorically rule that out. . . . We wouldn't be comfortable running an oil company. . . . We're far better off having decisions made through Conoco's management."†

Motivations for the first four types of combinations were discussed when optimal firm size was considered in the previous section. Each of these combinations results from a perception of the acquiring firm's management (and often that of the acquired firm's management or stockholders as well) that their firm can be run more profitably or efficiently because of the merger.

HISTORICAL PERSPECTIVE ON MERGER ACTIVITY

A typical growth strategy of a firm involves expanding activities into closely related lines. The combination that best allows this expansion of activity is the product extension. Table 17.1 shows that in the post-World War II era, 43% of large acquisitions—more than any other type—were of that sort.

Another typical growth strategy, usually for larger firms, is to diversify activity away from the products and services offered by the firm. This strategy indicates diversified activity combinations. Table 17.1 indicates that diversified activity conglomerate mergers have accounted for a significant proportion of mergers. Over one-fourth of the acquisitions in the period 1948–1979 were of this type; further, in the period 1967–1978, slightly less than one-third of the acquisitions were diversified, and in 1979 diversified activity mergers accounted for nearly one-half of all combinations.

It is clear that business managements believe that there are good reasons for expanding operations out of their firms' traditional fields, at least in the last three decades. Likewise, analysis of the major periods of merger activity in the American economy illustrates that merger activity is often a specific response to the distinct sets of economic forces that prevail. How economic forces and the business climate influence merger activity will be discussed next.

---

† "DuPont at a Discount—and Then Some," *Financial World* (April 1, 1982), p. 22.

TABLE 17.1
Number and Percentage Breakdown of Large Acquisitions.

Type of Acquisition	Number			
	1948–1978	1967–1978	1978	1979
Horizontal	326	163	22	5
Vertical	196	86	13	5
Product extension	829	486	37	41
Market extension	76	36	0	2
Diversified activity	499	368	39	44
Total	1,926	1,139	111	97

Type of Acquisition	Percentage			
	1948–1978	1967–1978	1978	1979
Horizontal	16.9	14.3	19.8	5.2
Vertical	10.3	7.6	11.7	5.2
Product extension	43.0	42.7	33.3	42.3
Market extension	3.9	3.2	0	2.1
Diversified activity	25.9	32.2	35.2	45.2
Total	100.0	100.0	100.0	100.0

Source: Federal Trade Commission, Bureau of Economics. Statistical Report on Mergers and Acquisitions (Washington D.C.: July 1981), p. 109.

Prior to the present high level of merger activity, the American economy had experienced three major periods of merger or combination, each with its own distinctive features.

First Period (1889–1903)

The important factors in the first period of combination include relaxation of business laws to permit corporations to hold stock in other corporations; achievement of combinations without violating the Sherman Antitrust Act of 1890, which prohibited collusive activities but permitted combinations if monopoly was not an issue; development of transportation facilities and national markets; improvements in management techniques; and development and expansion of the financial markets.

The first wave of business combination was typified by horizontal combinations. Accordingly, destructive competition was greatly reduced, and the stage was set for cost reductions, price increases, and profit expansion. Very little thought was given to diversification in this period, with management's apparent aim being to reduce costs and to obtain better control over markets. Contrary to the legends of a wide-open era characterized by flamboyant and unscrupulous promoters, this period provided much of the base of modern investment banking and proved to be generally beneficial to consumers, who were able to obtain better and more plentiful goods and services.

Second Period (1920–1931)

The predominant factor in the mergers of the 1920s was the stock market boom, which provided the ability to sell the securities of new combinations. Expansion was generally necessary for firm growth in response to increased consumer demand. Expansions made possible an adequate supply of raw materials and the formation and use of effective advertising, selling, and distribution organizations. In this second merger period, economies of scale were basic, that is, savings in buying raw materials and selling finished goods and in the use of personnel. However, the stock market's boom made promotional opportunities and underwriters' profits important factors for mergers as well, irrespective of economic realities.

The background for this merger movement is the economic legacy of World War I, when firms were pressured to combine in order to raise production by increasing efficiency in the use of labor and capital. The government insisted on standardization of products and elimination of competition among agencies purchasing war supplies, and even went so far as resorting to price fixing. The combinations of the 1920s continued such expansion under private control and for private profit. Many of the vertically combined corporate giants of today were conceived in this movement, among them oil companies, all of the automotive firms, and retail chain stores.

Third Period (1950–1971)

The third historic movement in merger activity was typified by a predominance of product extension and diversified activity combinations. Vertical and horizontal combinations waned; such mergers had been primarily based on a desire to secure market control. The giant integrated firms formed in the earlier movements could not expand their market control further without risking vigorous enforcement of the antitrust laws. Merger in this period seemed to be motivated by tax advantages, relatively low prices for the common stock of many companies, and the perception of a need for diversification in product lines so as to stabilize income over the business cycle. Another factor motivating diversification was that technology and consumer tastes were changing so rapidly that a one-product company could go out of business nearly overnight. Therefore, the aim in the third period was not to achieve growth, as much as to ensure financial strength and the flexibility to survive uncertain events and economic conditions through a variety of products and offerings.

	TABLE 17.2	
	Mergers Completed and Their Dollar Values, 1980–1982.	
Year	**Number of Mergers**	**Dollar Value of Mergers in Millions**
1980	1,583	$36,331.7
1981	2,414	$73,226.3
1982	2,321	$66,099.6

Source: Information for Industry. *Mergers & Acquisitions, Almanac & Index.* (Philadelphia, Pa.: 1982), p. 6; (1983), p. 16.

Present Period

Table 17.2 shows the number of value of acquisitions completed during 1980, 1981, and 1982. While the third historic movement ended in 1972, merger activity has rebounded since 1977. In fact 1981 and 1982 show a level of merger activity that has been described by some analysts as "mania." The number of acquisitions in these years was approximately 27% greater than the previous all-time high at the peak of the third merger movement in 1968. Over $73 billion in assets were acquired in 1981, almost 50% more than the $48 billion acquired in 1968. Because book values of assets are not adjusted for inflation, this increase is still quite meaningful even in view of the inflation that occurred over the same period.

MAXIMIZING THE RATE OF RETURN: SYNERGY

This section describes a qualitative phenomenon frequently cited as the motive behind the current high level of merger activity: synergy.

Assume that there are two firms: A, with assets of $2 million and an after-tax expected rate of return of 24%, and B, with assets of $1 million and an after-tax expected rate of return of 18%. If the two firms were combined, the resulting firm, C, would have assets of $3 million and an expected rate of return that is the weighted sum of the rates of return of A and B, or 22%. In general, expected rates of return are additive.

It is possible, however, that the expected rate of return for the combined firm C could be greater than 22%. A rate of return of a combination that is expected to be greater than the weighted average of the two entities' returns is called *synergistic.* **Synergy**, then, is a "one plus one equals three" effect. It describes the quantitative effect upon rates of return brought about by complementary factors. Synergy may be responsible for most of the merger activity since the mid-1970s. There are several consequences of mergers that may cause synergy.

Undervalued Stock

The low market value of a firm's stock is frequently cited as a principal motive for merger as well as a primary cause of synergy. *Undervalued* in this sense means that the market price of a firm's stock is perceived to be significantly less than the cost of replacing the firm's assets. For example, George M. Keller, chairman of the board of Standard Oil of California (Socal), has been quoted as regarding mining companies as "prime candidates for acquisition because they are still selling for great discounts from the underlying value of their assets."† Keller was further quoted as saying that his firm was willing to face "four or five years of earning dilution" to acquire a mining concern, because he viewed the mining industry as a "long-term component" of Socal's business.‡

At first, such a concession might seem to contradict the idea of synergy, that is, that the combination of Socal and a mining company would result in *lower* expected returns for several years. It is not a contradiction, however; central to the modern concept of synergy is the idea that strategic decisions to acquire businesses with different activities are synergistic in the long term. Amax, the mining firm in question, had a bleak outlook for the near term in 1981. Acquisition by Socal could do little if anything to change this outlook. However, the management of Socal apparently believed that the integration of metal mining and resource-holding activities that acquisition of Amax would provide would enhance the long-term prospects for the oil company. The stockholders of Socal would benefit if the market perceived a stronger, more well-rounded firm with integration of the new resource base. Further, the shareholders of Amax would benefit, because they would participate in the brighter near-term picture of the oil company.

Measuring Undervalued Stock: Q-ratio

The relationship between the market value of a firm's assets and the replacement cost of those assets was quantified by James Tobin in the 1960s with a ratio that was termed the **Q-ratio.**§ A Q-ratio greater than 1 means that each dollar invested by the firm will result in more than a dollar increase in the market value of the firm; a Q-ratio lower than 1 means that each invested dollar will increase the market value of the firm by less than a dollar. Hence,

---

† "What Oil Will Sacrifice for Resource Security," *Business Week* (August 24, 1981), p. 30.

‡ *Ibid.*, p. 31.

§ See, for example, James Tobin and William Brainard, "Asset Markets and the Cost of Capital," in *Economic Progress, Private Values and Public Policies: Essays in Honor of William Fellner*, ed. B. Belassa and R. Nelson (Amsterdam: North-Holland, 1977). For a discussion of current usage, see Seymour Zuker, "The Q-Ratio: Fuel for the Merger Mania," *Business Week* (August 24, 1981), p. 30.

if a firm's Q-ratio is lower than 1, the wealth of the shareholders is maximized by management's retaining investment funds in cash assets or by distributing the funds to the stockholders. In such a case, the shareholders' position can also be enhanced by using the investment funds to acquire the assets of other firms, if the Q-ratio of the target firms is also lower than 1.

Not only does a low Q-ratio appear to make a firm a desirable acquisition candidate, as in the Socal–Amax example, but there is also evidence that a low Q-ratio may motivate a firm to seek acquisitions itself.

The following example will illustrate how the shareholders benefit if a firm with a Q-ratio lower than 1 acquires another firm with new investment capital instead of undertaking internal expansion. Table 17.3 shows the Q-ratio, market value, and replacement cost of physical assets of two firms, X and Y.

Suppose firm X undertakes a $100,000 expansion and decides upon internal expansion. The market, if it applied the same Q-ratio, would now see the replacement cost of X's assets as the original $1 million plus the new $100,000. The market value of X would then be expected to rise to $9.90 ($1,100,000 × .90). If, however, X used the $100,000 to acquire all the outstanding shares of Y, the replacement cost of the combined physical assets would be $1,125,000. Applying the same Q-ratio of .90 to the firm after the acquisition, the stock price would be $10.125 ($1,125,000 × .90). Hence, the shareholders would gain $0.225 per share by the acquisition, as opposed to internal expansion.

Even if the market were to adjust X's Q-ratio after the merger, a gain would still accrue. For example, if the market believed that the postacquisition Q-ratio should be the weighted average of the prevailing preacquisition ratios for the two firms, the stockholders would still be better off.

Q-ratio estimation forms one of the bases of merger arbitrage. In arbitrage, brokers and speculators seek to gain from the changes in the market price of the two firms. To arbitrage the merger in the previous example, the arbitrageur would sell shares in Y short, using the proceeds to buy shares in X. Just prior to the merger, he or she would cover this short position in Y and reap the profit in the increased value of X's shares. It must be stressed that this method is hardly foolproof; often the announcement of a merger sparks a bidding war,

TABLE 17.3
Q-ratio, Market Value, and Replacement Cost of Assets of Two Firms.

	Firm X	Firm Y
Q-ratio	.90	.80
Market value	$900,000	$100,000
Replacement cost of assets	$1,000,000	$125,000
Stock price (100,000 shares)	$9.00	$1.00

and the stock price of the target firm rises as new offers are made. For example, the DuPont bid price for Conoco was about $68; Seagram subsequently bid $92 for the same shares. Any arbitrageur who positioned Conoco short before the Seagram offer is not richer today.

In fact, there are other arbitrage strategies, based on just such occurrences, that advise the reverse position. In such a case, an arbitrageur would sell the stock of X short and buy the stock of Y, anticipating higher offers for Y from other firms.

Financing

Sometimes it is possible to finance external purchases of business assets when it is not possible to issue securities in the capital markets. Loans to undertake an acquisition may be secured by the stock of the acquired company or its assets. In other words, the financing for the merger may become available only because of the merger; this situation could be considered a type of synergy. Further, the lenders may easily include foreign sources of capital, while the issue of securities in foreign countries could be difficult or even impossible.

Taxation

Corporate income tax regulations have made it desirable, in some cases, for profitable companies to acquire those in which there has been a loss. Under the provisions of the Internal Revenue Code, net operating losses of corporations may be carried back 3 years and carried forward 15 years to reduce taxable income. After an acquisition has been completed, amended tax returns can be filed for the years in which the carry-back is applicable. Also, when the firm showing past losses is merged into a profitable one, the carry-forward of those losses can reduce the future taxable income of the surviving firm. Such an accounting effect can be deemed to be synergy.

When much of the stock of a smaller firm is in the hands of a few individuals, such as the members of the founding family, the death of the founder might force the family to seek an acquisition in order to pay the inheritance taxes. In such a case, the terms of sale could make the firm's stock, and the subsequent control of the firm attractive as an acquisition.

FINANCIAL EFFECTS OF MERGERS

In contemplating a merger, stockholders of both firms are most concerned with the effect upon the market price and EPS of the stock after the merger. If the terms of a merger are known, the effect upon EPS can be derived. The effect upon the market price of the shares of the surviving or combined firm, however, cannot be predicted with such certainty.

Effect on Earnings per Share

EPS can be determined by considering the PE ratios of the two firms prior to a merger. In general, if firm A acquires firm B through an exchange of common stock, A's EPS will increase if A's PE ratio was greater than B's. Conversely, if A's PE ratio had been less than B's, its EPS will fall, or be diluted, after the merger. To illustrate this, consider the following example.

In this example, a high-growth firm acquires a lower-growth firm. For simplicity, the market price per share is the same for both firms: $120. It is assumed, therefore, that firm A exchanges 1 million of its shares for the 1 million shares of B outstanding. The immediate consequence is the change in EPS: for firm A, an increase of $1.17 per share; for firm B, a decrease of $5.83 per share. Note that the increase in A's EPS multiplied by the original 5 million shares exactly equals the dilution of the EPS of B multiplied by its original 1 million shares, except for rounding error.

This example should indicate that there is no magic in the increase in EPS of the high PE ratio firm. In reality, one of the two parties to a merger will always experience an increase in EPS, while the other will experience a decrease, when measured in terms of the premerger shares. The only exception to this rule occurs if the two firms had been selling in the market at exactly the same PE ratios.

Since one party to a merger always experiences a dilution of EPS, one might wonder why the management or shareholders of that firm would ever permit the merger. The answer is found by recalling that a shareholder is interested in personal wealth; in other words, the shareholder is concerned with the market price of his or her shares, not just EPS.

Effect on Market Price

The market price of the stock of the surviving firm in a merger is not determined easily beforehand. This is because the market price of a share of stock is jointly determined by the firm's present earnings, its dividend payout ratio, the expected growth rate of earnings, and the market's capitalization rate. Even if the earnings after the merger are the sum of what the separate earnings would have been had the two firms not merged, the postmerger growth rate of earnings is not necessarily systematically related to the growth rates of the two premerger firms. Further, the postmerger capitalization rate, the cost of equity capital discussed in Chapter 4, may be greater or less than the capitalization rates of the premerger firms, depending on whether the merger is perceived by the capital markets to have increased or decreased the risk of the combined firm.

In the example in Table 17.4, suppose that the acquisition is synergistic: The growth rate of the firm after the merger is 18%. Further, suppose that there is no change in the cost of equity capital to the new firm: The growth

TABLE 17.4
Acquisition of a Low-Growth Firm by a High-Growth Firm.

	Acquiring (Firm A)	Target (Firm B)	Post-acquisition
Total earnings	$40,000,000	$15,000,000	$55,000,000
Dividends paid	$24,000,000	$ 9,000,000	$33,000,000
Number of shares	5,000,000	1,000,000	6,000,000
Earnings per share	$8	$15	$9.17
Price/earnings ratio	15:1	8:1	n.a.
Market price	$120	$120	n.a.
Payout ratio	0.6:1	0.6:1	0.6:1
Growth rate	17%	7.5%	n.a.
Capital cost	21%	15%	n.a.

rate remains at 21%. Then, from the footnote below, it can be determined that the market would assign a PE ratio of 20; in this case, the stock price would then jump to over $180 per share.

In analyzing a merger or considering management's motivation to merge, the EPS increase or dilution is not sufficient. In a sense, the effect of a merger on EPS is little more than an accounting effect. What is important is the effect of the merger on the value of the stockholders' shares.†

AN ECONOMIC RATIONALE FOR COMBINATION: DIVERSIFICATION

Most traditional business firms produce items closely related to their original product lines, which employ the firm's experience, expertise, technology, and markets. Studies have shown that the unit cost tends to fall in relation to the number of units the firms has produced since the inception of the business; in other words, there appears to be some return on experience in production.

---

† The relationship between risk and capitalization rate is based on the formula for the cost of equity capital developed in Chapter 4. The basic formula there was derived from the model of price:

$$P = \frac{D_1}{K_e - g}.$$

If E is defined as earnings, b as the percentage of earnings paid in dividends (the payout ratio), g as the growth rate of earnings, and K as the capitalization rate, then

$$P = \frac{bE}{K - g}.$$

Therefore the PE ratio is jointly determined by b, g, and K.

$$\frac{P}{E} = \frac{b}{K - g}.$$

By external combination, a firm can not only quickly obtain the necessary facilities to embark on an unrelated line of business, but usually it also acquires a going concern with an experienced staff, outlets for the products, ready markets, and goodwill.

Present enforcement of the antitrust laws by the federal government has made it easier for corporate management to acquire noncompetitive companies in other industries. An economic rationale, however, must exist for a firm to acquire another firm whose line of business is radically different. One motivation seen most recently has been a desire for diversification.

Recall that the principal goal of a firm's management is to maximize the wealth of the shareholders. In the terminology of microeconomics, this goal also could be stated as the desire to maximize the utility of the shareholders. Increasing the rate of return to the stockholders of the firm clearly increases their utility. Minimizing the variability (or risk) of the rate of return, however, also increases the utility of the typical stockholder. If external expansion serves to increase the expected return to the stockholders, it can be considered consistent with management's primary goal. Likewise, if external expansion serves to decrease the variability of the rate of return, it can be considered to meet the utility-maximizing goal. In fact, one of the advantages of external expansion most often cited is that acquisition across lines of business can maximize the firm's rate of return through synergy.

Diversification also results in synergy in terms of the variability of rates of return. What causes this synergy is the mathematical properties of the variance of a sum of random variables. When two assets are combined, the variance of the portfolio is a function of the variance of each asset *plus* the covariance between the assets. If the correlation is not perfect, the portfolio variance will be less than the weighted average of the two original variances.†

This is another purported rationale for the merger of diverse lines of business: While the expected rates of return on a judicious combination of different lines of business will be the weighted average of the expected rates of the individual lines of business, the *riskiness* of the new firm's rate of return, as measured by the standard deviation, will be less than the weighted sum of the standard deviations of the individual lines.

From the standpoint of maximizing shareholder wealth, however, merger for the sake of diversification alone is questionable. It may be dangerous to spread the talents of management and the financial resources of the firm over too many diverse activities. This may result in a loss of management control

---

†The variance of the sum of two random variables is given by

$$\sigma_p^2 = X_1^2 \sigma_1^2 + X_2^2 \sigma_2^2 + 2X_1 X_2 \operatorname{cov}(1, 2).$$

Since $\operatorname{cov}(1, 2)$ can be written $\rho_{12}\sigma_1\sigma_2$, we see that the variance of a portfolio is a function of the correlation between the assets. If $\rho_{12} < 1$, σ_p^2 will be less than the weighted average of the individual variances. (See Appendix 4A for elaboration.)

that could overshadow any benefits to be derived from reduction of risk through diversification.

An argument against diversification for the sake of risk reduction is that it reduces the portfolio decision process of the firm's shareholders. That is, if the stockholders themselves wish to reduce risk in their own portfolios, they may do so themselves by their own selection of securities in other firms. In general, their own decisions will serve to increase their utility more than would diversification by the firm.

What is certain, however, is that diversification should be considered only when the expanding firm's management can forecast a rate of return on the investment that is higher than its cost of capital.

INSTITUTIONAL FACTORS IN BUSINESS COMBINATIONS

This section focuses on the ways in which business combinations come about. We will discuss how firms seeking mergers find firms with the characteristics they want, and then describe the common forms that business combinations take.

The acquisition of corporations and their operating assets is often initiated by professional promoters or investment bankers. While the promotion of mergers is not the primary activity of investment banking firms, they are uniquely equipped to perform such functions efficiently. Once a firm makes it known, often privately, that it is considering an acquisition, its investment bankers are in a position to help. Investment banking houses have broad experience in securities matters and are in close contact with many different firms. Large investment banking houses, such as Lehman Brothers or Salomon Brothers, may have 50 or more of their directors or staff on the boards of other firms, and they may act in an advisory capacity to perhaps several hundred other large corporations; therefore they may be as familiar with a firm's management as any insider. For this reason, they would be able to suggest a merger to two firms that they know are both willing to merge and that meet each other's specifications. Once acquisition negotiations have begun, the investment banker can also provide advice, legal counsel, and securities market services to one or both of the firms.

Those who negotiate a merger are seldom the ones who will operate the surviving firm after the merger. Therefore, the successful promotion and consummation of a merger does not necessarily ensure the success of the new operating firm. The promoter or investment banker simply acts as an intermediary, or, in a sense, as a salesperson who will be compensated for his or her efforts. The intermediary responds to the desires of the management of the firms; unless the management and stockholders of the two firms are correct in their assessment of the justification of a merger, it may be doomed to failure, or at least will damage the wealth position of both sets of stockholders.

When two or more existing corporations are combined, a major concern to the promoters, those within the subject firms, and their outside advisors is to select the form of combination. Consideration must be given to the arrangement of financing, the degree to which management control is altered, the effectiveness of the organization after the combination, and the attitude of the management and stockholders of the firm.

FORMS OF COMBINATIONS

The combinations discussed in this section include leasing, holding company, and consolidation or merger.

Lease Arrangement

The least expensive method of combination is by means of a lease. A lease transaction is the easiest form to organize and one of the most flexible. One firm simply leases the assets of a second company in order to use them. The lease arrangement will not change the existing tax structure of either firm significantly, since no assets are transferred on either firm's books. No cash may be needed by the acquiring firm, and negotiations may be extremely simple, since only the consent of the leased firm's stockholders is required. The intercorporate lease may include all the property of the leased firm, including the real estate and working capital.

The terms of a lease agreement may permit the leasing company to assume the corporate powers of the firm whose assets are leased, leaving the latter firm as little more than a passive recipient of lease revenues. The leased firm will, however, continue to hold annual meetings, maintain its stock transfer books, elect a board of directors, and pay dividends to its shareholders out of the lease revenues. Lease arrangements are often used when a firm has a protected technology or specialized equipment, as well as in the case of small mining firms that may find it more profitable to lease their claims and improvements to larger firms than to work the deposits themselves.

One clear advantage of a lease arrangement is that it does not need to be permanent; after the expiration of the lease, the terms may be renegotiated, or one firm may decide not to renew the lease at all. Of course, depending upon the circumstances, this could also be a disadvantage to either party to the lease.

Drawbacks to the lease combination are that (1) it may result in high fixed charges that may adversely affect the leasing firm's credit in the same manner as if that firm had taken on debt; and (2) property acquired through a lease is not allowed to be used as security or collateral, since title remains in the hands of the firm leasing the property. One exception to this restriction can occur in the case of an exclusive lease on a protected technology that could be transferred to another firm; in such a case, the lease itself could have a value, and hence be used as collateral. A final disadvantage is that the tax situation could be unfavorable because two corporate taxpayers are involved. Other than those instances cited, little use of lease arrangements is made. The tax disadvantages have been an important factor in the termination of many leases and the merger of the firms involved.

Holding Company

Firms that control one or more companies through the ownership of voting stock are called **holding companies.** Control of a firm technically entails the ownership of more than 50% of the voting stock; control of a widely held company can actually require ownership of as little as 20% of the voting stock. The Public Utility Holding Company Act of 1935 states that a holding company is one that "directly or indirectly owns, controls, or holds with power to vote, 10 percentum or more of the outstanding voting securities of a public utility company."

While holding companies are sometimes perceived as relics of the 1920s, their use remains quite pervasive. Many large industrial corporations are holding companies; further, most large banks are subsidiaries of holding companies.

In its simplest form, a holding company has assets that consist primarily of the voting stock of its subsidiaries. The holding company often acts as the finance company of the subsidiaries; the individual subsidiaries may sell bonds or stock entirely to the holding company (the parent), and the parent may then arrange and manage the outside financing. These activities can serve to intensify holding company control over subsidiaries that are not wholly owned. Holding companies may be preferred over mergers or other consolidations for widely varied reasons.

Simplified securities transactions. It is not necessary to obtain the approval of stockholders of either firm before or after the control of a company has been achieved. Sometimes an investment banker may be able to arrange the sale or exchange of a large block of stock of controlling size. Although the stock could be purchased in the open market, such a large purchase might tend to raise the price of the stock; further, it might take considerable time to acquire the shares. An alternative method of acquiring controlling shares is to offer a price for the stock that is above the market price, thereby pursuading individual stockholders to sell or tender their shares directly.

The bid made by Seagram for Conoco is an example of a tender offer made for cash. Further, it is evident that Seagram intended to remain as a holding company, rather than to consolidate Conoco's assets into the Seagram corporate structure.

The holding company strategy further allows conservation of cash, since there are no legal requirements that dissenting shareholders of the acquired firm must be paid, as is the case in consolidations and mergers.

Autonomy. In holding company acquisitions, the acquired firm typically retains its own name, management, assets, and liabilities. Usually the holding company does not guarantee or assume responsibility for the debts of its subsidiaries. The holding company is a stockholder like any other, and it enjoys the limited liability that such status provides. Therefore the parent company is insulated from extreme liability. Further, if a holding company were required to dispose of its shares in a company, due to legal or regulatory decisions like those that led to the breakup of the American Telephone and Telegraph Company, the autonomous structure means that no effective change in the corporate structure of either firm is necessary. Further, the disposal of a subsidiary is little more than a complex securities transaction, which is far simpler than even the most straightforward division of the assets, liabilities, and personnel of an integrated firm. Finally, the holding company structure may allow a firm to circumvent regulatory restrictions on lines of business. For example, a bank may create a holding company in a unit banking state to allow it to carry on branch banking; a bank holding company may also be able to engage in activities not legally permitted to a bank.

When a parent corporation is guilty of mismanagement of a subsidiary, it cannot avoid responsibility for the debts of the subsidiary that might have arisen from that misconduct. This is analogous to "piercing the corporate veil," so that one can hold managers or stockholders of a corporation liable for willful misconduct. Individual liability in the case of mismanagement or unfair treatment of a subsidiary is a matter of civil law, and the degree of responsibility of the parent must be determined by the courts.

On the other hand, in order to ensure that the parent cannot be held liable for the debts of the subsidiary, management must take the following precautions: (1) the subsidiary should be set up as an autonomous unit that is strong enough to bear its own economic risks; (2) the subsidiary and the parent should function separately, maintain arm's length transactions as much as possible, and maintain separate financial records; and (3) outside parties with whom both corporations deal should be made aware that the two are separate legal entities.

Multijurisdiction operation. The holding company form makes it easy to do business in different states or in foreign countries. For example, if one activity carried on by a corporation is subject to state regulation, it is possible that all activities of the corporation might be subject to review and regulation by the state. This can be avoided if the corporation maintains the regulated activity as the sole business of a subsidiary.

If American corporations or banks operating abroad conduct business as foreign subsidiaries, they may enjoy more goodwill as well as avoid discriminatory regulations that many nations impose on foreign business activity. Further, if the parent firm allows local investors to purchase the stock of the subsidiary, it may create thereby a base of economic and political support for the firm's activities that otherwise might not exist.

The greatest disadvantage of a holding company structure is possible double taxation of a subsidiary's earnings. If the parent does not own 80% of a subsidiary's voting stock, as well as 80% of each class of nonvoting common stock, then it cannot file consolidated financial statements. A consolidated tax return has the advantage of canceling out intercompany transactions. If the parent's holdings in the subsidiary are less than 80%, however, then 15% of the dividends paid by the subsidiary to the parent will be subject to tax. Of course, the funds with which the subsidiary pays the dividends come from after-tax income. That is, they have already been taxed, and they will be taxed again as income to the holding company, which results in double taxation.

Consolidation or Merger

The current trend in acquisition in business combinations is the formation of one company, rather than the maintenance of several legal corporate entities. **Consolidation** is the true merger, although this term is used to refer to most acquisitions. In the merger form of combination, the surviving company is the only taxpayer. Merger avoids some of the tax disadvantages of the holding company form. Further, when the merger is accomplished by an exchange of stock, no capital gains or transfer tax is involved. Any capital gains tax for which the stockholders of the merged firms would be responsible will be deferred until each owner disposes of his or her stock in the new entity.

One problem of consolidation is that two sets of stockholders must be satisfied before the transaction takes place. This may make the merger difficult to organize. If any stockholders dissent from approval of the merger, which they have a statutory right to do, their claims will need to be settled for the fair value of their stock. Procedures to handle settlement of dissenting stockholders' claims are spelled out in state statutes. In general, while dissent to a merger will not itself delay the transaction, the courts will determine the compensation if the corporation and the dissenting stockholders cannot agree on the fair market value of the shares.

Creditors have no voice in the decision of a firm to consolidate unless fraud or illegal actions occur. Secured creditors retain the same liens on assets that they had before the merger; that is, their claims follow the assets into the surviving corporation. The surviving corporation assumes the obligations, penalties, and liabilities of the former corporations, including judgments of any pending lawsuits.

SUMMARY

In this chapter, we have discussed the topic of planning and structuring the growth of a business firm.

A firm should seek to expand whenever its management judges that growth will serve the goal of maximizing the value of the firm. That is, the firm should grow only to its optimum size. Optimum size is determined by a combination of the value of the firm's final product, the technological base of the industry, the organization of the product's markets, the ability to use a process by-product, capital costs, and management's perception of the proper size of the firm.

A firm can expand either through internal or external growth. Internal growth involves the use of either retained earnings or outside capital. It avoids valuation problems, avoids problems of integrating the policies and personnel of another firm after a merger, allows new facilities to be built, and avoids the necessity to seek stockholder approval for growth projects. A primary drawback to internal growth is that it may take a long time for a project to become profitable. Another possible drawback is that internal expansion of facilities adds to the total capacity of an industry, which may make marketing more difficult as the supply of products is increased.

External growth is known as merger or acquisition. A primary advantage of external expansion is that the waiting period before expansion becomes profitable is reduced or eliminated. Further, it is much easier for a firm to acquire a business different from its own than it is for the firm to build that new business.

External expansion is categorized according to the primary economic relationship between the business activities of the merging firms. There are five forms: horizontal, vertical, product extension, market extension, and diversified activity. The last three forms define conglomerate mergers.

Synergy describes a situation in which the value of the whole is greater than the sum of its parts. Causes of synergy can be undervaluation of the market price of stock, financing techniques, and taxation effects. Synergy is commonly held to be a motive behind the current high level of merger activity.

The most obvious financial effect of a merger is the effect on EPS. Stockholders in one firm always experience an increase in EPS, and stockholders in the other firm always experience a decrease. Actually, the important result is the *value of the stock* after the merger, which is determined by the effects of the merger on the capitalization and growth rates of the new firm.

Diversification in lines of business is often cited as a rationale for conglomerate merger. That is, diversification may reduce the risk of the firm.

Business combinations are often promoted by investment bankers. One matter with which the promoters are concerned is selection of the form of combination. Forms typically employed include lease arrangements, holding companies, and consolidations or mergers.

QUESTIONS AND REVIEW ACTIVITIES

1. Compare the factors that determine optimal firm size with the factors that you believe limit the growth and ultimate size of a firm. Do these factors argue for internal or external growth? Explain.

2. A variation of an old saying is, "What is good for the goose may not be good for the flock." Why might external expansion be contrary to a national policy of spurring capital expansion and increasing productive capacity?

3. If Firm X were a supplier to Firm Y prior to a vertical integration in which X becomes Y's subsidiary, would X be justified in raising the price to Y? Would X be justified in lowering the price to Y?

4. What kinds of problems can occur in conglomerate mergers with respect to (a) management, (b) labor relations, (c) financing, and (d) production?

5. How has inflation motivated mergers and acquisitions? What kinds of companies become more desirable in inflationary times?

6. Using the formula in the footnote on p. 515, determine the effect on a firm's PE ratio of changes in (a) the cost of equity capital, (b) the growth rate of the firm, and (c) the earnings retention rate.

7. Explain how and why it may be cheaper to acquire control over a second corporation by stock ownership than by merger or outright purchase.

8. Is the use of debt in a holding company's capital structure more risky than the use of debt in an operating company? Explain.

9. Rumors of merger often cause the market price of both companies' stock to rise. Why? Does merger necessarily increase the value of both companies' stock?

10. In order for a merger to be profitable, must the combination be synergistic? Explain.

PROBLEMS

1. Compute the earnings available to Holding Company X if its operating company pays out all earnings in dividends, using the following information:

Holding Company X:	
Percentage of common stock in operating firm	60%
Operating Company	
Total assets	$250,000
Debt (8% average rate)	$125,000
Preferred stock (6% dividend)	$25,000
Earnings before interest and taxes	$75,000
Effective tax rate	40%

2. Engulf Resources is considering V. Little to determine whether it might be a merger partner. The following information is given:

	Engulf	Little
Total earnings	$20,000	$ 5,000
Number of shares outstanding	10,000	10,000
Earnings per share	$2.00	$0.50
Market price	$40.00	$5.00
Price-earnings ratio	20:1	10:1

Engulf's investment banker suggests that a tender offer be proposed in which one share of Engulf would be exchanged for five shares of Little.

a) Determine the effect of this offer on (i) the market price of Little as soon as the tender offer is announced, (ii) the PE ratio of Engulf after the acquisition, and (iii) the overall effect on the position of Little's stockholders.

b) Would you argue for the merger if you were the merger counsel for Engulf? If you were the merger counsel for Little?

3. National Corp. is contemplating the acquisition of Local Coal Co. Local's earnings over the last few years have averaged $100,000. National believes that Local's stock should have a PE ratio of 10; its earnings are $2.50 per share. What valuation should National place on Local?

4. There is a faction among National's stockholders who will not support an acquisition proposal unless the Q-ratio of the target firm is lower than .80. On the basis of the value determined in the previous question, what would the minimum replacement cost of Local's assets have to be in order for Local to meet this criterion?

5. Southwestern Diversified Holdings has two wholly owned operating companies, Southco and Westco. The balance sheets of both operating companies are identical, as of December 31, 1981, as follows:

Current assets	$12	Current liabilities	$ 2
Fixed assets	8	Bonds (10%)	4
		Preferred stock (8%)	4
		Common stock	8
		Retained earnings	2
Total assets	$20	Total claims	$20

Each operating company earns $2 million annually before taxes and before interest and preferred dividends. A 40% tax rate is assumed.

a) What is the annual rate of return on each subsidiary's net worth (common stock plus retained earnings)?

b) If Southwestern Diversified has fixed interest charges of $1 million, how much will be available annually for distribution to its stockholders?

c) A fourth company, Leveraged Brothers, acquired 30% of Southwestern Diversified, and thereby control, for $3 million. What percentage is this of the total assets of the operating companies?

ADDITIONAL READINGS

Alberts, W. W., and J. E. Segall (eds.). *The Corporate Merger*. Chicago: University of Chicago Press, 1966.

Beman, L. "What We Learned from the Great Merger Frenzy," *Fortune* (April 1973), pp. 70 ff.

Franks, J. R., R. Miles, and J. Bagwell. "A Review of Acquisition Valuation Models," *Journal of Business Finance and Accounting* (Spring 1974), pp. 35–53.

Gort, M. *Diversification and Integration in American Industry*. Princeton, N.J.: Princeton University Press, 1962.

Kintner, E. W. *Primer on the Law of Mergers*. New York: The Macmillan Company, 1973.

Lewellen, W. G. "A Pure Financial Rationale for Conglomerate Merger," *Journal of Finance* (May 1971), pp. 93–113.

Reinhardt, U. E. *Mergers and Consolidations: A Corporate-Finance Approach*. Morristown, N.J.: General Learning Press, 1972.

Scott, J. H. "On the Theory of Conglomerate Mergers," *Journal of Finance*, (September 1977), pp. 1235–50.

Shick, R. A., and F. C. Jen. "Merger Benefits of Shareholders of Acquiring Firms," *Financial Management* (Winter 1974), pp. 45–53.

TYPES OF BUSINESS FAILURE
COMMON CAUSES OF BUSINESS FAILURE
REMEDIES FOR BUSINESS FAILURE
LIQUIDATION—CHAPTER 7
REORGANIZATION—CHAPTER 11
ADJUSTMENT OF DEBTS—CHAPTER 13

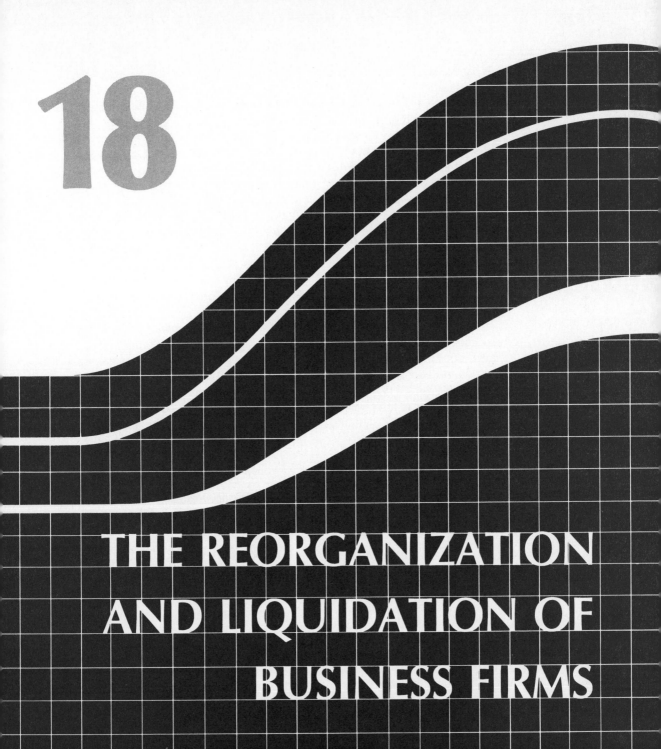

18

THE REORGANIZATION
AND LIQUIDATION OF
BUSINESS FIRMS

So far we have focused on the financial management of business firms as successful, ongoing enterprises. Even the most casual observer, however, is aware that it is not unusual for the management of a business to discontinue or reorganize some or all of the firm's operations. Despite the diligent application of management's entrepreneurial and professional business skills, the firm may fail.

The measure of what constitutes failure is a relative one. Failure may occur if any activity, operation, division, or the entire firm is unable to provide a sufficient return on investment. While the firm or subdivision of the firm may be successful in the sense that it is able to honor liabilities as they become due and continues to provide positive cash flows, management or shareholders may consider that the firm is a failure if its return on invested capital is less than the opportunity cost of these funds. Alternatively, the bankruptcy laws define a failed firm as one that generally is not paying debts as they become due. Sometimes a firm that has failed according to legal definitions may continue business operations by agreement with its creditors or under the protection of the bankruptcy laws.

Financial managers, in general, prefer to think in terms of opportunities for success rather than dwelling on risk and the possibility of failure. Failure, however, does occur, and it is important that management be aware of the legal procedures entailed, as well as what remedies are available to the firm. Such knowledge will help the firm minimize losses to creditors, stockholders, and others. The same information is important when the firm becomes a creditor of a bankrupt firm. Understanding the procedures of reorganization and liquidation may help a creditor to recover as much as possible on an unpaid account.

After careful study of this chapter, you should

1. Be familiar with much of the vocabulary associated with the reorganization and liquidation of business firms.
2. Understand the ways in which a business is considered to have failed.
3. Be knowledgeable about the most frequent causes of failure.
4. Understand the remedies available to bankrupt firms and their creditors on both a voluntary and an involuntary basis.

TYPES OF BUSINESS FAILURE

A firm may discontinue operations if management decides that it will be unable to provide adequate returns in the future. In the sense of not continuing operations, the firm fails. The more common measure of failure, though, is that the firm generally does not pay its debts as they become due. A firm is said to be technically insolvent when assets exceed liabilities, but the assets are held in a form that cannot be converted to cash readily. The complete term **insolvency in bankruptcy** or simply *insolvency* means that the firm's liabilities exceed the fair market value of its assets. Both failures are treated in the same way by the bankruptcy courts. Under the current laws, all that is necessary for a firm to fail is that it generally is not paying debts as they become due. This guide, used by the bankruptcy court, allows the court some flexibility in determining when a firm is bankrupt.

Failure to Earn an Adequate Return

A firm that is unable to earn a return equal to or greater than its cost of capital is a failure from the stockholders' position. Even though a firm may have been successful in the past, prospects for its future profitability may be so dismal that stockholders would fare better if the firm were liquidated before the losses absorb its remaining financial resources. Often the loss may be confined to one line of business or division. In such a case, firms commonly discontinue division operations when returns are inadequate, allowing real-location of resources to more promising activities.

By the definition of failure, as inadequate returns, a firm may be able to generate enough cash flow through operations, depreciation, recovery of past tax payments through income averaging, and other sources to avoid defaulting on its debts. It is considered to be a failure, however, because it is unable to provide stockholders with a return equal to the cost of the capital.

Technical Insolvency

Technical insolvency occurs when the firm is unable to obtain funds to pay debts as they become due even though the fair market value of the firm's assets exceeds its liabilities. The bankruptcy laws do not distinguish between failure when assets exceed liabilities and failure when assets are less than liabilities. From an economic viewpoint, however, there is a significant difference. Often a firm that is technically insolvent may be able to pay its debts and emerge as a financially viable entity if the creditors allow it to continue operating. The forbearance of creditors may be arranged informally or formally under the protective umbrella of the bankruptcy courts. Many firms that are technically insolvent may also be candidates for reorganization.

Insolvency in Bankruptcy

Insolvency in bankruptcy occurs when liabilities exceed the fair market value of a firm's assets. Some of the assets may be liquid or may become liquid if the firm is allowed to continue operations. In the short term, however, the firm is unable to meet maturing obligations. If a firm's financial condition has deteriorated to the point where it is insolvent in bankruptcy, the firm may be liquidated and the remaining funds distributed among the creditors.

COMMON CAUSES OF BUSINESS FAILURE

Some of the factors that may cause a successful firm to reach a point where future profits will be inadequate or even become losses include

- Changes in technology to which a firm is unable to adapt.
- Expiration of patents, licensing arrangements, franchises, concessions, and related contractual or legal competitive advantages.
- Death, retirement, or other loss of key personnel.
- Industry deregulation.
- Unaffordable pollution control requirement or other government regulations making profitable operations difficult.
- Increases in the cost of key inputs to the production process, such as raw materials, energy, or labor, that cannot be recovered through price increases.

In almost all instances, business failure can be traced to actions management took or should have taken but did not. Sometimes, of course, the reason for failure was beyond management's control. The most common causes can be classified as either managerial inadequacy or economic misfortune.

Managerial Inadequacy

Management can be inadequate in numerous ways. Dun and Bradstreet describes managerial inadequacy in terms of lack of experience in the line of business, lack of managerial experience, unbalanced experience (meaning that key managers lack well-rounded experience in various phases of the business), and incompetence. Usually, business failure results from actions management took that later proved to be errors or actions management failed to take that might have helped avoid failure. As Table 18.1 shows, some form of inadequacy in management is by far the largest cause of failure across a wide range of business activities.

Economic Misfortune

The term *economic misfortune* encompasses a number of external factors that are beyond the direct control of management. At the macroeconomic level, a recession reduces the total level of business activity. Despite the best efforts of management to conduct the firm's affairs efficiently, there may be little that can be done to avoid financial failure short of discontinuing business activities. Some industries, such as residential construction, basic industries (e.g., iron and steel, automobiles, and coal mining), and capital goods manufacturing, are especially sensitive to downturns in economic activity. On a

TABLE 18.1
Causes of 16,794 Business Failures in 1981.

Underlying Causes	Manufacturers	Wholesalers	Retailers	Construction	Commercial Services	All Firms Total
Neglect	0.4%	0.9%	0.7%	0.6%	0.4%	0.7%
Fraud	0.4	0.8	0.3	0.1	0.4	0.3
Lack of experience in the line	11.3	8.9	15.6	5.8	7.8	11.1
Lack of managerial experience	10.7	11.2	12.7	14.0	12.6	12.5
Unbalanced experience†	18.3	20.1	19.2	18.0	21.1	19.2
Incompetence	50.1	50.0	41.7	51.4	40.9	45.6
Disaster	0.7	0.6	0.5	0.2	0.3	0.5
Reason unknown	8.1	7.5	9.3	9.9	16.5	10.1
Total	100.0%	100.0%	100.0%	100.0%	100.0%	100.0%
Number of failures	2,224	1,708	6,882	3,614	2,366	16,794
Average liabilities per failure	$1,065,834	$660,792	$226,464	$235,689	$442,022	$414,147

† Experience not well rounded in sales, finance, purchasing, and production on the part of the individual in a proprietorship, or of two or more partners or officers constituting a management unit.
Source: Dun and Bradstreet. *The Business Failure Record* (New York: 1983), p. 12. By permission of Dun and Bradstreet Credit Services, a company of the Dun and Bradstreet Corporation.

smaller scale, individual firms or industries may be influenced by factors beyond management's control. Advances in technology may produce substitute products with which a firm cannot compete. Retail firms sometimes find that competitors have overexpanded and saturated a local market so that there is not enough business to go around. The failure or closing of a major employer may force many suppliers and local firms out of business.

In most cases, of course, it is far easier to look back and identify the causes of failure than it is to look forward and anticipate situations that could lead to financial distress. It is more valuable, however, to forecast a problem in advance, and thereby avoid failure, than it is to try to salvage a failing firm once a problem is allowed to develop. Altman† and, later, others developed statistical models for predicting bankruptcy using financial ratios. Whether using a formal model or relying on common sense, management must monitor the firm's financial condition. Further, managers should watch the condition of their major customers so that the warning signs of financial failure can be detected as early as possible. Unfortunately, even the most diligent monitoring may not prevent a firm from becoming involved in some form of failure. Once failure occurs, management should be aware of the possible remedies.

REMEDIES FOR BUSINESS FAILURE

A firm that fails by becoming technically insolvent or bankrupt may be able to reach a voluntary out-of-court settlement with its creditors. If voluntary arrangements cannot be made or maintained, formal reorganization or liquidation under the Bankruptcy Act becomes the final remedy. Usually, a voluntary settlement is better for all parties since the costs of formal bankruptcy proceedings can be avoided.

Voluntary remedies for insolvency and bankruptcy are intended to avoid a court settlement. By eliminating the cost of bankruptcy proceedings, creditors and owners have a better chance of recovery. Further, if all parties cooperate, a voluntary settlement can avoid the costly delays and extended litigation associated with court settlements. In a voluntary settlement, the management of the debtor firm has a better chance of obtaining a settlement that will permit it to survive or, if the firm is liquidated, have assets disposed of in a manner that allows the owners of the firm to recover as much of their investment as possible. To start the process, the debtor arranges a meeting with its creditors.

The meeting is often planned with the aid of a local credit or trade association. At this meeting, the creditors appoint a committee with representatives for both the large and small claimants. This **creditors' committee**

---

† Edward I. Altman, *Corporate Bankruptcy in America* (Lexington, Mass.: Heath Lexington Books, D. C. Heath and Company, 1971).

then arranges for an investigation of the debtor's financial condition. When an adjustment bureau of a local credit association assists, the bureau may have its own investigators who can be charged with gathering the necessary information. If the debtor and the creditors' committee can agree on a plan for reorganizing or liquidating the firm, the terms of the agreement are stated in a formal contract.

A major motivation for cooperation among creditors is that a smaller settlement may result if the bankruptcy court becomes involved. A problem, though, is that the refusal of even a single creditor to participate can legally prohibit the remaining creditors from enacting the arrangement. Sometimes larger creditors will pay off a smaller recalcitrant creditor to reach agreement on a plan. Approval of a plan is influenced by

- The management's reputation for honesty and integrity.
- The potential for achieving financial recovery.
- The economic outlook for the industry.

Four types of voluntary agreements are widely used: the extension, the composition, creditor control, and some combination of these approaches.

Extension

With an **extension,** the debtor is required to pay the full amount of all outstanding debts, but the time for payment is extended. The immediate problem with an extension is that the firm may not be able to obtain new working capital or trade credit with the overhanging claim of old debts. As a consequence, the firm may not be able to operate without new sources of funds. For this reason, the extension contract may allow for the subordination of existing debt while the extension is in effect. In exchange for accepting subordination, the creditors may place a number of controls on the firm's management. Often a trade creditor may require the debtor to pay cash for all new purchases but allow it to retire the outstanding balance over an extended period. Other common controls include assigning the firm's assets to a creditors' committee for the extension period and requiring stockholders to place their shares in escrow with the committee. Cash disbursements may be controlled by requiring prior approval or even the cosignature of checks. The advantage of an extension to the current managers should be clear: They retain control of the firm.

Composition

In a **composition** agreement, creditors agree to accept less than full payment, receiving instead partial payment on a *pro rata* basis. A creditor's incentive for accepting this arrangement is a practical one. An investigation of the debtor's financial affairs may make it apparent that the creditor can obtain more by entering into a composition agreement than by liquidating the firm. Avoiding the substantial legal fees, administrative expenses, and inflexibility of bankruptcy is the main reason encouraging the debtor and creditors to reach a composition agreement. Also, the debtor's management maintains control of the firm, avoiding the stigma associated with bankruptcy.

A substantial problem with a composition is that dissenting creditors may insist on more favorable treatment. The options open to the nondissenting creditors are to pay the dissenters in full, allowing the latter to recover a higher percentage of their claims, or to liquidate the firm. In a reorganization, dissenters may be forced to accept certain provisions known as a *cram down*, but in a voluntary settlement they may be able to prevent an agreement from being reached. Ultimately, their ability to extract more favorable treatment from other creditors depends on the difference in value between the firm as a going concern and as a property in liquidation. This difference depends on the line of business, but in general firms in service-related industries have few marketable assets compared with manufacturing firms.

Creditor Control

Occasionally control of the debtor firm is transferred to the creditors' committee until all claims are settled. This can happen when the investigation of the creditors' committee shows that the firm has a chance to survive if the operating management is monitored. Rather than liquidating the firm, the creditors may insist that a new management be installed before additional credit is extended. The creditors may be able to bring in expertise that the debtor firm could not acquire otherwise and institute controls and procedures that make recovery possible. Although the creditors may need to invest more time and professional assistance, they may succeed in collecting outstanding debts and establishing a valuable relationship with the debtor firm.

A problem with creditor control agreements is that stockholders of the firm may institute lawsuits alleging mismanagement by the creditors. Even though the suit may be utterly without merit, the prospect of potential litigation acts as a deterrent to creditors accepting the responsibility for control. Also, the interests of creditors and stockholders differ, and decisions benefiting one group may be detrimental to the other. For these reasons, creditors are usually reluctant to take over the management of a debtor firm.

Combination of Approaches

It is likely that when the creditors' committee completes its investigation and recommends a plan, not all parties will find the plan acceptable. Through negotiation the creditors may be able to devise some workable combination of an extension, composition, and creditor control. Many combinations of the basic types of plans are possible. A plan might be a composition in requiring the debtor to pay 80 cents on the dollar, an extension by calling for repayment in four equal annual installments, and a form of creditor control in which creditors agree to extend credit to the firm on 30-day terms if certain changes in management are made. The main concern of the creditors, however, is to collect the outstanding debts. If it appears that a greater return can be obtained by liquidating the firm than is expected from sustaining it, liquidation becomes the appropriate course of action. In many situations, a voluntary settlement calling for a private liquidation may be the best remedy.

Private Liquidation

To this point, our treatment of voluntary arrangements has focused on arrangements allowing a firm to continue operations. An investigation of the firm's finances, however, may reveal that the prospects for a return to profitability are poor. The creditors' committee may then recommend **liquidation** rather than continued operations as the best way to minimize losses. Once the decision to liquidate is reached, the only question is whether to arrange a private liquidation or to use the bankruptcy courts. When cooperation can be arranged among creditors and the debtor, a voluntary liquidation may be possible. The advantage of a private liquidation is that it is quicker and should result in higher settlements because it avoids the expenses of litigation. Since all parties must agree, firms with only a few creditors have a better chance of being liquidated this way.

The motivation for agreeing to a voluntary liquidation is to recover as much as possible for creditors and, after the creditors have been paid, for the stockholders. Often the same adjustment bureau or trade association that helped organize the creditors will liquidate the debtor firm's assets. A widely used procedure is for the creditors to *assign* their interest to a third party. This *assignee* is often a specialist at liquidating assets and may be associated with the adjustment bureau or trade organization. Whenever possible, the liquidator will attempt to dispose of the firm or its remaining profitable operations *in toto*, since most assets are worth more as part of a going concern. The remaining assets are typically sold at auction. After the assets are liquidated, whatever funds were recovered are distributed among the creditors and, if any funds remain after satisfying creditors' claims, to stockholders. When final payment is made, creditors will sign a release of their claims. If a creditor holds out for more than the liquidation may reasonably provide, the case may end up in the bankruptcy court.

Formal Remedies

Despite the best efforts of the creditors' committee and the adjustment bureau or trade organization, it may not be possible to agree upon a voluntary settlement. The firm may initiate bankruptcy proceedings itself, or it may be forced into bankruptcy by its creditors. Once in bankruptcy, the firm may be reorganized or liquidated. Even after bankruptcy proceedings begin, it still may be possible to reach a voluntary settlement and withdraw the bankruptcy petition.

Normally, creditors attempt to reach a settlement with a debtor firm without incurring the expenses and delay of court proceedings. A settlement is more likely to be reached if the firm has a reasonable probability of returning to profitability. A firm that has been reorganized under bankruptcy will have a certain stigma associated with it that tends to lessen its chance for a successful recovery. When a firm files a voluntary petition for reorganization, it may be trying to gain time in order to develop a plan for survival.

Bankruptcy legislation began with the American *Bankruptcy Act of 1800*. A number of repeals and reenactments followed, but it was not until the *Bankruptcy Act of 1898* that the basis of the present law was established. The only major revision since then resulted in the *Chandler Act of 1938*. More recently, however, there has been widespread belief that the interests of creditors and debtors are out of balance and that the process is overly cumbersome. The *Bankruptcy Reform Act of 1978* enacted major changes in the law intended to provide for more equitable treatment of all parties involved and to resolve cases more quickly and efficiently. Also, a special set of bankruptcy courts was established in the federal court system.

There are eight odd-numbered chapters in the Bankruptcy Code, but the key sections are Chapters 7, 11, and, to some extent, 13. Chapter 7 covers liquidations and can be invoked if there is no apparent basis for a reorganization that meets the test of being fair and equitable. Chapter 11 provides procedures for reorganization and applies whether the petition was voluntary or involuntary. Should a workable plan for reorganization not be obtained, or should the plan fail, procedures are provided for liquidation. Chapter 13 covers individuals with regular income and is usually thought of as applying to wage earners. However, many small business firms may qualify for use of the Chapter 13 provisions.

LIQUIDATION—CHAPTER 7

Chapter 7 of the Bankruptcy Code provides for liquidation. It applies to any corporation, individual, or partnership that is not specifically excluded from coverage. (Exceptions include municipalities, railroads, domestic banks and insurance companies, and foreign banks and insurance companies.) Cases filed under Chapter 7 may be either voluntary or involuntary. While no allegations of nonpayment from creditors are necessary for a firm to file a voluntary petition, an involuntary petition requires that the petitioning creditor(s) allege either that the debtor generally is not paying debts as they become due or that a custodian (a third party) was appointed or took possession of the debtor's assets within 120 days preceding the petition.

As soon as possible after the petition or Order for Relief is filed, the bankruptcy court appoints an interim trustee. Within a reasonable time after filing, a meeting of creditors is held in which one person is elected to serve as trustee. The debtor has the obligation to file a list of creditors and a financial statement listing assets and liabilities, to surrender all assets not specifically excepted to the trustee, and to appear at all meetings of the creditors. Even after the Order of Relief has been filed, the debtor has the right to convert from a liquidation case under Chapter 7 to a reorganization case under Chapter 11 or an individual repayment case under Chapter 13.

Order of Priority

The trustee then attempts to convert the debtor's assets to cash as expeditiously as is consistent with the best interest of all parties. The property is then distributed to holders of provable claims using the following order of priority:

1. Expense of administering the bankrupt firm.
2. Wages not exceeding $2,000 per worker earned within the three months immediately preceding the filing for bankruptcy.
3. Unpaid employee fringe benefits that are due within six months before the firm discontinued business operations or filed for bankruptcy, whichever occurred first. The sum of unpaid wages and benefits is not to exceed $2,000 per worker.
4. Up to $900 each for claims of unsecured customers.
5. Unpaid taxes due to the federal government, state government, or other governmental taxing jurisdiction such as a municipal authority.
6. Claims of secured creditors paid from the liquidation of collateralized assets. Should liquidation of the collateral assets be inadequate to pay secured creditors' claims in full, the unpaid amount is treated as an unsecured claim.
7. Claims of general unsecured creditors filed within six months of the first creditors' meetings. Claims are paid on a *pro rata* basis from available funds.
8. Claims of general unsecured creditors who filed their claims late.
9. Any interest due on claims paid to this point.
10. Preferred stockholders up to the par or stated value of the preferred stock.
11. Common stockholders are to receive any remaining funds on an equal per share basis.

The order of priority allows certain parties to enjoy a higher claim than that of secured creditors. In practice, however, these claims are often small compared to the collateralized assets of the secured creditors. A simple example illustrates the application of priorities under this rule of absolute priority.

Liquidation—An example.   At the meeting of creditors, the company to be liquidated presents the balance sheet shown in Table 18.2. On closer examination, it is found that none of the claims for wages, unpaid employee benefits, and unsecured claims of customers exceeds the statutory limitation for these categories. The total cost of administering the bankrupt firm is estimated at $700,000. Also, an investigation of the indenture for the subordinated debentures reveals that they are subordinated to the claims of the bank. The mortgages are secured by liens on the fixed assets.

After the liquidation is completed, the trustee reports that $3,000,000 was received from current assets and $2,400,000 from the sale of fixed assets. The distribution of the proceeds to the various creditors is shown in Table 18.3.

As Table 18.3 shows, the funds available for distribution to general creditors and for the unsatisfied portion of the second mortgage amount to $1 million. The total claims, however, amount to $3 million. From this it can be seen that the firm actually is bankrupt in the sense that liabilities exceed the fair market value of assets. The *pro rata* share due to each creditor is determined by the ratio of available funds to total claims: $1,000,000/$3,000,000. What a creditor actually receives may be different. In this example, the claims of the debenture holders are subordinated to the claim of the bank. No funds are to be distributed until the bank is paid in full. If, as is the case

---

TABLE 18.2
Busted Flat Company: Balance Sheet at Filing Date.

Assets		*Liabilities and Stockholders' Equity*	
Cash	$ 5,000	Accounts payable	$ 500,000
Accounts receivable	1,200,000	Notes payable—bank	1,000,000
Inventories	3,000,000	Accrued wages	400,000
Prepaid expenses	50,000	Unpaid employee benefits	200,000
Total current assets	$4,255,000	Unsecured customer claims	100,000
		Taxes payable	500,000
Land	$1,500,000	Total current liabilities	$ 2,700,000
Net plant and Equipment	2,000,000	First mortgage bonds	2,000,000
Total fixed assets	$3,500,000	Second mortgage bonds	1,000,000
		Subordinated debentures	1,000,000
		Total long-term debt	$ 4,000,000
		Preferred stock (10,000 sh.)	500,000
		Common stock (50,000 sh.)	4,000,000
		Retained earnings	(3,445,000)
		Total stockholders' equity	$ 1,055,000
Total	$7,755,000	Total	$ 7,755,000

TABLE 18.3 Distribution of Funds from Liquidation of Busted Flat Co.	
Proceeds from liquidation	$5,400,000
Priority claimants	
Expenses of administering bankrupt firm	700,000
Unpaid wage claims	400,000
Unpaid employee benefits	200,000
Unsecured customer claims	100,000
Unpaid taxes	500,000
Funds remaining for creditors	$3,500,000
First mortgage bonds, paid from $2,500,000 received from sale of fixed assets	2,000,000
Second mortgage bonds, partial payment of $500,000 from funds not needed to satisfy first mortgage claim	500,000
Funds remaining for general creditors	$1,000,000

here, the full amount of the bank's claim remains unsatisfied even after subordination of the debenture holders' claims to the bank, the owners of the debentures receive nothing. Clearly, subordination makes the debentures more risky for the bondholders.

Before the Bankruptcy Reform Act of 1978, an individual, partnership, or corporation could receive a discharge from all provable debts, or certification that no more was owed, other than debts specifically excepted. The new code, however, allows only an individual to receive a discharge. The reason for the change is to prevent trafficking in corporate shells and bankrupt partnerships.

While a number of provisions exist in the Bankruptcy Code whereby an individual may not be discharged, a discharge generally will be granted if the petition was not fraudulent, if assets were not concealed, and if the debtor has not been granted a discharge in a case beginning within six years of the date of filing for the present case. Some debts cannot be discharged under Chapter 7 proceedings. Among these are certain taxes; alimony, maintenance, and support payments to a spouse, former spouse, or child; and fines and penalties due to governmental units. Also, unless a loan first became due more than five years before filing, debts for education loans from a governmental unit or nonprofit institution of higher education usually cannot be discharged.

REORGANIZATION—CHAPTER 11

Rather than liquidate a firm, its financial structure may be **reorganized** in a way that will permit continued operation. Thus, it may be possible to provide continued employment, pay creditors, and still produce a return to stockholders. Like liquidation under Chapter 7, a petition to reorganize under Chapter

11 may be voluntary or involuntary. A voluntary case may be commenced even if the firm has not reached insolvency.

There are several reasons why a debtor firm would prefer to seek protection from its creditors under Chapter 11. First, the chapter provides for an automatic stay to permit the debtor time to work out a reorganization. Once the petition is filed, not even a secured party can move to liquidate the debtor's assets without approval from the bankruptcy court. In addition, the trustee is appointed by the court rather than elected by the creditors' committee. Often a trustee is not appointed; instead, the debtor in possession assumes most of the trustee's powers. In this way, the current management is often allowed to remain in control of the firm and to conduct business as if the bankruptcy case had not begun.

One of the first duties of the trustee, or current management if a trustee is not appointed, is to establish whether the firm is worth more dead or alive. If the firm's projected value based on anticipated future earnings is less than its liquidation value, the firm may be liquidated under Chapter 7, or a reorganization plan can be accepted that amounts to liquidation under Chapter 11. If future earnings are estimated to exceed the value obtained by liquidation, a reorganization plan is attempted.

Should no trustee be appointed, the debtor has 120 days to file a plan for reorganization and another 60 days to obtain acceptance from the creditors. When a trustee is appointed, a plan not filed within 120 days, or acceptance of the plan not obtained in 180 days, other parties with a vested interest may submit plans. Under the *Bankruptcy Reform Act of 1978*, the old **"absolute priority rule"** was abandoned in favor of a more flexible **fair and equitable** rule.

This rule provides that to secure confirmation for a plan by the court, each class of creditors (each claimant) must have accepted the plan or received at least as much value as would have been obtained if the debtor were liquidated quickly on the date of the plan. Each member of a secured class of creditors is entitled to receive property of no less value than the value of the creditor's interest in the collateral. Every class of creditors must either accept the plan or have its claims unimpaired under the plan. Should a class of creditors be impaired in that the full value of its claim will not be honored under the plan and refuse to accept the plan, an alternative procedure known by the legal term **cram down** can be used.

Cram down permits acceptance of a plan over the objections of an impaired class of creditors if the objecting class and all classes junior in priority are treated according to the absolute priority rule. When the absolute priority rule is applied, it is possible that a dissenting class of creditors would receive nothing. In such a case, the dissenting class is deemed to have received fair and equitable treatment if no senior class has been allowed more than 100%

of its claims. A class of secured creditors is subject to the cram down provision, too. Any one of several tests may be applied, but the important point is that secured creditors receive at least as much value in the reorganization as the collateralized assets were worth on the effective date of the plan.

Unless provisions to the contrary are specified in the plan, confirmation of the plan discharges the debtor from any debt incurred before the date of confirmation. As with liquidation, certain debts cannot be discharged in reorganization. Examples include money obtained by false representation, alimony and child support payments, and most educational loans.

In determining what the capital structure should be, the size of anticipated earnings and the capital structure of other firms in the industry are important guidelines. One way to establish the amount of debt the reorganized firm can support is to capitalize earnings. For example, study of similar firms in the same line of business may reveal that most have a capitalization rate of 12.5% on after-tax income. The implication is that the reorganized firm's capital structure should be scaled down until it represents eight times estimated future earnings. The capital structure of the reorganized firm is usually divided between debt and equity in the same proportion as the industry average. First mortgage holders, however, are often given a secured claim in reorganization equal to the prudent loan-to-value ratio of the collateral. As an example, if a parcel of land and the improvements on it are valued at $1 million, and the prevailing, prudent first mortgage loan on similar parcels is 75%, then first mortgage bonds of $750,000 in the reorganization would be appropriate.

Reorganization—An Example.　A company filing for reorganization under Chapter 11 presents the balance sheet illustrated in Table 18.4. Within a reasonable time, a meeting of creditors is held and two points are established. First, the reasonable future earnings of the firm exceed its value in liquidation; second, the firm's earnings are sufficient to support a financial structure of $12 million. The $12 million is consistent with the capitalization of other firms in the industry based upon its expected earnings after reorganization. This amount is 50% of the total liabilities now outstanding.

Before the 120-day period has passed, the management of the debtor firm submits the reorganization plan shown in Table 18.5, along with the proposed security revisions of Table 18.6. Even if all groups of creditors do not accept the reorganization plan, the bankruptcy court is likely to approve it. Creditors would receive more than they would under a quick liquidation of the firm's assets, and as the plan conforms to the absolute priority rule, the distribution would be considered fair and equitable under the provisions for cram down.

Examination of the capital structure of other companies in the same industry has shown that a one-third debt to two-thirds equity ratio is typical. The plan presented splits each debt category (accounts payable, notes payable, and first mortgage bonds) into two parts: half to the original debt claim and half to an equity security. As a result, the original $4 million claim for accounts payable is reduced to $2 million in

TABLE 18.4
In Big Trouble Corp.: Balance Sheet at Filing Date.

Assets

Total current assets	$ 5,000,000
Net plant and equipment	20,000,000
Other assets	1,000,000
Total assets	$ 26,000,000

Liabilities and Stockholders' Equity

Accounts payable	$ 4,000,000
Unsecured notes payable	6,000,000
Total current liabilities	10,000,000
First mortgage bonds	4,000,000
Subordinated debentures†	10,000,000
Total long-term liabilities	14,000,000
Total liabilities	$ 24,000,000
Common stock (50,000 shares)	$ 1,000,000
Paid-in capital	9,000,000
Retained earnings	(8,000,000)
Total equity	2,000,000
Total liability and stockholders' equity	$ 26,000,000

†Subordinated to mortgage bonds.

TABLE 18.5
In Big Trouble Corp.: Reorganization Plan.

Class of Creditor	Amount of Creditor Claim	50% of Claim	Claim after Subordination
Accounts payable	$ 4,000,000	$ 2,000,000	$ 2,000,000
Notes payable	6,000,000	3,000,000	3,000,000
First mortgage bonds	4,000,000	2,000,000	4,000,000
Subordinated debentures†	10,000,000	5,000,000	3,000,000
	$24,000,000	$12,000,000	$12,000,000

† Subordinated to mortgage bonds.

the reorganization. While the holders of accounts payable may be unhappy with the downgrading of their claim, $2 million is a larger amount than they could expect to receive from liquidation. Of the remaining $2 million, this class of creditors receives $1 million in accounts payable and $1 million in common stock. The purpose of this allocation is to ensure that the capital structure of one-third long-term debt to two-thirds equity will be obtained. Table 18.7 presents the revised financial structure.

TABLE 18.6
In Big Trouble Corp.: Proposed Securities in Reorganization Plan.

Old Security Class	New Security Class	Amount
Accounts payable	Accounts payable	$ 1,000,000
	Common stock	1,000,000
Notes payable	Preferred stock	1,500,000
	Common stock	1,500,000
First mortgage bonds	First mortgage bonds	2,000,000
	Subordinated debentures	1,000,000
	Preferred stock	1,000,000
Subordinated debentures	Common stock	3,000,000
		$12,000,000

TABLE 18.7
In Big Trouble Corp.: Financial Structure after Reorganization.

Accounts payable	$ 1,000,000
First mortgage bonds	2,000,000
Subordinated debentures	1,000,000
Preferred stock	2,500,000
Common stock	5,500,000
	$12,000,000

Protection against Potential Liabilities

Until July 1982, the provisions of the Federal Bankruptcy Code has been used only by companies with known liabilities. At that time, however, UNR Industries, Inc., and Uncerco, a metal fabricating company bought by UNR in 1970, made legal history by filing for protection against existing and potential asbestos lawsuits under Chapter 11. In August 1982, a much larger asbestos maker, Manville Corp., used the same approach, and in November 1982, Amatex, a third asbestos company, did the same. It is estimated that 20 or more companies that have been consistent targets of lawsuits may use this approach.

The unprecedented legal move by UNR is intended to find some way to deal with the possible liabilities represented by future claimants. The problem faced by companies that used asbestos is that no one knows how many people may eventually suffer from lung disease or cancer caused by exposure to the material. It can take up to 40 years for asbestos-related disease to appear. Faced with the possibility of endless lawsuits, the companies are unable to determine how extensive future claims might be. At the time of filing,

Manville estimated these claims at $2 billion. When the filing was made, no court had ever decided whether future liabilities can be resolved in advance in a bankruptcy case.

ADJUSTMENT OF DEBTS—CHAPTER 13

Some small-business owners may qualify for reorganization under the provisions of Chapter 13 of the Bankruptcy Reform Act of 1978. Chapter 13 applies to the **adjustment of debts** of an individual with regular income. Before the 1978 revision, application under this section was restricted to wage earners. The new law allows individuals with regular income, unsecured debts of less than $100,000, and secured debts of less than $350,000 to apply for relief under its provisions. Many small-business owners, especially those in service industries, may have debts below these ceilings, allowing them to qualify for the expeditious remedy made available under Chapter 13.

Rather than following strict reorganization standards, Chapter 13 allows for adjustment of debts. A debtor who owns and operates a business is permitted to continue doing so. Only the debtor, and not the creditors, can propose a plan. The plan can be an extension or a composition. Normally, it provides for payment over a three-year period, but the time allowed can be increased up to five years if the court decides that sufficient reason exists. Further, if the debtor either pays 100% of the allowed unsecured claims or pays 70% of these claims, but had proposed the plan in good faith as his or her best effort, a discharge can be obtained. A discharge in debt secured in this manner does not require a six-year wait before another petition for bankruptcy can be filed, as other sections of the Bankruptcy Code do.

Secured creditors have some advantages under Chapter 13. As the proceedings are fairly rapid, the cost of litigation is less than in a reorganization. Also, secured creditors cannot be forced to accept substitute collateral, and there is no opportunity for haggling among creditors or for acceptance of a plan. A significant disadvantage from their point of view, however, is that unsecured creditors have no voice in the confirmation process. Secured creditors are only permitted to receive payment based on the value of the collateral as of the effective date of the plan even if their claims exceed the value of the collateral. Should the value of the collateral subsequently increase, Chapter 13 contains no provision for revaluation of the claim. Once confirmed, the provisions of the plan bind the debtor and creditors.

In addition, there is a unique provision allowing the court to grant a discharge even if the payments specified under the plan are not completed. This "hardship" discharge may be given if failure to complete the plan resulted from circumstances beyond the debtor's control, if the creditors have received more than they would have under liquidation, and if it is not practical to modify the plan.

Because of the liberal benefits Chapter 13 offers, it has been termed a debtor's paradise. The flexibility in adjusting debts certainly makes Chapter 13 an attractive choice to a small-business owner experiencing difficulties, but in truth it provides benefits to both debtors and creditors.

SUMMARY

One of the consequences of economic competition is that some business enterprises fail. The reallocation of resources from unsuccessful ventures to more promising activities is an important factor in maintaining a workable economic system. In any firm, it is important that the persons responsible for financial management be aware of the causes of and remedies for financial failure. Such awareness is important for detecting the early signs of failure, not only within the firm itself but also in firms that have been extended credit.

Failure may be defined in several ways. Managers or owners may consider a firm a failure if it cannot provide a return sufficient to justify the owners' investment. By this standard, failure may result in sale of the firm and liquidation of its assets or, at least, sale or discontinuation of unprofitable operations. The better-known forms of failure are technical insolvency and bankruptcy. A firm is considered technically insolvent if assets exceed liabilities but it does not have the liquidity to pay debts as they become due. Bankruptcy occurs when the fair market value of the assets is less than the liabilities. The bankruptcy laws, however, do not distinguish between technical insolvency and bankruptcy; to be considered bankrupt, a firm must merely fail to pay its bills as they become due. Almost all instances of business failure can be attributed to some form of economic hardship or to managerial inadequacy.

Once failure occurs, the firm can pursue a remedy either by seeking a voluntary settlement with its creditors or by resorting, voluntarily or involuntarily, to the bankruptcy court. Typically, the debtor firm initiates negotiations with creditors to seek a voluntary settlement. The services of an adjustment bureau or trade organization are sometimes used. Voluntary settlements typically involve either an extension, a composition, some form of creditors' control, or a combination of these. With an extension, creditors receive full payment over an extended period of time. In contrast, when a composition is used, creditors agree to accept a *pro rata* distribution that is less than the full amount due. Should creditors' control be used, the creditors or their representatives become involved in the management of the firm. The advantage of a voluntary settlement is that the expenses and delays of formal bankruptcy proceedings can be avoided, leaving more resources available to creditors and possibly stockholders.

Should a firm that has failed be unwilling or unable to arrange a voluntary settlement, a remedy can be pursued under the bankruptcy laws. The filing of a petition for an Order of Relief is voluntary when filed by the firm or involuntary when filed by the firm's creditors. When the firm files, it usually requests reorganization rather than liquidation. The important chapters of the bankruptcy laws relating to the typical business firm are Chapter 7, which provides the procedures for liquidation; Chapter 11, which deals with reorganization of a bankrupt firm; and Chapter 13, which allows for the adjustment of debts for an individual. Many small-business owners can use the expedient provisions of Chapter 13 to continue operating while arranging for an adjustment of their debts.

Under Chapter 7, a trustee is appointed by the creditors' committee to convert the debtor's property to cash. The funds raised by disposing of the assets are distributed according to the priority of claimants. Claims for the expenses of administering the bankrupt firm, wages, unpaid employee benefits, certain claims by customers, and unpaid taxes actually are paid before claims of secured creditors. Unsecured general creditors and stockholders receive whatever, if anything, remains. After the trustee completes the disposal of assets, and if no objections are filed, a discharge is granted from all unpaid debts.

The feasibility of reorganization under Chapter 11 is determined by comparing the estimated value of the firm as a going concern with the value of the firm in liquidation. If reorganization is feasible, the trustee or debtor in control will submit a plan to the creditors. To be confirmed by the court, a plan must be approved by all classes of creditors. If some creditors do not approve it, the plan may be confirmed under the cram down provisions if it can be shown that these creditors would receive at least as much value as they would have if the absolute priority rule were applied to a quick liquidation of assets. Usually, the plan involves recapitalization and an exchange of securities. A successful plan discharges the firm from unpaid debts and allows it to continue operating as a viable economic entity.

With the reforms enacted in 1978, a trustee may be appointed; or, if there is no trustee, the debtor in possession is allowed to remain in control. Frequently, in reorganization the current management is allowed to continue operating the firm.

Chapter 13 applies to individuals with regular income and allows for an adjustment of their debts. Many small-business owners may qualify under the provisions of this chapter. The adjustment of debts is much like a reorganization except that creditors have no voice in approving the plan. As might be expected, the changes in Chapter 13 have been among the more controversial aspects of the Bankruptcy Reform Act of 1978.

QUESTIONS AND REVIEW ACTIVITIES

1. It has been said that the definition of failure is relative. Why would the owners of a firm have a different standard of failure from that of creditors?

2. Distinguish between a technically insolvent and a bankrupt firm.

3. What distinction do the bankruptcy courts make between technical insolvency and bankruptcy?

4. Firms fail for many reasons. What are the major reasons commonly suggested for failure?

5. When is a voluntary settlement appropriate? What is the major problem in arranging a successful voluntary settlement?

6. Distinguish between an extension and a composition.

7. What would motivate the management of a firm to agree to a voluntary liquidation?

8. Identify the chapters of the Bankruptcy Reform Act of 1978 that are most relevant to a typical business firm.

9. What is necessary for creditors to file an involuntary petition for bankruptcy against a firm?

10. Why does the management of a firm often prefer to file voluntarily for reorganization under Chapter 11 rather than to take its chances if creditors file an involuntary petition against the firm?

11. Under what circumstances might secured creditors receive a distribution in liquidation that is less than their claim even though the secured asset was sold for more than the amount needed to honor the claim?

PROBLEMS

1. The capital structure of the XYZ Co., in thousands of dollars, is as follows:

Short-term debt:	
Accounts payable	$ 1,000
Notes payable	2,000
Long-term debt:	
First mortgage, 11%	2,000
Second mortgage, 12%	4,000
Preferred stock, par value $100	1,000
Common stock, par value $10	2,000
Paid-in capital	1,000
Retained earnings	$(3,000)

The aggregate market value of the firm's assets is $10 million. The value of the fixed assets on which both mortgages have a lien is $4 million.

Develop a plan of reorganization that meets the statutory requirements of being "fair and equitable."

2. On December 31, 1983, the ABC Co. filed a voluntary petition in bankruptcy under Chapter 11. At that time, it had the balance sheet of Table 18.8. The ABC Co. can probably earn $600,000. It is determined that 10% is an appropriate rate of capitalization.

Outline a reorganization plan for the firm.

TABLE 18.8
ABC Co.: Balance Sheet, December 31, 1983 (in 000s).

Cash	$ 100	Accounts payable	$ 1,000
Accounts receivable	500	Notes payable, 7%	1,000
Inventory	1,400	First mortgage, 6%	2,000
Fixed assets	10,000	Debentures, 7%	3,000
		Preferred stock	1,000
		Common stock	2,000
		Retained earnings	2,000
Total assets	$12,000	Total claims	$12,000

TABLE 18.9
S.W. Co.: Balance Sheet Prior to Liquidation.

Cash in bank	$ 10,000	Accounts payable	$ 30,000
Accounts receivable	80,000	First mortgage bond	25,000
Inventories	40,000	Second mortgage bond	15,000
Plant and equipment	70,000	Debentures	20,000
		Common stock	100,000
		Retained earnings	10,000
Total assets	$200,000	Total claims	$200,000

3. The Air-Space Corp. has been liquidated and its assets sold for $200,000 cash. Given the corporation's liabilities and stockholders' equity shown, make a cash distribution plan for investors and creditors. (Assume that all debt is unsecured.)

Debentures	$ 300,000
Accounts payable	100,000
Preferred stock	200,000
Common stock	3,000,000

4. The Hardy Co. was forced to liquidate its assets, which were sold for $40,000 cash. What portion of the cash would you have distributed to each class of investors and creditors? Assume that the bank loan is unsecured and that the corporation's balance sheet before liquidation contained the following:

Bank loan	$15,000
Accounts payable	15,000
Debentures	20,000
Preferred stock	30,000
Common stock	50,000
Property taxes	5,000

TABLE 18.10
Tucson Co.: Balance Sheet Prior to Liquidation.

Cash on hand	$ 2,000	Bank loan (First National)	$ 6,000
Bank deposit (First National)	1,000	Accounts payable	12,000
		Common stock	1,000
Accounts receivable	3,000	Retained earnings	4,000
Inventory	5,000		
Equipment	12,000		
Total assets	$23,000	Total claims	$23,000

5. The S.W. Co. is forced to liquidate (see Table 18.9). The liquidation brings in $40,000 from fixed assets, $25,000 from accounts receivable, and $22,000 from inventories. The first and second mortgage bonds are secured by the plant and equipment. Describe the distribution of cash among the firm's creditors.

6. Tucson Co. is being liquidated. Table 18.10 is its balance sheet before liquidation. In liquidation the following amounts were realized, and the accounts receivable were pledged to the bank to secure its loan.

Cash	$ 2,000
Accounts receivable	2,000
Bank deposit	1,000
Inventory	3,000
Equipment	4,000
Total	$12,000

a) What dollar amount will the bank receive in final payment of the loan?

b) What would the bank have received if it had not had a lien on the accounts receivable?

c) In each case, what do the trade creditors and common stockholders receive?

ADDITIONAL READINGS

Altman, E. I. "Corporate Bankruptcy Potential, Stockholder Returns and Share Valuation," *Journal of Finance* (December 1969), pp. 887–900.

Altman, E. I., R. Haldeman, and P. Narayanan. "ZETA® Analysis: A New Model to Identify Bankruptcy Risk of Corporations?" *Journal of Banking and Finance* (June 1977), pp. 29–54.

Altman, E. I., and T. McGough. "Evaluation of a Company as a Going Concern," *Journal of Accounting* (December 1974), pp. 50–57.

Beaver, W. "Financial Ratios as Predictors of Failure," *Empirical Research in Accounting: Selected Studies, 1967, Supplement to Journal of Accounting Research*, pp. 71–102.

Moyer, R. C. "Forecasting Financial Failure: A Re-examination," *Financial Management* (Spring 1977), pp. 11–17.

Newton, G. W. *Bankruptcy and Insolvency Accounting: Practice and Procedure*, 2nd ed. New York: John Wiley & Sons, Inc., 1981.

Schnepper, J. A. *The New Bankruptcy Law: A Professional's Handbook*. Reading, Mass.: Addison-Wesley Publishing Company, 1981.

Scott, J. H., Jr. "Bankruptcy, Secured Debt, and Optimal Capital Structure," *Journal of Finance* (March 1977), pp. 1–21.

Warner, J. B. "Bankruptcy Costs: Some Evidence," *Journal of Finance* (May 1977), pp. 339–49.

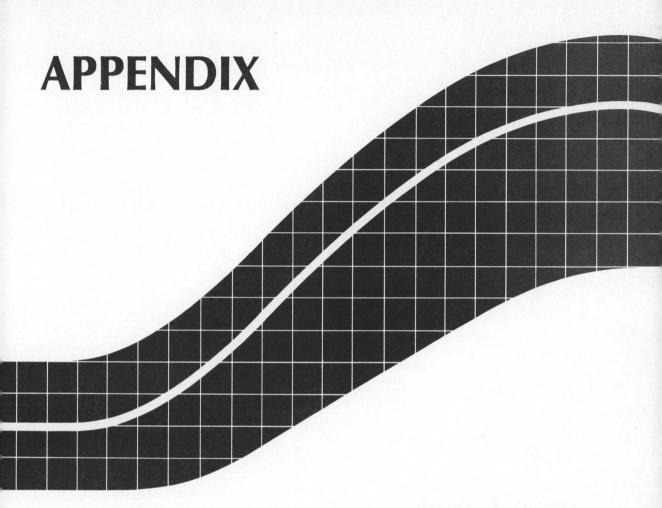

APPENDIX

FEDERAL
INCOME TAXES

This appendix includes three major sections. The first section discusses the various legal forms of business organization and how their tax treatment varies. Anyone selecting a form of business must consider its tax status, the tax rates applicable to the entity, and the way the entity's taxable income is determined.

The second section provides an overview of the tax considerations pertaining to each tax entity: sole proprietorship, partnership, corporation, and Subchapter S corporation. The filing requirements imposed upon each by the Internal Revenue Service (IRS) are described here.

The third section provides detailed illustrations and completed tax forms for each type of taxpayer. Those who want only a general overview of taxes may skip this section.

A disclaimer is in order. Tax laws are changed periodically by Congress and are constantly reinterpreted by the IRS and the courts. As a consequence, any tax summary is obsolete to some degree almost as soon as it is completed. The coverage here was current and accurate at the beginning of 1983. Also, this appendix cannot be a substitute for a tax course. Tax courses not only provide a more detailed explanation of tax issues but also teach the research methods necessary to determine what current tax law is, as defined by the most recent court and IRS interpretations. A financial management student should consider additional study in this area.

After careful study of this appendix, you should know

1. The distinctions between the different forms of business organizations and how a firm's legal and tax status is defined.

2. What is meant by a progressive tax schedule and how this affects individuals and corporations in the United States.

3. The general formulas for determining the federal income tax liability of individuals and corporations in the United States.

4. The three different types of gains and losses a business may have for tax purposes, and why the distinctions are important.

5. How depreciation and capital recovery allowances reduce taxes.

6. The differences between business and personal deductions.

7. How tax credits can save taxes and encourage businesses to invest in capital equipment.

8. The difference between regular (Subchapter C) and Subchapter S corporations.

9. What net operating losses are, and how tax law handles such losses.

10. The purpose and effect of the corporate dividend-received deduction.

11. What the tax returns of individuals, partnerships, and corporations look like.

FORMS OF BUSINESS ORGANIZATION

While thorough examination of the legal forms of organization is beyond the scope of this textbook, tax considerations in organizing one's business are important for financial planning. The most often encountered legal forms of businesses are sole proprietorships, general and limited partnerships, and corporations. A **sole proprietorship** is a business carried on by an individual under a separate name, thereby separating business affairs from personal affairs. The individual maintains separate accounting records for each group of interrelated activities but has unlimited personal liability for all business debts. Thus, the sole proprietorship and the individual who owns it are viewed as a single entity from the standpoint of legal liability.

A **general partnership** may be described as a *collection* of sole proprietorships unified to pursue a given business venture. In short, general partnerships are made up of several individuals, each of whom assumes unlimited personal liability for the combined business debts of the partnership—that is, what is known as "joint and several" liability. To reduce the legal exposure of some of its members, a partnership may consist of both general and limited partners (a **limited partnership**). Limited partners usually contribute only capital and limit their potential losses to that amount. In return for loss limitation, limited partners forgo their right to manage the business. The general partner or partners manage the business and risk personal losses beyond the amounts they may have invested in the partnership.

Another way business owners can limit their liability is through incorporation. By incorporating, owner-shareholders create a separate legal entity, a *corporation*, with separate legal rights. The corporate form offers advantages to both small, closely held businesses and large conglomerates. Owners of corporations have limited personal liability (their risk is limited to the amount paid for shares of the company) in addition to the right to manage the business (not curtailed, as in a limited partnership). Larger businesses may incorporate to help raise capital; they may sell stock to the general public.

An individual selecting the form his or her business should take must consider taxes. Tax law recognizes only two entities, the individual and the corporation. In the first case, an individual may do business as (1) a sole proprietor, (2) a member of a partnership, or (3) a shareholder of a Subchapter S corporation. The owner's share of the business income or loss will be attributed to the owner in the year of occurrence, when the tax on such income is paid for the year. It is the *individual*, not the business, who is liable for any taxes on the earnings of such businesses,† although the three forms of businesses file tax returns for information purposes.

---

† The Subchapter S corporation is an exception; it may be directly liable for taxes on net capital gains in some cases.

TABLE A.1
Tax Rate Schedules for Married Taxpayers Filing Joint Returns and Qualifying Widows and Widowers.

If taxable income is		The 1983 tax will be			The 1984 (and thereafter) tax will be		
Over	But not over	Amount	+ % of	Excess over	Amount	+ % of	Excess over
$ 3,400	$ 5,500	$ 0	+ 11%	$ 3,400	$ 0	+ 11%	$ 3,400
5,500	7,600	231	+ 13%	5,500	23	+ 12%	5,500
7,600	11,900	504	+ 15%	7,600	483	+ 14%	7,600
11,900	16,000	1,149	+ 17%	11,900	1,085	+ 16%	11,900
16,000	20,200	1,846	+ 19%	16,000	1,741	+ 18%	16,000
20,200	24,600	2,644	+ 23%	20,200	2,497	+ 22%	20,200
24,600	29,900	3,656	+ 26%	24,600	3,465	+ 25%	24,600
29,900	35,200	5,034	+ 30%	29,900	4,790	+ 28%	29,900
35,200	45,800	6,624	+ 35%	35,200	6,274	+ 33%	35,200
45,800	60,000	10,334	+ 40%	45,800	9,772	+ 38%	45,800
60,000	85,600	16,014	+ 44%	60,000	15,168	+ 42%	60,000
$ 85,600	$109,400	$27,278	+ 48%	85,600	$25,920	+ 45%	$ 85,600
For 1983 only, over $109,400		$38,702	+ 50%	$109,400			
$109,400	$162,400				$36,630	+ 49%	$109,400
over $162,400					$62,600	+ 50%	$162,400

In the second case, shareholders of a regular Subchapter C corporation pay no taxes on the earnings of the corporation except those on the dividends they receive, which are taxed as ordinary income. The corporation itself, however, is subject to taxes on its earnings for the year, regardless of whether such earnings are distributed. Consequently, corporate profits are doubly taxed; the same income is taxable for both the corporation and the shareholders. To offset the effect of such double taxation, lower tax rates apply to corporations than to individuals, although the difference was reduced following the Economic Recovery Tax Act of 1981.

Individuals are subject to **progressive** tax rates that begin at 0% and reach a maximum of 50% of taxable income. An example of a tax rate schedule is shown in Table A.1.† Corporate tax rates are also progressive, as Table A.2 shows. Note that the highest individual rate is only four percentage points

---

† There are four classes of individual taxpayers. In order of preferential treatment, these are (1) married couples filing joint returns, (2) heads of households, (3) single individuals other than heads of households, and (4) married couples filing separate returns.

TABLE A.2
Corporate Tax Rates.†

If taxable income is		The tax is		
Over	But not over	Amount +	% of	Excess over
$ 0		$ 0	15	$ 0
25,000	$ 25,000	3,750	18	25,000
50,000	50,000	8,250	30	50,000
75,000	75,000	15,750	40	75,000
$100,000	$100,000	$25,750	46	$100,000

† Effective as of January 1, 1983.

greater than the top corporate rate (50% for individuals as opposed to 46% for corporations).

The tax base differs for each type of tax entity. Both legal and tax considerations must be assessed when selecting a form of business organization. Tax case law has identified the characteristics an organization should possess to qualify as a corporate tax entity: (1) associates, (2) the objective of carrying on a business for profit, (3) continuity of life, (4) centralized management, (5) limited liability, and (6) free transferability of interests. Of the six, the last four are central; a business must possess more than two of these four attributes to qualify as a corporation. All other forms of organization are considered noncorporate.

INCOME TAXES

This section defines and discusses taxable income for individuals and corporations. Although the discussion touches on partnerships and Subchapter S corporations as tax entities, you must recognize that their income, or loss, ultimately passes through to the individual partners and shareholders, who incur the tax liability for business profits.

INDIVIDUALS

The general formula used to determine the income tax liability of an individual taxpayer may be summarized as follows:

Inflow of assets
− Return of capital
= Net inflow of assets (income broadly conceived)
− Exclusions
= Gross income
− Deductions to arrive at adjusted gross income
= Adjusted gross income (AGI)
− Deductions from AGI (excess, if any, of itemized (personal) deductions over the zero bracket amount)
− Personal and dependent exemptions
= Taxable income
× Applicable tax rate(s)
= Gross tax
− Tax credits and prepayments
= Net tax payable

Inflow of Assets

Inflow of assets consists of all money or property rights received by a taxpayer. These inflows may result from (1) exchanges, such as cash or receivables from a sale, and (2) nonreciprocal transfers, such as gifts or prizes. Increases in wealth resulting from nontransfers, for example, an increase in the market value of an investment, are not recognized by the taxing authorities. Some of the more familiar inflows of assets include wage and salary income, dividend and interest income, proceeds from the sale of capital assets, and net business income derived from operation of a sole proprietorship, partnership, or Subchapter S corporation.

Return of Capital

Return of capital is the cost of the asset in an exchange in which other assets are received. In the case of productive assets, the initial cost is allowed to be increased by any improvements the taxpayer has made between the time of acquiring the asset and disposing of it, and to be decreased by any depreciation, amortization, or depletion taken. This "new cost" is the asset's adjusted basis (book value); it is used to determine the gain or loss realized on the exchange. The excess (or deficiency) of the fair market value of the assets received over the book value of the property given constitutes a realized gain (or loss) on the exchange.

Net Inflow of Assets

The difference between inflow of assets and return of capital may be termed *net inflow of assets* or "income broadly conceived." An example is the sale of land purchased at a cost of $1,000 and sold for $4,000: $4,000 is the inflow of assets, $1,000 is the adjusted basis, and the difference is the net inflow of assets, $3,000. Gross profit is another example of a net inflow of assets. The difference between sales (an inflow of assets) and the cost of goods sold (a return of capital) is the net inflow.

Exclusions

Certain types of inflows are not taxed and are **excluded** from gross income. As an example, lump-sum life insurance proceeds received upon the death of the insured generally are excluded. Another exclusion allows the first $100 of an individual's dividend income to go untaxed (or $200 for a stock held jointly by married individuals filing jointly). Other net inflows of assets excluded from taxation include gifts and inheritances, many prizes and awards, and scholarship and fellowship grants.

Gross Income

The Internal Revenue Code defines **gross income** as follows:

General Definition—Except as otherwise provided in this subtitle, gross income means all income from whatever source derived, including (but not limited to) the following items:

(1) Compensation for services, including fees, commissions, and similar items;

(2) Gross income derived from business;

(3) Gains derived from dealings in property;

(4) Interest;

(5) Rents;

(6) Royalties;

(7) Dividends;

(8) Alimony and separate maintenance payments;

(9) Annuities;

(10) Income from life insurance and endowment contracts;

(11) Pensions;

(12) Income from discharged indebtedness;

(13) Distributive share of partnership gross income (as reported by the individual partnership);

(14) Income in respect of a decedent; and

(15) Income from an interest in an estate or trust.

In effect, gross income is all net inflows of income to the taxpayer, less specific items that are excluded from taxation.

Deductions to Arrive at Adjusted Gross Income

Individuals can take two types of deductions: "deductions to arrive at adjusted gross income," and "deductions from adjusted gross income." The latter are personal deductions to be discussed later.

Deductions to arrive at adjusted gross income (AGI) include expenses related to running a business or profession, 60% of net long-term capital gains, losses on exchanges, expenses related to the generation of rental income, moving expenses, employee business expenses, and alimony paid.

These deductions are generally analogous to the deductions of a partnership or corporation filing a separate return. The deductions are essentially the business expenses of the individual taxpayer.

If an individual engages in a business or practices a profession as a sole proprietor, the net profit or loss from this business activity is shown on a separate schedule filed with the tax return (Form 1040, Schedule C). (See Exhibit 3 at the end of this appendix.) The format followed in reporting income and expenses for a certified public accountant is illustrated in Table A.3.

TABLE A.3
John Q. Taxpayer: Profit from Operating Able Accounting Services.

Gross billings		$50,000
Expenses		
Advertising	$ 500	
Bad debts	800	
Car expenses	600	
Depreciation	6,000	
Dues/publications	250	
Insurance	1,500	
Interest	5,000	
Legal fees	2,000	
Office supplies	400	
Rent	1,200	
Repairs	200	
Travel and entertainment	1,000	
Utilities/telephone	2,500	
Wages	7,000	
Taxes (other than income)	1,000	
Miscellaneous	50	
Total expenses		30,000
Net profit		$20,000

Note that only the net amount (revenues less expenses) is included as gross income. Business expenses incurred by a sole proprietorship are deductions to arrive at AGI, because they directly reduce revenue that would otherwise be part of gross income.

Tax Treatment of Gains and Losses

Gains and losses may result from either (1) sales or exchanges or (2) other dispositions of property. The distinction is important for tax purposes, because certain sales or exchanges qualify for special tax treatment.

Three types of gains are recognized by the tax law, and each is accorded different treatment: (1) ordinary gains and losses, (2) capital gains and losses, and (3) Section 1231 gains and losses. While the tax treatment of these gains differs, the amount to be reported is the same for all three: the difference between the fair market value of the property received and the adjusted basis of that property given up. *Adjusted basis* usually refers to the cost of the asset, plus any capital additions and reduced by depreciation. For some items, such as inventories and other assets that do not qualify for depreciation, adjusted basis is cost.

Determining gains and losses—An example.   The X sole proprietorship purchased an asset three years ago for $1,000 with an estimated useful life of five years. It has been depreciated using straight-line depreciation since its acquisition; the asset's book value is $400. What would be the gain or loss if X were to sell the asset for the following prices: (1) $500, (2) $350, (3) $100 plus a machine with a fair market value of $350; total $450?

The gain or loss would be computed as follows:

	(1)	(2)	(3)
Fair market value of property received	$500	$350	$450
Adjusted basis of property given up	400	400	400
Gain (loss)	$100	$ (50)	$ 50

Ordinary gains and losses.   Ordinary gains and losses are best described as those gains and losses that are neither capital nor fall under Section 1231. This category includes inventory and real and depreciable business property owned for a year or less. Ordinary gains are taxed at the appropriate marginal tax rate for individuals, and ordinary losses are deducted as business expenses.

Capital gains and losses.   A capital asset is defined by exclusion. It is an asset other than inventory or other property held for sale during the normal course of business, accounts or notes receivable, depreciable property and real property used in a trade or business, copyrights and other creations in the hands of the creator, and short-term U.S. securities sold at a discount. The principal capital assets for individuals are investments (stocks and bonds) and personal property (jewelry and homes). It must also be noted that the way any given taxpayer intends to use an asset is a major determinant of whether capital asset status obtains; for example, real property may be used in the normal course of operating a trade or business, or it may be held for speculative investment.

It is important to determine whether a capital transaction is short-term or long-term. If more than a year passes between the date of acquisition and the date of sale, a transaction is long-term and receives beneficial treatment. Capital transactions are accounted for as follows:

1. All short-term transactions are totaled.
2. All long-term transactions are totaled.
3. The two totals are netted against each other.
4. If the net long-term capital gain is greater than the net short-term capital loss, the taxpayer is allowed a **net-capital-gain deduction** for AGI equal to 60% of the excess of the net long-term gain over the net short-term capital loss. The balance is included as taxable income.
5. If the total is negative, the taxpayer can use the negative balance to offset other income to a maximum of $3,000. Short-term capital losses offset other income dollar for dollar. Long-term losses offset 50 cents of other income for each dollar of loss. If the taxpayer has losses of both types, short-term losses are applied first.
6. Any unused losses are carried forward as the first entries in calculating next year's capital gains and losses.
7. The losses can be carried forward until exhausted, retaining their short- and long-term character and offsetting ordinary income, subject to the prevailing limits, in each year.

Section 1231 Assets

Section 1231 of the Internal Revenue Code deals with the gains and losses from the disposition of depreciable assets. The amount of the gain or loss depends upon the sale price and the book value of the asset. The asset's book value is its cost plus the cost of any improvement minus any depreciation taken. Recent changes in the tax law have materially changed depreciation calculations.

Depreciation and the accelerated cost recovery system. **Depreciation** may be defined as the systematic allocation of an asset's cost to the periods in which benefits are to be derived from its ownership. Accelerated depreciation is one way of allocating these costs. More rapid depreciation or write-off helps compensate for sudden changes in demand or in technology that make fixed assets obsolete prematurely, as well as for premature wearing out of fixed assets because of abnormal activity or use.

For assets acquired before January 1, 1981, the law regarding depreciation allows a taxpayer wide latitude in choosing depreciation methods, as long as the asset to be depreciated is used in a trade or business or for the production of income. The Internal Revenue Code allows specifically for the use of (1) the straight-line method, (2) any declining-balance method whose results do not exceed 200% of the straight-line method, (3) the sum-of-the-years-digits method, or (4) any other rational and systematic method that, in the first two-thirds of the useful life of the asset, does not exceed the allowance granted under the double-declining-balance method without economic justification. There are exceptions to these rules, the most notable being the depreciation of buildings. No matter what method of depreciation is selected, however, no more than the cost of a fixed asset may be deducted as an expense over the life of the asset.

While there is a limit on the aggregate depreciation deduction that may be taken over the life of the asset, the selection of one depreciation method over another depends on the timing. Table A.4 illustrates how different depreciation methods provide different tax savings over time.

Note that, while the double-declining-balance method yields the greatest tax savings in earlier years, which allows the firm to retain more case for reinvestment, over 7% of the cost of the asset remains unrecovered at the end of its five-year useful life. To mitigate this effect, tax law allows the taxpayer to change from a declining-balance method to the straight-line method at any time during the useful life of the asset.

Assets acquired after January 1, 1981, are governed by the Accelerated Cost Recovery System (ACRS). The depreciation system just described continues to apply to assets acquired before January 1, 1981. Thus, taxpayers who hold depreciable assets acquired both before and after this date will need to comply with two *different* depreciation statutes.

ACRS came into being with the passage of the Economic Recovery Tax Act of 1981. Recovery property is subdivided into broad classes, each subject to a different rate of accelerated depreciation. The first class is tangible personal property and depreciable real property with a useful life of 12.5 years or less. A 150% declining-balance method applies to assets in this group. However, individual depreciation amounts vary as a function of cost and useful life. This first class contains four subclasses of useful life, ranging from 3 to 15 years. ACRS ignores salvage values.

The second class is depreciable real property with a useful life of more than 12.5 years. This type of property is assigned a standardized useful life of

TABLE A.4 ○			
Depreciation of a $500 Asset with a Useful Life of Five Years Zero Salvage Value at a 46% Tax Rate.			
Year	Depreciation Deduction	Total Cost Recovered	Depreciation Tax Savings
Straight-Line			
1	$100	$100	$46
2	100	200	46
3	100	300	46
4	100	400	46
5	$100	$500	$46
Sum-of-the-Years-Digits			
1	$167	$167	$77
2	133	300	61
3	100	400	46
4	67	467	31
5	33	$500	$15
Double-Declining Balance			
1	$200	$200	$92
2	120	320	55
3	72	392	33
4	43	435	20
5	$ 26	$461	$12

15 years. A 175% declining-balance method is used to calculate depreciation for this classification.†

Before enactment of ACRS, taxpayers were allowed to take extra depreciation the first year they owned an asset. Now a taxpayer may elect to expense 100% of the cost of depreciable, tangible personal property up to an aggregate limit of $5,000 for 1983 (increasing to $7,500 for 1984 and 1985 and $10,000 for 1986 and thereafter).‡

ACRS should stimulate capital investment. Other than enactment of capital gains legislation, no other single change in the tax law has the potential for providing such marked incentive for capital investment. Early write-offs have increased substantially, which should allow businesses to replace productive assets more quickly.

---

† Short-lived property is allowed to use the half-year convention; property bought before six months of the year pass is allowed full depreciation, and that bought after six months a half-year's depreciation. Longer-lived property is not allowed this break.

‡ This election reduces the taxpayer's allowed investment tax credit.

Section 1231 gains and losses.   **Section 1231** provides special treatment for **gains and losses** resulting from the sale or exchange of 1231 assets. However, only certain portions of the gains or losses are accorded this special treatment. This amount is determined by netting out gains and losses from all of these exchanges to arrive at a net gain or net loss. Net losses are deducted as ordinary losses. The treatment of a net gain, however, is somewhat more complicated. To the extent that depreciation has been taken on an asset sold, the gain realized is ordinary income—depreciation recapture. Any gain in excess of recapture is treated as a long-term capital gain and taxed accordingly.

Section 1231 gains and losses—An example.   The Y sole proprietorship purchased a machine for use in its business on January 1, 1980, for $10,000. The asset had a useful life of 10 years and was depreciated using the straight-line method. On December 31, 1984, the machine was sold. (Book value was then $5,000.) What would be the tax implications of the sale given the following prices: (1) $3,000; (2) $7,000; (3) $12,000?

1. A loss of $2,000 would be realized that could be deducted as an ordinary loss.
2. A gain of $2,000 would be realized. Because of the recapture of up to $5,000 of depreciation, this $2,000 would be taxed as ordinary income.
3. A gain of $7,000 would be realized. The recapture of $5,000 of depreciation causes $5,000 to be taxed as ordinary income. The remaining $2,000 would be treated as a long-term capital gain.

Other Pre-Adjusted Gross Income Deductions

Other deductions used to arrive at AGI include expenses related to the generation of rental income, moving expenses, employee business expenses, and alimony payments.

Tax-deductible expenses pertaining to rental property are almost identical to those allowed a sole proprietorship. Rental expenses are reported on Schedule E (Supplemental Income Schedule, Exhibit 5), and the net income or loss from rental properties is shown on line 18 of Form 1040, Exhibit 1. Moving expenses are viewed as allowable business deductions if they are incurred in connection with a move to a new principal job site that is at least 35 miles farther from the old residence than the old job site was.

Adjusted Gross Income

For an individual, **adjusted gross income (AGI)** is defined as gross income minus all allowable pre-AGI deductions. The subtotal appears on line 32 of Form 1040.

Deductions from Adjusted Gross Income

Schedule A of Form 1040 (Exhibit 2) enumerates the major categories of deductible personal expenditures. These include

1. Medical and dental expenses (subject to limitations).
2. Taxes, such as state income taxes and real estate property taxes.
3. Interest expense.
4. Charitable contributions (subject to various maximum limitations).
5. Casualty and theft losses (again, subject to limitations).
6. Miscellaneous expenses, including union dues and tax preparation expenses.

To be of benefit in offsetting income, total personal itemized deductions must exceed the appropriate zero bracket amount applicable to each given taxpayer classification. **Zero bracket amount** refers to the dollar amount of taxable income subject to a *zero* tax rate for each taxpayer designation ($3,400 for married couples filing a joint return or qualifying widows or widowers; $2,300 for heads of households and single individuals; and $1,700 for each married individual filing a separate return).

Both the tax rate schedules and the tax tables (to be used if taxable income is less than $50,000) allow for this amount in calculating the taxpayer's liability. Tax tables provided by the IRS simplify calculations; the taxpayer need only cross-reference his or her amount of taxable income with the filing status to determine the tax liability.

Personal and Dependent Exemptions

Each taxpayer is allowed a personal exemption of $1,000 from AGI for himself or herself, his or her spouse (if a joint return is filed), and any qualified dependents. Additional exemptions are allowed for taxpayers and their spouses who are either 65 years of age or older or legally blind as of the end of the tax year.

Taxable Income

Taxable income is the AGI of the taxpayer, less the zero bracket amount, excess itemized deductions and the personal and dependent exemptions that apply.

Applicable Tax Rates

Individual taxes are assessed at progressively higher rates up to a maximum rate of 50%. The amount at which this maximum rate first applies varies with the taxpayer's status. In 1983 for married couples filing a joint return, the maximum rate applies at an income of $109,400.

Gross Tax

Gross tax is the total amount of income tax due before it is reduced by any tax credits or prepayments.

Tax Credits and Prepayments

Tax credits are direct offsets to the gross tax liability on a dollar-for-dollar basis. They may be either nonrefundable (limited to the amount of the current income tax liability) or refundable. A refundable tax credit is received by the taxpayer as a refund even if the amount exceeds the tax liability for the year.

Nonrefundable tax credits. The most familiar **nonrefundable tax credit** is the **investment tax credit (ITC)** allowed by the Revenue Act of 1962. The dual purposes of the ITC were to stimulate the domestic economy and to make U.S. businesses more competitive internationally through tax provisions that encouraged the modernization of plants and equipment. Since its enactment, the ITC has been amended, suspended, reenacted, repealed, and reenacted regularly. Suspensions and repeals have resulted from the fear of inflation; reenactments were designed to counter economic slowdowns. In spite of its changeability, the ITC is an important tax factor in business planning. Much of its popularity can be traced to the fact that it is a direct offset to the tax liability rather than a deduction. Table A.5 compares two businesses (A and B). The only difference is that A has a deduction of $1,000 and B has an ITC of $1,000. B pays $850 less in taxes by using the ITC.

The ITC is 6% of the cost of "qualified investment" property with a useful life (class life) of three years under ACRS and 10% of the cost of all other qualified ACRS investment property. The ITC would normally be taken

---

TABLE A.5
Illustration of the Investment Tax Credit.

Sole Proprietorship A		Sole Proprietorship B	
Gross income	$20,000	Gross income	$20,000
Business deductions	1,000	Business deductions	0
Taxable income	19,000	Taxable income	20,000
Tax (15% × $19,000)	2,850	Tax (15% × $20,000)	3,000
Tax credit	0	Tax credit	1,000
Tax liability	$ 2,850	Tax liability	$ 2,000

in the year the investment is actually made. It is applicable to only depreciable, tangible personal property associated with business activities or operations entered into for a profit.

The ITC actually taken in any given year is subject to certain maximum limitations. Beginning in 1983, the ITC can entirely offset the gross tax liability up to $25,000, as well as 85% of the gross tax in excess of this amount. Any unused ITC may be carried back 3 years and carried forward 15 years, starting with the earliest year possible. The ITC is also subject to recapture (requiring taxpayer repayment of the taxes previously reduced) if the qualified property is not held for its appropriate ACRS class life period. The recapture is determined on a *pro rata* basis, with credit given for the partial period during which the assets are actually held.

Refundable tax credits and prepayments.   The best example of a **refundable tax credit** is the earned income credit. The taxpayer must be married and supporting a dependent child to qualify and may generate a maximum credit amount of $500. The credit is refunded to the taxpayer to the extent that it exceeds any tax liability.

The earned income credit has the same effect as any other prepayment made toward the satisfaction of an individual's income tax liability for a given year. Other prepayments include withholding, estimated tax payments, and Social Security overpayments.

Net Tax Payable

The difference between gross tax liability (net of all nonrefundable tax credits) and all prepayments including refundable tax credits is the amount owed.

PARTNERSHIP

For tax purposes, a **partnership** is defined as a syndicate, group, pool, joint venture, or other unincorporated organization through or by means of which any business, financial operation, or venture may be carried on. Generally, two or more persons have joined together to carry on a business or investment activity for their mutual benefit. The mere act of joining capital and/or effort to operate a single business venture is sufficient, from a legal standpoint, to create a partnership. An express oral or written agreement between parties is not necessary to create a partnership, although the presence of such an agreement may prove extremely useful to the partners in resolving disputes or disagreements that may arise.

For tax purposes, a partnership is viewed as an aggregation of its individual owners, rather than as a separate entity subject to taxation in its own right.

The partnership transmits all items of income, expense, gain, and loss directly to each of its individual partners, paying no federal income tax in its own name. The character of each item of income and expense remains unchanged when the items are passed through to the individual partner (e.g., capital gains of the partnership remain capital gains when attributed to each partner). The partnership prepares a Schedule K-1 for each partner (Exhibit 7), itemizing his or her *pro rata* share of income (or loss) earned by the partnership for the tax year in question. The partnership must file its own tax return for the year (Form 1065—Exhibit 6) as a source of cross-referenced information. Each partner is personally liable for the taxes on his or her share of partnership income, regardless of whether any assets have actually been distributed to the partner during the business year. Any withdrawal of property by a partner is tax-free to him or her at the time of receipt. All partners must report their share of partnership income on an accrual basis for purposes of federal income taxes.

CORPORATION

The **corporation** is a separate tax-paying entity that has a separate legal existence, distinct from the individual shareholders who own it. The formula used to determine a corporation's net tax payable is similar to that used by individuals, although the deduction calculations are simpler. The formula is as follows:

Income broadly conceived
− Exclusions

= Gross income
− Deductions

= Taxable income
× Applicable tax rate

= Gross tax
− Tax credits and prepayments

= Net tax payable

Unless otherwise noted in the following sections, the computation of each item in the corporate formula is essentially the same as for individuals.

Gross Income

Included within gross income is an item entitled *capital gain net income.* This is the difference between net short-term and net long-term gains and losses derived from the disposition of capital assets during the period. Net short-term capital gains are included in the corporation's ordinary income and taxed at the applicable corporate rates. Net long-term capital gains, however, are taxed at *either* regular corporate rates or at an alternative 28% capital gains rate, whichever produces the lower tax liability. Under the present corporate tax rate structure, if total taxable income is $50,000 or less, the regular tax calculation yields a lower tax liability. If corporate income is more than $50,000, the 28% tax may lower taxes.

Net capital losses, whether short-term or long-term, cannot be deducted for tax purposes but must be used to offset any capital gains of the period. Any excess of capital loss over capital gains for that year may be carried back three years and forward five years to be offset against capital gains from the earliest possible year. All losses carried over to other years are considered short-term capital losses for purposes of computing capital gains and losses for that year.

Capital gains and capital losses—An example.   The XYZ Corp. has made a number of sales of stock from its portfolio during 1983, and in trying to determine its tax liability with regard to these sales has gathered the following information:

Security held	Purchase Date	Purchase Price	Sales Date	Sales Price
ABC Corp.	12/22/82	$10,600	5/4/83	$ 8,000
Scramble Corp.	9/5/77	12,100	2/1/83	8,000
Williams Paint Store	3/21/53	9,300	4/15/83	15,100
Snyder Corp.	12/3/82	4,300	5/3/83	6,100

The short-term capital loss from the sale of the ABC Corp. stock should be netted out against the short-term capital gain from the Snyder Corp. stock sale. The result is a net short-term capital loss of $800. Likewise, the long-term capital loss from Scramble Corp.'s sale should be offset by the long-term capital gain resulting from the sale of Williams Paint Store stock. The result is a $1,700 net long-term capital gain. The net short-term capital loss of $800 is subtracted to give a net long-term capital gain of $900 for the year. This would be taxed at a rate of 28%, provided ordinary income is more than $50,000.

If, in this example, the net short-term capital loss had exceeded the net long-term capital gain, the difference would have been carried back three years and netted out against capital gains of that period.

Deductions

Corporations are entitled to two special deductions: the net operating loss (NOL) deduction and the dividends-received deduction. The NOL applies to all taxpayers who incur business losses, while the dividend-received deduction applies only to corporations.

Net operating loss (NOL) deduction. Under Code Section 172, the NOL of a corporation may be carried back 3 years and carried forward 15 years, with the loss applied to offset taxable income in the earliest years of that period in which taxable income was realized. An amended tax return must be filed for the year to which the carry-back applies, and the tax rates applicable to that year must be used. The purpose of this provision is to avoid unduly penalizing firms with widely fluctuating income and also to aid young firms during early development.

Table A.6 shows how carry-back and carry-forward provisions work, assuming that there are *no* NOLs in previous years that would affect the tax years in question.

Before 1954, when restrictions were put on NOL provisions, it was profitable for some corporations to acquire another corporation that was experiencing losses for the sole purpose of offsetting these acquired losses against its own profits. These restrictions prevent mergers solely for the purpose of taking advantage of the tax law. Also, for tax years starting after June 30, 1982, the net operating loss carry-over is partially reduced, depending upon the percentage change in ownership experienced over a three-year period.

Dividends-received deduction. Corporations are allowed a business deduction of 85% of all dividend income earned from domestic corporations. Thus, only 15% of the dividends is taxable income, although 100% of the amount

TABLE A.6
Example of Net Operating Loss.

Year	Taxable Income (Loss)	Amount of Carry-Back Applied	Adjusted Taxable Income
1976	$ 20,000		$20,000
1977	45,000	$(30,000)	15,000
1978	20,000		20,000
1979	15,000	(15,000)	0
1980	(30,000)		0
1981	0		0
1982	(40,000)		0
1983	35,000	(25,000)	10,000

is initially gross income for the year. For a company taxed at the highest corporate tax rate (46%), the tax would be only 6.9% of the total dividend amount. This explains why many corporations hold investment-grade preferred stocks rather than bonds; interest received on bonds is taxable, in total, as ordinary income, while dividends receive preferential tax treatment. This relief is granted to avoid the problem of multiple taxation of corporate profits (e.g., theoretically, income earned by a corporation can be taxed three times: first, when earned; second, when distributed to a corporate shareholder as a dividend; and third, when the corporate shareholder distributes dividends to its own shareholders).

Other Considerations

A corporation is entitled to various tax credits (foreign tax credits and ITCs) but is denied others that are allowed individual taxpayers, for example, the earned income credit and the credit for the elderly. In addition, the corporation generally pays its taxes on a pay-as-you-go basis through periodic estimated tax payments during the course of the business year. The annual return is due on the fifteenth day of the third month after the end of the fiscal year (with no grace period), when final payment of any remaining amounts owed must be made.

SUBCHAPTER S CORPORATION

The **Subchapter S corporation** is a product of tax law. Congress's intent in establishing the Subchapter S provisions was to relieve from double taxation small businesses that operated like partnerships or sole proprietorships, although they were legally corporations. This was accomplished by allowing corporations meeting certain requirements to elect to have corporate income pass through to the stockholders, to be taxed at the appropriate individual tax rates. While the intent was to help smaller firms, Subchapter S may now be even more advantageous for certain large corporations than for small ones.

An organization qualifying as a Subchapter S corporation must meet the following conditions (per the Subchapter S Revision Act of 1982):

1. The corporation must have no more than 35 shareholders.
2. Each shareholder must be an individual, an estate, or a specified trust.
3. No shareholder may be a nonresident alien.
4. Although the corporation may not have more than one class of stock, differences in voting rights may exist among the shareholders. All, however, must continue to exercise identical rights to the profits and assets of the corporation.
5. Corporations with accumulated earnings and profits must pay a 46% tax on all passive income (i.e., rents, royalties, dividends, interest, annuities,

and gains from the sale of stock or securities) that is greater than 25% of gross receipts.

6. The corporation may not own 80% or more of the stock of any subsidiary company.

7. All shareholders must agree to the Subchapter S election (although new incoming shareholders are not allowed to terminate this election on their entry into the corporation). Revocation by a shareholder holding more than one-half of the corporation's voting stock or failure to meet any of the previous requirements terminates the election. Once revoked, another election cannot be made for five years unless the IRS consents to an earlier election.†

For corporations meeting these requirements, the tax advantage of making a Subchapter S corporation election can be significant. The dollar benefits of the election can be seen in the following example. Another tax advantage of the Subchapter S corporation is that tax credits and NOLs can be passed through directly to the shareholders.

Subchapter S—An example. Mr. A, who is married and files a joint return, owns all the shares of stock in the X Corp., which meets all the requirements for a Subchapter S election. In 1983 his taxable income was $200,000. Because Mr. A lived the good life, he wanted to have all after-tax earnings distributed to himself. If he had elected Subchapter S status, his total tax liability would have been $84,002. Under standard corporation tax rules, his total liability would have been $119,777 due to double taxation. The calculations are as follows:

Tax Liability under Normal Corporate Rules	Subchapter S Corporate Tax Liability
$ 25,000 × .15 = $ 3,750	Tax on $109,400 = $38,702
25,000 × .18 = 4,500	90,600 × 50% = 45,300
25,000 × .30 = 7,500	Total tax (using Table A.2) $84,002
25,000 × .40 = 10,000	
100,000 × .46 = 46,000	
Corporate income tax $71,750	

After-tax distribution: $115,998

Amount left for distribution: $128,250
Amount taxable: $128,050 ($200 dividend exclusion).
       Tax on $109,400 = $38,702
         18,650 × 50% = 9,325
Personal Taxes (using Table A.1) $48,027

After-tax distribution: $80,223

---

† This rule does not apply to terminations that were effected under rules in existence prior to the Subchapter S Revision Act of 1982.

SUMMARY

Business firms can be classified in various ways, some of the more common being according to the legal form of organization, type of industry, chief product, geographical location, method of operation, and nature of ownership. Legal forms of organization include (1) sole or individual proprietorships; (2) partnerships; and (3) corporations. There are advantages and disadvantages inherent in each form of legal organization that must be carefully considered when organizing a business firm and selecting the form under which to operate.

Factors to be considered include ease of organization, simplicity of management, ease of financing, and liability of the owners for the debts of the firm. Serious consideration must also be given to the possibility of lowering the firm's federal income tax. Proprietors account for business profits through their individual returns by attaching a separate schedule detailing the business operation. A corporation files its own return. These two types of tax entities are subject to appreciably different tax rates and provisions.

A business firm that can be taxed either as a corporation or a partnership should determine which is more economical, which depends on management's policies regarding dividends and retained earnings and on owners' tax rates. The owner-organizers of business firms may decide initially on one form of legal organization and later make changes. When tax savings is the primary objective, the general rules are (1) incorporate if management plans to finance future needs by retaining earnings; do not incorporate if a major portion of earnings is to be distributed to owners; and (2) incorporate if high profits are anticipated during the early years of the business; do not incorporate if losses are anticipated during these early years. (This procedure would allow the entrepreneur to offset such losses against personal income rather than carrying the losses in the corporation.) General rules, however, can be misleading, and recent changes in the tax code have severely eroded their application. The existence of the Subchapter S alternative, for example, makes the corporation a more attractive choice for many small businesses. The prudent entrepreneur would be well advised to enlist competent tax counsel at this crucial stage of a business.

While the organizers of a small business firm may have considerable choice regarding the legal form under which to organize, a large firm usually finds it necessary to incorporate because of financial, managerial, and tax considerations. The corporate form of organization is best suited to raising the large sums needed to finance large business firms, because new capital may be raised by the sale of stock or bonds in the capital market. In addition, corporations usually have perpetual charters and are legal entities separate from the individuals who own them; stockholders are not responsible for the debts of their corporations, and they may transfer ownership simply by selling their shares. For these reasons, most large firms in the United States are organized as corporations.

Comprehensive tax illustrations—Examples. Sample tax returns for three classes of taxpayers are illustrated in this section: an individual taxpayer using Form 1040 and supporting schedules; a partnership using Form 1065 and Schedule K-1; and a regular (Subchapter C) corporation filing on Form 1120.

Individual. The following facts pertain to the tax status of John Q. Taxpayer, an individual filing a joint return for 1983. He is 43 years of age and married, with two dependent children. He lives in Michigan. John is a certified public accountant. Table A.3 is the income statement for his practice.

In addition, he received income from the following sources:

1. A 10% share of total ordinary income of $100,000 from the Land Ho! partnership.

2. $9,000 in gross wages earned by his wife, Ellen, as a part-time accountant.

3. $450 in interest on a passbook savings account at Local Savings and Loan.

4. Dividends on stocks:
   $250 from ZYX Corp.
   $500 from PD Corp.

5. $5,000 as a net long-term capital gain, consisting of the following transactions:

   a) Sale of XYZ Corp.'s securities for $12,000 on May 1, 1983, acquired at a cost of $5,000 on January 1, 1979.

   b) Sale of PD Corp.'s securities for $6,000 on November 1, 1983, acquired at a cost of $9,000 on January 1, 1983.

   c) A 10% share ($1,000) of a long-term capital gain derived from the sale of securities held by the Land Ho! partnership.

Additional personal expenses data are as follows:

1. Medical expenses
a) Doctor's bills (unreimbursed)	$ 800
b) Blue Cross/Blue Shield (health insurance)	450

2. Taxes paid
a) State and local income	1,400
b) Real estate	900
c) General sales (from tax tables)	333

3. Interest
a) On home mortgage	9,000
b) Credit card charges	450

4. Contributions
a) Interdenominational Church	650
b) Boy Scouts of America	100

5. Miscellaneous
a) Job search	250

Total cash tax payments made during the year include the following:

1. Estimated tax payments	$4,000
2. Withholdings on wife's earnings	1,200

His completed individual tax return and supporting schedules appear as Exhibits 1–5†

Partnership. The information return, Form 1065, and related K-1 distribution schedule for the Land Ho! partnership for 1983 appear as Exhibits 6 and 7. Note that no tax liability is computed with this information return.

Corporation. A corporate income tax return (Form 1120) is shown in Exhibit 8. It contains the following information for the 1983 tax year:

Income	
Sales of merchandise	$1,000,000
Interest income—customers	4,000
Interest income—City of Chicago municipal bonds	10,000
Dividends received on investment in Ford	
Motor Co. common stock	50,000
Expenses	
Cost of goods sold	$ 600,000
Salaries	125,000
Bad debts	12,000
Taxes	40,000
Interest expense	8,000
Depreciation	75,000
Advertising	25,000
Other (supplies, etc.)	10,000

The corporation has remitted $30,000 in estimated tax payments during the course of the year.

QUESTIONS AND REVIEW ACTIVITIES

1. Define or discuss
   a) Sole proprietorship.
   b) General partnership.
   c) Limited partnership.
   d) Regular (Subchapter C) corporation.
   e) Subchapter S corporation.
   f) Progressive taxation.
   g) Exclusions.
   h) Adjusted gross income.
   i) Zero bracket amount.

---

† See page 579.

    j) Personal and dependent exemptions.

    k) Taxable income.

    l) Nonrefundable tax credit.

    m) Refundable tax credit.

    n) Sixty percent net capital gain deduction.

    o) Section 1231 gains and losses.

2. Which forms of business organization are directly subject to tax? Why do the tax rate structures differ from one another?

3. What are exclusions? How do they benefit a taxpayer?

4. How may deductions to arrive at AGI and deductions from AGI best be distinguished?

5. What policy considerations are served by giving preferential tax treatment to net capital gains?

6. Compare and contrast individual and corporate capital gains treatment.

7. Briefly explain the concept of depreciation, and distinguish between its method of calculation for asset acquisitions both before and after December 31, 1980.

8. What is the significance of the zero bracket amount? What theory is served by its inclusion in the tax system?

9. What differential exists between a dollar of investment tax credit versus a dollar of business expense deduction for a taxpayer in the following tax brackets: (a) 20%; (b) 32%; (c) 50%?

10. What purpose is served by the provision of both a carry-back and a carry-forward of business net operating losses?

PROBLEMS

1. J. R. Robinson is married and has two children. His income for 1983 is $26,500. Most of this is salary ($26,000), but $500 of it is dividends received on stock his wife owns. Mr. Robinson files a joint return. He does not itemize deductions, taking only the zero bracket amount. Calculate his tax liability.

2. Mr. Brine owns and runs a car dealership as a sole proprietorship. He pays himself a $15,000 salary. The proprietorship has been making $40,000 per year after all expenses (but before income tax). Since it is a proprietorship, this amount includes the $15,000 salary Mr. Brine pays himself. He is considering incorporating the dealership; if so, he would own all the stock. Part of the reason for considering incorporation is that Mr. Brine is thinking of acquiring another dealership. If this occurs, he will double his income. Assume that Mr. Brine is married with no children, takes the zero bracket amount for personal deductions, and files in the 1983 tax year.

    a) With earnings of $40,000, what would Mr. Brine's total tax liability be if the firm operated as

i) A proprietorship?

ii) A corporation that distributes all after-tax earnings?

iii) A corporation that distributes no earnings?

b) What considerations, other than taxes, might be important?

3. Following is a summary of the capital gains transactions of six different taxpayers, classified long-term and short-term:

Taxpayer	Short-Term		Long-Term	
	Gains	Losses	Gains	Losses
1	$2,000	$3,000	$10,000	$ 5,000
2	5,000	2,000	0	1,000
3	5,000	2,000	10,000	5,000
4	1,000	6,000	1,000	0
5	1,000	0	2,000	10,000
6	0	1,000	2,000	10,000

Explain the tax treatment that would result in each case for

a) An individual taxpayer with ordinary income of $60,000.

b) A corporate taxpayer with ordinary income of $60,000.

4. The ABC Corp. purchased a new widget-making machine on January 1, 1980, for $5,000. What would be the tax liability on the sale of the machine on January 1, 1983, for $6,000 under the following circumstances, assuming other taxable income of $110,000?

a) The machine was held as a part of the firm's inventory for sale to customers.

b) The machine was used to produce widgets that were sold by the ABC Corp. The machine had a useful life of five years, depreciated on a straight-line basis with zero salvage value.

5. Jenny Smith, the treasurer of the MAC Corp., is trying to decide whether to invest $100,000 in high-grade corporate bonds or stock of other corporations. She has weighed all factors except after-tax yield and has found favorable effects of each to cancel the other out. The bond investment she is considering pays 8% interest per year, while $4,500 in dividends would be paid on the stock investment. Which selection should Smith make based on after-tax investment income, assuming taxable income from other sources of $120,000?

6. The MBA Corp. purchased a new machine for use in its business at the beginning of 1984 for $100,000. Its ACRS class life is five years, and the appropriate depreciation percentage for the first year of recovery (allowing for application of the half-year convention in the initial year of acquisition) is 15%. What is the minimum tax liability for the firm for this year, assuming that it uses the investment tax credit and maximum depreciation allowances available and that its taxable income exclusive of these calculations is $150,000?

7. Spaced-Out-Tronics, Inc., has a history of vacillating earnings. As a result, full advantage has been taken of the tax loss carry-back and carry-forward provisions. The company's taxable income (loss) for 10 years is given here. In this problem, assume the current corporate tax rates for all years (even though the rates actually have varied). What has been the firm's adjusted annual tax liability, allowing for the effect of any carry-backs and/or carry-forwards?

1975	$ 35,000	1980	(30,000)
1976	15,000	1981	0
1977	20,000	1982	5,000
1978	(20,000)	1983	10,000
1979	(35,000)	1984	50,000

ADDITIONAL READINGS

Davies, R. M., and M. H. Lawrence. *Choosing a Form of Business Organization.* Durham, N.C.: Duke University Law School, 1963.

Economic Recovery Tax Act of 1981. Chicago: Commerce Clearing House, Inc., 1981.

Federal Tax Coordinator, 2nd ed. New York: Research Institute of America, Inc., 1983.

Federal Taxes. Englewood Cliffs, N.J.: Prentice-Hall, Inc., 1983.

The RIA Complete Analysis of the '82 Tax Equity and Fiscal Responsibility Act. New York: Research Institute of America, Inc., 1982.

Sommerfeld, R. M. *Federal Taxes and Management Decisions.* Homewood, Ill.: Richard D. Irwin, Inc., 1978.

Sommerfeld, R. M., H. Anderson, and H. Brock. *An Introduction to Taxation.* New York: Harcourt Brace Jovanovich, 1982.

Standard Federal Tax Reporter. Chicago, Ill.: Commerce Clearing House, Inc., 1983.

U.S. FEDERAL INCOME TAX EXHIBITS

Exhibits

Exhibit 1

Form **1040**	Department of the Treasury—Internal Revenue Service **U.S. Individual Income Tax Return**	**1983**		

For the year January 1-December 31, 1983, or other tax year beginning _____ , 1983, ending _____ , 19 ____   OMB No. 1545-0074

Use IRS label. Other-wise, please print or type.

Your first name and initial (if joint return, also give spouse's name and initial)   Last name
JOHN Q AND ELLEN   TAXPAYER

Your social security number   **111 22 3333**

Present home address (Number and street, including apartment number, or rural route)
500 FIRST STREET

Spouse's social security number   **444 55 6666**

City, town or post office, State, and ZIP code
EAST LANSING, MICHIGAN 48823

Your occupation   **ACCOUNTANT**
Spouse's occupation   **ACCOUNTANT**

Presidential Election Campaign   ▶ Do you want $1 to go to this fund?   Yes ___ No ___
If joint return, does your spouse want $1 to go to this fund?   Yes ___ No ___

Note: Checking "Yes" will not increase your tax or reduce your refund.

For Privacy Act and Paperwork Reduction Act Notice, see Instructions.

Filing Status

Check only one box.

1 ☐ Single
2 ☒ Married filing joint return (even if only one had income)
3 ☐ Married filing separate return. Enter spouse's social security no. above and full name here.
4 ☐ Head of household (with qualifying person). (See page 6 of Instructions.) If the qualifying person is your unmarried child but not your dependent, write child's name here. _____
5 ☐ Qualifying widow(er) with dependent child (Year spouse died ▶ 19 ___). (See page 6 of Instructions.)

Exemptions

Always check the box labeled Yourself. Check other boxes if they apply.

6a ☒ Yourself   ☐ 65 or over   ☐ Blind
b ☒ Spouse   ☐ 65 or over   ☐ Blind

Enter number of boxes checked on 6a and b ▶ **2**

c First names of your dependent children who lived with you **MARY, WILLIAM**

Enter number of children listed on 6c ▶ **2**

d Other dependents:

(1) Name	(2) Relationship	(3) Number of months lived in your home	(4) Did dependent have income of $1,000 or more?	(5) Did you provide more than one-half of dependent's support?

Enter number of other dependents ▶ ☐

e Total number of exemptions claimed . . . .   Add numbers entered in boxes above ▶ **4**

Income

Please attach Copy B of your Forms W-2, W-2G, and W-2P here.

If you do not have a W-2, see page 5 of Instructions.

7	Wages, salaries, tips, etc.	7	9000
8	Interest income (also attach Schedule B if over $400 or you have any All-Savers interest)	8	450
9a	Dividends (also attach Schedule B if over $400) **750** ,9b Exclusion **200**		
c	Subtract line 9b from line 9a and enter the result	9c	550
10	Refunds of State and local income taxes, from worksheet on page 10 of Instructions (do not enter an amount unless you deducted those taxes in an earlier year—see page 10 of Instructions)	10	
11	Alimony received	11	
12	Business income or (loss) (attach Schedule C) ▶	12	20000
13	Capital gain or (loss) (attach Schedule D)	13	2000
14	40% capital gain distributions not reported on line 13 (See page 10 of Instructions)	14	
15	Supplemental gains or (losses) (attach Form 4797)	15	
16	Fully taxable pensions, IRA distributions, and annuities not reported on line 17	16	
17a	Other pensions and annuities, including rollovers. Total received 17a ___		
b	Taxable amount, if any, from worksheet on page 10 of Instructions	17b	
18	Rents, royalties, partnerships, estates, trusts, etc. (attach Schedule E)	18	10000
19	Farm income or (loss) (attach Schedule F) ▶	19	
20a	Unemployment compensation (insurance). Total received 20a ___		
b	Taxable amount, if any, from worksheet on page 11 of Instructions	20b	
21	Other income (state nature and source—see page 11 of Instructions) _____	21	
22	**Total income.** Add amounts in column for lines 7 through 21 . . . . ▶	22	42000

Adjustments to Income

(See Instructions on page 11)

23	Moving expense (attach Form 3903 or 3903F)	23		
24	Employee business expenses (attach Form 2106)	24		
25a	IRA deduction, from the worksheet on page 12	25a		
b	Enter here IRA payments you made in 1984 that are included in line 25a above ▶ _____			
26	Payments to a Keogh (H.R. 10) retirement plan	26		
27	Penalty on early withdrawal of savings	27		
28	Alimony paid	28		
29	Deduction for a married couple when both work (attach Schedule W)	29		
30	Disability income exclusion (attach Form 2440)	30		
31	**Total adjustments.** Add lines 23 through 30 . . . . . . ▶		31	

Adjusted Gross Income

32	**Adjusted gross income.** Subtract line 31 from line 22. If this line is less than $10,000, see "Earned Income Credit" (line 59) on page 16 of Instructions. If you want IRS to figure your tax, see page 3 of Instructions . . . . ▶	32	42000

Exhibit 1 (*Cont.*)

Form 1040 (1983)   Page **2**

Tax Compu-tation (See Instruc-tions on page 13)	33	Amount from line 32 (adjusted gross income)	33	42000
	34a	If you itemize, complete Schedule A (Form 1040) and enter the amount from Schedule A, line 28	34a	9683
		Caution: If you have unearned income and can be claimed as a dependent on your parent's return, check here ▶ ☐ and see page 13 of the Instructions. Also see page 13 of the Instructions if: • You are married filing a separate return and your spouse itemizes deductions, OR • You file Form 4563, OR • You are a dual-status alien.		
	34b	If you do not itemize deductions on Schedule A (Form 1040), complete the worksheet on page 14. Then enter the allowable part of your charitable contributions here	34b	
	35	Subtract line 34a or 34b, whichever applies, from line 33	35	32317
	36	Multiply $1,000 by the total number of exemptions claimed on Form 1040, line 6e	36	4000
	37	Taxable Income. Subtract line 36 from line 35	37	28317
	38	Tax. Enter tax here and check if from ☑ Tax Table, ☐ Tax Rate Schedule X, Y, or Z, or ☐ Schedule G	38	4622
	39	Additional Taxes. (See page 14 of Instructions.) Enter here and check if from ☐ Form 4970, ☐ Form 4972, ☐ Form 5544, or ☐ section 72 penalty taxes	39	—
	40	**Total.** Add lines 38 and 39. . . . . ▶	40	4622
Credits (See Instruc-tions on page 14)	41	Credit for the elderly (attach Schedules R&RP)	41	
	42	Foreign tax credit (attach Form 1116)	42	
	43	Investment credit (attach Form 3468)	43	
	44	Partial credit for political contributions	44	
	45	Credit for child and dependent care expenses (attach Form 2441)	45	
	46	Jobs credit (attach Form 5884)	46	
	47	Residential energy credit (attach Form 5695)	47	
	48	**Total credits.** Add lines 41 through 47	48	—
	49	**Balance.** Subtract line 48 from line 40 and enter difference (but not less than zero) . . . . . . ▶	49	4622
Other Taxes (Including Advance EIC Payments)	50	Self-employment tax (attach Schedule SE)	50	
	51	Alternative minimum tax (attach Form 6251)	51	
	52	Tax from recapture of investment credit (attach Form 4255)	52	
	53	Social security tax on tip income not reported to employer (attach Form 4137)	53	
	54	Uncollected employee social security tax and RRTA tax on tips (from Form W-2)	54	
	55	Tax on an IRA (attach Form 5329)	55	
06	56	**Total tax.** Add lines 49 through 55 . . . . ▶	56	4622
Payments Attach Forms W-2, W-2G, and W-2P to front.	57	Federal income tax withheld.	57	1200	
	58	1983 estimated tax payments and amount applied from 1982 return	58	4000	
	59	Earned income credit. If line 33 is under $10,000, see page 16 . .	59		
	60	Amount paid with Form 4868	60		
	61	Excess social security tax and RRTA tax withheld (two or more employers)	61		
	62	Credit for Federal tax on special fuels and oils (attach Form 4136)	62		
	63	Regulated Investment Company credit (attach Form 2439)	63		
	64	**Total payments.** Add lines 57 through 63 . . . . ▶	64	5200
Refund or Amount You Owe	65	If line 64 is larger than line 56, enter amount **OVERPAID** . . . . ▶	65	578
	66	Amount of line 65 to be **REFUNDED TO YOU** . . . . ▶	66	578
	67	Amount of line 65 to be applied to your 1984 estimated tax . . . . ▶	67		
	68	If line 56 is larger than line 64, enter **AMOUNT YOU OWE.** Attach check or money order for full amount payable to "Internal Revenue Service." Write your social security number and "1983 Form 1040" on it . . . ▶ (Check ▶ ☐ if Form 2210 (2210F) is attached. See page 17 of Instructions.) $	68	

Please Sign Here

Under penalties of perjury, I declare that I have examined this return and accompanying schedules and statements, and to the best of my knowledge and belief, they are true, correct, and complete. Declaration of preparer (other than taxpayer) is based on all information of which preparer has any knowledge.

▶ *John Q Taxpayer* | 4/13/84   ▶ *Ellen Taxpayer*
Your signature   Date   Spouse's signature (if filing jointly, BOTH must sign)

Paid Preparer's Use Only	Preparer's signature ▶		Date		Check if self-employed ☐	Preparer's social security no.
	Firm's name (or yours, if self-employed) and address ▶				E.I. No.	
					ZIP code	

Exhibit 2

SCHEDULES A&B (Form 1040) Department of the Treasury Internal Revenue Service	**Schedule A—Itemized Deductions** (Schedule B is on back) ▶ Attach to Form 1040. ▶ See Instructions for Schedules A and B (Form 1040).			OMB No. 1545-0074 **1983** 07

Name(s) as shown on Form 1040
JOHN Q & ELLEN TAXPAYER

Your social security number: 111 22 3333

Medical and Dental Expenses (Do not include expenses reimbursed or paid by others.) (See page 18 of Instructions.)	1 Medicines and drugs	**1**		
	2 Write 1% of Form 1040, line 33	**2**		
	3 Subtract line 2 from line 1. If line 2 is more than line 1, write zero	**3**		
	4 Other medical and dental expenses:			
	a Doctors, dentists, nurses, hospitals, insurance premiums you paid for medical and dental care, etc.	**4a**	1250	
	b Transportation	**4b**		
	c Other (list—include hearing aids, dentures, eyeglasses, etc.) ▶			
		4c		
	5 Add lines 3 through 4c	**5**	1250	
	6 Multiply amount on Form 1040, line 33, by 5% (.05)	**6**	2100	
	7 Subtract line 6 from line 5. If line 6 is more than line 5, write zero	**7**		0
Taxes (See page 19 of Instructions.)	8 State and local income	**8**	1400	
	9 Real estate	**9**	900	
	10 a General sales (see sales tax tables)	**10a**	333	
	b General sales on motor vehicles	**10b**		
	11 Other (list—include personal property) ▶	**11**		
	12 Add lines 8 through 11. Write your answer here ▶	**12**		2633
Interest Expense (See page 20 of Instructions.)	13 a Home mortgage interest paid to financial institutions	**13a**	9000	
	b Home mortgage interest paid to individuals (show that person's name and address) ▶	**13b**		
	14 Credit cards and charge accounts	**14**	450	
	15 Other (list) ▶	**15**		
	16 Add lines 13a through 15. Write your answer here ▶	**16**		9450
Contributions (See page 20 of Instructions.)	17 a Cash contributions. (If you gave $3,000 or more to any one organization, report those contributions on line 17b.)	**17a**	750	
	b Cash contributions totaling $3,000 or more to any one organization. (Show to whom you gave and how much you gave.) ▶	**17b**		
	18 Other than cash (attach required statement)	**18**		
	19 Carryover from prior year	**19**		
	20 Add lines 17a through 19. Write your answer here ▶	**20**		750
Casualty and Theft Losses	21 Total casualty or theft loss(es) (attach Form 4684) (see page 20 of Instructions) ▶	**21**		
Miscellaneous Deductions (See page 21 of Instructions.)	22 Union and professional dues	**22**		
	23 Tax return preparation fee	**23**		
	24 Other (list) ▶ JOB SEARCH	**24**	250	
	25 Add lines 22 through 24. Write your answer here ▶	**25**		250
Summary of Itemized Deductions (See page 21 of Instructions.)	26 Add lines 7, 12, 16, 20, 21, and 25	**26**		13083
	27 If you checked Form 1040 { Filing Status box 2 or 5, write $3,400; Filing Status box 1 or 4, write $2,300; Filing Status box 3, write $1,700 }	**27**		3400
	28 Subtract line 27 from line 26. Write your answer here and on Form 1040, line 34a. (If line 27 is more than line 26, see the Instructions for line 28 on page 21.) ▶	**28**		9683

For Paperwork Reduction Act Notice, see Form 1040 Instructions.   Schedule A (Form 1040) 1983

Exhibit 2 (*Cont.*)

Schedules A&B (Form 1040) 1983   **Schedule B—Interest and Dividend Income**   08   OMB No. 1545-0074   Page **2**

Name(s) as shown on Form 1040 (Do not enter name and social security number if shown on other side)   Your social security number

JOHN Q & ELLEN TAXPAYER   111 22 3333

Part I
Interest Income

(See pages 9 and 21 of Instructions.)

Also complete Part III.

If you received more than $400 in interest or you received any interest from an All-Savers Certificate, you must complete Part I and list ALL interest received. If you received interest as a nominee for another, or you received or paid accrued interest on securities transferred between interest payment dates, see page 22.

Interest income other than interest from All-Savers Certificates		Amount
1 Interest income from seller-financed mortgages. (See Instructions and show name of payer.) ▶	1	
2 Other interest income (list name of payer) ▶		
LOCAL SAVINGS & LOAN		450
	2	
3 Add lines 1 and 2	3	450

Interest from All-Savers Certificates (ASCs). (See page 22.)		Amount
4	4	
5 Add amounts on line 4	5	
6 Write the amount of your ASC exclusion from the worksheet on page 22 of Instructions .	6	
7 Subtract line 6 from line 5	7	
8 Add lines 3 and 7. Write your answer here and on Form 1040, line 8 ...... ▶	8	

Part II
Dividend Income

(See pages 9 and 22 of Instructions.)

Also complete Part III.

If you received more than $400 in gross dividends (including capital gain distributions) and other distributions on stock, or you are electing to exclude qualified reinvested dividends from a public utility, complete Part II. If you received dividends as a nominee for another, see page 22.

Name of payer		Amount
9 XYZ CORP.		250
PD CORP.		500
	9	
10 Add amounts on line 9	10	750
11 Capital gain distributions. Enter here and on line 15, Schedule D.*	11	
12 Nontaxable distributions. (See Instructions for adjustment to basis.)	12	
13 Exclusion of qualified reinvested dividends from a public utility. (See page 22 of Instructions.)	13	
14 Add lines 11, 12, and 13	14	—
15 Subtract line 14 from line 10. Write your answer here and on Form 1040, line 9a . ▶	15	750

*If you received capital gain distributions for the year and you do not need Schedule D to report any other gains or losses, do not file that schedule. Instead, enter 40% of your capital gain distributions on Form 1040, line 14.

Part III
Foreign Accounts and Foreign Trusts

(See page 22 of Instructions.)

If you received more than $400 of interest or dividends, OR if you had a foreign account or were a grantor of, or a transferor to, a foreign trust, you must answer both questions in Part III.	Yes	No
16 At any time during the tax year, did you have an interest in or a signature or other authority over a bank account, securities account, or other financial account in a foreign country? (See page 23 of the instructions for exceptions and filing requirements for Form 90-22.1.)		
If "Yes," write the name of the foreign country ▶		
17 Were you the grantor of, or transferor to, a foreign trust which existed during the current tax year, whether or not you have any beneficial interest in it? If "Yes," you may have to file Forms 3520, 3520-A, or 926		

For Paperwork Reduction Act Notice, see Form 1040 Instructions.   Schedule B (Form 1040) 1983

Exhibit 3

SCHEDULE C (Form 1040)	**Profit or (Loss) From Business or Profession** (Sole Proprietorship) Partnerships, Joint Ventures, etc., Must File Form 1065. ▶ Attach to Form 1040 or Form 1041. ▶ See Instructions for Schedule C (Form 1040).	OMB No. 1545-0074 **19 83** 09

Department of the Treasury
Internal Revenue Service

Name of proprietor	Social security number of proprietor
JOHN Q. TAXPAYER	111 22 3333

A Main business activity (see Instructions) ▶ ACCOUNTING, CPA ; product ▶

B Business name and address ▶ ABLE ACCOUNTING SERVICES
100 W WASHINGTON, LANSING, MI.

C Employer identification number

D Method(s) used to value closing inventory:
(1) ☐ Cost (2) ☐ Lower of cost or market (3) ☐ Other (attach explanation)

E Accounting method: (1) ☒ Cash (2) ☐ Accrual (3) ☐ Other (specify) ▶ ....

	Yes	No
F Was there any major change in determining quantities, costs, or valuations between opening and closing inventory? . . . If "Yes," attach explanation.		X
G Did you deduct expenses for an office in your home?		X

PART I.—Income

1 a Gross receipts or sales	1a	50000
b Less: Returns and allowances	1b	—
c Subtract line 1b from line 1a and enter the balance here	1c	50000
2 Cost of goods sold and/or operations (Part III, line 8)	2	
3 Subtract line 2 from line 1c and enter the **gross profit** here	3	50000
4 a Windfall Profit Tax Credit or Refund received in 1983 (see Instructions) . .	4a	
b Other income	4b	
5 Add lines 3, 4a, and 4b. This is the **gross income** . . . . . . ▶	5	50000

PART II.—Deductions

6 Advertising	500	**23** Repairs		200
7 Bad debts from sales or services (Cash method taxpayers, see Instructions) .	800	**24** Supplies (not included in Part III) . .		
8 Bank service charges		**25** Taxes (Do not include Windfall Profit Tax here. See line 29.) .		1000
9 Car and truck expenses	600	**26** Travel and entertainment		1000
10 Commissions		**27** Utilities and telephone		2500
11 Depletion		**28 a** Wages	7000	
12 Depreciation and Section 179 deduction from Form 4562 (not included in Part III)	6000	**b** Jobs credit		
		c Subtract line 28b from 28a		7000
13 Dues and publications	250	**29** Windfall Profit Tax withheld in 1983		
14 Employee benefit programs . . .		**30** Other expenses (specify):		
15 Freight (not included in Part III) . . .		**a** Misc		50
16 Insurance	1500	**b**		
17 Interest on business indebtedness . .	5000	**c**		
18 Laundry and cleaning		**d**		
19 Legal and professional services . .	2000	**e**		
20 Office expense	400	**f**		
21 Pension and profit-sharing plans . .		**g**		
22 Rent on business property	1200	**h**		
		i		
31 Add amounts in columns for lines 6 through 30i. These are the **total deductions** . . . . ▶		**31**		30000

32 Net profit or (loss). Subtract line 31 from line 5 and enter the result. If a profit, enter on Form 1040, line 12, and on Schedule SE, Part I, line 2 (or Form 1041, line 6). If a loss, go on to line 33 . . | **32** | 20000

33 If you have a loss, you must answer this question: "Do you have amounts for which you are not at risk in this business (see Instructions)?" ☐ Yes ☐ No
If "Yes," you must attach Form 6198. If "No," enter the loss on Form 1040, line 12, and on Schedule SE, Part I, line 2 (or Form 1041, line 6).

Exhibit 3 *(Cont.)*

PART III.—Cost of Goods Sold and/or Operations (See Schedule C Instructions for Part III)

1 Inventory at beginning of year (if different from last year's closing inventory, attach explanation)	**1**	
2 Purchases less cost of items withdrawn for personal use	**2**	
3 Cost of labor (do not include salary paid to yourself)	**3**	
4 Materials and supplies	**4**	
5 Other costs	**5**	
6 Add lines 1 through 5	**6**	
7 Less: Inventory at end of year	**7**	
8 Cost of goods sold and/or operations. Subtract line 7 from line 6. Enter here and in Part I, line 2, above. . . .	**8**	

For Paperwork Reduction Act Notice, see Form 1040 Instructions.   Schedule C (Form 1040) 1983

Exhibit 4

SCHEDULE D (FORM 1040) Department of the Treasury Internal Revenue Service	**Capital Gains and Losses** (Examples of property to be reported on this Schedule are gains and losses on stocks, bonds, and similar investments, and gains (but not losses) on personal assets such as a home or jewelry.) ▶ Attach to Form 1040. ▶ See Instructions for Schedule D (Form 1040).	OMB No. 1545-0074 19**83** 11

Name(s) as shown on Form 1040: JOHN Q & ELLEN TAXPAYER   Your social security number: 111 22 3333

PART I.—Short-term Capital Gains and Losses—Assets Held One Year or Less

a. Description of property (Example. 100 shares 7% preferred of "Z" Co.)	b. Date acquired (Mo., day, yr.)	c. Date sold (Mo., day, yr.)	d. Gross sales price	e. Cost or other basis, plus expense of sale	f. LOSS If column (e) is more than (d) subtract (d) from (e)	g. GAIN If column (d) is more than (e) subtract (e) from (d)
*1 PD CORP. (STOCK)	1-3-83	11-1-83	6000	9000	3000	

2	Short-term gain from sale or exchange of a principal residence from Form 2119, lines 7 or 11	2		
3	Short-term capital gain from installment sales from Form 6252, line 21 or 29	3		
4	Net short-term gain or (loss) from partnerships, S corporations, and fiduciaries	4		
5	Add lines 1 through 4 in column f and column g	5	(3000)	
6	Combine columns f and g of line 5 and enter the net gain or (loss)	6		(3000)
7	Short-term capital loss carryover from years beginning after 1969	7		( )
8	Net short-term gain or (loss), combine lines 6 and 7	8		(3000)

PART II.— Long-term Capital Gains and Losses—Assets Held More Than One Year

a. Description of property	b. Date acquired	c. Date sold	d. Gross sales price	e. Cost or other basis	f. LOSS	g. GAIN
9 XYZ CORP. (STOCK)	1-2-79	5-1-83	12000	5000		7000

10	Long-term gain from sale or exchange of a principal residence from Form 2119, lines 7, 11, 16 or 18	10		
11	Long-term capital gain from installment sales from Form 6252, line 21 or 29	11		
12	Net long-term gain or (loss) from partnerships, S corporations, and fiduciaries	12		1000
13	Add lines 9 through 12 in column f and column g	13	( )	8000
14	Combine columns f and g of line 13 and enter the net gain or (loss)	14		8000
15	Capital gain distributions	15		
16	Enter gain from Form 4797, line 6(a)(1)	16		
17	Combine lines 14 through 16	17		8000
18	Long-term capital loss carryover from years beginning after 1969	18		( )
19	Net long-term gain or (loss), combine lines 17 and 18	19		8000

Note: *Complete the back of this form. However, if you have capital loss carryovers from years beginning before 1970, do not complete Parts III or V. See Form 4798 instead.*

For Paperwork Reduction Act Notice, see Form 1040 instructions.   Schedule D (Form 1040) 1983

Exhibit 4 *(Cont.)*

Schedule D (Form 1040) 1983   Page **2**

PART III.—Summary of Parts I and II

20 Combine lines 8 and 19, and enter the net gain or (loss) here	**20** *5000*

Note: *If line 20 is a loss, skip lines 21 through 23 and complete lines 24 and 25. If line 20 is a gain complete lines 21 through 23 and skip lines 24 and 25.*

21 If line 20 shows a gain, enter the smaller of line 19 or line 20. Enter zero if there is a loss or no entry on line 19 . . . .   **21** | *5000*

22 Enter 60% of line 21	**22** *3000*

If line 22 is more than zero, you may be liable for the alternative minimum tax. See Form 6251.

23 Subtract line 22 from line 20. Enter here and on Form 1040, line 13	**23** *2000*

24 If line 20 shows a loss, enter one of the following amounts:

   a   If line 8 is zero or a net gain, enter 50% of line 20;

   b   If line 19 is zero or a net gain, enter line 20; or

   c   If line 8 and line 19 are net losses, enter amount on line 8 added to 50% of the amount on line 19 . . . . .   **24**

25 Enter here and as a loss on Form 1040, line 13, the smallest of:

   a   The amount on line 24;

   b $3,000 ($1,500 if married and filing a separate return); or

   c   Taxable income, as adjusted   **25**

PART IV.—Complete this Part Only if You Elect Out of the Installment Method And Report a Note or Other Obligation at Less Than Full Face Value

☐   Check here if you elect out of the installment method.
     Enter the face amount of the note or other obligation   ▶ . . . .
     Enter the percentage of valuation of the note or other obligation   ▶

PART V.—Computation of Post-1969 Capital Loss Carryovers from 1983 to 1984

(Complete this part if the loss on line 24 is more than the loss on line 25)
Note: *You do not have to complete Part V on the copy you file with IRS.*

Section A.—Short-term Capital Loss Carryover

26 Enter loss shown on line 8; if none, enter zero and skip lines 27 through 30 then go to line 31.	**26**
27 Enter gain shown on line 19. If that line is blank or shows a loss, enter zero	**27**
28 Reduce any loss on line 26 to the extent of any gain on line 27	**28**
29 Enter smaller of line 25 or line 28	**29**
30 Subtract line 29 from line 28. This is your short-term capital loss carryover from 1983 to 1984	**30**

Section B.—Long-term Capital Loss Carryover

31 Subtract line 29 from line 25 (**Note:** *If you skipped lines 27 through 30, enter amount from line 25*)	**31**
32 Enter loss from line 19; if none, enter zero and skip lines 33 through 36	**32**
33 Enter gain shown on line 8. If that line is blank or shows a loss, enter zero	**33**
34 Reduce any loss on line 32 to the extent of any gain on line 33	**34**
35 Multiply amount on line 31 by 2	**35**
36 Subtract line 35 from line 34. This is your long-term capital loss carryover from 1983 to 1984	**36**

Exhibit 5

SCHEDULE E (Form 1040)	Supplemental Income Schedule	OMB No. 1545-0074
Department of the Treasury Internal Revenue Service	(From rents and royalties, partnerships, estates, and trusts, etc.) ▶ Attach to Form 1040. ▶ See Instructions for Schedule E (Form 1040).	1983 12

Name(s) as shown on Form 1040 JOHN Q & ELLEN TAXPAYER

Your social security number 111 22 3333

PART I.—Rent and Royalty Income or Loss

1 Are any of the expenses listed below for a vacation home or other recreational unit (see Instructions)? . . . . . . ☐ Yes ☐ No

2 If you checked "Yes" to question 1, did you or a member of your family occupy the vacation home or other recreational unit for more than the greater of 14 days or 10% of the total days rented at fair rental value during the tax year? . . . ☐ Yes ☐ No

Description of Properties (Show kind and location for each)

Property A ....

Property B ....

Property C

Rental and Royalty Income		Properties			Totals (Add columns A, B, and C)
		A	B	C	
3 a Rents received					} 3
b Royalties received					

Rental and Royalty Expenses						
4 Advertising	4					
5 Auto and travel	5					
6 Cleaning and maintenance	6					
7 Commissions	7					
8 Insurance	8					
9 Interest	9					
10 Legal and other professional fees . . .	10					
11 Repairs	11					
12 Supplies	12					
13 Taxes (Do **not** include Windfall Profit Tax here. See Part III, line 37.)	13					
14 Utilities	14					
15 Wages and salaries	15					
16 Other (list) ▶						
....						
....						
....						
....						
....						
....						
....						
....						
17 Total expenses other than depreciation and depletion. Add lines 4 through 16 . . .	17					17
18 Depreciation expense (see Instructions), or depletion	18					18
19 Total. Add lines 17 and 18	19					
20 Income or (loss) from rental or royalty properties. Subtract line 19 from line 3a (rents) or 3b (royalties)	20					

21 Add properties with profits on line 20, and write the total profits here 21

22 Add properties with losses on line 20, and write the total (losses) here . . . . 22 ( )

23 Combine amounts on lines 21 and 22, and write the net profit or (loss) here 23

24 Net farm rental profit or (loss) from Form 4835, line 49 24

25 Total rental or royalty income or (loss). Combine amounts on lines 23 and 24, and write the total here. If Parts II, III, and IV on page 2 do not apply to you, write the amount from line 25 on Form 1040, line 18. Otherwise, include the amount in line 39 on page 2 of Schedule E 25

For Paperwork Reduction Act Notice, see Form 1040 Instructions.   Schedule E (Form 1040) 1983

Exhibit 5 (Cont.)

Schedule E (Form 1040) 1983   **12**   Page **2**

Name(s) as shown on Form 1040 (Do not enter name and social security number if shown on other side) | Your social security number

JOHN Q & ELLEN TAXPAYER   *III 22 3333*

PART II.—Income or Losses from Partnerships, Estates or Trusts, or S Corporations

If you report a loss below, and have amounts invested in that activity for which you are not at risk, you may have to file Form 6198. See instructions.

(a) Name	(b) Check if foreign partnership	(c) Employer identification number	(d) Net loss (see instructions for at-risk limitations)	(e) Net income
LAND Ho!				*10000*

Partnerships

26 Add amounts in columns (d) and (e) and write the total(s) here . . . . . **26** ( ) *10000*

27 Combine amounts in columns (d) and (e), line 26, and write the net income or (loss) **27**

28 Deduction for section 179 property (from Form 1065, Schedule K-1). (See Instructions for limitations.) **28** ( )

29 Total partnership income or (loss). Combine amounts on lines 27 and 28. Write the total here and include in line 39 below **29** *10000*

Estates or Trusts

30 Add amounts in columns (d) and (e) and write the total(s) here . . . . . **30** ( )

31 Total estate or trust income or (loss). Combine amounts in columns (d) and (e), line 30. Write the total here and include in line 39 below **31**

S Corporations

32 Add amounts in columns (d) and (e) and write the total(s) here . . . . . **32** ( )

33 Combine amounts in columns (d) and (e), line 32, and write the net income or (loss) here . . . **33**

34 Deduction for section 179 property (from Form 1120S, Schedule K-1). (See Instructions for limitations.) **34** ( )

35 Total S corporation income or (loss). Combine amounts on lines 33 and 34. Write the total here and include in line 39 below **35**

PART III.—Windfall Profit Tax Summary

36 Windfall profit tax credit or refund received in 1983 (see Instructions) **36**

37 Windfall profit tax withheld in 1983 (see Instructions) . . . . **37** ( )

38 Combine amounts on lines 36 and 37. Write the total here and include in line 39 below **38**

PART IV.—Summary

39 TOTAL income or (loss). Combine lines 25, 29, 31, 35, and 38. Write total here and on Form 1040, line 18 ▶ **39** *10000*

40 Farmers and fishermen: Write your share of GROSS FARMING AND FISHING INCOME applicable to Parts I and II **40**

PART V.—Depreciation Claimed in Part I.—Complete only if property was placed in service before January 1, 1981. For more space, use Form 4562. If you placed any property in service after December 31, 1980, use Form 4562 for all property; do NOT complete Part V.

(a) Description of property	(b) Date acquired	(c) Cost or other basis	(d) Depreciation allowed or allowable in prior years	(e) Depreciation method	(f) Life or rate	(g) Depreciation for this year
Property A						
Totals (Property A)						
Property B						
Totals (Property B)						
Property C						
Totals (Property C)						

Exhibit 6

Form **1065**	**U.S. Partnership Return of Income**	OMB No. 1545-0099
Department of the Treasury Internal Revenue Service	▶ For Paperwork Reduction Act Notice, see Form 1065 Instructions. For calendar year 1983, or fiscal year beginning _____ 1983, and ending _____ 19__	19**83**

A Principal business activity (see page 4 of Instructions)	Use IRS label. Other-wise, please print or type.	Name LAND HO!	**D** Employer identification number
B Principal product or service (see page 16 of Instructions)		Number and street 100 E. ELMIRA	**E** Date business started 1-1-78
C Business code number (see page 16 of Instructions)		City or town, State, and ZIP code PHOENIX, ARIZONA	**F** Enter total assets at end of tax year $

		Yes	No
G Check method of accounting: (1) ☒ Cash (2) ☐ Accrual (3) ☐ Other	**N** (1) Was there a distribution of property or a transfer of a partnership interest during the tax year?		X
H Check applicable boxes: (1) ☒ Final return (2) ☐ Change in address (3) ☐ Amended return	(2) If "Yes," is the partnership making an election under section 754? If "Yes," attach a statement for the election. (See page 4 of the Instructions before answering this question.)		
I Check if the partnership meets *all* the requirements shown on page 4 of the Instructions under **Question I** . . . . . ▶ ☐	**O** At any time during the tax year, did the partnership have an interest in or a signature or other authority over a bank account, securities account, or other financial account in a foreign country (see page 4 of Instructions)?		X
J Number of partners in this partnership ▶ _____	**P** Was the partnership the grantor of, or transferor to, a foreign trust which existed during the current tax year, whether or not the partnership or any partner has any beneficial interest in it? If "Yes," you may have to file Forms 3520, 3520-A, or 926. (See page 5 of Instructions.)		X
K Is this partnership a limited partnership (see page 3 of Instructions)?			X
L Is this partnership a partner in another partnership?			X
M Are any partners in this partnership also partnerships?	**Q** Are there any specially allocated items of income, gain, loss, deduction, credit, etc. (see page 5 of Instructions)?		X

Income

1a	Gross receipts or sales $ 250,000 **1b** Minus returns and allowances $ — Balance ▶	**1c**	250,000
2	Cost of goods sold and/or operations (Schedule A, line 7)	**2**	100,000
3	Gross profit (subtract line 2 from line 1c)	**3**	150,000
4	Ordinary income (loss) from other partnerships and fiduciaries	**4**	
5	Nonqualifying interest and nonqualifying dividends	**5**	
6a	Gross rents $ _____ **6b** Minus rental expenses (attach schedule) $ _____		
c	Balance net rental income (loss) . . . . ▶	**6c**	
7	Net income (loss) from royalties (attach schedule)	**7**	
8	Net farm profit (loss) (attach Schedule F (Form 1040))	**8**	
9	Net gain (loss) (Form 4797, line 14)	**9**	
10	Other income (loss)	**10**	
11	**TOTAL** income (loss) (combine lines 3 through 10)	**11**	150,000

Deductions

12a	Salaries and wages (other than to partners) $ 19,000 **12b** Minus jobs credit $ _____ Balance ▶	**12c**	19,000
13	Guaranteed payments to partners (see page 6 of Instructions)	**13**	
14	Rent	**14**	6,000
15a	Total deductible interest expense not claimed elsewhere on return (see page 6 of Instructions) . . . **15a**		
b	Minus interest expense required to be passed through to partners on Schedule K-1, lines 13, 20a(2), and 20a(3) and Schedule K, lines 13, 20a(2), and 20a(3) (if Schedule K is required). **15b**		
c	Balance . . . . ▶	**15c**	20,000
16	Taxes	**16**	2,000
17	Bad debts (see page 7 of Instructions)	**17**	
18	Repairs	**18**	
19a	Depreciation from Form 4562 (attach Form 4562) $ _____ **19b** Minus depreciation claimed on Schedule A and elsewhere on return $ _____ Balance ▶	**19c**	3,000
20	Depletion (*Do not deduct oil and gas depletion.* See page 7 of Instructions.)	**20**	
21a	Retirement plans, etc. (see page 7 of Instructions)	**21a**	
b	Employee benefit programs (see page 7 of Instructions)	**21b**	
22	Other deductions (attach schedule)	**22**	
23	**TOTAL** deductions (add amounts in column for lines 12c through 22)	**23**	50,000
24	Ordinary income (loss) (subtract line 23 from line 11)	**24**	100,000

Please Sign Here	Under penalties of perjury, I declare that I have examined this return, including accompanying schedules and statements, and to the best of my knowledge and belief it is true, correct, and complete. Declaration of preparer (other than taxpayer) is based on all information of which preparer has any knowledge.	
	▶ O. E. Deel Signature of general partner	▶ April 1, 1984 Date

Paid Preparer's Use Only	Preparer's signature ▶	Date	Check if self-employed ☐	Preparer's social security no.
	Firm's name (or yours, if self-employed) and address ▶		E.I. No. ▶	
			ZIP code ▶	

Exhibit 6 (Cont.)

Form 1065 (1983)   Page **2**

SCHEDULE A.—Cost of Goods Sold and/or Operations (See Page 7 of Instructions.)

1	Inventory at beginning of year	1	800,000
2	Purchases minus cost of items withdrawn for personal use	2	200,000
3	Cost of labor	3	
4	Other costs (attach schedule)	4	
5	Total (add lines 1 through 4)	5	1,000,000
6	Inventory at end of year	6	900,000
7	Cost of goods sold (subtract line 6 from line 5). Enter here and on page 1, line 2	7	100,000

8a Check all methods used for valuing closing inventory:

   (i) ☒ Cost

   (ii) ☐ Lower of cost or market as described in regulations section 1.471-4 (see page 8 of Instructions)

   (iii) ☐ Writedown of "subnormal" goods as described in regulations section 1.471-2(c) (see page 8 of Instructions)

   (iv) ☐ Other (specify method used and attach explanation) ▶ ....

  b Check if the LIFO inventory method was adopted this tax year for any goods (if checked, attach Form 970)   ☐

  c If you are engaged in manufacturing, did you value your inventory using the full absorption method (regulations section 1.471-11)? ☐ Yes ☐ No

  d Was there any substantial change in determining quantities, cost, or valuations between opening and closing inventory? ☐ Yes ☒ No

    If "Yes," attach explanation.

SCHEDULE B.—Distributive Share Items (See Pages 8, 10-11, and 15 of Instructions.)

(a) Distributive share items		(b) Total amount
1 Net long-term capital gain (loss)	1	10,000
2 Other net gain (loss) under section 1231 and specially allocated ordinary gain (loss)	2	
3a If the partnership had income from outside the United States, enter the name of the country or U.S. possession ▶		
b Total gross income from sources outside the United States	3b	

SCHEDULE L.—Balance Sheets
(See Pages 4 and 8 of Instructions and Question I on Page 1 Before Completing Schedules L and M.)

	Assets	Beginning of tax year (a)	(b)	End of tax year (c)	(d)
1	Cash				
2	Trade notes and accounts receivable				
a	Minus allowance for bad debts				
3	Inventories				
4	Federal and State government obligations				
5	Other current assets (attach schedule)				
6	Mortgage and real estate loans				
7	Other investments (attach schedule)				
8	Buildings and other depreciable assets				
a	Minus accumulated depreciation				
9	Depletable assets				
a	Minus accumulated depletion				
10	Land (net of any amortization)				
11	Intangible assets (amortizable only)				
a	Minus accumulated amortization				
12	Other assets (attach schedule)				
13	**TOTAL** assets				
	Liabilities and Capital				
14	Accounts payable				
15	Mortgages, notes, and bonds payable in less than 1 year				
16	Other current liabilities (attach schedule)				
17	All nonrecourse loans				
18	Mortgages, notes, and bonds payable in 1 year or more				
19	Other liabilities (attach schedule)				
20	Partners' capital accounts				
21	**TOTAL** liabilities and capital				

SCHEDULE M.—Reconciliation of Partners' Capital Accounts (See Page 8 of Instructions.)
(Show reconciliation of each partner's capital account on Schedule K-1, Item F.)

(a) Capital account at beginning of year	(b) Capital contributed during year	(c) Ordinary income (loss) from page 1, line 24	(d) Income not included in column (c), plus nontaxable income	(e) Losses not included in column (c), plus unallowable deductions	(f) Withdrawals and distributions	(g) Capital account at end of year

Exhibit 7

SCHEDULE K (Form 1065)	Partners' Shares of Income, Credits, Deductions, etc.	OMB No. 1545-0099
Department of the Treasury Internal Revenue Service	▶ File this form if there are more than ten Schedules K-1 to be filed with Form 1065. Do not complete lines 6, 8, 21b, and 21c. The amounts for these lines are shown on Schedule B, Form 1065. ▶ Attach to Form 1065. ▶ See Instructions for Schedule K (Form 1065).	1983

Name of partnership LAND Ho !

Employer identification number

	a. Distributive share items		b. Total amount
Income (Loss)	1 Ordinary income (loss) (page 1, line 24)	1	100,000
	2 Guaranteed payments	2	
	3 Interest from All-Savers Certificates	3	
	4 Dividends qualifying for exclusion	4	
	5 Net short-term capital gain (loss) (Schedule D, line 4)	5	
	6 Net long-term capital gain (loss) (Schedule D, line 9)		
	7 Net gain (loss) from involuntary conversions due to casualty or theft (Form 4684)	7	
	8 Other net gain (loss) under section 1231		
	9 Other (attach schedule)	9	
Deductions	10 Charitable contributions (attach list): 50% _____ 30% _____ 20% _____	10	
	11 Expense deduction for recovery property (section 179) from Part I, Section A, Form 4562	11	
	12a Payments for partners to an IRA	12a	
	b Payments for partners to a Keogh Plan (Type of plan ▶ _____)	12b	
	c Payments for partners to Simplified Employee Pension (SEP)	12c	
	13 Other (attach schedule)	13	
Credits	14 Jobs credit	14	
	15 Credit for alcohol used as fuel	15	
	16 Credit for income tax withheld	16	
	17 Other (attach schedule)	17	
Other	18a Gross farming or fishing income	18a	
	b Net earnings (loss) from self-employment	18b	
	c Other (attach schedule)		
Tax Preference Items	19a Accelerated depreciation on nonrecovery real property or 15-year real property	19a	
	b Accelerated depreciation on leased personal property or leased recovery property other than 15-year real property	19b	
	c Depletion (other than oil and gas)	19c	
	d (1) Excess intangible drilling costs from oil, gas, or geothermal wells	19d(1)	
	(2) Net income from oil, gas, or geothermal wells	19d(2)	
	e Net investment income (loss)	19e	
	f Other (attach schedule)	19f	
Investment Interest	20a Investment interest expense:		
	(1) Indebtedness incurred before 12/17/69	20a(1)	
	(2) Indebtedness incurred before 9/11/75, but after 12/16/69	20a(2)	
	(3) Indebtedness incurred after 9/10/75	20a(3)	
	b Net investment income (loss)	20b	
	c Excess expenses from "net lease property"	20c	
	d Excess of net long-term capital gain over net short-term capital loss from investment property	20d	
Foreign Taxes	21a Type of income _____		
	b Foreign country or U.S. possession		
	c Total gross income from sources outside the U.S. (attach schedule)		
	d Total applicable deductions and losses (attach schedule)	21d	
	e Total foreign taxes (check one): ▶ ☐ Paid ☐ Accrued	21e	
	f Reduction in taxes available for credit (attach schedule)	21f	
	g Other (attach schedule)	21g	

For Paperwork Reduction Act Notice, see Form 1065 Instructions.

Schedule K (Form 1065) 1983

Exhibit 7 (Cont.)

SCHEDULE K-1 (Form 1065)	Partner's Share of Income, Credits, Deductions, etc.	OMB No. 1545-0099
Department of the Treasury Internal Revenue Service	For calendar year 1983 or fiscal year beginning _____, 1983, and ending _____, 19___	1983

Partner's identifying number ▶

Partnership's identifying number ▶

Partner's name, address, and ZIP code

JOHN Q. TAXPAYER
500 FIRST STREET
EAST LANSING, MICHIGAN

Partnership's name, address, and ZIP code

LAND HO!
200 E. ELMIRA
PHOENIX, ARIZONA

A Is partner a general partner (see page 3 of Instructions)? . . . . ☒ Yes ☐ No

B Partner's share of liabilities (see page 10 of Instructions):
Nonrecourse . . . . $ _____
Other . . . . $ _____

C What type of entity is this partner? ▶ INDIVIDUAL

D Enter partner's percentage of:

	(i) Before decrease or termination	(ii) End of year
Profit sharing	10 %	10 %
Loss sharing	10 %	10 %
Ownership of capital	10 %	10 %

E IRS Center where partnership filed return ▶ UTAH

F Reconciliation of partner's capital account:

(a) Capital account at beginning of year	(b) Capital contributed during year	(c) Ordinary income (loss) from line 1	(d) Income not included in column (c), plus nontaxable income	(e) Losses not included in column (c), plus unallowable deductions	(f) Withdrawals and distributions	(g) Capital account at end of year

	(a) Distributive share item	(b) Amount	(c) 1040 filers enter the amount in column (b) on:
Income (Loss)	1 Ordinary income (loss)	10,000	Sch. E, Part II, col. (d) or (e)
	2 Guaranteed payments		Sch. E, Part II, column (e)
	3 Interest from All-Savers Certificates		Sch. B, Part I, line 4
	4 Dividends qualifying for exclusion		Sch. B, Part II, line 9
	5 Net short-term capital gain (loss)		Sch. D, line 4, col. f. or g.
	6 Net long-term capital gain (loss)	1,000	Sch. D, line 12, col. f. or g.
	7 Net gain (loss) from involuntary conversions due to casualty or theft . .		See attached instructions
	8 Other net gain (loss) under section 1231		Form 4797, line 1
	9 Other (attach schedule)		(Enter on applicable lines of your return)
Deductions	10 Charitable contributions: 50% _____, 30% _____, 20% _____		See Form 1040 instructions
	11 Expense deduction for recovery property (section 179)		Sch. E, Part II, line 28
	12 a Payments for partner to an IRA		See Form 1040 instructions
	b Payments for partner to a Keogh Plan (Type of plan ▶ _____).		Form 1040, line 26
	c Payments for partner to Simplified Employee Pension (SEP)		Form 1040, line 26
	13 Other (attach schedule)		(Enter on applicable lines of your return)
Credits	14 Jobs credit		Form 5884
	15 Credit for alcohol used as fuel		Form 6478
	16 Credit for income tax withheld		See Form 1040 instructions
	17 Other (attach schedule)		(Enter on applicable lines of your return)
Other	18 a Gross farming or fishing income		See attached instructions
	b Net earnings (loss) from self-employment		Sch. SE, Part I
	c Other (attach schedule)		(Enter on applicable lines of your return)
Tax Preference Items	19 a Accelerated depreciation on nonrecovery real property or 15-year real property.		Form 6251, line 4c
	b Accelerated depreciation on leased personal property or leased recovery property other than 15-year real property. . . .		Form 6251, line 4d
	c Depletion (other than oil and gas)		Form 6251, line 4i
	d (1) Excess intangible drilling costs from oil, gas, or geothermal wells .		See Form 6251 instructions
	(2) Net income from oil, gas, or geothermal wells		
	e Net investment income (loss)		Form 6251, line 2e(2)
	f Other (attach schedule)		See attached instructions

For Paperwork Reduction Act Notice, see Form 1065 Instructions.

Schedule K-1 (Form 1065) 1983

Exhibit 7 (*Cont.*)

		(a) Distributive share item	(b) Amount	(c) 1040 filers enter the amount in column (b) on:
Investment Interest	**20 a**	Investment interest expense:		
		(1) Indebtedness incurred before 12/17/69		Form 4952, line 1
		(2) Indebtedness incurred before 9/11/75, but after 12/16/69 .		Form 4952, line 15
		(3) Indebtedness incurred after 9/10/75		Form 4952, line 5
	b	Net investment income (loss)		See attached instructions
	c	Excess expenses from "net lease property".		Form 4952, lines 11 and 19
	d	Excess of net long-term capital gain over net short-term capital loss from investment property		Form 4952, line 20
Foreign Taxes	**21 a**	Type of income _____		Form 1116, Checkboxes
	b	Name of foreign country or U.S. possession _____		Form 1116, Part I
	c	Total gross income from sources outside the U.S. (attach schedule) .		Form 1116, Part I
	d	Total applicable deductions and losses (attach schedule)		Form 1116, Part I
	e	Total foreign taxes (check one): ▶ ☐ Paid ☐ Accrued		Form 1116, Part II
	f	Reduction in taxes available for credit (attach schedule).		Form 1116, Part III
	g	Other (attach schedule)		Form 1116, instructions
Property Eligible for Investment Credit	**22**	Unadjusted basis of new recovery property **a** 3-Year		See attached instructions
		b Other		See attached instructions
		Unadjusted basis of used recovery property **c** 3-Year		See attached instructions
		d Other		See attached instructions
	e	Nonrecovery property (see page 15 of Instructions) (attach schedule)		Form 3468, instr., line 2
	f	New commuter highway vehicle		Form 3468, line 3
	g	Used commuter highway vehicle		Form 3468, line 4
	h	Qualified rehabilitation expenditures		Form 3468, line 6a,b,or c

		Properties:	A	B	C	
Property Subject to Recapture of Investment Credit	**23 a**	Description of property (state whether recovery or nonrecovery property)				Form 4255, top
	b	Date placed in service				Form 4255, line 2
	c	Cost or other basis				Form 4255, line 3
	d	Class of recovery property or original estimated useful life				Form 4255, line 4
	e	Date item ceased to be investment credit property				Form 4255, line 8

Exhibit 8

Form 1120
Department of the Treasury
Internal Revenue Service

U.S. Corporation Income Tax Return

For calendar year 1983 or other tax year beginning _____, 1983, ending _____, 19 _____

► **For Paperwork Reduction Act Notice, see page 1 of the instructions.**

OMB No. 1545-0123

1983

Check if a—
A. Consolidated return ☐
B. Personal Holding Co ☐
C. Business Code No. (See page 9 of Instructions)

Use IRS label. Otherwise please print or type.

Name **BARTAL CORPORATION**

Number and street **350 W. ALEX STREET**

City or town, State, and ZIP code **SAN FRANCISCO, CA**

D. Employer identification number

E. Date incorporated **1-1-75**

F. Total assets (see Specific Instructions) $

G. Check box if there has been a change in address from the previous year . . . . ► ☐

Gross Income	1 (a) Gross receipts or sales $ **1,000,000** (b) Less returns and allowances $ _____ Balance ►	1(c)	**1,000,000**
	2 Cost of goods sold (Schedule A) and/or operations (attach schedule)	2	**600,000**
	3 Gross profit (subtract line 2 from line 1(c))	3	**400,000**
	4 Dividends (Schedule C)	4	**50,000**
	5 Interest	5	**4,000**
	6 Gross rents	6	
	7 Gross royalties	7	
	8 Capital gain net income (attach separate Schedule D)	8	
	9 Net gain or (loss) from Form 4797, line 14(a), Part II (attach Form 4797) . .	9	
	10 Other income (see instructions—attach schedule).	10	
	11 TOTAL income—Add lines 3 through 10 and enter here . . . . . ►	11	**454,000**
Deductions	12 Compensation of officers (Schedule E)	12	
	13 (a) Salaries and wages $ **125,000** (b) Less jobs credit $ _____ Balance ►	13(c)	**125,000**
	14 Repairs (see instructions)	14	
	15 Bad debts (Schedule F if reserve method is used)	15	**12,000**
	16 Rents	16	
	17 Taxes	17	**40,000**
	18 Interest	18	**8,000**
	19 Contributions (not over 10% of line 30 adjusted per instructions)	19	
	20 Depreciation (attach Form 4562) 20 **75,000**		
	21 Less depreciation claimed in Schedule A and elsewhere on return . . 21(a) ( )	21(b)	**75,000**
	22 Depletion	22	**25,000**
	23 Advertising	23	
	24 Pension, profit-sharing, etc. plans (see instructions)	24	
	25 Employee benefit programs (see instructions)	25	
	26 Other deductions (attach schedule)	26	**10,000**
	27 TOTAL deductions—Add lines 12 through 26 and enter here . . . . ►	27	**295,000**
	28 Taxable income before net operating loss deduction and special deductions (subtract line 27 from line 11)	28	**159,000**
	29 Less: (a) Net operating loss deduction (see instructions—attach schedule) . 29(a)		
	(b) Special deductions (Schedule C) . . . . . 29(b) **42,500**	29	**42,500**
	30 Taxable income (subtract line 29 from line 28)	30	**116,500**
Tax	31 TOTAL TAX (Schedule J).	31	**33,340**
	32 Credits: (a) Overpayment from 1982 allowed as a credit.		
	(b) 1983 estimated tax payments **30,000**		
	(c) Less refund of 1983 estimated tax applied for on Form 4466 ( )		
	(d) Tax deposited with Form 7004		
	(e) Credit from regulated investment companies (attach Form 2439). .		
	(f) Federal tax on special fuels and oils (attach Form 4136). . . .	32	**30,000**
	33 TAX DUE (subtract line 32 from line 31—If line 32 is greater than line 31, skip line 33 and go to line 34). See instruction C3 for depositary method of payment . . . . . . (Check ► ☐ if Form 2220 is attached. See instruction D.) ► $ _____	33	**3,340**
	34 OVERPAYMENT (subtract line 31 from line 32)	34	
	35 Enter amount of line 34 you want: Credited to 1984 estimated tax ► | Refunded ►	35	

Please Sign Here

Under penalties of perjury, I declare that I have examined this return, including accompanying schedules and statements, and to the best of my knowledge and belief, it is true, correct, and complete. Declaration of preparer (other than taxpayer) is based on all information of which preparer has any knowledge.

► *Farley Able* Signature of officer | Date **2/23/84** | Title **V.P. Finance**

Paid Preparer's Use Only

Preparer's signature ► *Gerald Large* | Date **3/1/84** | Check if self-employed ► ☐ | Preparer's social security number **777 88 9999**

Firm's name (or yours, if self-employed) and address ► **LARGE & WEALTHY, CPA's** | E.I. No. ► | ZIP code ►

Exhibit 8 (Cont.)

Form 1120 (1983)   Page 2

SCHEDULE A.—Cost of Goods Sold
(See instructions for Schedule A)

1 Inventory at beginning of year.	1	1,100,000
2 Merchandise bought for manufacture or sale.	2	200,000
3 Salaries and wages	3	
4 Other costs (attach schedule).	4	
5 Total—Add lines 1 through 4.	5	1,300,000
6 Inventory at end of year.	6	700,000
7 Cost of goods sold—Subtract line 6 from line 5. Enter here and on line 2, page 1	7	600,000

8 (a) Check all methods used for valuing closing inventory:
    (i) ☐ Cost
    (ii) ☐ Lower of cost or market as described in Regulations section 1.471–4 (see instructions)
    (iii) ☐ Writedown of ''subnormal'' goods as described in Regulations section 1.471–2(c) (see instructions)
    (iv) ☐ Other (Specify method used and attach explanation) ▶ ------------------------------
  (b) Check if the LIFO inventory method was adopted this tax year for any goods (if checked, attach Form 970) . . . . ☐
  (c) If the LIFO inventory method was used for this tax year, enter percentage (or amounts) of closing inventory computed under LIFO
  (d) If you are engaged in manufacturing, did you value your inventory using the full absorption method (Regulations section 1.471–11)? . . . . ☐ Yes ☐ No
  (e) Was there any substantial change in determining quantities, cost, or valuations between opening and closing inventory? ☐ Yes ☐ No
    If ''Yes,'' attach explanation.

SCHEDULE C.—Dividends and Special Deductions
(See instructions for Schedule C)

	(A) Dividends received	(B) %	(C) Special deductions: multiply (A) X (B)
1 Domestic corporations subject to 85% deduction	50,000	85	42,500
2 Certain preferred stock of public utilities		59.13	
3 Foreign corporations subject to 85% deduction		85	
4 Wholly-owned foreign subsidiaries subject to 100% deduction (section 245(b))		100	
5 Total—Add lines 1 through 4. See instructions for limitation			42,500
6 Affiliated groups subject to the 100% deduction (section 243(a)(3))		100	
7 Other dividends from foreign corporations not included in lines 3 and 4			
8 Income from controlled foreign corporations under subpart F (attach Forms 5471)			
9 Foreign dividend gross-up (section 78)			
10 DISC or former DISC dividends not included in line 1 (section 246(d))			
11 Other dividends			
12 Deduction for dividends paid on certain preferred stock of public utilities (see instructions)			
13 Total dividends—Add lines 1 through 11. Enter here and on line 4, page 1 ▶	50,000		
14 Total deductions—Add lines 5, 6 and 12. Enter here and on line 29(b), page 1 ▶			42,500

SCHEDULE E.—Compensation of Officers (See instruction for line 12, page 1)
Complete Schedule E only if your total receipts (line 1(a), plus lines 4 through 10, of page 1, Form 1120) are $150,000 or more.

1. Name of officer	2. Social security number	3. Percent of time devoted to business	Percent of corporation stock owned		6. Amount of compensation
			4. Common	5. Preferred	
		%	%	%	
		%	%	%	
		%	%	%	
		%	%	%	
		%	%	%	
		%	%	%	
		%	%	%	

Total compensation of officers—Enter here and on line 12, page 1 . . . .

SCHEDULE F.—Bad Debts—Reserve Method (See instruction for line 15, page 1)

1. Year	2. Trade notes and accounts receivable outstanding at end of year	3. Sales on account	Amount added to reserve		6. Amount charged against reserve	7. Reserve for bad debts at end of year
			4. Current year's provision	5. Recoveries		
1978						
1979						
1980						
1981						
1982						
1983						

Exhibit 8 (Cont.)

Form 1120 (1983)   Page **3**

SCHEDULE J.—Tax Computation
(See instructions for Schedule J on page 7)

1 Check if you are a member of a controlled group (see sections 1561 and 1563) . . . . ▶ ☐			
2 If line 1 is checked, see instructions and enter your portion of the $25,000 amount in each taxable income bracket:			
(i) $ _ _ _ _ _ _ _ (ii) $ _ _ _ _ _ _ _ (iii) $ _ _ _ _ _ _ _ (iv) $ _ _ _ _ _ _ _			
3 Income tax (see instructions to figure the tax; enter this tax or alternative tax from Schedule D, whichever is less). Check if from Schedule D ▶ ☐	**3**	33,340	
4 (a) Foreign tax credit (attach Form 1118).	4(a)		
(b) Investment credit (attach Form 3468).	(b)		
(c) Jobs credit (attach Form 5884)	(c)		
(d) Employee stock ownership credit (attach Form 8007)	(d)		
(e) Research credit (attach Form 6765)	(e)		
(f) Possessions tax credit (attach Form 5735)	(f)		
(g) Alcohol fuel credit (attach Form 6478)	(g)		
(h) Credit for fuel produced from a nonconventional source (see instructions)	(h)		
5 Total—Add lines 4(a) through 4(h)	**5**	33,340	
6 Subtract line 5 from line 3	**6**		
7 Personal holding company tax (attach Schedule PH (Form 1120))	**7**		
8 Tax from recomputing prior-year investment credit (attach Form 4255)	**8**		
9 Minimum tax on tax preference items (see instructions—attach Form 4626)	**9**		
10 Total tax—Add lines 6 through 9. Enter here and on line 31, page 1	**10**	33,340	

Additional Information (See page 8 of instructions)	Yes	No		Yes	No
H Did you claim a deduction for expenses connected with:			**(e)** Enter highest amount owed to you by such owner during the year ▶ _ _ _ _ _ _ _		
(1) Entertainment facility (boat, resort, ranch, etc.)? . . .			**(Note:** For purposes of I(1) and I(2), "highest amount owed" includes loans and accounts receivable/payable.)		
(2) Living accommodations (except employees on business)? . .					
(3) Employees attending conventions or meetings outside the North American area? (See section 274(h)) . . .			**J** Refer to page 9 of instructions and state the principal: Business activity ▶ _ _ _ _ _ _ _ _ _ _ _ Product or service ▶ _ _ _ _ _ _ _ _ _ _ _		
(4) Employees' families at conventions or meetings? . . . . If "Yes," were any of these conventions or meetings outside the North American area? (See section 274(h))			**K** Were you a U.S. shareholder of any controlled foreign corporation? (See sections 951 and 957.) If "Yes," attach Form 5471 for each such corporation.		
(5) Employee or family vacations not reported on Form W-2? . .			**L** At any time during the tax year, did you have an interest in or a signature or other authority over a bank account, securities account, or other financial account in a foreign country? (See page 8 for exceptions and filing requirements for Form 90–22.1.) . . . . If "Yes," write the name of the foreign country ▶ _ _ _ _ _ _		
I (1) Did you at the end of the tax year own, directly or indirectly, 50% or more of the voting stock of a domestic corporation? (For rules of attribution, see section 267(c).) . . . If "Yes," attach a schedule showing: (a) name, address, and identifying number; (b) percentage owned; (c) taxable income or (loss) before NOL and special deductions (e.g., If a Form 1120: from Form 1120, line 28, page 1) of such corporation for the tax year ending with or within your tax year; (d) highest amount owed by you to such corporation during the year ; and (e) highest amount owed to you by such corporation during the year.					
(2) Did any individual, partnership, corporation, estate or trust at the end of the tax year own, directly or indirectly, 50% or more of your voting stock? (For rules of attribution, see section 267(c).) If "Yes," complete (a) through (e)			**M** Were you the grantor of, or transferor to, a foreign trust which existed during the current tax year, whether or not you have any beneficial interest in it? . . . . If "Yes," you may have to file Forms 3520, 3520-A or 926.		
(a) Attach a schedule showing name, address, and identifying number.			**N** During this tax year, did you pay dividends (other than stock dividends and distributions in exchange for stock) in excess of your current and accumulated earnings and profits? (See sections 301 and 316) . . .		
(b) Enter percentage owned ▶ _ _ _ _ _ _ _			If "Yes," file Form 5452. If this is a consolidated return, answer here for parent corporation and on Form 851, Affiliations Schedule, for each subsidiary.		
(c) Was the owner of such voting stock a person other than a U.S. person? (See instructions). . . . . If "Yes," enter owner's country ▶ _ _ _ _ _ _			**O** During this tax year did you maintain any part of your accounting/tax records on a computerized system?		
(d) Enter highest amount owed by you to such owner during the year ▶			**P** Check method of accounting: (1) ☐ Cash (2) ☐ Accrual (3) ☐ Other (specify) ▶		

Exhibit 8 *(Cont.)*

Form 1120 (1983)   Page **4**

SCHEDULE L.—Balance Sheets

Assets	Beginning of tax year		End of tax year	
	(A)	(B)	(C)	(D)
1 Cash				
2 Trade notes and accounts receivable				
(a) Less allowance for bad debts				
3 Inventories				
4 Federal and State government obligations				
5 Other current assets (attach schedule)				
6 Loans to stockholders				
7 Mortgage and real estate loans				
8 Other investments (attach schedule)				
9 Buildings and other depreciable assets				
(a) Less accumulated depreciation				
10 Depletable assets				
(a) Less accumulated depletion				
11 Land (net of any amortization)				
12 Intangible assets (amortizable only)				
(a) Less accumulated amortization				
13 Other assets (attach schedule)				
14 Total assets				

Liabilities and Stockholders' Equity				
15 Accounts payable				
16 Mortgages, notes, bonds payable in less than 1 year				
17 Other current liabilities (attach schedule)				
18 Loans from stockholders				
19 Mortgages, notes, bonds payable in 1 year or more				
20 Other liabilities (attach schedule)				
21 Capital stock: (a) Preferred stock				
(b) Common stock				
22 Paid-in or capital surplus				
23 Retained earnings—Appropriated (attach schedule)				
24 Retained earnings—Unappropriated				
25 Less cost of treasury stock	(	)	(	)
26 Total liabilities and stockholders' equity				

SCHEDULE M-1.—Reconciliation of Income Per Books With Income Per Return

Do not complete this schedule if your total assets (line 14, column (D), above) are less than $25,000.

1 Net income per books			7 Income recorded on books this year not included in this return (itemize)	
2 Federal income tax				
3 Excess of capital losses over capital gains			(a) Tax-exempt interest $ _____	
4 Income subject to tax not recorded on books this year (itemize) _____				
5 Expenses recorded on books this year not deducted in this return (itemize)			8 Deductions in this tax return not charged against book income this year (itemize)	
(a) Depreciation . $ _____			(a) Depreciation . . . $ _____	
(b) Contributions carryover $ _____			(b) Contributions carryover $ _____	
			9 Total of lines 7 and 8	
6 Total of lines 1 through 5			10 Income (line 28, page 1)—line 6 less line 9 . .	

SCHEDULE M-2.—Analysis of Unappropriated Retained Earnings Per Books (line 24 above)

Do not complete this schedule if your total assets (line 14, column (D), above) are less than $25,000.

1 Balance at beginning of year			5 Distributions: (a) Cash	
2 Net income per books			(b) Stock	
3 Other increases (itemize) _____			(c) Property	
			6 Other decreases (itemize) _____	
			7 Total of lines 5 and 6	
4 Total of lines 1, 2, and 3			8 Balance at end of year (line 4 less line 7) . .	

GLOSSARY

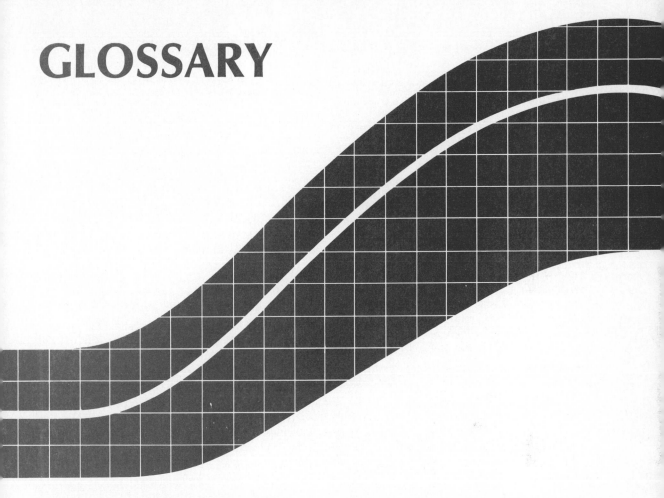

Absolute priority The rule stating that all senior claimants must be completely satisfied before junior claimants receive payment.

Acceptance A time bill of exchange (essentially a check) drawn on a bank or purchaser by the selling firm as payment for goods or services.

Accounts receivable A short-term asset representing credit sales to customers.

Accrued income taxes A current liability representing taxes payable on income but not yet due.

Acid test (quick) ratio A stringent liquidity ratio; a test of a firm's short-term bill-paying ability calculated by dividing current assets, excluding inventory, by current liabilities.

Activity ratios Measures of how well a firm's assets are being employed. The comparison is between the level of activity (sales) and the investment in some type of asset.

Adjusted gross income (AGI) The arithmetic difference between gross income and deductions for AGI. The latter constitute essentially the direct business expenses of the individual taxpayer.

Adjustment of debts A reorganization plan for individuals with regular income. The plan can be an extension or a composition.

Aging schedule A listing of accounts receivable balances by the period of time during which they have been outstanding. The usual practice is to show the percentage of all receivables outstanding for 30 days or less, 30–60 days, and so on.

Alternatives   The courses of action available in making a decision.

Amortize   To repay a loan on a periodic basis. A typical house mortgage is amortized monthly over a 20- to 30-year period.

Annual percentage rate (APR)   The interest rate on a loan. The Truth in Lending Act requires all lenders to indicate the cost of a loan, which usually is different from the simple interest rate specified in the loan agreement. The APR is the per-period rate times the number of periods per year; e.g., $1\frac{1}{2}\%$ per month is $1\frac{1}{2} \times 12 = 18$, an APR of 18%.

Annuity   A series of equal cash payments with equal amounts of time between each payment. In a deferred or ordinary annuity, the payments occur at the end of each period. With an annuity due, the payments occur at the beginning of each period.

Annuity due   An annuity in which the first payment is immediate, not being one period delayed, as with an ordinary annuity.

Arbitrage   The attempt to earn a riskless profit by simultaneously buying and selling the same security or currency in two different markets.

Arrearage   Overdue dividend payments to preferred stockholders.

Asked price   Price at which a market participant is offering a security for sale.

Asked rate   The exchange rate for buying foreign currency from a bank or currency dealer.

Asset   Any item a firm owns that is expected to generate future benefits and is measurable in dollar terms.

Available funds balance   Reflects the amount of cash that can be withdrawn from a demand deposit account. Also called the *good funds balance.*

Average collection period   A ratio used to evaluate the level of investment in receivables versus sales, calculated as accounts receivable divided by net sales per day. Where comparisons are available, the denominator should be credit sales per day.

Average rate of return (ARR)   A nondiscounted cash flow approach to capital budgeting. It is the average annual net income after taxes divided by the average investment.

Balance of trade   Difference between the imports and exports of a country.

Balance sheet   A formal report showing a firm's assets, liabilities, and net worth.

Balloon payment   A payment on a loan larger than the preceding payments, typically made at the end of a loan period to retire the loan.

Bank cash investment services   A service offered to businesses in which a bank pools investment funds from several demand deposits and invests them in money market securities. The service enables smaller businesses that cannot afford to buy money market securities directly to earn an acceptable return on excess cash balances.

Bankers' acceptance   A draft drawn on and accepted by a bank. The bank is obligated to ensure payment of the acceptance on presentation (sight draft) or at maturity (time draft).

Basis points   One hundredth of a percentage point. Used to express changes in interest rates. For example, a change from 8 to 8.4% is a 40-basis-point change.

Best efforts basis   The sale of an issue of securities in which the investment banker acts as an agent for the issuing corporation and receives a commission based upon the number of shares actually sold. The banking firm signs no underwriting or purchase agreement.

Beta   A measure of a security's systematic (non-diversifiable) risk. Beta is the percentage change in an individual security's return for a 1% change in the return of the market.

Bid price   The price at which a market participant is willing to buy a security.

Bid rate   The exchange rate at which foreign currency can be sold to a bank or currency dealer.

Bill of exchange   A legal instrument that presupposes a debtor/creditor relationship between two parties and contains an order or promise to transfer funds from the debtor to the creditor.

Bill of lading   A contract signed by a goods carrier to deliver goods to a third party (consignee). An order bill of lading is made to the order of the consignee or the bearer and controls title to the goods. It is negotiable. A straight bill of lading is a contract for shipment only, in which the goods can be delivered to the consignee without surrender of the bill of lading.

Blue Sky laws   State securities laws that regulate securities transactions occurring within the state.

Bond   A long-term debt instrument representing a promise to repay a specified amount of money at a future time.

Bond issue   The sale of debt obligations by a corporation consisting of a series of similar credit instruments, all of which may or may not be of the same denomination and maturity.

Bond trustee   An impartial party who represents the bondholders in their dealings with the bond issuer. The trustee's responsibility is to ensure that the bond issuer fulfills all the provisions of the trust indenture.

Book value of common stock   The accounting value of common stock, which is calculated by dividing the common stock equity by the number of shares outstanding.

Budgets   Financial statements used to plan allocation of resources, facilitate control of resources, and evaluate past performance.

Call option   A contract created by individual investors that allows the buyer to purchase 100 shares of a specified stock from the seller for a specified price (exercise price) any time during the life of the option.

Call premium   The amount by which the call price of a bond exceeds the face value.

Call price   The amount the bond issuer must pay to the bondholder if the bonds are to be called. The call price is frequently equal to the principal amount plus one year's nominal interest.

Call provision   A feature of the trust indenture of a bond that allows the bond issuer to repurchase outstanding bonds at a given price from the bond holders after a given date.

Capital asset pricing model (CAPM)   A mathematical relationship indicating the expected return on an asset as a function of its systematic risk (beta), the expected return on the market, and the return on the riskless asset.

Capital budget   The total anticipated capital expenditures for one fiscal period.

Capital investment   The investment of a firm in fixed assets, such as plant and equipment.

Capital market line (CML)   The relationship between risk and return in well-diversified portfolios.

Capital rationing   A situation in which a firm limits new investment to less than that which is economically justifiable; positive net present value investments are not undertaken. Capital rationing may be externally or internally imposed.

Capital structure   The composition of the firm's long-term financing represented by long-term debt, preferred stock, and common stock.

Carrying costs   Expenses incurred in holding inventory over a given time period.

Cash   Relative to a business, all coin and currency possessed by the firm plus good funds balances in demand deposits.

Cash budget   A schedule showing expected cash receipts and disbursements for a firm over a specified period.

Cash dividend   A cash payment made by a firm to its shareholders.

Cash flow   The inflow of cash from an investment, assuming that it is purchased outright and there are no changes in working capital; defined as net income plus depreciation.

Certainty equivalents (CE)   A formal adjustment technique used in capital budgeting to allow for variations in projected risk (or uncertainty). The CE approach adjusts risky cash flows downward to the point at which an individual would be indifferent to either the risky or the adjusted (certain) cash flow. Certain cash flows are discounted at the riskless rate.

Class voting   The requirement to obtain the consent of current preferred stockholders before any major changes in preferred stock can occur.

Classified boards Boards whose term of office for directors is longer than one year.

Coefficient of variation (CV) A summary statistic used to relate an alternative's measure of risk (standard deviation) to its expected value. This statistic is particularly useful in comparing alternatives with different expected returns.

Collateral trust bond A bond secured by pledges of stocks and bonds.

Collection float The time between deposit of a check and the point at which good funds from the check are credited to the account.

Collection risk Uncertainty regarding collection for sales made on credit.

Commercial paper Unsecured promissory notes sold by large, financially sound companies. They have a maturity of less than nine months and usually yield a return above that of Treasury bills.

Common size statement Accounting statement expressed as a percentage of sales or assets to aid comparison. In common size balance sheets, all entries are expressed as a percentage of total assets. In common size (operating) income statements, all entries are expressed as a percentage of net sales.

Common stock Shares in the ownership of a firm. Common stockholders are the last to receive any distribution of earnings or assets.

Compensating balance The amount of cash a firm must keep in its demand deposit account as part of the requirement for a loan from the bank. It may be calculated as an absolute amount or as the daily average cash balance during the month.

Competitive bidding The process of bidding on an issue of securities by investment banking firms. The firm with the highest bid purchases the securities.

Composition An agreement by creditors to accept less than full payment in order to retire the debt.

Compound interest A situation in which interest earned on an investment is added to the principal at the end of each compounding period and earns interest for each future compounding period.

Compounding Calculating the future value of a series of cash flows when it is assumed that periodic interest payments are added to the principal and begin earning interest.

Concentration bank A bank to which a company transfers (concentrates) daily all good funds balances.

Consent voting The requirement to obtain the consent of preferred stockholders when considering a distribution of the corporation's assets or when proposing changes in the rights and privileges of these stockholders. Preferred stockholders vote as a class.

Consol A bond with no maturity date; a perpetuity.

Consolidation The combination of two or more firms into a completely new firm.

Continuous compounding (or discounting) A situation in which interest is added to the principal continuously rather than at discrete time intervals.

Controlled disbursing A cash-disbursing technique in which a firm pays creditors with checks written on a bank located in a different region of the country from that of the creditor. The purpose is to increase the collection float. Also called *remote disbursing*.

Conversion period The time period during which a convertible security may be exchanged for common stock.

Conversion price The price that each share of common stock will cost when purchased with a convertible security valued at par. A $1,000 (par) convertible bond will purchase 20 shares of stock if the conversion price is $50.

Conversion ratio The number of shares of common stock that each convertible security will purchase. A conversion ratio of 20 means that one bond will purchase 20 shares.

Convertible bond A bond that pays fixed interest payments and has a specified maturity, just like an ordinary bond, but differs in that it can be exchanged at the discretion of the bondholder for a specified number of shares of common stock during a defined time period.

Convertible preferred stock Preferred stock that can be exchanged for common stock of the same issuer at the discretion of the preferred stockholder.

Convertible security Either bonds or preferred stock that can be converted into common stock of the issuing corporation at the discretion of the holder.

Corporation A legal entity separate from its owners, generally created for the purpose of conducting business. A corporation functions under its own name and is solely liable for its legal obligations, including the taxes on its income.

Correlation coefficient A value between +1 and −1 that indicates the strength of the association between two variables. A perfect positive correlation is indicated by a correlation coefficient of +1.

Cost of capital The minimum rate of return that can be accepted on new investments in order to maintain the value of the firm.

Covered interest arbitrage An attempt to earn a riskless profit by taking advantage of mispricing between the spot and forward rates of two currencies. For example, if the forward rate on dollars to pounds were too high, a U.S. investor would borrow dollars, convert them to pounds in the spot market, and invest the pounds in England. At the same time, the investor would sell pounds forward at the current forward rate. When the forward contract came due, the investment would be sold and the pounds used to satisfy the forward contract. Because the forward exchange rate was too high, the investor would have a riskless profit after repaying the U.S. loan.

Coupon rate A bond's stated rate of interest.

Cram down The acceptance of a reorganization plan over the objections of a class of creditors. Cram down can occur if the objecting class and all classes junior in priority are treated according to the absolute priority rule.

Credit period The time period within which a credit purchase must be paid for.

Credit policy Company regulations concerning the minimum financial strength of firms that can purchase on credit, the terms of credit sales, and the collection efforts that will be used.

Credit standards Criteria used to determine which customers are extended credit. Credit standards usually require an examination of the customer's credit rating, credit references, outstanding debt, and financial statements.

Credit terms Payment procedures to be followed by firms granted credit.

Creditors' committee A group of individuals representing both large and small claimants of a bankrupt firm. The committee oversees the reorganization or liquidation of the firm.

Cumulative dividends A feature of some preferred stock that states that all prior unpaid preferred stock dividends must be paid before any common stock dividends can be paid.

Cumulative voting A voting system in which a stockholder may cast votes equal to the number of shares he or she owns times the number of directors to be elected. The votes may be cast for only one director or in any combination.

Current assets Assets that will be converted into cash within the next 12 months, for example, cash, marketable securities, accounts receivable, and inventory.

Current liabilities Liabilities that will be paid within the next 12 months, for example, notes payable, accounts payable, taxes payable, and accrued wages.

Current ratio The most commonly used liquidity ratio, calculated by dividing current assets by current liabilities.

Debenture A debt obligation not secured by specific property but backed by the general credit of the issuing corporation.

Decision making under certainty An alternative choice situation in which the future state of nature is known; that is, its probability is 1.

Decision making under risk An alternative choice situation in which one of several states of nature may occur and the probability of each state can be specified.

Decision making under uncertainty An alternative choice situation in which several states of nature are possible but the probabilities of the states are unknown.

Decision tree A worksheet for decision making under risk. A separate limb is provided for each event on which the event's value and probability can be indicated. The probability of each series of branches and the value of each series can be calculated. Summing all possible series provides the expected payoff for the risky event(s).

Degree of financial leverage (DFL) The percentage change in earnings per share for a 1% change in operating earnings at a given level of output.

Degree of operating leverage (DOL) The percentage change in operating earnings (EBIT) for a 1% change in sales volume at a given level of output.

Degree of total leverage (DTL) The percentage change in earnings per share for a 1% change in sales at a given level of output.

Depository transfer check (DTC) An instrument used to transfer funds between financial institutions.

Depreciation The accounting process by which the cost of a productive asset is allocated (written off) against the revenues it helps to produce.

Devaluation A reduction in the value of one currency compared to another currency.

Direct placement Sale of securities directly by the issuing firm to the end purchaser rather than through a financial intermediary.

Dirty float Floating exchange rate system in which central banks intervene in foreign exchange markets to control the exchange rate of their currency.

Disbursement float Use of funds paid to someone else until they are removed from the payer's demand deposit account.

Disbursement float analysis Examination of the time required for each check written by the firm to clear the firm's demand deposit account. A technique used in cash management.

Disbursement float balance The difference between the number of checks issued and the number that have cleared the demand deposit account on which they were written.

Disclosure The Securities Act of 1933 requires a company wishing to sell its securities to the public to provide comprehensive background information in the form of documents known as a prospectus and a registration statement.

Discount rate The interest rate used to find the present value of a stream of payments.

Discounted loan A borrowing arrangement in which interest is deducted from the cash proceeds to the borrower at the time the loan is established.

Discounting In capital budgeting, the process of calculating the present value of expected cash flows.

Diversified activity combination The merger of two unrelated firms.

Dividend payout ratio The proportion of earnings paid out in dividends.

Dividend policy Determines the amount of earnings to be retained or paid out by the firm.

Dividend yield The yearly dividends paid by a stock divided by the current price of the stock.

Draft A bill of exchange. It may be payable on sight (sight draft) or at some future date (time draft). See *Bill of exchange.*

Due diligence The responsibility of all persons involved in the sale of a securities issue to ensure that all information required in the registration statement and prospectus is disclosed and factual.

DuPont return-on-investment (ROI) system A model relating the firm's return on investment (net income/net worth) to its activity, sales margin, and use of debt financing.

EBIT Earnings before interest and taxes.

Economic order quantity (EOQ) model A mathematical technique used to calculate the order size that will minimize inventory costs.

Effective interest rate The true interest rate being paid on a loan. It is the discount rate that equates the payments on the loan to usable funds received when the loan is established. See *Internal rate of return.*

Efficiency measure The basis of choice (decision variable) used to select among alternatives.

Efficient markets Markets are efficient if the items traded are exchanged at correct prices; that is, there are no bargains. Attributes of efficient markets include low transaction costs, freely accessible information, lack of monopolistic control, and quick price corrections. Evidence suggests that U.S. securities markets are efficient.

Equivalent annual economic profit (EAEP) A modified net present value analysis for mutually exclusive projects that have unequal lives. EAEP is the *equal* annual cash flow that would have the same net present value as a project's current cash flows.

Eurobond A debt instrument denominated in a currency different from the currency of the country in which it is sold.

Eurodollars Dollar-denominated deposits in financial institutions outside the United States.

Exchange rate The price of one currency in terms of another currency.

Exchange rate risk Uncertainty regarding the amount of domestic currency involved in a transaction in which future cash flows are denominated in a foreign currency.

Exclusions Certain forms of income that are not included in the concept of gross income. Consequently, these items are not subject to taxation, as they are simply omitted from reporting on the taxpayer's income tax return for the year in question. Exclusions have arisen in response to a variety of policy considerations, such as equity and the subsidization of lower-level (i.e., state and local) governmental units.

Ex-dividend Ownership without the right to a dividend about to be paid by a firm.

Exercise price Regarding a warrant, the contract price at which the stock can be purchased from the company. Regarding an option, the price at which the stock can be purchased from (in the case of a call) or sold to (in the case of a put) the option writer.

Expected value (Ê) A statistical measure of central tendency, the mean of a probability distribution, calculated by multiplying the numerical value of each event by its probability and summing over all events.

Expiration date The last day on which an option or warrant can be exercised.

Ex-rights Ownership without the privilege of receiving rights. A share of stock is ex-rights if it

does not entitle the owner to a right that is about to be issued by a firm.

Extension Lengthening of the time allowed the debtor to pay the full amount of the outstanding debt.

External growth Expansion of the size or scope of activities of the firm through acquisition of existing firms.

Factor A financial institution that purchases or loans money against the accounts receivable of other firms.

Factoring of accounts receivable The sale of accounts receivable to a financial institution called a *factor* to obtain cash.

Fairness and equitable rule The requirement that in a reorganization each class of creditors receive at least as much value as would have been received if the debtor were liquidated quickly on the date of the plan. This doctrine holds that claims must be recognized in the order of their contractual priority.

FASB No. 13 Issued by the Financial Accounting Standards Board in November 1976 in order to standardize the accounting procedures for leases. The requirements vary with the type of lease but are much more stringent than in the past.

Field warehouse A storage location on the borrower's premises that contains inventory items pledged as security for a loan.

Field warehousing arrangement A procedure in which inventory pledged as loan collateral is stored on the property of the borrower (in the field) in a segregated area controlled and supervised by the lender.

Finance The study and practice of making dollar-denominated decisions. As a discipline, finance can be classified into three main areas: investments, markets and institutions, and financial management.

Financial break-even point The level of sales at which two alternative financing plans produce the same EPS.

Financial institutions Establishments that do business in the financial market—buying, selling, and/or aiding in the buying and selling of securities. Included are banks, brokers, investment bankers, pension funds, and savings and loan associations.

Financial (capital) lease A lease contract that is noncancellable and has a lease period shorter than the useful life of the asset being leased. The full cost of the asset is recovered through periodic payments during the contract's life.

Financial leverage The effects of debt financing on shareholders' claims on future earnings.

Financial management The study and practice of dollar-denominated decision making in a business firm. Financial management's functions are the allocation and acquisition of funds.

Financial markets The places and procedures through which buyers and sellers of financial assets (securities) transact business.

Financial risk Variability in the earnings stream of a company that results from the company's use of debt.

Financial structure The entire right-hand side of the balance sheet, which includes both current and permanent sources of financing.

Finished goods inventory Completed items awaiting sale.

Fixed assets Capital assets of a firm, for example, plant and equipment.

Fixed exchange rate system A monetary system in which the exchange rate is fixed by the government. Changes are made infrequently and only by governmental action. The Bretton Woods Agreement of 1944 established a fixed-rate international exchange system that lasted until 1971.

Float Cash items in the process of collection.

Floating exchange rate system A monetary system in which the exchange rate is allowed to vary continuously in response to market forces. Most major countries have been operating under a floating exchange rate system since 1973.

Floating lien A legal claim by a creditor on the entire inventory of a firm.

Floating lien agreement A legal contract in which a borrower gives a lender a general claim on the firm's entire inventory as collateral for a loan.

Flotation costs Costs associated with the issuance of new securities.

Forced conversion An attempt by the company to force the holders of convertible securities to convert to common stock when the market price of the common stock is above the conversion price of a convertible security. This is accomplished by issuing a call notice so that convertible security holders will convert to common stock rather than tendering the securities for the lower call price.

Foreign bond A debt instrument issued by a foreign borrower, with interest and principal denominated in the local currency.

Foreign exchange Currency of another country.

Forward market A market in which foreign currency or commodities can be bought or sold for delivery at a future date.

Fully diluted earnings per share Calculated by dividing earnings available to common stockholders by the number of common shares outstanding, plus the number of shares that would be issued if all warrants or convertible securities were exchanged for common stock.

Funds management In a foreign business operation, the movement of cash balances between subsidiaries in different countries to take advantage of expected currency fluctuations or to create hedged positions.

Future value The future worth of a series of cash flows.

Future value interest factor (FVIF) The value of $(1 + i)^n$, where i is the interest rate and n is the number of time periods. The interest factor is multiplied by a current dollar amount, P_0, to determine a value n periods from today.

Future value interest factor of an annuity (FVIFA) Equivalent to the expression

$$\sum_{t=1}^{n} (1 + i)^{n-t},$$

where n equals the number of compounding periods and i is the interest rate per period.

General partnership Two or more individuals engaged in a business activity for joint profit. Each partner is personally liable for the debts of the partnership.

Good funds balance The balance in a firm's demand deposit account that can be withdrawn from the account. It is equal to or less than the ledger balance, which includes deposited checks that have not cleared through the banking system.

Gordon model A widely known valuation model that is often used to determine the cost of equity calculated as dividend yield plus expected growth.

Gross income A tax term defined by the Internal Revenue Service (IRS) to mean all income derived from all sources except those specifically excluded by the IRS tax code.

Gross spread The difference between the price at which newly issued securities are to be offered to the public and the amount to be paid to the corporation.

Holder-of-record date The date as of which all security holders listed in company records are noted to receive the forthcoming cash or stock dividend when it is paid.

Holding company A firm owning a controlling interest in one or more other corporations.

Holding period yield Rate of return earned from holding an asset during a given time period and calculated as the ending period price, P_1, plus the dividend, D, minus the beginning-of-the-period price, P_0, divided by the beginning-of-the-period price, P_0.

Horizontal combination The merger of two firms in the same business.

Hung convertible An issue of convertible securities that cannot be forced into conversion because the stock price has not risen above the conversion price.

Immediate annuity A series of equal cash flows with an equal amount of time between payments in which the cash flows occur at the end of each period.

Income bonds Debt obligations specifying that interest is to be paid only when the corporation has earnings sufficient to cover the interest payments.

Income statement A report summarizing a firm's operations for a given accounting period, showing revenue less expenses and the resulting income.

Indenture A contract specifying the legal requirements between the bond issuer and the bondholders.

Insolvency in bankruptcy A situation in which the firm is unable to obtain funds to pay debts as they become due and the firm's liabilities exceed the fair market value of its assets.

Installment loan A loan arrangement in which principal and interest are repaid over the life of the loan.

Interest rate parity theorem An economic principle that holds that the differential in interest rates between countries is the only determinant of the difference between the spot and forward currency rates.

Interest rate risk Uncertainty about the future value of a debt instrument caused by fluctuations in interest rates.

Internal growth Expansion of the size or scope of the activities of the firm caused by the use of retained earnings.

Internal rate of return (IRR) A capital budgeting technique. The IRR is the discount rate such that a project's net present value equals zero.

International Development Association (IDA) An affiliate of the World Bank which was established in 1960 to provide credit to the least developed nations.

Intrinsic value of a warrant Difference between the exercise price and the current market price of the stock. If the stock's market price is $37, one warrant which allows the purchase of one share of stock for $30 will have an intrinsic value of $7.

Inventory The company's stock of goods including raw materials, work in process, and finished goods completed and ready for sale.

Inventory turnover An activity ratio used to evaluate the appropriateness of the firm's inventory investment, generally calculated by dividing sales by inventory. Theory suggests that the numerator should be the cost of the goods sold.

Investment The allocation of resources to a project or security. Investments courses typically concentrate on the evaluation of corporate common stocks.

Investment banking The act of underwriting and selling new securities by a financial intermediary called an *investment banking firm.*

Invoicing float The time required for a firm to send a bill to customers who purchased on credit.

Joint venture In foreign trade, an arrangement in which both foreign and domestic firms contribute equity and earn a *pro rata* share of profits.

Leads and lags of payments Timing payments flows between subsidiaries or between the parent and the subsidiaries so as to take advantage of exchange rate movements.

Lease An extended rental agreement in which the lessee (user) pays the lessor (owner) of the asset rent for a number of time periods in exchange for the right to use the asset.

Ledger balance Relative to a demand deposit account, deposited checks that have not yet cleared the payee's bank. Ledger balances cannot be withdrawn from the account.

Lessee The user of a leased asset.

Lessor The owner of a leased asset.

Letter of credit A document issued by a bank indicating the bank's willingness to extend credit to a second party. It is provided to a seller to enable the buyer to obtain goods on credit. It may be *revokable* or *irrevokable* by the issuing bank, and if a second bank adds its promise to pay, it is called *confirmed* letter of credit. The strongest document is a confirmed, irrevocable letter of credit.

Leverage Use of fixed-cost assets or funds by a firm in anticipation of generating higher earnings for common stockholders.

Leverage ratios Ratios that measure the extent to which a firm is financed with debt; the two types are balance sheet and income statement leverage ratios. The latter are called *coverage ratios.*

Liabilities Debts that the firm owes to others.

Licensing In international operations, an arrangement in which a foreign company is allowed to manufacture a domestic firm's product in its own country.

Limited partnership A partnership in which partners are designated as general or limited. The former manages the ongoing affairs of the business venture; the latter merely invest capital in the enterprise. Consequently, limited partners are liable only for the amount of their personal investment. That is, "joint and several" personal liability for all debts of the partnership pertains only to the general partners, not to the limited partners.

Line of credit An informal borrowing arrangement in which a business may obtain funds up to a maximum amount merely by indicating its requirement to the bank. Under ordinary circumstances, a bank is not obligated to meet a firm's request for funds. A *revolving line of credit,* however, legally obligates the bank to lend money to the firm.

Liquidation The sale of a firm's assets when the corporation is dissolved.

Liquidity Amount of cash or near-cash items relative to the cash liabilities of the firm.

Liquidity ratios Ratios used to evaluate a firm's ability to satisfy creditors in the immediate future. These ratios compare the assets available for meeting current obligations with the level of those obligations.

Listing of securities The right to trade a registered security on an organized security exchange if it meets all exchange requirements. A security traded on an organized exchange is "listed." "Dual listing" occurs if the security is traded on two established exchanges.

Lockbox A post office box to which credit customers mail payments. A bank will empty the lockbox daily and deposit all checks, thus reducing the processing and collection float.

Mail float The time a cash item (i.e., invoice or check for payment) spends in the mail between a firm and its customer.

Majority voting A voting system in which the number of votes a stockholder may cast for any director may not exceed the number of shares he or she owns or controls through proxies.

Market extension combination The merger of two firms producing the same products but selling them in different geographic markets.

Market price The current selling price of a security.

Marketable securities Securities with less than one year to maturity (e.g., Treasury bills, bankers' acceptances). Marketable securities have little risk and are appropriate investments for excess cash balances. Also called *money market securities.*

Matching principle The strategy of financing assets with liabilities having a maturity equal to the life of the assets. It implies that current assets should be financed with current liabilities and fixed assets with long-term sources of funds.

Maximax A decision rule for uncertainty according to which one should take the alternative that offers the highest possible payoff.

Maximin A decision rule for uncertainty according to which one should take the alternative that offers the highest minimum payoff.

Merger The combination of two or more firms in which one firm retains its identity.

Methodology An analysis of the procedures of inquiry in a particular field.

Model The formal relationship between observable events and the event being forecast.

Money market mutual fund An institution that pools investors' funds to buy money market securities.

Money market security A security with less than one year to maturity. Typical securities are Treasury bills, repurchase agreements, negotiable certificates of deposit, and bankers' acceptances. Also called *marketable securities.*

Mortgage bond A bond secured with a lien on real property.

Multinational corporation A business with investments and operating facilities in more than one country.

Negotiable certificate of deposit (NCD) A security issued by a bank with an average maturity of four months and a minimum denomination of $100,000. A secondary market exists for these securities.

Negotiated issues Stock issues that are purchased under the terms of a contract between an investment banking firm and an issuing corporation.

Net capital gain deduction Sixty percent of the excess of the net long-term capital gain over the net short-term capital loss that is excluded from taxation for the individual taxpayer. Only the remaining 40% is subject to taxation (at ordinary marginal tax rates).

Net financial asset exposure The amount invested in a foreign business that can change in value when exchange rates fluctuate.

Net present value (NPV) A discounted cash flow capital budgeting technique—the present value of future cash flows minus cost.

Net working capital Current assets minus current liabilities. Net working capital provides information about a firm's liquidity.

Net worth The book value of owners' claims on a corporation; equal to total assets minus total liabilities.

Nominal interest rate The interest rate stated on the loan agreement. Nominal means "in name only." The nominal interest rate probably is not the effective rate of interest that the borrower pays on the loan unless it is a simple interest loan.

Noncumulative dividends A feature of some preferred stocks that states that dividends not paid in one period cannot be collected in a later period.

Nonrefundable tax credit A dollar-for-dollar reduction of the gross tax liability of the taxpayer, allowed as an incentive to promote a particular economic, political, or social goal. A nonrefundable tax credit can only reduce this tax liability to zero, however; it can never generate a cash refund to the taxpayer.

Nonsystematic risk The random element in a security's return that is unrelated to the market and can be eliminated through diversification.

Offering price The price at which newly issued securities are offered to the general public or, in some instances, to current stockholders.

Open account A trade credit arrangement in which the buyer receives the goods or services but does not have to remit payment until an invoice is received or until the end of the credit period allowed by the seller.

Operating income statement An income statement in which each expense and revenue item is expressed as a percentage of net sales.

Operating leases Less binding than a financial lease. It entails rental payments totaling less than the purchase price of the asset and generally includes a renewal option.

Operating leverage The effect of fixed operating costs on earnings when sales revenue change.

Opportunity cost of funds The return that could be earned on the next best investment.

Optimal order size The appropriate size of each order that enables the firm to minimize inventory costs. Usually it is determined using the EOQ formula. Also called the *optimal order quantity.*

Optimal reorder point The inventory level at which a new order should be placed. Inventory costs will be minimized if the optimal order size is ordered at the optimal reorder point.

Optimum firm size The size that enables the firm to produce most efficiently and at the lowest possible unit cost.

Option pricing model (OPM) A theoretical valuation model for contingent claims securities.

Ordering costs All costs incurred when an order is placed for inventory items.

Origination of public issues The acquisition of a public issue of a corporation by an investment banking firm.

Overhanging issue An issue of convertible securities that cannot be forced into conversion because the convertible price is not sufficiently below the market price of the common stock.

Par value The face value of a security. The par value of a bond indicates its worth at maturity. The par value of common stock represents the legal liability of the equity holders; it is usually less than the market price.

Participating preferred dividend A dividend beyond the stated dividend received by participating preferred stockholders, who share in earnings with common stockholders.

Partnership See *General partnership* and *Limited partnership.*

Payable-through-draft An instrument, similar to a check, drawn against the company rather than the company's bank.

Payback period A nondiscounted cash flow capital budgeting technique that determines the estimated time it will take to recover the original investment in a project.

Permanent current assets The level of current assets required to support the minimum sales of the firm.

Perpetuity An investment that promises an infinite stream of equal payments.

Personal and dependent exemptions A $1,000 reduction in taxable income for the individual taxpayer, spouse, and each qualified dependent. In addition, the taxpayer and spouse each receive an additional exemption if either or both are blind and/or over the age of 65.

Pledging Using accounts receivable or inventory as collateral for a loan.

Political risk Uncertainty about future government actions that may impede foreign business transactions.

Portfolio management The construction of a multiple-security investment combination in an effort to obtain improved risk and return characteristics in line with an investor's investment objectives.

Preauthorized check (PAC) An instrument used to transfer funds between demand deposit accounts.

Preemptive right A provision in the corporate charter or in state law that allows the existing stockholders to purchase additional shares of stock before they are offered for sale to the public. This allows existing stockholders to maintain their proportionate ownership in the firm.

Preferred stock A type of equity that has a claim against earnings and assets before common stockholders but after debt holders.

Present value The current worth of a future sum considering the time value of money.

Present value interest factor (PVIF) The value of $1/(1 + i)^n$ where i is an interest rate and n is time periods, which when multiplied by a future cash flow indicates the present value of the cash flow.

Present value interest factor of an annuity (PVIFA) Equivalent to the expression

$$\sum_{t=1}^{n} \frac{1}{(1 + i)^t},$$

where i is the discount rate and n is the number of discounting periods.

Price earnings (PE) ratio The current price of a stock divided by the previous year's earnings.

Primary earnings per share (EPS) Calculated by dividing the earnings available to common stockholders by the number of common shares outstanding. No allowance is made for convertible bonds, preferred stock, or warrants that have not been converted into common stock.

Prime rate The lending rate charged by banks to their most creditworthy customers.

Private placement A securities issue offering made to institutional investors. Securities issues to be privately placed are not registered with the Securities and Exchange Commission if they meet certain restrictions.

Probability The expected frequency of occurrences of a particular event.

Probability density function (PDF) A probability distribution for a continuous variable in which the probability of an event can be calculated as a mathematical function of the numerical value of the event.

Probability distribution (PD) A rule relating all possible events and their expected frequency of occurrence. The probabilities of all possible events must sum to 1.

Processing float The time between receipt of payment by the billing firm and deposit of the check for collection.

Product extension combination The merger of two firms that have related production and/or distribution activities but products that do not compete directly with one another.

Profitability index (PI) A discounted cash flow approach to capital budgeting; the ratio of the present value of a project's benefits to its cost.

Profitability ratios Measures of a firm's ability to generate a profit in relation to some base figure, such as sales or assets.

***Pro forma* balance sheet** A projected balance sheet for future periods based on estimates of anticipated sales and income. The *pro forma* income statement and the cash budget are used as inputs into the *pro forma* balance sheet.

***Pro forma* income statement** A projected income statement for future periods based on forecasts and assumptions about sales and costs.

Progressive taxation A tax system in which the rate of taxation increases as the amount subject to tax (i.e., the tax base) increases (i.e., higher incomes are subject to progressively higher taxes). This type of system is based on the criterion of ability to pay.

Promissory note A legal contract formally recognizing a borrower's obligation to repay a specified sum to a lender.

Prospectus Information provided to potential investors in a new securities issue detailing all pertinent facts concerning the securities to be offered. The prospectus also contains the firm's annual Securities and Exchange Commission Form 10-K.

Proxy   A document that a stockholder gives to another party for the purpose of voting the shares.

Purchasing power parity   A principle stating that comparable goods should sell for equivalent prices regardless of the currency used to price the goods.

Put option   A contract created by individual investors that permits the buyer to sell 100 shares of a specified stock to the seller for a specified price (exercise price) any time during the life of the option.

Q-ratio   The relationship between the market value of a firm's assets and the replacement cost of the assets. Computed by dividing the market value of a firm's assets by the replacement cost.

Quick ratio   See *Acid test ratio.*

Ratio analysis   A method of analyzing accounting statements in which accounting numbers are implicitly compared through the calculation of ratios.

Raw materials inventory   Basic items required to produce a finished product.

Receivables   Obligations due to the firm, primarily from sales; uncollected accounts outstanding.

Refundable tax credit   A tax credit in which cash refunds in excess of the tax liability due can be paid to the taxpayer up to certain specified limitations.

Refunding   Sale of new debt obligations to retire old debt obligations.

Registration of securities   The requirement that all corporations issuing securities register those securities with the Securities and Exchange Commission. The corporation, not the investment banking syndicate handling the issue, is responsible for fulfilling this requirement.

Registration statement   A document filed with the Securities and Exchange Commission each time new securities are offered to the public.

Regression analysis   A statistical method for forecasting the value of one variable (dependent variable) on the basis of information about one or more variables (independent variables). The

most common estimation procedure is that of least squares.

Regular (Subchapter C) corporation   A legal entity separate from its owner-shareholders and subject to a separate corporate federal income tax. All income and expense remains locked in at the corporate level; shareholders are taxed only upon receiving distributions from the corporation or disposing of their stockholdings.

Reinvestment rate   The investment rate at which the interim cash flows from a project are assumed to be reinvested. The net present value approach and the profitability index assume reinvestment at the project's cost of capital. The internal rate of return approach assumes reinvestment at the internal rate of return.

Reinvestment rate risk   Uncertainty about the rate of return that will be earned by future cash flows from an investment.

Reorganization   Changes in the asset structure and financial structure of a firm to reflect the true value of the firm. All claims against the firm are settled, and the company continues its operations.

Repurchase agreement (repos)   A contract to buy and sell back specific securities. The maturity of most repos varies from overnight to 30 days.

Required rate of return   The minimum acceptable return on a new investment. A project's required rate of return is synonymous with its discount rate and/or its cost of capital.

Retained earnings   The portion of after-tax earnings not paid out as dividends. The figure appearing on the balance sheet is the sum of all earnings retained by the firm throughout the company's history.

Return on net worth   A profitability ratio calculated by dividing net income after taxes by net worth (assuming that no preferred stock is outstanding). The ratio is normally adjusted if the firm has preferred stock outstanding. Also called *return on equity.*

Return on sales   A profitability ratio that measures the percentage profit on each dollar of sales.

Return on total assets A profitability ratio that measures the return on the firm's total asset base.

Revaluation An increase in the value of one currency compared to another.

Revolving credit agreement An arrangement between a bank and a borrower in which the bank is legally required to provide credit to the borrower, up to a stipulated amount.

Right An option offered to present stockholders when a company is coming to market with a new issue of stock. Rights allow these stockholders to maintain proportional ownership in a firm by purchasing additional stock before it is offered to the public.

Rights-on-ownership The privilege of receiving rights. A share of stock is rights-on if it entitles the owner to a right that is about to be issued by a firm.

Risk Uncertainty about the future outcome of a particular event. Risk is potential forecast error.

Risk, degree of The potential error in a forecasted outcome, for example, uncertainty about future income to be earned from an investment. Total risk in an investment is measured by the standard deviation of returns.

Risk-adjusted discount rate (RADR) A formal risk-adjustment technique used in capital budgeting. Higher RADRs are used for more risky investments and lower RADRs for less risky ones.

Rule of 72 A mathematical approximation stating that any product with an interest rate and time that equal 72 produces a compound value interest factor of 2, representing a doubling of the original investment. For example, money deposited at 10% will double in a little more than 7 years (7.2 years × 10 = 72).

Safety stock Extra inventory held as a hedge or protection against the possibility of a stock-out.

Sale and leaseback A procedure in which the owner of an asset sells the asset to investors and simultaneously leases the asset back.

Salvage value The worth of an asset at the end of its useful life.

Scenario planning An analysis of the effects on sales and income under a specific set of circumstances.

Section 1231 gains and losses Gains and losses from the disposition of assets used in a trade or business that have been owned for more than one year. Net 1231 gains are treated as net long-term capital gains, whereas net 1231 losses are treated as ordinary losses for the year.

Secured creditor An individual or firm whose claim against another firm has collateral.

Securities A general term for all types of financial claims created by corporations, governments, and financial institutions, for example, stocks, bonds, convertibles, warrants, and options.

Security analysis The evaluation of a financial asset's risk and return characteristics in the context of existing economic and industry conditions.

Security market line (SML) The relationship between a security's return and its beta. Every security should earn an expected return equal to the risk-free rate plus (or minus) a risk premium proportional to its beta.

Selling group A group of investment bankers and stock brokerage firms formed to sell a securities issue. Members of the selling group are paid on a commission basis.

Sensitivity analysis An analysis of changes in operating income when individual causal variables are altered.

Serial bonds Debt obligations issued at the same time with differing maturity dates. The bonds may have the same coupon rate for all maturities or differing coupon rates for each maturity.

Shelf registration Securities and Exchange Commission Rule 415, which allows companies to register all securities they plan to issue over the following two years. The companies may then sell any part of those securities whenever they choose.

Short-term fixed-amount loan A loan arrangement in which a specified amount is borrowed for a period of one year or less. Generally used to finance working capital or to fund a specified asset of the firm.

Simple interest loan   A loan agreement in which the borrower agrees to repay the principal plus interest at the end of the borrowing period.

Simulation   The use of computer models to predict the outcome of alternative decisions. Simulation models allow the analyst to incorporate simultaneously many variables that can affect the results.

Sinking fund   A deposit or investment account into which borrowers make periodic deposits of cash to redeem bonds or long-term notes before or at maturity.

Sole proprietorship   The conduct of a business by a single individual. Unlimited personal liability exists for all of the debts of the sole proprietorship.

Speculative premium   The difference between the market value of an option-type security and the cash flow that can be generated by its immediate exercise. Convertible securities, warrants, and options contain a speculative premium. For example, a warrant that can be used to purchase stock for $20 when the stock is at $25 will generate $5 in income if exercised. If the warrant is selling for $7, then the price contains $2 of speculation premium, also called *nonintrinsic premium*.

Spot market   A market in which foreign currency or goods can be bought or sold for immediate delivery.

Stabilization period   The period of time between the offering of the security to the public and the final distribution, during which the underwriting firm maintains the market price of the security at the offering price. Stabilization periods typically last for 30 days.

Standard deviation (σ)   A statistic used to measure dispersion about an expected value. A high (low) standard deviation is associated with high (low) risk. Standard deviation is the square root of the variance.

Standby underwriting   A contract between the firm and an investment banking syndicate. It requires the investment banking firm to purchase the unsold portion of an issue for which old shareholders have not subscribed.

State of nature   Each possible future set of circumstances that might occur. Each state of nature has a related probability of occurrence.

Statistic   A summary description of numerical data. Frequently used statistics include the mean, median, standard deviation, variance, and skewness.

Stock   See *Common stock.*

Stockholder of record   The owner of a share of stock as stated on the back of the stock certificate. All dividends/rights are paid/offered only to the stockholder of record.

Stock-out cost   Any cost incurred because inventory is depleted. Typical stock-out costs include lost sales and production delays.

Straight financial lease   Synonymous with financial lease except that it makes explicit that the transaction is not a sale and leaseback.

Striking price   Relative to a call option, the price at which the buyer can obtain the stock from the seller. Relative to a put option, the price at which the buyer can sell the stock to the seller.

Subchapter S corporation   A corporation meeting certain tax code requirements and electing to be treated as a partnership for tax purposes; a tax variant of the regular (Subchapter C) corporation. All items of income, expense, gain, and loss pass directly to the individual shareholders, regardless of any asset distributions actually made by the Subchapter S corporation. Because it is a corporation, each shareholder's personal liability is limited. Special conditions must be met to obtain this tax status.

Subordinated debentures   Debentures whose holders have a claim on the firm's assets only after the holders of senior debt have been paid.

Subscription price   The price at which shares may be purchased from the issuing company by the use of a stock right.

Subscription warrant   A certificate issued by the corporation stating the conditions under which existing stockholders may purchase additional stock from a new stock issue.

Syndicate   A collection of lenders who jointly assume the responsibility for making a large loan or purchasing a large block of securities for resale. Several banks may form a syndicate to make a large loan to one firm, or several investment banking firms may underwrite one security issue.

Syndicate manager   The investment banking firm overseeing the underwriting of a securities issue.

Syndicated loan   A loan that is extended by several banks or lenders who jointly assume responsibility for the loan.

Synergy   An increase in the performance measures of two merged companies that exceeds the sum of the two premerger companies.

Systematic risk   Also referred to as *relevant* or *nondiversifiable risk*. That component of a security's risk that diversification does not eliminate. Beta measures a security's market sensitivity (systematic risk).

Tax shield   The tax saving afforded by a given tax-deductible expense.

Taxable income   For an individual taxpayer, the amount of adjusted gross income for the year, less itemized deductions above the zero bracket amount and personal and dependent exemptions. For a corporation, the amount of gross income less all allowable deductions. Taxable income serves as the basis for computing the gross tax liability in both cases.

Technical insolvency   Inability of a firm to obtain funds to pay debts as they become due even though the firm's assets exceed its liabilities. This occurs in firms whose assets are not easily converted into cash.

Temporary current assets   Investment in current assets that rises and falls to meet seasonal or cyclical expansion of sales.

Term loan   A loan with a maturity greater than one year. Typical term loans by banks range in maturity from one to five years, whereas loans made by insurance companies and pension funds may have a term greater than 25 years.

Term structure of interest rates   The relationship between yield and time to maturity of a debt instrument.

Terminal warehouse   A public warehouse used for the storage of goods.

Terminal warehousing arrangement   A procedure in which inventory pledged as loan collateral is maintained in a public warehouse by a third party.

Theory   A plausible or accepted explanation of a phenomenon or set of relationships.

Times-interest-earned ratio   A coverage ratio showing how well a firm has covered its interest obligations, calculated as earnings before interest and taxes divided by the interest expense.

Tombstone ads   Advertisements about a pending security issue that indicate the characteristics about the security and list the members of the investment banking syndicate. These ads can be found constantly in the *Wall Street Journal.*

Total asset turnover   An activity ratio that measures how well a firm is utilizing its total resources; the ratio of net sales to total assets.

Trade acceptance   A time bill of exchange drawn against the buyer of goods by the seller. Trade acceptances are widely used to finance agricultural and international transactions.

Trade credit   Short-term financing provided by a firm's suppliers. It is shown as accounts payable on the balance sheet of the borrowing firm.

Transfer pricing   Costs charged one subsidiary by another. In international operations, transfer pricing can be used to move currencies between countries to take advantage of changes in exchange rates.

Transit stock   Inventory that would be used (or sold) between the time an order is placed and the time it is delivered.

Treasury bill   An obligation of the U.S. government issued with a maturity of less than one year. Treasury bills are sold at a discount, and their interest rate is considered to be an approximation of the risk-free rate.

Treasury stock   Common stock that has been repurchased by the company that originally issued it.

Trend analysis   Comparison of financial ratios over several time periods to detect changes in the firm's financial situation.

Trust indenture A document describing the bondholder's rights and claims on the corporation's assets. It is frequently referred to as an *indenture.*

Trust receipt A document that gives a lender title to goods held in trust by a borrower and that is used for the purpose of financing inventory.

Uncertainty, degree of The potential error in a forecasted outcome; synonymous with *risk.*

Underwriting A guarantee by investment banking firms to an issuing corporation that a definable sum of money will be paid on a specified date for the issue of stocks or bonds.

Underwriting spread The fee paid to the investment banking syndicate for handling a securities issue. The underwriting spread is a negotiated percentage of the total face value of the issue.

Unsystematic risk The component of a security's risk that is not related to the market. Unsystematic risk can be eliminated through diversification. The market does not reward unsystematic risk.

Valuation (*n*), the worth of an economic asset. (*v*), the process of determining the worth of such an asset.

Value-additivity principle (VAP) The premise that a firm's total value is the sum of value of its investments, that is, that the whole equals exactly the sum of the parts.

Variance (σ^2) A statistic that measures dispersion about the expected value. High (low) variance is associated with high (low) risk. The variance equals the standard deviation squared.

Vertical combination The merger of two firms involved in successive stages of production of the same product.

Voting rights Vary with the type and class of the stock issue. Typically, one share of common stock has one vote on corporate matters. Preferred shares may or may not have voting rights.

Warehouse receipt A legal document acknowledging storage of goods and specifying the terms on which they can be removed from the warehouse.

Warrant A security issued by a company, usually attached to a bond, giving the holder the right to buy a specified number of shares of the company's common stock at a specified price during a given time period. A warrant may be *nondetachable*, in which case it cannot be removed from the bond and traded independently, or *detachable*, meaning that it can be traded as a separate security.

Weighted average cost of capital (WACC) A cost of capital formula in which the cost of each source of capital is weighted in proprotion to how much of each type of capital is employed by the firm.

Wholly owned foreign subsidiary An international business arrangement in which a domestic company owns a foreign facility responsible for the total production and sale of the firm's products.

Wire transfer Electronic bank-to-bank transfer of funds.

Work in process Items in various stages of the production cycle but not yet ready for sale.

Working capital Current assets of the firm directly related to the firm's production cycle. Typically consists of cash and marketable securities, accounts receivable, and inventory.

Working capital cycle The flow of cash through the working capital accounts of the firm. The cycle begins when cash is received by a business. It is then invested in inventory, which produces sales resulting in accounts receivable. Collection of accounts receivable produces a cash inflow and completes the working capital cycle.

Working capital turnover Ratio of sales to current assets. The higher the ratio, the greater efficiency the firm displays in using its current assets.

World Bank Also called the International Bank for Reconstruction and Development. Provides long-term credit to underdeveloped countries at below-market rates.

Yield Rate of return earned by an investment as determined by the internal rate of return.

Yield curve A graph relating interest rates and time to maturity of debt obligations that are identical, except for their maturity. The yield curve is a pictorial representation of the term structure of interest rates.

Yield to maturity The discount rate that makes the present value of a bond's interest and principal equal to its current price. The yield to maturity will not equal the coupon rate when the bond is selling at a premium or a discount.

Zero balance account (ZBA) A subaccount of a demand deposit account in which a company maintains a zero balance. Checks written against the ZBA are covered at the end of each day with funds taken from the master demand deposit account.

Zero bracket amount The amount of taxable income subject to a zero tax rate. This amount varies depending upon the filing classification of the individual taxpayer.

Zero coupon bond A bond that earns no annual interest payments. The difference between the purchase price and the par value at maturity represents interest to the bondholder.

TABLES

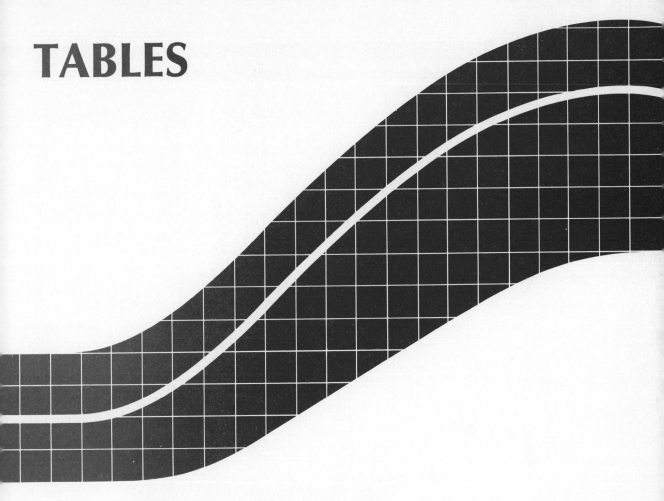

TABLE A
Present Value of $1, PVIF.

Year	1%	1½%	2%	4%	5%	6%	7%	8%	9%	10%
					Rate					
1	0.990	0.985	0.980	0.962	0.952	0.943	0.935	0.926	0.917	0.909
2	0.980	0.971	0.961	0.925	0.907	0.890	0.873	0.857	0.842	0.826
3	0.971	0.956	0.942	0.889	0.864	0.840	0.816	0.794	0.772	0.751
4	0.961	0.942	0.924	0.855	0.823	0.792	0.763	0.735	0.708	0.683
5	0.951	0.928	0.906	0.822	0.784	0.747	0.713	0.681	0.650	0.621
6	0.942	0.915	0.888	0.790	0.746	0.705	0.666	0.630	0.596	0.564
7	0.933	0.901	0.871	0.760	0.711	0.665	0.623	0.583	0.547	0.513
8	0.923	0.888	0.853	0.731	0.677	0.627	0.582	0.540	0.502	0.467
9	0.914	0.875	0.837	0.703	0.645	0.592	0.544	0.500	0.460	0.424
10	0.905	0.862	0.820	0.676	0.614	0.558	0.508	0.463	0.422	0.386
11	0.896	0.849	0.804	0.650	0.585	0.527	0.475	0.429	0.388	0.350
12	0.887	0.836	0.788	0.625	0.557	0.497	0.444	0.397	0.356	0.319
13	0.879	0.824	0.773	0.601	0.530	0.469	0.415	0.368	0.326	0.290
14	0.870	0.812	0.758	0.577	0.505	0.442	0.388	0.340	0.299	0.263
15	0.861	0.800	0.743	0.555	0.481	0.417	0.362	0.315	0.275	0.239
16	0.853	0.788	0.728	0.534	0.458	0.394	0.339	0.292	0.252	0.218
17	0.844	0.776	0.714	0.513	0.436	0.371	0.317	0.270	0.231	0.198
18	0.836	0.765	0.700	0.494	0.416	0.350	0.296	0.250	0.212	0.180
19	0.828	0.754	0.686	0.475	0.396	0.331	0.277	0.232	0.194	0.164
20	0.820	0.742	0.673	0.456	0.377	0.312	0.258	0.215	0.178	0.149
21	0.811	0.731	0.660	0.439	0.359	0.294	0.242	0.199	0.164	0.135
22	0.803	0.721	0.647	0.422	0.342	0.278	0.226	0.184	0.150	0.123
23	0.795	0.710	0.634	0.406	0.326	0.262	0.211	0.170	0.138	0.112
24	0.788	0.700	0.622	0.390	0.310	0.247	0.197	0.158	0.126	0.102
25	0.780	0.689	0.610	0.375	0.295	0.233	0.184	0.146	0.116	0.092
26	0.772	0.679	0.598	0.361	0.281	0.220	0.172	0.135	0.106	0.084
27	0.764	0.669	0.586	0.347	0.268	0.207	0.161	0.125	0.098	0.076
28	0.757	0.659	0.574	0.333	0.255	0.196	0.150	0.116	0.090	0.069
29	0.749	0.649	0.563	0.321	0.243	0.185	0.141	0.107	0.082	0.063
30	0.742	0.640	0.552	0.308	0.231	0.174	0.131	0.099	0.075	0.057
31	0.735	0.630	0.541	0.296	0.220	0.164	0.123	0.092	0.069	0.052
32	0.727	0.621	0.531	0.285	0.210	0.155	0.115	0.085	0.063	0.047
33	0.720	0.612	0.050	0.274	0.200	0.146	0.107	0.079	0.058	0.043
34	0.713	0.603	0.510	0.264	0.190	0.138	0.100	0.073	0.053	0.039
35	0.706	0.594	0.500	0.253	0.181	0.130	0.094	0.068	0.049	0.036
36	0.699	0.585	0.490	0.244	0.173	0.123	0.088	0.063	0.045	0.032
40	0.672	0.551	0.453	0.208	0.142	0.097	0.067	0.046	0.032	0.022
45	0.639	0.512	0.410	0.171	0.111	0.073	0.048	0.031	0.021	0.014
48	0.620	0.489	0.387	0.152	0.096	0.061	0.039	0.025	0.016	0.010
50	0.608	0.475	0.372	0.141	0.087	0.054	0.034	0.021	0.013	0.009

						Rate					
11%	**12%**	**13%**	**14%**	**15%**	**16%**	**18%**	**20%**	**22%**	**24%**	**25%**	**30%**
0.901	0.893	0.885	0.877	0.870	0.862	0.847	0.833	0.820	0.806	0.800	0.769
0.812	0.797	0.783	0.769	0.756	0.743	0.718	0.694	0.672	0.650	0.640	0.592
0.731	0.712	0.693	0.675	0.658	0.641	0.609	0.579	0.551	0.524	0.512	0.455
0.659	0.636	0.613	0.592	0.572	0.552	0.516	0.482	0.451	0.423	0.410	0.350
0.593	0.567	0.543	0.519	0.497	0.476	0.437	0.402	0.370	0.341	0.328	0.269
0.535	0.507	0.480	0.456	0.432	0.410	0.370	0.335	0.303	0.275	0.262	0.207
0.482	0.452	0.425	0.400	0.376	0.354	0.314	0.279	0.249	0.222	0.210	0.159
0.434	0.404	0.376	0.351	0.327	0.305	0.266	0.233	0.204	0.179	0.168	0.123
0.391	0.361	0.333	0.308	0.284	0.263	0.225	0.194	0.167	0.144	0.134	0.094
0.352	0.322	0.295	0.270	0.247	0.227	0.191	0.162	0.137	0.116	0.107	0.073
0.317	0.287	0.261	0.237	0.215	0.195	0.162	0.135	0.112	0.094	0.086	0.056
0.286	0.257	0.231	0.208	0.187	0.168	0.137	0.112	0.092	0.076	0.069	0.043
0.258	0.229	0.204	0.182	0.163	0.145	0.116	0.093	0.075	0.061	0.055	0.033
0.232	0.205	0.181	0.160	0.141	0.125	0.099	0.078	0.062	0.049	0.044	0.025
0.209	0.183	0.160	0.140	0.123	0.108	0.084	0.065	0.051	0.040	0.035	0.020
0.188	0.163	0.141	0.123	0.107	0.093	0.071	0.054	0.042	0.032	0.028	0.015
0.170	0.146	0.125	0.108	0.093	0.080	0.060	0.045	0.034	0.026	0.023	0.012
0.153	0.130	0.111	0.095	0.081	0.069	0.051	0.038	0.028	0.021	0.018	0.009
0.138	0.116	0.098	0.083	0.070	0.060	0.043	0.031	0.023	0.017	0.014	0.007
0.124	0.104	0.087	0.073	0.061	0.051	0.037	0.026	0.019	0.014	0.012	0.005
0.112	0.093	0.077	0.064	0.053	0.044	0.031	0.022	0.015	0.011	0.009	0.004
0.101	0.083	0.068	0.056	0.046	0.038	0.026	0.018	0.013	0.009	0.007	0.003
0.091	0.074	0.060	0.049	0.040	0.033	0.022	0.015	0.010	0.007	0.006	0.002
0.082	0.066	0.053	0.043	0.035	0.028	0.019	0.013	0.008	0.006	0.005	0.002
0.074	0.059	0.047	0.038	0.030	0.024	0.016	0.010	0.007	0.005	0.004	0.001
0.066	0.053	0.042	0.033	0.026	0.021	0.014	0.009	0.006	0.004	0.003	0.001
0.060	0.047	0.037	0.029	0.023	0.018	0.011	0.007	0.005	0.003	0.002	0.001
0.054	0.042	0.033	0.026	0.020	0.016	0.010	0.006	0.004	0.002	0.002	0.001
0.048	0.037	0.029	0.022	0.017	0.014	0.008	0.005	0.003	0.002	0.002	0.000
0.044	0.033	0.026	0.020	0.015	0.012	0.007	0.004	0.003	0.002	0.001	0.000
0.039	0.030	0.023	0.017	0.013	0.010	0.006	0.004	0.002	0.001	0.001	0.000
0.035	0.027	0.020	0.015	0.011	0.009	0.005	0.003	0.002	0.001	0.001	0.000
0.032	0.024	0.018	0.013	0.010	0.007	0.004	0.002	0.001	0.001	0.001	0.000
0.029	0.021	0.016	0.012	0.009	0.006	0.004	0.002	0.001	0.001	0.001	0.000
0.026	0.019	0.014	0.010	0.008	0.006	0.003	0.002	0.001	0.001	0.000	0.000
0.023	0.017	0.012	0.009	0.007	0.005	0.003	0.001	0.001	0.000	0.000	0.000
0.015	0.011	0.008	0.005	0.004	0.003	0.001	0.001	0.000	0.000	0.000	0.000
0.009	0.006	0.004	0.003	0.002	0.001	0.001	0.000	0.000	0.000	0.000	0.000
0.007	0.004	0.003	0.002	0.001	0.001	0.000	0.000	0.000	0.000	0.000	0.000
0.005	0.003	0.002	0.001	0.001	0.001	0.000	0.000	0.000	0.000	0.000	0.000

TABLE B
Present Value of an Annuity of $1, PVIFA.

Year	1%	1½%	2%	4%	5%	6%	7%	8%	9%	10%
					Rate					
1	0.990	0.985	0.980	0.962	0.952	0.943	0.935	0.926	0.917	0.909
2	1.970	1.956	1.942	1.886	1.859	1.833	1.808	1.783	1.759	1.736
3	2.941	2.912	2.884	2.775	2.723	2.673	2.624	2.577	2.531	2.487
4	3.902	3.854	3.808	3.630	3.546	3.465	3.387	3.312	3.240	3.170
5	4.853	4.783	4.713	4.452	4.329	4.212	4.100	3.993	3.890	3.791
6	5.795	5.697	5.601	5.242	5.076	4.917	4.767	4.623	4.486	4.355
7	6.728	6.598	6.472	6.002	5.786	5.582	5.389	5.206	5.033	4.868
8	7.652	7.486	7.325	6.733	6.463	6.210	5.971	5.747	5.535	5.335
9	8.566	8.361	8.162	7.435	7.108	6.802	6.515	6.247	5.995	5.759
10	9.471	9.222	8.983	8.111	7.722	7.360	7.024	6.710	6.418	6.145
11	10.368	10.071	9.787	8.760	8.306	7.887	7.499	7.139	6.805	6.495
12	11.255	10.908	10.575	9.385	8.863	8.384	7.943	7.536	7.161	6.814
13	12.134	11.732	11.348	9.986	9.394	8.853	8.358	7.904	7.487	7.103
14	13.004	12.543	12.106	10.563	9.899	9.295	8.745	8.244	7.786	7.367
15	13.865	13.343	12.849	11.118	10.380	9.712	9.108	8.559	8.061	7.606
16	14.718	14.131	13.578	11.652	10.838	10.106	9.447	8.851	8.313	7.824
17	15.562	14.908	14.292	12.166	11.274	10.477	9.763	9.122	8.544	8.022
18	16.398	15.673	14.992	12.659	11.690	10.828	10.059	9.372	8.756	8.201
19	17.226	16.426	15.678	13.134	12.085	11.158	10.336	9.604	8.950	8.365
20	18.046	17.169	16.351	13.590	12.462	11.470	10.594	9.818	9.129	8.514
21	18.857	17.900	17.011	14.029	12.821	11.764	10.836	10.017	9.292	8.649
22	19.660	18.621	17.658	14.451	13.163	12.042	11.061	10.201	9.442	8.772
23	20.456	19.331	18.292	14.857	13.489	12.303	11.272	10.371	9.580	8.883
24	21.243	20.030	18.914	15.247	13.799	12.550	11.469	10.529	9.707	8.985
25	22.023	20.720	19.523	15.622	14.094	12.783	11.654	10.675	9.823	9.077
26	22.795	21.399	20.121	15.983	14.375	13.003	11.826	10.810	9.929	9.161
27	23.560	22.068	20.707	16.330	14.643	13.211	11.987	10.935	10.027	9.237
28	24.316	22.727	21.281	16.663	14.898	13.406	12.137	11.051	10.116	9.307
29	25.066	23.376	21.844	16.984	15.141	13.591	12.278	11.158	10.198	9.370
30	25.808	24.016	22.396	17.292	15.372	13.765	12.409	11.258	10.274	9.427
31	26.542	24.646	22.938	17.588	15.593	13.929	12.532	11.350	10.343	9.479
32	27.270	25.267	23.468	17.874	15.803	14.084	12.647	11.435	10.406	9.526
33	27.990	25.879	23.989	18.148	16.003	14.230	12.754	11.514	10.464	9.569
34	28.703	26.482	24.499	18.411	16.193	14.368	12.854	11.587	10.518	9.609
35	29.409	27.076	24.999	18.665	16.374	14.498	12.948	11.655	10.567	9.644
36	30.108	27.661	25.489	18.908	16.547	14.621	13.035	11.717	10.612	9.677
40	32.835	29.916	27.355	19.793	17.159	15.046	13.332	11.925	10.757	9.779
45	36.095	32.552	29.490	20.720	17.774	15.456	13.606	12.108	10.881	9.863
48	37.974	34.043	30.673	21.195	18.077	15.650	13.730	12.189	10.934	9.897
50	39.196	35.000	31.424	21.482	18.256	15.762	13.801	12.233	10.962	9.915

						Rate					
11%	12%	13%	14%	15%	16%	18%	20%	22%	24%	25%	30%
0.901	0.893	0.885	0.877	0.870	0.862	0.847	0.833	0.820	0.806	0.800	0.769
1.713	1.690	1.668	1.647	1.626	1.605	1.566	1.528	1.492	1.457	1.440	1.361
2.444	2.402	2.361	2.322	2.283	2.246	2.174	2.106	2.042	1.981	1.952	1.816
3.102	3.037	2.974	2.914	2.855	2.798	2.690	2.589	2.494	2.404	2.362	2.166
3.696	3.605	3.517	3.433	3.352	3.274	3.127	2.991	2.864	2.745	2.689	2.436
4.231	4.111	3.998	3.889	3.784	3.685	3.498	3.326	3.167	3.020	2.951	2.643
4.712	4.564	4.423	4.288	4.160	4.039	3.812	3.605	3.416	3.242	3.161	2.802
5.146	4.968	4.799	4.639	4.487	4.344	4.078	3.837	3.619	3.421	3.329	2.925
5.537	5.328	5.132	4.946	4.772	4.607	4.303	4.031	3.786	3.566	3.463	3.019
5.889	5.650	5.426	5.216	5.019	4.833	4.494	4.192	3.923	3.682	3.571	3.092
6.207	5.938	5.687	5.453	5.234	5.029	4.656	4.327	4.035	3.776	3.656	3.147
6.492	6.194	5.918	5.660	5.421	5.197	4.793	4.439	4.127	3.851	3.725	3.190
6.750	6.424	6.122	5.842	5.583	5.342	4.910	4.533	4.203	3.912	3.780	3.223
6.982	6.628	6.302	6.002	5.724	5.468	5.008	4.611	4.265	3.962	3.824	3.249
7.191	6.811	6.462	6.142	5.847	5.575	5.092	4.675	4.315	4.001	3.859	3.268
7.379	6.974	6.604	6.265	5.954	5.668	5.162	4.730	4.357	4.033	3.887	3.283
7.549	7.120	6.729	6.373	6.047	5.749	5.222	4.775	4.391	4.059	3.910	3.295
7.702	7.250	6.840	6.467	6.128	5.818	5.273	4.812	4.419	4.080	3.928	3.304
7.839	7.366	6.938	6.550	6.198	5.877	5.316	4.843	4.442	4.097	3.942	3.311
7.963	7.469	7.025	6.623	6.259	5.929	5.353	4.870	4.460	4.110	3.954	3.316
8.075	7.562	7.102	6.687	6.312	5.973	5.384	4.891	4.476	4.121	3.963	3.320
8.176	7.645	7.170	6.743	6.359	6.011	5.410	4.909	4.488	4.130	3.970	3.323
8.266	7.718	7.230	6.792	6.399	6.044	5.432	4.925	4.499	4.137	3.976	3.325
8.348	7.784	7.283	6.835	6.434	6.073	5.451	4.937	4.507	4.143	3.981	3.327
8.422	7.843	7.330	6.873	6.464	6.097	5.467	4.948	4.514	4.147	3.985	3.329
8.488	7.896	7.372	6.906	6.491	6.118	5.480	4.956	4.520	4.151	3.988	3.330
8.548	7.943	7.409	6.935	6.514	6.136	5.492	4.964	4.524	4.154	3.990	3.331
8.602	7.984	7.441	6.961	6.534	6.152	5.502	4.970	4.528	4.157	3.992	3.331
8.650	8.022	7.470	6.983	6.551	6.166	5.510	4.975	4.531	4.159	3.994	3.332
8.694	8.055	7.496	7.003	6.566	6.177	5.517	4.979	4.534	4.160	3.995	3.332
8.733	8.085	7.518	7.020	6.579	6.187	5.523	4.982	4.536	4.161	3.996	3.332
8.769	8.112	7.538	7.035	6.591	6.196	5.528	4.985	4.538	4.162	3.997	3.333
8.801	8.135	7.556	7.048	6.600	6.203	5.532	4.988	4.539	4.163	3.997	3.333
8.829	8.157	7.572	7.060	6.609	6.210	5.536	4.990	4.540	4.164	3.998	3.333
8.855	8.176	7.586	7.070	6.617	6.215	5.539	4.992	4.541	4.164	3.998	3.333
8.879	8.192	7.598	7.079	6.623	6.220	5.541	4.993	4.542	4.165	3.999	3.333
8.951	8.244	7.634	7.105	6.642	6.233	5.548	4.997	4.544	4.166	3.999	3.333
9.008	8.283	7.661	7.123	6.654	6.242	5.552	4.999	4.545	4.166	4.000	3.333
9.030	8.297	7.671	7.130	6.659	6.245	5.554	4.999	4.545	4.167	4.000	3.333
9.042	8.304	7.675	7.133	6.661	6.246	5.554	4.999	4.545	4.167	4.000	3.333

TABLE C
Future Value of $1, FVIF.

Year	Rate												
	1%	1½%	2%	4%	5%	6%	7%	8%	9%	10%	11%	12%	13%
1	1.010	1.015	1.020	1.040	1.050	1.060	1.070	1.080	1.090	1.100	1.110	1.120	1.130
2	1.020	1.030	1.040	1.082	1.103	1.124	1.145	1.166	1.188	1.210	1.232	1.254	1.277
3	1.030	1.046	1.061	1.125	1.158	1.191	1.225	1.260	1.295	1.331	1.368	1.405	1.443
4	1.041	1.061	1.082	1.170	1.216	1.262	1.311	1.360	1.412	1.464	1.518	1.574	1.630
5	1.051	1.077	1.104	1.217	1.276	1.338	1.403	1.469	1.539	1.611	1.685	1.762	1.842
6	1.062	1.093	1.126	1.265	1.340	1.419	1.501	1.587	1.677	1.772	1.870	1.974	2.082
7	1.072	1.110	1.149	1.316	1.407	1.504	1.606	1.714	1.828	1.949	2.076	2.211	2.353
8	1.083	1.126	1.172	1.369	1.477	1.594	1.718	1.851	1.993	2.144	2.305	2.476	2.658
9	1.094	1.143	1.195	1.423	1.551	1.689	1.838	1.999	2.172	2.358	2.558	2.773	3.004
10	1.105	1.161	1.219	1.480	1.629	1.791	1.967	2.159	2.367	2.594	2.839	3.106	3.395
11	1.116	1.178	1.243	1.539	1.710	1.898	2.105	2.332	2.580	2.853	3.152	3.479	3.836
12	1.127	1.196	1.268	1.601	1.796	2.012	2.252	2.518	2.813	3.138	3.498	3.896	4.335
13	1.138	1.214	1.294	1.665	1.886	2.133	2.410	2.720	3.066	3.452	3.883	4.363	4.898
14	1.149	1.232	1.319	1.732	1.980	2.261	2.579	2.937	3.342	3.797	4.310	4.887	5.535
15	1.161	1.250	1.346	1.801	2.079	2.397	2.759	3.172	3.642	4.177	4.785	5.474	6.254
16	1.173	1.269	1.373	1.873	2.183	2.540	2.952	3.426	3.970	4.595	5.311	6.130	7.067
17	1.184	1.288	1.400	1.948	2.292	2.693	3.159	3.700	4.328	5.054	5.895	6.866	7.986
18	1.196	1.307	1.428	2.026	2.407	2.854	3.380	3.996	4.717	5.560	6.544	7.690	9.024
19	1.208	1.327	1.457	2.107	2.527	3.026	3.617	4.316	5.142	6.116	7.263	8.613	10.197
20	1.220	1.347	1.486	2.191	2.653	3.207	3.870	4.661	5.604	6.727	8.062	9.646	11.523
21	1.232	1.367	1.516	2.279	2.786	3.400	4.141	5.034	6.109	7.400	8.949	10.804	13.021
22	1.245	1.388	1.546	2.370	2.925	3.604	4.430	5.437	6.659	8.140	9.934	12.100	14.714
23	1.257	1.408	1.577	2.465	3.072	3.820	4.741	5.871	7.258	8.954	11.026	13.552	16.627
24	1.270	1.430	1.608	2.563	3.225	4.049	5.072	6.341	7.911	9.850	12.239	15.179	18.788
25	1.282	1.451	1.641	2.666	3.386	4.292	5.427	6.848	8.623	10.835	13.585	17.000	21.231
26	1.295	1.473	1.673	2.772	3.556	4.549	5.807	7.396	9.399	11.918	15.080	19.040	23.991
27	1.308	1.495	1.707	2.883	3.733	4.822	6.214	7.988	10.245	13.110	16.739	21.325	27.109
28	1.321	1.517	1.741	2.999	3.920	5.112	6.649	8.627	11.167	14.421	18.580	23.884	30.633
29	1.335	1.540	1.776	3.119	4.116	5.418	7.114	9.317	12.172	15.863	20.624	26.750	34.616
30	1.348	1.563	1.811	3.243	4.322	5.743	7.612	10.063	13.268	17.449	22.892	29.960	39.116
31	1.361	1.587	1.848	3.373	4.538	6.088	8.145	10.868	14.462	19.194	25.410	33.555	44.201
32	1.375	1.610	1.885	3.508	4.765	6.453	8.715	11.737	15.763	21.114	28.206	37.582	49.947
33	1.389	1.634	1.922	3.648	5.003	6.841	9.325	12.676	17.182	23.225	31.308	42.092	56.440
34	1.403	1.659	1.961	3.794	5.253	7.251	9.978	13.690	18.728	25.548	34.752	47.143	63.777
35	1.417	1.684	2.000	3.946	5.516	7.686	10.677	14.785	20.414	28.102	38.575	52.800	72.069
36	1.431	1.709	2.040	4.104	5.792	8.147	11.424	15.968	22.251	30.913	42.818	59.136	81.437
40	1.489	1.814	2.208	4.801	7.040	10.286	14.974	21.725	31.409	45.259	65.001	93.051	132.782
45	1.565	1.954	2.438	5.841	8.985	13.765	21.002	31.920	48.327	72.890	109.530	163.988	244.641
48	1.612	2.043	2.587	6.571	10.401	16.394	25.729	40.211	62.585	97.017	149.797	230.391	352.992
50	1.645	2.105	2.692	7.107	11.467	18.420	29.457	46.902	74.358	117.391	184.565	289.002	450.736

				Rate				
14%	15%	16%	18%	20%	22%	24%	25%	30%
1.140	1.150	1.160	1.180	1.200	1.220	1.240	1.250	1.300
1.300	1.323	1.346	1.392	1.440	1.488	1.538	1.563	1.690
1.482	1.521	1.561	1.643	1.728	1.816	1.907	1.953	2.197
1.689	1.749	1.811	1.939	2.074	2.215	2.364	2.441	2.856
1.925	2.011	2.100	2.288	2.488	2.703	2.932	3.052	3.713
2.195	2.313	2.436	2.700	2.986	3.297	3.635	3.815	4.827
2.502	2.660	2.826	3.185	3.583	4.023	4.508	4.768	6.275
2.853	3.059	3.278	3.759	4.300	4.908	5.590	5.960	8.157
3.252	3.518	3.803	4.435	5.160	5.987	6.931	7.451	10.604
3.707	4.046	4.411	5.234	6.192	7.305	8.594	9.313	13.786
4.226	4.652	5.117	6.176	7.430	8.912	10.657	11.642	17.922
4.818	5.350	5.936	7.288	8.916	10.872	13.215	14.552	23.298
5.492	6.153	6.886	8.599	10.699	13.264	16.386	18.190	30.288
6.261	7.076	7.988	10.147	12.839	16.182	20.319	22.737	39.374
7.138	8.137	9.266	11.974	15.407	19.742	25.196	28.422	51.186
8.137	9.358	10.748	14.129	18.488	24.086	31.243	35.527	66.542
9.276	10.761	12.468	16.672	22.186	29.384	38.741	44.409	86.504
10.575	12.375	14.463	19.673	26.623	35.849	48.039	55.511	112.455
12.056	14.232	16.777	23.214	31.948	43.736	59.568	69.389	146.192
13.743	16.367	19.461	27.393	38.338	53.358	73.864	86.736	190.050
15.668	18.822	22.574	32.324	46.005	65.096	91.592	108.420	247.065
17.861	21.645	26.186	38.142	55.206	79.418	113.574	135.525	321.184
20.362	24.891	30.376	45.008	66.247	96.889	140.831	169.407	417.539
23.212	28.625	35.236	53.109	79.497	118.205	174.631	211.758	542.801
26.462	32.919	40.874	62.669	95.396	144.210	216.542	264.689	705.641
30.167	37.857	47.414	73.949	114.475	175.936	268.512	330.872	917.333
34.390	43.535	55.000	87.260	137.371	214.642	332.955	413.590	1192.533
39.204	50.066	63.800	102.967	164.845	261.864	412.864	516.988	1550.293
44.693	57.575	74.009	121.501	197.814	319.474	511.952	646.235	2015.381
50.950	66.212	85.850	143.371	237.376	389.758	634.820	807.794	2619.996
58.083	76.144	99.586	169.177	284.852	475.505	787.177	1009.742	3405.994
66.215	87.565	115.520	199.629	341.822	580.116	976.099	1262.177	4427.793
75.485	100.700	134.003	235.563	410.186	707.741	1210.363	1577.722	5756.130
86.053	115.805	155.443	277.964	492.224	863.444	1500.850	1972.152	7482.970
98.100	133.176	180.314	327.997	590.668	1053.402	1861.054	2465.190	9727.860
111.834	153.152	209.164	387.037	708.802	1285.150	2307.707	3081.488	12646.219
188.884	267.864	378.721	750.378	1469.772	2847.038	5455.913	7523.164	36118.865
363.679	538.769	795.444	1716.684	3657.262	7694.712	15994.690	22958.874	134106.817
538.807	819.401	241.605	2820.567	6319.749	13972.428	30495.860	44841.551	294632.676
700.233	1083.657	670.704	3927.357	9100.438	20796.561	46890.435	70064.923	497929.223

TABLE D
Future Value of an Annuity of $1, FVIFA.

Year	1%	1½%	2%	4%	5%	6%	7%	8%	9%	10%	11%	12%
1	1.000	1.000	1.000	1.000	1.000	1.000	1.000	1.000	1.000	1.000	1.000	1.000
2	2.010	2.015	2.020	2.040	2.050	2.060	2.070	2.080	2.090	2.100	2.110	2.120
3	3.030	3.045	3.060	3.122	3.152	3.184	3.215	3.246	3.278	3.310	3.342	3.374
4	4.060	4.091	4.122	4.246	4.310	4.375	4.440	4.506	4.573	4.641	4.710	4.779
5	5.101	5.152	5.204	5.416	5.526	5.637	5.751	5.867	5.985	6.105	6.228	6.353
6	6.152	6.230	6.308	6.633	6.802	6.975	7.153	7.336	7.523	7.716	7.913	8.115
7	7.214	7.323	7.434	7.898	8.142	8.394	8.654	8.923	9.200	9.487	9.783	10.089
8	8.286	8.433	8.583	9.214	9.549	9.897	10.260	10.637	11.028	11.436	11.859	12.300
9	9.369	9.559	9.755	10.583	11.027	11.491	11.978	12.488	13.021	13.579	14.164	14.776
10	10.462	10.703	10.950	12.006	12.578	13.181	13.816	14.487	15.193	15.937	16.722	17.549
11	11.567	11.863	12.169	13.486	14.207	14.972	15.784	16.645	17.560	18.531	19.561	20.655
12	12.683	13.041	13.412	15.026	15.917	16.870	17.888	18.977	20.141	21.384	22.713	24.133
13	13.809	14.237	14.680	16.627	17.713	18.882	20.141	21.495	22.953	24.523	26.212	28.029
14	14.947	15.450	15.974	18.292	19.599	21.015	22.550	24.215	26.019	27.975	30.095	32.393
15	16.097	16.682	17.293	20.024	21.579	23.276	25.129	27.152	29.361	31.772	34.405	37.280
16	17.258	17.932	18.639	21.825	23.657	25.673	27.888	30.324	33.003	35.950	39.190	42.753
17	18.430	19.201	20.012	23.698	25.840	28.213	30.840	33.750	36.974	40.545	44.501	48.884
18	19.615	20.489	21.412	25.645	28.132	30.906	33.999	37.450	41.301	45.599	50.396	55.750
19	20.811	21.797	22.841	27.671	30.539	33.760	37.379	41.446	46.018	51.159	56.939	63.440
20	22.019	23.124	24.297	29.778	33.066	36.786	40.995	45.762	51.160	57.275	64.203	72.052
21	23.239	24.471	25.783	31.969	35.719	39.993	44.865	50.423	56.765	64.002	72.265	81.699
22	24.472	25.838	27.299	34.248	38.505	43.392	49.006	55.457	62.873	71.403	81.214	92.503
23	25.716	27.225	28.845	36.618	41.430	46.996	53.436	60.893	69.532	79.543	91.148	104.603
24	26.973	28.634	30.422	39.083	44.502	50.816	58.177	66.765	76.790	88.497	102.174	118.155
25	28.243	30.063	32.030	41.646	47.727	54.865	63.249	73.106	84.701	98.347	114.413	133.334
26	29.526	31.514	33.671	44.312	51.113	59.156	68.676	79.954	93.324	109.182	127.999	150.334
27	30.821	32.987	35.344	47.084	54.669	63.706	74.484	87.351	102.723	121.100	143.079	169.374
28	32.129	34.481	37.051	49.968	58.403	68.528	80.698	95.339	112.968	134.210	159.817	190.699
29	33.450	35.999	38.792	52.966	62.323	73.640	87.347	103.966	124.135	148.631	178.397	214.583
30	34.785	37.539	40.568	56.085	66.439	79.058	94.461	113.283	136.308	164.494	199.021	241.333
31	36.133	39.102	42.379	59.328	70.761	84.802	102.073	123.346	149.575	181.943	221.913	271.293
32	37.494	40.688	44.227	62.701	75.299	90.890	110.218	134.214	164.037	201.138	247.324	304.848
33	38.869	42.299	46.112	66.210	80.064	97.343	118.933	145.951	179.800	222.252	275.529	342.429
34	40.258	43.933	48.034	69.858	85.067	104.184	128.259	158.627	196.982	245.477	306.837	384.521
35	41.660	45.592	49.994	73.652	90.320	111.435	138.237	172.317	215.711	271.024	341.590	431.663
36	43.077	47.276	51.994	77.598	95.836	119.121	148.913	187.102	236.125	299.127	380.164	484.463
40	48.886	54.268	60.402	95.026	120.800	154.762	199.635	259.057	337.882	442.593	581.826	767.091
45	56.481	63.614	71.893	121.029	159.700	212.744	285.749	386.506	525.859	718.905	986.639	1358.230
48	61.223	69.565	79.354	139.263	188.025	256.565	353.270	490.132	684.280	960.172	1352.700	1911.590
50	64.463	73.683	84.579	152.667	209.348	290.336	406.529	573.770	815.084	1163.909	1668.771	2400.018

				Rate					
13%	14%	15%	16%	18%	20%	22%	24%	25%	30%
1.000	1.000	1.000	1.000	1.000	1.000	1.000	1.000	1.000	1.000
2.130	2.140	2.150	2.160	2.180	2.200	2.220	2.240	2.250	2.300
3.407	3.440	3.472	3.506	3.572	3.640	3.708	3.778	3.812	3.990
4.850	4.921	4.993	5.066	5.215	5.368	5.524	5.684	5.766	6.187
6.480	6.610	6.742	6.877	7.154	7.442	7.740	8.048	8.207	9.043
8.323	8.536	8.754	8.977	9.442	9.930	10.442	10.980	11.259	12.756
10.405	10.730	11.067	11.414	12.142	12.916	13.740	14.615	15.073	17.583
12.757	13.233	13.727	14.240	15.327	16.499	17.762	19.123	19.842	23.858
15.416	16.085	16.786	17.519	19.086	20.799	22.670	24.712	25.802	32.015
18.420	19.337	20.304	21.321	23.521	25.959	28.657	31.643	33.253	42.619
21.814	23.045	24.349	25.733	28.755	32.150	35.962	40.238	42.566	56.405
25.650	27.271	29.002	30.850	34.931	39.581	44.874	50.895	54.208	74.327
29.985	32.089	34.352	36.786	42.219	48.497	55.746	64.110	68.760	97.625
34.883	37.581	40.505	43.672	50.818	59.196	69.010	80.496	86.949	127.913
40.417	43.842	47.580	51.660	60.965	72.035	85.192	100.815	109.687	167.286
46.672	50.980	55.717	60.925	72.939	87.442	104.935	126.011	138.109	218.472
53.739	59.118	65.075	71.673	87.068	105.931	129.020	157.253	173.636	285.014
61.725	68.394	75.836	84.141	103.740	128.117	158.405	195.994	218.045	371.518
70.749	78.969	88.212	98.603	123.414	154.740	194.254	244.033	273.556	483.973
80.947	91.025	102.444	115.380	146.628	186.688	237.989	303.601	342.945	630.165
92.470	104.768	118.810	134.841	174.021	225.026	291.347	377.465	429.681	820.215
105.491	120.436	137.632	157.415	206.345	271.031	356.443	469.056	538.101	1067.280
120.205	138.297	159.276	183.601	244.487	326.237	435.861	582.630	673.626	1388.464
136.831	158.659	184.168	213.978	289.494	392.484	532.750	723.461	843.033	1806.003
155.620	181.871	212.793	249.214	342.603	471.981	650.955	898.092	1054.791	2348.803
176.850	208.333	245.712	290.088	405.272	567.377	795.165	1114.634	1319.489	3054.444
200.841	238.499	283.569	337.502	479.221	681.853	971.102	1383.146	1650.361	3971.778
227.950	272.889	327.104	392.503	566.481	819.223	1185.744	1716.101	2063.952	5164.311
258.583	312.094	377.170	456.303	669.447	984.068	1447.608	2128.965	2580.939	6714.604
293.199	356.787	434.745	530.312	790.948	1181.882	1767.081	2640.916	3227.174	8729.985
332.315	407.737	500.957	616.162	934.319	1419.258	2156.839	3275.736	4034.968	11349.981
376.516	465.820	577.100	715.747	1103.496	1704.109	2632.344	4062.913	5044.710	14755.975
426.463	532.035	664.666	831.267	1303.125	2045.931	3212.460	5039.012	6306.887	19183.768
482.903	607.520	765.365	965.270	1538.688	2456.118	3920.201	6249.375	7884.609	24939.899
546.681	693.573	881.170	1120.713	1816.652	2948.341	4783.645	7750.225	9856.761	32422.868
618.749	791.673	1014.346	1301.027	2144.649	3539.009	5837.047	9611.279	12321.952	42150.729
1013.704	1342.025	1779.090	2360.757	4163.213	7343.858	12936.535	22728.803	30088.655	120392.883
1874.165	2590.656	3585.128	4965.274	9531.577	18281.310	34971.419	66640.376	91831.496	447019.389
2707.633	3841.475	5456.005	7753.782	15664.259	31593.744	63506.490	127061.917	179362.203	982105.588
3459.507	4994.521	7217.716	10435.649	21813.094	45497.191	94525.279	195372.644	280255.693	1659760.743

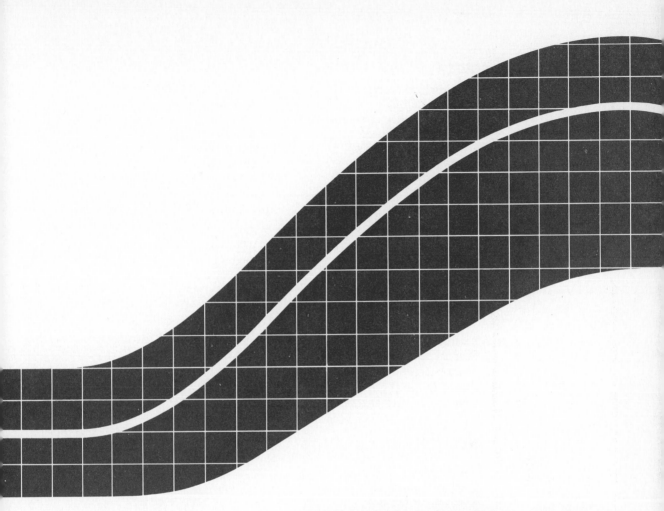

ANSWERS TO
SELECTED PROBLEMS

Chapter 2

1. Able Mfg. Co. (only)
   a) Current ratio   3.58 times
   b) Average collection period   53.3 days
   c) Inventory turnover   4.43 times
   d) Debt to total assets   .455 or 45.5%
   e) Net profit to sales   .05 or 5%
   f) Times interest earned   8.1 times
   g) Return on net worth   .115 or 11.5%
   h) Operating ratio   .903 or 90.3%

2.
Current assets	$ 600,000
Fixed Assets	400,000
Total Assets	$ 1,000,000
Current liabilities	$ 400,000
Term debt	100,000
Net worth	500,000
Total	$ 1,000,000
Total sales	$ 2,000,000
Cost of goods sold	(1,000,000)
Gross profit	$ 1,000,000 (50%)
Other expenses	(800,000)
Net Profit after Taxes	$ 200,000

4. Selected ratios

	Industry	Wynot
Current ratio	2.5	2.4
Total asset turnover	3	2.5
Inventory turnover	6	4.2
Days sales	30	45
Return on sales	3.5%	6.0%
Return on net worth	15.0%	30.0%

Chapter 3

1. a) $1,216, b) $1,360, c) $1,464.   3. 6 yrs. $1\frac{1}{3}$ mos.
5. $30,725.   7. $15,937.78.
9. a) $10,820, $10,900; b) 8.2%.
11. $1,670,843.80.
14. b) PV of X = $1,208.90; PV of Y = $1,065.10. 17. 6%.
18. a) W = 12%, X = 13.25%, Y = 13%, Z = 10%;
    b) PV of W = −$2.69; PV of X = $463.75.
20. $1,996.63.

Chapter 4

1. a) 5.6%, b) 11.4%, c) 12.3%, d) 12.0%.
2. 10.14%. **4.** 9.49%. **5.** 10.86%. **6.** 1.42.
7. a) 1.68, b) .2344 or 23.4%, c) 16.5%.

Chapter 5

2.

	X	Y	Z
Payback	4	5	6 years
NPV	$2,274	$4,995	$2,150
PI	1.57	1.56	1.17

3. X, 7%, Y, 32%, Z, 20%.
4. a) 5.2 years and 18.8%, b) $9,021, c) 1.176, d) ≈14% (approximately).
5. a) $5,349, b) 1.273, c) ≈16%.
6. a) $4,367, b) 1.223, c) ≈19%.
9. a) NPV = $1,355, b) PI = 1.028.

11.

	EAEP
Cheapie	$1,686
HDWW	$1,359

Chapter 6

1. a) $2,000, b) $866, c) .43.
4. a) Arcade, laundromat; b) the arcade;
   c) Alternative $(\hat{C}, \sigma, CV)$,
      Laundromat ($3,000, $1,000, .33),
      Arcade ($3,650, $3,350, .92).
5. Accept B. **6.** Yes. **7.** Reject A; accept B; accept C.
8. $N\hat{P}V$ = $4,897; σ = $4,008; CV = .82.

Chapter 7

1. $1,530. **2.** No. **3.** Total assets = $2,375.
4. No. The firm is short $9,725. **5.** Net loss = $3,125. **6.** Total assets = $94,600.

Chapter 8

2. a) Net Income Plan G, $36,466.50;
      Net Income Plan T, $37,466.50;
      Total Assets Plan G, $382,667;
      Total Assets Plan T, $383,667.

b) Plan G: NWC = $166,667   Plan T: NWC = $113,667
             WC = $292,667   WC = $296,667
             Current = 2.25   Current = 1.63

c) Plan T.

Chapter 9

1. $54,794.53.   **3.** a) Yes, $3,623.01 increase in before-tax profit;   b) $9,863.01.
5. a) $44,375,   b) $50,000.
7. Yes, increased profit exceeds costs by $64,520.63.
8. No, net change in profit is −$30,282.54.
9. EOQ = 2,000 units;   20 orders.
11. 100,000.

Chapter 10

1. $12,000, $10,000.   **3.** b) 36.73%, d) 24%.
5. Yes, borrowing cost of 12% versus 18.18% on the discount.
7. a) $45,000,   b) $60,000,   c) 10.67%.
9. $9,950,   24.36%.
11. 14.45%.

Chapter 11

1. Present value cost of leasing, $32,179; borrowing, $29,488. Borrowing is cheaper in present-value adjusted terms.
2. Present value cost of leasing, $54,421; borrowing, $62,760. In this case leasing is cheaper.

Chapter 12

1. a) Reduced,   c) No change,   e) Worse.
2. a) If interest rates fall to 8%; present value = $1,212.20.
   b) Change in interest rates or business risk.
3. NPV = −$192,949.
4. EPS rises from $1.40 to $1.70.
5. a) $881.06,   c) $1,340.96.
6. a) $1,098.62.
7. b) $1,746.
8. a) $8,250,000,   c) Yes: NPV = $8,191,329.
9. b) Sales = $621.667.
10. a) $3.806.   c) DOL = 2; DTL = 2.63.

Chapter 13

1. $2.00.   **2.** a) 50,000 shares, c) 35.2¢, d) $4.93.
3. a) 1,000,000, c) 50¢.
4. a) 60¢.   **5.** a) 20,001 shares.   **6.** 1.
7. a) 1,501 shares to elect 2, b) 3,001.
8. b) 1.   **9.** New EPS = $4.36.
10. Invest in (a) and (b).   **12.** (a) $12 per share.
13. Preferred, after tax income = $37,600.
14. X = 5.4%; Y = 7.5%; Z = 5.5%.

Chapter 14

1. a) $35.55 per share.
3. a) At $25, bond = $500; no.
   At $55, bond = $1,100; may.
   b) At $25 no; at $55 yes.
   c) at $1,000 or the yield price.
5. a) $62.50, b) 16, c) $800, d) 80,000
7. a) Stock return, 27.27%; warrant return, 300%.
   b) Stock return, −22.73%; warrant return, −100%.

Chapter 15

1. Invest in Comfort-Last. Return on investment = 15.2%.
2. a) EPS = $1.92; c) EPS = $2.00.
3. Equity EPS = $.895.
4. a) Debt EPS = $2.16; c) Common stock EPS = $2.40.
5. a) $1,500,000
6. c) DOL = 7; DFL = 1.15, DTL = 8.02 for current operations. Times interest earned = 7.86 for current operations.
7. Standby: $9,000,000; best efforts: $8,100,000.
8. Private placement.
9. a) $49.25 million; c) $750,000.

Chapter 16

1. $1.5385, $1.0526, $.9091, $.6667.   **3.** a) $57,000, b) $55,200.
5. a) (Eq. 16.5) = −.05273; invest in U.S.
   c) 25.754%.
7. a) $250,000, b) $302,500.
8. a) $40,000, b) $36,000, c) Sell francs forward or restructure balance sheet by borrowing.
   d) Yes, because dollar value in 30 days is $32,000.
      No, because dollar value in 30 days is $44,000.
9. b) −700 SF.

Chapter 17

1. $22,500 common stock dividend.   **2.** An $8.33 per share of Little.
3. $25 per share.   **4.** $800,000.   **5.** a) 6.4%, c) 7.5%.

Chapter 18

3. Accounts payable = $50,000; Debentures = $150,000.
4. Property taxes = $5,000; Bank loan = $10,500; Debentures = $14,000.
5. First mortgage bond = $25,000; Second mortgage bond = $15,000; Accounts payable = $28,200; Debentures = $18,200.
6. a) $4,500,   b) $4,000,
   c) Trade creditors in each case receive, respectively, $7,500 and $8,000; common stockholders receive nothing.

Appendix A

1. $3,127.   **2.** a) i) $7,604,   ii) $10,029,   iii) $5,086.
4. a) Taxes due = $460; b) taxes due = $1,660.
5. Bonds would yield $4,320 after tax versus $4,189 on the stock.

INDEX

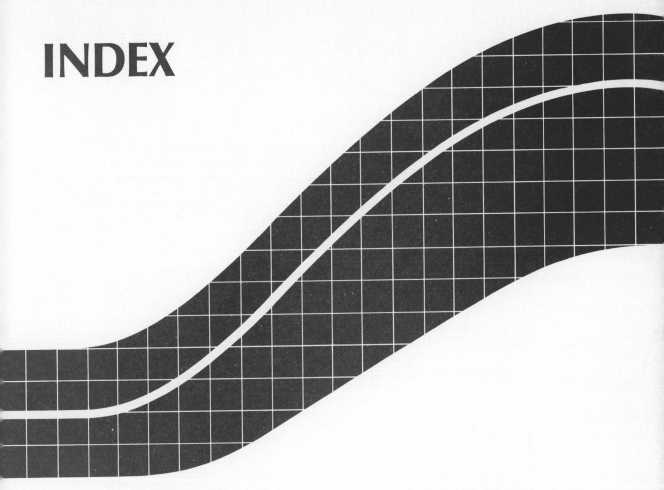